ROGER B. TANEY

By

CARL BRENT SWISHER

NEW YORK
THE MACMILLAN COMPANY
1935

To

RUSSELL M. STORY

ACKNOWLEDGMENTS

So MANY people have contributed in one way or another to the writing of this book that individual acknowledgments of indebtedness to each of them can not be made here. Materials of value have been gathered in at least one-fourth of the states of the Union, and in each of them libraries or historical societies or individuals have rendered assistance. For most of them, unfortunately, a general expression of gratitude must suffice. To some, however, a special indebtedness must be acknowledged. Many months of service were rendered in the manuscript and periodical divisions of the Library of Congress, and in the former the service was not merely routine but was characterized by an obvious desire to be helpful. Mr. A. V. Sullivan aided in the discovery of rich materials in the files of the Secretary of the Treasury. The Maryland Historical Society, the Historical Society of Pennsylvania, the New York Historical Society, the Massachusetts Historical Society, the New York Public Library, and a number of other societies and libraries provided assistance which is further acknowledged in the Bibliography and in footnotes when quotations have been made.

Mr. Edward S. Delaplaine made available the materials in the Taney House at Frederick, Maryland, and some in his own possession, and aided in securing photographs for reproduction. Professor Alester G. Holmes supervised the copying of many letters from the Calhoun manuscripts at Clemson College. Descendants of William M. Beall kindly permitted the use of a number of valuable Taney letters, and so many other people contributed a few letters or information as to where letters might be found that it is unfortunately impossible to mention them, save as documents quoted are cited in the footnotes. Detailed research over many weeks was conducted by my wife, Idella Gwatkin Swisher, and she conducted interviews through which many valuable original manuscripts were discovered. She also aided in the final revision of the book.

Every major piece of work of this kind is almost inevitably characterized by a period of intellectual isolation for the author, a period when his efforts have little meaning to anyone except himself. Many friends have aided in dispelling the loneliness in this case, by participating in the discussion of facts of obscure interpretation and by reading chapters well in advance of the time when they reached their finished form. For such helpfulness I am deeply grateful to many of my student friends at Columbia University, who kindly submitted to imposition prior to the time when I dared make use of my busy colleagues. Professor Carter Goodrich read the bank war chapters shortly after the first tentative synthesis was made. Professor Harry Carman read and appraised the entire manuscript in an early draft, and Professor Schuyler Wallace performed the same service at a later date. Dr. Dwight Miner rendered invaluable service by criticizing the manuscript page by page in great detail.

Finally, although the preparation of the book has been in the main an independent project, I am indebted to the Columbia University Council for Research in the Social Sciences for awards covering part of the expenditures for research.

CARL BRENT SWISHER

COLUMBIA UNIVERSITY
    September, 1935

CONTENTS

ILLUSTRATIONS

ROGER B. TANEY

CHAPTER I

THE HERITAGE OF A SOUTHERN GENTLEMAN

ON THE crest of a low hill in the western part of Calvert County, in southern Maryland, stands the house in which Roger Brooke Taney [1] was born. It is a large, rectangular building of three stories. A hallway runs through it from front to back, dividing it into the great rooms which once sheltered the Taney family and the fox-hunting crowds of southern aristocrats who long ago were accustomed to gathering there. Tall trees surround the house, through the branches of which it looks down a rolling slope to the placid Patuxent River. The Patuxent, a tidewater stream some two miles wide at this point, glistens and glimmers in the sun as its waters move slowly southward toward the Chesapeake Bay, or backward toward the fountainhead of the stream, depending on the action of the tides.

The river marks the eastern boundary of Calvert County down to the point a score of miles away where it flows at an angle into the bay. The angle is such, indeed, that the bay marks the western boundary of the county, so that the region has much the appearance of a peninsula as it juts southward between the two bodies of water. For a century or more after it was settled they constituted its principal highways, both for local transportation and travel and for bringing in European goods and carrying away tobacco, the principal product of the community.

The soil of the rolling hills of southern Maryland, like that of the adjoining state of Virginia, was very fertile. It was well adapted to the growth of the weed which Sir Walter Raleigh had taught his fellow Englishmen how to use with great pleasure. At an early date the economy of the region, into which settlers poured thick and fast

[1] The name is pronounced as if spelled T-a-w-n-e-y.

I

during the second third of the seventeenth century, became predominantly a tobacco economy, in which indentured and slave labor was concentrated on the production of this valuable commodity for sale abroad. Except for the land itself tobacco was the principal form of wealth, and tobacco, or warehouse receipts for it, largely took the place of money as a medium of exchange.

The planters usually sold not directly to foreign consumers, but to merchants and shippers. These merchants and shippers had virtual monopolies both of credit and of shipping facilities. They were therefore in position to dictate the prices which planters received for their product, and also the prices to be paid for imported goods. They made full use of their powers, creating in the planters a deep distrust and dislike for the mercantile and creditor class.

Society in the tobacco region in the early years was extremely heterogeneous. There was a sprinkling of wealthy aristocrats from abroad, who had received grants of huge tracts of land. More numerous were men and women from the impoverished rank and file, who came as indentured servants with the hope of bettering their lot in the new world. Added to them were political offenders and criminals of one sort or another, who came likewise as indentured servants, receiving allotments of land at the end of their periods of indenture. Below them in the social scale were negroes. In the early years many of the negroes who came had reason for expecting to be set free, but in the later period most of those who came were slaves for life, and their descendants with them.

Many of the white men who had acquired minimum tracts of land worked it themselves until they were able to buy indentured servants or slaves, then added to their crops, so that even with their meager money profits they were able to acquire more land, until ultimately they or their descendants found themselves the proud owners of great estates, on which the work was done for them by slaves. These rulers of agricultural domains evolved gradually into a planting aristocracy, merged with the families of immigrant aristocrats, and developed consciousness of class no less keen than that to be found in any society on the globe. They constituted an aristocracy largely without money, it is true, due to the cost of old world supplies and of land, servants, and slaves, and to the effectiveness with which merchants and shippers depressed the prices they received for their product. The purses of all planters were in much the same condition, however, and they found that money, while highly desirable, was not indispensable to aristocracy.

They built fine plantation homes. They fashioned, borrowed, or stole coats of arms. They bred blooded fox hounds with which they scoured the country in the company of those of their neighbors who had likewise achieved the status of "gentlemen." Traveling up and down the streams of southern Maryland, they visited and entertained in great style, stimulating their awareness of the fact that they were the cream of society. By them the negro was usually thought of as property, which he was. The poor white man who failed to get ahead was mildly despised, both by white men and by negroes. The mercantile and creditor class, who did not live among them, were usually disliked with a considerable amount of vigor, save perhaps by those families who happened to have close relatives among the enemy. It was permissible to marry into the "moneyed aristocracy." Otherwise, to be respectable, marriages had to be made within the landed aristocracy itself.

Roger Taney descended from a line of Taneys all of whom, within the Maryland history of the family, had borne the name of Michael. His father was the fifth in the line. The first Michael Taney came to Calvert County about 1660. Although there is no clear proof of the fact, there is good circumstantial evidence to show that he came from some place in England. His condition was evidently impoverished, for, like many other founders of distinguished families in Maryland, he came as an indentured servant. The colonial records tell little of his period of indenture. It may have been less eventful but probably differed little otherwise from the experience of his brother, John, who had arrived in the country about 1652. John was sold at least twice during the four or five years which he was required to serve to pay for his passage to the new world. His value was estimated in tobacco, the only currency available, to the amount of eleven hundred pounds.[2] At the end of his period of service, after suing for it, he received from his owner the usual minimum equipment, in the form of three barrels of corn, a waistcoat, a pair of canvas drawers, a pair of shoes and stockings, a hat or cap, a weeding hoe and a falling axe.[3] He received likewise an allotment of at least fifty acres of land, on which to begin his new life of freedom.

It is possible that by 1660 John was able to afford an indentured servant, and that he bought his brother Michael, but if so the fact is not revealed by the records. At any rate, Michael served out his period, and received land, prospered, bought more land, prospered further, and continued to buy. The rent rolls of the county list for him tracts bearing the names of Taney's Reserve, Taney's Right, Taney's Ease, Taney's Delight, Littleworth, Blind Tom, Long Point, Wooden Point, and Berry. The latter was the estate on which the ancestral Taney home was to be located. His success as a planter made it possible for him to import a wife and indentured servants, and with every person brought in he acquired the right to fifty additional acres. He became a man of prestige in the community. He established himself with Lord Baltimore and other colonial leaders, and was made sheriff of the county, in which position he added substantially to his income if not to his popularity. His status is indicated by the fact that he came to be referred to as "Michael Taney, Gentleman."

Michael and his wife, Mary Taney, were members of the Church of England, and according to tradition were very devout. It is said that he was accustomed to taking his spiritual reading from a text in the original Latin.[4] The two of them worked zealously in the interest of the religious life of the community, urging its needs upon the king and upon the leaders of the church. A number of letters remain, one signed by both Mary and Michael and the others only

[2] *Archives of Maryland*, X, 436.

[3] *Ibid.*, pp. 505–506.

[4] G. A. Tawney to Mrs. Katharine Taney Silverson, Aug. 25, 1927, MS. Where not otherwise cited the materials here presented are gathered from the *Archives of Maryland*, the *Maryland Calendar of Wills*, the wills and administration books, the rent rolls and other similar records.

by the former, in which the dignitaries are humbly petitioned for aid. Charles II had sent Bibles and other church books, but the minister had died, and the people, because of the king's customs on tobacco, were unable to provide another. The want of religious ministration, wrote Mary, was a misery under which she and her numerous family and many others had groaned. They were seized with horror when they thought that for want of the gospel their children were in danger of being condemned to infidelity or apostasy. Mary begged that for religious purposes a certain amount of tobacco be freed from customs, or that a church and a minister be directly provided.[5]

Two clergymen were eventually sent out from England, presumably in part as the result of the efforts of Mary Taney. Michael was made one of the trustees of a fund left by Captain Richard Ladd, "Gentleman," to support a clergyman and build a church at the "Clifts." [6] It was not until a later generation that the family deserted the Church of England and embraced the Catholic faith, which was to be the faith of Roger Taney.

The local troubles of the years immediately following the revolution of 1688 showed the sternness of the stuff of which Michael Taney was made. The Catholic Calverts had been careful to avoid discriminations based on religion, but with the accession of William and Mary a group of Protestants sought to make the religious issue a reason or excuse for seizing control of the government. Under the leadership of John Coode they demanded an election for members of the Assembly. Michael Taney and many other Protestants objected, declaring that the king and queen would ultimately look to the welfare of the colony, and that the election would cause unnecessary expense.

When urged as sheriff of the county to call the election, Taney refused. Thereupon he and Richard Smith, who was supporting him, were seized and imprisoned by the Coode forces, and the election was held in spite of them. Coode ordered Taney brought before the

[5] See the Library of Congress transcripts of manuscripts in the Bodleian Library, Oxford, England.

[6] *Maryland Calendar of Wills*, IV, 235.

new Assembly to answer for his offenses. Taney, instead of pretending humility to secure his release, demanded to see the authority by which the order was given. "What!" shouted Coode wrathfully. "This is like King Charles, and you are King Taney. Take him away!"[7] Taney was returned to prison, to be released only after Coode's power had begun to wane.

Michael Taney died May 22, 1692, leaving his second wife, Margaret, and three sons and a daughter. To his heirs he left numerous tracts of land in Calvert County, running into thousands of acres. He left personal property appraised at more than eight hundred pounds, not including 162,825 pounds of tobacco, the value of which was not estimated. The inventory included five indentured servants and eleven negro slaves. Measured by the prevailing standards, the success of his life was unqualified. He had established a family, a family name, and a family estate. He had buried the record of his indenture in a position of unquestioned aristocracy, leaving to posterity all the prestige which any ancestor in such a locality could have handed down.

His second son, also named Michael and now usually referred to as Michael II, inherited the estate overlooking the Patuxent, where generation after generation other Michaels were to live. He married Dorothy Brooke, a descendant of Robert Brooke, who traced his aristocratic ancestry back to William the Conqueror. Brooke had brought his large family to Maryland in 1650, along with the accoutrements of a country gentleman in the form of a pack of fox hounds of fine pedigree. He settled at Delabrooke, on the opposite side of the Patuxent from what was to become the Taney estate, and quickly made himself a man of importance in the community. A branch of his family into which the Taneys were to marry at least four times settled on the same side of the Patuxent but to the southward, on the opposite side of Battel Creek, or Battle Creek. The stream was so named, it seems, from Battel, in Sussex, England, which had once been the home of Robert Brooke.

The fact that Michael II did little more to distinguish himself

---

[7] Narrative of Barbara Smith, Dec. 30, 1689, *Archives of Maryland*, VIII, 154.

than the making of this family alliance may be explained by the fact that he died at an early age, in 1703. His son, Michael III, passed on the name and the estate by marrying Mary Neale, of a family of no less prestige than the Brookes. His second wife bore the name of Sarah Brooke. He likewise left no other record of important achievement. At his death, in 1743, he left the Taney plantation to Michael IV, who married Jane Doyne. This Michael likewise failed to distinguish himself. He died in 1758, and is of interest here chiefly because he left the ancestral estate to Michael V, who was to be the father of Roger B. Taney.

In each generation there were two or more children to inherit the property of the parents, but the home estate was always left to a Michael. The other children were not necessarily treated unfairly, but they had to be satisfied with land which from time to time was acquired in other localities. Each Michael, it seems, was able to accumulate about the amount of property necessary to leave to each of his descendants the amount which he himself had received from his father. As seen in the perspective of later years, therefore, life at the Taney home flowed on uneventfully from generation to generation. Certain problems of course arose again and again. Husbands and wives for the younger Taneys had to be selected from the best families. Land had to be acquired and rented out to tenants for planting, and rentals had to be collected in the customary currency. Tobacco had to be sold for shipment abroad, with careful scheming to prevent strategically powerful merchants from taking all the profits for themselves—no easy task in those days.

Even though they left no permanent imprint upon local history, the fact that these Taneys of the middle period continued to acquire land and slaves in spite of the difficulties is evidence of abilities far from meager in each succeeding generation. Whether any of the Michaels had a deep desire still further to better his position we do not know. The records show only that each lived much as his father had lived, maintaining himself approximately at the social and economic level achieved by his first American ancestor.

At some time between the first and the fourth Michaels, however, one important change took place. The Taneys became Catholics. They did so in spite of legislation which deprived them of political rights, limited their privileges of worship, and prohibited the establishment and maintenance of Catholic schools. Whether the change was made as an incident to marriage into a Catholic family is not clear, or whether it represented a step upward socially—since many of the more prominent people were Catholics, who adhered to their faith in spite of persistent governmental discrimination against them. The Brooke family, too, sometime within the same period, underwent the same transition. The more intangible results of being isolated into a highly self-conscious minority, which was persecuted for its religion and envied for social and economic prestige, are not to be measured. More direct results were apparent in the field of education. Catholic girls, if they had hitherto been educated formally at all, were now left to such training as the home could provide. The same was true of the sons of indigent families. The sons of wealthy families were often sent abroad to school.

The Carrolls and others of the more prominent Maryland aristocrats patronized an English Catholic school which had been established at Saint Omer, in France. Michael V, in order that he might be in every sense worthy of his position in the family line, was sent to the same place, about 1760, some two years after the death of his father. His education, however, like his life in many other respects, proved chaotic. The Jesuits were becoming more and more unpopular in France, and it was suddenly discovered, in 1762, that the authorities were about to be banished and the school turned over to secular teachers. To prevent such a disaster the entire school fled secretly into Belgium and established itself at Bruges. It remained there in a state of uncertainty and was ultimately compelled to move again, though not until Taney had taken his leave.

In this peripatetic and uncertain fashion Michael V obtained a classical education. He returned to Maryland to take charge of the family plantation. He followed the precedent established by his forefathers by taking a wife from a distinguished family, when Monica Brooke, daughter of Roger Brooke, from the opposite side of Battle

Creek, became the mistress of his home. Outwardly there was little evidence of approaching change in the life of the family, yet beneath the surface forces were working which carried forebodings of disaster. Some of them, indeed, seem to have been in the personality of Michael V himself. He was able enough, no doubt, both intellectually and physically, but from between the lines of the sketchy records comes evidence that he was hot-tempered, impatient, and arrogant, rather than shrewd and stable as a man in his position needed to be. It was as if the family had experienced too long the isolation of aristocracy, which was exaggerated by religious isolation as well, and needed to merge itself in the ranks once more to restore its balance. The chaos of external events was likewise to aid in bringing to an end the traditional life of the Taney family.

Early in the 1770's Monica Taney gave birth to the sixth, and, as we now know, the last of the Michaels—the last, at any rate, to preside at the old home, for Michael VI, after a drab and undistinguished early life, was to pass utterly into oblivion. A daughter preceded or followed the birth of the sixth Michael, and then, on March 17, 1777, was born Roger Brooke Taney, about whose life this account is woven. During the years which followed, two other sons and two other daughters were born, making seven in all. Traditionally Michael VI would remain at the home estate. Michael V would acquire land elsewhere and additional slaves with which to establish Roger and his two younger brothers in the way of living which the family had followed for generations. The sisters would marry gentlemen.

It was in this period, however, that the American colonies, driven to desperation by clashes of interest with the mother country, were uniting to make themselves independent. Such struggles are not conducive to the maintenance of the status quo. Recent English trade restrictions had hurt the sale of tobacco in rural Maryland, and that which hurt the tobacco trade struck at the vitals of the planter society. Most of the planters, including the Taneys, united in the cause of freedom. Michael Taney served as a first lieutenant [8] in the state militia, defending the coasts of the county against the forays of British privateers and of local pirates who took advantage of the war to plunder in their own interest. His brother Joseph, who in 1776 had married Dorothy Brooke, Michael's wife's sister, was made an ensign in a Calvert County company.[9] True, the Taneys participated only in unspectacular local defense, not in the more dramatic scenes of the war. It was a necessary service, however, and it is not necessarily a criticism of their patriotism that they were absent from Yorktown and other points at which stirring events of history took place.

The planters suffered heavily from the war. Their tobacco was tied up in warehouses. If a ship ventured out with a cargo it was quickly gobbled up by the enemy. The local militia had to supply its own provisions, and Calvert, like other counties, was heavily assessed for the support of the continental army. The records are replete with entries of bushels of wheat and quantities of beef and other products which the commissary, Patrick Sim Smith, was called upon to collect. The money which he was authorized to pay for the supplies was usually depreciated state or continental currency, in the value of which there was no stability. Some of it had practically no value at all, except for the payment of taxes. He was instructed to buy the provisions, nevertheless, if the owners would sell, but to take them if necessary, taking first those most in danger of being seized by the enemy. As a result of this policy the people were still further impoverished.

The governor of Maryland directed Smith to apply to the people for loans in the form of money. As should have been expected, his collections were exceedingly small. "They say they would willingly lend, could they command the money," Smith replied to the governor, "but their sole dependence is on the sale of their tobacco to raise it, which the present stagnation of that business renders impracticable. They are looking forward to the payment of their assessments, and I am well convinced three fourths of the inhabitants have no way of making their payments but by the sale of tobacco. A few individuals

[8] *Archives of Maryland*, XXI, 37.
[9] *Ibid.*, p. 290.

I believe have cash by them for that purpose but will not part with [it] for any other." [10]

With the defeat of Cornwallis in the autumn of 1781 the war came virtually to an end, relieving the people from the demands for supplies; but the troubles of the tobacco planters were not at an end. England refused for a number of years to make a commercial treaty with the United States, and the tobacco trade continued to languish. Such credit as was available was supplied more and more by American rather than British capitalists, and the carrying trade was taken over largely by Baltimore merchants. The planters found the merchants of Baltimore quite as willing to take advantage of their necessities as the English merchants had been, and conflicts of interest provoked deep antagonisms, in spite of such sympathies of class as may have developed between the aristocracies of land and of liquid and movable wealth through intermarriage and association.

To make matters worse, the payment of interest on state debts was demanded, and principal ultimately fell due. Harassed and overburdened debtors and taxpayers began to think of the printing press as a cure for their ills. Michael Taney, no longer disfranchised because of his Catholicism, was one of the majority in the House of Delegates who in 1785 voted for the emission of bills of credit. The measure failed because of rejection by the Senate, but through no fault of Taney and many others who saw no other way to help themselves.

The Taneys may not have been subjected to actual distress during this period. They retained their land, and they retained and perhaps added to their slaves. They were not able to acquire much additional property, however, and there seemed to be no prospect of being able to establish all the sons on estates of their own, if, indeed, in view of the depression of the tobacco business, it would have been desirable to do so. The fact that such conditions prevailed among great numbers of families may have been responsible for the repeal of the law of primogeniture, whereby landed estates descended through eldest sons,

[10] Patrick Sim Smith to Governor Thomas Sim Lee, June 1, 1780 (or 1781), *Archives of Maryland*, XLIII, 508.

so that they might be divided among the heirs. Michael Taney opposed the bill in the legislature. When it was passed in spite of his opposition he declared stubbornly that whatever the law his own estate would go to his own eldest son, following the custom of many generations. It was not that he intended to leave his younger sons unprovided for. He would give them a liberal education and make it possible for them to study a profession, but after that they would have to take care of themselves.[11] Thus he retrenched somewhat upon the customary family program, but it would go on essentially unchanged in that a Michael would continue to own the undiminished home plantation.

It was during these turbulent years of change, which threatened the disappearance of the old order, that Roger Taney made his boyhood adjustments to life. Not much evidence remains to throw direct light upon him during this period. Scattered facts which touch upon him at intervals over a considerable number of years indicate that he had in his make-up a mixture, and at times a poorly coördinated mixture, of the diverse qualities of his father and his mother. He was a slender, flat-chested youngster, apparently impetuous and hot-tempered like his father, with a physique too frail to house a stormy disposition. On the other hand he had, or was to develop, a nature warmly sympathetic, like that of his mother.

Monica Taney, like other Catholic women of the times, had little formal education. She did not concern herself with public affairs. She would not, like the wife of the first Michael, have belabored kings and bishops with petitions to lower customs on tobacco and make

---

[11] "It was no part of my father's plan to give my elder brother a classical education," wrote Roger Taney. "He was, at that period of his life, strongly imbued with the English notion of perpetuating the family estate in the eldest son. And he gave us all to understand, as early as we were capable of understanding it, that his landed estate would go to my elder brother; and that his younger sons would have a liberal education and the means of studying a profession, and, after that, we must rely on ourselves for support. And carrying out this plan, which proved to be an unfortunate one for my elder brother, he designed to give him nothing more than a good English education, that would fit him for the business of a landed gentleman cultivating his own estate, and qualify him to associate upon equal terms, as to education and information, with the gentlemen of the county."—Roger B. Taney, "Early Life and Education," in Samuel Tyler, *Memoir of Roger Brooke Taney*, p. 34.

grants to build churches and supply ministers. She had other qualities, however, which were more deeply needed in the wives and mothers of Taney men. "She was pious, gentle, and affectionate, retiring and domestic in her tastes," Roger Taney wrote of his mother. "I never in my life heard her say an angry or unkind word to any of her children or servants, nor speak ill of any one. When any of us or the servants about the house who were under her immediate control (all of whom were slaves) committed a fault, her reproof was gentle and affectionate. If any one of the plantation servants committed faults, and were about to be punished, they came to her to intercede for them; and she never failed to use her influence in their behalf, nor did she ever hear of a case of distress within her reach that she did not endeavor to relieve it. I remember and feel the effect of her teaching to this hour." [12]

There is every reason for believing that the gentle and loving disposition of his mother did much, over a long period of years, to iron out of Roger's disposition the intenseness and harshness produced by poorly disciplined emotions, and the social snobbery which was almost inevitable in a boy brought up as he was among the planter aristocracy. At any rate it is worth running ahead of the story to say that/harshness and narrowness and snobbery/did at times appear during the years immediately ahead, but that with the advancing years they were more and more to disappear. In his personal relationships he was to develop the lovable and gentle traits of his mother, though with evidence in the background of an unrelenting will. It was doubtless from her that he learned personal kindness even to slaves. He said in later years that before he manumitted his own slaves he treated them like children, and it seems that he did not exaggerate. He was never at any stage in his life an abolitionist, but in this there was no inconsistency. The slaves who were provided for on his father's plantation, and chidden and protected by his mother, were not legitimate objects of pity. They were better off than many free negroes who were trying to get along under a white man's economy, and were more to be envied, indeed, than some of the poor whites in the neighborhood.

[12] *Ibid.*, pp. 26–27.

The fact that he withheld any sympathies arising from the mere fact that the negroes in question were slaves should occasion no surprise.

Michael Taney had great zest for active, outdoor life. In their early boyhood he taught his sons to ride, taught them how to swim, fish and row and sail in summer, and how to skate and shoot wild ducks and geese in winter. He perhaps did much to make the countryside the delight which it was to remain throughout Roger Taney's life, though except for riding the son abandoned most of the forms of exercise as soon as he escaped from his father's hand. He had not as a boy, and was never to have, the stalwart physique necessary for a physically strenuous life. Daydreaming on a hillside or beside a quiet stream fitted him much more happily.

Michael Taney, in spite of his superior education, as education went among the planters, had not the temperament for training immature minds. He left that task to others, many of whom were far from competent. In the beginning, on days when the weather was fair, young Michael and Roger and their elder sister trudged three miles to the only school in the neighborhood. It was taught by a man whose academic qualification was his ability to read and write and do arithmetic as far as the rule of three. The Bible was used as one of the texts, not for its subject matter, in the teaching of which there might have been some difficulties as far as the young Catholics were concerned, but for training in spelling and pronunciation. It was Dillworth's spelling book that made the deeper impression on Roger. "I remember yet," he wrote in 1854, "the pleasure which I felt when I was able to read and understand the fable of the boy and the frogs, and the wagoner praying to Hercules, etc., etc., in the spelling book and admired the wretched woodcuts with which it was embellished." [13]

Upon exhausting the resources of this school Michael and Roger were sent to board at a grammar school ten miles away, where Roger took up the study of Latin. Unfortunately the teacher's mind was unbalanced, and his belief that he could walk unharmed upon the surface of water led to his being drowned in the deep channel of the Patuxent. Following the custom of the wealthier planter families, the father

[13] *Ibid.*, p. 28.

then hired a tutor for his children. The tutor died of tuberculosis within the year. Another was hired, but he had to be dismissed because of inadequate knowledge of foreign languages. Finally the position was given to David English, a graduate of Princeton and an able teacher, under whom Roger studied until he was ready for college.

If it was financially possible to send Roger to the school which his father had attended, it was for other reasons not feasible to do so. That institution had experienced a precarious few years at Bruges, had then found it necessary to move to Liége, and was now on the verge of another move, with prospects of a troubled future ahead of it. There was no Catholic institution in the United States which would serve as an adequate substitute. As a member of the legislature Michael Taney had worked energetically and consistently for the support of St. John's College, at Annapolis, but at this time no Maryland institution seemed to him adequate for the education of his son. Two Calvert County families were sending sons to Dickinson College, a Presbyterian institution recently established at Carlisle, Pennsylvania, under the direction of Dr. Charles Nisbet. They spoke highly of the school, and Michael Taney was persuaded that this was the place to send Roger.

So it was that Roger, at the age of fifteen, left his home for the first time. One day in autumn in 1792, with another student who was returning to Dickinson after the summer vacation, he boarded a merchant schooner at the landing below the Taney home. As the wind filled its sails the schooner moved slowly down the Patuxent to the junction with the Chesapeake Bay. It turned northward on the bay in the direction of Baltimore, moving sluggishly because of the lack of wind, and taking an entire week for the trip. Since no stage ran between Baltimore and Carlisle, Roger and his companion put up at an inn in the small but thriving mercantile town until they could find someone making the trip in a wagon who would take their trunks for them and allow them an occasional ride. The trunks were precious articles of baggage, for in them was packed enough money, in coin, to pay expenses until the following year. In terms of distances and modes of transportation at the time, Carlisle was located in a far country. Its merchants would not be satisfied with tobacco warehouse receipts, or even with Maryland paper money. The traveler had to take currency with intrinsic value. Thus equipped, the boys set out beside the wagon which was to bring them to Carlisle.

The town of Carlisle, situated in the Cumberland valley in central Pennsylvania, had a population of not more than two thousand people. Although it is now within a comfortable driving distance of Harrisburg, conditions in 1792 were such as to make it appear cut off from the outside world. Its chief claim to fame was the fact that during the War of the Revolution it had been the site of a camp into which the captured mercenaries of the enemy had been herded. The surrounding country was thinly settled. Most of the population were Scotch-Irish, who ably took their own part in clashes with the heterogeneous and despised German immigrants who were beginning to pour in.

The Scotch-Irish were for the most part strict Presbyterians, and Carlisle was the center of a Presbyterian community. They were shrewd in things political as well as religious, and had established Dickinson College during the preceding decade in part for the purpose of perpetuating their influence. The Presbyterians must withdraw a little from political offices, declared Dr. Benjamin Rush, the leader among the founders, since their prominence had occasioned jealousy and opposition, and entrench themselves in schools of learning, which were the true nurseries of power and influence.[14]

The college was incorporated in 1783, with a charter which provided that at least one-third of the forty trustees must be clergymen. It was by virtue of the fact that they knew only his good points and thoroughly misunderstood him in other respects that the trustees, under the leadership of Dr. Rush, chose as head of the college Dr. Charles Nisbet, a Presbyterian minister of Montrose, Scotland. Dr. Nisbet was a brilliant man, a master of many languages and learned in their literatures, and an excellent teacher. During the American

---

[14] Hints for Establishing a College at Carlisle in Cumberland County, Pennsylvania. Rush MSS., Library Company of Philadelphia.

Revolution he had endeared himself to his American friends by his vociferous support of their cause, both by letter and from his pulpit at Montrose. He was not interested in serving any religious group or political clique, however, and in spite of his brilliance he was opinionated, vituperative, and notoriously lacking in tact. He had accepted the invitation to Dickinson, it is quite evident, with the idea of becoming the leader of the cultured and liberal thought of an intellectually disciplined people who eagerly awaited his leadership.

Great was his disillusionment. He discovered that the college was located in a two-story building of four rooms located on an alley, in a dismal little town which was buried in the wilderness, and was dominated by the petty ambitions of ministers and politicians. He met no intellectual geniuses eager for his words of wisdom, but found even the community leaders bound up in the minutiae of their own concerns. He ranted and raved at the college, the trustees, the town and the country as a whole, making himself thoroughly unpopular with everybody except the students, whom he drew to him and taught successfully in spite of his lack of tact in dealing with mature people.

He tried by sharp criticisms to bring about the improvement of conditions. "You know," he wrote to Dr. Rush a few weeks after Roger Taney's arrival in Carlisle, "that the town is situated in a deep clay swamp, which is almost impassable for a great part of the year, and that the houses are few and small, and not likely to increase by which means the students, who are excluded from the best houses, are obliged to lodge in small, narrow and inconvenient apartments, unfit for study and unfriendly to the health, by which means they are not only crowded, and kept from following their studies to advantage, but are exposed to low company and vicious habits, which often counteract the best moral instruction that their teachers can give them." The college could not expect to grow in its present quarters, he declared, since it had inadequate lodging facilities even for the sixty-five students now in attendance.[15]

He succeeded only in antagonizing many of the trustees and other pioneer leaders of Pennsylvania. He basked in the friendship of his

[15] Nisbet to Rush, Nov. 28, 1792, Rush MSS.

students, however, save that some of them were doubtful about his political doctrines. His early parlor radicalism in the cause of democracy having given way in the face of the excesses of the French Revolution and the crudeness of the American system, he showed now a deep hostility to all leveling tendencies. His lectures were interspersed with exposures of the fallibility and prophecies as to the impermanence of the new government. "These opinions," wrote Taney, "were monstrous heresies in our eyes. But we heard them in good humor, without offending him by any mark of disapprobation in his presence. We supposed they were the necessary consequence of his birth and education in Scotland. Yet many, I believe a majority of the class, would not write down these portions of his lectures; and, if the opinions had been expressed by any other professor, the class would probably have openly rebelled." [16]

Such sympathy as he had with the ideals of any political group in the United States was with the Federalists, who represented for the most part the large propertied interests of the country, and favored a strong central government. He was bitter in his denunciation of their opponents. Dr. Rush was disturbed by the possibility that Nisbet's caustic comments would turn Democrats away from the college. Tuition funds, he declared, were neither Federalist nor Republican. Students ought to be allured to the college by the silence of the teachers on subjects which did not belong to the essence of good government. [17] Nisbet, however, was not given to that kind of strategy. He flatly refused to be silenced, either at the threat of the loss of his position or at the threat of the destruction of his property by the Whiskey Rebellion Democrats whom he had the temerity to denounce in a political sermon.

Roger Taney spent much time at Nisbet's house. His father had sent Nisbet a letter asking him to act as guardian to this youth who for the first time was venturing away from home, and Nisbet had taken the plea more seriously than such requests are often taken. As a result, many evenings during the ensuing three years found the boy

---

[16] Taney, *op. cit.*, p. 41.
[17] Rush to John Montgomery, June 21, 1799, Rush MSS.

in his home, talking with and listening to the brilliant conversation of a man of rare intellect and learning, who had the capacity of imparting unobtrusively to immature students much of the richness of his own culture. It was in his associations with Nisbet, either informally in the home or formally in classes in ethics, metaphysics, logic, and criticism, that Taney's college experience was of more than ordinary significance in his life. He may not have remembered the details of the scores of pages of notes which he took in Nisbet's classes. He grasped, however, his teacher's belief in the aristocracy of learning, his dislike for mediocrity, his dislike for pettiness in human relations, and his belief that government should be in the hands of men of culture, intellect, and vision, to be administered for the good of all. These beliefs were readily to be grounded upon the accepted doctrines of the landed aristocracy from which Taney came—that men were essentially different in breeding and capacity, and that even in a society professing to be democratic the aristocrats should rule. With this background of home and college training it is not surprising that Taney ultimately found his way to leadership in the Federalist party, and revealed in that position much of the breadth and narrowness characteristic of his training.

He took work in other subjects than those taught by Nisbet, including languages, mathematics, and geography, and seems to have done well in them. He liked most of his teachers, though in common with many of his fellows he was disgusted with the obvious narrowness and egotism of one. He lived with seven other students in the home of the teacher of mathematics, and apparently enjoyed normally friendly relations with them. In his account he mentioned college sports only incidentally, by remarking that the students amused themselves in the lot back of the school building by playing bandy, and that he gladly joined in their athletic sports and amusements while still finding time to do a good deal of reading beyond the assignments made for his classes.

Whether he made friends in the town or surrounding country other than students, the records do not show. Gossip persists even to this day that he was not fundamentally different from other southern gentlemen among whom a rigid and scrupulous chastity was more of an ideal than a reality, and that a certain buxom lass of German origin remained forever unmarried because a young hero from Maryland went away and never returned. The story, while plausible and not out of character, is apparently undocumented, and must be taken only for the vague tradition which it is.

At last in 1795 Taney and his classmates passed their oral examinations before the faculty and members of the board of trustees. Out of the group two members were to be chosen for honors, but the choice was made not by the faculty but by the students. Student politics was dominated by the two literary societies, the Belles Lettres and the Philosophical, secret organizations which included most but not all of the students in the college. The membership in each was about equal, and three or four boys in the graduating class were allied with neither of them. The choice was therefore likely to be close.

Taney's name was urged in his society, the Belles Lettres, for the position of valedictorian. He won the society nomination, over an older and at that time perhaps an abler person, but one who had not made himself so intimately and clannishly a member of the group. He won in the general election also by a narrow margin of two votes, whereas the candidate of his society for the other honor was defeated. He attributed his success in this, his first political contest, not to any superior popularity, but to the fact that a loyal friend had aided him by an intensive campaign of electioneering. Whether or not the disclaimer was a product of undue modesty, we have no means of knowing.

The elation of victory faded into grim forebodings of failure in a task to be performed. The subject and outline of the valedictory address were always provided by Nisbet himself. He prepared for Taney the skeleton of an address on the utility of seminaries of learning, in which it may be assumed that the ideas and prejudices of the teacher found ample expression, some of them conflicting sharply with those of the trustees. In great trepidation Taney set about developing the outline into an oration. He had learned to speak informally before his friends in the literary society, but he had done so only from notes. The college offered no courses in composition, and he had always disliked the manual task of writing. So it was that the writing out and memorizing of a formal address to be delivered before a mature audience seemed a formidable undertaking.

"This oration cost me much trouble and anxiety," Taney declared. "I took great pains with it, and perhaps should have done better if I had taken less. I remember well that my greatest difficulty was how to begin it; and the first two or three sentences gave me nearly as much trouble as all the rest of it put together. I am quite sure that I spent hours upon them, and wrote them over at least a dozen times. However, the speech was worked out at last, and submitted to Dr. Nisbet; and I was much relieved when he returned it to me with only one or two slight verbal alterations.

"But now came my severest trial. The Commencement was held in a large Presbyterian church, in which Dr. Nisbet and Dr. Davidson preached alternately. A large platform of unplaned plank was erected in this church in front of the pulpit, and touching it, and on a level with its floor. From this platform the graduate spoke, without even, I think, a single rail on which he could rest his hand while speaking. In front of him was a crowded audience of ladies and gentlemen; behind him, on the right, sat the professors and trustees in the segment of the circle; and on the left, in like order, sat the graduates who were to speak after him; and in the pulpit, concealed from public view, sat some fellow student, with the oration in his hand, to prompt the speaker if his memory should fail him. I evidently could not have been very vain of my oration, for I never called on my prompter for it, and have never seen it since it was delivered, nor do I know what became of it. I sat on this platform, while oration after oration was spoken, awaiting my turn, thinking over what I had to say, and trying to muster up courage enough to speak it with composure. But I was sadly frightened, and trembled in every limb, and my voice was husky and unmanageable. I was sensible of all this, much mortified by it; and my feeling of mortification made matters worse. Fortunately, my speech had been so well committed to memory, that I went through without the aid of the prompter. But the pathos of leavetaking from the professors and my classmates, which had been so carefully worked out in the written oration, was, I doubt not, spoiled by the embarrassment under which it was delivered.

"Perhaps it may be thought," Taney continued, "that the honor of speaking the Valedictory, in the manner in which the task was executed, was hardly worth the pain and mortification which it brought with it. Philosophically considered, this is true; for I might have gone home, after my examination, without further labors, or trials, or mortifications.

"And as a mere calculation of interest, my college honor was of no consequence in my future pursuits. I doubt whether a dozen persons out of my own family connection, in the new world upon which I was afterwards to enter, even knew that this mark of distinction had been awarded to me. Yet in the little world of a college, it is as much valued, and as much the object of ambition, as the high offices of government in the great political world. And I confess that I would, at that time, have endured much more than I did rather than not have obtained it. Such is ambition in the little world and the great, and so early do our teachers and instructors plant it in our hearts. I do not say that it is wrong. For when it is properly regulated, and directed to proper objects, it often leads the possessor to great personal sacrifices for the benefit of others. But I doubt whether it promotes often his own happiness, however successful he may be." [18]

When the ordeal was over, Taney, doubtless viewing it much less philosophically than he was able to do sixty years later when the comment quoted was written, set out once more for Calvert County. He had visited his home only once since his departure three years earlier. He had left home an immature boy. He returned still immature in a sense, but a college man, and apparently with something

[18] Taney, *op. cit.*, pp. 52–54.

of the swagger of a young man of the world. The consciousness of being a "gentleman," in the sense of breeding and culture rather than of morality, had been intensified by his three years of training. He was a member of the elect, of the class born to distinction, born to rule.

CHAPTER II

PURSUIT OF A CAREER [1]

TANEY returned from college to spend a winter of recreation in fox hunting, the supreme sport of the planters of southern Maryland. It was the custom of the planters to come together periodically with their hounds at the home of a member of the group, making that home the pivotal point for a series of forays into the foxes' lairs. When they gathered at the Taney home young Roger rode with them over the rolling hills of southern Maryland with the enjoyment of a man of long experience, save that the heavy breakfasts washed down with egg-nog which preceded each trip provided embarrassing discomfort. After pursuing agile red foxes throughout the day the parties returned at evening to dine in great sociability and sit by the fireside in conversation or playing whist. Those of the guests who were familiar with life at Annapolis often told anecdotes of Luther Martin and William Pinkney and other prominent lawyers, for they knew that Michael Taney had high ambitions for his son in that field.

The gatherings often lasted as long as a week, the guests leaving for their own homes only after making arrangements to meet at some other place. When no large parties were in progress Michael Taney and his sons set out alone, spending many days in exultant outdoor exercise. It was a fine, health-building experience for the not too husky younger man, and perhaps deepened his love of nature, which in his mature years was to minister often to his recovery from the exhaustion of professional labors.

In the spring of 1796, at nineteen years of age, young Taney went

[1] The materials of this chapter, where not otherwise cited, are taken for the most part from Taney, "Early Life and Education," in Tyler, *Memoir of Roger Brooke Taney*.

to Annapolis to begin reading law in the office of Jeremiah Townley Chase, one of the three judges of the General Court. The General Court was an institution of great importance in those days. It had jurisdiction in a great variety of cases, both large and small. At its sessions held in Annapolis it served all of that part of Maryland which lay west of the Chesapeake Bay. Jurors were summoned from each of the counties of that section, and lawyers likewise came from all points. The quality of the court was maintained by the fact that its metal was repeatedly tested by the best lawyers in the state, and the lawyers, in competition with one another, were likewise kept at their best as they would not have been had their operations been confind to isolated local county courts.

On the advice of Judge Chase, Taney spent much time in the court room observing the techniques of counsel and making notes on points of law. He was much impressed by the scenes wherein such men as Luther Martin, Philip B. Key, John T. Mason, Arthur Shaaff and others crossed verbal swords before the scarlet-robed judges. There was no moot court for the many law students who, like Taney, were being trained in the offices of local lawyers and judges. It was the prevailing belief that premature argument of legal points led to slipshod methods in court, and that young men should not argue legal points until they knew what they were talking about. Taney and others organized a debating society to develop skill at verbal combat, but they confined themselves for the most part to non-legal topics.

Reading in the office of a judge rather than a practicing lawyer had both advantages and disadvantages. It gave more time for uninterrupted study, but it provided no instruction in the ordinary routine of practice, or information as to forms and manner of pleading, except such as could be gathered from books. "In the office of a lawyer in full practice," Taney wrote in later years, "the attention of the student is daily called to such matters, and he is employed in drawing declarations and pleas, special and general, until the usual forms become familiar to his mind, and he learns, by actual practice in the office, the cases in which they should be respectively used, and what averments are material, and what are not." [2]

The want of this practical knowledge proved a serious inconvenience to Taney. For some time after beginning practice he dared not draw a declaration or a plea without a precedent before him. If the cause of action required a declaration varying in any degree from the precedents at hand he found it necessary to examine the principles of pleading which were applicable. It was no easy task, he declared, "for an inexperienced young lawyer to satisfy himself upon a question of special pleading. Chitty had not made his appearance, and you were obliged to look for the rule in Comyn's Digest, or Bacon's Abridgment, and the cases to which they referred; and I have sometimes gone back to Lilly's Entries and Doctrina Placitandi in searching for a precedent.

"Although this deficiency gave me so much trouble, it, perhaps, in the end made me a better pleader; for the consciousness of my want of knowledge, and that I had no office experience to rely on, made me study the subject the more carefully, whenever a case was likely to present a question of pleading; for in that day strict and nice technical pleading was the pride of the bar, and I might almost say of the court. And every disputed suit was a trial of skill in pleading between the counsel, and a victory achieved in that mode was much more valued than one obtained on the merits of the case." [3]

Intensely ambitious, Taney read law week after week for periods of twelve hours a day. He admitted in later years that it would have been better had he greatly reduced his schedule of formal study and spent more time in thinking out the principles, and had he taken more time for society from which he might have learned many things which the law books could not teach.

[2] *Op. cit.*, p. 60.

[3] *Ibid.*, pp. 60–61. So it was that the interests of the parties in the cases were often submerged in the lawyers' trials of skill on technicalities which were hardly more than matters of professional etiquette. Taney himself became highly adept in that field. Whatever may be said of it otherwise, this training was to fit him admirably for the important task of systematizing chaotic and conflicting rules of practice in the Supreme Court of the United States. The problems were not necessarily identical but there was the same need for mastery of technical niceties.

In spite of his long hours of labor he formed friendships with young men which proved valuable at the time or in later years. He roomed for a year with William Carmichael, who was reading law in another office, and spent many evenings discussing professional matters with him and relieving his mind of the mass of material which he had memorized. The two were later members of the state Senate at the same time, and in their old age were to meet at Virginia summer resorts and discuss the experiences of their youth.

In the office of Judge Gabriel Duvall, which was near that of Judge Chase, studied William H. Winder, who throughout his life was to be another of Taney's friends. He is known to history chiefly as the man who engineered the unsuccessful defense of Washington against the British in 1814. At a later date Taney helped bring about his election to the state Senate.

Another friend was Frank Key, who in his enjoyment of such pranks as tearing about the campus of St. John's College on the back of a surprised and aggrieved cow was quite unburdened by the fact that he was to live through the ages as Francis Scott Key, the author of a national anthem. He was the son of John Ross Key, the owner of Terra Rubra, a large estate in Frederick County, and the nephew of Philip B. Key, an able lawyer and politician of whom Taney saw a great deal in Annapolis. More important, he was the brother of Anne Key, who some years later became Taney's wife.

Taney made other influential friends among law students, students at St. John's College, and the sons of prominent people who came to Annapolis for the season. Among them was William Potts, who planned to be a merchant in Baltimore. Young Potts was the son of Judge Richard Potts, of Frederick, who was to be one of the promoters of Taney's professional and political career. Another was John Hanson Thomas, likewise from Frederick, who was to be a close personal and political friend until they were divided by the issues of the War of 1812.

The formal records and such fragmentary bits of personal evidence as are to be found provide a picture of Taney and his friends in Annapolis which at best is dim. There is some reason for believing

that they alternated the prankishness of typical boyhood with affecta-
tions of the social superiority thought to belong to people of their
class. They evidently drank a bit, and pretended to drink a great
deal more than they did, thinking it a mark of superior manhood to
do so. They perhaps indulged in other petty vices without ever becoming quite as wicked as they pretended to be. Taney and many
of his friends were undoubtedly interested in their work and spent
long hours in mastering the basic materials of their profession, and
this fact, rather than the froth of post-adolescent living, is of primary
importance.

In the spring of 1799, after three years with Judge Chase, Taney
was admitted to the bar. Two days after his admission he delivered
his maiden speech, in defense, he wrote grandiloquently to William
Potts, "of as great a scoundrel as ever lived, who was indicted for a
felony. However, what he had done was only a private fraud, and
not a felony in the eyes of the law, so that I felt myself perfectly
justifiable in defending him, as every man ought to be punished only
according to the laws of his country. As he had not done what
amounted to a felony he ought not to have been punished for a
felony. He was acquitted. Watts and I defended him. But the fellow was too poor to give us any fees." [4]

Taney's 1854 account of his first speech at the bar so differs from
this contemporary statement as to indicate that the one above mentioned had then been crowded out of his mind by another which had
been more harrowing. According to the later account his first effort
was made in the Mayor's Court of Annapolis. He and another novice
at the bar defended a man who had been indicted for assault and
battery in a fight in which neither party was much hurt. The mayor
was a good-natured old gentleman who had never studied law, and
Taney assumed that his own legal knowledge was more ample than
that of any other person likely to be present.

Doubtless with something of a swagger, therefore, Taney and his
friend empaneled the jury and proceeded with the trial. They were

---

[4] Taney to William Potts, July 2, 1799, from a copy from the original provided by Miss
Eleanor Johnson, of Frederick, Md.

suddenly terrified by the appearance of Judge Gabriel Duvall, of the General Court. Duvall was recorder of the Mayor's Court, but he was not accustomed to appearing at trials unless his advice was needed on legal problems of unusual difficulty. The two fledgling lawyers were thoroughly abashed at the thought that he had come to compare their amateur performances with the finished work of the lawyers who habitually appeared before the General Court.

It was a good case for a speech. The fight had taken place in the midst of an excited crowd, and the testimony was so conflicting as to leave the facts deeply in doubt. Yet Taney, in the face of Judge Duvall, felt anything but adequate to the occasion. "I watched the testimony carefully as it was given in," he recounted, "turning in my own mind the use that might be made of it. I took no notes, for my hand shook so that I could not have written a word legibly if my life had depended on it; and when I rose to speak, I was obliged to fold my arms over my breast, pressing them firmly against my body; and my knees trembled under me so much that I was obliged to press my limbs against the table before me to keep me steady on my feet; yet, under all these disadvantages, I determined to struggle for composure and calmness of mind, and by a strong effort of the will I managed to keep possession of the reasoning faculties, and made a pretty good argument in the case, but in a tremulous and sometimes discordant voice, and inferior to what I could have made under more auspicious circumstances." [5]

He won his case, but the verdict hardly consoled him for the timidity and lack of poise he had demonstrated. This experience, similar to his commencement experience at Dickinson College, was not to be the last of its kind. It was followed by others before the Maryland Court of Appeals, and before the Supreme Court of the United States. Even in the lower courts, with which he became thoroughly familiar and where he was regarded as the leader of the bar, the same feeling of paralyzing terror often came back to him when his health was poor, although he learned better how to conceal

[5] Taney, "Early Life and Education," in Tyler, *op. cit.*, pp. 77–78.

it.[6] "Indeed," he wrote reflectively when he was Chief Justice of the United States, "this morbid sensibility was so painful to me, in the first years of my practice, that I am not sure that I should not have abandoned it, if I had been rich enough to have lived without it; but, as things were, I never for a moment thought of engaging in any other pursuit. I knew that my father and family had formed high hopes of my future eminence, and that a good deal of money had been spent on my education. So I determined from the first to march forward in the path I had chosen, and, whatever it might cost me, to speak on every occasion, professional or political, when my duty required it. A firm and resolute will can do a great deal, yet I knew in many instances I fell far short of what I was capable of performing, had I been perfectly calm and self-possessed.

"The source of this misfortune," Taney continued, "was my delicate health. It was infirm from my earliest recollection; my system was put out of order by slight exposure; and I could not go through the excitement and mental exertion of a court, which lasted two or three weeks, without feeling, at the end of it, that my strength was impaired and I needed repose." [7]

Taney continued for a time at Annapolis, trying to find enough work to justify his remaining there, but with little success. The city in which in future years he was to win substantial fees seemed to have no place for him now. He put aside vocational problems, however, long enough to celebrate the Fourth of July. A mimic battle was to be staged at the wharves to commemorate the recent victory of Commodore Truxton, commander of the American frigate *Constellation* in a brush with the French *Insurgente*. "Take notice I mean to celebrate the 4th of July in high glee," Taney wrote to William Potts. "I must however keep myself sober in order to see the engagement between the *Constellation* and *Insurgente*, which is to be exhibited at the theatre on that evening. I intend to put myself

---

[6] One of his early associates at the bar remembered his difficulty as in the nature of an impediment of speech. See E. F. Ellet, *Court Circles of the Republic*, p. 193.

[7] Taney, *op. cit.*, pp. 79–80.

only in a humor to be highly patriotic, and to join with warm enthusiasm in bestowing praise on the gallant Truxton." [8]

Unable to support himself in Annapolis, Taney returned to Calvert County, where he was admitted to the bar, but where likewise there was little work for a young lawyer. His father, however, had plans for him. After an absence of some years Michael Taney had returned to Annapolis each of the two preceding years as a member of the House of Delegates. He wished now to send his lawyer son in his place. He was convinced that he was influential enough in the county to do it, in spite of the fact that Roger was only twenty-two years of age, had been away from home most of the time for six years, and was not personally well known to the voters.

Each county in the state was entitled to four seats in the lower house of the legislature. Votes for members were cast *viva voce* at the respective court houses, over periods of four days. The elections were often gala affairs, providing opportunities for the farmers of the county to get together at one place. Booths were set up and refreshments served near the polls. The backers of particular candidates met voters riding in from long distances, and doubtless turned many votes by the judicious use of foaming steins. Votes were influenced also by the fact that every man had to call out his choices so that they might be heard. Prominent planters were often able to sway the votes of people who were dependent upon them. It is therefore not surprising that Michael Taney, with a number of friends to aid him, believed that he could put a relatively unknown boy into an office supposed to be filled by popular choice.

The four-day election period was not an easy time for the candidates. Competing slates of candidates were not put forth by opposing parties, but five men sought the four positions. "The candidates, during the election," wrote Taney, "sat on a raised bench immediately behind the sheriff, so that each of them could see and be seen by every voter. It was an exciting scene to an inexperienced young man like myself. When a voter came up, every candidate began to

---

[8] Taney to William Potts, July 2, 1799, from a copy from the original provided by Miss Eleanor Potts, of Frederick, Md.

solicit his vote, and press his own name upon him; and, as many of the voters cared very little about the candidates, except the particular favorite he came to support, I think it very likely that the skillful in these struggles sometimes obtained votes that would otherwise have been given to another. These scenes were occasionally enlivened by sallies of wit between the voter and the candidate, and sometimes the voter gave a pretty hard hit to a candidate whom he happened to dislike. But, however hard the hit, the candidate was obliged to take it in good humor, and treat it as a joke. I made no great figure in this part of the contest, for I was not experienced in it, nor hardened to it, and knew very few of the voters even by name. Some of my friends saw my deficiency, and stood near me and spoke for me." [9]

The poll books being open before the candidates, they were aware of the number of votes they had received, and of the ebb and flow of their prospects. The election was closer than Taney's friends had expected, and he was greatly relieved when he saw that he was elected. He was fully aware that he owed his election not to the speeches he had made but to the active support of his friends. When the results had been proclaimed he made a speech of thanks, whereupon he was raised to the shoulders of the crowd and carried in triumph about the court-house green. The other candidates were also cheered, but none, Taney proudly observed, was cheered so vigorously as he.

The ensuing session of the legislature, which began in November, 1799, provided one of the most profitable experiences of Taney's life. Although a substantial proportion of his colleagues were of the landholding aristocracy, masters of fox-hunting techniques and quite at home in rural drawing rooms, they were awed and helpless in the face of legal problems and parliamentary procedure. Taney, in spite of his youth, had many advantages over them in this respect. He lost much of his embarrassment and morbid sensibility in addressing men less able in discussion than he, and began to find enjoyment in his work. Through his contacts with legislators he broadened his as-

[9] "Early Life and Education," in Tyler, *op. cit.*, pp. 82–83.

sociations, and mixed somewhat in the mature society of the capital. His lack of parlor finesse, however, coupled with a defect of eyesight which made it difficult to recognize people at a distance, prevented any very profound enjoyment of social life. He was much more at home playing the game of politics in the House of Delegates.

The work of framing and reporting bills was done at that time not by standing committees but by special committees, appointed by the speaker, the man who asked leave to bring in the bill usually being made chairman. Taney served on many committees, some of them of considerable importance, and he held at least one important chairmanship.[10] Most of the work of the session, as of any ordinary legislative session, was routine in nature and without lasting significance either for the state or for the lawmakers. Two movements of deep significance for the story of Taney's life were under way, however. One was a struggle between the rural areas of the state and Baltimore, which was a phase of the perennial struggle between the planters and the merchants. The other was a movement in the direction of democracy which in certain of its aspects threatened the dominance of planters and employers over elections.

The particular struggle with Baltimore, of some years' standing, was over the building of a canal to connect the Chesapeake and Delaware Bays. Baltimore opposed the project because it would enable Philadelphia to compete for the trade of the Chesapeake Bay region, of which Baltimore now had a virtual monopoly.[11] The farmers of the region, more interested in better bargains than in enriching merchants and building up a state metropolis, urged the construction of the canal. Michael Taney, in earlier years, had given his full support. Roger Taney followed his lead, and had the good fortune to see the measure enacted into law. It was presumably his first skirmish in the intermittent warfare which his forefathers had waged with mercantile interests. It indicated the alignment to which he was to

---

[10] Data concerning the session of the legislature, where not otherwise cited, are drawn for the most part from the *Votes and Proceedings of the House of Delegates*, for 1799.

[11] See Taney's opinion in *Perrine* v. *Chesapeake and Delaware Canal Co.*, 9 Howard 172 (1850).

adhere throughout his life, when in various more influential positions he came in contact with what he regarded as mercantile cupidity.

In connection with the various measures to promote democracy in elections Taney was likewise true to his class. He showed himself opposed to the secret ballot. He fought unsuccessfully against a measure to divide counties into electoral districts in which all the voting would be done on one day, instead of on four days at the court house. Unsuccessfully, likewise, he opposed a provision for a fine of five hundred dollars and imprisonment for buying or making gifts for votes, and for setting up booths at the polls to give out food or drink. The system by which country gentlemen kept control of county elections seems to have been quite satisfactory to him. It might be said that he showed democratic tendencies to the extent of supporting a movement for a constitutional amendment removing the property qualification for voting. This movement, however, was at least incidentally in the interest of sons of planters who like himself had no property, and could not vote or hold office without the aid of their fathers, and in supporting it Taney was in no sense running counter to the interests of his class.[12]

At the close of the session Taney returned to Calvert County convinced that he had become a man of importance in the state, and that his political future was assured. He confidently expected to be re-elected to the legislature the following year. Having little opportunity for the practice of law, he read in cursory fashion from history and literature, and did some thinking on the needs of the state in preparation for later work in the legislature. Most of the time, however, he seems to have done nothing at all. "Indeed," he commented in mature life, "I have always loved the country and coun-

[12] Unfortunately the records do not show Taney's position on the provision, which was made a part of the amendment as passed at a later session, limiting voting to free white males. It is improbable that any free negro voted in Calvert County even while there was no constitutional prohibition, and sentiment and customs differed little in the other counties of the state. Yet it may have seemed best to have the matter determined finally by law. There is reason for believing that Taney thought that both negroes and white people would be better off if suffrage was frankly limited to the ruling race. The evidence can be better presented, however, in connection with the dramatic events of later years.

try scenes too much to study, except in the long nights of winter. When the weather permitted, I was always out, wandering on the shore of the river or in the woods, much of the time alone, occupied with my own meditations, or sitting often for hours together under the shade, and looking almost listlessly at the prospect before me. There was always a love of the romantic about me, and my thoughts and imaginings when alone were more frequently in that direction than in the real business of life." [13]

He soon discovered, however, that it was a bad time to neglect what he called "the real business of life," for events were shaping themselves in such a way as to interfere drastically with his plans. State elections had hitherto turned for the most part on local issues, but the strife connected with the national campaign of 1800 now threatened to become a determining factor in the choice of state officers. The Federalist party, largely pro-British in sympathy, had been responsible for the enactment and enforcement of the memorable alien and sedition laws. The Republicans, on the other hand, had leanings toward the French, hated the repressive legislation enacted by the Federalist party, and opposed its policy of centralizing power. The Federalists were seeking to return John Adams for another four years as President, while the Republicans were supporting Thomas Jefferson.

The Taneys had aligned themselves with the Federalists, perhaps quite as much because the Federalist party was the party of aristocrats as for any other reason. They supported the party candidate in spite of the fact that they had no warmth of feeling for him, and saw no reason why this fact should affect Roger Taney's return to the legislature.

It was a movement begun in Virginia which carried national issues into state politics. Presidential electors in that state had hitherto been chosen by districts. Some electors might therefore be chosen for one presidential candidate and some for another. The legislature, which was predominantly Jeffersonian, changed the law so that electors would be chosen by that body, with the result that Virginia

[13] "Early Life and Education," in Tyler, *op. cit.*, p. 87.

would vote unanimously for Jefferson. In Maryland the choice of electors had likewise hitherto been by districts, and the districts at this election seemed likely to divide on the candidates. The legislature at the preceding term had been predominantly Federalist. The Federalists expected to remain in power at the ensuing session. A number of them, therefore, began to clamor for a special session of the legislature, to change the law so that electors would be chosen by that body—which would mean that all the electors would vote for Adams, and thus counteract the results of the movement of Virginia. The plan for a special session was given up as too expensive and too dangerous in view of the opposition it might incur, but the issue was carried into the October election of members to the legislature, with the idea that the new legislature would change the law and choose the electors.

For some time the plan was kept quiet, and Taney, daydreaming on the banks of the Patuxent, knew nothing at all about it. He learned about it when he and other Federalists received copies of a pamphlet supporting the program which had been written by Robert Goodloe Harper,[14] but which bore the signature, "A Bystander." Party tickets were nominated on the issues defined, and Taney, whatever his convictions in the matter, fell into line.

The strategy was discussed on both sides in terms of doctrinaire arguments. Republicans declared that the people would be deprived of their rights if the legislature took from them the opportunity of choosing electors. Taney made what was presumably the typical reply, that since the people chose the members of the legislature the choice of electors by the legislators was indirectly their act, and they were therefore deprived of no rights by the change in machinery. It was obvious, however, in spite of Federalist web-spinnings on the subject, that the plan would deprive predominantly Republican districts of the right to choose electors from their own party.

[14] Harper was an eloquent, sharp-tongued politician who had formerly been a member of Congress from South Carolina. He had at first been a Republican, but because of expediency, temperament, or conviction had become one of the most haughty of the Federalists. He had now moved to Baltimore, where he practiced law and became the son-in-law of Charles Carroll of Carrollton, the wealthiest man in the state and a leader of the Federalist aristocracy.

It soon became apparent that the state election would turn largely on this issue, which, as the campaign progressed, produced a fairly clear alignment, with the wealthier and more aristocratic element on one side and the common people with less property on the other. The point of view of the Federalists was illustrated by the comments of Charles Carroll of Carrollton, to whom through the Brooke family Taney was distantly related. Jefferson, Carroll declared, was too theoretical and fanciful a statesman to direct the affairs of this growing confederacy. He might safely try his experiments in the little republic of San Marino, but not here. "I once saw a letter of his, in which, amongst several others, was contained this strange sentiment,—'that to preserve the liberties of a people, a revolution once in a century was necessary.' A man of this way of thinking may be said to be fond of revolutions." [15]

Apart from his wealth and his distinguished family lineage Carroll's chief claim to fame lay in the fact that he had participated in one revolution by signing the Declaration of Independence; but one revolution had evidently been quite enough. His chief interest now was in the preservation of his property and the prevention of all disturbing change. "I much fear," he lamented, "that this country is doomed to great convulsions, changes and calamities. The turbulent and disorganizing spirit of Jacobinism, under the worn out disguise of equal liberty and right, and equal division of property, held out to the indolent and needy, but not really intended to be executed, will introduce anarchy, which will terminate here, as in France, in a military despotism." [16]

Taney was the only Federalist candidate who made speeches in the defense of the party, and he went to the polls confident of success. The result was tragic. He was heckled in humiliating fashion for being an aristocrat, and although one member of the party was elected in the county it was not Taney. Many other Federalists, including men much more prominent than he, were defeated in the

[15] Carroll to Alexander Hamilton, April 18, 1800, in Kate M. Rowland, *Life and Correspondence of Charles Carroll of Carrollton*, II, 235–236.
[16] Carroll to Hamilton, Aug. 27, 1800, *ibid.*, pp. 238–241.

state, with the result that the party was in the minority in the next legislature, but Taney and his father were not consoled by the fact that in their misfortune they had the best of company.

Taney was too little known to receive attention from the press, but comments of the opposition papers on other candidates indicate the significance of the political reversal of which he was the victim. "The interesting and grateful prospect before us," exulted a Republican paper in Baltimore, "the recent successes of the friends of freedom in this state, and the overturn of a faction which aimed a vital blow at the bosom of liberty, in an attempt to destroy one of the most precious rights obtained by our revolutionary struggle, absorbs every other feeling, and fills reflection with the most pleasing and animating sensations. The expulsion of Key, of Carroll, of Ridgely, the Thomas's, with the whole mass of fungus that too long has corroded our state legislature, is such a happy omen of the total purification of the body politic of this state from the leprosy of aristocracy, as to give the best hopes that the real sentiments of a large majority of the people of Maryland will never again be the mere play things, the absolute punchinelloes of a set of designing and awkward state jugglers." [17]

Federalist leaders were greatly discomfited. Charles Carroll of Carrollton meditated on the gloomy possibility that he might in a few years be driven into exile by an execrable faction and be forced to dwell in a poor hovel the remainder of his life.[18]

Although some of the more prominent Federalist politicians were taken care of by appointments in Washington before the party retired from power, Taney could not expect recognition of this sort. He had to find some means of taking care of himself. He was too restless to remain at home in the hope that his political fortunes would be better the following year. His father proposed that he go to Baltimore, where there was more work for lawyers than at any other place in the state, but Taney feared that as a stranger in the city he would be unable to get a start. He was informed, however,

[17] Baltimore *American*, Oct. 20, 1800.
[18] Carroll to Charles Carroll, Jr., Oct. 23, 1800, in Rowland, *op. cit.*, II, 245–246.

that two elderly members of the bar were retiring from practice in Frederick, and his young friends in that vicinity urged him to come and make a place for himself there. So it was that in March, 1801, Taney again set out from the place of his birth, which was never again to be his home.

Two historical parallels are significant. First, as Taney set out to make a place for himself the Republican party was taking over the reins of government in Washington. The Federalist party as a nationalist organization was doomed. It retained its strength for a time in a number of states, and Taney's experience was for some years interwoven with its fluctuating and decadent fortunes. It remained to be seen whether, when the party and its principles were irrevocably obsolete, Taney would have the versatility and ingenuity to align himself with new organizations and new ideas.

The second parallel was in the fact that at approximately the same time John Marshall, to whose place Taney was to succeed thirty-five years later, was beginning his work as Chief Justice of the United States. During the years when Taney was acquiring prestige as a lawyer and statesman Marshall was building the Supreme Court into one of the most powerful institutions in the country.

CHAPTER III

LIFE IN FREDERICK

THE town of Frederick,[1] which was to be Taney's home for more than twenty years, had in 1801 a population of about three thousand people. It was located in the heart of a fertile valley in western Maryland, and served as a marketing place for the surrounding country. Numerous articles for local use were manufactured there. Much of the land of Frederick County had been taken up around the middle of the preceding century by men of property and foresight then living in other parts of Maryland, such as the Carrolls, Dulanys, Johnsons, and Keys. Raphael Taney, a descendant of one of the early Michaels, had given his name to Taney Town, the location of which was then within the borders of Frederick County, and Joseph Taney, Roger Taney's uncle, now lived near that place.

With the coming of new residents many of the great tracts had been broken up into small farms or town lots, and sold at handsome profits or rented out. Frederick was located on part of a grant which had been made to Patrick Dulany, whose name has been preserved in Patrick Street, one of the principal thoroughfares. A great manor owned by Charles Carroll of Carrollton, on which lived many tenants, was only a short distance away, and other similar tracts might be named throughout the surrounding country. The land was fertile and attractive to settlers, particularly to the large numbers of Germans who poured in.

The people of the county, like those in the vicinity of Taney's home, included aristocrats, common people, and slaves, although slaves made up a smaller proportion of the total than in southern

[1] The official name at that time was Frederick Town. Since the word "Town" was frequently omitted, and since in letters to be quoted hereafter Taney used the abbreviated form, which is the name now in vogue, it seems best to use it here.

Maryland. A leader of the aristocracy was Thomas Johnson, formerly of Calvert County and an old friend of Michael Taney. He had been the first governor of the state and had held other positions of local and national prominence, including for a brief period that of justice of the Supreme Court of the United States. He lived now in retirement at Rose Hill, a short distance from Frederick, and was to come often to Taney's office to give him advice and tell anecdotes of old times.

More actively prominent at the time of Taney's arrival was Judge Richard Potts, the father of his Annapolis friend, William Potts. Judge Potts had held many offices, including positions in the Continental Congress and the United States Senate. The latter body had not the prestige it was later to acquire, and at the request of his neighbors he resigned to take a local judicial position, from which he was later promoted to a place on the Maryland Court of Appeals. He owned extensive tracts of land, and was a leader of the local Federalists. He was a valuable friend for a young man with aspirations for success in law and politics, and Taney was to owe much to him and his family.

Another influential citizen was Dr. Philip Thomas, who seems to have been quite as much concerned with his large estates and the fortunes of the Federalist party as with the practice of medicine. Taney and his son, John Hanson Thomas, had become close friends in Annapolis. "What happiness I should not expect," the pompous young Thomas wrote to William Potts a year before Taney moved to Frederick, "if we three [Potts, Taney, and himself] can only spend a few days together once more. It would be a triumvirate far more joyful and honest, I believe than any of ancient Rome or that of modern France." [2] He had deplored the fact that the young men of Frederick could afford him "little pleasure by their company, or little improvement by their conversation," [3] and was doubtless much pleased when Taney arrived to preserve him from ennui.

The Potts and Thomas families and most other prominent people

[2] Thomas to Potts, Feb. 12, 1800, MS., Maryland Historical Society.
[3] Thomas to Potts, Sept. 4, 1799, *ibid.*

of the community were members of the Episcopal church. The other churches, including the Catholic, were left largely to the Germans and the undifferentiated mass of common people. Taney preserved his Catholic affiliation, but he made most of his friends among people allied with the Episcopal organization.

Social life in Frederick was varied. Fox hunting was less popular than in southern Maryland, but people came together socially in other ways. Picnics and barbecues were frequent on holidays and as incidents of political campaigns. Leisurely visiting was common. Before Taney's arrival John Hanson Thomas had written of a dance at the home of Judge Potts at which he and other young men "were sober enough to dance till twelve o'clock at night," and of subscription balls to be held throughout the winter.[4]

To entertain the common people an occasional magician came to town. In the midst of a show he might permit a member of the audience to cut off the head of a cock, which he would immediately restore, so that the cock would live and crow again, "to the surprise of every beholder." Such performances were apt to begin at the respectable hour of six o'clock in the evening. The "elocutionary exercises" of the local Academy were open to the public, or rather to the fifty or sixty persons who could be crowded into the building at fifty cents a ticket. Taney took an interest in this institution, was made a member of the board of visitors in 1802, and attended the meetings regularly for twenty years.

The Cumberland Road, which passed through Frederick from Baltimore to the West, added greatly to the variety of life, bringing the stagecoaches, the mail, and travelers with news of the outside world. Presumably the ladies of Frederick peered discreetly from behind curtains at passing equipages and waited for the news to be brought by the opposite sex, but the men, young and old, rich and poor, aristocratic and common, found excuse or reason for being near such places as Mrs. Kimboll's Lamb Inn, identified by a huge sign of a golden lamb, when the stage came clattering up to the door. The gossip which flowed with foaming steins gave spice and zest to

---

4 Thomas to Potts, Jan. 16, 1799, *ibid*.

the social life of the community. For how else could the inhabitants learn so quickly of social events or market trends in Baltimore, or of the doings of Napoleon and the ever changing façades of the turmoil in France? Or how else could they so easily gather gossip about the doings of the new President, who in the muddy-dusty little town on the Potomac was manipulating the reins of government?

Taney was admitted to the bar in Frederick soon after his arrival. His friend Arthur Shaaff invited him to speak in one of his cases, to give him the opportunity of appearing in public. From that time he worked his way into the profession in Frederick, was admitted to the bar in adjoining counties and secured clients there, and became ultimately the most prominent lawyer in that section of the state. His cases grew out of the problems of the community in which he lived. In no small part they had to do with the determination of boundaries and titles to land, partly because land was one of the major commodities of ownership and exchange, and partly because of the vagueness of many of the original grants. He did not attempt to specialize, however, and took criminal cases and cases of every other kind as they came to him.

Much of the local legal business at that time was carried to the General Court in Annapolis. There was increasing resentment, however, at the necessity of taking witnesses, jurors, and lawyers to such a distant point, and after the broadening of the electorate by the abolition of the property qualification for voting, the Republican legislature forced the abolition of the old system. In its place was set up a system of district courts, each having three judges, and each district embracing at least three counties. The chief justices of these local courts made up the Court of Appeals, which sat at Annapolis. Taney increased his local practice under the new system, and built up an extensive practice before the Court of Appeals.

His exuberant young friend, Frank Key, was also practicing in Frederick when Taney went there. The fact that their names were later found scratched on a window in Market Street has been taken by some to indicate that they roomed together for a time—for the Key estate of Terra Rubra was too far distant to permit young Key to reside at home while working in Frederick. Key was also a relative of the Potts family and may have aided Taney in establishing himself with the family.

It was largely through John Hanson Thomas, however, that Taney worked his way back into politics. Thomas had studied law for a time in the office of Robert Goodloe Harper, in Baltimore. After the defeat of the Federalists in the election of 1800, Harper had aided in the establishment of the Baltimore *Anti-Democrat,* and had sent Thomas back to Frederick with the idea that the Frederick Federalists should also set up an anti-democratic organ. The result was the establishment by Thomas' father, Judge Potts, and others, of the *Frederick Town Herald,* with John P. Thompson, a graduate of Dickinson College, as its editor.

The *Herald* made its appearance June 19, 1802. It launched at once into a vindictive campaign of ridicule and denunciation of the Jefferson administration and of the opposition candidates for the House of Delegates. It was noised abroad by the Republicans, with apparent truth, that much of the writing was done not by Thompson but by Taney and young Thomas—the latter being referred to never by his own name but as "Sancho."

The only Republican paper in the town with any vigor was Matthew Bartgis' *Hornet,* which announced its purpose each week in the jingle,

> To true Republicans I'll sing,
> Aristocrats shall feel my sting.

The *Hornet* republished from another paper [5] an article written from Frederick mentioning by name and denouncing three of the founders of the *Herald.* "Good men ought to be warned against such a junto," the writer concluded, "and upright men cautioned against the insidious wiles of a persevering aristocracy that winds its course in every direction in search of a place to make a stand to destroy the liberties of the people." Two articles in hot defense appeared soon

[5] Philadelphia *Aurora,* April 26, 1802.

afterward in the *Herald*,[6] one of which in particular was written in a style closely resembling that of Taney. There is reason for believing that he entrenched himself in the good graces of the leaders of his party by loyally defending their reputations and their cause.

On August 4, 1803, the Federalist convention meeting in Frederick nominated Taney and John Hanson Thomas as two of the four candidates of the party for the House of Delegates. These two, declared the *Hornet*, were generally believed to be writers and directors of that dirty sheet, the *Herald*, and had been in the practice of attacking and slandering in the most villainous manner every man or thing that was Republican, from the President down to the levy court. They had now become fair game, and their names and pretensions should be brought into the public view.[7]

In the ensuing campaign, however, which was to be memorable in Taney's life, the *Hornet* faded into the background, outdone as it was by John B. Colvin's recently established *Republican Advocate*, compared with which the *Hornet* was an insect with no sting at all. Colvin opened fire by classifying the four Federalist candidates. Robert Cummings was a violent partisan, an Adams man who had once been a Tory. John Troxel had been nominated because it was necessary to have a German on the ticket to appeal to the German vote. Young Thomas had been nominated because his father wanted his son to make some noise before federalism was entirely dead. It was disgusting to have such a "thing" as a candidate, a boy, and not a smart boy either! As for Taney, it was no use to discuss his principles, Colvin pretended, because he had been heard to say he would not run for office even if nominated. Two weeks later he warned that he was still waiting for Taney to resign. "If he does not do it in the course of another week, we must bring him out at full length, as Dr. Kent says"—referring to Taney's unhappy experiences with heckling at the Calvert County election.

The exciting campaign turned on personalities and group loyalties rather than on the political principles avowed by the candidates. It

[6] Frederick *Herald*, July 3 and 24, 1802.
[7] Frederick *Hornet*, Aug. 15, 1803.

was conducted by public gatherings and barbecues as well as through the press. Some six hundred persons were present at a Republican barbecue September 9 at Middletown, in the heart of a German district. Taney and Thomas appeared at the barbecue, stating that one of the managers had invited them to attend.[8] People formed in clusters to discuss the presence of the two men. "It was impossible," declared the vindictive Colvin, "for many not to remember that Taney and Sancho were the impudent and principal scribblers for the *Herald*. It was impossible for them to forget the base and unfounded calumnies of that paper, which every one believes to proceed from Taney and Sancho. It was therefore hinted to the lads that they might vanish as soon as they pleased. The youths took the hint, and they instantly became invisible at the dinner place." [9]

Having dined in town instead of at the barbecue, Taney and Thomas remained there throughout the afternoon discussing politics with the people as they straggled in from the Republican celebration. They attempted, declared Colvin venomously, to delude the people into believing that they were Republicans. "Such a miserable cheat, we sincerely believe, was never before attempted. Taney and Sancho both, were evidently in a high flow of spirits. The former was heard repeatedly to say, 'I am a *Republican!* a *true* Republican. My name is *Taney*—and now *wont* you—wont you—my *dear* dear fellow *wont* you vote for me.' " [10]

Toward nightfall a crowd assembled at Stemple's Tavern, and one of the Republican candidates was listened to with attention by the predominantly Republican audience. Thomas arose to reply, but was

---

[8] Frederick Stemple was said to have invited them through a friend, apparently with the idea that a debate would ensue. Major Joseph Swearingen, a prominent Republican, had vowed that if Taney and Thomas appeared they would be thrown into John Swearingen's mill dam (affidavit of Thomas Marlow, *Herald*, Oct. 1); but when they did appear he merely stamped away from the grounds declaring that there were too many damned Federalists about.— *Herald*, Sept. 17.

[9] Frederick *Republican Advocate*, Sept. 17, 1803. The Federalists of course pictured the withdrawal of Taney and Thomas as much more dignified. The two announced that as one of the managers had left on account of their coming they would not remain to break up the harmony of the company, and anyway they could not reconcile their feelings to remaining after the rudeness they had suffered. Therefore, with a few friends, they walked back to town for their dinners.—*Herald*, Sept. 17.

[10] Frederick *Republican Advocate*, Sept. 14, 1803.

shouted down time after time, whereupon he repeatedly proclaimed his satisfaction at seeing the opposition thus disgrace itself, "upbraiding them for their meanness in trying to drown the voice of truth." When Thomas had finished, Taney mounted the platform. Descriptions by the political enemy indicate that he experienced his old difficulties with public speaking. "So confused, so confounded, so overpowered were his faculties," wrote Colvin, "that he could only vociferate, 'now *do* hear me—and *pray* hear me,' and so forth. Now and then, indeed, he would squeeze in an expression, against the Republican administration—but would directly again introduce his prayer of 'now *do* hear me; O *pray* hear me,' &c. the people listening all the time very quietly to hear what the gentleman *would* say: But alas! Taney seemed to have taken leave of his senses, for his whole incoherent discourse was errant nonsense." [11]

So the day ended, not too happily for the Federalist candidates. Taney and Thomas pretended to return good for evil by inviting the Republicans to a Federalist banquet to be held near Frederick the following Saturday. Why should Republicans go to Federalist barbecues? demanded Colvin. "To hear the wonderful harangues of orator Taney (who was fairly laughed out of Calvert County in 1800 or 1801 for being an aristocrat), or to listen to the impertinent gabble of his little man Sancho, who follows him through the county, begging the people to make him a representative? . . . Mr. Taney owes it to the people of this county to give some account of himself before he goes about spouting. Before he accuses others, let him tell the people who he is. What do the people of Frederick County know of Roger B. Taney? What do the farmers know of him? Or what does he know of the interests of the farmers? Why does he not tell the people how Dr. Kent served him? Precious representatives, indeed, would the people have in such men as Roger B. Taney and his little man Sancho!" [12]

The Federalists held their barbecue as scheduled, but the Republicans, instead of attending, competed by having another of their

[11] *Ibid.*
[12] *Ibid.*

own. Toward night, recorded Colvin, a cavalcade of persons on horse and on foot marched noisily into Frederick from the Federalist barbecue, "headed by Taney in all his glory, and brought up in the rear by Potts and Thomas." They proceeded to the court house, made speeches some of which were said to be well flavored with intoxicating spirits, and brought the day to a close by engaging in a small riot with interfering Republicans.[13]

This was the first election in the state to be held by secret ballot and without a property qualification for voting. The Federalists were worried about the effects of their loss of direct control over elections through the changes in machinery. Colvin declared that every ligament was stretched to preserve their dominance. Even Charles Carroll, "that hoary-headed aristocrat," had gone down to the Manor, doubtless with a view to influence the tenants on his place.

"Shall the people be dictated to by this lordly nabob," Colvin demanded, "because he has more pelf than some others? Has he more virtue, more honor, or more honesty, than a good, industrious farmer? Dares he, with his British monarchical and aristocratical politics, come into Frederick County to cajole, to swindle the people out of their rights? Why does he not confine himself to the place of his residence? Cannot the people judge for themselves? Is he, old in iniquity as he is, to be the chief director of the people of the Manor? Citizens of Frederick County, set Charles Carroll at defiance. The Republicans have secured to you the right to vote by ballot. You may vote the true sentiments of your mind without his knowing anything about it. If he has oppressed or insulted you by threats, now is your time to rally around republicanism and the constitution, and triumph over his mean and dastardly advantage he would take of your poverty. Rise, people of the Manor! Rise like a giant in his strength, and destroy the tricks of your oppressing landlords. Show that you have independence of mind; that you have virtue and fortitude enough to hold in contempt Carroll's vile arti-

---

[13] *Ibid.*, Sept. 24, 1803. Colvin followed his account with cutting gibes at Taney: "Why is candidate Taney like a bladder of wind? Because, when he opens his mouth, it emits nothing but empty sound." "Why has candidate Taney got a *down* look? Because he is not an *upright* man. The gentleman stoops in his shoulders."

fices, and that you scorn the revengeful threats of the enemy to your country." [14]

Taney and his fellow candidates were defeated by a majority of about six hundred votes, out of a total of forty-eight hundred. It was not a humiliating defeat, but it was more decisive than that experienced by their predecessors of the preceding year. The changes in qualifications and methods of voting doubtless had their effect. The tirades and demagogic appeals of Colvin's *Republican Advocate* played their part. The lack of finesse on the part of the Federalist candidates is also to be noted. It is apparent that Taney was oppressed by his old platform deficiencies, and that he was ineffective as a political orator who had to endure the heckling and follow the moods of outdoor political audiences. He was only gradually learning that as a politician his place was behind the scenes, working with political leaders, writing unsigned articles, preparing political handbills, and making individual contacts.

The lashing which he took from the opposition, particularly from the pen of Colvin, had importance in at least two respects. First, it solidified him all the more firmly with the Federalist leaders of the community who were traduced along with him, so that he was thereafter regarded as belonging to the inner councils of the party. Second, it to a degree hardened him to endure the far greater abuse which, time after time in the years to come, was to be poured out upon him, even though he continued to fret intensely at the prickings of the opposition. [15]

In the meantime Taney was looking forward to the establishment of a home. While at Annapolis he had met Anne, the charming sister of Frank Key. After moving to Frederick he rode many times to Terra Rubra, the Key estate, where an old brick mansion was set

[14] *Ibid.*, Sept. 30, 1803.

[15] The score with Colvin was to a degree evened some months later. He was caustic in his comments about the lottery for the completion of the Catholic Church, and about the fact that the local priest, John Dubois, had secured an amendment to a legislative act to make Taney a member of the board of managers. The managers were all Federalists, and although they advertised the lottery widely throughout the state, no contract was offered to Colvin's *Republican Advocate.*—See the issue of March 9, 1804.

in the midst of a broad lawn and surrounded by trees and a terraced garden of shrubs and flowers. "A copious spring of purest water, where young people loved to retire, and sit under the sheltering oaks in summer, was at the foot of the hill. A meadow of waving grass spread out toward the Catoctin Mountain, which could be seen at sunset curtained in clouds of crimson and gold." [16]

Taney fell deeply in love with the girl, whose gracious and kindly temperament was much like that of his mother. He withdrew for a time from active politics and concentrated on his law practice with such success that by 1806 he felt able to marry. The wedding took place on January 7 of that year. It was a happy marriage and most fortunate for Taney. It seems probable, in view of his fragile health and easily shattered nervous system, that his long life and professional achievements would have been impossible without the solicitous care and devotion of his wife and the daughters who were born to them.

Matters of religion may have seemed a threat to happiness, since Taney was a Catholic while his wife was a member of the Episcopal Church. A tradition is still vouched for throughout the Frederick community to the effect that the couple made a premarital agreement that all sons born to them should be brought up as Catholics and all daughters as Protestants. [17] Catholics have been reluctant to believe that Taney would make such an agreement. They report that one of his relatives once asked him if he had done so, and that he replied that he could not have done so as a Catholic. [18] The reply indicates nothing definite except his unwillingness to discuss the matter.

The marriage was performed by a Catholic, and the birth and baptism of the first child are said to have been recorded by the Catholic Church in Taney Town. [19] Only one of the six daughters accepted Taney's faith, however, and she did so rather late in life.

[16] Tyler, *Memoir of Roger Brooke Taney,* p. 101.

[17] A great-grandson, Roger Brooke Taney Anderson, who became a Protestant minister, told the same story.

[18] "Did Taney Make a Pre-Nuptial Agreement with his Wife?" *American Catholic Historical Researches,* Jan., 1912, p. 88.

[19] G. A. Tawney to Clifford A. Taney, Oct. 30, 1914.

The only son died in infancy. Between husband and wife complete trust and understanding seem to have existed on matters of religion. Mrs. Taney was so little fearful of the influence of her husband's faith that she would urge that one of the daughters accompany him to vespers.[20] On the other hand the Taney pew in the All Saints' Protestant Episcopal Church stood in Taney's own name. Protestants in the community still tell with relish the story that when a priest calling on the family pressed too zealously his religious views upon the feminine members Taney courteously but firmly reminded him that such matters were not debated in his home.

In a domestic atmosphere of harmony and affection the tenseness and stiffness of Taney's make-up began to disappear, and the more lovable side of his nature, inherited perhaps from his mother, came to the fore. He became a gracious host to his friends, and a citizen of the community whom it was a delight to know. Although the family lived simply their expenses seem to have been high. They were generous in giving, and relatives on both sides of the family were frequent visitors. Taney could not therefore, like his rural ancestors, live leisurely and let a great estate supply his needs. He had to be in constant attendance upon his profession.

Although his profession for some years left him no time to seek a political office which would take him from home, he continued to be interested in politics, and to be regarded as a leader of his party. It was the custom of each party, at the elections which were held every five years, to support fifteen of its most eminent men for the state Senate. The Senate was chosen not directly but by electors, much as the President of the United States was chosen. Since the electors from each party voted always for members of their own organization the Senate was made up of the slate picked by the electors of the majority party, but the minority nevertheless honored men within its ranks by nominating a slate of its own. The Republicans elected the Senate in 1806, but Taney, Charles Carroll of Carrollton, John Eager Howard, Judge Potts, and others were marked for distinction within the Federalist party by the receipt of the votes of the

[20] B. C. Steiner, *Life of Roger Brooke Taney*, p. 45.

Federalist electors. For a man of his age and position Taney was in an eminently respectable group.

The Federalist leadership chose Taney for the position of presidential elector in 1808, and in 1811 he again received the votes of the representatives of his party for the state Senate. He seemed to be firmly entrenched with the party and with the class of people which most closely approximated the class in which he had been born and brought up. Yet surface appearances did not tell the whole story. Fleeting traits of heretical democracy were occasionally apparent in Taney, while the dominant members of the Federalist party were growing steadily more inflexible, more arrogant, and more narrow in their political ideas. As they demonstrated a growing incapacity to see any interests but their own and those of the minority group to which they belonged, Taney was growing in his conceptions of human welfare and of the rights of the masses of the people. Such a divergence of trend must inevitably at some point bring disaster. It came with the Federalist schism during the War of 1812.

CHAPTER IV

THE FEDERALIST SCHISM

MANY issues between the two political parties in the United States during the first decade of the nineteenth century had to do with the conflict between France and England, in which the United States was in constant danger of becoming embroiled. Both nations were guilty of such extensive depredations on American shipping that Thomas Jefferson declared, "The one is a den of robbers, and the other of pirates." [1] Neither country seemed much concerned about what the United States might think or do about its conduct. The Republicans were in general sympathetic with France, and the Federalists with England. Republicans were particularly resentful at the search of American merchant ships by the British and the kidnaping of American sailors, while the Federalists thought the matter of too little importance to justify the destruction of profitable business by a war with England.

The Jefferson administration, believing that the offenders could be coerced by the withdrawal of American products, resorted to embargoes and non-intercourse measures of which the disastrous effects upon American merchants and shippers were more obvious than the good effects abroad. The Federalists, among whom mercantile and shipping interests were heavily represented, fought the administration program with vigor and venom. They blamed the administration itself for the unsatisfactory relations existing between foreign countries and their own.

The Federalists paused in their defense of Great Britain, however, when a public vessel of the United States was attacked. On June 22, 1807, the British *Leopard* fired on the United States frigate *Chesa-*

[1] Jefferson to John Adams, Jan. 21, 1812, *Writings of Thomas Jefferson*, VI, 37.

peake, compelling her to surrender, and taking from her three American sailors who had escaped the British after impressment, and one deserter who was a British subject. It was a far more serious offense than stopping and searching privately owned merchant vessels. Indignation meetings were held throughout the country in which Federalists and Republicans joined in denunciation of the attack, and in pledging support to the government in any measures which might be necessary. It is significant that the New England Federalists were a bit slow in expressing themselves, though most of them ultimately did so. As a forerunner of his approaching break with his party John Quincy Adams was among the first and most vigorous in denouncing the British, while Timothy Pickering forecast from the opposite extreme his leadership of the near secessionist Federalists of the War of 1812 by having nothing to do with any of the protests.

A nonpartisan meeting was held at Frederick on July 4, at which a Republican was chairman and a Federalist was secretary. Roger Nelson, a Republican, moved the reading of the President's proclamation ordering all British armed vessels to leave America, and followed the reading with an address calling for the whole-hearted support of the President. Roger B. Taney then arose, stated a reporter, and addressed the meeting in such a manner as to evince his contempt of the perpetrators of the outrage. He was of the opinion that, however men might differ with respect to the management of the internal affairs of the country, there would be but one sentiment in case of foreign aggression. He mentioned the injuries that could be done to Great Britain if necessary, and recommended the adoption of energetic measures to secure redress of the injury done. The man who would not support such measures was a traitor to his country, and undeserving of the confidence of its citizens.[2]

Taney's speech was loudly applauded. Thereafter he and Judge Potts and Dr. Thomas served on a committee which drafted resolutions viewing with abhorrence the "unprovoked and dastardly attack," and declaring that "we pledge our lives and fortunes to cooperate with the government in obtaining redress for this unex-

[2] Frederick *Independent American Volunteer,* July 8, 1807.

ampled insult to our national honor, and that we will at all times prefer prompt and decisive war, to dishonorable peace." [3]

The President, it seems, could have led the country into war at this time with hearty support from all groups. He hoped to avoid war, however, and relied upon less drastic embargo measures instead. The Federalists denounced this anti-mercantile program. A local newspaper announced in the autumn of 1808 that Taney and David Lynn, who were presidential elector candidates, would not support the candidacy of "any character favorable to embargo measures." [4]

In a long and forceful address delivered at Hagerstown a few days later Taney attacked the laying of the embargo, though not, perhaps, in the manner in which a more rabid partisan would have done it. The necessity for the embargo act, he declared, had arisen from the fact that the government had not in the beginning taken a firm stand against the French decrees affecting American shipping. Some of the provisions of the act were in any case unnecessary. There was no reason why American ships should not trade in the open ports of countries not at war or under the control of the warring powers.

Before closing his address Taney spoke on another political issue on which unfortunately he was inadequately reported. He repelled Republican charges that the Federalists wished to infringe the rights of suffrage which had been conferred by the legislation of recent years, and tried to vindicate his own illiberal conduct on these matters while a member of the legislature. [5]

Other Federalists showed no evidence of restraint in their attacks upon the methods of the administration in the conduct of foreign affairs. Timothy Pickering, Secretary of State under John Adams, and now a member of the United States Senate, flooded the country with copies of "A Letter from the Hon. Timothy Pickering, a Senator of the United States from the State of Massachusetts, exhibiting

[3] Frederick *Bartgis' Republican Gazette*, Sept. 16, 1809.
[4] Hagerstown *Maryland Herald*, Oct. 28, 1808.
[5] From a summary in the Hagerstown *Maryland Herald*, Nov. 4, 1808.

to his Constituents a View of the Imminent Danger of an Unnecessary and Ruinous War." Dr. Philip Thomas, although he had aided in the drafting of the Frederick resolutions on the *Chesapeake* affair, now engaged in circulating copies of the letter among local Republicans. He thought it might do some good among the more moderate members of that party, but that most of the members would be swayed from the policy of hostility to England only by divine interposition.[6]

Partly no doubt because of the unpopularity of the embargo, Federalists elected the Frederick County members of the legislature in 1808, with John Hanson Thomas as one of the successful candidates. He was reëlected the following year, and revealed himself as intensely pro-British in a speech of two and a half hours against resolutions approving the acts of the federal government.[7] Taney, on the other hand, refrained from participating in the process by which his close associates worked themselves into a frenzy. He did not break with them, but merely withdrew into his practice of law, for which he had all the excuse that was necessary. In one of his most important cases of the period, indeed, he acted jointly with John Hanson Thomas.[8] It was the final coming of war with England, forced on the country by a variety of circumstances, which made it necessary for Taney to make a choice between his convictions and his loyalty to the friends who had taken him in and given him position and prestige in the Federalist party.

It was Taney's disapproval of attempts of certain Federalists to circulate the pro-British *Federal Republican* resulting in the famous Baltimore riot of 1812, that first turned his old friends against him. Or, more particularly, it was the publication of a letter written by his brother, Augustus Taney, giving it as Taney's opinion that the forcible reëstablishment of the *Federal Republican* newspaper in Baltimore might legitimately result in serious criminal charges.

The rabidly partisan paper in question had been established in

---

[6] Charles W. Upham, *Life of Timothy Pickering*, IV, 133.
[7] Baltimore *Evening Post*, Jan. 3, 1810.
[8] The court-martial of James Wilkinson, in Frederick in 1811.

Baltimore in 1808 by Alexander Contee Hanson, a patrician descendant of celebrated old families, and a cousin of John Hanson Thomas. As editor-in-chief Hanson employed Jacob Wagner, who had been chief clerk under his devoted friend, that ardent Federalist Timothy Pickering. The paper's criticism of the administration was so persistent and so violent as to lead to the remark made many times that in case of war with England the Federalist paper would have to be silenced.

War with England was proclaimed June 19, 1812, and on June 20 the *Federal Republican* published an editorial entitled "Thou Hast Done a Deed Whereat Valour Will Weep." It bitterly denounced the administration and vowed to oppose the conduct of the war in every way possible. Such an article, published after the declaration of war, sounded treasonable in the ears of Republicans and loyal citizens. Two days later a mob, made up of indignant citizens and of the rougher element of what was to be known as "the mob city," completely destroyed the office of the paper.

The Federalist leaders were enraged at this interference with freedom of the press, even though it was a time of war.[9] Hanson and Wagner established their paper temporarily in Georgetown, and Hanson began gathering around him a group of hardy Federalists who would aid him in resuming publication in Baltimore. His friends cheered him on, though his cousin in Frederick had a sick wife and could not go, another friend had a cold and a headache and had to buy some cattle, and still others had other excuses.[10]

The center of recruitment was at Rockville, the county seat of Montgomery County, a few miles from Washington. Rockville was the place where Taney's young brother Augustus was making his home and practicing law. Taney was very fond of this young

---

[9] In Frederick, John Hanson Thomas, using a pen name, wrote for the *Herald* an indignant article which he suggested Hanson should have copied in other papers. "The late infamous enormities in Baltimore," he wrote to Hanson, "and the scandalous submission to the prevalence of an atrocious, damnable mob, have filled me with equal indignation and astonishment. . . . It is a most awful and fearful consideration if the press can be thus prostrated and silenced."—Thomas to Hanson, June 28, 1812, Baltimore *Federal Gazette,* Aug. 8, 1812.

[10] See the several letters published in the Baltimore *Federal Gazette,* Aug. 8, 1812.

brother, whom he had brought to this section of the state and to whom he had doubtless taught the rudiments of his profession, and although Augustus had agreed to join the Hanson expedition to Baltimore Taney advised him to stay at home. Augustus wrote Hanson a letter telling him that he could not go because his brother advised against it, and it was this letter which was later published, embarrassing the Federalists involved in the expedition and discrediting Taney in their eyes.

Young Taney wrote that he had entered with reluctance into the plan to reëstablish the paper in Baltimore by the use of such force as might be necessary. Furthermore, he had assumed that the only danger involved was the danger of injury in battle, and had not thought it possible that the defense of the paper would result in actions which would be regarded as criminal. "But upon conversing with my brother," Augustus Taney continued, "he seems clearly of opinion that to fire on the assailants before other means of putting them out of the house have been used, would be unlawful, and subject us to the punishment of manslaughter. Thus in protecting the laws we should be violating them. To wait until the mob have entered, would not do, because then numbers would overpower us; nor do I consider this a part of the plan as developed to me; besides with a Democratic judge to direct a Democratic jury, as to the law, he considers our conviction of murder as far more than probable. . . . My opinion is formed upon authorities I have looked into with my brother, and if such were not my opinion, I would not act contrary to his. . . . This will seem too much like a plan to provoke an attack, that we may take into our own hands the sword of justice, and you know that this the law will not allow." [11]

In spite of the desertions, Hanson and twenty-one other Federalists, all reputable citizens, entered Baltimore with arms and ammunition, and, under the leadership of General Henry Lee, barricaded themselves in a house in Charles Street. From this house they distributed copies of the *Federal Republican* denouncing the mayor, the police, and the people for the destruction of the Baltimore office of

[11] A. Taney to Hanson, July 24, 1812, *ibid.*

the paper. Amid great excitement a mob assembled and attacked the house. A member of the mob was killed and others were injured. The besieged party surrendered to the local authorities on promise of protection, and were taken to jail.

The jail was inadequately guarded. The mob broke in, assaulted and tortured the prisoners, and stacked the writhing bodies outside the door. General James M. Lingan, a popular Revolutionary veteran, a friend of Taney and Frank Key, was killed. General Lee was crippled for life. Hanson, pretending to be dead when tortured to discover if he still lived, slipped away into the crowd.

The brutal massacre turned the Hanson crusaders into martyrs. The Federalists, shedding tears over the fate of the much loved Lingan, shed them no less freely because they watered Federalist political prospects and cast the war party into disrepute. Political meetings were held all over the state to denounce the rioters, the suppression of free speech, and the conduct of the war, and to urge the election of Federalists to all offices. At the October elections the Federalists in Frederick County elected all candidates to the House of Delegates, and in the state as a whole they elected a majority of that body. Hanson won a seat in Congress in the election held in November.

Taney, who was also a candidate for Congress, labored under difficulties. Presumably his nomination had been decided upon before it was known how fully he disagreed with his party in its opposition to the war, or else the nomination was made in the hope of securing his support thereby. His name was announced beneath the slogan, "An Honorable Peace, Union, Free Trade." Taney and other candidates were said to be friends of peace, union, and commerce, and opposed to an unnecessary war. A saving clause was included, however, to the effect that if peace could not be obtained on honorable terms the war was to be prosecuted with foresight, energy, and vigor.[12]

Emotional scenes based on the Baltimore riot, and particularly upon "the blood of Lingan," constituted the most effective sort of

[12] Hagerstown *Gazette*, Sept. 12, 1812.

campaign material for the Federalists. Yet Taney could not well use this type of appeal, since in the investigation of the riot the letter of his brother was discovered and published. He had said that the Baltimore expedition looked too much like an attempt to provoke an attack, and that the members might be punished for murder if any of the attackers were killed. He could therefore hardly display the misfortunes of Hanson and his crowd as reasons for voting for Federalists.

The Federalist leaders gave Taney at least nominal support, and attempted to show that his brother's letter had been "perverted to an unjust and infamous purpose." [13] It was embarrassing, however, to have published an indirect statement by their candidate that the Baltimore martyrs, whose martyrdom was to bring success to the party, had been little more than criminals. Taney lost the election. He lost also the friendship of many of his former associates, including John Hanson Thomas, and incurred the enmity of Hanson and others connected with the *Federal Republican.*

Taney made matters worse by refusing to support De Witt Clinton, who, although a Democrat, had been endorsed by the Federalists as their candidate to oppose the reëlection of James Madison to the presidency. The Clinton opponents among the Federalists were called Coodies, sometimes derisively, no doubt, though not always so. The title was coined from the name of Abimelech Coody, a character created by Gulian C. Verplanck, one of Clinton's sharp-tongued enemies in New York. Abimelech Coody first came into prominence when a letter was widely published alleged to have been written by Coody, a simple shoemaker, to his congressman, to find out what he should do with a large sum of money which he had won in a lottery. He had been hopelessly bewildered by the advice of members of the opposing political parties not to trust this or that bank or enterprise because of some ludicrous danger connected with politics.

"It is thus," wrote Verplanck as anonymous publisher of the letter, "that the good sense of the real American people is blinded, while their passions are heated, till at length, almost forgetting the

---

[13] J. T. Scharf, *Chronicles of Baltimore,* p. 331.

original subject of difference, instead of one great people, united by every bond of common principle and of mutual interest, they find themselves arrayed under the banners of opposing factions, and contend with all the rancorous and deep-rooted hostility of rival nations." [14]

Opposing all demagogy as he did, Abimelech Coody became a prominent character. When Verplanck, believing Clinton to be a dangerous demagogue and disliking him for personal reasons as well, attacked Clinton as a presidential candidate, Abimelech Coody did him good service. Those who stood with him were called Coodies, and Taney, being the leader of this group in Maryland, was nicknamed King Coody. The name and the party division continued throughout the war and for a number of years thereafter. The opposition partisans were called "blue light" Federalists, because of the accusation that they aided enemy ships at night by signaling to them with blue lights.

Since much of Maryland was in the theater of war, many of the anti-war Federalists had to fight because their homes and properties were in danger. They raised troops and voted appropriations to the accompaniment of bitter denunciations of the national government which was responsible for their predicament. Among the prominent opponents of the war was Charles Carroll of Carrollton, who displayed great uneasiness as to the safety of his person and his property. Another was his son-in-law, Robert Goodloe Harper. At a dinner at Annapolis, given in honor of Alexander C. Hanson, the owner of the *Federal Republican*, Harper offered as a toast, "No *French alliance*, but a speedy termination to an unnecessary and wasteful war."

The presiding officer at the Hanson dinner was a prominent young Federalist, Virgil Maxcy, the son-in-law of John Galloway, who after this strife was over was to become one of Taney's close friends. Dur-

[14] *Letter to the Hon. Saml. L. Mitchell, M.D., Representative in Congress from the City of New-York; Professor of Natural His. &c. On the Danger of Putting Money into the U. States' and Manhattan Banks, with Sundry Novel Speculations on Insurance Stock, Domestic Manufactures, and the Best Mode of Vesting a Capital "So As to Make Both Ends Meet." By Abimelech Coody, Esq., Ladies' Shoemaker. New-York: Published at the Literary Exchange. 1811.*

ing the war Maxcy served on a resolutions committee of a local political meeting which demanded the early termination of the war, and urged the formation of corresponding committees to work for the election of persons pledged to procure "an honest peace and the restorations of the blessings of commerce." Taney's father, in the legislature, supported the attacks made by his party on the administration. Michael VI, who succeeded his father at an ensuing term, did likewise.

The *Federal Republican* had been unable to return to Baltimore, but it continued from Georgetown its attacks upon the administration and upon the conduct of the war. The Frederick *Herald,* lamenting the breaking up of homes and the destruction of property and the apparent inability of the government to develop an efficient army, indirectly advocated surrender. "Every man in his senses," it declared, "may now see how much better it is, to yield for a time to lesser evils, than to plunge desperately into unprepared and unreasonable war, regardless of the thousand fold disaster and calamity which assuredly follow. The only remaining cause for the declaration of war is the impressment of seamen, a small part of whom were American citizens; and thousands are now suffering from the evils of the war without any, even the remotest prospect, of preventing the exercise of the right of impressment in the future." [15]

This almost plaintively negative attitude lacked the vigor pleasing to the more dynamic leaders among the "blue light" Federalists. A new paper therefore, the *Plain Dealer,* to which Hanson and his cousin John Hanson Thomas contributed, was published in Frederick during the period of the war to purvey some of the spirit of the *Federal Republican.*

During the summer of 1813 Timothy Pickering, who seems to have been the political ideal of Thomas, Hanson, and other ultra-Federalists, stopped in Frederick on his way home from Washington to Massachusetts. Accompanied by Hanson, he put up at the Thomas home. A grand gathering of Federalists was held at Mrs. Kimboll's, a "kissing scene," a local opposition paper called it. Dr. Philip

[15] Frederick *Herald*, quoted, Baltimore *Federal Gazette*, May 13, 1813.

Thomas presided. Many toasts were drunk. Hanson proposed one, "Our rulers have organized falsehood into a system,—and Federalism expects every man to do his duty, without regard to clamor, cant or personal hazard." A prominent local Federalist proposed another, "Alexander Contee Hanson—The hope and ornament of Maryland." The local papers made no mention of the presence of Taney in this group of which a year or two earlier he would have been a prominent member.

While Taney remained quietly at home, critical both of his party and of the inefficient way in which the war was conducted, but saying little except to his close friends, John Hanson Thomas was chosen at the ensuing election to the House of Delegates. He went triumphantly to Annapolis to declaim against the government and preside over the "Committee on the defenseless and unprotected situation in which the state has been left by the General Government."

The conduct of the war was a lamentable performance. Ignoble failures were often to be traced partly to inefficient political and military leadership, but deeper causes lay in the fact that the country was not in sentiment organized for war, and the intense individualism of leaders and citizens prevented the necessary submergence of everything in the common cause. When the British blockaded the coast and began with small forces of men to commit depredations far inland, the emotions of the people, particularly in Maryland, were mixtures of fear for the loss of life and property, indignation at the enemy, and often greater indignation at the government which had committed the country to the war.

People along the coast often buried their valuables or shipped them to inland points. The Baltimore banks sent large quantities of specie to be stored in Frederick. The Farmers' Bank of Maryland, of the Frederick branch of which Taney was a director, closed its central house in Annapolis for a time and transacted all its business in Frederick. Quantities of material from the government archives in Washington were sent to Frederick for storage. Terrorized by the rapacious conduct of British soldiers, women fled from the danger area. When the enemy, pillaging and burning, moved up the Patuxent River, Taney's mother left Calvert County to take refuge in his home in Frederick. While there, in the latter part of 1814, she fell ill and died. To her grave in the little Catholic cemetery Taney left a beaten path when some years later he removed to Baltimore.

The defense of the country was left for the most part to the militia raised by the states, which were in many cases poorly trained and disciplined. The commanders knew little beyond the simplest military techniques, and the privates of many companies had the habit of performing chiefly when and as their moods inclined. Taney's eldest brother, Michael VI, served for a time as a private in the militia which coöperated with Commodore Barney's attempts to prevent the British from advancing up the Patuxent. When the commander, not having been paid for his services, resigned his position, Michael Taney succeeded him. He was faced with a difficult situation. The people in the community were much alarmed, he wrote to Governor Levin Winder on June 8, 1814. A British frigate with several smaller vessels was reported moving up the Patuxent in pursuit of Barney's flotilla, which had taken refuge in St. Leonard's Creek. "Your Excellency will afford us all the assistance you can or may deem necessary. Tents, camp kettles, and canteens, are very much wanting." [16]

In spite of the efforts of Taney and his regiment of Calvert County militia, the British captured and destroyed property on both sides of the Patuxent. The county was impoverished for years to come by the loss, chiefly of tobacco, which according to the *Federal Republican* would have been worth $1,500,000 if sold in Europe. Calvert Town, lying at the foot of the hill below the Taney home, was wiped out. The court house and the jail at Prince Frederick were destroyed. Finally, the enemy crowded Barney's flotilla of

---

[16] Michael Taney to Governor Levin Winder, June 8, 1814, Annapolis *Maryland Republican,* June 9, 1814.

gunboats to the point where the commander had to blow them up to prevent their capture, and a British land force which had been carried up the Patuxent unmolested set out for Washington.

Michael Taney was bitterly criticized by a prominent Republican paper for his inefficiency. "The militia," it declared, "were encamped within one and a half miles of the enemy, and every night an attack was apprehended—indeed expected. During four or five days he was in camp but once, and then in such a style as to excite nothing but laughter. Indeed had his character not been known, we should have taken him for any thing else but the commander of a regiment. Without sword, without pistols, without uniform, without everything that constitutes the equipment of a soldier or entitles him to the regard or respect of his inferiors, he seemed prepared for any thing but to fight the enemies of his country. They were frequently in the practice of landing in the very face of his troops and burning houses and destroying other property with impunity, but the Colonel was never there to meet them. He did not like the situation, the quarters were too hot for him. He preferred his mother's chimney corner to the field of battle, and felt more personal security in feeding the pigs and driving the ducks to water than in encountering the dangers in defense of his country's rights or protecting the property of his fellow citizens." [17]

The criticism is obviously biased. It may have been in part the product of personal dislike, or the reaction of party prejudice, of which it is quite typical. Nevertheless it is true that his regiment was highly ineffective. Perhaps the commander did lack military qualifications, as he seems to have lacked qualifications as a member of the legislature. He was not entirely to blame, however, for the lack of equipment and the lack of discipline and training which characterized the militia of the state. That he was discontented with what he was able to do is indicated by the fact that when in desperation the state finally made provision to establish a regular force to take the place of the militia during the emergency he begged for a

[17] Annapolis *Maryland Republican*, July 23, 1814.

position in the new organization. He was "completely sick" of his present command in the militia, he declared.[18]

As British forces penetrated inland, forebodings grew concerning the safety of Washington. The military district around Washington was placed in the command of William H. Winder, the nephew of the governor of Maryland and one of the friends of Roger Taney's years as a law student. Taney, made deeply anxious by the apathy of the people and the indolence and inefficiency of the militia, wrote to Winder, asking the latter to urge his uncle, the governor of Maryland, to go about among the people and persuade them to rally round him in the nation's defense. The capture of Washington would be most disastrous to Maryland, Taney declared, and in the present unhappy state of the public mind he doubted whether the Union would survive the shock.

Something must therefore be done to improve the attitude of the militia. If the militia were suffered to remain in their present state of apathy, evading or disregarding calls when danger was distant, and seeking safety at home when the enemy approached, there would be little hope of effectual resistance. "The two great parties who divide the country," he continued, "are too busy quarreling with one another and preparing for the ensuing elections to bestow much thought on defending the country against the common enemy. Scarcely any one marches willingly, or encourages others to march, and this state of public feeling is likely to [be] continued, unless some measures shall be taken to rouse the people, and animate them with the spirit of resistance. If those who are in authority at Washington, will give themselves a little trouble they might easily make their political friends ashamed of abandoning them in the midst of the perils, into which they have encouraged them to go." [19]

The letter expressed, either directly or by implication, the full position of the Coodies. It left aside all opinions of the President, of the Republican party, and of the merits of the war itself. These

---

[18] Michael Taney to Governor Levin Winder, Feb. 7, 1815, MS.

[19] Taney to General Winder, Aug. 4, 1814, Force transcript of W. H. Winder MSS., Library of Congress. The transcript uses the name Wilder instead of Winder—which from the context would seem to be an error.

matters were irrelevant at the moment. What was essential was that partisanship of every sort be put aside, and the people unite for the purpose of saving the Union. It was very different from the policy of persistent heckling indulged in by the "blue light" Federalists, even when for the protection of their property they had to participate in the conflict which they so bitterly denounced.

It is a matter of history that the British overcame the shamefully ineffective resistance of Winder's forces and the more stubborn resistance of a few hundred sailors under Joshua Barney, marched into Washington and desecrated the capital as fully as their imaginations showed them how.[20] The records of the event, which have been reworked by historians again and again, indicate that Winder was an incompetent commander of unorganized and untrained forces, whose defeat before British regulars was almost inevitable.

Taney was no doubt right in his belief that many men high in office shared the responsibility of failure to defend the capital. It seems, however, another example of his loyalty to his friends which led him to write to Winder's son in later years that "every one who lived at that time, and was near enough to know what was passing and who were the actors in the scenes that were passing, knew perfectly well that not the slightest blame could attach to General Winder." [21] This appraisal seems to have been correct only in the sense that men are not to blame when after doing their best they fail in positions which they are not properly equipped to fill.

Soon after the British land forces withdrew from Washington, British ships made their way up the Potomac to Alexandria, and plundered the town of tobacco and other property. It was feared that a similar marauding attack might be made on Washington and Georgetown. Frank Key lived in Georgetown and was a volunteer in the light infantry organized for local defense. Mrs. Key, in spite of the danger, refused to leave him. The Taneys and Key's parents worried about her safety, and Taney made a trip to Georgetown to persuade her to go to a place of greater safety. Fortunately, instead

[20] See Henry Adams, *History of the United States*, VIII, 146–147.
[21] Taney to William H. Winder, July 18, 1849, Winder MSS.

of attacking, the British sailed down the Potomac soon after Taney's arrival, and the danger seemed to be over.

They took with them as prisoner, however, a Dr. Beanes, who was one of Key's intimate friends. Key sent his family to Frederick in Taney's care, and set out to negotiate for his friend's release. He overtook the enemy ships and arranged successfully for the release, but the British, being at the point of attacking Baltimore, refused to permit even Key to leave until the battle was over. He was therefore on board a British vessel in sight of Fort McHenry while the fort was being bombarded.

The bombardment having ceased some time before daybreak, Key waited with deep anxiety to discover whether the fort had surrendered. Peering through his glasses as the dawn crept in, he at last discovered that the stars and stripes still fluttered above it. A little later, thrilled at the fact that the British had given up the siege, he phrased on the back of a letter part of an exuberant song about the "Star-Spangled Banner." A day or two later the song was completed and printed, and it quickly achieved the popularity of a national anthem.[22]

In spite of the reversal of British fortunes indicated by the failure to capture Baltimore, there was still ground for the fears of Taney and others that the Union would not survive after the taking of the capital. On December 15, 1814, the Hartford Convention of the New England states assembled. The discussions were carried on in secret, and the public was convinced that disunion was being plotted. Before it closed the convention made a report attacking the record of the Republicans from 1801 to date. It declared that New England was the victim of sectional misrule, and demanded the restoration of her rights and the termination of Republican abuses. It recommended secession only as a last resort, but the threat of nullification was implicity made, particularly in connection with the plan of the government to raise an army by conscription.

The report was mild as compared with the speeches of Timothy Pickering and others, but many suspicious people were convinced

[22] See Taney to Charles Howard, March 12, 1856, Tyler, *op. cit.*, pp. 109–119.

that the convention had done and said far more about secession than the report disclosed. Republicans, naturally enough, were hostile. Although a few of the ultra-Federalists of the South, like Alexander C. Hanson, were pleased with the report, the Coodies and some of the milder friends of Hanson bitterly resented the threat of New England to desert at a time when Maryland and other sections of the South were almost in the grip of the enemy. The Hartford Convention, therefore, in what it did and was suspected of doing, struck a fatal blow at the Federalist party as an organization having anything like national unity.

Early in 1815 the war blundered its way to an inglorious close, thereby removing the danger that it would result in the dissolution of the Union. The close of the war, oddly enough, was a misfortune for the Federalists then in power in Maryland, for it deprived them of their most valuable issues. Soon afterward they suffered other misfortunes and embarrassments. Prominent among them was the death of John Hanson Thomas, of Frederick, whom they had planned to send to the United States Senate. Realizing that the end was coming, Thomas disconcerted the "blue light" leaders of his party by calling Taney to his bedside and effecting a reconciliation with the king of the Coodies.

Hanson, lamenting the death of Thomas, gave evidence of his continued dislike for the Coody leader by the remark that it was "given to none to know with certainty, who may not be impelled by ambition, jealousy or envy to abandon and betray a friend." [23] The implication was that Taney had used Thomas and other friends in winning position and prestige for himself, and had then been disloyal to them in refusing to coöperate with them in their relentless opposition to the conduct of the war. It was characteristic of the group of Federalists to which he belonged that Hanson had no tolerance for political ideas or loyalties different from his own, or for the men who held them.

In the emergency created by the death of Thomas the Federalists

[23] *Federal Republican*, quoted, Annapolis *Maryland Gazette*, May 18, 1815.

shifted their support to Robert Goodloe Harper for the position in the United States Senate, and set out to secure sufficient representation in the state legislature to insure Harper's election. They had no more than committed themselves to Harper when they were disconcerted by the publication of a letter declaring that the British were right on important issues of the war. "It will be a bitter pill for Mr. Madison," Harper had written, "to acknowledge the British right of impressment, and their doctrine of perpetual allegiance; but he must swallow it. He will squall and kick and make wry faces but down it must go. The thing is right in itself, and though disgraceful to him, not in the least dishonorable to the nation." [24]

Many Federalists felt that they had already been labeled too often as disloyal, in spite of the fact that they privately agreed with Harper's sentiments, and argued that for the sake of winning the election the sentiments ought to be disavowed. Hanson, who, whatever his faults, attempted to be consistent, expressed his disgust with such a policy of temporizing. "When I first became enamored of political pursuits," he wrote to Harper, "it was my delight to contrast the public and private qualities of the individuals in general composing the two parties. I considered Federalism all that was pure, disinterested and exalted and Democracy exactly the reverse. Experience has shown me that the shades of difference between the two parties are but slight, with some few distinguished exceptions among the prominent men on both sides." [25]

The Federalists won a substantial majority in the state legislature without a disavowal of the letter on Harper's part. Some Republicans still believed, or pretended to believe, that the legislature would not choose the writer of the letter for the senatorial position. A Hagerstown Republican suggested to the Federalists that they choose "a man who is eminently worthy of your choice, a man of whom any party might be justly proud, a man who is not merely an ornament to his country, but to human nature itself, who is candid, liberal, and

[24] Harper to George Baer, Oct. 10, 1814, Annapolis *Maryland Gazette* (Extra edition), Sept. 14, 1815.
[25] Hanson to Harper, Sept. 22, 1815, copy, Virgil Maxcy MSS.

enlightened, whose presence in the Senate of the United States will never be a disgrace to Maryland, will never cause dislike, nor suspicion, even among those who may be opposed to him in some leading points. But after this short description I need scarcely name him. Some of you must already have recognized him to be no other than Roger B. Taney, of Frederick." [26]

Like most recommendations from the camp of the enemy, this one received little attention from the Federalists. The man upon whom they conferred distinction would not be the leader of the hated Coodies. The Federalists in the legislature took orders from the party caucus, and elected Harper.

In one respect luck had been against the Federalists in state politics. The state Senate had been chosen in 1811 before the issues of the war became dominant, the Republicans had won a majority of the electors, and as a result the entire membership of the Senate was Republican. That body had therefore been in a position throughout the war to defeat exclusively partisan measures of the Federalist House of Delegates and to force compromises. A new membership was to be chosen in the autumn of 1816. The Federalists were eager at this time to capture the Senate for themselves, since at best they would then be able to dominate the legislature without restraint from the Republicans, and at the worst they would control the upper house of the legislature for the period of five years.

So important was the winning of this election that the Federalists resorted to various types of strategy and compromises in the struggle. For instance, it was certain that there would be an evenly matched battle over the one elector to be chosen by the city of Annapolis, which by a small majority was normally Republican. Six months residence was necessary for voting in any locality. About the first of March the people of Annapolis were surprised to discover some forty persons at the taverns of the city, mostly laborers, who claimed to be in search of work. Although no work was found, they continued to dwell contentedly in the taverns. Republican leaders grew suspicious, investigated, and discovered that Federalists had

[26] Hagerstown *Maryland Herald,* Nov. 15, 1815.

hired the men for twenty dollars a month and board to establish residence in Annapolis and vote the Federalist ticket. The exposure of the plan stirred such indignation that the men were discharged.[27]

Another interesting bit of strategy was connected with raising funds for the campaign. Some Baltimore merchants wished the federal government to send William Pinkney to Naples to negotiate for compensation for property seized some years earlier. A Federalist member of the United States Senate for a time held up the confirmation of the Pinkney appointment, but later permitted it to go through. The explanation was said to lie in a promise made by the Baltimore merchants that if the mission was provided for there would be funds for the state election. Otherwise there would be none.[28]

A compromise of another sort was forced upon the leaders of the Federalists. If they were to be sure of winning the election it was important that the breach in the ranks of the party should be closed. The dissent of the Coodies, even though they constituted a minority, might bring defeat. The restoration of harmony seemed feasible, since the termination of the war had removed the issues on which the party had divided. The barrier to unity of action, if any, lay now not in issues but in personalities, in the personal bitterness and antagonism stirred by the conflict.

The details of the restoration of outer harmony did not find their way into permanent records. The results, however, indicate that the Coodies exacted a high price for their support of the party ticket. They forced the nomination of a number of candidates whose sympathies had been with the Coodies more than with their opponents. This was true, for instance, in the choice of party candidates for the House of Delegates from Frederick County, where at least two of

---

[27] J. B. McMaster, *History of the People of the United States*, IV, 367.

[28] See Christopher Gore to Rufus King, Oct. 9, 1816, King MSS., New York Historical Society. The details of such transactions are seldom available for examination, and only a few are available here. It seems that Robert Oliver, a wealthy merchant, had bought up for a trifle some millions of dollars in claims for damages against Naples, and had offered Pinkney an enormous fee to collect for him. Senator Robert H. Goldsborough apparently changed his position, under pressure from Oliver, and Oliver presumably underwrote the Federalist campaign expenses. Pinkney failed to collect, and the scandal caused Oliver much irritation and embarrassment.—See A. C. Hanson to Rufus King, Sept. 8, 1818, King MSS.

the four, young Richard Potts and Ignatius Davis, seem to have been friendly to the Coodies. It is to be presumed that Taney, who worked in the inner councils, was in no small part responsible for their choice. He probably had at least no objection to another of the four, his uncle, Joseph Taney, who had served in the legislature during the two preceding terms.

The party leaders paid an additional price for party harmony, in the nomination of King Coody himself for the position of senatorial elector, along with John Grahame, who was at least friendly to the Coodies. The electors themselves, of course, did not automatically become senators, but merely elected the senators. The leaders, even though they had had experience with Taney as a political manipulator behind the scenes, presumably had no conception of the concession they were making when they accepted him as a candidate.

At the September election substantially more than half of the senatorial electors chosen were Federalists. All of the senators would therefore be chosen from the majority party. "The Battle of Waterloo," declared an exuberant correspondent, "was not more important in Europe, than the last election to the state of Maryland. Proud is the small state of Maryland of the right which nature has given her; she disdains to be governed by a mob, and all the money of Baltimore, cannot induce the good citizens of Maryland to continue in bondage; we shall have in the next representation a Senate of fifteen Federal members, not one of James Madison's men on the floor for the next five years." [29]

Having won a victory over the Republicans, the Federalist leaders attempted to limit the concessions they had made to the Coody faction by working for the choice of senators from within their own ranks. Taney and other Coodies had been among the victorious candidates for the positions of electors, however, and they refused to be mere rubber stamps for the men by whom they had been maligned through the years of the war. They insisted on the choice of a certain number of senators from their own group. They proved success-

[29] *Poulson's American Daily Advertiser,* quoted, Baltimore *Federal Republican,* Sept. 11, 1816.

ful strategists, and when the party slate of senators was announced the names of Taney himself and certain of his friends were on the list. He had been made an elector by the votes of the people, and his fellow electors had made him a senator.

Having consolidated their victory in the choice of a number of senators, the Coodies now carried factional warfare into the campaign for the election of members of the House of Delegates which was to be held during the following month. Their opponents had reluctantly consented to the nomination of Richard Potts, son of the late Judge Richard Potts, in Frederick County, but thereafter a number of them withdrew their support from him. The Coodies engineered his election in spite of the opposition.

The Coodies themselves attacked and set out to defeat their most bitter enemy, who was a party nominee in Montgomery County. The war being over, Alexander C. Hanson arranged to reëstablish his paper in a more profitable location in Baltimore, after having published it in Georgetown since the summer of 1812. To keep in politics and to add to the influence of his paper he sought election to the House of Delegates, and sought and received the nomination of the party in Montgomery County. Since the Coodies were not strong enough to prevent the nomination there was no reason for believing that they could elect a candidate of their own on an independent ticket. They determined to throw the election to the Republican nominee, however, rather than permit Hanson to win. They therefore nominated another candidate, divided the Federalist vote, and brought about the election of Hanson's Republican opponent. Augustus Taney, doubtless encouraged by his brother, was one of the Coody leaders who successfully plotted Hanson's defeat.[30]

[30] Writing anonymously in the third person as "A Faithful Federalist," Hanson denounced the scheme: "You all know that the opposition to Mr. Hanson was got up by young lawyer Taney, the brother of the electoral candidate in Frederick County. You know also, for you have it from his own hand published four years ago in mob times, that this young gentleman never acts contrary to the opinion and advice of his brother. Know then that I have seen a certificate in Mr. Hanson's possession, signed by Mr. G. Gaither, that young *Taney*, who leads the *Federal* opposition declared, 'it would be proper now and then to let a Democrat be elected in Federal counties.' After this, can you any longer doubt, or hesitate to give a name to the designs of these men, who have combined with the Democrats?"—A pamphlet attributed to Hanson, Annapolis *Maryland Republican*, Sept. 14, 1816.

Factional strife continued among the Federalists during the ensuing term of the legislature. Since Hanson had been foiled in his attempt to secure a seat in the legislature, an arrangement was made whereby Robert Goodloe Harper should resign from the United States Senate, and Hanson should be chosen to take his place. When the notice of Harper's resignation was received Taney began lining up members of both houses to support his friend General William H. Winder for the vacancy, hoping doubtless to serve a friend and strike a blow at an enemy at the same time. He got a majority of the Senate votes for Winder, and thought he had a sufficient number of votes in the lower house to ensure Winder's election. He lost the support of some of the men on whom he had counted, however, and Hanson won by a majority of seven. There was only limited consolation in the fact that he was able soon afterward to bring about Winder's election to a vacancy in the state Senate.[31]

Nothing which Taney had previously done had enraged the Hanson Federalists more than his successful attempt to block the removal from office of a large number of Republican judges. Because their own party controlled the Senate these judges had been safe hitherto, even though the Federalists had been dominant in the House of Delegates. Now that they had a majority in both houses the Federalists were eager to clear out the positions which in their estimation had become political nests for incompetent Republicans, and to fill them with Federalists. The governor and council, by whom judicial appointments were made, were Hansonians. Taney knew that if the Republican judges were removed at this time the offices would be filled with members of the opposing faction. Either because he preferred to favor Republicans rather than his enemies within his own party, or because he hoped at a later date to be able to fill the places with Coodies, Taney organized enough of an opposition to block the movement, justifying his action on the ground that the Federalists had always stood for the independence of the judiciary. He won thereby a victory which was quite as important as

[31] Taney to W. H. Winder (Jr.), Dec. 21, 1848, Winder MSS.

his previous defeat in connection with the election of Hanson to the United States Senate.

"He furiously opposed a reform of the judiciary," raged a Hansonite paper, the *Star of Federalism*, "because he himself will not be eligible as a judge for five years, and because none of his friends, unless it be a few honest Democrats, could get on the bench. This gives us the sum total of Mr. Taney's honesty and moderation as a politician. Self interest, malice, revenge are what he seeks to gratify at the expense of the character and welfare of the party to which he hypocritically professes still to belong. How he can belong to a party which he always opposes, and has acted with on no occasion of notoriety for the last six years, we are at a loss to comprehend." [32]

Both in the strategy connected with popular elections and in the strategy of legislative manipulation Taney had now demonstrated his ability to hold his own against his Federalist enemies. Another test was yet to be met. Shortly after the beginning of the legislative term which took him away from home for a number of weeks, friends of Hanson established the *Star of Federalism* in Frederick, one of the principal aims of which seems to have been to malign and discredit the Coodies in general and their leader in particular. It began its career with the promise to "untie the mystical knot of knavery" and expose the "consummate craft and dark dissimulation" used by Taney and his friends to prostrate the Hanson faction.[33]

So malignant and so relentless were the attacks made upon him that Taney violated a rule to which he adhered most of his life, and answered them publicly. Upon his return to Frederick he published a twelve-page defense which he called "An Address to the People of Frederick County," in which, using all the techniques of democratic appeal, he roundly denounced his enemies. He was appealing to the people, he declared, not for votes but in defense of his reputation which had been foully traduced. Summarizing the story of the series of attacks made upon him, he told why he had been so victimized:

"It is because when I was a private citizen, I could not be made

[32] *Star of Federalism*, Feb. 15, 1817, quoted, Frederick *Herald*, April 19, 1817.
[33] *Star of Federalism*, quoted, Frederick *Political Examiner*, Dec. 18, 1816.

to flatter and fawn and play the sycophant to those who fancied they had the power to dictate to the people. It is because I would not coöperate in measures that in my conscience I believed to be wrong. It is because I have asserted the rights of a freemen, and been always prepared to resist dictation from whatever quarter it might come. It is because I dared to accept a nomination, which another had expected and was eager to obtain. It is because I dared to accept a seat in the Senate when others were rejected who were anxious to get there. In short it is because I dared to obtain the confidence of the people without having first obtained the permission of a few men who claim the right to rule freemen. . . .

"It was my conduct as an elector that roused up all this increased malignity. I would not in the electoral college be made the instrument of their ambition. I would not suffer them to govern and control me in choosing the Senate. I preferred the public good, to the favor of these men. This is my great offense in their eyes. If, in electing the Senate, I had assisted the ambitious views of these men and endeavored to put all power in their hands; then I should have been as much praised by them as I am now abused. . . .

"I address you to bring before you the conduct and views of these men who have established here 'The Star of Federalism.' I address you to warn you of their designs; to guard you against the mischief they wish to accomplish. What they are now doing to me they would do to any one of you who stood in the way of their insatiable ambition and thus roused their malignity. It is the spirit of independence which they are endeavoring to overthrow and crush. They wish to make the people the mere instruments of their power and to rule you at their will. And money, violence, noise and slander, are the weapons by which they hope to effectuate their purposes.

"For my own part I hold in utter disdain the slanderers and their slander. I disregard the efforts of the whole band of conspirators with all the yelpers who follow at their heels. . . . They will find that wealth, rudeness, noise, violence and slander combined together cannot awe you into submission. They will find that you still dare, to elect and reject whom you please without asking the permission or fearing the resentment of those who wish to be dictators." [34]

The address had its sequel some weeks later when several hundred Federalists from all parts of the county assembled in Frederick to decide whether they would support one faction or the other, or merely make a futile recommendation of harmony. Taney and his friends were victorious, and secured an overwhelming endorsement of their program, including a resolution in favor of the independence of the judiciary.[35]

Taney played a leading part in the selection of candidates for the House of Delegates for the following year. He vetoed the nomination of the one Hansonian who had been elected from Frederick County the preceding year. Republicans, making the most of the strife in the camp of the enemy, joined the Hansonians in denouncing this act of the Coody leader. Taney's reason for denouncing the Hansonians as a band of conspirators, it was said, was the fact that they revered the memory of a successful rival. The vengeance which Taney could not wreak on his rival was hurled at his rival's admirers. "Such," it was scornfully declared, "is the man who assumes to govern this county and the state. Unknown in the political world until the kindness of friends (whom he betrayed), and fortuitous circumstances thrust him forward, like the scorpion which had been nurtured by the fireside of his benefactor during the winter, and turned his sting on him in the spring, Mr. Taney has no sooner grown into greatness by the fostering care of friends, than he sets to undermining their reputations and destroying their political existence. And all the while he has as many smiles, and bows, and apish tricks as a Frenchman. 'A man may smile and smile and be,'—what Mr. Taney is." [36]

In directing the political campaign Taney frequently met his fellow workers at the office of the Frederick *Herald*, which now gave him full support. The enemy declared that the king of the Coodies

[34] R. B. Taney, *An Address to the People of Frederick County,* Feb. 27, 1817.
[35] Frederick *Herald*, April 19, 1817.
[36] "Cato," Frederick *Political Examiner*, Sept. 21, 1817.

held his court there each day. His prime minister and menials were said to be wholly submissive to his demands. Royalty was exhibited in miniature. It was thought, however, that the court would adjourn *sine die* on the first Monday in October—the day of the election.[37]

The prediction came near to being correct, for the kingdom of King Coody was about to be dissolved. The Federalists elected only one of the four delegates from Frederick County. True, the party had a majority in the state as a whole, and this time the Hansonites, or "Big Bugs," as they were often called by the Coodies, were ousted from the governor's council, but the prospects for the future looked gloomy. With the disappearance of the party as a national organization it was increasingly difficult to maintain it in the state. Furthermore, the Coodies had outmaneuvered the enemy within the party, but they were unable to maintain control and effect a reconciliation at the same time. In 1818 they placed on the Frederick County ticket the name of the man whom they had rejected the preceding year, but in spite of this concession they were decisively defeated in the county; and in the state as a whole the Republicans elected ten more delegates than the Federalists. It was only by virtue of the unanimous vote of the Federalist Senate on the joint ballot that they were able to choose the governor.

After 1818 Federalist representation in the House of Delegates dropped year by year to an increasingly insignificant minority, and by the end of Taney's term in the Senate the party organization was virtually a thing of the past. King Coody and his subjects, and their Big Bug enemies, had to seek new alignments. It remained to be seen whether the new alignments would be made in terms of vital public issues, or of the personalities of leaders, or of the interests of squabbling factions.

Taney's experiences in connection with the Federalist schism indicated that he had grown or changed a great deal since the time when

---

[37] The following advertisement was published by the enemy: "*Wanted*, about fifty horses, mules or *asses*, to send on electioneering expresses. None but such as are perfectly tame and submissive, will be employed. If they are given to kicking up, they will not be received on any account. Apply to KING COODY."—Frederick *Political Examiner*, Oct. 1, 1817.

his father and his friends had forced his election to the House of Delegates upon voters who were at least not more than passively interested in him. He had been largely content with the system then, and had been content to carry out the will of the dominant people of his community. In 1812, however, although the ties of blood and friendship, and to an extent the ties of class, linked him to the Federalist leaders who were bitter enemies of the war, he refused to permit these ties to bind him. In so doing he made himself exceedingly unpopular with his associates of the preceding decade, he ruined his immediate chances for political advancement; and his professional opportunities, improving though they were, were doubtless adversely affected by his defiance of men of property and influence.

It is significant of his capacity as a political leader that he was able to build up a following strong enough ultimately to seize control of the party from the hands of the men whom he had defied. He did it in part, no doubt, through the warmth of his personality, through skillful maneuvering in conference, and through a type of appeal to the people which was more characteristic of the party of Thomas Jefferson than of that to which he belonged. His "Address to the People of Frederick County," in so far as it stresses his reliance on the judgment of the people, sounds so clearly the keynote of the new party of which he was ultimately to be a member—the party of Andrew Jackson—as to seem like a product of Old Hickory himself.

It is not to be assumed, on the other hand, that Taney had made a complete break with the past. For some years the Federalist party had been becoming more and more obviously the party of New England and of the merchant and shipping class in other parts of the country. The opposition to the War of 1812 came predominantly from these interests. Between these interests and those of the planter community from which Taney came there was traditional rivalry, and, to a degree, enmity. It is therefore not greatly surprising that, amid the excitement of the merchants and those allied with them over the damage done to them by the war, he remained comparatively calm. No great class indignation stirred him to aid in their vindictive opposition to the acts of the government. Even the continuation of the Federalist party was a matter of no great importance to him if it was to act as the tool of a hostile interest. It was therefore, it seems, with some equanimity that he watched its gradual dissolution, expecting to realign himself with some organization more clearly representative of the interests which he had at heart.

CHAPTER V

PROBLEMS OF LOCAL STATESMANSHIP

IMPORTANT as it was in Taney's career, the struggle between the two factions of the Federalist party provided only one significant aspect of his experience during the years from 1816 to 1821 when he was a member of the Maryland Senate. Few periods in the history of the state ever offered better opportunities for reflection, experimentation, and growth in connection with significant problems of statesmanship. For many years the threat of war, and then the war itself, had provoked the concentration of interest on foreign affairs. The termination of the war and the disappearance of the prospect of further international conflict made it possible to give attention to problems more definitely local. Some of them, such as those having to do with negroes, both free and slave, had come about by a slow process of evolution. Others, including banking and currency problems, had been rendered more complex by the financial stress created by the war. His work in connection with both these types of problems aided greatly in educating Taney for his subsequent responsibilities as an officer of the federal government.

The conditions of banking and the nature of the currency in circulation had been in process of change ever since the time of the formation of the federal government. The people were novices in their attempts to keep the banks stable and safe, and the currency sound. Much of the paper money issued during the Revolution depreciated hopelessly, causing losses to everybody except shrewd speculators. For many years thereafter no type of paper was issued which was accepted generally at its face value throughout the United States. Much of the currency with which Taney was familiar in his boyhood days was in the form of warehouse receipts which were issued by private individuals or firms on the basis of tobacco deposited. When he went to Dickinson College, in 1792, there was no type of currency in circulation in Calvert County, either private, state, or national, which would have been acceptable in the central part of the adjoining state. He had to take specie instead, presumably in the form of Spanish coins.

When in 1789 the new Constitution became the supreme law of the land the country had only three banks. The first Bank of the United States, established largely as the result of the efforts of Alexander Hamilton, provided much needed banking facilities, and its notes provided a certain amount of relatively sound currency during the twenty years for which it was chartered. The national institution supplied by no means all banking and currency needs, however, and in the several states new local banks were established from time to time, with power to make discounts and to issue notes to circulate as money. The notes of the strong state banks circulated at or near their face value in the area in which they were located, and at various degrees of depreciation elsewhere.

Taney grew up at a time when the banking system, or systems, of his state and of the country were in their adolescence. He saw the first Maryland banks established by mercantile interests in the mercantile center of Baltimore. He doubtless shared in the beliefs of other rural Marylanders that the Baltimore bankers controlled credit for the benefit of local interests, and sympathized with the struggles of the farmers to secure from the legislature charters for banks in the smaller towns of the state. In 1807 he was one of five persons in Frederick who were chosen to sell in that place one thousand shares in a newly established bank in Hagerstown.

In the same year the Farmers' Bank of Maryland, which had been established at Annapolis for the benefit of farmers in spite of the opposition from Baltimore, opened a branch in Frederick. A local paper announced ungrammatically, "For the accommodation of those who have business to transact with the *Farmers' Bank of Maryland*, is opened in the upper story of the new brick house now occupied by *Roger B. Taney, Esq.* as an office, three doors south of the post office." [1] Taney served as a director of this Frederick branch from 1810 to 1815, years which included the trying period of the war with England.

The charter of the first Bank of the United States expired in 1811. Hostile interests were strong enough to prevent its renewal, leaving the state banks in control of the field. These banks proved inadequate for the needs of the country during the war period. When, in the state of panic which followed the capture of Washington, the people began to withdraw and hoard their gold and silver the banks were forced to suspend specie payments, whereupon their irredeemable paper, together with the paper issued by other corporations and individuals, made up the circulatory medium. The banks in many instances found it more profitable to do business with currency of fluctuating value than to return to a specie basis, and their influence was so great that the state governments proved unable to compel them to redeem their notes in specie.

The federal government itself was much embarrassed by the situation, since a great deal of the gold and silver which it owned was tied up in the banks. In the collection of taxes it had to accept notes of state banks in spite of their irredeemable and depreciated quality, since there was no better type of money to be had. Reluctantly the Republican Congress provided in 1816 for the creation of a second Bank of the United States, in the hope that it would provide a sound currency acceptable everywhere, and that it would aid in the difficult task of transferring funds from point to point. The project was so popular in Maryland that the state provided approximately half the subscribers to the stock of the bank, though its percentage of the total amount subscribed was much less. [2]

It took time to establish the bank, however, and the government needed sound money at once. Furthermore, there was doubt as to whether the national bank could perform the functions expected of it unless the state banks were forced to release specie through the redemption of their notes. Congress therefore provided by joint resolu-

---

[1] Frederick *Republican Advocate*, March 6, 1807.
[2] J. B. McMaster, *History of the People of the United States*, IV, 313.

tion that after February 20, 1817, all payments to the government must be made in coin, in Treasury notes, in notes of the Bank of the United States, or in the notes of state banks which on demand made specie payments. It was recognized that most of the people could not meet taxes and other obligations in specie unless the state banks released it, but it was the hope of Congress that the measure would force these banks to resume payments.

Taney seems to have favored the early resumption of specie payments and the establishment of the Bank of the United States, but, devoted as he was to the interests of the farmers, he disliked the coercion of banks by the indirect means of trying to get tax money from the farmers in specie which they did not possess. According to a hostile newspaper he played up the issue during his campaign for the position of presidential elector in 1816.

"Mr. Thompson, in his paper,[3] and Mr. Taney, from the stump, informed the farmers that their houses and lands were to be knocked off by the auctioneer to satisfy the rapacity of the government; specie, specie, must be paid to the collector, to obtain which property was to be sacrificed, and farmers turned houseless from their doors. There was only one way to prevent these mischiefs—*elect Mr. Taney and his friends*—they would make the government tremble and compel it to receive rags for taxes."[4]

Fortunately, because of the pressure of government debtors and of public opinion in general, and the threat of the government to refuse their notes, the state banks capitulated and began at least nominally to redeem them. Taxpayers and debtors were therefore able to meet their obligations in the type of currency to which they were accustomed.

The people of the rural districts and small towns, however, were still in difficulties from lack of adequate banking accommodations. They demanded, therefore, the creation of more local banks. Taney joined in the movement, and during his second year in the Senate aided in securing a charter for the Frederick County Bank, which

[3] The Frederick *Herald*.
[4] Frederick *Political Examiner*, Sept. 24, 1817.

was to be established with a capital of $500,000. Four other new banks were chartered at the same time.[5] The result was doubtless to aid somewhat the cause of those who sought "easy money," who hoped to improve the condition of debtors by depreciating the entire circulatory medium. In view of Taney's firm belief in sound money, however, which was to be disclosed in later years, it seems probable that he was interested not in depreciation but in protecting farmers and inland business men against the mercantile interests of Baltimore who had been the traditional rivals of the planter class to which he belonged.

Even the establishment of additional banks did not give all the protection needed against Baltimore. The balance of trade was against the rural areas. The notes of the rural banks therefore drifted toward Baltimore for payment for excess purchases. Brokers and speculators found ways of depreciating these notes on the exchange even though issued by thoroughly sound banks, after which they presented the notes to the banks of issue and demanded and received specie for them at their face value. The rural people who expended these notes, therefore, paid tribute to the speculators to the amount of the depreciation.

Taney tried to eliminate this evil, and also the evils resulting from the circulation of notes of banks of doubtful safety, by introducing in the Senate a bill entitled "An act to prevent the passing of bank notes within the state at a rate below their nominal value." [6] It provided that persons passing notes at less than their face value should pay treble the amount involved, one half to go to the informer and the other half to the state. It was intended that the notes of sound banks should circulate at par, while those of banks of questionable solvency would be driven out of circulation.

The bill stirred heavy opposition. The brokerage business as then conducted would hardly have survived such an attack. This might have been no deterrent from Taney's point of view, but the business was linked with important financial interests which objected. There

[5] Frederick *Political Examiner,* Sept. 24, 1817.
[6] See a copy of the bill, *ibid.,* Jan. 6, 1819.

were probably objections from weak banks, too, which preferred to have their notes circulate at depreciated figures rather than not circulate at all. Furthermore, the bill was somewhat paternal in character, protecting the people from the ingenuity of sharp traders. It was out of harmony with the belief that a man had only himself to blame if he were worsted in a business deal.

In spite of these and other objections Taney was able to get the bill through the Senate. Such an interference with a popular form of gambling was too severe for the House of Delegates, however, and when the sponsors refused to accept devitalizing amendments it was voted down, to the accompaniment of ridicule from both political parties. Later in the session a somewhat emasculated form of the bill was passed by both houses as "An act to relieve the people of this state, as far as practicable, from the evils arising from the demands made on the banks of this state for gold and silver by brokers, and to prohibit the officers of the different banks from buying and selling the notes of the banks of this state at a less price than their nominal value."

In supporting another ill-fated bill, "to regulate the several incorporated banks in this state," Taney introduced an amendment providing that all bank charters previously granted should be modified to harmonize with the provisions of the act. It was a coincidence, of course, that twelve days later Chief Justice Marshall stamped such legislation as unconstitutional by holding that a charter was a contract which a state might not impair.[7]

The circulation of large quantities of paper money of amounts of less than one dollar provided varied abuses. Along with many other citizens of Frederick, Taney objected to it. He introduced a bill to prohibit the circulation of such notes in the state. He was defeated, but his action was indicative of the distrust of paper money which characterized him in later years. He was apparently hostile to any kind of money which fluctuated in value and made it possible for adventurers to take advantage of the people. At the last session of his five-year term in the Senate he proposed the abolition of all notes

[7] *Dartmouth College* v. *Woodward*, 4 Wheaton 518 (1819).

for circulation of amounts less than five dollars, and of denominations between five and ten dollars. He failed again, but his effort provided another illustration of the same attitude. Throughout this period, both in the Senate and as a director of the Frederick County Bank, to which position he was chosen as soon as it was established, he was active in his efforts to solve the money and banking problems of the state.

The downward sweep of the business cycle which occurred during this period added to the complexity of legislative tasks. Much temporary legislation was necessary, such as that staying executions and protecting insolvent debtors. No more at this time than at any other did Taney reveal himself as a fanatical friend of the debtor class, but he did show liberal tendencies to the extent of supporting legislation to discourage imprisonment for debt by making creditors responsible for the support of persons so imprisoned.[8]

It was these same conditions of financial crisis which revealed the fact that the Bank of the United States, which was supposed to add to the soundness of the currency and check speculative abuses on the part of the state banks, might be so managed as to constitute as much of a menace as a benefit to the country. Instead of acting conservatively, and coercing state banks into doing likewise by refusing to accept their notes or calling on them for specie when they expanded too rapidly, the national bank began its career by lending too heavily itself. When the depression came it had speedily to contract its loans. In doing so it had to call on state banks, which were already embarrassed, for the redemption of their notes. It thereby speeded the failure of some of these banks, perhaps caused the failure of others which might otherwise have survived, and made trouble for some which did not fail.

The Bank of the United States therefore provided a focal point for the wrath of distressed people and distressed state banks. This sentiment resulted, in a number of states, in legislation hostile to the bank and to its branches. The Maryland legislature passed an act to discourage the business of the Baltimore branch by requiring it to pay a

[8] See the Hagerstown *Maryland Herald*, Feb. 20, 1821.

tax on its notes or to pay an annual lump sum to the state. Taney, not yet ready to join the enemies of the bank, voted against the measure. Presumably he still regarded the bank as the defender of the people against the irresponsible conduct of the more powerful state banks, and as the source of a currency sounder than that which the state banks could provide. It is possible that he believed the Maryland law to be unconstitutional, as the Supreme Court was to hold a year later through the opinion of Chief Justice Marshall,[9] but probably he was thinking in terms of policy rather than constitutionality.

The conduct of the bank was such, however, that Taney ultimately turned against it, and became one of its most bitter enemies. Certain of the abuses of which he disapproved occurred during this period, in connection with the branch of the bank which had been established in Baltimore. The president and the cashier of the Baltimore branch, and a member of the board of directors of the parent bank, so manipulated a huge block of stock as to be able to borrow on it from the parent bank and other sources an amount far greater than its par value. They were able to conceal their activities until hard times forced a sharp decline in the value of the stock. Then certain Baltimore citizens who were members of the parent board demanded an investigation, and the trickery of the officers was discovered.

The managers of the parent bank were in a quandary, fearing that if the abuses of the Baltimore officers were made known the safety of the bank might be endangered. They kept the matter secret for a time, and demanded that the culprits find security for their good conduct, the two officials continuing in the meantime in their positions with the Baltimore branch. So it was that James W. McCulloch, the cashier, acting as if still in good standing with the institution which he had virtually robbed, went about persuading sixteen Baltimore merchants to become his security for $12,500 each. When he presented the security to the bank the directors assumed that they were now protected to a substantial amount from losses due to his past misconduct, and promptly discharged him.

Some time later a demand was made on McCulloch for part of the

[9] *McCulloch* v. *Maryland*, 4 Wheaton 316 (1819).

debt which he owed to the bank. He was unable to pay. Payment was then demanded of Solomon Etting, a prominent Jewish merchant of Baltimore, who had endorsed a security bond. Etting indignantly refused to pay, declaring that the bank had voided the contract by concealing the fact of McCulloch's fraudulent conduct until the security was provided. The bank brought suit against Etting in a lower federal court, and won its case. Etting then appealed the case to the Supreme Court of the United States, with Taney and Daniel Webster as his counsel.

The members of the court looked forward to the argument. "Hitherto we have had but little of that refreshing eloquence which makes the labors of the law light," wrote Justice Story; "but a cause is just rising, which bids fair to engage us all in the best manner. It is a great question of legal morality, which, after all, is very sound morality. Webster, Wirt, Taney (a man of fine talents, whom you have not probably heard of), and Emmet, are the combatants, and a bevy of ladies are the promised and brilliant distributors of the prizes." [10]

Webster and Taney sought to prove that by keeping McCulloch in office while he sought security the bank had suppressed facts material to the contract, even though Etting had not made inquiry at the bank as to the cashier's character. "It was a positive deceit by acts though not by words," they declared. ". . . It was a case of industrious concealment. By continuing the cashier in office, the defendants in error gave him a fictitious credit which they knew did not belong to him. It was analogous to the ordinary case of fraudulent misrepresentation of the credit of another. It had been said there was no inquiry. Why was there none? Because the very continuance of the officer in office was evidence that they thought him honest." [11]

The judges divided equally on the legal question involved. It was for this reason that the decision of the court below was affirmed, rather than because of the opinion expressed by Chief Justice Mar-

[10] Joseph Story to Samuel P. P. Fay, March 8, 1826, in W. W. Story (ed.), *Life and Letters of Joseph Story*, I, 493.

[11] Reporter's summary, 11 Wheaton 67.

shall, a devoted friend of the bank, that those who had acted for the bank could not have contemplated anything legally or morally wrong, and that their names could never be connected with actual fraud.[12] Quite possibly it was with this uniquely prejudiced opinion on the part of the Chief Justice that Taney began to question the soundness of the decisions of the court with respect to the bank.

Apparently it had been agreed by the parties that if the judgment resulted from an even division of the court it should not be enforced until another case had been tried in Baltimore before a jury. Another case was tried in a lower court, and the bank was again the victor. Preparations were being made for argument of an appeal before the Supreme Court when the parties finally compromised for less than half the amount claimed by the bank.

The controversy, which dragged along until 1830, put the bank in a light anything but favorable with Taney. The issue was, as Justice Story had put it, one of legal morality. And, in spite of the whitewashing comments of Chief Justice Marshall, it is clear that the bank had engaged in sharp practice in retaining McCulloch temporarily as if he still were a bona fide cashier while he persuaded unsuspicious individuals virtually to underwrite his obligations. The only justification for its conduct lay in the belief that an immediate disclosure of what amounted to defalcations by officers of the bank would destroy the bank and injure the public. Such an argument was not a high recommendation for the judgment and integrity of the most powerful banking institution in the country, which had been set up in part to coerce smaller institutions into treading the straight and narrow path.

The scandals connected with the institution led to the transfer of both the parent bank and the Baltimore branch to other hands. The men in power in Baltimore thereafter were Robert Oliver, his son-in-law R. L. Colt, John McKim, William Patterson, and others. They were shrewd financiers who were perhaps less likely to make way with the funds of the bank than their predecessors. They were not likely to use it as an agent of mercy, however, or broadly for the

[12] *Etting* v. *Bank of the United States,* 11 Wheaton 59 (1826).

public good, if they saw other ways of making more money either for the bank or for themselves.[13] They were of the money-minded mercantile class, with narrow conceptions of social interest, which had been the traditional rival or enemy of the planter class from which Taney had come. This fact presumably provided an additional reason for Taney's growing dislike for the bank.

At no time had he desired that state banks, with which he had been connected for many years, should be placed at the mercy of an irresponsible national institution. Presumably he had hoped for healthful regulation, but for nothing more. After his removal to Baltimore, in 1823, he had occasion to observe the conduct of the Bank of the United States on many occasions. Some of them involved its relations with the Union Bank of Baltimore, for which Taney argued many cases. The president of the Union Bank, Thomas Ellicott, a shrewd and ambitious Quaker, became his close friend. Before the selection of Nicholas Biddle as president of the Bank of the United States Ellicott had been discussed in Baltimore as a candidate for that office. When the position was conferred on another man he gave all his energies to the Union Bank, which on a small scale was a rival of the larger institution. His own hostility to the national bank, whether or not it was wholly justified, doubtless aided in persuading Taney that the Bank of the United States was a dangerous institution whose wings needed to be clipped. The clipping process, in which under the Jackson administration he was to participate, was to be a dramatic affair, with lasting significance both in Taney's life and in the history of the country.

During the years when Taney was a member of the Maryland Senate the state was in a turmoil over problems very different from

[13] Oliver, for instance, who was a wealthy man for his time, was in 1818 characterized by Alexander C. Hanson as follows: "He will do anything for money and has become the veriest Jew and Shylock on our exchange. Having abandoned commerce and turned broker and shaver, his income, in this way, owing to the great distress which the operations of the new bank has occasioned all classes, has become enormous. His gains are never below twenty per cent and often exceed it, and $500,000 employed in this way yield him more than he knows what to deal with. He is far from the man he has long passed for at home and abroad."—Hanson to Rufus King, Sept. 9, 1818, King MSS.

those of currency and credit, problems having to do with the several thousands of negroes, both freemen and slaves, who lived in the state. Slavery, though sanctified by many generations of acceptance, was a perennial cause of worry and discontent. There were people who questioned whether in the long run it was economically profitable for the state, and there were many more who regarded it as a sinful institution which ought to be abolished whether it was profitable or not. Both abolitionists and slave owners agreed that the presence of free negroes within a society of white people, where other negroes were held as slaves, constituted a menace to public well-being.

Many years of discussion of the problem of the free negro culminated in the latter part of 1816 in the organization of "The American Society for the Colonization of Free People of Color of the United States," which labored for many years to have free negroes transplanted to a colony in Africa. Frank Key was among the prominent and enthusiastic workers for the organization. He freed a number of his own slaves and attempted to persuade his friends to do likewise, but the colonization movement itself was carefully distinguished from the abolitionist movement. It was an attempt to remove from the country free persons whose presence was regarded as embarrassing both by slave owners and by the enemies of slavery.

Taney, like most other sons of Maryland planters, had been brought up in the midst of slaves, with pickaninnies as playmates, and had accepted the condition of the black people as normal and right. He owned slaves himself at an early age. He too, however, recognized the restlessness among slaves caused by the presence of free negroes, and the difficulties of free negroes in maintaining themselves in a white men's society. Although he was never as active as Key, he supported the colonization movement at least to the extent of holding the office of vice president of a local organization for a time.

[He supported both state legislation and extra-governmental attempts to protect free negroes from abuses which were growing more and more evident.] As with the expansion of cotton production the value of slaves increased in the cotton belt, the stealing of free negroes for sale outside the state became more and more common. Those who were not stolen outright were subject to seizure and imprisonment if they were unable to produce papers to prove their status, and if not claimed by an alleged owner might thereafter be sold for jail fees. Common items in local newspapers were advertisements that negroes of certain descriptions were being held to await the claims of owners, and if not claimed would be sold to pay the expenses incurred by the county. Some negroes held in this way were indeed slaves fleeing from their owners, but many free persons were likewise deprived of their liberty.

To remedy these abuses a society was formed in Baltimore in 1816, for the announced purpose of suppressing the kidnaping of free negroes and protecting free persons imprisoned for want of papers to prove their freedom. Taney served as a councilor of a rural branch of this organization.

In other ways he showed his interest in the welfare of colored people. On one occasion he and Frederick A. Schley aided a free negro in the purchase of his slave wife by advancing the price of the slave and permitting him to bind himself to them for that amount. The negro repaid the money, and the family was given its freedom. During the same period Taney manumitted his own slaves, providing that they should become free some years hence, doubtless on the assumption that education for freedom was necessary before they could be trusted to take care of themselves. He continued to support those who were too old to earn their living, and to watch carefully over their interests. To each of the older servants he gave a wallet, which was brought each month to him or to a member of his family for replenishment. Some negroes knew too little of mathematics to be aware when they were short-changed by merchants, and there were merchants who in making change intimidated negroes into accepting less than was due them. As a protection against these abuses Taney gave his monthly allowances in small silver pieces with which the negroes were familiar, none of them exceeding fifty cents in value.

During this period in which Taney served as a member of a colonization society and as councilor for a negro protective organization, and in which he was liberating his own slaves, he delivered also his argument in a famous case arising out of slavery issues. Slavery had long been prohibited in the adjoining state of Pennsylvania, and negroes held in bondage in the South had been encouraged to take refuge within its borders. Toward the end of Taney's first session in the Maryland Senate the legislature adopted a resolution that the governors of Pennsylvania and Delaware be requested to recommend legislation to prohibit such abuses. Nothing was done immediately, however, and friction between the states continued to develop.

The feeling already aroused was stirred to fever pitch in the summer of 1818 when Jacob Gruber, a Methodist minister from Pennsylvania, delivered a sermon at Hagerstown, Maryland, in which he bitterly attacked the institution of slavery and made derogatory comparisons between Maryland and Pennsylvania. The occasion was that of a Methodist camp meeting, to which people, both black and white, had come from many miles around. Some twenty-six hundred white people were gathered together before the open-air speaker's stand, and behind it, according to custom, were placed the negroes in attendance, about four hundred in number. The minister who had been scheduled to speak was unable to appear, and Gruber, who was in charge of the meeting, had to substitute for him on the spur of the moment. He began an address, therefore, after the customary prayers and singing of hymns, on the subject of "national sins."

In good old-fashioned Methodist manner Gruber orated his condemnation of infidelity, intemperance, and profanity. Now warmed to his subject, he came to the topic of slavery. "We live in a free country," he proclaimed. According to the Declaration of Independence all men were created equal, and had certain inalienable rights, such as life, liberty, and the pursuit of happiness. It was gross inconsistency to hold articles of liberty and independence in one hand, and a bloody whip in the other, while a negro stood trembling, with his back cut and bleeding.[14]

Humane though they may have been in their treatment of their own slaves and in their efforts to protect the rights of free negroes,

[14] See W. P. Strickland, *Life of Jacob Gruber*, pp. 146–165, 171–187.

the white people in the congregation wanted no such doctrines expounded to them from the pulpit, particularly in the presence of slaves who might thereby be stirred to rebellion. They were further offended by Gruber's derogatory comments about their native state:

"We Pennsylvanians think it strange," he declared, "and it seems curious, to read the prints or newspapers, from some states, and find —*For sale, a plantation, a house and lot, horses, cows, sheep, and hogs; also, a number of negroes—men, women, and children—some very valuable ones; also, a pew in such and such a church.* In this inhuman traffic and cruel trade the most tender ties are torn asunder, the nearest connections broken." [15]

In excitement and hot indignation for weeks thereafter the people discussed the offensive sermon of the visiting minister. Charges were brought against Gruber at the next meeting of the grand jury, and he was indicted for attempting to incite slaves to insurrection and rebellion. Beene S. Pigman, who practiced extensively both in Hagerstown and in Frederick, and who like Taney was a councilor for the society for the protection of free negroes, secured Taney's services for the defense of Gruber. To escape the hostile excitement prevailing in Hagerstown they had the trial transferred to Frederick. Even there the odds seemed to be against them. It was necessary to appear before a jury on which a number of slaveholders might be expected to sit, and to defend a man who in local estimation was almost a foreigner and who was charged with attacking local institutions. The occasion promised to be one for the exercise of all of Taney's well known tact and ingenuity.

He made his appeal on grounds of free speech as guaranteed by Maryland laws. Under those laws no man could be punished for preaching the articles of his religious creed unless they were immoral and calculated to disturb the peace and order of society. Furthermore, to convict Gruber of the offense charged it would be necessary to prove not only that his doctrines were dangerous but also that he had preached them for the purpose of disturbing the peace. This accusation could not be proved. Gruber, a minister for many years in

[15] Samuel Tyler, *Memoir of Roger Brooke Taney,* p. 126.

the Methodist Episcopal Church, in which no slaveholder could be a minister, had preached the doctrine of his church that slavery should be done away with by peaceful abolition. Methodist ministers were accustomed to preaching on the subject of the injustice and oppressions of slavery. If the Maryland slaveholders objected to the expression of such ideas in the presence of their slaves, they should not have brought them to the meeting. Gruber had not gone to the slaves. They had come to him. They could not have come without the consent of their masters.

Furthermore, declared Taney in language which was to embarrass him in later years, there was no law which forbade men to speak of slavery as they thought of it. "Any man has a right to publish his opinions on that subject whenever he pleases. It is a subject of national concern, and may at all times be freely discussed. Mr. Gruber did quote the language of our great act of national independence, and insisted on the principles contained in that venerated instrument. He did rebuke those masters, who, in the exercise of power, are deaf to the calls of humanity; and he warned them of the evils they might bring upon themselves. He did speak with abhorrence of those reptiles, who live by trading in human flesh, and enrich themselves by tearing the husband from the wife—the infant from the bosom of the mother: and this I am instructed was the head and front of his offending. Shall I content myself with saying he had a right to say this? That there is no law to punish him? So far is he from being the object of punishment in any form of proceeding, that we are prepared to maintain the same principles, and to use, if necessary, the same language here in the temple of justice, and in the presence of those who are the ministers of the law. A hard necessity, indeed, compels us to endure the evil of slavery for a time. It was imposed upon us by another nation, while we were yet in a state of colonial vassalage. It cannot be easily, or suddenly removed. Yet while it continues it is a blot on our national character, and every real lover of freedom confidently hopes that it will be effectually, though it must be gradually, wiped away; and earnestly looks for the means, by which this necessary object may be best attained. And until it shall be accomplished: until the time shall come when we can point without a blush, to the language held in the Declaration of Independence, every friend of humanity will seek to lighten the galling chain of slavery, and better, to the utmost of his power, the wretched condition of the slave. Such was Mr. Gruber's object in that part of his sermon, of which I am now speaking. Those who have complained of him, and reproached him will not find it easy to answer him: unless complaints, reproaches and persecution shall be considered an answer." [16]

After the examination of witnesses and the speeches of his colleagues Taney spoke again for an hour in a concluding address, which has been lost to history because his persistent ill health in the following months prevented his arranging his materials for publication. At the close of the address the jury retired, and quickly returned with a verdict of "Not guilty." The credit for the verdict was for the most part given to Taney, and it was said that for years thereafter the Roman Catholic lawyer, who in his old age was accused of saying that the negro had no rights which the white man was bound to respect, was remembered with a warm sense of gratitude by the Methodists of western Maryland.

Taney's speech was of course phrased primarily for the purpose of winning his case, and it did not, therefore, necessarily represent fully his own opinions concerning slavery. Other evidence, however, makes it a plausible assumption that he believed it to be a "blot on our national character," which should be peaceably removed as rapidly as circumstances might permit. In addition to the activities previously mentioned he supported legislative measures to prevent the sale for jail fees of negroes who had been imprisoned on suspicion of being slaves. He supported other measures to prevent negroes entitled to freedom from being taken outside the state to be held in permanent servitude, and indicated generally his desire to protect the rights of the unfortunate people.

In spite of his generally humanitarian attitude toward negroes,

[16] David Martin, *Trial of the Rev. Jacob Gruber, Minister in the Methodist Episcopal Church, at the March Term, 1819, in the Frederick County Court, for a Misdemeanor* (1819), pp. 42–44.

however, one event of the period showed that his position was qualified, and bore ominous significance for the distant future. Congress
was debating the admission of Missouri into the Union. Abolitionists
urged that the state be admitted only on condition that slavery be
outlawed, and the proslavery element hotly objected to any such condition. The issue was much discussed and debated throughout the
country. In December, 1819, the Maryland Senate received from the
House of Delegates a resolution providing as follows:

"Our Senators and Representatives in Congress are requested to
use their utmost endeavors, in the admission of new states into the
Union, to grant to such states all the rights and privileges of the
states heretofore admitted, without requiring, as a condition of their
admission, the inhibition of involuntary servitude, or any other condition limiting their sovereign powers in a greater degree than the
sovereign powers of the original states forming the Union are limited
and restrained." [17]

Taney voted against this resolution, which was sponsored by slavery
interests. Tradition has it, however, that he opposed the Missouri
Compromise which was ultimately adopted, and which provided that
other states carved from the Louisiana Purchase within a certain area
should be admitted only on the condition of prohibiting slavery. His
objection to the resolution before the state Senate seems to have been
based on the theory that the legislature had no right to give directions
to members of the House of Representatives, who were representatives of the people and not of the legislature. His old friend and colleague, William Carmichael, introduced a substitute resolution to the
effect that the legislature had no authority over Congress in the matter but that the members individually thought the new states should
have all the powers of the old. The resolution was defeated without a
record vote, but there is reason for believing that it was supported by
Taney, Carmichael, and the three other members of the Senate who
opposed the original resolution.

It was in this manner that Taney was first confronted with the
principle of the Missouri Compromise, more than a third of a century

[17] *Votes and Proceedings of the Senate of Maryland,* 1819, p. 31.

before the time when, in the Dred Scott case, he was to hold that it
had been unconstitutional. The evidence is too intangible to provide
a basis for broad generalization. It may be, however, that already he
was growing fearful of the use of the federal government to interfere with the institutions of the section of the country of which he was
a product. It may be that at this early date his sympathies with the
South in the growing sectional struggle were beginning to qualify the
expression of his humane sympathies for the enslaved members of an
unfortunate race. The conflict between these sympathies was one
which he was never fully able to resolve.

Throughout his five years in the state Senate Taney dealt in various ways with these issues and others of lesser importance. No drastic
and conclusive action was taken in connection with any of them. Yet
the experience was invaluable, in that it provided a background of
preparation for more important activities as an officer of the federal
government in years yet to come. For a full understanding of Taney
and his work the fact can not be too often recalled that in his dealings
with the problems of statesmanship his heritage as a southern gentleman was always apparent. He saw currency and banking problems
from the point of view of farmers and the residents of small communities, rather than from that of merchants or urban people generally. He saw the problems of slavery from the point of view of the
residents of communities where slavery was a tradition and where
negroes, free or slave, continued to dwell among the members of the
ruling class. He had a warm paternal attitude toward negroes individually, but he knew the problems created by their presence, and felt
that they must be solved locally and gradually, rather than by decisive action from the federal government, which was apt to be
dominated by people from sections unfamiliar with the intricacies of
the problems.

Chapter VI

CHANGING SCENES

Taney lived in Frederick and practiced law there during a period of seventeen years after his marriage to Anne Key in January, 1806. The events of the period were for the most part the normal events of the life of a family man with a growing reputation, a growing income, and a growing household. The first child, Anne, was born in the summer of 1808. Thereafter, at intervals averaging about two years, occurred the births of Elizabeth, Ellen, Augustus, Sophia, and Maria. Eight years later, in 1827, occurred the birth of Alice, the youngest of the children. It was not until 1815 that Taney was able to own the house in which he lived. He bought one at that time not so much because he wanted that particular property as because it was necessary to collect a debt from the previous owner. It was a house on Bentz Street, in that part of Frederick which was colloquially known as Bentztown, where the inhabitants were German rather than gentry. The house, which is now preserved as a memorial to Taney, was of two stories, with an attic room, a cellar, and outhouses for slaves. It was an unpretentious dwelling in an unpretentious locality, and was none too large for the family and the relatives who gathered there as guests.[1]

Presumably Taney was normally eager for the birth of sons who would grow up to distinguish the family name. Fate in this respect was unkind. Six of his seven children were girls. It is possible that the one son inherited something of his own physical frailty and that of Mrs. Taney, or it may be that the boy fell victim to one of the contagious diseases which the family was unable to guard against. At any rate he died in 1818, when only three years of age, leaving no one

[1] Interesting relics of the family are the low beds in which the children slept, beds which were so constructed that they could be gotten rid of in the daytime by the simple expedient of pushing them under the beds of the adults.

in the family to perpetuate the name of Taney. His death was doubtless a blow in another respect, for he was to have been brought up in the Catholic faith of his father, while his sisters accepted the church of the mother's choice. All the younger members of the family were therefore Protestants until, some time in middle life, Sophia accepted Catholicism.

So poor was their health and so ominous was the threat of epidemics of uncontrolled disease that the lives of the parents and the remaining children were many times in danger. The following letter, written by Taney in the autumn of 1820 soon after the crisis in the illness of his eldest daughter, illustrates the type of incidents which appear again and again in accounts of the life of the family:

"You will have heard my dear Madam before this reaches you of the illness of our dear child, and I am sure you will rejoice to hear she is recovering. On Saturday and Sunday last we had scarcely a hope that she would recover. It has pleased Heaven in the fullness of mercy to raise her up again, and save us from the severe chastisement with which we were threatened. She has been well enough to ride out yesterday and today and we hope will be strong enough by Monday next to undertake a journey to the sulphur spring near Martinsburg in Virginia, where Anne and myself received much benefit a few years ago, and where we intend to spend a week or two in this month if the weather continues good. And as we all need change of air and exercise we shall probably go on westward until the cold weather drives us back. Mrs. Taney . . . has not . . . recovered her strength, and frequently suffers from headaches, and the fatigue and agitation produced by the illness of our dear Anne has enfeebled her a good deal. As to my own health it is hardly worth complaining about. It has been so long bad I have got used to it, but if I am not able to add a little to my strength before the cold weather sets in, I fear I shall have a bad winter of it." [2]

Taney's gloom was doubtless deepened by the disgrace which his father had recently brought upon himself and the family. After the death of Monica Taney in 1814 old Michael lived on at the ancestral

[2] Taney to Mrs. Anne Key, Sept. 6, 1820, Etting Coll., Historical Society of Pennsylvania.

home on the Patuxent. It would seem that he was irascible, opinionated, and restless, his life left harsh and unhappy through the loss of the qualities of home which his wife had provided. The story of the catastrophe which befell him is told with chaotic variations through which truth filters but vaguely. The essential facts seem to be that on July 1, 1819, John Magruder, who lived on a neighboring plantation, had dinner with other guests at the Taney home; he and Michael Taney quarreled over a woman; they fought, and Taney stabbed Magruder so that he died; and Taney fled from the community to escape prosecution.

Some accounts have it that Taney quarreled with Magruder, a much younger man, over the possession of a lady's favors, the quarrel beginning at the dinner table where the men had perhaps partaken too freely of wine. Arrangements were made for a duel in the front yard. The contestants discovered that the pistols had not been loaded, the seconds having attempted to prevent a fatal outcome. Taney, undaunted, attacked Magruder with a dirk. Coming to his senses after stabbing his enemy, he helped move the wounded man into the house. Discovering that the wound was fatal, he slipped from the dining room by way of an entrance into the negro quarters in the cellar, and with the aid of his slaves made his escape across the Patuxent and fled into Virginia.

According to a version more acceptable to the Taney family, Magruder offered at the table a toast insulting to a young woman who was an orphan and a relative of Taney's. Taney, always the gentleman when a woman's honor was at stake, challenged him. When Magruder discovered that the pistols were not loaded he accused Taney of being party to the arrangement to leave them unloaded, and attacked Taney. The latter defended himself with the only weapon available, a knife, with results fatal to Magruder.[3]

[3] The Baltimore *Federal Gazette*, July 14, 1819, quotes the Annapolis *Maryland Republican* as follows: "Died on the first inst *Mr. John M. Magruder*, of Calvert County, in consequence of a stab with a dirk, given by Michael Taney, sen, on the same day—as a jury of inquest have declared on oath." For varying accounts see T. J. C. Williams, *History of Frederick County, Maryland*, II, 197–199; Swepson Earle, *The Chesapeake Bay Country*, pp. 168–169; James Hungerford, *The Old Plantation*, pp. 300–302.

Whatever the truth as to details, Michael Taney fled secretly from the estate which for generations had been the home of ancestors bearing the same name as his own, and took refuge in Loudoun County, Virginia, which adjoined Frederick County, Maryland. Soon afterward, perhaps accompanied by Roger Taney, he went quietly to Alexandria, then in the District of Columbia, to place his property in the hands of his heirs. The act marked the defeat of the old man's cherished hopes. The property went not to Michael VI, through whom he had planned to pass to succeeding generations of Michael Taneys the Calvert County home, but to his sons Roger and Octavius, who were to hold it as trustees.[4]

The fragmentary records fail to show why Michael VI failed to take his place in the line of succession. He disappeared from history with the close of the War of 1812. He may have died between that date and the tragedy of July 1, 1819. He may have given up hope of inheriting from his father before he himself grew old, and gone off to the Southwest, to which, according to an unverified rumor, he at some time did go. He may have been implicated in the quarrel along with his father, so that he too had to flee from the law and the wrath of the Magruders. At any rate, while his father was hiding in the wilds of Virginia he too was conspicuously absent.

About a year after his flight old Michael was thrown from a horse and killed. The family, evidently believing that the hostility of his enemies was no longer to be feared, had the body taken back to Calvert County for interment beside the bones of his ancestors. A vindictive brother of the deceased Magruder is said to have insisted on opening the casket to see whether a funeral had been faked to persuade him to give up the search for the criminal. Rage filled him as he looked on the familiar though dead features of Michael Taney, and he seized a stone and battered it down upon the face of the corpse.

Only the youngest son, Dr. Octavius C. Taney, remained in the county and attempted to live down the disgrace. In his immediate neighborhood he seems to have become a man of reputation both as a

[4] See the Frederick County (Md.) Land Records, J. S. 10, p. 617.

physician and as a politician. He represented his county in the House of Delegates, and was a member of the state Senate in 1832 when death cut him off before he reached his prime. He was then attempting to solve some of the race problems of his state, and it is possible that he might have achieved prominence had his life been prolonged. After his death the old home was sold outside the family, and the name of Taney ceased to appear in the records of Calvert County, save as an occasional negro served as a reminder of the past by claiming it as his own.

Augustus Taney, who had established himself in politics and law at Rockville, may have given as much promise of distinction as did his elder brother in Frederick. After building up a successful practice his reputation began to spread, and he sought a more lucrative business in Georgetown, near the national capital. He died in 1823 before he had had time to make himself an outstanding figure, and his name found no place in the history of the country. His only son, Joseph Augustus, became a respected member of a Montgomery County community, but, perhaps because of the early death of his father and the cramping hand of penury, he too failed to achieve distinction.

Of Roger Taney's sisters not much is known. One died in early womanhood. The other two, Dorothy and Sophia I. Taney, shared in the property distributed after their father's death, and seem thereafter to have lived either with or near the Roger Taney family. Neither of them was married in 1836 when Dorothy made a will leaving to Sophia the income from shares of stock and other property which she possessed, and providing that after Sophia's death the property should go to Roger.[5] Dorothy died early in 1837.[6]

The available records prove nothing as to the subsequent life of Sophia. An odd bit of circumstantial evidence suggests either that at middle age or later she may have married, or that the eldest brother, Michael VI, whose name had disappeared from the records and who seems not to have participated in the settlement of the family estate,

[5] Baltimore Wills, Folio 251, Book 16.

[6] *Ibid*. See also Taney to W. M. Beall, March 20, 1837, MS., Taney House, Frederick, Md.

was still alive as late as 1846. Early in that year Roger Taney wrote
to his son-in-law, J. Mason Campbell, of a letter which he had received from his "brother." [7] If the man referred to was indeed his
brother it must have been Michael VI, for Augustus and Octavius had
been many years in their graves. The term was often loosely used,
however, to include brothers-in-law, and the reference may have been
to Sophia's husband, whose name, if indeed he existed, remains a
mystery.

Since his father, who had aspired to see the name of Taney preserved as a mark of aristocracy, had himself discredited it, and since
his brothers and sisters failed to bring it distinction, it was left to
Roger Taney, with a frail physique and without male descendants, to
give it place in history. His own hopes seem for a time to have flick-
ered low. The early years of the 1820's brought news of the deaths of
his father-in-law, John Ross Key, his friend William H. Winder, and
John Eager Howard and other friends or persons prominent in the
state. "So many of our friends have been the victims of this fatal
season," Taney wrote to Virgil Maxcy, his former colleague in the
Maryland Senate, "that I am the more anxious about those that remain. . . . For myself I am much as you left me, perhaps rather
better. Yet from my office window I can see the faded leaves falling
from the trees, and have no reason to suppose that my hold of life is
much firmer than theirs." [8]

Other influences than those provocative of gloom were, however,
playing upon Taney's life. The passing years witnessed the growth of
his reputation as an honest and able lawyer. At first he practiced
chiefly in the courts of Frederick and the adjoining counties of Washington and Montgomery. As he became better known he was called
more and more to counties at a distance for the argument of impor-

---

[7] "I received your letter this morning, and begin my answer by saying that the acceptance
of my brother's note is right, and I enclose herewith a check payable to your order (dated
the 9th inst) with which please take up the draft at once and keep it until I return. I have
received a letter from my brother explaining why the draft was drawn at that time, but was
not to be presented until he heard from me."—Taney to J. Mason Campbell, Feb. 7, 1846,
Campbell MSS.

[8] Taney to Virgil Maxcy, Oct. 21, 1822, MS., New York Public Library.

tant cases. In carrying to the Court of Appeals cases in which he had appeared in lower courts he established a reputation at Annapolis. As a result he was often called on to argue appealed cases with which he had had no previous connection. He showed himself thoroughly competent as the colleague and as the opponent of the best known lawyers in the state.

Gradually his services came to be sought in Baltimore, the most fruitful locality in the state for lawyers of reputation. With the death or retirement of a number of the more prominent members of the Baltimore bar it was only natural that he should consider leaving Frederick, where he had already achieved unquestioned leadership, and seeking a new position in an urban center where the owners of great estates, the bankers, and the merchants paid fees for legal services too high to be collected in rural areas.

With feelings of mingled regret and anticipation, he prepared early in 1823 to leave the place which had been his home for more than a score of years. To that place he had brought his bride; there his children had been born and his mother and son had died, and there he had made his reputation both in politics and in law. It would have been possible for him to vegetate in Frederick throughout the remainder of his life. He was forty-six years of age, and, in terms of the standards of the community, he was a success. Nothing more could be required of him. Yet now, as in his days as a schoolboy, he stirred to the call of ambition. He sold his house on Bentz Street and much of his household goods, left his local practice to Frederick A. Schley and his business affairs to William M. Beall, and moved his family to Baltimore.

The metropolis of Maryland had a population of diverse groups, including the rough element usually found in seaport towns, the tradesmen and small merchants found in any urban center, and a mercantile aristocracy intermixed with landed gentry who had drifted there. The respectable lawyers whom he knew were numerous enough for Taney quickly to find himself at home, though not in the warm, informal sense that he had been at home in Frederick. He rented a house in a respectable neighborhood in South Gay Street, from which he later moved to another which he purchased in Lexington Street near St. Paul, which was to be his permanent home until after the death of Mrs. Taney in 1855. The Taneys had no desire for a place in gay society, even if the care of a family of five small girls, between the ages of four and fifteen, had left them time for it. Yet in his gracious and kindly manner Taney steadily added first to the circle of his acquaintants and then to that of his personal friends, including among them members of the mercantile class for whose business methods and systems of ethics he had little sympathy. He played a responsible part in civic affairs, and came gradually to be looked upon as one of the leading citizens of Baltimore.

His new associations brought him new business. He appeared before county courts, the Court of Appeals, the federal District Court, and the federal Circuit Court. In the latter he faced with equanimity Judge Gabriel Duvall, who had been the cause of his memorable fright in the Mayor's Court in Annapolis in 1799. In 1825 he appeared for the first time before the Supreme Court of the United States in two now unimportant admiralty cases, addressing John Marshall and Joseph Story, and other judges of less distinction. Even at this late date he experienced the shattering and enervating stage fright which had characterized other important initial experiences. He was ill throughout his stay in Washington, and wrote miserably to his daughter Sophia that he did not feel as if he should be well until he was back home.[9] No record remains to show whether or not his nervous condition destroyed the effectiveness of his argument. At any rate he had now made his beginning before the highest court in the land, and his arguments at later terms were to be heard with deep respect.

He was unique in his appearance at the bar and in his manner of presenting cases. He was tall and flat-chested, with broad and stooping shoulders. His face was long, his features uneven, his mouth large, and his tobacco-stained teeth irregular and prominent. Dressed in black, ill-fitting clothes, his description calls to mind oftentimes the picture of Abraham Lincoln, in spite of his deficiency in physical

[9] Taney to Sophia Taney, Feb. 22, 1825, *Maryland Historical Magazine*, XIII, 171.

vigor. He spoke usually without gestures, without emphasis, and in a low, hollow voice. In this era of pompous oratory at the bar he avoided all high-sounding phrases, and made no quotations from the masters of literature. He talked simply, earnestly, and directly to judges and juries, with a minimum of verbal display. Yet his method was tremendously effective. William Pinkney declared, he could answer Taney's argument, he was not afraid of his logic; but "that infernal apostolic manner of his" there was no replying to.[10] In simple and familiar language he made the most difficult problems seem clear. He was a man with a moonlight mind, declared William Wirt, a mind which, like moonlight of the arctics, "gave all the light of day without its glare." [11] One of his friends declared that "I have often heard jurors, our plain unlettered farmers, say, that even when discussing a mere point of law before the court, his argument was distinguished by so much clearness, such apt and striking illustrations, such plain, common sense views, that they listened with pleasure and benefit." [12]

Another friend attributed much of his success with juries to the integrity which he was known to possess. "The people knew that he was sincere and honest, they knew that he was a composer of strifes and controversies, whenever the opportunity was afforded, and that he never promoted any; and they also knew that whilst he was earnest, strenuous and indefatigable in his efforts to secure for his clients their full and just rights, yet he never sought to gain from the other party any unjust advantage. He was an open and fair practitioner. He never entrapped the opposing counsel by any of the maneuvers of the artful attorney, and he contemned, above all things, the low tricks of the pettifogger." [13] He was eminently generous with his colleagues, particularly the younger men associated with him. A number of young men had the rich experience of reading law in his office, as he had studied under Judge Chase. They remained thereafter his grateful friends and enthusiastic admirers.

10 See Semmes, *John H. B. Latrobe and His Times*, p. 203.
11 Van Santvoord, *Lives of the Chief Justices*, pp. 477–478.
12 Frederick *Herald*, quoted, Washington *Globe*, Oct. 16, 1833.
13 William Schley, Baltimore *Sun*, Oct. 15, 1864.

He accepted cases of all kinds, in some of which the chances of winning were doubtless very slight. He was of course defeated many times. Whatever the prospects, he gave his best efforts to every case, and when the argument was completed he promptly dismissed it from his mind. When asked how he was able to achieve such calmness while a decision was pending he replied that having done his best to win he would not thereafter worry his interiors into fiddle strings over results.[14]

Although it was by no means the most important controversy which he participated in, the celebrated Gilmor divorce case throws light upon Taney from a number of different angles. Sarah Gilmor was a striking and headstrong member of the family of a wealthy Baltimore merchant, the senior Robert Gilmor. Without the consent of her parents she married the energetic but evidently uncouth David S. Barnum, the proprietor of Barnum's Hotel. The marriage was not a success. Evidently Barnum was not received into the wealthy and aristocratic set to which his wife's family belonged, and was resentful and jealous of her associations. Her conduct may or may not have been above just reproach. At any rate, Barnum scandalized the city by bringing in the legislature, where all such actions at that time had to be brought, an action for divorce, charging his wife with adultery.

The "best people" of Baltimore, many of whom were related by blood or by marriage to the accused woman, flew to her defense. Taney was numbered among her friends, and he, along with Jonathan Meredith and young John H. B. Latrobe, was employed as counsel in her defense. Shortly before the legislative committee began its hearings Taney was asked to appear before the Supreme Court of the United States in a case which had to do with the title to a great deal of property in Washington,[15] and in which his appearance would add both to his prestige and to his income. In a revealing letter to Richard S. Coxe, the lawyer who asked his assistance, he explained his predicament:

"A petition has been presented to the legislature of this state for

[14] F. J. Nelson, Frederick *News*, April 11, 1893.
[15] *Van Ness* v. *Mayor . . . of Washington*, 4 Peters 232 (1830).

a divorce upon grounds which implicate the character of a lady, who is closely allied to many of the most respectable members of the society of this place, and in whose defense it has become my duty to appear not merely as counsel but as a friend. Under such circumstances and in such a case, may I ask for indulgence until the latter end of February by which time this petition must be disposed of? You will at once feel that it is impossible for me to desert a case like the one I speak of, whatever may be the sacrifice. And I hope and believe that you and General Van Ness will think me justified in considering it my first duty to appear in behalf of an injured woman, placed in this painful situation by a brutal husband and his associates in iniquity." [16]

Taney and his colleagues and Barnum's counsel summoned many witnesses, who offered before the legislative committee a mass of highly scandalous testimony. Barnum's petition was denied. His wife then retaliated by submitting a petition on her own part for a divorce *a mensa et thoro*, the equivalent of a legal separation. After further battles the legislature granted her petition, and her counsel went home victorious, with time still available for Taney's appearance before the Supreme Court in Washington. [17]

This was the end of Taney's direct participation in the Gilmor divorce case, but it was not the end of the controversy, and Taney was made to suffer embarrassment from it. The aggrieved wife wanted not merely a legal separation but a complete divorce. Taney, a good Catholic in this respect, had always opposed divorces which completely dissolved the marriage bond. Yet he had never attempted officiously to force his beliefs upon his friends, and in so far as possible had avoided all differences based upon religious creed. He was not asked to conduct the case, since he was at that time living in

[16] Taney to Coxe, Jan. 25, 1830, MS., copied with permission of the owner, Barnet J. Beyer, 5 East 52nd Street, New York City.

[17] Local scandalmongers sought to profit from the case by publishing as much of the evidence as they could get, together with the arguments of counsel. Taney and his colleagues indignantly refused, however, to permit this use of their materials, and the Gilmor faction was influential enough to prevent the filing of the evidence in the archives of the legislature. See Jonathan Meredith to J. H. Milbourn, March 14, 1830, copy, Meredith MSS., Library of Congress.

Washington as Attorney General of the United States, but he was asked for advice and assistance.

Few men could go farther than Taney with people with whom they disagreed, without sacrificing their own principles, but the dilemma left him badly puzzled. He attempted to work his way out of it by a vaguely phrased letter. He concurred, he stated, in the plan which had been adopted. He would send letters if he thought they would induce any persons in the House of Delegates to take an interest in the matter, but he knew no one there who would be influenced by his opinion. If at a later date Miss Gilmor's agent thought it would be helpful if he wrote to particular members he would consider the matter and decide whether or not the letters would be of service. He closed with the phrase, "Sincerely wishing that the object you have in view and which I think a most desirable one may be accomplished. . . ." [18]

Taney quite evidently hoped that the matter would be dropped as far as he was concerned, but the Gilmors pressed him to write to the Baltimore members of the House of Delegates, and he was finally forced to clarify his position. As a member of the Senate, he declared, he had voted against all applications for complete divorces not only from his religious opinions but because he believed them wrong on the score of policy as well. He held the same opinion now, and if he wrote to any member of the legislature it would be his duty to express it.

With an ingenuity which leads the reader to question whether he stretched consistency more than it would endure, he explained why he had advised the application and had promised to write letters. Since he had left the Senate the granting of divorces had become a part of the ordinary business of the legislature. He had not expected that his friends should be guided by his own religious and political opinions, and he felt that if divorces were granted at all, one would be justified in this case. By his promise to write letters he had meant only that if he could clarify the facts in the minds of some legislators who might be in doubt as to them he would do so, if such a state-

[18] Taney to ———, Dec. 27, 1832, MS.

ment would be helpful in a letter in which he would have to say that as a matter of principle he was opposed to all divorces. The Baltimore delegates might be presumed to be as familiar with the facts as he, and he could not therefore with propriety address a letter to them. "I have given this detailed explanation," he concluded, "amid many urgent engagements, because I am unwilling that Sarah or her friends should believe that I have lost any of the sincere interest which I have heretofore taken in her welfare." [19]

The letters reveal the capacity which he had developed as a legalist for making fine-spun distinctions. Perhaps he overdid it here, permitting his principles to be too deeply submerged for a time by his loyalty to his friends and his desires for their happiness, or by his unwillingness to offend them. On the other hand it might be thought that he demonstrated a commendable agility in preventing religious dogmatism from interfering with the lives of other people and with his friendship for them. As far as his actual conduct was concerned, he adhered to his convictions. He did not, however, rationalize his own convictions into universals and attempt to force them on his friends. To this extent, certainly, he exercised a commendable self-restraint, a tolerance not too often characteristic at that time of people of his own or other faiths.

Although it was true in general that, as his reputation increased, Taney's clients were more and more apt to be men or institutions able to pay relatively high prices for his services, his practice was nevertheless exceedingly varied. He participated in the councils of his church, and gave professional advice to its leaders. He drew a will for Charles Carroll of Carrollton and prepared codicils to it, and defended his interests before the courts. He was one of the many eminent lawyers who engaged in the fight for settlement of the great Ringgold estate in western Maryland, which was one of the memorable legal battles of the period. He added not merely to his reputation as a lawyer by his work for the Union Bank of Maryland, but also to the stock of facts and ideas which he later used in the struggle with the Bank of the United States. He argued many

[19] Taney to ———, Jan. 27, 1833, MS., Taney House, Frederick, Md.

admiralty cases, preparing himself unknowingly for his subsequent judicial decisions in this branch of the law.

The case of greatest permanent importance in which he appeared was perhaps that of *Brown* v. *Maryland*,[20] in which Chief Justice Marshall announced his "original package doctrine," a doctrine which was to be highly influential in the development of the constitutional law of the country. The legislature, which had previously required a license of all persons retailing merchandise of certain kinds, enacted a law requiring a similar license of wholesalers. The wealthy mercantile firm of Alexander Brown and Sons, importers of huge quantities of goods, contested the law, arguing that it was unconstitutional as a state tax on imports and as a regulation of foreign commerce. Taney and Reverdy Johnson argued for the state that after the goods had arrived in Maryland they were neither imports nor articles of foreign commerce, but were subject to state control and state taxation.

Taney lost his battle with the mercantile interests. The Supreme Court held that while imported goods were in the hands of the importers and in the "original packages" they remained imports and articles of foreign commerce, and were therefore exempt from state taxation. Taney officially admitted in later years when he was himself Chief Justice of the United States that the line marked out by his predecessor was the best that could be drawn to delimit commerce of a particular kind.[21] The case was significant in Taney's life in that it represented one of his many struggles with mercantile interests. It was significant also in the fact that in spite of his Federalist heritage he appeared here as the defender of the rights of a state against the restraining hand of the federal government. At a strategic moment in a time of political transition he demonstrated his ability in defense of decentralized power, and called himself prominently to the attention of state rights politicians.

Some months later, during the summer of 1827, a vacancy occurred in the office of Attorney General of Maryland. Small re-

[20] 12 Wheaton 419 (1827).
[21] *License Cases*, 5 Howard 504 (1847).

muneration was connected with the office, but it had usually been held by lawyers of renown, and appointment to it conferred a mark of high distinction. So high was Taney's standing at the bar of his state at this time that the governor, although a political opponent, named him for the office. Deeply grateful for the honor, Taney accepted the position and held it until his resignation in 1831 to become Attorney General of the United States. The duties were light, however, and most of them could be delegated to subordinates, so that the appointment wrought little change in his professional life.

He was deeply interested in the much discussed subject of public improvements. Roads and canals were being built all over the country to facilitate the marketing of farm products and the distribution of manufactured goods, and the developments were entangled with national and local politics. Taney, his brother Augustus while he lived, and Frank Key discussed methods and finances in many internal improvements conventions. Taney vigorously supported the plan for a canal along the Potomac River to connect the West with the Atlantic coast. It was an immense project, however, and he believed that no private corporation would be adequate for the task, or ought to be trusted with the immense sums to be spent. He thought the work should be done under the supervision of the federal government or under the joint supervision of the governments of the United States, Maryland, and Virginia.[22]

His attitude provides another illustration of his distrust of great aggregates of property in the hands of a few individuals. At a time when theories of laissez faire were becoming dominant in American thinking, he preferred the risks of a certain amount of paternalism to those of individualism uncontrolled save by competition. The task, nevertheless, was left to a private corporation, which never carried it to completion. The difficulties were too great, and it ultimately gave way before the competition of the Baltimore and Ohio Railroad.

Either because he believed it the more feasible project or because it offered him employment as counsel, or for both reasons, Taney

[22] Frederick *Political Examiner*, Dec. 28, 1825.

early gave his support to the railroad. He aided in the preparation of the case and in the first argument of a suit between the railroad and the canal company over a strip of land along the Potomac which seemed essential to the success of each project. The railroad was victorious in the lower state court, and the canal company took the case to the Court of Appeals. There certain judges seem to have juggled the handling of the case for the benefit of particular interests, in a way which inevitably brings courts into disrepute. At the time when the case was advanced for argument Taney, who had been made Attorney General of the United States, was for some reason unable to attend, and William Wirt, one of his colleagues, was absent because of illness. One of the six judges, also, was absent because of illness. There was ample justification, therefore, for the postponement of the case.

The judges, however, had apparently made up their minds on the case before the argument, and were divided three to three. A decision on such an alignment would have confirmed the decision of the court below, which had been in favor of the railroad. The judge who fell ill, however, was one of the three friends of the railroad. The three opposing judges, being in the majority during his absence, insisted that the case be argued at approximately the date which had been set. Two eminent lawyers, Daniel Webster and Reverdy Johnson, presented the railroad argument, but they lost the decision by a vote of three to two.[23]

The defeated lawyers long continued their wrathful sputtering at the treatment accorded their client by the Court of Appeals. It was difficult to write on the subject, declared Taney to one of his colleagues, without saying what he thought about the conduct of the three judges who seemed to have been determined to decide the case against the railroad and resolved to do it when the absence of one of the judges made it possible. An attempt was made to secure action from the legislature which would make possible a rehearing of the case. Taney predicted failure. It was useless to nourish false hopes,

---

[23] *Chesapeake & Ohio Canal Co.* v. *Baltimore & Ohio Railroad,* 4 Gill & Johnson 1 (1832).

he declared. Judges who had used despotic power in this fashion would find means to use it again. The argument had been a solemn farce, and the judges had reached a decision without taking time to think out reasons for it.[24]

Although he may not have lobbied directly with congressmen for federal funds for the railroad while Attorney General of the United States, Taney watched with interest and criticized the strategy of those who urged its claims. He gave advice to Senator Samuel Smith as to the best mode of action. In a letter to John H. B. Latrobe, permanent counsel for the railroad, he disapproved of the methods used when a deputation had been sent to Washington for lobbying purposes. "You who know the deep interest I take in the road," he wrote, "will readily imagine how vexatious it is to see those who are its friends falling into mistakes which might have been so easily avoided." He wished that Latrobe or the president of the company would come to Washington and discuss matters with him.[25]

Taney's interest, however, seems not to have been primarily in the enrichment of the railroad company, but in the benefit to the community to be derived from this and other internal improvements when successfully completed. True, he may not have been wholly consistent in his attitude of distrust toward powerful corporations, which was to be more clearly revealed somewhat later. A corporation which employed his services may have seemed less of a menace to public welfare than others with which he had no connection. Yet, to repeat, it seems probable that his major interest was in the promotion of the public welfare by the building of the railroad, rather than in the corporation, and that since the government itself had not undertaken the project he regarded the corporation as a necessary instrument for the achievement of the desired ends.

The varied cases mentioned here were only a few of the many in which Taney participated after his removal from Frederick to Baltimore. His professional work took most of his time, leaving him little opportunity for public activities other than those mentioned, to-

[24] See Semmes, *John H. B. Latrobe and His Times*, pp. 344–345.
[25] Taney to Latrobe, Jan. 31, 1832, Latrobe MSS., Maryland Historical Society.

gether with a limited participation in politics. He did find time, however, for the promotion of one other form of civic activity, that of public education. A committee of the legislature, reporting on the University of Maryland in February, 1826, listed him and six other persons as members of the faculty of law. David Hoffman was the only professor listed, however.[26] Presumably Taney and the other persons did little more than give advice concerning the work in law, and perhaps participate in examinations.

When the legislature, dissatisfied with the way in which the university was managed, abolished the board of regents, Taney was chosen as one of the twenty-two trustees. The governor of the state was made *ex officio* president of the board, but at the first meeting Taney was chosen vice president. He presided thereafter over the meetings at which university policies were discussed and determined. On the death of the provost of the university Taney was chosen to fill that office, and he held it at least nominally for some years, in spite of the burden of other duties.[27]

Outside his law practice, however, it was politics that interested him most deeply and that brought out the abilities and traits which were dominant in his work as a national figure. The next segment in the story of his life, therefore, is the account of the realignment of political parties in Maryland, and of the beginning of Taney's allegiance to a colorful and dynamic leader, Andrew Jackson.

[26] Baltimore *American*, March 9, 1826.
[27] Thomas W. Griffith, *Annals of Baltimore*, p. 268; Eugene F. Cordell, *The University of Maryland*, 1807-1907, I, 93.

CHAPTER VII

IN THE RANKS WITH ANDREW JACKSON

THE Federalist party had been in process of slow decay since 1800, when friction within its ranks aided Thomas Jefferson in defeating John Adams, its candidate for the presidency. It declined in membership in the years which followed because of the narrowness of the interests it represented, and because of the scarcity of patronage resulting from its inability to win a sufficient number of the higher offices of the government. The issues of the War of 1812 weakened the party by dividing it, and the fact that one wing of the party was at this time branded with disloyalty tended to cut off from it the new membership which was necessary for its survival.

Furthermore, with the passing of the years the issues which had formerly divided the parties tended to disappear, or at least they ceased to constitute dividing lines. Foreign relations issues so changed as to have little bearing on party alignments. The conflict over the extent to which the federal government should promote internal improvements was within each of the two parties, rather than between them. The Democrats took over much of the nationalist program of the Federalists by chartering a Bank of the United States, and by levying protective tariffs. Robert Goodloe Harper, leader of the old "blue light" Federalists, admitted in 1823 that the Democrats, under James Monroe, had destroyed the Federalist party. They had done it, however, he declared, by the only method by which it could be destroyed; namely, by the adoption of its principles.[1]

Political parties die, however, only to be born again, or to be supplanted by others. The Federalist organization had no more than

[1] Annapolis *Maryland Republican*, Feb. 15, 1823.

disappeared when that of the victorious opposition split asunder to form in groups around rival personalities, each of whom sought to capture or create an organization for the advancement of his own political ambitions. Three of the leaders, John Quincy Adams, William H. Crawford, and John C. Calhoun, were members of Monroe's cabinet. Henry Clay and Andrew Jackson also promised effective competition, and others were only less prominent.

The struggle for leadership in the congressional caucus of the party in 1824 resulted in the nomination of Crawford for the presidency. He won thereby the support of the party machine, but at the same time he antagonized many people who were hostile to the caucus system of nominating candidates and to the custom of nominating candidates from the cabinet of the President then in power. Adams, Clay, and Jackson ran independently, each having some chance of success. Calhoun recognized the fact that his own position was weak, and contented himself for the time by running for vice president. The differences among the opposing candidates were for the most part differences of personality and personal ambition, rather than of political or economic issues. The latter were not wholly absent, but they were pretty thoroughly submerged.

With the expiration of the five-year term in the Maryland Senate for which he had been chosen in 1816 Taney's political career had been temporarily closed. He had been suggested as the man to fill the vacancy in the state's representation in the United States Senate, but the Federalists had been too weak in the legislature to bring about the choice of one of their number. For a time after his removal to Baltimore he paid little attention to politics. He had to give all his energies to establishing himself in a strange community, and he lacked the intimate contacts with people which he had had at Frederick, and which were necessary to a person of his type of ability if he was to exercise political influence. "I am perhaps too old," he wrote to a friend in Frederick, "and too much of an invalid to form such close intimacies here as I had in Frederick with a few tried friends, tried in scenes of great excitement, in warm conflict, and towards whom one feels very differently from the cold associations of every day acquaintances." [2]

Nevertheless, participation in politics had been an important feature of his life too long to be entirely abandoned, and as general interest began to develop in the presidential campaign of 1824 he found himself discussing the topic at length in his letters to his old friends. The Baltimore Federalists had debated the advisability of once more nominating a candidate, or of acting as a unit in support of one of the candidates already in the field. "For my own part," Taney declared, "I have been very willing to wait for I am not very full of zeal on the subject. But I am perfectly convinced that the party cannot unite in any man and that it would be idle to attempt it. Some are for one and some for another, and it will result in every one taking his own course for there is no party feeling on either side, and perhaps it is best so. Crawford, Adams, and Jackson must be the three highest. The rest are out of the question. Indeed I believe Crawford's chance to be desperate, and that the chief contest will be between Adams and Jackson. As matters now stand, however, neither would have votes enough to be elected by the electors and the election must go to Congress. But from all I hear and see Jackson is gaining ground most rapidly, and for myself I am a good deal inclined to go with the rest for Old Hickory.

"But I have not yet taken sides with anybody. Jackson is not indeed the man I would name for President, if it rested with me to choose from the whole United States. But compared with his competitors he stands on strong ground. He is honest, he is independent, is not brought forward by any particular class of politicians, or any sectional interest. He is not one of the Secretaries. He is taken up spontaneously by the people, and if he is elected will owe obligations to no particular persons. It is a way in which a President ought to come in, for he is then unfettered by secret promises and may act independently. I am sick of all Secretary candidates, and would be glad to see it understood that a man might be elected without the

[2] Taney to William M. Beall, March 19, 1824, Beall MSS., in possession of Miss Nannie Floyd, Frederick, Md.

patronage of the President for the time being, or the power of members of Congress, or a combination of mercenary presses, or local interests."

He felt no zeal in the matter, however, Taney assured William M. Beall, to whom he was writing, and had not even made up his mind finally as to whom he would support. "You must set down this long letter to the pleasure I take in delivering myself up to a talk with my old friends and almost forgetting for the time, that I am not by the stove in my old office, and not writing either a handbill or a paragraph for Thompson." [3]

Although Jackson had presumably never heard of King Coody, he won Taney's devotion in 1824 when letters were published in which he had denounced the disloyal wing of the Federalist party, the group which had included Taney's enemies. Had he commanded the military department when the Hartford Convention met, Jackson declared in his correspondence with James Monroe, he would have punished the principal leaders even if it had been the last act of his life. These men, he continued, "although called Federalists, are really monarchists, and traitors to the constituted authorities. But I am of opinion that there are men called Federalists that are honest and virtuous, and really attached to our government; and although they differ in many respects and opinions with the Republicans, still they will risk everything in its defense." He recommended, therefore, that Monroe make appointments from among these Federalists as well as from his own party. [4]

Taney gave Jackson his full support, though he took no prominent part in electioneering. Others of the old Federalists did likewise, partly perhaps because of the belief that Jackson would not discriminate against them and partly from positive dislike of his competitors. As Taney had predicted several months before the election, neither of the candidates won a majority of the electoral votes, and the selection of a president devolved upon the House of Repre-

[3] Taney to Beall, April 13, 1824, *ibid*. The Thompson referred to was John P. Thompson, editor of the Frederick *Herald*.

[4] Tyler, *op. cit.*, pp. 157–158.

sentatives. Jackson had received much the largest popular vote. A number of the Federalist leaders who had supported him, including Taney and Charles Carroll of Carrollton, tried to aid him further by the warning that if Adams were elected he would be vindictive enough to proscribe Federalists in the making of appointments. When approached on the matter Adams denied that he would take any such course, and expressed regret that Taney, of whose talents he had heard high encomiums, should harbor such opinions of him.[5] It is doubtful if the assurance or the flattery had any effect upon Taney, but a number of Maryland Federalists drifted thereafter into the Adams camp.

Henry Clay determined the outcome of the battle in the House of Representatives by throwing his support to Adams, giving him thereby the number of votes needed to win. Adams, in turn, in the face of the charge that he had made a bargain with Clay in the matter, appointed him Secretary of State, seemingly bringing him in immediate line for the presidency. The Adams-Clay factions accepted the arrangement with satisfaction, denying scornfully that any agreement had been made. The Jackson politicians on the other hand raged impotently over the alleged corrupt bargain by which their hopes had been defeated and the popular will flouted.

Calhoun and his friends were likewise deeply disgruntled. Calhoun had been elected to the vice presidency, and now found himself part of an administration with which he had no sympathy, and which was thought to be grooming Clay to succeed Adams in the position which above all things Calhoun desired. The administration was soon torn by hidden strife between the Vice President and the Secretary of State, and the former, finding himself at a hopeless disadvantage, eventually aligned himself with the forces of Jackson for the battle of 1828.

Taney's friend, Virgil Maxcy, who was also a close friend and admirer of Calhoun, initiated the Jackson-Calhoun party movement in Maryland, in which Taney was to participate as chairman of the state Central Committee. Maxcy, a young man with a New England

[5] *Memoirs of John Quincy Adams*, VI, 499.

background, had come to Baltimore and begun the practice of law. He met and married the daughter of John Galloway, a member of an old Maryland family and the proprietor of a great estate near Annapolis called Tulip Hill. Upon his marriage he gave up his practice in Baltimore, and retired to the estate to carry on as a country gentleman. He won position in the Federalist party, and during the period of Taney's membership he was elected by the Maryland Senate to fill a vacancy in its own ranks. Taney visited many times at Tulip Hill while in the Senate and when at Annapolis for the argument of cases, and in this manner the friendship developed into one of close personal intimacy.

In 1826 Maxcy announced his candidacy for a seat in Congress, but the administration threw its weight against him, presumably because of his alignment with Calhoun. Calhoun told him of the intentions of the Adams organization, and asked him to come to Washington for a conference.[6] The outcome was the withdrawal of Maxcy from the congressional race and the issuance of an address to the people of his congressional district attacking the political methods of the administration.[7] "When Maryland in 1826 was quietly floating down the united corrupt stream of federal and state patronage," Maxcy wrote to Calhoun at a later date, "I first roused the attention of the people here to the importance of the principles, to the violation of which they were yielding without opposition, by my address to my congressional district, in making which I sacrificed a prospect, as certain as such things can be, of a seat in Congress, and by proclaiming openly my opposition to the reëlection of Mr. Adams and the reasons of it brought upon me bitter hostility and much reproach." [8]

Taney, though not a close friend of Calhoun as was Maxcy, gave the latter his full support, and the attack upon the administration created quite an uproar. The *National Journal*, the leading Adams

[6] Calhoun to Maxcy, June 6, 1826, Maxcy MSS.
[7] Maxcy letter, July 14, 1826, Annapolis *Maryland Republican*, July 29, 1826.
[8] Maxcy to Calhoun, April 6, 1829, J. Franklin Jameson (ed.), "Correspondence of John C. Calhoun," *Annual Report of the American Historical Association for the Year 1899*, II, 797. Hereafter cited as "Correspondence of John C. Calhoun."

paper in the capital, predicted that Maryland was to undergo a terrible and distressing convulsion. "Mr. M[axcy] has given impetus to the ball. He is now directing his creatures, and his influence, limited as it is, to procure the election of members unfriendly to the present administration; and if he should succeed in his election as a representative in the state legislature, all his efforts will be directed to the election of R. B. Taney, who is decidedly hostile to the powers that be." [9]

The plan to elect Taney to the United States Senate, if indeed there was such a plan, did not work out. The organization of the opposition party was continued, however, and Maxcy and Taney and others made arrangements for a state Jackson convention, to be held in Baltimore in May, 1827, to stir enthusiasm and set up machinery for use in the 1828 election. In the preceding February a local convention met at the Fountain Inn in Baltimore, at which Taney and seven others were appointed to represent the city at the state convention. Similar appointments were made in other localities. Maxcy assured Calhoun that the coming Jackson convention in Maryland would bring together as respectable and weighty a set of names as had ever been witnessed in the state.

The Jackson convention, heralded as the body which was to unify public sentiment against the administration which had come into power through a corrupt bargain, assembled at the Atheneum in Baltimore on May 21, 1827. Taney called it to order, and, according to Maxcy, could have had the presidency of the convention had he desired it.[10] He insisted, however, on the choice of General Thomas M. Foreman, a Revolutionary War veteran and a prominent Democrat from the Eastern Shore, whose name would carry weight with hesitant Democrats in his section. Taney's close friend, William M. Beall, was chosen secretary.

Maxcy had prepared an address to be adopted by the convention in which he denounced the "bargain" and the flouting of the popular

---

[9] *National Journal*, Aug. 4, 1826, quoted, Annapolis *Maryland Republican*, Aug. 12, 1826.

[10] Maxcy to Calhoun, May 7, 1829, "Correspondence of John C. Calhoun," p. 805.

will, and outlined the issues of the campaign. The fundamental questions at issue, he declared, were not those of tariffs, or internal improvements, or commercial treaties. They were rather questions as to whether the presidency was to be obtained through intrigue and bargain, and whether the system of electing the president should be changed to give the people the right to vote directly, in order to prevent the recurrence of the present abuses.[11] The address was adopted as proposed, except that, to Maxcy's distress, a provision was expunged in which Vice President Calhoun was exonerated from all blame for administration misconduct.[12]

The convention set up a Jackson Central Committee of Maryland, to direct the campaign and provide campaign materials for county organizations. Taney, who was evidently regarded as head of the party in the state, was made chairman of the committee. Using his ill health as an excuse, he guarded against the charge of Federalist domination by securing the appointment of James Mosher, "a most respectable Democrat," as vice president and active assistant.[13]

The records do not show how much Taney had to do with making up the materials of the campaign, which was one of the most venomous in American history. There is no evidence as to his conduct at any time to justify the assumption that he sanctioned the grossly false charges which were made against Adams, or looked with favor upon the dirty battles of mud-slinging in which both parties engaged. One of his comments made in later years indicates that the methods almost invariably used in the heat of political campaigns filled him with deep discomfort. "You have I think done wisely," he wrote to his son-in-law during the period of another such struggle, "in determining to remain in the country until after the election and also in refusing to make speeches. The excitement is now so high that nothing will take but very bitter speeches, and no one when the excitement is over thinks with any pleasure upon speeches of that

[11] Washington *United States Telegraph*, May 30, 1827.
[12] See Taney to Maxcy, July 1, 1827, Maxcy MSS.
[13] Maxcy to Calhoun, May 7, 1829, "Correspondence of John C. Calhoun," p. 805.

sort and most commonly would be glad that he had not made them." [14]

If, however, Taney and his friends did wink at or aid somewhat in spreading offensive false charges against Adams, they were not without provocation. The military hero in whose cause they had united suffered abuse such as few presidential candidates have been called upon to endure. The charge which wounded him most deeply and most enraged his friends, was directed at his wife. She was accused of having lived with Jackson while she was the wife of another man. The accusation was all the more damaging because there was a slight amount of truth in it, so that if discussed at all by the Jackson partisans it had to be explained rather than flatly denied. Jackson had married her after he believed his wife's first husband had secured a divorce from her. When he later discovered that the divorce proceedings had not been completed at the time of the wedding he at once had the ceremony performed again. His irregular conduct was obviously the product of error rather than design, but it provided lurid campaign material, nevertheless, when in the hands of unscrupulous persons, and it was used to the full. It was often easier for the Jackson men to hurl countercharges which were almost as gross and equally false than to explain away the charge against the Jacksons.

Taney, always at his best when working behind the scenes, demonstrated his ability at tactful manipulation by preventing a serious breach within his own party. George Winchester had been the Jackson candidate for the position of presidential elector from the vicinity of Baltimore in 1824. He had continued as an active leader of the party, and hoped for the nomination again. He had incurred the enmity of Maxcy, however, and perhaps of other friends of Calhoun within the party, by a motion to expunge the portion of the Jackson convention address which spoke kindly of Calhoun. The Calhoun faction therefore opposed his nomination. Taney ended the strife by arguing persuasively that to capture the maximum number of votes it might be well to nominate Benjamin C. Howard, a promi-

[14] Taney to J. Mason Campbell, Sept. 27, 1844, Campbell MSS.

nent local politician and the son of General John Eager Howard. By "a good deal of delicate and excellent management on the part of Taney," Maxcy later declared, Winchester was induced to stand aside and let Howard be the candidate.[15] When Taney had settled the matter in private a nominating meeting was held, and Howard was chosen by a unanimous vote of the delegates.[16]

Although he made no speeches, Taney visited the communities in which he was best known to work for the Jackson party. In the place which had been his home for twenty years he received a rough handling from an opposition paper which must have reminded him of the campaigns of his youth. Reporting on a Jackson barbecue, a "Citizen of Frederick" wrote as follows:

"The rostrum was erected—the ajax [Francis Thomas, of Frederick] mounted and beside him to the astonishment of the spectators, R. B. Taney, the Attorney General of the state, took a seat beside the champion of the Jacksonians. And as soon as the Attorney General took his seat on the stand it was audibly said, he is electioneering, he's ambitious, he's desirous of supplanting Mr. Wirt, the present Attorney General of the United States, and many other observations were heard circulating through the crowd. . . . The Attorney General at first smiled assent to what Thomas said in justification of himself, but when he entered upon the merits and justification of General Jackson he seemed to look abashed, hung his head and finally descended from the pulpit, no doubt seeing many of his former political friends eying him and marking the changes of his countenance—he could not withstand their piercing gaze and observations." [17]

The national campaign came to an end with the election at which a substantial majority of the electors were chosen for Jackson. A sectional division of the country was clearly apparent, Adams having run well in the North and East, but having won no electoral votes at all south of the Potomac and the Ohio. Maryland, a border state, was

---

[15] Maxcy to Calhoun, April 9, 1829, "Correspondence of John C. Calhoun," p. 796.
[16] Baltimore *Republican*, quoted, Annapolis *Maryland Gazette*, Nov. 29, 1827.
[17] For this and similar comments see the Baltimore *Patriot*, Sept. 19, 1828.

almost evenly divided. Adams received a slightly heavier popular vote than Jackson, and six of the eleven electoral votes.

The result did not mean that the efforts of Taney and his fellows had been without avail. With the use of the patronage during the preceding four years Adams might have been expected to achieve a substantial advantage over Jackson. This he failed to do. Presumably his failure was due in no small part to the efforts of the Jackson organization. Within Maryland, as elsewhere, there were of course conflicts of economic interests, conflicts of a type usually highly influential in politics. For the most part Maxcy was right, however, in his draft of the address of the Jackson convention, in declaring that such matters did not constitute the issues of this campaign. On these economic questions the friends of both Adams and Jackson were divided. The real issues had to do with personal conduct, and with the mode of filling the presidential chair. The period was one of the breaking down of old political alignments. It was only as new and permanent lines began to be drawn that economic factors reasserted themselves as determining influences.

In view of the personal animosities which were created or made more intense by the venomous campaign it is not surprising that the victory of the Jackson forces was accompanied by an unprecedented clamor for the spoils of office. Nothing was more natural than that "rascals," who in the excitement of the occasion seemed to be most of the people holding federal office, should be turned out to make place for an army of loyal Jacksonians. Unfortunately, however, the victory was no more than won when the victors began a series of big and little wars among themselves. Calhoun, with an eye to the future, tried to get as many of his friends as possible into important positions. Opposed to him was the faction formerly led by his political enemy in the South, William H. Crawford. One of the most influential members of this faction was Martin Van Buren, of New York, who vied with Calhoun in his hope of winning the presidency, and who was influential enough to persuade Jackson to appoint him as secretary of state rather than the man favored by Calhoun. In the face of the growing wrath of Calhoun he secured the appointment of a number of his friends to positions which were eagerly sought by Calhoun men.

The most influential Crawford leader in Maryland was the aged United States Senator Samuel Smith. With the defeat of Crawford in 1824 Smith had announced his intention never again to take a prominent part in a presidential election. He adhered to this policy in 1828. He shrewdly gave the Jackson leaders the impression that he was with them, however, and when the election was over he seems to have hurried away to Washington to give the impression that he had been one of the leaders of the Jackson party, and ought therefore to have the distribution of the patronage. He succeeded in blighting the hopes of a number of men who relied on the support of Taney and other actual leaders of the party, or of Calhoun.

Virgil Maxcy, for instance, looked confidently to his own appointment as treasurer of the United States. Calhoun assured him that with the exception of Taney he knew of no one in Maryland who could be considered Maxcy's competitor for the higher offices of the government.[18] Smith prevented the appointment by making it appear that Taney, Maxcy, and others who were active for Jackson were now trying to seize an undue number of offices for old Federalists, and perhaps by assuring Van Buren that Maxcy ought not to be trusted because of his friendship with Calhoun. It was not until the following year, when the position of Solicitor of the Treasury was created, probably with the aid of Calhoun and with the understanding that Maxcy was to fill it, that a berth was finally found for him.

Taney concerned himself chiefly with federal appointments in Baltimore. On the day on which the warrior from the West took the oath of office, to the acclaim of the masses and to the disgust of those who held themselves superior, Taney and others sought an interview with the new Secretary of the Treasury to urge him to sweep the Adams men out of the custom house in Baltimore and replace them with Jacksonians.[19] With the purging of the custom house he made recommendations as to the filling of the vacancies, and suc-

[18] Calhoun to Maxcy, Jan. 13, 1829, Maxcy MSS.
[19] Maxcy to Calhoun, May 7, 1829, Calhoun MSS., Clemson College.

ceeded in part in determining the choices, in spite of the interference of the Crawford faction.

Although Taney was mentioned as a possible candidate for the position of Attorney General of the United States, Taney at this time seems not to have desired federal office, and made no attempt to get it. The hazards of office holding were great. If he were to go to Washington for a four-year term he would lose in income rather than gain, and the profitable practice which he had carefully built up might dwindle away. As for the honor of a federal appointment, it would not be much greater in the eyes of the people whose opinion he valued than the honor of his position as Attorney General of Maryland.

Taney was for the time quite satisfied with that position as a symbol of his rank and with his private practice as a source of income. When Jackson took over the reins of government there seemed no reason to expect that Taney would soon hold an office of national importance. Fate, however, dealt her cards unexpectedly. The whole course of his life was about to be changed by the warfare between Calhoun and Van Buren, and, incidentally, by the stormy social career of a former barmaid of informal manners and questioned morals.

Chapter VIII

THE JACKSON CABINET

THREE months after his victory at the polls, grieved and embittered because of the recent death of his wife, which he attributed to brutal slander by his political enemies during the campaign, Andrew Jackson entered Washington to take up the reins of government. He was quickly surrounded with a horde of hungry office-seekers, more of them, Daniel Webster cynically remarked, than could be fed without a miracle.[1] The selection of a cabinet came first. Calhoun desired the appointment of Littleton W. Tazewell of Virginia as Secretary of State; but the services of Martin Van Buren, Calhoun's future rival, had been so outstanding as virtually to dictate his selection. Calhoun was largely responsible, however, for the choice of Samuel D. Ingham of Pennsylvania for Secretary of the Treasury, John Branch of North Carolina for Secretary of the Navy, and John M. Berrien of Georgia for Attorney General. He thus disappointed Van Buren, who hoped to have his friend Louis McLane of Delaware placed in one of these positions, and could doubtless have selected for the other positions persons more pleasing to himself than were the adherents of Calhoun.

For the position of Secretary of War, Jackson chose his friend John H. Eaton of Tennessee. He had intended to retain as Postmaster General John McLean, of Ohio, who during the preceding campaign had got the reputation of being for Jackson by refusing to work for Adams. When McLean demurred at removing subordinate post-office officials to make room for loyal Jacksonians, however, Jackson transferred McLean to the Supreme Court and gave the

---

[1] Webster to Mrs. Ezekiel Webster, Feb. 19, 1829, *Writings of Daniel Webster*, XVII, 470.

cabinet position to William T. Barry, a mediocre statesman from Kentucky.

Jackson yielded to the political necessity of filling his cabinet positions with men who for the most part were neither personal friends nor trusted advisers. From the first, however, he looked for guidance not so much to his official family as to the "Kitchen Cabinet," the political henchmen in whom he had put his trust during the campaign. Prominent among them were William B. Lewis of Tennessee and Amos Kendall of Kentucky. These men were quick to fathom the political importance of the rivalry between Calhoun and Van Buren. They saw their political fortunes as more secure under Van Buren than under Calhoun, and the astute Van Buren eagerly welcomed their support.

Jackson and Calhoun worked together smoothly for a time, and Jackson was uncommitted as to his choice of a successor. For more than ten years, however, Jackson had been kept in ignorance of the fact that Calhoun, as Secretary of War, had recommended that Jackson be disciplined for drastic and unauthorized measures in the campaign against the Seminole Indians in 1818. William H. Crawford, brooding in retirement over his own political misfortunes, maliciously circulated the story. Lewis is said to have seen that it reached Jackson, and he and other Van Buren men undoubtedly played up its importance. Jackson, a man of iron integrity, detested duplicity of every sort. He called on Calhoun for the truth of the matter. Instead of meeting the issue with a frank admission, by which he might have preserved peace with Jackson, Calhoun temporized, and was maneuvered into a position in which his influence with Jackson was virtually destroyed.

Calhoun was forced into an almost untenable position in the administration even before this controversy reached a crisis by his disagreement with Jackson on the issue of southern rights, in connection with tariff legislation highly injurious to the South. Sectional friction grew more and more intense after the adoption of the "tariff of abominations" in 1828, culminating in the celebrated Webster-Hayne debate in the Senate in January, 1830. The followers of Calhoun threatened nullification unless the South were relieved of oppression. Jackson said nothing during the period of the debates, and his position was in doubt. At the Jefferson Day dinner, however, in the following April, he struck a blow at nullification by offering a toast, "Our Federal Union: it must be preserved." Calhoun likewise offered a toast to the Union, but with the lame attenuation, "next to our liberty the most dear," and with the warning that the Union could be preserved only by the preservation of state rights and by the equal distribution of benefits and burdens. Jackson's toast came as a surprise, and it was an omen of defeat for Calhoun.

Still another controversy added to Van Buren's prestige and damaged that of Calhoun, and led eventually to the elimination of Calhoun men from Jackson's cabinet. It was the ludicrous social squabble which Van Buren labeled the "Eaton malaria." In appointing as Secretary of War his friend John H. Eaton, Jackson had brought into official circles Eaton's wife, who was of lowly origin and was considered not good enough to associate with the people whom she met there. Six years earlier Jackson had come to Washington as a member of the United States Senate, and had been taken by Eaton, his colleague, to a boarding house with which he was greatly pleased. It was at the home of a Mr. O'Neal, he wrote to Mrs. Jackson, "whose amiable pious wife and two daughters, one married and the other single, take every pains in their power to make us comfortable. . . . I can with truth say I never was in a more agreeable and worthy family. When we have a leisure hour in the evening we spend it with the family. Mrs. Timberlake, the married daughter, whose husband belongs to our Navy, plays on the piano delightfully, and every Sunday evening entertains her pious mother with sacred music, to which we are invited." [2]

Most unfortunately, Mrs. Timberlake, formerly Peggy O'Neal but now the wife of a purser who spent much of his time away from home, was not credited by local gossips with any high degree of piety. Perhaps her impetuous temperament provoked misunderstand-

---

[2] Jackson to Mrs. Jackson, Dec. 21, 1823, J. S. Bassett (ed.), *Correspondence of Andrew Jackson*, III, 218.

ing. She had never merely liked or disliked anybody, she wrote in her autobiography. "I think I always hated everybody I did not love, and have always loved everybody I did not hate." [3] At any rate it was commonly declared that she had less praiseworthy methods of entertaining guests than that of playing the piano, and that her methods had much to do with the presence of lonesome legislators in her father's boarding house. Her name was frequently linked with that of Senator Eaton in unconventional comment. After the death of her husband Eaton heard of the gossip, and went to Jackson for advice. Jackson, having just emerged from the campaign in which he believed the slimy gossip of his political enemies to have been the cause of the death of his wife, advised Eaton to marry the woman and defy her detractors. Eaton took his chief's advice. Hence the introduction of the much discussed lady into cabinet circles.

Jackson declared that the uproar over the elevation of Mrs. Eaton was caused by disappointeed office-seekers and troublesome women. "If I had a tit for every one of these pigs to suck at," he sputtered, "they would still be my friends. They view the appointment of Eaton as a bar to them from office, and have tried here, with all the tools of Clay helping them on, to alarm and prevent me from appointing him. . . . I did not come here to make a cabinet for the ladies of this place, but for the nation." [4]

He would sink in honor to his grave before he would abandon his friend Eaton, he declared on another occasion,[5] and again, "I will never abandon an old and well tried friend for new ones, for slight or trivial causes, nor will I ever be silent when female character is wantonly assailed." [6] He severely lectured an old army friend who had circulated offensive stories about Mrs. Eaton without being able to prove them, and whose motives may have grown out of the fact that he had himself made advances to the lady, and had been repulsed.[7] He demonstrated the falsity of certain ugly charges made

[3] *Autobiography of Peggy Eaton*, p. 18.
[4] Jackson to J. C. McLemore, April, 1829, *Correspondence of Andrew Jackson*, IV, 21.
[5] Jackson to McLemore, May 3, 1829, *ibid.*, p. 31.
[6] Jackson to R. K. Call, July 5, 1829, *ibid.*, p. 53.
[7] Referring to General Call, Jackson to W. B. Lewis, Sept. 10, 1829, *ibid.*, p. 72.

by the minister of the church which he had been accustomed to attending while in Washington.[8] When the reverend gentleman refused to permit his conduct to be influenced by the facts, Jackson arranged thereafter to attend divine services elsewhere.

The families of Vice President Calhoun and Secretaries Ingham and Branch and Attorney General Berrien, who had been appointed in part as a result of the influence of Calhoun, refused to grant social recognition to Mrs. Eaton, thereby further exasperating Old Hickory. The wife of his nephew and private secretary, Andrew J. Donelson, who lived at the President's House, endured Mrs. Eaton for a time. She discovered, however, that whatever the state of the lady's chastity she was a very crude person, and thereupon likewise blacklisted her. Jackson put pressure upon Mrs. Donelson to compel her to support him, but rather than yield she refused to return to Washington after a visit to Tennessee in the summer of 1830. Jackson and his nephew, both residing in the same house, wrote each other long letters in unsuccessful attempts at a solution.

When he heard that Ingham, Branch, and Berrien not only ignored Mrs. Eaton but planned to persuade other persons of social prominence in Washington to do likewise, Jackson called them in and lectured them on the subject.[9] He would not part with Major Eaton from his cabinet, he declared, and those who could not harmonize with him had better withdraw, for harmony he must and would have. The three replied that they would be the last to do anything to injure the feelings or character of Major Eaton and his family, but that they could not undertake to control their own families in the matter. Jackson was at an impasse, for he could hardly dismiss members of his cabinet because their wives refused to associate with the wife of a colleague. As he had said, he had formed a cabinet for the country, and not for the women of Washington.

He never swerved, however, in his loyalty to the Eatons, and his voluminous correspondence on the subject continued to pile up. At first he threw much of the blame on Henry Clay, and then, as fric-

[8] Jackson to E. S. Ely, Sept. 3, 1829, *ibid.*, p. 67.
[9] See J. P. Taylor to John McLean, Dec. 28, 1830, McLean MSS., Library of Congress.

tion developed between himself and Calhoun, the latter was credited with being the chief instigator. In truth, it seems that every politician who could do so turned the affair to his own advantage, but there is no evidence that any major portion of the trouble flowed from any one malignant source.

Van Buren, being a widower with no daughters, was free from the handicaps of most of his colleagues, and shrewdly made the most of the situation. Without joining in the fray to the extent of incurring the hostility of either party he paid courteous attention to Mrs. Eaton, thereby winning the gratitude of Jackson. When he had thoroughly entrenched himself with the president and his advisers he delivered the master stroke which led to the removal of himself and all other members of the cabinet, with the exception of the Postmaster General. Van Buren was quite content for the time being to withdraw from the cabinet and slip behind the political scenes, for in taking a stand as Secretary of State on any of a number of highly controversial issues with which the administration must deal he might demolish his prospects for achieving the presidency itself. On the other hand, if he could bring about a complete reorganization of the cabinet he could save himself from these embarrassments, the friends of Calhoun would be eliminated from cabinet positions, and there would be no reason to fear that Calhoun would have any influence in the selection of the new appointees.

Van Buren therefore reminded Jackson that the administration was suffering from the friction in the cabinet, and suggested that since he and Eaton were the immediate causes of the friction they ought to resign. If they resigned Jackson could then call for the resignation of the other members, on the ground that the resignations made it seem advisable entirely to reconstitute the cabinet. If Ingham, Branch, and Berrien were removed and their enemies retained, public hostility would be stirred, but if all factions went out at once nobody would have any legitimate complaint. When Jackson saw the strategy by which he would be able to get rid of men whom he regarded as Calhoun's trouble makers he agreed to the plan. He saw nothing but high altruism on Van Buren's part, and apparently was quite unaware that Van Buren hoped actually to strengthen himself by the measure, and at the same time avoid responsibilities which might embarrass his own political future.

Eaton was therefore persuaded to resign, on April 7, 1831. Four days later Van Buren sent in his own resignation, with a cleverly written letter in which he discussed for public consumption the political dissensions in the cabinet and their bad effects upon the administration. Jackson then informed the other members of his cabinet of the resignations, mentioned his plan for reorganizing the cabinet completely, and intimated that, pleased as he was with their services individually, it would gratify him if they would voluntarily withdraw.

The scheme worked. Ingham and Branch left the cabinet with little disturbance, and it was privately understood that Berrien was to go at such later date as seemed best. Jackson, elated that he and Van Buren had outwitted his enemies, set about the formation of a new cabinet. He offered the position of Secretary of War to Hugh L. White of Tennessee, in the hope that the legislature would elect Eaton to White's place in the United States Senate, but White declined the offer. Jackson then appointed Lewis Cass, a westerner who had served with distinction in the War of 1812, and had later been governor of Michigan Territory. To succeed Van Buren as Secretary of State he chose Edward Livingston, of the New York family of that name, an able lawyer who had served under Jackson at the battle of New Orleans. To the position of Secretary of the Treasury he appointed Louis McLane of Delaware, a friend of Van Buren for whom Van Buren had desired better things but who until now had had to be satisfied with the position of minister to London. Levi Woodbury of New Hampshire, another Van Buren man, was made Secretary of the Navy. William T. Barry, who had taken little part in the cabinet strife, was retained as Postmaster General.

If Jackson was impervious to Van Buren's deeper motives, his enemies were less blind. "Did you ever read such a letter as Mr. Van Buren's?" Clay scornfully inquired. "It is perfectly characteristic of the man—a labored effort to conceal the true motives, and to assign assumed ones, for his resignation, under the evident hope of profiting by the latter. The 'delicate step,' I apprehend, has been taken, because, foreseeing the gathering storm, he wished early to secure a safe refuge. Whether that will be on his farm, or at London, we shall see." [10]

Calhoun likewise perceived Van Buren's strategy as soon as Virgil Maxcy informed him of the sequence of events. "It is a Van Buren move," he declared, "and has for its object the increase of his control in the movements of the government and at the same time to diminish his responsibility. It was a great point for him to remove Ingham and Branch, while his own presence could be dispensed with at Washington. He has so surrounded the President with his creatures that his affairs can be safely administered in his absence." [11]

Jackson arranged to place Van Buren at the ministerial post which McLane was leaving vacant at London, and turned to the filling of the last of the important positions at home, that of Attorney General. It was variously rumored that Berrien might be retained, that James Buchanan of Pennsylvania might be chosen, and that Philip P. Barbour, a state-rights Virginian, would fill the office. Other names, including that of Taney, were frequently mentioned. Taney was probably not well known to Jackson at the time. He must have been aware of Taney's leadership in the campaign by which he was elected, but he may have desired assurance that Taney was not, like Virgil Maxcy, primarily a Calhoun man.

Furthermore, McLane, a former Federalist, had now been appointed Secretary of the Treasury, and it weighed against Taney that Jackson was unwilling to place another Federalist in the cabinet. Taney's friends overcame this obstacle by stressing Taney's loyalty to the Union during the War of 1812,[12] and gave assurance that Jackson could count on his full support. He made inquiries, and then sent for Frank Key, Taney's brother-in-law, who lived in

[10] Clay to Francis Brooke, May 1, 1831, Calvin Colton (ed.), *Works of Henry Clay*, IV, 299–300.

[11] Calhoun to Maxcy, May 16, 1831, Maxcy MSS.

[12] See Tyler, *Memoir of Roger Brooke Taney*, p. 167.

Georgetown. Key was an enthusiastic Jackson man, who was branded by John Quincy Adams as a pious informer when he frustrated the desire of a neighbor for a magistrate appointment by telling Jackson that the man had opposed his election.[13] Jackson told Key that he knew Taney's doctrines to be sound on leading constitutional questions, and that from Judge Baldwin, whom he had appointed to the Supreme Court, and from others, he knew of Taney's standing in the court. He would like to have him in the office of Attorney General. He wished Key to find out whether Taney would accept the position.

"I believe it is one of the instances in which the General has acted from his own impulses," Key wrote to Taney, "and that you will find yourself, both as to him and his cabinet, acting with men who know and value you, and with whom you will have the influence you ought to have, and which you can do something efficient with. As to your business, you can be as much in Baltimore as you would find necessary or desirable, with the understanding that you would come over whenever wanted. This would only be when you were wanted at a meeting of the cabinet, or anything important. On ordinary occasions, and applications for opinions from the Departments, they could send you the papers to Baltimore, and you could reply from there. As to the Supreme Court, it would of course suit you entirely, and the increase in your business there would make up well for lesser matters." [14]

Taney, who at the time was attending the Court of Appeals at Annapolis, replied that he would accept the position if he could do so without violating his obligations to his clients. Key reported, in turn, that Jackson was greatly pleased, as was also Barry, the Postmaster General. The office need not interfere with Taney's engagements in court or with his affairs in Baltimore. He need not even change his residence unless he wished to do so.[15] The Secretary of State officially notified Taney of his appointment June 21, 1831, and

---

13 *Memoirs of John Quincy Adams*, VIII, 313.
14 Key to Taney, June 14, 1831, Tyler, *op. cit.*, p. 171.
15 Key to Taney, June 16, 1831, *ibid.*, p. 172.

Taney accepted three days later. On June 23 Jackson, having his usual difficulties with matters of spelling, reported to Van Buren as follows:

"I have appointed mr Tauney atto. Genl." [16]

Taney was at this time widely known only in his own state, and to a lesser extent in the states adjoining. Hence most of the comments on the appointment which did more than merely announce it were published in Maryland and Virginia. "We congratulate the state, the administration, and the country, upon this selection," declared the Baltimore *Republican*. "With all parties it is recognized as one which will strengthen the administration and do honor to the public service. A lawyer surpassed by none in the country, a gentleman whose name is identified wherever it has been heard, with everything that is pure and elevated in character, a ripe scholar, a sound, discreet, orthodox politician, gentle in manners and uniformly courteous in deportment.—Mr. Taney will be found a safe and firm counsellor, and valuable public servant to the state which sends him, and the Union which receives him, may justly be proud.—The change can hardly advance the pecuniary interests of Mr. Taney. The great extent and value of his practice in his profession, must make a change of his arrangements, and a removal to Washington, a matter of much inconvenience. But no man ever thought less of personal considerations, when placed in competition with public duties." [17]

Other comments by political friends and foes were similarly approving. "Censure for once is dumb," boasted the Richmond *Enquirer*. "The opposition press of his own state is as loud in praise of his talents and virtue, as the friends of the administration. All that he wants to make himself universally known, is what Decatur wished to his brother officer, viz 'opportunity.' The more conspicuous theatre on which he is now placed furnishes him with this 'opportunity.' " [18]

Taney's own account of his appointment as Attorney General, al-

[16] Jackson to Van Buren, June 23, 1831, *Correspondence of Andrew Jackson*, IV, 302.
[17] Baltimore *Republican*, quoted, in Richmond *Enquirer*, July 1, 1831.
[18] Richmond *Enquirer*, July 31, 1831.

though written nearly two decades later and perhaps colored by the feelings stirred by later events, reveals something of his attitude toward the change in his political fortunes. The only office he had ever deeply coveted, he declared, was that of Attorney General of Maryland, the position which he held at the time of his appointment to the federal office. "It had been most commonly filled by highly gifted and eminent men; and my family on both the father and mother's side have been for so many generations Maryland people, that I have always felt strong Maryland attachments; and having no desire for political distinction in power, my highest ambition was to receive the highest bar honor in my native state; and to be thought worthy of succeeding the distinguished lawyers who had held the office before me."

He left this office with reluctance, he declared. He had no particular connection with the public affairs of the United States, and little acquaintance with the leading men of the government except those from Maryland. Yet such were his feelings for the President that when a request came for his assistance he felt under obligation to grant it, even though his law practice would inevitably suffer and his income be reduced. He and other men who had supported Jackson in his political campaigns, and had in this way brought on him the vindictive assaults against his character and against that of his wife, were under obligation to stand by him, to the extent of making real personal sacrifices. "Such sacrifices seemed to me to be necessary where new enemies were combining with old ones, to wage war against him in the same fierce spirit of personal hostility. . . .

"In a country like ours where exciting political subjects follow each other in rapid succession, some of the influences under which we have at times acted pass away from our own minds and cannot easily be understood or appreciated by those who come subsequently upon the stage and did not mingle in the conflict. But the feelings which I entertained toward General Jackson, and which strongly influenced my decision to accept the place of Attorney General of the United States were at that period common to thousands of those who had supported him in the warm and exciting contests which began in 1824, and ended in his election in 1828, and we gathered around as personal friends who felt and resented the cruel destruction of his domestic happiness." [19]

Taney went to Washington as soon as his work was completed at Annapolis, and took the oath of office July 20, 1831. The Secretaries of State, Treasury, War, and Navy were at that time entitled to salaries of $6,000 per annum, the Postmaster General received $4,000, and the Attorney General was entitled to a direct salary of $3,500. The act of 1830 which created the office of Solicitor of the Treasury required the Attorney General to give the Solicitor advice in certain matters, and added $500 to his salary, making a total of $4,000 in all. There was at that time no Department of Justice to be supervised by the Attorney General, and it had been expected that men filling this office would add to their incomes by continuing private practice. Taney's previous income, though not to be determined with exactness, was far in excess of the amount of the salary—sufficiently in excess to permit him not only to continue heavy current expenditures but also to purchase for $11,000 the property at Lexington and Courtland streets which was to be his home for a quarter of a century. He did not agree to the suggestion that he should continue to reside in Baltimore while serving as Attorney General—which may account for the fact that the number of his cases before the Maryland Court of Appeals steadily fell off, although he continued a substantial private practice until he became Secretary of the Treasury. He rented his house in Baltimore and moved his family to a dwelling on the east side of Lafayette Park, in Washington. One reason for moving may have been devotion to the duties of his office, but it is also probable that with his frail physique he would have found numerous trips over the rough roads between Baltimore and Washington excessively burdensome.

For a time after his arrival in Washington he filled two cabinet positions, his own and that of the Secretary of War, Lewis Cass not having arrived. He was commissioned as Acting Secretary of War on July 21, 1831, and presumably served until Cass was sworn in

[19] Taney, Bank War MS., pp. 31–34.

August 9. Since the second office paid a higher salary than his own he secured added compensation from it, thereby laying himself open to ultimate political attack, though apparently there was no just cause for criticism.

The demands of his own office were varied and heavy. Taney considered it the most laborious in the government, with the exception of that of the President.[20] William Pinkney, who had held it some years earlier, had expressed a similar opinion. Judge Peter V. Daniel, who refused it in 1833 when Taney resigned to become Secretary of the Treasury, called it the most troublesome office in the government. "With the duties of a cabinet minister," he declared, "with the liability of being called on for instructions by every bureau, with the necessity of encountering not one or two, but every one in succession of the ablest counsel in the nation, each separately and deliberately prepared on every varied department of jurisprudence foreign and domestic, the office of the Attorney General is decidedly the most onerous in the government. The salary of that office ought to be ten thousand dollars in just proportion to the salaries of the heads of other departments." [21]

Office seekers were of course among the first to make demands on his time. He had little patronage, since a clerk and a messenger made up his staff, but his support was desired for various purposes. James Buchanan wished him to make public his appointment as minister to Russia, and thus correct the popular impression that he had been politically shelved. Jackson had insisted on keeping the appointment secret until John Randolph, who had not been too successful in the office, had returned to the United States. Taney replied with a friendly letter, but shifted responsibility to Secretary of State Livingston, who in turn conferred with Jackson and then informed Buchanan that he must wait.[22] A Baltimore acquaintance asked his aid in getting a position under Livingston, either in the Department of

[20] Taney, Bank War MS., p. 34.
[21] P. V. Daniel to John Y. Mason, July 19, 1845, Polk MSS., 2d series, Library of Congress.
[22] Taney to Buchanan and Livingston to same, Aug. 2, 1831, Buchanan MSS., Historical Society of Pennsylvania.

State or in the Foreign Service. Taney replied diplomatically that he could not interfere with the arrangements of another member of the cabinet, but made the ambiguous promise, "If, however, Mr. Livingston or any other gentleman should do me the honor of asking my knowledge of you, it will give me pleasure to speak of you as you deserve." [23] A minister who had served with Taney in the Federalist party in earlier years, and who had been ejected from St. John's College because he had voted for Jackson and would certainly so vote again, begged for a chaplaincy,[24] with results which are not revealed by the records.

One application for political support brought a letter from Taney revealing democratic ideas in sharp contrast with the aristocratic beliefs which had characterized him and his father as leading Federalists many years before. Robert Gilmor, a wealthy and influential Baltimore merchant and an intimate of the group with which Taney associated, asked his aid in securing a position for Charles Carroll Harper, the son of Robert Goodloe Harper and the grandson of Charles Carroll of Carrollton. The position was that of commissioner under the treaty which was to settle long-pending claims of the United States against France.

Taney replied frankly that he could not encourage Harper's application for the position. "It is a post not only of honor, but of labor and profit and will be sought altogether on account of the emolument annexed to it. The known wealth of Mr. Carroll would I think be regarded as a decisive objection to the appointment of his grandson to an office of this description, for it would you know be impossible to enter an explanation on this subject with the public, to satisfy them that the state of his finances justified him in seeking the office. The appointment will no doubt be desired by many professional men of high standing, advanced in life, and whose pecuniary situation would be known to be such as to render the salary a matter of importance to them. I do not think the President could with propriety appoint Mr. Harper in preference to such men, especially as

[23] Taney to Thomas W. Griffith, Aug. 11, 1831, MS., Maryland Historical Society.
[24] Henry L. Davis to Taney, Aug. 3, 1831, MS.

he has been so long abroad and is looked upon by the community as a gentleman of fortune traveling for his own amusement." [25]

The letter suggests the belief that public office and the rewards thereof belonged to the deserving and needy, rather than to the elect. It does not say that public opinion ought always to be permitted to rule in such matters, but it shows an awareness of the force of public opinion, and of the fact that the administration must of necessity take such a force into account. This is hardly a philosophy of aristocracy. Yet it doubtless represented in part an outgrowth of the experience of an aristocracy of a particular kind, the aristocracy of family and of land, of which the members might be poor in terms of liquid wealth and in need of salaries if they were to hold public office.

Taney was called upon by the Departments and by the President for opinions on a great variety of subjects, most of which were of transient importance. One of his first formal opinions was an interpretation of the federal bankruptcy law, which proved displeasing to James Buchanan and Daniel Webster, who had had much to do with its enactment. "With the most unfeigned respect for the opinions of the Attorney General," Webster declared, "I cannot persuade myself to think that he has taken the right view of the provisions of the act. If he has done so, we were very clumsy law-makers." [26] The question as to who was right is no longer important. It is of interest, however, that at this early date in his career as a federal officer Taney disagreed with "the Godlike Daniel," with whom in succeeding years he was to clash again and again in battles in which Webster ceased even to pretend that he had respect for Taney's opinions.

If there was little permanent significance attached to many of the problems to which Taney was required to give attention, one type of problem, that of the rights of negroes, was a striking exception. In spite of many varied attempts to solve it, the negro problem had grown more and more difficult of solution since the period of a

---

[25] Taney to Gilmor, Sept. 7, 1831, Dreer Coll., Historical Society of Pennsylvania.
[26] George T. Curtis, *Life of Daniel Webster*, I, 405–406.

decade earlier when Taney had been much concerned with it. The lower South, specializing more and more in the production of cotton, needed an increasing supply of slave labor, and southern statesmen forgot their former doubts as to the wisdom and morality of preserving the institution. The North, moving steadily in the direction of industrialization, and using diverse methods of production for which slavery could not easily be adapted, became increasingly critical of it. The states with interests in harmony with those of the North grew sufficiently populous to force the adoption of tariff legislation which the South found oppressive, and back of southern resentment of the tariff lay the fear that sooner or later the North would use the power of the federal government to interfere with its "peculiar institution."

The southern states feared and resented the spread of abolitionist sentiment within their borders, by whatever means it was brought about, and adopted laws excluding free negroes from other states and from foreign countries, on the ground that they might provoke uprisings among the slaves. A South Carolina law provided that free negroes employed on foreign vessels which came into the ports of the state should be seized and held in prison while the vessel was in port. Upon the departure of the vessel the negroes would be released if the master of the vessel paid the costs of their imprisonment. Otherwise they would be sold to recover these costs. The British diplomatic officer in the United States objected to the seizure of colored subjects of the king, on the ground that it violated the treaty between Great Britain and the United States. The Secretary of State called upon Taney for his opinion in the matter.

The delivery of the opinion was postponed for many months, however, probably because of startling events which intervened. In August, 1831, Nat Turner, a slave who claimed to be a minister, made arrangements for a revolt, and massacred a large number of women and children in Southampton County, Virginia, while most of the men of the respective families were absent at a camp meeting. The news flashed quickly throughout the entire South, and white people were terrified by the belief that the long-dreaded uprising of slaves was upon them. Strange negroes or negroes seen acting strangely were shot on sight. Those who had participated in the revolt were killed, and Nat Turner was tried, sentenced to death, and hanged; but the South remained stricken with fear. The vigilance committee of Columbia, South Carolina, offered a reward of $1,500 "for the apprehension and prosecution to a conviction, of any white person who may be detected in distributing or circulating within the state the newspaper called 'The Liberator,' printed in Boston, or the pamphlet called 'Walker's Pamphlet,' or any other publication of a seditious tendency." [27] A great impetus was given to the movement to colonize free negroes in Liberia.

Taney's youngest brother, Dr. Octavius C. Taney, the only member of the family still residing among the tobacco planters of Calvert County, was elected to the Maryland Senate in September of the same year. During the ensuing term he introduced a resolution stating that "recent occurrences in this state, as well as in other states of our Union, have impressed more deeply upon our minds the necessity of devising some means, by which we may facilitate the removal of the free persons of color from our state, and from the United States." Since the states would be relieved of the heavy tax burden if an appropriation for the purpose was secured from Congress, he urged that such an appropriation be sought. If Congress could not constitutionally make such an appropriation he recommended that the Constitution be amended.[28]

Dr. Taney was made chairman of a committee to confer with the committee on grievances and courts of justice on "the condition of the colored population in this state." Although Dr. Taney died before all the memorials on the subject had been considered and recommendations worked out, the report of the committee was in harmony with his point of view. It revealed a total colored population in Maryland of 155,932, of which 52,938 were free. The free population was increasing, while the slaves were decreasing in number. Many more slaves would undoubtedly be set free if the state would

[27] *Niles' Weekly Register*, Oct. 29, 1831.
[28] *Journal of the Proceedings of the Senate of Maryland*, 1831, p. 55.

provide for their transportation to Africa. The report recommended that citizens of other states be forbidden to bring slaves into Maryland, that manumission should not be permitted without transportation, and that the state transport all free negroes capable of becoming parents, thus solving the problem in one generation.

The Marylanders were deeply concerned about the fact that land values and the white population had increased much more rapidly in the free state of Pennsylvania than in Maryland where slaves and free negroes worked in competition with white labor, and hoped to capture the prosperity of their neighbors by eliminating the handicap. "Her position near the free states, will enable her to make the change contemplated in her laboring class, with ease and success. The free white labor of these states, the overflowing of which now turns in another course, will be gradually poured into her territory, and as the slave retires from her fields, they will smile in renewed luxuriance, under the labor of the free man." [29]

Thus Maryland and many other states, all highly sensitive on the subject, were attempting in their own ways to deal with the exceedingly delicate problems arising out of the presence of negroes within their borders. Octavius Taney recommended individually that the national government be asked to supply funds to deport free negroes, but he did not suggest that the federal government interfere to determine policy, and even the recommendation which he did make was not supported by the committee. The southern states on the whole, already fearful of the federal government as the tool of the North, preferred to solve their own problems by their own methods.

Under the circumstances it is not surprising that Taney postponed his answer to the question as to whether South Carolina laws affecting alien negroes violated the treaty with Great Britain. Fortunately, or so it must have seemed at the time, it became possible to answer the question not directly but by implication through the answer to another, without offending either the North or the South. A man from Philadelphia who was interested in the West India trade asked Secretary Livingston whether the slaves on colonial vessels flying the

[29] *African Repository*, VIII, 52–55, April, 1832.

British flag were covered by that flag while in ports of the United States, or whether they were subject to the laws of the states.[30] The matter was important to the merchants because some states had decreed that slaves brought into their ports should immediately become free. Livingston referred the inquiry to Taney.

Taney replied that the treaty with Great Britain contained no express provision on the subject. The engagement for mutual freedom and liberty of commerce could not be construed to imply the obligation to protect slave property. Certainly Great Britain had not so construed it, for it was said to be a fixed principle of the law of England that a slave became free as soon as he touched her shores. Furthermore, the liberty of trade guaranteed by the treaty was conferred subject to the laws of the country, and within their respective borders the laws of the states constituted part of the laws of this country.

"If therefore," Taney continued, "by the laws of any of the states a slave becomes free, as soon as he is brought within the limits of the state, . . . and is there taken by the state authorities from the possession of his owner and declared to be free, the General Government is under no obligation to interfere in behalf of the master, and he has no right to call on the United States to support him in his claim of property. It is perhaps unnecessary now to inquire whether the United States could by treaty control the several states in the exercise of this power. I think they could not. But the decision of that question is not material in the present state of things, for there is no conflict between the stipulations in the treaty and the laws of those states which forbid the introduction of slaves within their limits, and declare that persons of that description, when introduced, shall become free." [31]

In this manner Taney upheld the claims of the abolitionists on the one hand, and on the other asserted the right of the states to legislate on the subject of property rights in slaves, in spite of any treaty made

[30] Samuel Brooks to Livingston, Nov. 18, 1831, Miscellaneous Letters, Department of State.
[31] Opinion of Dec. 6, 1831, 2 Official Opinions of the Attorneys General 475.

by the federal government. His suggestion that the treaty-making power of the federal government could not be used to interfere with the powers of the states in the matter, while it protected the right of the northern states to prohibit slavery within their borders, was still more deeply satisfying to slave owners who feared that the federal government might interfere with the control of the "peculiar institution" of the South.

This opinion, without mentioning the South Carolina law which provided for the imprisonment of free negroes who entered the ports of the state on foreign ships, clearly implied that the subject was one with which the federal government could not interfere. Evidently Taney preferred not to discuss the matter further in an official opinion. The enforcement of a North Carolina law similar to that of South Carolina provided additional friction, however. Charles Bankhead, the British chargé d'affaires in Washington, wrote to Livingston protesting against "the power of a state to enact any law which has for its object the forcible detention of British subjects, under circumstances altogether at variance with the freedom of commercial intercourse between nations, and unauthorized by any treaty or convention between Great Britain and the United States." [32]

Livingston promised to investigate, but there the matter rested until the following May, when in a letter vigorous almost to the point of insolence Bankhead again remonstrated against the North Carolina law, reminded Livingston that William Wirt had as Attorney General pronounced such a law void, declared that the states had not "shown any disposition to repeal their obnoxious enactments," and demanded effective measures to secure their immediate repeal. [33]

It was true that Wirt had declared the laws invalid, but Berrien, his successor, had held otherwise. Livingston naturally desired the opinion of his own legal adviser on the point immediately in question before stating his position to the British chargé. Upon receipt of Bankhead's peremptory demand, therefore, he sent a formal note to

[32] Bankhead to Livingston, Nov. 7, 1831, Great Britain Notes, Department of State.
[33] Bankhead to Livingston, May 14, 1832, *ibid.*

Taney to call attention to his letter of August 9, 1831, "and to request the Attorney General's answer." [34] Taney replied on May 28, 1832, reminding Livingston that the latter was aware of the circumstances supposed to render unnecessary a reply to his letter of the preceding August, but admitting that Bankhead's renewed application seemed to require the government to come to a definite conclusion on the subject. He followed with a discussion some four thousand words in length, and on June 9, having worked it out in the midst of his handling of cases before the Court of Appeals at Annapolis, he sent in a supplement which ran more than half the length of the original document.

It is significant that when some years later the compilation of the Official Opinions of the Attorneys General was begun, neither this opinion, nor the supplement, nor any form of it, was included. The opinion on the power of states to free slaves brought into their ports was included, but the existence of the opinion delivered on the more delicate subject was not mentioned. The excuse may have been that it was never put into finished form for publication. The quotations which follow from the original document are taken from a draft in Taney's hand, much interlined and with many passages crossed out,[35] which does leave much to be desired as a piece of finished composition. The manuscript of the supplement which is followed here is in the hand of a copyist, with occasional changes in Taney's hand.[36] The opinion throughout is similar not so much to Taney's finished work as to his efforts at intermediate stages wherein by repeating, rephrasing, and reworking he clarified his own ideas.

It seems probable however, that the content rather than the condition of the opinion was chiefly responsible for the fact that it was left unpublished. It abounds with comments on controversial questions as to the historical condition and the historic legal rights of negroes, including, indeed, important materials which did not appear

---

[34] Livingston to Taney, May 19, 1832, Domestic Letters, Department of State.

[35] This draft is in the Attorney General MSS., which at the time of this writing are in the Library of Congress.

[36] This copy is filed with a letter, Taney to Livingston, June 9, 1832, Miscellaneous Letters, Department of State.

publicly over Taney's signature until twenty-five years later in connection with the Dred Scott decision. It analyzes and narrows the interpretation of one of John Marshall's famous decisions in a manner which might have proved highly embarrassing to Taney as Marshall's successor. Finally, it suggests doubts as to the sufficiency of Supreme Court decisions as precedents to determine administrative policy—which, to say the least, would be regarded as gross heresy in any Chief Justice of the United States. These characteristics, of course, however legitimately they may have operated to prevent the publication of the opinion, do not detract from and in many respects they add to its value as material for the study of the development of Taney's ideas on these important subjects.

As in his earlier opinion, Taney declared that the rights conferred by the treaty with Great Britain were granted subject to the restraints of the laws of the country, among which the laws of the states were included. The law of South Carolina had been assumed to be constitutional, and no judicial tribunal of competent authority had declared otherwise. No foreign government could be allowed in its negotiations with the United States to question the interpretation given to the Constitution by the people and their constituted authorities. If any individual British subject wished to contest the constitutionality of the law he could do so by bringing the subject before the judicial tribunals of the country for decision. Under the circumstances, however, it seemed best that he should himself discuss the constitutional question, about which his two immediate predecessors in office had disagreed.

It was his opinion that any slave state had the right to guard itself from the dangers thought to arise from the introduction of free negroes among its slaves, and that this right had not been surrendered by the adoption of the Constitution of the United States. This right, he believed, could not be abrogated by federal laws or federal treaties. The Constitution, it was true, declared that a treaty should be the supreme law, but the treaty would itself be void if it came in conflict with the reserved rights of the states. The negroes themselves had no constitutional rights in the matter.

"The African race in the United States even when free, are every where a degraded class, and exercise no political influence. The privileges they are allowed to enjoy, are accorded to them as a matter of kindness and benevolence rather than of right. They are the only class of persons who can be held as mere property, as slaves. And where they are nominally admitted by law to the privileges of citizenship, they have no effectual power to defend them, and are permitted to be citizens by the sufferance of the white population and hold whatever rights they enjoy at their mercy. They were never regarded as a constituent portion of the sovereignty of any state. But as a separate and degraded people to whom the sovereignty of each state might accord or withhold such privileges as they deemed proper. They were not looked upon as citizens by the contracting parties who formed the Constitution. They were evidently not supposed to be included by the term *citizens*. And were not intended to be embraced in any of the provisions of that Constitution but those which point to them in terms not to be mistaken."

In this fashion Taney stated his doctrine as to the social and legal position of negroes in the United States, the doctrine which was to be so hotly condemned twenty-five years later when announced in his opinion in the Dred Scott case. He produced still other arguments to show that the slave states at the time of the adoption of the Constitution had had no intention of conferring equal rights upon free negroes, and had obviously not sanctioned the Constitution with the expectation that it could give to negroes the rights guaranteed to citizens. "Our constitutions were not formed by the assistance of that unfortunate race nor for their benefit. They were not regarded as constituent members of either of the sovereignties and were not therefore intended to be embraced by the terms, *citizens of each state.*" Neither had the states, by the more general phrases of the Constitution, such as that dealing with the power to make treaties, surrendered their full control over negroes within their borders. The state laws would therefore be valid even if in direct conflict with a federal treaty.

It had been said that the South Carolina law was more severe and oppressive than was necessary for the protection of the state. Taney confessed his own opinion that milder measures would have achieved the desired object and created less dissatisfaction. Since the state had the power to protect itself from the danger in question, however, the methods used must be a matter of legislative discretion, even though they proved oppressive.

Had this particular conclusion been made public it would have been highly pleasing to the state-rights doctrinaires of the South. One of Taney's illustrations, however, would have been highly displeasing to the same group. He was not presenting a narrow state-rights argument, but was merely contending that a legislature was the sole judge as to the proper exercise of the powers which belonged to it. Congress, for instance, through its power of regulating commerce, might impose a tariff for the protection of domestic industry. This power might be oppressively exercised so as to throw an unequal and unjust burden on one portion of the country in order to enrich another. Yet, Taney declared, in a statement clashing with the doctrines of Calhoun, the law would be constitutional and everybody bound to obey it, since Congress had the power and the discretion as to its use.

The argument in its broader aspects, however, was more devastating for the doctrines of the nationalists than for those of their opponents, for by implication it limited the power of the judiciary, which under the leadership of John Marshall had become the nationalist stronghold. Indeed, with superb deftness, Taney utilized one of Marshall's most significant nationalist opinions to demonstrate his point that the the courts could not interfere with the discretion of a legislature in exercising the powers conferred upon it. In *McCulloch* v. *Maryland* [37] Marshall had shown that Congress had the implied power to establish a bank. In reply to the argument that the bank established was unnecessarily large and in other respects not within the scope of the Constitution, he declared that such questions were not open to judicial inquiry. They were legislative in character, and belonged within the province of the legislature.

[37] 4 Wheaton 316 (1819).

Taney was resorting to a much used technique of logical combat. He was using Marshall's generalizations to support contentions which Marshall would have refused to accept. He was suggesting a possibility—which in other arguments made during the same period he attempted to show to be a fact—that the Bank of the United States had in certain respects been organized in violation of the Constitution. The Supreme Court had upheld its rights in *McCulloch* v. *Maryland* not because it was in every respect constitutionally organized, but because the court had no power to prescribe the kind of bank which Congress might create.

It is a matter of history, however, that in the case cited Marshall had been interested in defending the Bank of the United States pretty much as it stood, and in protecting in from the necessity of proving that in all the many details of its organization it was "necessary and proper" in the constitutional sense. There is no reason for believing that he intended to make any broad surrender of the power of judicial review, as Taney implied, and to leave solely to Congress the decision as to how powers granted should be exercised. Certainly he would not have followed Taney all the way in his contention that state legislatures were unrestrained by judicial power in their control over negroes within their borders, federal laws and treaties to the contrary notwithstanding.

The only remedy for legislative abuses, Taney declared, was in the electorate. "To deny the sufficiency and safety of this tribunal is to question the political axiom on which the general and state governments of this country are all founded. . . . Experience as well as theory proves that no tribunal can be formed so likely to come to just conclusions on all questions of legislative discretion as the great body of the people themselves."

He admitted finally, however, that, convinced as he was of the correctness of his own argument, the Supreme Court might not agree with him. Indeed, he thought it highly probable that the court would declare the law of South Carolina null and void if contrary to the stipulations of the treaty, should the question come before it. He was not prepared to admit, however, that a constitutional interpretation made by the court should be regarded as permanently binding upon other branches of the government if they believed it erroneous. "If the judgment pronounced by the court be conclusive it does not follow that the reasoning or principles which it announces in coming to its conclusions are equally binding and obligatory." Certainly he would not advise the Executive to adopt a wrong construction of the Constitution merely because the Supreme Court might be expected to adopt it at some time in the future. Judgment could be postponed as to what ought to be done should the court later declare the law to be void.

This opinion, unique in many ways, has interest for lawyers in its attempt to narrow the range of judicial review, and in its heretical suggestion that the Executive was not bound to accept the principles asserted by the Supreme Court—for it was written by a man who four years thereafter was to be Chief Justice of the United States. It will be clear to lawyers and laymen alike that Taney was attempting to mold legal doctrines, quite as much as to follow them. He was faced with a situation wherein the southern states, supersensitive on the subject, were attempting to solve their own problems arising out of slavery. The federal government was regarded with distrust as far as these problems were concerned. Yet a foreign diplomat was pressing the federal government to interfere with the enforcement of southern laws. Taney agreed with the southerners that only the states could and should deal with the problems in question. He argued, therefore, that the federal government had no power to interfere, and selected and interpreted historical facts and constitutional doctrines accordingly. He was acting as a realist, though he had to conceal his realism behind the verbiage of law.

His technique is further revealed by the disparity between his argument here and that which he had delivered in defense of Jacob Gruber in 1819. While slavery continued, he had declared before the Frederick County court, it was a blot on our national character. Every real lover of freedom hoped that it would be effectually wiped away. "And until it shall be accomplished," he had continued, "until the time shall come when we can point without a blush, to the language held in the Declaration of Independence, every friend of humanity will seek to lighten the galling chain of slavery . . ." [38]

In 1832, however, he considered the Declaration of Independence irrelevant as evidence of the status of the negro. "Our Declaration of Independence," he argued in the supplement to his opinion, "we know was drawn by a distinguished citizen of a slave holding state. And when it was asserted in that instrument 'that all men are created equal; that they are endowed by their Creator with certain unalienable rights; that among these are life, liberty and the pursuit of happiness; that to secure these rights, governments are instituted among men, deriving their just powers from the consent of the governed;'—no one ever supposed that the African race in this country were entitled to the benefit of this declaration, nor did any one imagine that they had a right to claim the extension of that great principle to themselves."

It would be beside the point to discuss at length the extent to which the signers of the Declaration of Independence intended it to apply to negroes. Furthermore, it would be propagating error to pretend that between 1819 and 1832 Taney had grown callous in his feelings toward negroes. Toward them personally he still had the same feeling of warm solicitude which he had revealed many times in the past, as was shown, for example, by his efforts on behalf of a negro boy named Cornelius. Cornelius, the slave of a Major Hughes, had been permitted by his master to earn small sums of money toward the purchase of his freedom, and to educate himself above the level of most slaves, so that he was able to write letters. Taney in some way became interested in the boy, and discussed with his friend William M. Beall, of Frederick, the possibility of buying the boy and setting him free as soon as he was able to earn the remaining amount necessary to cover the purchase price.

"Major Hughes it seems," Taney wrote to Beall, "is willing to let Cornelius go for $450, and he has but a hundred and fifty of his own. Cornelius is a good boy and I am willing to aid him, and there-

[38] See Chapter V.

fore send a check payable to your order." [39] The purchase was made, and Taney not only made the boy a free person in effect from the beginning, but looked after him from that time on almost as if he were a member of the family. Yet, believing as he did that the problems of slavery were so intricate and so peculiarly local as to require local handling, he felt it his duty as Attorney General so to interpret law as to leave the control of the subject in local hands, even though some negroes suffered thereby. Doubtless he would have said, as he did say on other occasions, that even the negroes, on the whole, since they were in the country, were better off under the prevailing system of control than they would have been under a system or lack of system brought about by outside interference.

Perhaps fortunately for the country, though unfortunately for those deeply interested in the intricacies of judicial processes, the Supreme Court did not have occasion in this period to pass upon the highly controversial issues which Taney had discussed, and although history has it that President Jackson defied the Supreme Court in connection with matters about which the country was less sensitive, he had no occasion to do it as far as the southern negro laws were concerned. Taney's opinion, however, remains as a landmark in the story of the government's attempts to deal with slavery problems, and it is of prime importance for the light which it throws on Taney's political and legal methods, and on his point of view.

[39] Taney to Beall, April 22, 1832, MS. in the possession of Miss Nannie Floyd, Frederick, Md.

CHAPTER IX

THE BEGINNING OF THE BANK WAR

TANEY's appointment as Attorney General of the United States was approximately coincident with the beginning of one of the major political and economic conflicts which this country has experienced, the struggle between the Jackson administration and the Bank of the United States. Like Jackson and most other statesmen of the period, Taney seems at this time to have had little conception of the extent of the impending conflict, little conception, indeed, that a conflict of importance was impending at all. Quickly, however, it became a subject of strife in the cabinet, in Congress, and in the country as a whole. Taney was involved in it throughout the three years which he served in the Jackson cabinet, first as Attorney General and later as Secretary of the Treasury. It was responsible for his appointment to the second position. In Taney's life the struggle was second in importance only to his achievements as Chief Justice of the United States, and many of his conceptions of constitutional law which were applied from the bench were worked out or modified in the midst of the warfare with the bank.

The parts played by Taney and his colleagues in the cabinet were colored and at times almost wholly determined by personal rivalries, jealousies and prejudices—for by changing his cabinet Jackson did not fully achieve his desire for peace within his official family. The most intense friction developed between Taney and Louis McLane, the Secretary of the Treasury, who aspired to a position on the Supreme Court and feared that his hopes might be frustrated by the appointment of Taney instead of himself when a vacancy occurred.

McLane, like Taney, had formerly been a Federalist. With the disintegration of his party he aligned himself with the Crawford faction, however, and became a close friend of Van Buren. The Van Buren organization supported him for a cabinet position at the beginning of the Jackson administration, but by securing a number of cabinet positions for his own friends Calhoun forced McLane to be satisfied with the ministerial post at London. Van Buren secured from Jackson a promise that McLane would be appointed to the Supreme Court in the event of the death or resignation of Justice Gabriel Duvall, who was assigned to the circuit including Maryland and Delaware—the latter being McLane's own state. At McLane's request Van Buren asked Jackson to appoint McLane in case Justice Henry Baldwin, of Pennsylvania, fulfilled a threat to resign. It was the custom to appoint judges from the circuits they were to serve, but Jackson promised to choose McLane if he could consistently do so.

When the cabinet was reorganized Van Buren secured the Treasury post for McLane, and advised him to accept it. He did so, but persuaded Van Buren to write to Jackson that he still desired a position on the Supreme Court. Van Buren wrote the letter,[1] and gave it to McLane for delivery in person. Upon arriving in Washington, McLane concluded that it would create a bad impression to apply directly for another office at the moment of becoming head of the Treasury Department. He returned the letter to Van Buren, urging him to change the date and send it to Jackson by mail. He was deeply agitated on the subject, for he had found a rival in the new cabinet. Taney was from the same state as Justice Duvall, and McLane was convinced that Taney had his eye on the Supreme Court position. "You must not ascribe it to suspicion," he urged in his letter to Van Buren, "when I assure you that Mr. Taney *fights shy* of me. He was the only one of the cabinet who kept off and *him I did not see until we met yesterday at the President's in council*. We were always on good terms and I know of no cause of separation now but his fears on a certain subject. Therefore do not fail to send the letter."[2]

---

[1] Van Buren to Jackson, Aug. 3, 1831, John C. Fitzpatrick (ed.), *Autobiography of Martin Van Buren*, p. 578.

[2] McLane to Van Buren, early August, *ibid.*, p. 579.

McLane grew more and more anxious as he pondered on the menace of Taney's rivalry, and wrote again to Van Buren to urge the importance of pressing his case with Jackson. "The designs in another quarter," [3] he declared, "are not to be disregarded and there is no other quarter than you from which it would be possible for me to intimate my wishes. You may invent what pretext you please for your letter, but on no account neglect it." [4]

Van Buren sent his original letter to Jackson, and told its history. "Mr. McLane is delighted with your reception of him," he added, "and will in all respects come up to your expectations. Between us, in strict confidence, he apprehends that another member of your cabinet may desire the same place that he does. Talk to him freely about it if you please and he will be at ease. It has been a very unpleasant matter for me to press this subject upon your attention at this moment but I could not well avoid it, and it is best that you should know all." [5]

In spite of McLane's suspicions there is no proof that at this early period Taney had any deep desire for a place on the Supreme Court. The suspicions produced stiffness and friction between them, however, and the growing friction led them to take opposite sides on issues which they might have been able to meet together—including issues both in connection with the struggle with the Bank of the United States and elsewhere. Taney's appraisal of McLane, written many years later, gives some indication of his opinion of the man during this early period:

"Mr. McLane was an ambitious man; loved power, and aspired to the presidency which he confidently expected to reach. He had been many years in Congress; and was for some time Chairman of the Committee on Ways and Means, which had made him familiar with the financial concerns of the country. This circumstance gave his opinions weight in the cabinet and he was sensible of it. He had always been in favor of a Bank of the United States, and his close in-

3 "The 'other quarter' spoken of by Mr. McLane, referred to Mr. Taney, the Attorney General, as is plainly enough intimated in the first note."—Van Buren, *ibid.*, p. 580.
4 McLane to Van Buren, Aug. 11, 1831, *ibid.*, p. 579.
5 Van Buren to Jackson, Aug. 15, 1831, *ibid.*, p. 580.

timacy with Mr. Biddle and with the Barings in England made him perhaps more zealous in its support. He was an accomplished diplomatist, and exercised as much diplomacy in Washington to carry his measures as he would at a foreign court; and he had a remarkable talent at managing men with whom he came in contact, who were inferior to himself in strength of mind or firmness of purpose. He had great tact, and always knew whether he should address himself to the patriotism, the magnanimity, the pride, the vanity, the hopes or the fears of the person on whom he wished to operate. And he thus always had a clique about him wherever he was in power over whose opinions he exercised a controlling influence." [6]

The personalities of the other members of the new cabinet were not such as to lead them to take vigorous parts in struggle such as that which developed with the Bank of the United States. Livingston was a man of literary tastes who was interested in historical researches and in the application of principles of international law, but he had neither the knowledge nor the interest in finance possessed by Taney and McLane. Lewis Cass, the Secretary of War, had had a varied and honorable career in the West, but he was much at sea as far as the intricacies of banking were concerned. The caution produced by an awareness of his own ignorance was further sanctioned by his fear of doing anything which might defeat his aspirations for the presidency.

Levi Woodbury, Secretary of the Navy, was characterized by Taney as a trained politician. "He was perfectly familiar with the operations of the bank," Taney declared, "and had no doubt carefully examined the principles on which the charter had been justified. He had been much engaged in public life and was familiar with all the proceedings of the general government. But he was a singularly wary and cautious man, unwilling to commit himself upon any opinion upon which he was not obliged immediately to act, and never further than that action required. And if he expressed an opinion upon a measure he most commonly added to it so many qualifications and limitations and doubts, that he sometimes appeared to take it

[6] Taney, Bank War MS., pp. 77–78.

back again. He was a man of a strong and astute mind; of great industry, who carefully gathered together all the information that could be obtained upon any subject before him, even to the smallest matter of detail. He had I presume his own opinions and views well defined in his own mind, but did not deem it prudent to disclose them too distinctly even to his friends and associates. . . . But whatever his opinions were, they were certainly his own, and never impressed upon him by the influence of others. In this respect he was entirely unlike General Cass. It was said however that like him he aspired to the presidency. I rather think he did, but if he had any views of that sort he kept them to himself, and determined to work them out in his own way and in his own time, and in a manner that would not bring him prematurely into rivalship or conflict with the other aspirants." [7]

Barry, the Postmaster General, was the least competent of the members of the cabinet, and his support or opposition was a matter of little importance. It was left to Taney and McLane therefore, who had deep convictions on the subject, and between whom rivalry already existed on other grounds, to lead in the struggle to determine administration policy toward the bank.

It is no easy task to discover the right and the wrong of the struggle between the administration and the Bank of the United States, which resulted in the ultimate defeat and dissolution of the bank. The task is made more difficult because of the fact that most competent writers on the subject, even in recent years, have permitted their judgments to be molded by abstract theories of finance, rather than by detailed knowledge of what the Bank of the United States actually was, and what it did. Modern theories of banking, sympathetic as they are to a large extent with centralized control of money and credit, lead to the conclusion that the termination of the life of the Bank of the United States was a tragedy. A judgment arrived at from a study of the whole situation can not be so simple. It must take into account not merely so-called laws of money, but also

[7] *Ibid.*, pp. 83–85.

the actions, the motives, the emotions, and perhaps the illusions of such men as Andrew Jackson and Nicholas Biddle, Thomas H. Benton and Daniel Webster, James K. Polk and Henry Clay, Amos Kendall and John Quincy Adams, Roger B. Taney and Louis McLane, and a host of others who were involved in the conflict. Information on these subjects is to be acquired only by painstaking study of the scattered but extremely numerous fragmentary records which remain. None of the participants left a complete record of the struggle. In addition to briefer documents of importance, however, Taney left a long manuscript account, written some years after his retirement from active political life, which is immeasurably valuable for a study of the events of the period. Because of its value and its unique character, quotations will be made from it at length in the following pages in appraisal of the Bank of the United States and its friends and enemies.

It will be recalled that among the purposes for which the Bank of the United States had been established had been the creation of a sound currency, the checking of dangerous speculative overexpansion by state banks, and the facilitating of the transfer of money from one part of the country to another, all of which would add to the prosperity of the country and aid the federal government in the performance of its functions. The bank and its branches established throughout the country succeeded in providing a currency which circulated more widely with less depreciation than the notes of any of the state banks. By demanding or threatening to demand specie for the state bank notes which it took in, or by refusing to receive them altogether, it did tend to check excessive expansion on the part of state banks. By means of its several branches strategically located it did facilitate the transfer of funds from point to point.

Yet there were abuses and dangers which ought not to be ignored even by the most ardent admirers of the bank. After the unfortunate experiences of the first years of its life the bank came under the control of a new president, Nicholas Biddle, an able and ambitious financier, who was also an able politician, although, to his misfortune and that of the bank, he was less able in the latter field than he believed.

Before assuming the presidency he expressed the belief that the government should have no influence direct or indirect over the bank. This was in spite of the fact that the government had provided one-fifth of the capital of the bank, that the charter provided that the government should choose five of the twenty-five directors for the obvious purpose of watching over the interests of the government, and that the government was by far the heaviest depositor. He admitted that it would be not unwise to consult to a certain extent the feelings of the government where the great interests of the bank might depend so much on its countenance and protection; but beyond that point, he insisted, the bank should go its own way, without government interference.[8]

It was with this conception of its independence of the government that he managed the bank, adding to its strength and bringing about in no small degree the performance of the functions which it had been chartered to perform. It was in the same spirit, however, that he authorized measures which to many seemed abuses of the privileges granted by the government to the bank, which qualified the performance of its desirable functions, and which stood out as a threat to state banks and private businesses should the bank be rechartered and thereby be freed from the necessity of asking favors from the government for a period of years. In his account of the bank war, written in 1849, Taney described at length the processes by which the bank functioned and the abuses which appeared to him to be most dangerous:

"The bank was undoubtedly capable of exercising great influence and possessed powers with which no corporation can be safely trusted in a republican government. It had already established branches at the principal places of business throughout the United States. These branches were all governed by the central power in Philadelphia and of course always acted in perfect harmony and concert. And the bank could make itself felt at the same moment in every part of the United States.

[8] Biddle to ———, Oct. 29, 1822, R. C. McGrane (ed.), *Correspondence of Nicholas Biddle*, pp. 25–26.

"It issued notes payable at some one of these branches, and for which specie could be demanded nowhere else. Yet as these notes were by the charter of the bank made receivable everywhere in payment of public dues, they readily circulated all over the Union, no matter how distant from the place at which they were made payable. It was the policy of the central bank and its branches to put in circulation as far as they could notes made payable at distant places. And it was enabled by this means to keep out a larger circulation and transact a much larger business, than its actual subsisting means of redemption would have justified. Discounts were freely made at the southern and western branches, where it was known that the notes would be disbursed in the importing cities when the revenue was collected. Unless these discounts exceeded all reasonable bounds, there could be little danger of a run upon the mother bank or any one of its branches.

"The pledges of the government to receive them in payment for duties, lands and all other public demands made the United States in effect responsible for the payment of every note issued. This guaranty of the United States sustained the credit of these notes, at the most distant places. And if by any means a large amount accumulated in the hand of an individual for which he desired to obtain specie, it was always his interest to submit to a small discount rather than incur the expense and hazard of sending for the specie to a distant branch.

"Upon examining the accounts of the bank it will be found, that a very large amount of these notes were made payable at places to which the course of trade would hardly ever return them. There was a very large amount of them I recollect made payable at the branch at Fayetteville, in North Carolina. And before the invention of railroads, very few would have been willing to travel to Fayetteville for specie, from any one of the principal importing cities, and would have preferred paying a considerable discount. These branch notes and the guarantee of the government, gave the bank great power over the business concerns of the country. It enabled it to expand its issues suddenly and to an immense amount when it desired to create an abundance in the circulating medium. And could create a pressure by as suddenly contracting, when a pressure upon the public was a part of its policy. This immense machine in all its parts moved at the same moment according to the unchecked will of one man.

"These privileges would not have been so formidable, if the bank and its branches had not been the depositories of the public. This daily filled its vaults and those of its branches with the notes of different state banks paid in for duties or for lands; or the public demands. And as the mother bank and branches were not bound to redeem notes made payable at another branch, they were not obliged to receive them in the settlement of their accounts with the state banks. They might demand the specie from the state banks although actually debtor to it, provided the notes it offered were not made payable at that particular branch. And this power was freely exercised, especially toward the banks which it did not choose to patronize.

"These privileges combined placed every state bank in the commercial cities at its mercy. It could shake the credit of any state bank and cripple its business, by refusing its notes in payment of duties upon the ground that it did not regard it as safe. And it could compel any one of them to stop payment by holding up for a time its notes received for revenue at the various branches and then suddenly demanding specie and refusing to receive its own notes in exchange, if not payable at that place.

"The bank itself was fully aware of this power. In a letter of Mr. Biddle to a chairman of a committee of the Senate written some time before the question of recharter was brought before Congress he states with great confidence, that it had always been in the power of the Bank of the United States to break any state bank it pleased; and the tone of his letter seemed to imply that he thought himself entitled to credit for his forbearance.[9]

"This statement of the power of the bank ought in my opinion to have been of itself sufficient to prevent the renewal of the charter. It certainly would have been a most dangerous experiment to continue the existence of a monster admitted to be capable of swallowing up the whole of the state banks. It made the existence of the state institu-

[9] See the *Register of Debates in Congress*, 21st Cong., 1st sess., Appendix, p. 103.

tions dependent upon the will of a single individual. And all the advantages ascribed to the Bank of the United States if they had been really founded in truth, would not have compensated for the destruction of the hundreds of millions of property invested in stocks of state banks, and the notes they had issued.

"As to its forbearance, it had been so crippled by its own misconduct in the early years of its existence that its power over the state banks for some time was not very formidable. For a time indeed it needed their good will and support. And after it had recovered and reestablished its strength, its charter had but a few years to run; and it was not a time to bring upon itself the united hostility of the state institutions and the multitude of persons interested in them when it must soon ask for a renewal of its own existence. What would have happened if a recharter for twenty or thirty years had been obtained it is impossible now to say. But I believed as soon as I read Mr. Biddle's letter and believe now, that it would gradually have compelled every state bank in the Union to wind up. His statement shows that the matter had been thought of, and that the manner in which it could be done was well understood." [10]

The power of the bank was increased, Taney continued, by the number of individuals who came under its influence. The directors of the parent bank and of the branches throughout the country naturally enough gave it their support. Each office of the bank employed one or more eminent lawyers, who in effect became lobbyists for it. Persons who received loans from the bank wished their privileges continued, and therefore favored the extension of the charter. The establishment of new branches added to the business and therefore to the influence of the bank, at the same time costing it little, because of the method of circulating notes far from the point at which they had to be redeemed in specie on demand. The circulation of notes with little depreciation gave a false impression of superior management in the bank, since it was the guarantee of the government which

[10] Taney, Bank War MS., pp. 10-16. In this document, as in some others quoted, the word 'deposit' is spelled with a final 'e'. For the sake of uniformity the spelling has been changed to the form now in use.

protected their value—the provision that they should be accepted in payment of all debts due to the government.

The bank used its false prestige to extend further its power over the circulatory medium, and consequently over the state banks and business generally, by what Taney called a palpable evasion of one of the provisions of its charter. The charter authorized the issue of notes of a denomination as low as five dollars, but the notes had to be signed by the president of the bank, and counter-signed by the cashier. A large portion of the paper in circulation as money was in the form of five-dollar notes. In theory it was possible for the Bank of the United States to supply any amount of these notes, but in practice it could supply nowhere near all of them, since the burden of signing them, as provided in the charter, would have been too great.

"Certainly," declared Taney, "Mr. Biddle with his aspiring views and gigantic plans was not a man to sit at his desk month after month to sign five-dollar notes in number sufficient to supply the wants of the whole Union for that description of paper. It had therefore been supplied for some years by the local banks. But it was for the interest of the bank to engross if it could this circulation. For it would enable it to keep in circulation a much larger amount of paper, and thus increase its business and its profits. And what was still more important to it with its views of obtaining power over the business of the country it would give it more effectually the control of the currency, and make its power more sensibly and universally felt when it thought proper to increase or diminish the circulating medium.

"It therefore contrived, in place of the five-dollar notes authorized by its charter to issue what it called branch drafts: that is, one of its branches drew a bill on another branch for five dollars, payable to some person or bearer, or perhaps in some instances payable to one of its own officers or to his order and indorsed by him in his official character. . . . They were printed on paper and in type so as to look like bank notes. And without being ever accepted by the branch on which they were drawn, they were paid out and put in circulation as money, like their other notes. These drafts made by the branches upon each other did not upon the face of them bind the bank to pay them at any place, for as I have said they were not generally, if ever, accepted by the branch on which they were drawn, and there might have been some difficulty in maintaining a suit for them against the branch that issued them or anyone else. For they were passed from hand to hand for years without being presented to the branch on which they were drawn; and the one that drew them could not be sued; for it was not a corporation.[11]

"The bank itself, that is to say the corporation, was not a party to them, and neither drew, nor accepted nor promised to pay them. Yet it had influence enough to obtain an order from the Treasury Department directing them to be received in all cases as money in payment for government dues. And when this was done, they readily passed current in individual transactions; and shared in the general confidence reposed everywhere in the notes of the bank. . . . And it is no small proof of the power which the bank had acquired, that it was able to circulate as many of these issues, obviously in fraud of the law to which it owed its existence and for the payment of which it was difficult to say who was responsible, or where the holder had a right to apply.

"It was however," Taney continued, revealing his own distrust of paper currencies in general, "one of the usual fruits of a currency entirely of paper. For when that is the case, men in their ordinary business take anything they find circulating in the form of paper money, without inquiring whether it will be paid or not, and indeed often without the means of ascertaining the fact if they were disposed to inquire. The party takes it, not because he supposes it will be paid on demand; for he does not intend to demand payment: but because he supposes he can pay it away as money when he proposes to use it. This is one of the many evils of a paper currency. Notes of no real value are confounded with the good ones, and the unwary and ignorant cheated."[12]

[11] The branches, Taney implies, were created by the parent bank without such sanction by law as would make them legal entities with the capacity to sue and be sued before the courts.

[12] Taney, Bank War MS., pp. 20–24.

Such was the portion of Taney's indictment of the Bank of the United States which was wholly applicable to the conduct of the bank prior to the beginning of its struggle for the renewal of its charter. Discussion of plans for renewal began at an early period, however, while its enemies began scheming to prevent its success. Philip P. Barbour of Virginia, later to be Taney's colleague on the Supreme Court, initiated one of the early skirmishes in the House of Representatives in 1827 by proposing that the government sell its one-fifth of the stock of the Bank of the United States. One of the effects of such a measure would have been to demonstrate the really private character of the bank to the thousands who looked upon it as in a large sense a government institution. The scheme failed, but it stimulated the alignment of politicians for and against the bank. Richard Rush, Secretary of the Treasury in the Adams administration, painted in his final annual report a glowing picture of the achievements of the bank, for the purpose of aiding it in securing the renewal of its charter. He intended to send copies abroad, he wrote to Biddle, not merely to prominent statesmen, but also to "some of those capitalists and bankers who can make the pecuniary world heave, in both hemispheres, by holding up a finger, at the Royal or stock exchange." [13] Biddle was of course much pleased with the report.

Except possibly at isolated points the bank issue played no prominent part in the election at which Jackson defeated Adams. True, many of the Jackson partisans were known to be hostile to the bank, but Jackson himself came into office uncommitted on the matter of renewing the charter, and Biddle was convinced that after the publication of the highly favorable Rush report the administration would not dare act in hostile fashion. He was therefore unpleasantly surprised when Jackson, in his first message to Congress, suggested a critical inquiry into the bank situation. "Both the constitutionality and the expediency of the law creating this bank," Jackson declared, "are well questioned by a large portion of our fellow-citizens, and it must be admitted by all that it has failed in the great end of establishing a

13 Rush to Biddle, Dec. 10, 1828, Biddle MSS.

uniform and sound currency." [14] Biddle chose at this time to be lenient with Jackson. "My impression," he wrote to Alexander Hamilton [15] of New York, "is that these opinions expressed by the President are entirely and exclusively his own, and that they should be treated as the honest though erroneous notions of one who intends well." [16]

Whatever the source of his opinions, however, Jackson adhered to them, and in his second annual message to Congress, delivered in December, 1830, he again called attention to the subject, and suggested the establishment of a new bank with narrowly limited powers, with no power to make loans or to issue notes, which should operate as a branch of the Treasury Department. "The states," he declared, "would be strengthened by having in their hands the means of furnishing the local paper currency through their own banks, while the Bank of the United States, though issuing no paper, would check the issues of the state banks by taking their notes in deposit and for exchange only so long as they continue to be redeemed with specie. In times of public emergency the capacities of such an institution might be enlarged by legislative provisions." [17]

By this time Biddle was thoroughly disturbed. It seemed to him that Jackson had turned the subject into an electioneering topic. "By inviting the state governments to strengthen themselves by usurping the whole circulating medium of the country, he will probably excite them to instruct their delegations in Congress to oppose the charter, and it is to be presumed that in no event will he sanction a bill for the recharter." [18] Some thought, however, that Jackson would not veto an act to recharter the bank if certain minor modifications were made, even though he might not wholly approve of it. It was in this state of uncertainty, with both sides scheming for advantage, that the matter stood when the new cabinet came into office.

Louis McLane, immediately upon taking office as Secretary of the

[14] J. D. Richardson, (ed.), *Compilation of Messages and Papers of the Presidents*, II, 462.

[15] The son of the man responsible for the founding of the first Bank of the United States.

[16] Biddle to A. Hamilton, Dec. 12, 1829, President's Letter Book, Biddle MSS.

[17] *Messages and Papers of the Presidents*, II, 529.

[18] Biddle to Joseph Hemphill, Dec. 14, 1830, President's Letter Book, Biddle MSS.

Treasury, threw the weight of his influence on the side of the bank. "If the old Chief would consent to recharter the bank," he wrote to Senator Samuel Smith, the Crawford leader of Maryland, who was also a friend of the bank, "what a glorious operation I could make for him! But be discreet by all means." [19] Soon afterward, on their way to pay a visit at the home of Charles Carroll of Carrollton, McLane and Jackson discussed the bank. McLane did not get from the President any commitment as to policy, though Jackson did remark on the inconsistency of those who wished to destroy the bank in order that they might set up another, and he admitted that he saw no force in the argument against the bank which was based on the fact that much of its stock was held by foreigners.[20]

At Carroll's home, however, according to Roswell L. Colt of Baltimore, a tireless collector of gossip and information for Biddle, Jackson spoke of the bank with sharp disapproval. "I have started for the second election," Colt reported him as saying, "upon the principle of putting the bank down, and will risk my election on that question —no bank and Jackson—or bank and no Jackson." This looked positive, Colt remarked, but Jackson was unstable, "and let it be supposed that by this opposition he jeopardizes his popularity, and he will kiss and make friends with the bank." [21] Colt's opinion of Jackson, which was similar to that still held by many others, showed how little the stubbornness of the old general's character was understood. The outburst, doubtless, was not well received by the Carrolls, for they had heavy investments in the stock of the bank.

Soon afterward McLane and Livingston met with Jackson to discuss the annual message to be delivered at the forthcoming session of Congress. McLane persuaded Jackson that after his expressions in two former messages on the subject of the bank it would be better this time to say nothing about it. Having secured Jackson's reluctant assent, he then unfolded his plan for praising the work of the bank in his own report to Congress with the recommendation that its

---

[19] McLane to Smith, Aug. 24, 1831, Samuel Smith MSS., Library of Congress.
[20] Biddle memorandum, Oct. 19, 1831, *Correspondence of Nicholas Biddle*, p. 132.
[21] Colt to Biddle, Oct. 3, 1831, Biddle MSS.

charter be continued. Jackson, liking independence in his subordinates, up to a certain point at least, sanctioned McLane's program in spite of his disagreement with McLane's ideas. McLane reported all this to Biddle. Biddle was pleased with the program as far as it went, but suggested that it would be still better if instead of ignoring the subject of the bank Jackson should say that having on former occasions brought the subject to the attention of Congress, he would now leave it, without further comment, to the representatives of the people.[22] McLane then attempted to persuade Jackson to include such a provision in his message, and succeeded in bringing about the use of words substantially to that effect in the draft of the message which was to be read and discussed in cabinet meeting.

It was Jackson's custom to begin the preparation of his messages to Congress by calling on the heads of the departments for statements on current problems within their respective fields. These statements, together with some directions as to the embodiment of his own views, were turned over to some individual who was competent as a literary draftsman and in whom he had confidence, to be worked into a message. This work was usually done by Livingston while he was Secretary of State. When the writing had been completed the cabinet was called together, and parts to which any member objected were freely discussed in the presence of the President, as a result of which he might or might not make changes.

Taney, not being the head of any department, was not called upon to write any part of the message. Somewhat surprisingly, since he professed to doubt the constitutionality of the bank charter, Jackson had never discussed the bank question with his new Attorney General. It is possible, though there seems to be no proof of the fact, that McLane had created suspicions in Jackson's mind as to Taney's motives, which resulted in his being ignored, while the Secretary of the Treasury had ready access to the presidential ear. Taney, with all his distrust of the bank, had recently told Robert Oliver, a wealthy Baltimore merchant, that he favored the recharter of the bank, but with modifications in the charter one of which was so drastic as to

[22] Biddle memorandum, Oct. 19, 1831, *Correspondence of Nicholas Biddle*, p. 132.

forbid the establishment of branches without the consent of the states in which they were to be set up.[23]

Taney listened with anxiety as the message was read aloud to the cabinet by Andrew J. Donelson, the President's nephew and private secretary. He knew that the subject of the bank came within the field of the Secretary of the Treasury, and he suspected that McLane's friendship for the bank had found its way into the message. If so, it would be a serious matter politically, since it would create the impression that the new cabinet had persuaded Jackson to abandon his opposition to the bank. Donelson read through what was to be nearly fourteen printed pages of the message without any mention of the bank. Then, in next to the last paragraph, came a statement in approximately the following words:

"Entertaining the opinions heretofore expressed in relation to the Bank of the United States as at present organized, I felt it my duty in my former messages frankly to disclose them, in order that the attention of the Legislature and the people should be seasonably directed to that important subject, and that it might be considered and finally disposed of in a manner best calculated to promote the ends of the Constitution and subserve the public interests.[24] Having conscientiously discharged a constitutional duty I deem it proper without a more particular reference to the subject to leave it to the investigation of an enlightened people and their representatives."

Taney was startled by the paragraph, even though he was in no position to know that it had had its origin in a suggestion of the president of the Bank of the United States. It seemed to him to imply that Jackson, though still opposed to the bank, would acquiesce in any decision which Congress arrived at concerning it. Somewhat hesitantly, perhaps, but yet firmly, he declared his opposition to the paragraph. "It was my first conflict in the cabinet," he wrote in retrospect some years later. "I stood alone in it; and in opposition to Mr. Livingston and Mr. McLane who were experienced politicians, and

[23] R. L. Colt to Biddle, Oct. 3, 1831, Biddle MSS.
[24] The paragraph thus far is from the *Messages and Papers of the Presidents* II, 558. The remainder is as Taney remembered it at a later date. See his Bank War MS., p. 72.

in both of whom I knew that the President at that time reposed the highest confidence. The duty of making this objection I felt to be an unpleasant one and the whole scene is yet strongly impressed on my memory." [25] He stated what he believed the general interpretation of the paragraph would be, and added that people would think the President had been won over by his new cabinet and friends of the bank.

Livingston supported the message as it stood, and doubted that the inference suggested by Taney would be drawn from it. Livingston's principal object, Taney believed, was to avoid any decided step with reference to the highly controversial subject until after the election of the following year, at which Jackson was to be a candidate for another term. He showed no depth of feeling with regard to the merits of the bank issue itself.

The discussion in support of the paragraph in question was conducted chiefly by McLane, who vigorously objected to any alteration. Cass, a friend of Biddle,[26] and to some extent of the bank, and as usual subject to the influence of McLane, thought he agreed with the latter, though he seemed confused about it all. Woodbury expressed no opinion directly upon the subject. He suggested changes in words and phrases which he thought might reconcile the differences between McLane and Taney and be acceptable to them and to the President, but he did not commit himself as to what he believed should be said. As usual, he was riding the fence. Barry said nothing at all.

From the earnestness with which McLane defended the paragraph it seemed obvious to Taney that he had drafted it originally, and Livingston had inserted it in the message as it had been written. Taney continued his efforts to have it modified until he saw that the President was worried and desired the discussion to end. Jackson, says Taney's account, "had interposed occasionally as it went on, and my objection was evidently new to him and unlooked for. He finally said that he certainly did not mean to have it understood that he was

[25] Taney, Bank War MS., p. 73.
[26] See Cass to Biddle, Aug. 13, 1831, Biddle MSS.

prepared to sign any bill that Congress might pass for continuing the bank; nor did he think it necessary to say at that time that he would veto it. It would be time enough when he saw the act and its provisions, if one should be passed. But he intimated that the clause in question did not appear to him to be liable to the objection I had taken, and he did not at that time seem to be disposed to make any alteration, and I left the cabinet meeting, when it broke up, with the belief that I had failed and that no alteration would be made, and with strong doubts also whether under the influence of his new advisers he would not be persuaded to consent to the recharter of the bank with some plausible but unsubstantial restrictions on its power. But I did not then know General Jackson as well as I afterwards knew him. If I had, these doubts would never have been entertained." [27]

On the following day when Taney called at the President's house on business, Donelson showed him an alteration of the paragraph on the bank, saying that Jackson had directed that it be called to his attention. The alteration was slight, and might not avoid the construction which Taney feared, and in any case was far short of what he desired. "I wished him," he declared, "after stating that he still entertained the opinions set forth in his former messages, to recommend to Congress to make some provision by law for the safe keeping, disbursement of the public money and its transmission from place to place to take effect when the charter of the bank should expire. This would have shown his fixed opinion that the bank was not to be continued, and would have been understood to imply, that he would feel himself bound to exercise all his constitutional powers to prevent it." [28]

Taney had to be satisfied with the consoling fact that Jackson had made a gesture of friendliness in his direction by changing McLane's language in the message, even though the import seemed to be much the same. It was a small concession, but it was something.

As far as the bank issue was concerned the message created much

[27] Taney, Bank War MS., p. 87.
[28] *Ibid.*, p. 94.

the impression which Taney had feared. The impression was deepened when McLane's annual report as Secretary of the Treasury was published. In this document McLane destroyed the remaining effects of Jackson's former messages by praising the work of the bank and recommending the renewal of its charter. It was generally assumed that he would not have spoken on so important a matter without the sanction of his chief, and that Jackson had reversed his position.

Biddle was much pleased. "Mr. McLane's report," he wrote to a clerk in the Treasury Department, "is all that his friends could wish —enlarged, liberal, wise, and statesmanlike. It is much fitter for a President's message than *the* President's message itself and I wish with all my heart that the writer of it was President. The style of the paragraph in that message about the bank, with the commentary of the *Globe*, the Richmond *Enquirer*, and the *Standard*, I confess shake my confidence much. It is not in such an ambiguous tone that a President should speak or suffer his dependents to speak." [29]

Thus Biddle applauded McLane for his support of the bank, touched his vanity on the subject of the paragraph which had been rewritten because of Taney's objections, and stimulated his ambitions still further by suggesting bank support for McLane as a candidate for the presidency. The administration papers criticized by Biddle were bitterly hostile to the bank, and they sharply denounced McLane's report. Francis P. Blair and Amos Kendall, who edited the *Globe*, the organ of the administration in Washington, were so violent in their denunciation that McLane threatened to resign if a proposed paragraph on the subject was published. To prevent another cabinet crisis the paragraph was modified.[30]

Jackson sent a copy of his message to Van Buren, in London. McLane differed with him on the subject of the bank, he remarked. Still, it was an honest difference of opinion. McLane had acted fairly in his report, and Jackson, as he had intended, was left uncommitted. He liked McLane's candor and frankness. "He is a fair, honorable man, with whom I am much pleased, and will get on with very well

[29] Biddle to Asbury Dickins, Dec. 20, 1831, President's Letter Book, Biddle MSS.
[30] Robert Gibbes to Biddle, Dec. 11, 1831, *ibid.*

—in short my whole cabinet are harmonious, and I have no doubt but we will succeed well." [31]

It was with quite different feelings that Van Buren, whose support had placed McLane in the cabinet, read his report. It suggested that McLane was seeking indirectly to supersede Jackson as head of the government, and that Jackson was in danger of being humiliated before his enemies.[32] Shrewd politician that he was, he may also have begun to suspect at this time that the Supreme Court was not the only goal which McLane had in mind, and that in nursing McLane's ambitions for high office he had unwittingly been grooming a rival. Such, at any rate, was the truth, whether or not Van Buren was at this time aware of it.

Some of Biddle's friends advised him that it would be good strategy to apply for the recharter of his bank at this time, on the ground that Jackson, desirous of another term as President, would not dare oppose it. Other and more cautious friends warned him that the trend of public sentiment was in his favor, and that it would be better to wait, rather than make a political issue of the matter. Among the latter was Senator Samuel Smith of Maryland. He had talked with McLane, he declared, who had advised against taking steps immediately. The message showed that the Chief was wavering. The increase in the number of the friends of the bank ought to have its effect. Full play should be given to the members of the administration, "every one of whom (except Taney) are favorable; his opposition, I think, arises out of the mistaken idea that the bank has operated politically. Can you give me the means of conquering that idea?" [33]

Ten days later Smith wrote again to Biddle, saying that "Mr. Taney (to my astonishment he having been a warm friend of it) is the only member of the cabinet hostile to the bank and I can account for it in no way except (that he is a partisan) that he thinks that the bank has interfered with elections. I never have had any conversation

---

[31] Jackson to Van Buren, Dec. 6, 1831, *Correspondence of Andrew Jackson*, IV, 379.
[32] *Autobiography of Martin Van Buren*, p. 581.
[33] Smith to Biddle, Dec. 7, 1831, Biddle MSS.

with him on the subject. *All,* I say, *all* his friends differ with him. I think I will talk with him and try to know his reasons. He is an amiable man, and highly esteemed." [34]

Thomas Cadwalader, whom Biddle had sent to Washington to inquire into the advisability of applying for the renewal of the charter of the bank at this time, likewise reported that Taney was the only member of the cabinet who was hostile to the bank. "He is latterly *radical* on all points—*par example,* he thinks the judges ought to hold their appointments only for four or five years." [35] If Taney had really made such a statement regarding judicial tenure it may have been an unconsidered utterance delivered when he learned that Justice Baldwin, sitting in the United States Circuit Court in Pennsylvania, had decided that the drafts issued by the branches of the Bank of the United States to circulate as money had been legally issued.[36] Taney himself was thoroughly convinced to the contrary,[37] and he had little respect for any judge who justified what he regarded as a clear violation of the charter of the bank.

In spite of the efforts of many of the friends of the administration to keep the bank issue out of the presidential campaign, the opposing party forced it forward. The National Republican party, which was the party of John Quincy Adams, of Clay, of Webster, and of Nicholas Biddle, met in convention in Baltimore on December 12, 1831, and nominated Henry Clay for President and John Sergeant for Vice President. Clay had long been counsel for the bank in the West, and was a bitter enemy of Jackson. Sergeant was a friend of Biddle, and was counsel for the bank in Philadelphia. The convention pledged vigorous support to the bank, and attacked Jackson for his opposition to it.

It seems probable, indeed, that the National Republicans viewed with uneasiness the friendliness of McLane and other members of the administration toward the bank. The issue seemed to them most

[34] Smith to Biddle, Dec. 17, 1831, *ibid.*

[35] Cadwalader to Biddle, Dec. 21, 1831, *ibid.*

[36] See a clipping from the Detroit *Journal,* filed with a letter of John Norvall to Biddle, Dec. 8, 1831, Biddle MSS. See also the Philadelphia *National Gazette,* Nov. 15, 1831.

[37] See his Bank War MS., pp. 20–24.

promising for political purposes, and they were at that time more interested in having it used as an instrument to return them to power than in having the enemy capitulate to the bank without a struggle. While McLane, in order to preserve the united front of the Jacksonians, urged that the struggle for the renewal of the charter be postponed, Clay and Webster were writing to Biddle urging him to make application to Congress immediately. They assured him that Jackson would not at this time dare veto the bill, and that even if he did veto it he would injure himself so badly as to promote greatly the interests of the party which was friendly to the bank. [38]

Indeed, current political gossip had it that the matter had been put to Biddle even more strongly. "It was understood at the time," wrote Taney, "that Mr. Clay and Mr. Webster informed Mr. Biddle that if the petition was not presented and urged on at that session, that he must not count on their support at a future time, but must expect to meet their decided opposition, and that this had determined him to proceed. Such a communication was I believe certainly made by those two gentlemen to Mr. Biddle. The information came to me from sources which left no room for doubt. But my own opinion was and still is that Mr. Biddle was himself bent upon going on unless he was prevented by the directors or stockholders. He was offended with the course General Jackson had pursued toward the institution, and was strongly opposed to him. . . .

"He persuaded himself that General Jackson would hardly dare to meet the bill with an absolute and unqualified veto. But if he did, he felt confident that the popularity of the bank and the influence it could exercise would defeat his reëlection. And if he assented to the bill or appeared to temporize and evade the issue presented to him, it would be regarded as proof that he feared the bank, and destroy the high place he then held in the confidence and affections of the people. In either case his resentment would be gratified. I cannot believe he acted from any apprehension of hostility from Mr. Clay or Mr. Webster, or was influenced by their threats. Both of

[38] Clay to Biddle, Dec. 15, 1831; Webster to Biddle, Dec. 18, 1831, *ibid.*

these gentlemen had published and repeatedly expressed their opinions in favor of the bank, and maintained that it was a necessary agent in the collection of the revenue. The great majority of the stockholders as well as of the directors of the mother bank and its numerous branches and officers were the political friends of these two gentlemen, and members of the same party. And their leading paper, the *National Intelligencer*, was virtually owned by the bank and under its control. With a full knowledge of all these circumstances Mr. Biddle had obviously nothing to apprehend from the threats of Mr. Clay or Mr. Webster, and knew that they could not come out in opposition to a recharter without forfeiting the support of a majority of their party, and surrendering their hopes of political elevation. But whether he was prompted by his own inclinations or by fears of the hostility of the gentlemen above named, in either case the application at that time was a political movement leveled at General Jackson, and converted a corporation, which had been created as a fiscal agent and merely for the fiscal purposes of the government, into a powerful political partisan seeking to govern the government by controlling the election of its officers." [39]

Biddle postponed his final decision until early in January, when he threw to the winds any doubts which he may have had, and applied for the renewal of the charter of the bank. The Bank War was on! It was a fatal move on Biddle's part, as subsequent events were to prove. It was a mistake which he might not have made had the Jacksonians from the first presented a united front against the bank. Their lack of unity led him to believe that by forcing the issue he could further divide them and defeat those who opposed him. Jackson was himself to a degree responsible for the beginning of the battle at this time, in that he had chosen for his cabinet a number of men who differed with him radically on one of the major issues of the day. It was on the point of this political error that Taney criticized Jackson more severely than on any other aspect of his political life. His responsibility was qualified, of course, by the fact that at the time of the formation of the new cabinet the bank issue

[39] Taney, Bank War MS., pp. 108–110.

was only one of many which the administration had before it, and at that time it was not necessarily the most important. It would have been impossible to pick a cabinet of independent men who agreed with the President and with each other on every issue. Had he chosen men in full agreement as to the bank they might have been at swords' points as to the tariff, nullification, and the difficult negotiations then being conducted with France.

WHILE the measure for the renewal of the charter of the Bank of the United States was pending in Congress, a number of events occurred which had a bearing upon its fate. The first was the rejection of the nomination of Van Buren for the ministerial post at London. The followers of Calhoun united with those of Clay to bring about the defeat of a dangerous political opponent, and the casting vote of Calhoun himself determined the decision. "It will kill him, sir, kill him dead," boasted Calhoun. "He will never kick, sir, never kick." [1] It proved, however, to be a short-sighted move which stirred the wrath of the friends of the administration, and paved the way for Van Buren's nomination to the vice presidency. Jackson's rage at the Senate created doubt as to his approval of measures which it might adopt. One of Biddle's observers reported a comment from Jackson that "the majority of the Senate who acted on this nomination, were a political pack of scoundrels." [2]

Biddle turned every possible political situation to his own advantage. His friends secured from the Pennsylvania legislature resolutions urging the Pennsylvania representatives in Congress to support the bank measure. Biddle then suggested that George M. Dallas, a Pennsylvanian in the Senate who hoped to be the vice presidential candidate on the Jackson ticket, should take a vigorous stand for measures to which Van Buren was supposed to be hostile—particularly for the recharter of the Bank of the United States. With the Pennsylvania resolutions as an excuse Dallas should ask Jackson what modifications in the charter would be necessary to make it ac-

[1] Thomas H. Benton, *Thirty Years' View*, I, 219.
[2] R. M. Gibbes to Biddle, Feb. 7, 1832, Biddle MSS.

ceptable, and report the answer to the bank. The bank would then consent to the changes, and the act would pass as an administration measure.

Biddle had no notion of adhering to any group of politicians unless his doing so would help the bank. He cared for no party in politics or religion, he wrote in a rough draft of a letter to Charles J. Ingersoll, who at the time was working for him. He had no sympathy for Jackson, Clay, Calhoun, Van Buren, or other political leaders. He was "for the bank and the bank alone." He supposed the President had been made to believe the bank was hostile to him. The belief was unfounded. "For myself I do not care a straw for him or his rivals—I covet neither his man servant—nor even his maid servant, his ox nor any of his asses. Long may he live to enjoy all possible blessings, but if he means to wage war upon the bank— if he pursues us till we turn and stand at bay, why then—he may perhaps awaken a spirit which has hitherto been checked and reined in—and which it is wisest not to force into offensive defense." [3]

Ingersoll attempted to secure Jackson's coöperation through conferences with Livingston, who claimed to speak for the President in the matter. Livingston thought he could get the support of Woodbury and Cass for the measure. He was in doubt as to McLane, who though friendly to the bank was quite aware that the bank measure was being used to advance the interests of political enemies, and was therefore opposed to it. Livingston even hoped to convert Taney, who was frankly hostile to the measure on all grounds. He finally reported a list of changes which, he claimed, would make the charter acceptable to Jackson. Biddle was jubilant, and urged Ingersoll to get a public commitment from Jackson as soon as possible.

In the meantime the bank enemies were active in the House of Representatives. A resolution was adopted providing for the appointment of a committee to investigate the bank before action was taken on the bill for renewal of the charter. Legislation and negotiations were suspended during the six weeks of investigation. Then a majority of the committee reported against the bank, exposing a number

[3] Biddle to Charles J. Ingersoll, Feb. 11, 1832, *ibid.*

of abuses. A minority reported for it, and John Quincy Adams, with the concurrence of one of Biddle's handy men from Pennsylvania, wrote a separate report containing a scathing denunciation of the opposition to the bank.[4] None of these reports could have aided in winning Jackson's support for the bank, even if he had been willing to go along with Livingston in an attempt to reach a compromise— a fact which is by no means fully established. Bank negotiations with the administration were finally dropped, and the struggle in Congress was taken up in earnest.

Biddle appeared in Washington on May 20 to assume leadership of the bank forces, and on June 5 he was still working with unabated zeal. "It has been a week of hard work, anxiety and alternating hopes and fears," he wrote at the time, "but I think that we may now rely with confidence on a favorable result."[5] On June 11 the bill passed the Senate by a vote of twenty-eight to twenty, and Biddle, elated, went back to Philadelphia. The struggle in the House was likewise severe, and the outcome remained in doubt for some weeks. Declaring that Biddle was a host in himself and worth fifty or a hundred aids, one of his advisers urged him to return to Washington.[6]

Biddle apparently believed that the groundwork for victory had been laid, however, for he did not return until the evening of July 3, the day on which the bill passed the House. He "made his appearance in the House the next day," wrote Taney, "when the public business was for some time interrupted by the number of members leaving their seats and crowding about him, and shaking hands with him and congratulating him. It was a public triumph given him in the hall of the House. Nor did it end there. They crowded about him again that night at his lodgings when they feasted high and drank toasts and made speeches, and celebrated the victory, taking pains to make their rejoicing sufficiently vociferous to be heard in the

---

[4] The three reports are in the *Congressional Debates*, 22nd Cong., 1st sess., Appendix, pp. 33–73.

[5] Biddle to Thomas Cadwalader, June 5, 1832, Biddle MSS.

[6] R. L. Colt to Biddle, June 16, 1832, *ibid.*

streets and sufficiently public to make sure that it would reach the ears of the President." [7]

On July 5, the day after Biddle left Washington, Webster wrote to express to friends of the bank his sense of the value of Biddle's presence during the struggle. "We should have done but badly without him," declared Webster.[8]

Some of Biddle's methods of getting votes had to do with explaining away misunderstandings and demonstrating the services of the bank to the country. Others were of a different nature. Taney revealed one of them through a personal illustration. One day when riding in a hack on his way to the Supreme Court his only companion was a member of the House who was spoken of and treated as one of the President's warmest friends. He was well acquainted with Taney, and, saying that he planned to make a speech against the bank bill, he asked Taney for a list of points which he might safely make. Taney replied that he was extremely busy with his work in the Supreme Court, and furthermore that as a member of the cabinet he did not like to interfere with proceedings in the House. When the bank bill came to a vote he was surprised to discover that the man had voted for it. On seeking an explanation he found that the man had obtained a loan of twenty thousand dollars from the bank, and had changed his position.

"Now I do not mean to say," Taney continued, "that he was directly bribed to give this vote. From the character he sustained and from what I knew of him I think he would have resented anything that he regarded as an attempt to corrupt him. But he wanted the money, and felt grateful for the favor, and perhaps thought that an institution which was so useful to him, and had behaved with so much kindness, could not be injurious or dangerous to the public, and that it would be as well to continue it. Men when under the influence of interest or passion often delude themselves thoroughly, and do not always acknowledge even to themselves the motives upon

---

[7] Taney, Bank War MS., p. 116.

[8] Webster to Thomas Cadwalader, July 5, 1832, *Correspondence of Nicholas Biddle,* p. 193.

which they really act. They sometimes persuade themselves that they are acting on a motive consistent with their own self respect, and sense of right, and shut their eyes to the one which in fact governs their conduct. It was one of the dangers arising from this mammoth money power, that its very duties as collecting and disbursing agent brought it constantly in contact with members of Congress and other public functionaries and made it acquainted with their wants and enabled it to place them under obligations and create a feeling of dependency or even gratitude without the direct and offensive offer of a bribe. In cases when it intended to operate it was not very particular about the indorsers or the sufficiency of the securities offered. Its losses upon these political loans were enormous. How many received pecuniary favors during that session and during the 'panic war' we shall never know. I have heard many names mentioned, some of them high in influence. But it would be improper to repeat them as I have no absolute proof upon the subject." [9]

Taney had been extremely busy with the preparation of cases for argument before the Supreme Court during the early months of 1832, and had not discussed the bank bill with Jackson or any member of the cabinet. He assumed that of the cabinet he stood alone in his opposition to the measure, and, in spite of assurances to the contrary from some of his friends, he feared a lack of firmness on the part of the President, in view of his lenient attitude toward McLane's earlier discussion of the bank in his report to Congress. Many of Taney's friends urged him to advise the President to sign the bill, saying the President would hardly veto it in the face of a unanimous cabinet. Taney had no intention of being persuaded in the matter, however. Many of the political sponsors of the bill cared little what Jackson did. They felt that he was on the horns of a dilemma, and his chances for another term in office would be injured whether he signed the bill in spite of earlier criticisms of the bank, or made enemies by vetoing it.

Taney made no attempt to influence Jackson until some time in

[9] Taney, Bank War MS., pp. 111–114.

June, when he discovered that the bill would probably be passed and presented for the President's signature during ensuing weeks when he would be in Annapolis arguing cases before the Maryland Court of Appeals. Then he determined to state in writing his advice that the bill be met with an open and direct veto, so as to destroy all hope that the President would ever consent to the continuation of the bank. He knew that other members of the cabinet might advise a veto, but one which would temporize on the merits of the issue and condemn the bill merely because it was presented too long in advance of the time when the old charter was to expire. Taney wished Jackson to base the veto on the ground that the renewal of the charter was unconstitutional and inexpedient. "It appeared to me that a veto which placed the objections merely upon time, and evaded the direct issue, would be unworthy of him and would justly result in his overthrow." [10]

Taney wrote out his opinion just before leaving for Annapolis. He called on Jackson, expressed his belief that the bank bill would pass, and told Jackson that because of his own absence from the city he had decided to submit a written opinion on the subject. He said he was convinced that the bill should be met with a direct veto, and that his reasons would appear in the document. Jackson thanked him and replied that he would be glad to have the opinion; but he said nothing to indicate his own attitude on the subject, and Taney evidently thought it best not to ask for a commitment at the time. When he left for Annapolis, therefore, he was completely in doubt as to the policy which the President would pursue.

He was evidently dissatisfied with the draft of his opinion prepared for Jackson before he left Washington, and upon arriving at Annapolis he rewrote it or added to it so that it became a document of some nine or ten thousand words.[11] It was to be another of his important official opinions which did not appear in the published volumes. Whether it was omitted purposely, because of the constitu-

---

[10] *Ibid.*, p. 119.

[11] The copy of the opinion from which the following summary is made is dated Annapolis, June 27, 1832. It is in the hand of a copyist, with corrections and a signature in Taney's hand. It is filed with the Jackson MSS. in the Library of Congress.

tional doctrines expressed or because of its frank denunciation of the political activities of the bank, or whether it was at the time lost among the unorganized Jackson papers, does not appear. At any rate, point by point, on grounds both of constitutionality and of expediency, he argued against the renewal of the charter of the bank:

First, if a bank could be created by Congress for the performance of federal functions under the "necessary and proper" clause of the Constitution, it was not "necessary," at a time when the public revenues and expenditures were to be reduced, that the bank have a capital of thirty-five millions. The excess of capital, being unnecessary, could not be constitutionally justified.

Second, if a bank of this capital were constitutionally created, it could not be necessary that this particular bank have a monopoly for fifteen years of banking privileges under the government. This Congress could not, by granting a monopoly, prevent the creation at later sessions of other corporations as federal instruments. "There can be no necessity," he declared, "for tying up the hands of the government in this respect, and subjecting the people of this country to the evils and abuses which great moneyed monopolies have always occasioned."

Third, it could not be necessary, nor had Congress the power, to allow the bank to establish branches in every state, either with or without the consent of the states. If branches were needed as agents of the government it was the province of Congress to say where they should be established. By surrendering this power to the corporation it would enable the bank to establish branches for the purpose of obtaining political influence or for private profit, in places where they were not required for the purposes of the government. Congress could not constitutionally delegate this power and prevent the people from resuming it for a period of fifteen years.

Fourth, it was not necessary that the bank, as a fiscal agent, should have the great banking powers conferred upon it. The fact that the bank agreed to pay a large bonus for the renewal of its charter proved that it had privileges which were to be used for individual and private interests. If the establishment of the bank was justified on the ground that it was a convenient agent for governmental purposes, it was contrary to the spirit of the Constitution to sell such an office for money. Peculiar privileges to be used for private profit could not be sold by the government without violating the principles of our institutions.

Fifth, even if Congress could sell such privileges to individuals where the whole community had an equal opportunity to buy, it was an abuse of power and a violation of the principles of equality in terms of which all of our institutions had been framed, to select a favored body of individuals and confer valuable privileges upon them alone.

Even if the powers, privileges, and immunities before mentioned could be constitutionally granted, Taney argued, it was inexpedient to grant them. They were so vast and overwhelming, so liable to abuse, and so intimately connected with the prosperity and welfare of every portion of the United States that they ought never to be entrusted to an irresponsible corporation for use for private interests. Through its immense capital and its power of branching into every state the bank could make money plentiful or scarce at any point or at all points at the same time. It could bring ruin on any commercial city in the United States if it chose to do so. Its president had admitted that there were few state banks which it might not have broken had it been so inclined.

The bank had patronage connections of many kinds, and had the means of acquiring a corrupt influence in the councils of the states and of the federal government, and of influencing government activities. It concentrated and gave combined action to great money interests already sufficiently powerful to be dangerous. It thus "gives to a portion of the moneyed aristocracy as a separate class and a separate body a power in the government which is adverse to the first principles on which our institutions are founded."

The true object of making the application for a new charter at this time, Taney continued shrewdly, could not be mistaken. "We are upon the eve of an election for President, and the directors of the bank, feeling their great political power and influence, have brought forward their application in the hope that the President would yield up the opinions heretofore expressed by him in order to secure his election. And if his well known firmness and independence should disappoint their wishes, they hope, by combining with the other elements of opposition, to defeat his reëlection and secure a President of the United States who is favorable to their views. When a great moneyed institution attempts to overawe the President in the discharge of his high constitutional duties, it is conclusive evidence that it is conscious of possessing vast political power, which it supposes the President can be made to feel. And any institution clothed with such power will always be ready to use it, and is dangerous to the liberties of the country and ought not to be continued. . . .

"Upon the whole," Taney concluded, addressing Jackson personally in his shrewdly tactful manner, "I respectfully advise that the proposed bill be not approved. And as the frank and decided course which has marked your conduct through your whole life is, I have no doubt, not only the right one in morals but the wisest in public affairs I think the proposed charter ought to be met on every ground on which you may deem it liable to objection."

About a week after his arrival at Annapolis Taney learned from the newspapers that the bill had passed. Andrew Stevenson, speaker of the House of Representatives, wrote urging him to return at once. Jackson was said to be firm in his opposition to the bill, but he had no support from the cabinet members around him. Taney was eager to return but thought it unwise to do so without an invitation from Jackson. To his great relief he received a note from Jackson asking him to come back as soon as possible. He wound up his business at Annapolis, or placed it in the hands of other lawyers there, and hurried to Washington.

Jackson declared he was much pleased to see Taney, for he had been left in an embarrassing position. He agreed with Taney's advice on the bank bill, but the other members of the cabinet did not. They concurred in the opinion that he ought not to sign the bill, but they wished him to place his veto on grounds that would leave it open for him to sign a bill for the renewal of the charter at a later session. They offered to help write a veto message that would leave the subject open for future action, but refused to have anything to do with a flat veto. Jackson could not prepare a message of this kind without help. Amos Kendall had worked out a draft for him which Donelson, Jackson's nephew and private secretary, was now revising. Jackson asked Taney to go over the entire manuscript and suggest the changes which he thought desirable.

"I passed three days in this employment," wrote Taney, "the President frequently coming in, listening to the reading of different portions of it from time to time as it was drawn up, and to the observations and suggestions of Mr. Donelson and myself, and giving his own directions as to what should be inserted or omitted. . . . Mr. Donelson told me when I came in that no member of the cabinet had been in the room or offered any aid to him, since Mr. Kendall's draft had been placed in his hands. I saw none of them the first day; and it is possible that none of them knew I had returned. For I did not go to my office, as I did not wish to be interrupted by other business. Upon the second day Mr. Woodbury came in, and took part in the work, and continued with us until it was completed, when a fair copy was made, which after being examined by the President and approved and read in the cabinet, was transmitted to Congress. This is the history of my concern with the veto. I need not add that I cordially approved of it." [12]

One of Jackson's biographers, who wrote before Taney's manuscript on the bank war was discovered, stated that the veto message [13] had at the beginning and the end a number of pages which were poor economics but were shrewdly written, perhaps "by some such purveyor of balderdash as Isaac Hill or Amos Kendall," to win the masses to the support of the measure. In between these two parts was a constitutional argument which could have come from no other member of the anti-bank coterie than Taney. It was a veto message

[12] Taney, Bank War MS., pp. 125–126.
[13] See *Messages and Papers of the Presidents*, II, 576–591.

in itself, expressed in concise, legal style, "in contrast to the loose illogic of the rest of the document." [14]

This characterization of the message is accurate in part, but only in part. Kendall had written the original draft, and it is to be presumed that some evidence of his handiwork remained even after revision by Taney and others. Yet not all the political material can with certainty be attributed to him. Taney also was skilled in the writing of political articles. His touch was as sure in dealing with matters of this kind as in the phrasing of legal arguments. There is no way of telling where Kendall's work ends and Taney's begins. Furthermore, it is far from accurate to imply that the pages at the beginning and end of the message are "balderdash." There is exaggeration, and at one point at least the logic is extremely bad. Yet there is also the presentation of political and economic materials which had a profound relevance to the men and women whose welfare was affected by the activities of the bank, even though they might not fit well into the abstract reasoning of doctrinaire financiers.

The historian of the bank has declared that the reasoning of the message "is in the main beneath contempt." [15] Perhaps it is beneath the contempt of fundamentalist economists who have unquestioning faith in the working of economic laws, without reference to the particular situations in which they are to be carried into effect, and without reference to the particular men who are to bring about their efficient operation. But the financial problems of the United States in 1832 were not problems for cloistered halls, but for a nation extremely heterogeneous in character, with people who possessed the frailties of human nature along with its other traits. The widespread popular appeal of the message was doubtless due in large part to the awareness which it showed as to actual relations between the bank on the one hand and different groups and different sections of the country on the other.

In no small part the message was a rephrasing and an elaboration of the arguments which Taney had previously written out for Jack-

[14] J. S. Bassett, *Life of Andrew Jackson*, p. 619.
[15] R. C. H. Catterall, *The Second Bank of the United States*, p. 239.

son. While not denying altogether that the bank had produced some benefits to the country, it characterized the institution as the instrument of a class and of a section, by means of which other classes and other sections were made to pay tribute. The government owned only one-fifth of the stock. More than one-fourth of the privately owned stock was held abroad. Most of that owned in this country was held in the middle and eastern states. Profits made in the South and West flowed largely to the moneyed aristocracy of the East, or left the country altogether.

The market value of the stock was now above par, and the present stockholders had already profited greatly by the monopoly grant of banking privileges under the federal government. If the charter were renewed the stock would rise still higher, and in spite of the bonus to be paid by the bank to the government the act of renewal would operate to make a huge donation to the already favored few, who at best were no more deserving of government favors than were any other group of citizens. The foreign stockholders had no claim at all to the charity of the government, and the government had no right to enrich them at the expense of the American people.

The message repeated Taney's argument that the Supreme Court had not passed upon the constitutionality of the present Bank of the United States in all its aspects, but had merely decided that Congress had the power to establish a bank and that other questions were left to the discretion of Congress and were not subject to judicial inquiry. Even if the opinion of the court had covered the whole ground, however, the message continued, it ought not to control Congress and the Executive when it came to the enactment of a new law. The opinion of the judges had no more authority over Congress than the opinion of Congress had over the judges, and the President was independent of both when deciding upon constitutional grounds for sanctioning or vetoing proposed acts of legislation.

The statement on this subject, obviously written by Taney, was not as clear as it might have been. Its obscurity was probably due to the fact that Taney's ideas were unsettled at the time as to how far the President should permit past judicial decisions to govern his plans and his execution of the laws. Administration enemies, in good faith or for political purposes, interpreted the statement to mean that Jackson would not enforce legislation which he believed to be unconstitutional even though the Supreme Court had upheld it. This, declared Taney in later years, was not at all what was meant.[16] Jackson had in the past enforced the provisions of the existing charter of the bank even though he believed them to be unconstitutional, and he would have enforced the provisions of the new charter had it been granted over his veto and become effective during the period of his administration. But in so far as he participated in the making of new laws his oath to support the Constitution obligated him to follow his own judgment as to constitutionality, and to veto acts which he believed unconstitutional even though previous decisions indicated that the Supreme Court would disagree with him. Even this was heretical doctrine, however, as far as men of the Marshall school were concerned.

If some of the arguments were complex, the message closed with a summary and a personal appeal from Jackson that every man could understand. Congress had yielded to the demand of the privileged few for additional special privileges. It was the duty of government to protect the weak and strong alike, and give special privileges to none. The attempt to gratify the desires of rich men had arrayed section against section, interest against interest and man against man, in a fearful commotion which threatened to shake the foundations of the Union. A firm stand must be taken against measures of this kind. A general discussion of the issues would now take place, Jackson predicted. In the midst of the discussion a new Congress would be elected, by which he had no doubt a satisfactory settlement would be reached. He had now done his duty. If sustained by his fellow citizens he would be grateful and happy. If not, he would derive peace and contentment from the motives by which he had been guided.

The message, dated July 10, 1832, was sent to the Senate. After

[16] Taney to Van Buren, May 8 and June 30, 1860, Van Buren MSS.

the reading of part of it one of Biddle's Pennsylvania friends in the House of Representatives wrote that it was "a most wretched production, going far to weaken every principle of the government, assailing the Supreme Court, and almost denouncing the tariff itself. . . . If Jacksonism can stand this, it will stand anything and we may as well give up the rule to vulgarity and barbarism at once." [17]

It was clear that sufficient votes could not be secured to pass the bill over the veto, but a number of speeches attacking the message were delivered for campaign purposes. The first and most important was that of Daniel Webster, who discussed the message point by point. He ruthlessly exposed unbalanced statements and weak arguments. Going further, he skillfully twisted accurate statements and sound arguments to make it appear that the message was a truly pitiable document. Indeed, if the message at times stooped to the trickery of the demagogue, Webster's speech had the same fault in no less degree.

Among other things, he attacked with more bluster than conviction Jackson's charge that the bill would provide gratuities for the present stockholders of the bank. The statement that the value of the stock would go up if the bill were passed rested "on random estimate or mere conjecture," he declared, although he must have known that in so far as there was certainty in any economic forecasting there was certainty that if fifteen years were added to the life span of the institution whose future was now in doubt the market value of the stock would rise. He argued furthermore that outside parties should trust Congress to exact a bonus sufficient to make an adequate return for privileges conferred upon the bank.

In discussing questions of constitutionality Webster misinterpreted Jackson—or Taney—making it appear that Jackson had said he would not enforce a law which had been upheld by the Supreme Court if he himself thought it unconstitutional. He scorned the argument that though the establishment of a bank might be a constitutional means of exercising powers of the federal government many of the features of this particular bank were unconstitutional. No one,

[17] J. G. Watmough to Biddle, July 10, 1832, Biddle MSS.

he declared, not even the judges, would be able to agree on when a bank was constitutional if the constitutionality of all its different features was inquired into. The only satisfactory doctrine was that if a bank was constitutional all the features which might normally belong to it were also constitutional.

Webster's argument was a plea in behalf of a régime of centralized government under the control of an aristocracy of wealth and ability. Jackson claimed to believe in government by the masses of the people, and thought the people should be kept informed as to what their representatives were doing. Webster contended that the people should trust their representatives, and that discretion should be used in giving information to the people, lest they act rashly on matters too complex for their understanding. Yet if he was opposed to mass action in most instances he made one important exception. He sought to stir the wrath of the people against Jackson, and to bring about his defeat at the polls. In a climactic and concluding paragraph he declared that the message appealed to every prejudice which might betray men into mistaken views. It urged specious topics of state rights and nationalism against rightful and hitherto accepted measures. It sowed seeds of jealousy and ill will. It wantonly attacked whole classes of the people, and sought to turn the poor against the rich. It found no topic too exciting for its use, no passion too inflammable for its solicitation.

"It remains, now," Webster concluded, "for the people of the United States to choose between the principles here avowed and their government. These cannot subsist together. The one or the other must be rejected. If the sentiments of the message should receive general approbation, the Constitution will have perished even earlier than the moment which its enemies originally allowed for the termination of its existence. It will not have survived to its fiftieth year." [18]

Biddle printed and circulated thousands of copies of Webster's speech, at the expense of the Bank of the United States. One item in the bank records calls for 25,000 copies, another for 52,500, and

[18] See the *Register of Debates in Congress*, Senate, July 11, 1832, p. 1240.

another for 63,000. Such was presumably the purpose for which it was delivered. Taney declared that in spite of the fact that it was delivered on the floor of the Senate it was in tone, temper, and partisan character obviously the speech of counsel paid by the bank, "and of one, too, by no means scrupulous in his statement of facts. I do not know whether Mr. Webster received directly a fee from the bank for this speech in the Senate, and I will not therefore assert that he did. But I do know certainly that while this struggle was going on, he was, under the names of professional fees for services and loans, receiving a princely income from the bank, and that what was called loan was afterwards colorably paid by the transfer of property of trifling value and bearing no sort of proportion to his debt. This speech upon the face of it was made for distribution and to deceive the uninformed. And the same may be said both as to the inducement and object of many of the speeches made on that occasion and which appear by this report [19] to have been so extensively circulated." [20]

Webster knew the real source of the constitutional argument which he so scornfully denounced, and it is possible that Taney knew that he knew, and that the fact gave an added sharpness to Taney's criticism of Webster's speech. The two men had met at the bar on a number of occasions, both as associates and as opponents, but there is no evidence that they had ever been close friends. They were alike in that both were ambitious and both were able members of the profession, but they were ambitious and able in strikingly different ways. Webster was a nationalist doctrinaire of the school of Marshall. He had held high political office for many years and aspired to rise still higher, to the presidency. On the platform, at the bar, and even in private association he was a great showman. He staged every entrance, and dramatized every gesture and modulation of his voice. He was an artist, at least up to the point where the obviousness of his dramatization destroyed its character as art.

[19] Report of the government directors of the Bank of the United States to the President, Aug. 19, 1833, *Correspondence of Andrew Jackson*, V, 160–165.
[20] Taney, Bank War MS., pp. 136–137.

Taney on the other hand, Federalist though he had been, had never committed himself to the broad nationalism of Marshall. He was a believer in local government wherever it could be made to work effectively. He disapproved more and more of the extension of the powers of the federal government with the growth of the danger of its becoming the tool of moneyed interests in particular sections of the country, and as the Constitution came to be used to interfere with the states in the regulation of their own local affairs. If he was at this time politically ambitious in the same sense as Webster, that fact is not apparent from the records, yet in his own way he was highly sensitive about his professional prestige, and, perhaps without admitting it even to himself, he may have been jealous of Webster's impressiveness on the platform. If Taney was himself a platform artist, his form of art was at the opposite extreme from that of Webster. For where Webster was grand, ponderous, and impressive, Taney was simple, unaffected, direct, and clear. Webster was handsome and graceful, Taney was homely and awkward. Webster's voice was deep and sonorous, Taney's was flat and lacking in resonance. Webster, in society, was an animated object of grandeur, drawing the admiration of the crowd. Taney was humbly gracious, his irregular features and short-sighted dark eyes warmly alight, meeting men and women as individuals rather than part of a crowd, bowing before them according to the best manners of the old southern tradition.

Their very differences perhaps added to the sense of antagonistic rivalry felt by both men when they found themselves supporting opposing political causes, Webster therefore doubtless had personal as well as professional reasons for giving every possible ounce of weight to his speech against the veto message before releasing it for publication. He took his materials to Boston with him, and wrote a letter to his friend Joseph Story, of the Supreme Court of the United States, whose residence was in Cambridge. He was going to Marshfield, Webster stated. "I shall stay there some days, and intend, during that period, to correct the notes of my speech, on the *veto* message. You have seen that message. My wish is, to give a full answer to its *trash*, on the constitutional question. That is Taney's work. The argument, you perceive, is that *some* powers of the bank are not *necessary*, and so, not constitutional. Now, my dear sir, the object of this is, to request you to turn to the message, read this part of it, and give me, in a letter of three pages, a close and conclusive confutation, in your way, of all the nonsense in this particular. It will take you less than half an hour. Pray direct it to me at Marshfield, and let me have it, if possible, in two or three days." [21]

The scattered collections of Story letters do not reveal his reply to Webster, thereby disclosing the extent to which his published speech attacking the veto message was the product of one of the members of the Supreme Court. There is reason for believing that Story did not rebuff Webster for his violation of judicial decorum in asking for an opinion on a matter which had been and would again be before his court for interpretation, for during the following year Webster requested and received Story's opinion on another legal argument made by Taney.[22] Story may have been sufficiently discreet on the former occasion, however, to ask Webster not to make known his coöperation in the drafting of the document which was to be used in the ensuing presidential campaign and circulated at the expense of the bank. Story was a loyal advocate of the bank, and was warmly friendly toward Biddle. "If I shall have attained a little to your approbation by my labor as a public magistrate," he wrote to Biddle a few years later, "I shall have great consolation in the thought; for I know nothing, beyond the consciousness of a discharge of duty, which ought to gratify one more, than to have a place in the respect of the wise, the good, and the honored of our times." [23]

Congress adjourned a few days after the delivery of the veto message, and weary politicians fled from Washington to escape the oppressive heat and to prepare for the coming campaign. Jackson

---

[21] Webster to Story, July 21, 1832, Story MSS., Massachusetts Historical Society.
[22] *Post*, pp. 258–259.
[23] Story to Biddle, March 22, 1838, Etting Coll., Historical Society of Pennsylvania.

left for the Hermitage, his home in Tennessee. The Taneys packed the family plate for safe keeping and sent it to the vaults of the local branch of the Bank of the United States—revealing thus at least a minimum of faith in the "monster"—and fled likewise from the heat and from the cholera which was spreading in certain parts of Maryland. They rented the Waring place, near the Key home on Pipe Creek, in Frederick County, planning to remain there until October. Mrs. Taney's health was as usual a matter of grave concern, and Taney himself was in need of rest and the quiet of the country, in spite of the zest of his victory over his cabinet rival and over the bank. Unknown to himself perhaps, his reputation, hitherto for the most part local, was beginning to spread, largely because of his opposition to the bank. Living in retirement in his home in Virginia, James Madison heard of Taney, and persuaded one of Taney's friends to tell about him and about his opinions.[24] Madison was the President who with reluctance had consented to the chartering of the existing Bank of the United States. Now he was apparently among those who opposed the renewal of its life.

During the summer months the campaign simmered, while the friends of Jackson and Van Buren, and Clay and Sergeant, prepared for the autumnal battle. As Jackson and others had predicted, Van Buren had been nominated for Vice President at the Baltimore Convention held in May, in spite of the opposition of some who thought he would injure the ticket and others, including his friend Louis McLane,[25] who thought he might interfere with their own aspirations for the presidency. On August 1 Biddle wrote to Clay, the National Republican or Whig presidential candidate, that the veto worked as well as the friends of the bank could desire. In fact, he was delighted with it. "It has all the fury of a chained panther biting at the bars of his cage," Biddle declared. "It is really a manifesto of anarchy—such as Marat or Robespierre might have issued to the mob of the Faubourg St. Antoine: and my hope is that it will con-

---

[24] John H. B. Latrobe to Charles Carroll Harper, Aug. 4, 1832, Semmes, *John H. B. Latrobe and His Times*, p. 244.

[25] See the *Autobiography of Martin Van Buren*, pp. 581–590.

tribute to relieve the country from the dominion of these miserable people." [26]

Joseph Hopkinson, a well known Philadelphia lawyer and federal judge, reread the veto message and found it "a poorer piece of wickedness and imbecility" than he had thought it on first perusal. He was strongly tempted to "expose its ignorance, falsehoods, absurdities and vulgar slang," but feared that because of his judicial position he would be overwhelmed with reproaches for doing so. He urged Biddle to answer the message, however. It was particularly necessary to do this in Pennsylvania, where great pains had been taken to mislead the Germans on the subject of the bank.[27]

Jackson, at the Hermitage, was well satisfied. "The veto works well everywhere," he declared; "it has put down the bank instead of prostrating me." [28] The Jackson leaders continued to use the methods of the veto message. They wrote and spoke directly to the masses of the people, in terms of emotions they could feel and ideas they could understand. They portrayed Jackson as the leader of the common people, in a struggle with Clay and others who were labeled tools of banking or other propertied or sectional interests. Such, indeed, were the customary methods of so-called Jacksonian Democracy. Jackson did not wait until the people had expressed their desires and then seek to gratify them. Rather he acted on his own decisions, and then dramatized his actions to win popular acclaim and convince the people that he was acting at their behest.

The Whigs were not adept at the making of popular appeals. While Biddle and his friends were circulating thousands of copies of pretentious speeches of Daniel Webster, John Quincy Adams, and others, the Jacksonians won heavily in state and local elections in the West. Clay, realizing that much of the material provided was too profound and abstruse for campaign purposes, wrote to Biddle about it. "It is a common, sometimes fatal, error," he declared, "to suppose that the mass of the community is as well informed as the intel-

---

[26] Biddle to Clay, Aug. 1, 1832, President's Letter Book, Biddle MSS.
[27] Joseph Hopkinson to Biddle, Aug. 13, 1832, *ibid.*
[28] Jackson to W. B. Lewis, Aug. 18, 1832, *Correspondence of Andrew Jackson*, IV, 467.

ligent, respecting a given subject. It should be addressed as if it knew nothing about it, in plain, intelligible and forceful language." [29]

By means of the *Globe* Kendall and Blair spread the veto message far and wide, reiterating its arguments day after day with vigorous comments on the personalities involved. These materials were reprinted and spread more widely by other Jackson papers. The opposition press, including papers in some manner subsidized by the bank and others friendly for other reasons, campaigned with similar vigor though on the whole with less facility at persuading the common people. Speeches and essays poured forth directly or indirectly from the Bank of the United States. Taney declared that much money was spent by the bank for "anonymous publicity containing the grossest and coarsest libels upon the President, Col. Benton, and other distinguished opponents of the bank. And upon the order merely of Mr. Biddle, without disclosing the name of the person who received it or the service rendered." [30]

The bank made its influence felt in another way. Through 1831 and until May, 1832, it had expanded its loans, thereby increasing the number of persons dependent upon it and stimulating the expansion of business. After the veto of the bill to recharter the bank, using the veto as its excuse, it contracted its loans and put pressure upon state banks which were debtor to it. "By this means," said Taney, "Mr. Biddle succeeded in producing much distress and embarrassment in the cities, and ruined many enterprising men, who had been encouraged to enlarge their commercial operations by the abundance of money and the facility with which loans had been obtained while the bank was so rapidly expanding. . . . But the time between the veto and the election was too short to reach that large portion of the American people who are not accustomed in their business to rely on discounts at banks. It was not long enough to affect seriously the prices of produce or the wages of labor. Yet the pressure was severe in the commercial cities, and the outcry was great in that class of persons who depend upon bank accommodations

[29] Clay to Biddle, Aug. 27, 1832, Biddle MSS.
[30] Taney, Bank War MS., pp. 136–137.

to carry on their business. And as the distress followed after the veto it was imputed to the veto and General Jackson represented as responsible for the evils which Mr. Biddle himself was daily producing. Bold and profligate as this scheme was, it succeeded to a considerable extent. The politicians who opposed the reëlection of General Jackson, united with the agents of the bank in making the charge. . . . And this banking operation of Mr. Biddle undoubtedly deprived General Jackson of thousands and tens of thousand votes, which would otherwise [have] been cast for him." [31]

In addition to the banking interests Clay had the support of the broad constructionists of the Constitution, the industrial interests desiring tariff protection, and the advocates of internal improvements at the expense of the federal government. He had the assistance of many able politicians. The Jackson leaders were deeply concerned about the results of the election until returns began to come in from Pennsylvania, the stronghold of banking and industrial interests, showing that the state had been won for Jackson. The race was close in a number of states, but Jackson won an overwhelming majority of the electoral votes.

Biddle, however, was undaunted. His avowed reason for applying for a new charter four years before the expiration of the old one had been that if renewal was not to be granted the bank should at once begin a gradual withdrawal from business. After the veto he had contracted loans nominally because the threat of discontinuing the bank made contraction necessary, though according to Taney his real motive was his desire to influence the election. Now that the President who had blocked the renewal was returned to power, however, he announced: "The bank does not mean to commence any systematic reduction of its loans with a view to winding up its affairs. It does not mean to begin to close its concerns. It means to go on in its general business just as if no such event as the President's negative had ever happened." [32] It was clear, therefore, that the bank war was not yet over, had perhaps not even reached its crisis.

[31] *Ibid.*, pp. 133–134.
[32] Biddle to John Rathbone, Jr., Nov. 21, 1832, President's Letter Book, Biddle MSS.

CHAPTER XI

SKIRMISHES

THE Jackson victory at the polls in the autumn of 1832 marked the end of a major struggle. It marked also the beginning of a series of bickerings, feints, and skirmishes in which the bank issue was involved in one way or another, and which led eventually to the supreme test of strength between the administration and the Bank of the United States. The resumption of the bank war was preceded, however, by the events of a major national crisis, the threat of South Carolina to prevent the enforcement of tariff legislation in southern ports, and the arrangement of the federal government to meet nullification by force if necessary.

The story of the nullification crisis of this period has little place in an account of Taney's life. Although the issues later became of great importance in his thinking he at this time failed to participate in the struggle because he had too many other things to do. He was in Annapolis during most of the time when Livingston was writing Jackson's proclamation on nullification, and most of the days spent in Washington were taken up by illness or by the preparation of cases for the ensuing term of the Supreme Court. Some months earlier he had expressed to Livingston the opinion that a state had no constitutional right to disobey a tariff law adverse to its interests,[1] and he seems to have shared Jackson's distrust of Calhoun, and perhaps his active dislike. On the other hand his ideas were less strongly nationalistic than the doctrines which Livingston wove into the proclamation. The crisis came and passed, however, without involving him primarily in any way.

The records seem to indicate that Taney was much more interested in the cumulative disclosures of the abuses of the Bank of the

[1] *Ante,* p. 155.

United States than in nullification, and as soon as the nullification struggle was brought to an end Jackson and other members of the administration likewise turned their attention to their old enemy. Jackson had looked forward to the retirement of what remained of the national debt during the period of his administration. The officers of the Bank of the United States knew of this plan, but considered it a ridiculous idea that freedom from debt was something to be desired on the part of a national government. Personal dislike for Jackson and his friends probably had something to do with their attitude. Their unwillingness to surrender government funds on deposit to pay off the debt was no doubt of even greater influence, coupled with the fact that in the future government income and expenditure would be on a smaller scale, and would provide less business for the bank.

While knowing that the government planned to use its deposits to pay the debt, the bank during 1831 and the first half of 1832 continued to expand loans based in part on these deposits. The loans may have been needed, although there is a question as to whether they did not aid unhealthful business expansion. The money may have been safe. The bank loaned out the money, however, and kept it out, knowing that the government would soon call for it, and that only a severe contraction of the loans would make payment possible. It was governed presumably not merely by the desire for interest returns but also by the belief that expansion would make friends for the bank and aid in bringing about the renewal of its charter, while contraction would have the opposite effect.

On March 24, 1832, while the bill to renew the charter was before Congress, the Treasury Department informed Biddle that notice would be issued April 1 concerning the retirement of part of the government debt. The amount to be retired, on July 1, would run to six or seven million dollars, and constituted one-half of a series of three per cent loan certificates then outstanding. Biddle was asked if he had any objection to the plan.[2] He hurried to Washington for

---

[2] See J. K. Polk's minority report of the House Ways and Means Committee, *Register of Debates*, 22nd Cong., 2d sess., Appendix, p. 103.

a conference with McLane. He urged that since the government had already caused considerable pressure on the business community by other financial legislation it ought to be slow in requiring further contraction. Since approximately half the certificates to be retired were held abroad, the necessity for shipping gold would make the contraction particularly severe. He succeeded in persuading the administration to postpone payment of any portion of the debt until the first of October, though only after agreeing that the bank would protect the Treasury from loss by paying the interest during the intervening period.[3]

After the strife culminating in the enactment and veto of the bill to recharter the bank, the administration was in no mood to show further leniency toward Biddle. He was notified on July 19 that two-third of the three per cent certificates would be redeemed on October 5, and the remainder on January 5. In the meantime, knowing that the government would call on the bank for a large sum of money, he had been searching for a mode of escape from his predicament. He evolved a scheme whereby the foreign holders of several million dollars of the certificates would be dissuaded from presenting their certificates for payment in spite of the fact that the government would have ceased to pay interest. In that event the Bank of the United States would not have to surrender the funds deposited with it by the government.

To effect the arrangement Biddle sent his friend and a director of the bank, Thomas Cadwalader, to negotiate with foreign holders of the securities. The bank was to pay three per cent interest for the periods of three, six, and nine months for which the certificates were to be held, and a reasonable commission as well. Biddle had counted on getting about $3,000,000 of which the financial house of the Barings was agent for the owners, and $2,000,000 from other sources. The Barings, however, being merely agents and not owners, were not able to coöperate fully, and Cadwalader was unable to get control of the requisite number of certificates. He finally went beyond the letter of his printed instructions, and made a contract by which

[3] Taney, Bank War MS., pp. 143–144.

the Barings were to purchase certificates outright for the bank, hold them, and advance the bank money on them. In this way the British financiers were to aid the obstreperous Bank of the United States in defeating the fiscal policies of the United States government.

The government was quite unaware of the maneuvering of Biddle and his agents until October 11, 1832, when the New York *Evening Post* published a circular sent by the Barings to the holders of the certificates. In the excitement which followed, it was discovered that the purchase of certificates by the bank was a violation of its charter, and an offense probably serious enough to justify its revocation. Four days after publication of the circular Biddle wrote to the Barings disavowing the contract as not within Cadwalader's instructions or the powers of the bank. It is significant, however, that although he had known of the arrangement for some time he did not disavow it until publication of the circular had brought a storm of criticism.

The conduct of the bank was so bitterly denounced that Biddle arranged a four per cent loan with the Barings and directed that the certificates be sent in as soon as they were collected. Substantial amounts, however, which had been postponed under the strictly legal but not highly ethical arrangement by which the bank was to pay the interest, were not surrendered until well along in the following year, thus defeating Jackson's plan to redeem all the three per cent certificates before the termination of his first administration. Taney's comment that Jackson was "exceedingly indignant" [4] was probably stating the case altogether too mildly.[5]

In November, 1832, Jackson called a meeting of the cabinet at which hostilities between Taney and McLane were renewed, if indeed they had ever been suspended. Jackson declared the conduct of the bank had convinced him that a thorough examination would prove it to be insolvent. He therefore asked advice as to whether it would be better to seek the revocation of the charter or immediately to remove all government money deposited in the bank. McLane,

---

[4] *Ibid.*, p. 147.
[5] For a summary of events see the Washington *Globe*, Jan. 1, 1833.

friendly though he had been toward the bank, had been offended by its alignment with the Whig politicians, and was not averse to seeing it punished. He may have favored measures less drastic than those which Jackson proposed, however, and his choice may have been influenced by the belief that the method which he advocated could not be made effective. In any event it was a foregone conclusion that he and Taney would disagree in the matter. McLane urged that a *scire facias* be issued to forfeit the charter. The abuses of the bank amply justified such a measure, he declared. He did not favor the mere withdrawal of the government deposits.

"I was opposed to issuing a *scire facias*," said Taney, "and thought better to do nothing than adopt a measure of that kind. I said there were many things which we certainly knew in relation to the conduct of the bank, and upon which the Executive might properly act, but which it would be difficult if not impossible to establish by legal proof in a court of justice, and especially against an adversary so adroit and unscrupulous as the bank had shown itself to be. Besides, the case must be tried in Philadelphia, before a Philadelphia jury, with all the leading counsel of that city retained as counsel for the bank, and it would obviously be impossible to obtain a verdict against the bank in a case where the trial from its very nature must last some weeks, and the jury during all that time [be] exposed to the influences which the bank would not scruple to exercise; and that such an excitement would be got up through the local press and otherwise in its favor that even honest and incorruptible men on the panel most probably would not have the firmness to withstand it." [6]

With a realism born of experience Taney was likewise afraid of the particular judge before whom the case would be tried. Philadelphia was in the circuit of Justice Henry Baldwin, who "was known to be warmly in favor of the renewal of the charter and had held earnest and repeated conversations with me at my office, endeavoring to persuade me to advise the President not to veto the bill." [7] Baldwin was in some respects an able judge, but he was a very excit-

[6] Taney, Bank War MS., pp. 149–150.
[7] *Ibid.*, p. 150.

able person, and a combination of intensive study and deep feeling on a subject sometimes brought him to a state of actual insanity. Indeed, a few weeks after this meeting of the cabinet it was reported that he was confined in a hospital, probably the victim of incurable lunacy.[8] He was absent from the term of the Supreme Court which began in January, 1833, but later returned to the bench—and was to be Taney's colleague for a few years. Knowing Baldwin as he did, Taney thought it highly probable that in his charge to the jury he would reply to the veto message and lecture the President for his conduct in directing the *scire facias*.

McLane intimated in virtuous fashion that the implications of what Taney had said were disrespectful to the jury and to Judge Baldwin. Taney replied that there was nothing new in the suggestion that justice could not be had from a jury in a particular place. Usually a change of venue could be had in a case concerning which prejudice was apt to be strong in a particular locality, but the charter of the bank provided that this type of case against the bank should be tried in this court, and made no provision for change of venue. As for Judge Baldwin, his unhappy temperament was his misfortune rather than his fault. It should not be mentioned publicly, of course, but it was a fact well known to all who were present at the cabinet meeting, and it would be foolish to ignore it.[9]

Although he thought it bad strategy to attack the charter of the bank Taney urged that the government deposits be removed. The conduct of the bank in relation to the three per cent certificates seemed to indicate that it was financially embarrassed and might be an unsafe depository for public funds. But even if the bank were unquestionably solvent, its conduct in attempting to block the policies of the government and retain the use of government money, when it should be used in paying off the public debt, showed the bank to be an untrustworthy fiscal agent, and it ought not to be continued as such. Its interference with politics and elections, and its obvious use of corrupt means to obtain the renewal of its charter, were even

[8] Alexandria *Gazette*, quoted in the Richmond *Enquirer*, Jan. 5, 1833.
[9] Taney, Bank War MS., pp. 156–158.

more objectionable, and since the possession of the public deposits increased the powers it exercised for such improper and corrupt purposes, they ought to be withdrawn. Although the bank was now evidently much embarrassed, it would by means of its foreign connections be able to keep itself afloat, if the public deposits were continued, until after the next presidential election, and would keep the country continually disturbed by its struggle for a renewal. On the other hand, if the deposits were withdrawn and other methods of collecting and disbursing the revenue were adopted, the bank would give up the fight and would proceed to wind up its affairs at the proper time.[10]

McLane countered by urging that there should first be an investigation of the bank, and that the deposits should be removed only if they were proved to be unsafe. Otherwise the removal would be regarded as an unjust attack upon the bank, and Congress might very probably order the deposits restored to it. Taney replied that the books of the bank were kept in such a way that no one could tell from them whether the bank was solvent or not. He did not think Congress would go so far as to order the deposits restored, but if it did so the President could veto the bill, and he was convinced that the people would stand by the veto.[11] Jackson listened to the discussion, said little, and finally closed the meeting, saying that he would think the matter over and call it to the attention of the cabinet at a later date.[12]

In his annual message to Congress of December 4, 1832, Jackson referred to the bank's abuse of its powers, and suggested that Congress investigate to discover whether the deposits of the government were safe. McLane, having in the meantime made some investigations through an agent, Henry Toland, expressed in his report to Congress the belief that the deposits were safe, and recommended that they be not removed, particularly since the bank and its branches had been advertised as the medium through which the outstanding

[10] *Ibid.*, pp. 152–153.
[11] *Ibid.*, pp. 154–156.
[12] *Ibid.*, p. 158.

government certificates were to be redeemed. He suggested, however, that Congress might make further study of the safety of the government money if it so desired. John Quincy Adams declared testily in the House of Representatives that it was the business of the Secretary of the Treasury to know the affairs of the bank, and to remove the deposits if they were in danger, and report his reasons to Congress. He had no right to throw the responsibility upon Congress. Nevertheless the Committee on Ways and Means was directed to conduct an investigation.

In the meantime unpleasantness between Taney and McLane continued from another angle. Early in November, immediately after the election, McLane went to New York to see Van Buren. One of Biddle's observers reported that the visit was for the purpose of getting Van Buren's support in the event of the death of Chief Justice Marshall, or even in the case of the death of Justice Duvall.[13] The visit did concern the matter of a promotion for McLane, but this time it was not a position on the Supreme Court which he was seeking. It had been arranged that some time in the ensuing months Livingston should resign as Secretary of State and be sent as minister to France. McLane wished and expected to move to the Department of State, but he did not wish to move without knowing who was to succeed him in the Treasury Department—a post which was now one of more than usual importance because of the trouble with the Bank of the United States. Van Buren urged immediately that Taney be moved to the Treasury Department, and that Benjamin F. Butler of New York be made Attorney General. McLane declared that such an arrangement would be so distasteful to him as to bring about his retirement from public life. He much preferred having William J. Duane of Pennsylvania in the Treasury Department.[14] Van Buren issued no ultimatum, but suggested that since he did not know whether Butler was interested in an office nothing be said about him until more was known.

On November 26 McLane wrote to Van Buren again praising

[13] R. L. Colt to Biddle, Nov. 17, 1832, Biddle MSS.
[14] *Autobiography of Martin Van Buren*, pp. 593-594.

Duane as the ideal man for the place. "I am, both on personal and political grounds, so thoroughly satisfied of the propriety of this selection that I should clinch it at once and irrevocably but for an apprehension that it may create some disappointment in your quarter. I hope you need no assurance of my determination to promote Mr. Butler to anything; though I confess that the means you hinted to me [15] would be gall and wormwood; and, I frankly tell you, rob me of almost every inducement to continue in public life: it would rob me of all but the difficulty of making immediate provision for a large and helpless family. If that inducement could be removed my course, in the event referred to would be plain. . . . If Mr. B[utler] could be placed in the T[reasury] I should be fully satisfied; or if Mr. T[aney] could go abroad and thus accomplish your own view, I should be even better satisfied. However, this and one other act of patronage has given me more solicitude than I am willing now to express, and more than all the honors of cabinet place will ever repay." [16]

McLane won. On December 4 Jackson offered the position of Secretary of the Treasury to Duane, who, after he came into office the following June, was sufficiently the tool of McLane to cause the latter to be spoken of frequently as the head of two departments. Taney was ill part of the time during which the arrangement was being worked out, and was busy with the preparation of cases for argument in court. Whether under other circumstances he could have lobbied effectively enough with Jackson to secure his own promotion, or so as to secure the appointment of someone more in accord with his own point of view on critical issues, is a matter for speculation. Certain it is that Taney, if he tried lobbying in this matter, definitely failed, and that he had difficulties with McLane in the matter of pushing minor appointments as well.[17] It was Taney's recollection,

[15] Of making a place for Butler by moving Taney to the Treasury Department.

[16] *Autobiography of Martin Van Buren*, p. 597.

[17] In discussing a proposed appointment with Van Buren, McLane thought there would be no difficulty "but for the pressure by T[aney] in behalf of his relation Heath of Baltimore. God knows these family concerns have been carried far enough and will be more apparent in the final composition of the legation at Paris."—McLane to Van Buren, April 25, 1833, Van Buren MSS.

more than a quarter of a century later, that he had not desired the position at all, and had refused to permit his name to be presented for it.[18] Long-time recollections are apt to be faulty, however. Furthermore, it seems probable that even if he did not desire the post for himself he was disgruntled, along with Blair, Lewis, Kendall, and others, when the tireless political climber succeeded with his maneuvers.

Because of engrossing interest in the struggle over nullification little was heard of the bank controversy during the final weeks of Jackson's first administration. A ripple of uneasiness was created in bank circles when James K. Polk offered a bill in the House of Representatives providing for the sale of the government stock in the Bank of the United States, but the measure was defeated by a close vote. It was rumored that Taney had given McLane an official opinion to the effect that he had the power to sell the government stock without permissive legislation. Friends of the bank believed, however, that the rumor was spread by brokers who were short of stock and were seeking to acquire it through spreading misinformation.[19]

James A. Hamilton of New York passed on to Jackson information concerning the bank's malevolent plans for the future. It would guard its own loans closely, stimulate expansion on the part of state banks, and then, near the date for the expiration of its charter, bring about a crisis which would compel them to suspend specie payments. The desire of the people for a sound currency would bring about the recharter of the Bank of the United States.[20] Whether or not the bank leaders really had such a plan in mind, Hamilton's report kept Jackson aware of the fact that his enemy was still strong enough to be dangerous.

On March 1, 1833, the Ways and Means Committee of the House of Representatives made a report based on a superficial investigation of the bank. It concluded that the government deposits were safe. It

---

[18] Taney to Van Buren, March 8, 1860, Van Buren MSS.
[19] See R. L. Colt to Biddle, Dec. 26 and 27, 1832, Biddle MSS.
[20] Hamilton to Jackson, Feb. 28, 1833, *Correspondence of Andrew Jackson*, V, 22-23.

stated that although the purchase of government certificates by the bank had been illegal that act had been renounced, and most of the certificates postponed because of the arrangement of the bank had been turned in, and the bank now seemed sound and free from misconduct. The House adopted the report by a large majority. A minority report, presented by James K. Polk, set forth at length the evidence of the attempt of the bank to disrupt the fiscal plans of the government. It was a document of great importance, for it provided materials for most of the editorials and speeches directed against the bank in the months to come.[21]

After his second inauguration Jackson again took up the problem of dealing with the bank. On March 12, 1833, he and Taney discussed the feasibility of voiding the charter and removing the government deposits. When Taney left, Jackson asked him to provide in writing his opinion on the bank's violation of the law under which it had been chartered. That night Jackson read the reports made to the House of Representatives by the investigating committee, and wrote a note to Taney saying he was still of the opinion that the bank could not continue specie payments for one month after the payment of the public debt, and he would like to talk with Taney about the problem of finding safe places of deposit for the government funds. [22]

A few days later Jackson drafted a series of questions concerning the bank, with his own tentative conclusions appended, and sent copies to all members of the cabinet and to other advisers. The questions were: Was there still room for doubt as to the safety of the deposits? Could the bank be relied upon as an agent of the government? Should the bank under any circumstances be rechartered? If not, should another national bank be established in its place, and under what circumstances? And, how should the public revenues be collected and stored?

Jackson gave it as his own conclusion that the bank should not be rechartered under any circumstances. If a substitute were created it ought to be located in the District of Columbia, with a right to estab-

[21] See the report in the Appendix to the *Register of Debates*, 22d Cong., 2d sess.
[22] Jackson to Taney, March 12, 1833, *Maryland Historical Magazine*, IV, 297–298.

lish branches in the states only with the consent of the states and under conditions prescribed by them. The government should appoint the president and enough directors to control the bank, and should have the power to alter or repeal the charter at any time. No such institution should be created until an attempt had been made to get along without it. A system should be immediately devised for using state banks as government depositories, to be put into operation as soon as was thought advisable.[23]

Taney replied that he thought there was still doubt as to the financial stability of the bank, although the opinion of the House of Representatives was entitled to respect. But the ability of the bank to meet its obligations was not the only subject of inquiry. In view of the past conduct of the bank he thought it could no longer be relied upon as an agent of the government. He gave four illustrations of misconduct. First, by making excessive loans of money deposited with it the bank had made it necessary to postpone the payment on the public debt scheduled for July 1, 1832. Second, the bank had enormously increased its loans during 1831 and the first half of 1832 under circumstances which made it obvious that the purpose was to add to its political power and compel the renewal of its charter. Third, the conduct of the bank in attempting to prevent the payment of the public debt was alone a sufficient reason for refusing further to confide in it as the fiscal agent of the government. Fourth, an even more cogent reason for the withdrawal of government deposits from the bank was the use of bank money to secure newspaper support. To continue the bank in the confidence of the government would be to sanction conduct so pregnant with evil that it could not be too severely and pointedly reprobated.

He urged that this particular national bank should under no circumstances be rechartered, and opposed the creation of a substitute until an attempt had been made to get along without it. Ignoring Chief Justice Marshall's interpretation of the "necessary and proper" clause of the Constitution, he argued that the establishment of a national bank was not constitutional if the powers of the government

[23] *Correspondence of Andrew Jackson,* V, 32–33.

could be exercised without it. He was convinced that the bank was not a necessity for the government, and the implication was clear that he thought any national bank a menace to constitutional government.

Taney discussed briefly Jackson's last question, as to a substitute mechanism for the collection and disbursement of public revenue. He was convinced that state banks, judiciously selected, could act efficiently as fiscal agents. The details of the scheme could be worked out only on a basis of the facts as to where deposits would be needed by the government and where disbursements were likely to be made. The pledge of the government to receive everywhere the notes of these banks would afford a currency as sound and stable as that provided by the Bank of the United States.[24]

In addition to Taney's, Jackson received a number of replies to his questions. Outstanding among them was the long and able letter written by McLane.[25] McLane was in agreement with Taney that the present national bank should not be rechartered, but there was little agreement on anything else. "There are some strong points in this view—all ably discussed," Jackson noted at the end of McLane's opinion. How Taney felt about Jackson's favorable reception of McLane's report is not recorded, but members of the "Kitchen Cabinet" were greatly disturbed, and Francis P. Blair tried to counteract its effect by providing Jackson with a critical analysis of it.[26]

Taney's friend Thomas Ellicott, president of the Union Bank of Maryland, took an active part in the discussions. He urged, probably in part for the benefit of his own institution, that the government deposits be removed from the national bank to state banks. He aided in the discovery of a way around some of the more obvious difficulties. For instance, under existing law the government was required to accept the notes of the Bank of the United States in payment of debts until the expiration of the charter in 1836. In the event of a struggle the bank might circulate notes at particular points which

[24] Taney to Jackson, March, 1833, *ibid.*, pp. 33-41. (The document in the Jackson MSS. bears the penciled date of April 3, 1833.)

[25] McLane to Jackson, May 20, 1833, *ibid.*, pp. 75ff.

[26] *Ibid.*, p. 102.

were redeemable at distant branches. Local branches might refuse to redeem them, and the state banks chosen as government depositories would have no adequate means of getting their face value for them.

Ellicott found a solution in the fact that the law required the Bank of the United States to move money from point to point as needed by the government, and showed that if the bank refused to redeem its notes where they were circulated it could be required to move them to the places where redemption was prescribed. Ellicott wrote a letter outlining this theory for Jackson.[27] Jackson presumably referred it to Taney, who replied outlining the same theory in other words. If the bank refused to obey the order of the Secretary of the Treasury in the matter, he declared, the act would be a palpable forfeiture of the charter. The government might then refuse to receive its notes.[28]

In the meantime a new conflict developed between the government and the bank. Under a recent treaty with France a payment was due the United States for damages to American shipping during the Napoleonic wars. McLane consulted Biddle as to the best way to transfer the money from France to the United States. Biddle advised McLane to sell his bank a bill of exchange on France. While Mc-Lane hesitated the rate of exchange declined, to Biddle's sardonic amusement,[29] and the government lost substantially before the transaction was completed as advised by Biddle. Then the bank on its own books transferred the value of the bill to the credit of the government—the money remaining on deposit, however, and subject to the use of the bank without interest.

France unfortunately failed to pay, and the money credited to the government had to be retransferred to the bank. In addition the bank laid claim to interest and all expenses incurred in connection with the transaction, and a further amount of fifteen per cent damages on the amount of the bill of exchange. Since Taney was the legal adviser of all departments of the government McLane sent him the records

[27] Ellicott to Jackson, April 6, 1833, *ibid.*, p. 49.
[28] Taney to Jackson, April 29, 1833, *ibid.*, p. 67.
[29] See Biddle to Henry Clay, Feb. 28, 1833, Clay MSS.

of the transaction and asked his advice. Taney replied that the interest and expenses should be paid, but that the claim for fifteen per cent damages had "no foundation in law or in equity, and ought not to be paid by the government." [30] He was busy with other tasks and did not work out a statement of reasons for his conclusion, but promised to present such a statement at a later date.

At this stage of developments, about the first of June, 1833, came the shifts in cabinet positions which had been arranged some months earlier. Livingston withdrew from the State Department to prepare for his duties as minister to France, McLane moved from the Treasury to the position of Secretary of State, the highest in the cabinet, and his friend William J. Duane, son of the one-time firebrand editor of the Philadelphia *Aurora*, became Secretary of the Treasury. A number of historians have made what seems clearly an error in assuming that Jackson transferred McLane at this time because McLane was friendly to the bank and opposed to the removal of the deposits.[31] They have ignored the fact that arrangements for the cabinet changes were made during the later months of 1832,[32] when the indignation of McLane against Biddle and the bank seemed to compare well with that of Taney. To be sure, McLane had at that time announced his opposition to the removal of the government deposits as a means of disciplining the bank, but Jackson himself was not committed to the removal at that time or for some months thereafter. Although he opposed the measures favored by his rival, Taney, McLane also professed his opposition to the renewal of the charter of Biddle's bank, and Jackson was clearly persuaded that McLane was among its more vigorous enemies.

Jackson seems to have accepted Duane almost exclusively on Mc-Lane's recommendation. He did not ask Duane to commit himself on the bank problem. This was not strange, in view of the fact that while the President and all members of the cabinet were irritated or

[30] Taney to McLane, May 24, 1833, *Bank of the United States* v. *United States*, 2 Howard 716 (1844).

[31] See Channing, *History of the United States*, V, 448; McMaster, *History of the People of the United States*, VI, 187; Bassett, *Life of Andrew Jackson*, p. 632.

[32] *Ante*, pp. 214–215.

angered by the bank there was no agreement as to the measures to be adopted. The alignment for and against the removal of the deposits came during the months between the date of Duane's appointment and the time when he took up the duties of his office. When in office he revealed reluctance toward the removal of the deposits similar to that of McLane, and he was probably more friendly toward Biddle and the bank than even McLane had suspected. McLane probably believed that Duane would be guided by his advice. Biddle seems to have been equally confident that Duane could be counted on to serve the bank. If a choice had to be made McLane may have preferred to see Duane align himself with the bank rather than with Taney and the others of Jackson's advisers to whom McLane was hostile.

Three weeks after Duane took office, nothing having been done by the government about the bill for expenses and damages, Biddle sent a letter of inquiry to Duane. Duane replied that the expenses incurred by the bank in the unfortunate transaction would be paid, but that the Attorney General had given the opinion that the fifteen per cent damages had no foundation in law or equity—and enclosed a copy of Taney's letter.[33]

Biddle replied immediately, asking if Taney had yet fulfilled his promise to file with the Secretary a statement of the reasons for his opinion, and requesting that a copy be sent to him. The bank did not wish to press an improper claim, he declared, and the board of directors would give the most respectful consideration to Taney's views.[34] Duane, hearing that Taney had returned from Annapolis, sent him a statement of the correspondence,[35] evidently hoping that it would prod Taney into preparing the coveted opinion, but Taney ignored it. Biddle wrote to Duane again, and Duane sent a copy of the letter to Taney, with a peremptory intimation that he expected a reply.[36] Taney answered sharply that he would file his opinion in his own good time, implying that since he was employed by the govern-

---

[33] Duane to Biddle, June 21, 1833, Letters to Banks, Treasury Department.

[34] Biddle to Duane, June 24, 1833, Attorney General MSS.

[35] Duane to Taney, July 2, 1833, Cabinets and Bureaus, Treasury Department.

[36] Duane to Taney, Aug. 14, 1833, *ibid.*

ment, and not by the bank, the bank could get its legal advice from its own lawyers. He could not "imagine that it is the duty of the counsel for the United States to argue this question for the satisfaction of the president and directors of the bank whenever they may think proper to call on him to do so." [37] Duane countered lamely that he was only trying to find out whether Taney would provide the information which the bank desired. "All that I desire is, that there may be no misapprehension anywhere, and, that it should be understood, that I had done all that it became me to do, to comply with the request of the bank." [38]

Duane sent Biddle copies of all the letters which had passed between Taney and himself,[39] and here negotiations were suspended for a time, because of the growing conflict over the removal of the deposits. The controversy had only added to the bitter feeling existing between the bank and its enemies in the government, and it had convinced Taney and others who knew of the correspondence here cited that the Secretary of the Treasury was nothing more than the tool of the bank.

On June 1, 1833, the day on which he took the oath of office, Duane was visited by Reuben M. Whitney, who had at one time been a director of the Bank of the United States. He was now one of its bitter enemies, however, and hoped to get a paying job for himself in the war which was to be waged against the bank. Whitney told Duane that Taney and Barry favored removing the deposits as soon as possible, McLane opposed it, as probably did Cass, while Woodbury's position was "yes and no." Jackson had decided to take the step, Whitney declared, and Amos Kendall was even now preparing the order directing the Secretary of the Treasury to make the removal. Soon afterward Duane talked with Jackson, who assured him that he had not sent Whitney to discuss bank matters with him. Jackson, however, leaned toward removing the deposits, while Duane refused to agree. Jackson was not disturbed, said he liked frankness, and remarked that

[37] Taney to Duane, Aug. 16, 1833, *Bank of the United States* v. *United States*, 2 Howard 747 (1844).

[38] Duane to Taney, Aug. 16, 1833, Cabinets and Bureaus, Treasury Department.

[39] Duane to Biddle, Aug. 17, 1833, Letters to Banks, Treasury Department.

although he had disagreed with McLane on the subject they had got along quite amicably.[40]

On the morning of June 6, before setting out on a tour of the eastern part of the country, Jackson wrote to Van Buren that the matter of removing the deposits had given him much concern, and that he would like Van Buren's opinion before he acted. "I must meet it fearlessly," he declared, "as soon as I can digest a system that will insure a solvent currency and a sure system for the fiscal operations of the government." [41] Three days later Kendall wrote to Van Buren outlining the system which he hoped Van Buren would recommend to Jackson.[42] While on his trip Jackson, after conversations with Van Buren, who had joined him, had some member or members of his party working on a statement of reasons why the deposits should be removed. It was giving him some trouble, he admitted, because of the necessity of meeting the views which had been presented by Mc-Lane.[43] On June 26 he sent to Duane, from Boston, a long statement of reasons why the deposits should be removed, enumerating therein the grievances most of which had already been stated many times. It is significant that the letter of transmittal, in which he outlined a plan for organizing state bank depositories,[44] was identical in form and often in terminology with that which Kendall had urged Van Buren to recommend to Jackson. It is not clear whether Van Buren had vigorously supported Kendall's program—the wily "Red Fox" was always exceedingly hesitant about making recommendations for positive action on vital issues—or whether Kendall had exercised his influence directly.

During the ensuing weeks many letters passed between Jackson and Duane on the subject, the latter resisting all arguments for the removal. Prominent among his objections was his contention that the state banks, fearing the vengeance of the Bank of the United States,

---

[40] W. J. Duane, *Narrative of Correspondence Concerning the Removal of the Deposites* (1838), pp. 5–9.

[41] Jackson to Van Buren, June 6, 1833, *Correspondence of Andrew Jackson*, V, 106.

[42] Kendall to Van Buren, June 9, 1833, *ibid.*, p. 106.

[43] Jackson to Andrew Jackson, Jr., June 17, 1833, *ibid.*, p. 110.

[44] Jackson to Duane, June 26, 1833, *ibid.*, p. 111.

would not dare to accept deposits from the government. It was true that Thomas Ellicott, president of the Union Bank of Maryland, always eager to make the most of the war against the national institution, had written to Duane offering the services of his bank,[45] as had also the president of the Girard Bank in Philadelphia,[46] but experience of recent years had shown that most state bankers had hearty fears of the wrath of Biddle and his colleagues.

Amos Kendall, who had been waiting eagerly to start organization for the conflict, declared that he would be delighted to find out if the state banks would take the deposits. Jackson thought it a good idea, and Duane reluctantly made out instructions for Kendall's investigation. He appended a paragraph, however, in which he declared that in his judgment nothing had yet taken place which would justify the removal. Jackson, now beginning to lose the rather surprising amount of patience which he had used with Duane, told him he could not see the propriety of the paragraph, and asked if it meant that Duane would not remove the deposits if the President, upon the advice of his cabinet, decided that they were to be removed.[47] Duane replied that he had thought the investigation a mere inquiry, and not a step in the process of removal. As for his final action in the matter, he would either coöperate with Jackson or retire from office.[48] Jackson, grimly pleased with Duane's promise to coöperate or resign, directed Kendall to write out his own instructions, and sent him off to visit the state banks.[49]

Kendall left Washington the last week in July, and during the next few weeks he visited state banks in Baltimore, Philadelphia, New York, and Boston. He found a considerable number of banks eager to have the deposits, though not all were willing to give the security which was thought to be needed. He made frequent reports of progress to Jackson, always adroitly including comments calculated to stimulate Jackson's antagonism to the bank. He sent information that

---

[45] Ellicott to Duane, June 15, 1833, Letters from Banks, Treasury Department.
[46] James Schott to Duane, June 28, 1833, *ibid.*
[47] Jackson to Duane, July 22, 1833, *Correspondence of Andrew Jackson*, V, 140.
[48] Duane to Jackson, July 22, 1833, *ibid.*, p. 141.
[49] *Autobiography of Amos Kendall*, p. 379.

Henry Toland, who after investigation under instructions from Mc-
Lane had reported on December 4, 1832, that the Bank of the United
States was a safe depository for government funds, had on one occasion received a loan of $100,000 from the bank, and on another
occasion $45,000. He reported that Edward Livingston had recently
"got a loan of $18,000 upon a pledge of ground rents in New York
payable in produce, stock and poultry. Mr. Biddle stated at the Board,
that he would not go to France without it." [50]

Kendall also reported to Jackson a conversation in which he had
been told that McLane had procured the appointment of Duane as
Secretary of the Treasury so that he would really be head of two
departments instead of one.[51] Jackson told Van Buren that he could
not believe that McLane had recommended Duane knowing his
friendly sentiments toward the bank. In any case it would be unpleasant to differ with McLane and Duane, for whom he had high regard, but it was his duty "to put down this mammoth of corruption
and to separate it from being the agent of the government as early as
possible for the safety of its fiscal concerns." [52]

Kendall heard through one of the government directors of the
bank that there was an expense book which would reveal the expenditures which the bank had made in the previous election. Jackson
wrote to the government directors urging them to examine this book
and tell him of its contents. They transcribed for him the large sums
which had been spent by the bank to circulate articles and speeches
favorable to the bank, and other unidentified sums, presumably spent
for similar purposes, listed under the general head of "stationery and
printing." [53] This report further stimulated the zeal of the enemies
of the bank, and gave them additional ammunition for the war
against it.

In April, Biddle had declared it his opinion that the government
would not dare to remove the deposits. If such a step were taken,
however, it would be a declaration of war which could not be re-

[50] Kendall to Jackson, Aug. 11, 1833, *Correspondence of Andrew Jackson*, V, 151.
[51] *Ibid.*
[52] Jackson to Van Buren, Aug. 16, 1833, *ibid.*, p. 158.
[53] Government Directors to Jackson, Aug. 19, 1833, *ibid.*, p. 160.

called.[54] By the end of July he was less hopeful, speaking with enthusiasm only of the loyalty of his friend in the Treasury Department. "The gamblers are doing everything in their power to bend Mr. Duane to their purposes," he declared. "But he knows them and will not yield an inch. I feel entirely confident that he will do his duty, and will leave his place rather than prostitute it." [55] He urged Robert Lenox, in connection with the policies of the New York branch of the Bank of the United States, to keep within his income, and, without announcing that the policy was directed from Philadelphia, quietly to bring the state banks into his debt. "For when once we begin, we shall have many things to do, which will crush the Kitchen Cabinet at once." [56] In August the bank began to entrench itself for war by contracting its loans, and Biddle began again to send out materials to be used in articles and speeches in defense of the bank. "The truth is," he wrote to a Virginia politician enclosing such materials, "that by you and by such as you alone, can the bank and the country be saved from the gang of bankrupt gamblers who now wield the executive power and who are aiming to throw the country into disorder in hopes of plundering during the confusion." [57]

Late in July, Jackson set out to spend a month at his summer home at Rip Raps, Virginia. Before leaving Washington he discussed with Taney the problems connected with the removal of the deposits, intimated that he had about decided to take the step on October 1, and suggested that if Duane decided to resign rather than coöperate it might be necessary to make Taney Secretary of the Treasury. Taney declared he did not feel that he was qualified to fill the office, but the subject was dropped without any decision having been arrived at. On August 5 Taney wrote Jackson a letter [58] which was intended only for Jackson's eyes, or at least was not intended for the eyes of a coolly appraising public of a century hence, which might not

[54] Biddle to Daniel Webster, April 8, 1833, and a similar letter, April 10, 1833, Biddle MSS.
[55] Biddle to Lenox, July 30, 1833, President's Letter Book, *ibid.*
[56] *Ibid.*
[57] Biddle to James Barbour, Sept. 4, 1833, *ibid.*
[58] Taney to Jackson, Aug. 5, 1833, *Correspondence of Andrew Jackson*, V, 147.

have intimate and sympathetic knowledge of the personalities involved. The letter could not but be embarrassing to sweeping apologists for Taney, and it provides difficulties for the biographer who seeks to be fair and to be accurate. Taney referred to the fact that he had previously urged that the deposits be withdrawn if safe and convenient arrangements could be made with the state banks. "And I have advised," he continued, "that the step should be taken before the meeting of Congress because it is desirable that the members should be amongst their constituents when the measure is announced and should bring with [them] when they come here the feeling and sentiments of the people. I rely at all times with confidence on the intelligence and virtue of the people of the United States, and believing it to be right to remove the deposits, I think they will sustain the decision."

He remarked that obstacles which had recently come in the way—probably referring to the resistance of Duane—had strengthened the hand of the bank, but his opinion had not changed. "My mind has for some time been made up, that the continued existence of that powerful and corrupting monopoly will be fatal to the liberties of the people, and that no man but yourself is strong enough to meet and destroy it, and if your administration closes without having established and carried into operation some other plan for the collection and distribution of the revenue, the bank will be too strong to be resisted by anyone who may succeed you. Entertaining these opinions I am prepared to hazard much, in order to save the people of this country from the shackles which a combined moneyed aristocracy is seeking to fasten upon them."

He would not press the measure upon Jackson, however, Taney continued with smooth diplomacy. The bank was a powerful institution. He would feel deeply mortified if after a long life of civil and military victories Jackson should in the last term of his public life meet with defeat. It was perhaps not fair to ask him to take the risk. If Jackson had any doubts in the matter he should wait until the next session of Congress, and Taney would cheerfully acquiesce in his decision, and give him full support. He declared modestly, perhaps too modestly, that he did not think himself qualified for the position of Secretary of the Treasury, but would accept it if Jackson thought best.

This has been characterized by an unfriendly critic as "a sycophantic letter." [59] It does shriek praises of Jackson, not only in references to his past achievements and to the alleged fact that he is the only man strong enough to meet and destroy "that powerful and corrupting monopoly," but also by parroting his ideas on various matters. Taney's profession of faith in the virtue and intelligence of the people of the United States, for instance, and of confidence that they would support the removal of the deposits, was hardly more than a paraphrase of a comment which Jackson was accustomed to making when members of his cabinet expressed fear of the political effects of particular measures: "Never fear, the people will understand it, and if we do right Providence will take care of us." [60]

Again, when we recall the sniping at Taney of which McLane had been guilty, and also the belief of the enemies of the bank that McLane had worked Duane into the cabinet to serve as his own errand boy, it seems highly probable that Taney was giving thought to Jackson's sentiments rather than to his own when he declared that he should regret the necessity of any change in the cabinet. As for the suggestion that even Jackson, the only man living who was strong enough to meet the enemy, might go down in defeat before it, and that therefore he ought to think carefully before exposing himself, nothing could be better calculated to put the old war horse in a mood for battle. Taney's motive here was undoubtedly to get action, rather than to give a warning which Jackson might heed.

It is possible, however, to criticize Taney unfairly in the matter of this letter. It is evident from a great variety of materials that he and other men who worked closely with Jackson had deep affection for and loyalty to Old Hickory, and would have been deeply grieved to see him humiliated. It is true also that there was nothing halfhearted about Taney's affection for those whom he trusted as his

[59] William Graham Sumner, *Andrew Jackson*, p. 301.
[60] Taney, Bank War MS., p. 91.

friends, and in his attitude toward his family and the closest of his friends he was sufficiently demonstrative as to be regarded by his enemies as unpleasantly gushing. He may not have been conscious of any incongruity in writing as he did to Jackson.

Furthermore, Taney had been a politician all his mature years, and was a master of the art and the technique of persuading men to act as he desired. Certainly he was not demonstrating the worst aspects of political technique when by judicious flattery of a man for whom he had deep affection he sought to achieve ends which he thought socially desirable. It was his misfortune that in later years the letter fell into the hands of historians some of whom were both unsympathetic and unaware of the setting, and that it was used as evidence to support the charge that Taney, quite without regard to matters of principle, had flattered Jackson into accepting him as a subservient and humble tool.

Jackson replied August 11 that Taney's letter had been "perused with much pleasure." He was still of the opinion that the deposits ought to be removed, and he was not disturbed by the threats of the bank. If Duane withdrew, Taney could superintend the work. His nomination would not have to be sent to the Senate until near the close of the next session of Congress, by which time the fight would be over.[61] "Should Mr. Duane refuse to yield to the wishes of the Executive, and retire," wrote Jackson to Van Buren, "I pledge myself that no one superintends that Department hereafter but one whose whole opinions I *know* correspond with my own. I will give the agency to Mr. Taney who is right, and with me *in all points*." [62]

While at Rip Raps, Jackson began the preparation of a statement of reasons for removing the deposits which he intended to read to the cabinet before taking that step, and to put on file as its official justification. He sent it to Van Buren for comments and criticisms. Van Buren gave the desired assistance, but his letters revealed his characteristic reluctance to participate in decisive measures. He was not willing, as was McLane, to leave the matter exclusively in the hands

[61] Jackson to Taney, Aug. 11, 1833, Tyler, *Memoir of Roger Brooke Taney*, p. 198.
[62] Jackson to Van Buren, Aug. 16, 1833, *Correspondence of Andrew Jackson*, V, 159.

of Congress, but he was rather inclined toward a middle course, of leaving the deposits where they were until January 1, prior to which date Congress would have an opportunity to discuss the plan for removal. Jackson sent him a copy of the report of the government directors on the subject of the political expenditures of the Bank of the United States, and indicated his displeasure that Van Buren was not with him in his decision to remove the deposits on October 1, whereupon the Red Fox trailed into line.

On September 10 Jackson presented to the cabinet Kendall's report that there was a sufficient number of sound state banks which were willing to receive and give the desired security for government deposits. Jackson thought that a day should immediately be set for the removal, but no decision was reached. From this time on, the subject was up for almost constant discussion. A Baltimore observer for the Bank of the United States reported that the war in the cabinet began September 12. He had been told that Taney, Woodbury, and Cass argued for removal in a very warm debate, while McLane and Duane opposed it. Barry was absent.[63] Another of Biddle's Baltimore observers heard that Taney was very vindictive, that McLane and Duane were firm in opposition, and that the meeting broke up in anger. His informer, one of the Kitchen Cabinet, "said that McLane wanted to be a greater man than nature intended him for, and that he must mind his P and Q, or he would be sent to the right about." [64] On September 14 Jackson suggested to Duane that he resign as Secretary of the Treasury, and take another post, such as the mission to Russia. Duane replied obstinately that he had no desire for another office.[65] He continued to protest his doubts as to the legality of the removal of the deposits, whereupon Jackson told him to take Taney's opinion and follow it. "He being our legal adviser, his opinion of the law, where there were doubts, ought to govern the heads of the Departments as it did the President." [66] Duane agreed to see and converse with Taney.

[63] R. M. Gibbes to Biddle, Sept. 13, 1833, Biddle MSS.
[64] R. L. Colt to Biddle, undated but undoubtedly Sept., 1833, Biddle MSS.
[65] Duane, *Narrative and Correspondence*, pp. 98–99.
[66] Jackson to Van Buren, Sept. 15, 1833, *Correspondence of Andrew Jackson*, V, 187.

Jackson had placed in Taney's hands for criticism and correction his statement of reasons for removing the deposits. On September 15 he wrote a note to Taney asking him to hand the paper in as soon as possible. The subject had been too long pending, and a final decision should be made. If Duane did not agree with the conclusions arrived at, the sooner he withdrew the better.[67] Taney, who had been delayed in beginning his revision, set about his work with all possible speed. "The clock is now striking twelve," he wrote that night in a note to Donelson, Jackson's secretary, "and I am afraid my strength is not enough to allow me to work on much longer. I send you about the half of what you are about to copy, and will bring you the other as soon as I can finish it in the morning. I mean to lay aside other business and lock myself up in my office at home until I finish it." [68] He finished the task, and answered in a separate note Jackson's inquiry about the proper time for removing the deposits. He had talked with Kendall and Thomas Ellicott, he said, and thought the necessary arrangements could be made by October 1. "I am fully prepared to go with you firmly through this business," he concluded, "and to meet all its consequences." Jackson filed the letter away with the endorsement, "R. B. Taney Esqr private. Tuesday night 17th of Septbr 1833—to be filed with my private papers, as evidence of his virtue, energy and worth." [69]

Jackson's—or Taney's—statement of reasons for removing the deposits, [70] commonly known as "The Paper Read to the Cabinet," was presented September 18. Even Duane admitted that it was a strong paper, and Jackson was told, whether truthfully or not there seems to be some doubt, that Taney had drawn high encomiums from Mc-Lane. "Mr. Taney is a sterling man," Jackson wrote to Van Buren. "You would have been delighted with him had you been present." Duane had asked to have until the evening of the 20th to decide what he would do. "I have thought it right to indulge him and I expect *now* he will act with energy, or retire friendly, which to me is

---

[67] Jackson to Taney, Sept. 15, 1833, *ibid.*, p. 188.
[68] Taney to A. J. Donelson, Sept. 15, 1833, Donelson MSS.
[69] Taney to Jackson, Sept. 17, 1833, *Correspondence of Andrew Jackson*, V, 191.
[70] *Messages and Papers of the Presidents*, III, 5-19.

desirable. . . . If Mr. Duane retires, I will have the able and hearty aid of Mr. Taney who is not afraid of the Senate, or to meet with me, the question boldly." [71]

On September 20, in spite of Duane's protest, a brief notice was printed in the *Globe* stating that the government deposits would be moved from the Bank of the United States to certain state banks as soon as arrangements could be made, which would probably be about October 1. This did not mean, the notice explained, that the government funds in the vaults of the bank would at once be taken away. It meant that all government revenue collected in the future would be placed in the chosen state banks, while funds now with the Bank of the United States would be withdrawn gradually and only as needed to pay the expenses of the government. Hence the bank would not be justified in putting pressure upon the commercial community by suddenly contracting its loans on the ground that it had to make an immediate payment of a large sum to the government.

Being unable to postpone a decision any longer Duane wrote a long letter to Jackson giving a list of reasons why he could not remove the deposits, and implying that Jackson had been unfair to him. Jackson returned the letter, replying sharply that its contents were such that it could not be received. Many other letters passed between the two men during the next two days. Duane not only refused to remove the deposits but refused also to resign, announcing that his duty to the office forbade him voluntarily to give it up in such an exigency. When reminded that he had promised to coöperate or resign he replied that the publication of the notice in the *Globe* in spite of his protest had absolved him from his promise, and that anyway, if he had made any mistake at all it was in making the promise in the first place, rather than in refusing to keep it now.

Jackson was astonished at the mixture of truculence and whimpering obsequiousness which characterized Duane's communications. "He is either the weakest mortal or the most strange composition I ever met with," he declared.[72] Finally, seeing that Duane was determined

[71] Jackson to Van Buren, Sept. 19, 1833, *Correspondence of Andrew Jackson*, V, 203.
[72] Jackson to Van Buren, Sept. 22, 1833, *ibid.*, p. 206.

to be made a martyr, he sent him a letter—which seems probably to have been written by Taney—which closed by saying, "I feel myself constrained to notify you that your further services as Secretary of the Treasury are no longer required." [73] Taney was immediately appointed to fill the vacancy. Later on the same day Jackson wrote to Van Buren that he had dismissed Duane and appointed Taney, "who accepted, resigning the Attorney General's office, and unites with me heart in hand to meet the crisis. Mr. Taney is commissioned, sworn into office, and the business of the Treasury is progressing as though Mr. Duane had never been born." [74]

[73] Jackson to Duane, Sept. 23, 1833, *ibid.*, p. 206.
[74] Jackson to Van Buren, Sept. 23, 1833, *ibid.*, p. 207.

Chapter XII

REMOVING THE DEPOSITS

For a time after the announcement of the plan to remove the deposits it seemed as if the Jackson cabinet might again be torn asunder. The "Paper Read to the Cabinet" was turned over to Francis P. Blair for publication in the *Globe*. While it was in proof William B. Lewis told Blair that if the paper was published in such a way as to give the impression of cabinet responsibility for the decision Cass and McLane would resign. Blair reported the conversation to Jackson. Jackson was amused at the thought of Cass being held responsible for the measure, and remarked that if he and McLane wished to leave the cabinet they could do so. They could do no mischief either in the cabinet or out of it. However, he was willing to insert a sentence taking full responsibility upon himself, and with Blair's help he did so.

"The next morning," said Blair, "I went to Taney's house with the printed paper, and Donelson being there, Taney, putting a segar in his mouth and his feet upon the writing table, prepared to enjoy his first state paper in print, said 'Now, Mr. Secretary, let us hear how it reads for the public.' Donelson read on until he reached the responsibility passage when Taney stopped him with 'How under Heaven did that get in!' I told him the story and he said, 'This has saved Cass and McLane; but for it they would have gone out and have been ruined—as it is, they will remain and do us much mischief.' " [1]

In spite of the change in the "Paper," McLane and Cass called on Jackson to decide whether they ought not to resign because of lack of sympathy with the measure decided upon. Jackson reminded them that he had taken full responsibility, and promised that neither

[1] F. P. Blair to Van Buren, Nov. 13, 1859, *Autobiography of Martin Van Buren*, p. 608.

should be asked to act in violation of his principles. McLane's griev-
ance was probably due as much to Taney's accession to power as to
the removal of the deposits itself. He curbed his resentment, however, and both he and Cass retained their positions. Cass eventually
claimed part of the responsibility for the removal of the deposits
when he discovered the popularity of the measure.[2] McLane, deprived of his former influence, remained privately critical of administration policies, and in spite of official denials repeated rumors were
heard that he was on the point of resigning. He did ultimately resign, though not until the following spring.

Few comments of a personal nature were made by newspapers on
the appointment of Taney as Secretary of the Treasury. M. M. Noah,
in the first issue of his Washington *Star*, labeled Taney a Federalist
and declared he had been "engaged in the celebrated Baltimore
mob" of 1812. Friendly papers refuted the mob story, and declared
that Taney held doctrines of limitations upon federal power and hostility to monopolies and aristocracy which should gladden the heart
of a sterling Democrat.[3]

A comment in the Frederick *Herald*, the old Federalist organ at
Taney's former home, stung him severely. "The recent appointment
of Mr. Taney," the *Herald* declared, "is here termed the 'best joke'
of the administration, and has caused great cachinnation. That Mr.
Taney is a gentleman of legal talents all persons admit; but no man
in this community acquainted with his almost proverbial inattention
and indifference to pecuniary affairs, would have named him as head
of the Treasury Department without the risk of confinement in a
straight jacket." [4]

Upon reading the note in a copy of the paper sent to him Taney
wrote immediately to William M. Beall, his old friend in Frederick,
urging that his friends in the Frederick community do him justice.
He was sure the article had been written for reprint in other opposition papers as representative of his character in the place where he was

[2] *Ibid.*
[3] See the Baltimore *Gazette*, Sept. 28, 1833, and the Baltimore *Republican* as quoted in
the Washington *Globe*, Sept. 30, 1833.
[4] Frederick *Herald*, Sept. 28, 1833, quoted, Centreville *Times*, Oct. 5, 1833.

best known. Concerning the charge of indifference to pecuniary matters it was true that he had never spared his money when it was needed for his family or for charity, and he had emancipated his slaves and treated them with the indulgence of children. But he had never spent anything beyond his income. "I did not hoard money but I never went in debt. No merchant or mechanic that I recollect ever found it necessary to call on me a second time for his account unless the urgency of professional business prevented me from attending to it. And I believe that my punctuality in the payment of any accounts against me was as much relied on by the citizens of Frederick as the punctuality of its banks—or any banks—and while I lived there I never had a dispute with a merchant or mechanic about his bill." [5]

Taney's friends wrote for the *Citizen*, the Jackson paper in Frederick, a statement characterizing the *Herald* charges as unwarranted. [6] They even persuaded the editor of the *Herald* to explain away the most offensive portion of his comment, and to publish the letter of "A Citizen" in defense of Taney. "His business," the letter read in part, "though various and extensive, was conducted with the strictest regard to system; so much so that he made regular and minutely detailed entries of all his pecuniary transactions with his clients, and was especially particular to furnish them with full and satisfactory statements of their business, and promptly to pay over every cent to which they were entitled. Indeed he was so particular about all matters of account that his punctuality became proverbial. . . . His credit would compare with those [*sic*] of ten times his wealth. . . . Mr. Taney possesses that order of mind, that clearness of perception, those practical common sense views, that he can master almost any subject to which he gives a full share of his attention." [7]

Taney was pleased and grateful to his friends for their publications in his defense. [8] They were too late, unfortunately, to prevent the extensive circulation of the original article, and many people were

[5] Taney to Beall, Sept. 29, 1833, Taney House, Frederick, Md.
[6] Quoted, Washington *Globe*, Oct. 8, 1833.
[7] Quoted, *ibid.*, Oct. 16, 1833.
[8] Taney to Beall, Oct. 15, 1833, Beall MSS.

doubtless led to believe that the new Secretary of the Treasury was not fitted for his office. Even the defenses did not mention the many years which he had served as a director of banks in Frederick and as counsel for banks in Baltimore. Perhaps it was thought best to leave the subject unmentioned, lest in revealing his training in financial matters an impression of selfish prejudice toward state banking interests might be created. As between a national bank and local state banks he did consider the latter more desirable, but in spite of charges made at a later date there is reason for believing that his own pecuniary interest had little or nothing to do with his attitude.

Three days after his appointment as Secretary of the Treasury Taney announced that government deposits, instead of being made in the Bank of the United States or its branches, would be made in the Union Bank of Maryland in Baltimore, the Girard Bank in Philadelphia, the Mechanics Bank, the Manhattan Company, and the Bank of America in New York, and the Commonwealth Bank and the Merchants Bank in Boston. The new policy was to be instituted October 1, 1833. In a circular letter sent to the selected banks in New York—similar to other letters sent to other depositories selected now and later—he set forth a statement of policy:

"In selecting your institution as one of the fiscal agents of the Government, I not only rely on its solidity and established character as affording a sufficient guaranty for the safety of the public money intrusted to its keeping, but I confide also in its disposition to adopt the most liberal course which circumstances will admit towards other moneyed institutions generally, and particularly to those in the city of New York.

"The deposits of the public money will enable you to afford increased facilities to commerce, and to extend your accommodation to individuals. And as the duties which are payable to the Government arise from the business and enterprise of the merchants engaged in foreign trade, it is but reasonable that they should be preferred in the additional accommodation which the public deposits will enable your institution to give, whenever it can be done without injustice to the claims of other classes of the community." [9]

By October 10 at least eleven more banks had been selected as depositories. All were to give security whenever the deposits amounted to as much as one-half the capital stock paid in, and the government might if it chose demand security on smaller amounts. The banks were to make weekly reports to the Secretary of the Treasury, their books were to be open to examination by the government at all times, and if an extensive examination seemed necessary the banks were to pay as much of the cost as the government thought it proper to assess. The government might withdraw the deposits or the banks might surrender them at any time. The arrangements were regarded as temporary, to last until permanent regulations were prescribed by Congress.

At the end of the first two weeks of the new régime Taney seemed well satisfied with his achievement. The removal of the deposits promised to be one of the most popular acts of the administration. "The accounts from the commercial cities are most gratifying. It has relieved the pressure under which they were suffering, made the currency more sound and healthful than it was before by compelling the Bank of the United States to honor the notes of its distant branches, and appears from the letters I receive as well as from the elections to become daily more and more popular. It is I think the final blow to the Bank of the United States and its dissolution at the end of its charter is now inevitable." [10]

Taney was slow in selecting additional depositories, and banks which had not been so fortunate as to be chosen suggested jealously that in favoring a few banks he was putting down one monopoly but setting up another. He replied on one occasion to this criticism by saying that it was not possible to establish business relation with all sound banks. "It has been my desire in the first stages of the removal to confine my selection to as small a number as was compatible with

[9] Taney to the New York depositories, Sept. 26, 1833, Letters to Banks, Treasury Department.

[10] Taney to W. M. Beall, Oct. 15, 1833, Beall MSS.

safety and public convenience. And I have done so because I wished to see the operation of the plan in its simplest form. All of the arrangements heretofore made are to be regarded as temporary, and as soon as I can ascertain results of the plan I have adopted, by experience and observation, the number will most probably be enlarged, whenever the public convenience will permit it to be done. In contending against one monopoly, it is not my desire to create others. But you will perceive that I could not add to the number, on the ground that the selected bank gains more extensive credit, and in this respect enjoys advantages over other institutions equally entitled to confidence, because if I acted on this principle, it would compel me in some of the cities to increase the number far more than could be justified by a due regard to the convenience of the government." [11]

Although he had made a satisfactory beginning Taney quickly found himself in difficulties which were due chiefly to the cupidity and mismanagement of the "pet banks," the state banks which he had chosen as depositories. Fearing that the Bank of the United States might attack the deposit banks by presenting large quantities of their notes for redemption in specie, or might cause trouble by refusing to redeem its own notes except at the branches at which redemption was promised, he issued to each of several of the banks contingent drafts on the Bank of the United States which were to be cashed only in the event of such action by the latter institution. He sent $500,000 drafts to each of the depositories in New York and to the Girard Bank in Philadelphia. He sent a draft for $100,000 to the Union Bank of Maryland.

In Jackson's mind this arrangement constituted a superb bit of strategy. "A good general will always keep his enemy in check," he declared. "We have the bank now checkmated, [and] will treat her gently if she behaves well." [12] For the successful execution of strategic moves, however, a general must have dependable subordinate officers. The possession of uncashed drafts of large amounts proved too much for the self-restraint of a number of the depositories. The first to

[11] Taney to C. S. Stevenson *et al.*, Nov. 16, 1833, Letters to Banks, Treasury Department.
[12] Jackson to Van Buren, Sept. 29, 1833, *Correspondence of Andrew Jackson*, V, 213.

make trouble was Taney's friend Thomas Ellicott, president of the Union Bank of Maryland. Because of his possession of stock and other connections with the Union Bank, Taney had left to Jackson the selection of the Baltimore depository. For a number of reasons the selection of Ellicott's bank had, however, seemed the only wise choice.

Early in October Ellicott sent to Washington two friends of Taney's, Reverdy Johnson, counsel for the Union Bank, and David M. Perine, a director. They told Taney that one of the small banks of Baltimore was about to fail, that others might go with it, and that the Bank of the United States might take occasion to put the entire community at its mercy. Taney immediately wrote out two additional contingent drafts of $100,000 each on the Bank of the United States, to be used only in the event of the misbehavior of that institution. On October 5 Ellicott acknowledged the receipt of the drafts, and promised solemnly that Taney's instructions would be strictly complied with.[13]

Without Taney's knowledge, however, though with the connivance of Reverdy Johnson,[14] Ellicott had become involved in speculation with another institution bearing the name of the Bank of Maryland, which was now in difficulties. He cashed two of the $100,000 drafts immediately, in spite of his promise to Taney, and his bank at the same time became the owner of a huge allotment of Tennessee bonds formerly owned by the Bank of Maryland.

Taney demanded an explanation, saying he knew the conduct of the Bank of the United States since October 1 had not been such as to justify the use of the drafts. Ellicott replied in a long and devious letter saying that the conduct of the bank during the preceding month had been such as to make the use of the drafts necessary, and that his action had been within the spirit of Taney's instructions. In a formal letter to be used for public consumption if necessary Taney accepted the explanation, but called Ellicott to Washington to find

---

[13] For the correspondence concerning the drafts see Senate Document 16, 23rd Cong., 1st sess.

[14] See Johnson to the President and Directors of the Union Bank of Maryland, Oct. 5, 1833, U. S. Bank MSS., Library of Congress, and other documents in this collection.

out what his real motives had been. Amos Kendall, who was in Taney's office during the interview, reported that Ellicott was stammering and incoherent under Taney's questioning, and finally admitted that he had used the government funds to sustain speculation.[15]

Taney was in an ugly predicament. Ellicott's conduct had been such as to justify the withdrawal of the government deposits from his bank. Such a measure might have wrecked the bank, however, and would certainly have forced a curtailment of credit injurious to the community. Taney's system would have been labeled a failure, and public sentiment might have forced the restoration of the deposits to the Bank of the United States. He therefore merely sent Ellicott home with a reprimand, retaining $300,000 of the Tennessee bonds as security for government funds. Soon afterward, using measures of the Bank of the United States as an excuse, he authorized the use of the third of the drafts sent to the Union Bank. Reverdy Johnson had promised that Taney would pile up additional deposits in Baltimore, and Ellicott, apparently uncowed by the discovery of his duplicity, continued to scheme for more money.[16] Although not fully aware of the complexity and extent of corrupt banking activities in Baltimore, Taney refused to make any such concession. It was fortunate that he did so, for more trouble with Ellicott was yet to come.

The contingent drafts likewise caused trouble in other quarters. The President of the Girard Bank of Philadelphia, which had been second only to the Union Bank of Maryland in its haste to offer its services as a depository, seems to have been intoxicated by the possession of a draft of $500,000 on the Bank of the United States. It extended its discounts on the basis of the draft. The Bank of the United States now started a rapid curtailment which created distress, and the Girard Bank informed Taney that it would be necessary to cash the draft or curtail discounts and add to the crushing pressure on the financial community. Taney regretted the unwise extension of

[15] *Autobiography of Amos Kendall,* p. 389.

[16] See Ellicott to Taney, Nov. 2, 1833, in reply to Taney's letter to the deposit banks, Oct. 31, 1833, Letters to Banks, Treasury Department.

discounts and urged that the draft be cashed only if absolutely necessary. Some time later the Bank of the United States called on the Girard Bank for balances of $58,000 in specie. It was necessary to cash the $500,000 draft to get the money.[17]

One of the drafts sent to New York had to be cashed, partly because of the mismanagement of the Post Office Department. Barry, the easy-going and unmethodical Postmaster General, had allowed his department to get badly in debt. He had promised Taney not to borrow from the deposit banks, but he had allowed his subordinates to do so, and there were not sufficient appropriations to cover the loans. Taney took measures to avoid publicity on the scandalously poor business methods of his colleague, and quietly directed the deposit banks to make no more loans to the Post Office Department.[18]

On the whole Taney's strategy in issuing the contingent drafts, which Jackson had so much admired, was far more troublesome than helpful. In addition to aiding the deposit banks in misconduct it gave the Bank of the United States grounds for the charge of unfairness. It had been the custom of the Treasury Department to give the bank each week a list of the drafts drawn on it during the preceding week. The contingent drafts, although for large amounts, were not included in the lists which Taney submitted. They were omitted because it was hoped that they would not be presented for payment, and because of the expectation that if they were cashed it would be because of the misconduct of the bank, in which case it would merit no warning. When the drafts were presented without notice and without fault on the part of the bank it had just cause for complaint, and it did complain vigorously. Taney explained as best he could, but the bank was more interested in ammunition than explanations.

The coördination of the work of the deposit banks involved an immense amount of detail, much of which Taney had to handle in person. He wrote his letters in long hand, after which they were sometimes though not always copied by clerks. The task was exhausting in spite of such arrangements as that of writing to only one of

---

[17] For the correspondence see Senate Document 16, 23rd Cong., 1st sess.
[18] See the *Autobiography of Amos Kendall*, p. 390.

the New York banks and trusting its president to transmit the letter to the others. It seems to have been the original plan of the government to place the Washington depository, the Bank of the Metropolis, at the head of the system, with the expectation that Amos Kendall would be made president of the bank. According to Kendall he refused the position [19]—certainly wise if the statement was true, for he was better at writing fiery editorials than at dealing with complex problems of banking.

Reuben M. Whitney sought an appointment as coördinator of the deposit banks. The Bank of the Metropolis refused to employ him in that capacity as Kendall suggested, but he continued to seek the office. When Taney took all the work upon himself, instead of delegating it, Whitney seems to have written to the deposit banks suggesting a plan of coördination headed by himself. When Ellicott asked Taney if the plan had his approval Taney replied emphatically that it did not. He would not appoint such an agent at that time even if all the selected banks were to recommend it.[20] He gave similar assurance to Reverdy Johnson. No such position could be created without an act of Congress, and if the act were passed he would not appoint Whitney, in whom the public did not have confidence. "I will never mortify my friends by such a usurpation of power nor by such an injudicious appointment, where I have a lawful right to fill an office. The whole proceeding has been an indiscreet act of the party himself, and wholly unauthorized by me."[21]

Whitney was a most persistent person, and after Taney's retirement from the Treasury Department he persuaded some of the deposit banks to employ him as their agent in Washington. As long as he was Secretary of the Treasury, however, Taney carried alone the burden of communicating with and coördinating the activities of the several deposit banks.

In spite of the complex duties of his new office, Taney remained for a time responsible also for the office of Attorney General, which

---

[19] *Ibid.*, p. 389.

[20] Taney to Ellicott, Oct. 22, 1833 (here misdated 1836), *Niles' Weekly Register*, April 8, 1837.

[21] Taney to Reverdy Johnson, Oct. 24, 1833, *ibid.*

he had vacated. There were many aspirants for the position, but it was not easy to find a man who was well qualified, sympathetic with the major policies of the administration, and unobjectionable politically. Peter V. Daniel of Virginia declined the position, whereupon Jackson permitted Van Buren to offer it to his friend Benjamin F. Butler of New York.[22] In urging him to accept Van Buren reminded Butler that Wirt, Webster, Pinkney, and Taney would not have achieved more than passing notice outside their own states had they not entered national politics. Until his acceptance of federal office Taney had hardly been heard of. Now he was known and respected as a man of talents throughout the Union.[23] Butler accepted, and, without achieving notoriety, he became one of the more capable members of the cabinet, and relieved Taney of a portion of his responsibilities.

The Bank of the United States began the preparation of public sentiment for congressional restoration of the deposits by reducing its discounts far more rapidly than was necessary and creating financial pressure throughout the country. Biddle kept an eye on the politicians who might be won to his support, and the politicians made plans for turning the struggle to their personal advantage. Duff Green, a Calhoun editor in Washington, sought bank support for his leader. If the defeat of Jackson by the bank meant the ascendancy of Webster and Clay and the doctrines for which they stood, said Green, the Calhoun forces would leave the bank and Jackson to fight it out. "If on the other hand the friends of the bank cease their warfare on our principles and evince that confidence and reliance on us which our talents, public virtue and influence entitle us to *exact* in this emergency, the result will be placed beyond question and the defeat of our opponents is certain." [24]

Two days later Biddle, as if taking his cue from Green, wrote to a South Carolina politician that the removal of the deposits went even

---

[22] Not to be confused with the Benjamin F. Butler of Civil War notoriety.
[23] See W. A. Butler, *A Retrospect of Forty Years*, pp. 41–42.
[24] Green to Biddle, Sept. 22, 1833, Biddle MSS.

beyond Jackson's nullification proclamation in its centralizing tendencies. "It seems to me that we have never yet had any pretension equal to this of taking possession—into his own hands—of the whole revenue of the country. Cannot there be formed a union of parties to expel these people?"[25]

R. L. Colt, one of Biddle's Baltimore friends, urged him to meet administration policies by creating runs on state banks. One hundred thousand dollars spent in this way against New York country banks would bring some of them to a pause, he declared.[26] Biddle's first instructions to the New York branch were to do nothing spectacular, but to go on quietly reducing discounts. He advised Robert Lenox to redeem the notes of distant branches when presented, not from motives of fairness to the enemy but because the deposit banks might otherwise accumulate these notes and then embarrass the branches responsible for them by presenting them all at once.[27]

The board of directors of the Bank of the United States privately adopted resolutions providing for a policy of steady contraction of loans. The government directors of the bank tried to get copies of the resolutions to send to Taney, but the privilege was denied by unanimous vote of the private directors, and they were not even permitted to read the resolutions.[28] Taney learned about them, of course, but he did not get the text to use for counter propaganda purposes.

Both the bank and the administration party made systematic efforts to mold public opinion. Such influential newspapers as the *National Intelligencer* and the New York *Courier and Enquirer*, which by means of loans had been brought completely under the influence of the bank, carried great quantities of materials provided by the bank and its friends. The articles were widely copied by other papers throughout the country. Administration materials poured forth from the office of the Washington *Globe*, under the supervision of Blair

[25] Biddle to Thomas Cooper, Sept. 24, 1833, President's Letter Book, *ibid.*
[26] Colt to Biddle, Sept. 27, 1833, *ibid.*
[27] Biddle to Lenox, Oct. 1, 1833, President's Letter Book, *ibid.*
[28] H. D. Gilpin and Peter Wager to Taney, Oct. 4, 1833; Gilpin, Wager, Sullivan, and McEldery to Taney, Oct. 8, 1833, Letters from Banks, Treasury Department.

and Kendall. They were reprinted in other Jackson papers, along with local articles written in similar vein. People and papers formerly neutral were forced by the intensity of the conflict to take sides. Something of the feeling developed is indicated by the comment of a Miss Spear, evidently a person of some importance among the aristocrats of Baltimore, when Taney remarked to her that Biddle wanted to be a greater man than the President. She answered, with a delicacy all her own, that he had a right to be—that Biddle was a man of sense and a gentleman, while the President was a blackguard.[29]

Taney looked forward to the conflict. There was much to talk over, he wrote to Andrew Stevenson, speaker of the House of Representatives, two weeks before the beginning of the session of Congress. "We have a fiery contest before us, but we shall conquer the mammoth, with all the allies that are coming to its aid." He anticipated united action on the part of the leaders of the bank forces of the North and the nullifiers of the South, but he thought the administration would have a safe majority in the House of Representatives. "I certainly came into a storm of this sort very unwillingly," he continued. "But being there I have made up my mind to meet it with perfect good humor, and perhaps shall feel a little disappointed if I am not thought sufficiently important to be soundly abused. Having no political ambition I am afraid they may contrive to make a Vice President of me before they are done with me." [30]

Jackson and his aids, doubtless partly under Taney's supervision, were preparing the annual message which Jackson would deliver to Congress. Taney, as Secretary of the Treasury, wrote a report of his reasons for removing the deposits from the Bank of the United States. Both documents were sent to Van Buren for criticism. The Red Fox offered Taney two suggestions on strategy. Taney's report made much of the bank's recent policy of merciless contraction as a justification for removing the deposits. If Duane were to publish the correspondence on the subject the letter sent to him from Boston the

---

[29] Robert Oliver to Biddle (undated but postmarked Oct. 1, 1833), Biddle MSS.
[30] Taney to Stevenson, Nov. 16, 1833, Stevenson MSS., Library of Congress.

preceding June would show that Jackson desired the removal of the deposits long before the abuses given as reasons by Taney had taken place. It would be better to write the report in such a way as to show that the events of recent weeks justified a decision previously made.

Furthermore, continued Van Buren, all "high toned" positions which might give excuse for state rights agitation should be avoided. The nullifiers were seeking grounds for agitation. "Their old stories have become stale and unprofitable and we will I trust be too wise to give them fresh hobbies. I have communicated my views upon this point to the President. I am happy to think that he concurs in them very fully." [31]

The bank leaders were eager to learn the contents of Taney's report in order to speed up the preparation of a reply. J. G. Watmough, a Pennsylvania congressman who was a borrower from the bank and apparently a willing tool, tried to gain personal access to Taney. "I have ascertained," he wrote to Biddle, "that Taney has become extremely cautious and has but one individual in whom he confides. I am not without hope of being able to penetrate him sufficiently for our purposes by means of William B. Lewis—how I will explain to you shortly." [32] Although Lewis was not as enthusiastic as other administration advisers about the policy toward the bank, Watmough did not succeed in his venture.[33] Van Buren was said to have called Taney's report the greatest state paper produced since the organization of the federal government. John Quincy Adams remarked caustically that if Van Buren made such a statement it might be because he himself wrote the report, or a great part of it.[34]

Jackson's message to Congress was delivered December 3.[35] Among other comments on the bank he discussed the report of the government directors which revealed the efforts of the bank to control the preceding presidential election. "At this time," he continued, "the

[31] Van Buren to Taney, Nov., 1833, *Maryland Historical Magazine*, V, 32.
[32] Watmough to Biddle, Nov. 28, 1833, Biddle MSS.
[33] Watmough to Biddle, Dec. 3, 1833, *ibid.*
[34] *Memoirs of John Quincy Adams*, IX, 41.
[35] *Messages and Papers of the Presidents*, III, 19ff.

efforts of the bank to control public opinion, through the distresses of some and the fears of others, are equally apparent, and, if possible, more objectionable. . . . I am happy to know that through the good sense of our people the effort to get up a panic has hitherto failed, and that through the increased accommodations which the state banks have been able to afford, no public distress has followed the exertions of the bank, and it can not be doubted that the exercise of its power and the expenditure of its money, as well as its efforts to spread groundless alarm, will be met and rebuked as they deserve."

Jackson was talking for effect, meeting propaganda with propaganda, when he stated that there was no public distress. There was distress, and it was growing worse. Taney had realized that the Bank of the United States would have to contract its loans to some degree because of the gradual withdrawal of government funds, but he had given directions to his depositories to extend discounts correspondingly, with the idea that the credit situation as a whole need change but little. The mere changing of creditors was disturbing, however, and, furthermore, it was no part of Biddle's plan to permit the change to be brought about smoothly. He contracted so rapidly and made such extensive calls for specie that the state banks could not extend loans as needed. This part of the story, however, Jackson left for discussion in Taney's report.

The report [36] was presented to the House of Representatives on the day after the delivery of Jackson's message. In it Taney reiterated most of the charges previously made against the bank. He called attention to the fact that under the charter the deposits could be removed only by the Secretary of the Treasury, who was required to submit to Congress his reasons for doing so. The act of Congress chartering the bank did not say what reasons would justify removal, but Taney was convinced that if the public interest would be served that fact was a sufficient reason, even though the money on deposit might be in no actual danger. To support his argument he quoted from a letter written in 1817 by William H. Crawford, then Secre-

[36] *Register of Debates*, 23rd Cong., 1st sess., Appendix, pp. 59–68.

tary of the Treasury, in which Crawford said he would remove government deposits to certain state banks if necessary to protect them from attack by the Bank of the United States. Taney referred to other Crawford letters illustrating the same point, laying himself open to Clay's unjust charges of misinterpretation by not quoting in full.

Among his arguments that the public interest required the removal of the deposits Taney stated that the charter of the bank was to expire March 3, 1836, and the defeat of the banking interests at the preceding election indicated that a new charter would not be granted. In any event, therefore, the time before the removal must be short. Had the deposits been left until the expiration of the charter and then all transferred at once a serious disturbance would have been created. It was better to withdraw them gradually, as was now being done, so that no disturbance was necessary unless one was arbitrarily created.

He showed how the bank had offended through the regulation of its discounts. Early in 1832 it had applied for the renewal of its charter, justifying the early application on the ground that if the charter were not renewed the bank ought to begin at once a policy of contraction. Yet neither after the veto of the bank bill nor after the defeat of the friends of the bank at the election of 1832 did it institute such a policy. Its discounts on August 2, 1833, were $64,-160,349.14, as against $61,571,625.66 on the first of the preceding December. It had therefore continued to expand its loans until past the middle of 1833.

Then suddenly it changed its policy, and reduced its loans by more than four million dollars in two months. During those two months the government deposits in the bank increased more than two millions, so that the bank collected more than six millions from the community. It increased the pressure by demanding specie for the notes of state banks in its possession, adding more than six hundred thousand dollars to its supply during that period. To meet this demand for specie the state banks probably had to reduce their loans four or five times that much, extracting an additional enormous sum from the community. Had the government continued to deposit with the bank two months longer, Taney declared, and had the bank continued to demand specie from state institutions, bankruptcy and ruin would have prevailed throughout the country.

"Under other circumstances," he continued, with more outward plausibility than consistency with his private letter to Jackson the preceding August 5,[37] "I should have been disposed to direct the removal to take effect at a distant day, so as to give Congress an opportunity of prescribing, in the meantime, the places of deposit, and of regulating the securities properly to be taken. It is true, that the power given to the Secretary of the Treasury to remove the deposits from the Bank of the United States, necessarily carries with it the right to select the places where they shall afterwards be made. The power of removal cannot be exercised, without placing them elsewhere; and the right to select is therefore contained in the right to remove." Yet he would have preferred to wait for instructions from Congress had it seemed wise to do so.

In this manner Taney laid himself open to the charge of inconsistency, as Van Buren had warned, for a few days later Duane published the correspondence between himself and Jackson in which the deposit question was discussed.[38] The argument was plausible, however, and the masses of the people were probably little affected by the inconsistency. It was true likewise that the bank might not have instituted its policy of drastic contraction had it not been clear that the deposits were about to be removed. The removal did not make this degree of contraction necessary as a matter of finance, but from the point of view of the bank it did make it necessary as a weapon to force the restoration of the deposits. If the bank could create a panic and blame the panic upon the government, the people might force Congress to direct that the deposits be returned to the bank.

[37] "And I have advised that the step [removal of the deposits] should be taken before the meeting of Congress because it is desirable that the members should be amongst their constituents when the measure is announced and should bring with [them] when they come here the feelings and sentiments of the people."—Taney to Jackson, Aug. 5, 1833, *Correspondence of Andrew Jackson*, V, 147-148.

[38] See J. G. Watmough to Biddle, Dec. 5, 1833, Biddle MSS.

As one of the additional reasons for his action Taney emphasized the disclosure of the government directors of the bank that Biddle had persuaded the board of directors of the bank to permit the appointment of an "exchange committee," with himself at the head, with the power to transact important business without reporting to the board. In this manner the government directors were kept ignorant of the affairs of the bank, and the purpose of their appointment was defeated. "Would any individual of ordinary discretion," demanded Taney, "continue his property in the hands of an agent who had violated his instructions for the purpose of hiding from him the manner in which he was conducting the business confided to his charge? Would he continue his property in his hands, when he had not only ascertained that concealment had been practiced towards him, but when the agent avowed his determination to continue in the same course, and to withhold from him, as far as he could, all knowledge of the manner in which he was employing his funds? . . . The public money is surely entitled to the same care and protection, as that of an individual; and if the latter would be bound, in justice to himself, to withdraw his money from the hands of an agent, thus regardless of his duty, the same principle requires that the money of the United States should, under the like circumstances, be withdrawn from the hands of their fiscal agent."

Selected state banks, Taney declared, would be able to perform all the functions desired of the Bank of the United States, including the provision of a sound currency. At the same time these banks were free from the evils which accompanied the larger institution. The influence of each of them was limited to its own neighborhood, where it would be kept in check by other local banks. The directors of the deposit banks dwelt among the people whose lives were affected by its conduct, and could not be indifferent to the opinions and interests of these people.

On the other hand, he declared in a paragraph as cogent a century later as when written, a great corporation like the Bank of the United States "is continually acting under the conviction of its immense power over the money concerns of the whole country, and is dealing also with the fortunes and comforts of men who are distant from them, and to whom they are personally strangers. The directors of the bank are not compelled to hear daily the complaints and witness the sufferings of those who may be ruined by their proceedings. From the nature of man such an institution cannot always be expected to sympathize with the wants and feelings of those who are affected by its policy. And we ought perhaps not to be surprised, if a corporation like the Bank of the United States from a feeling of rivalry, or from cold calculations of interest or ambition, should deliberately plan and execute a course of measures highly injurious and oppressive, in places where the directors who control its conduct have no local sympathies to restrain them. It is a fixed principle of our political institutions, to guard against the unnecessary accumulation of power over persons and property, in any hands. And no hands are less worthy to be trusted with it than those of a moneyed corporation."

Taney's friends were elated with the report, as they had reason to be, for in spite of its defects it was the ablest document yet prepared on the subject of the bank. Biddle and some of his friends pretended to believe that it could be readily answered. Joseph Gales, one of the editors of the *National Intelligencer,* declared there were parts of it he could tear to flinders. He admitted, however, that other parts were worthy of abler hands, and asked Biddle for material for articles. He was particularly eager to know of things in the report which could be made ridiculous.[39] Robert Gilmor, a prominent Baltimore merchant and director of the Bank of the United States, remarked that the report was full of misstatements and contradictions which would perhaps "require some animadversions from the bank to defeat its effect upon the ignorance of the public, which will believe every word of it." [40]

Through a report of a committee of the private directors [41] the bank struck a counter blow at the administration and the government

[39] Joseph Gales, Jr., to Biddle, Dec. 7, 1833, *ibid.*
[40] Gilmor to Biddle, Dec. 9, 1833, *ibid.*
[41] *Register of Debates,* 23rd Cong., 1st sess., Appendix, pp. 289–305.

directors. They answered many incidental accusations, perhaps proved that some of the charges against the bank had been exaggerated, and placed different interpretations upon admitted facts. They did not deny that the bank had spent considerable sums defending its reputation, but they refused to see that this had anything to do with politics. They accused the government directors of disloyalty to the bank, and implied that directors who would reveal the secrets of the bank were not entitled to its confidence or to participation in its management.

It is clear that they thought of the bank exclusively as a private corporation, in spite of the fact that its charter could not have been conferred without the excuse that it was a necessary and proper agent of the government. They did not recognize the right of the government, the subscriber of one-fifth of the capital and a heavy depositor, to participate through its representatives on the board of directors in making the policies of the institution. In their estimation, apparently, the function of the government began and ended with its capacity as investor. Having given what was expected of it, it had no further rights and was expected not to interfere.

The government directors replied with a rebuttal report to Congress,[42] Biddle sent a protest against the removal of the deposits,[43] and so the volume of messages, reports, and protests flowed on, creating an inexhaustible store of materials for editors and orators. Although incidental defects were disclosed, the bank forces were never able to annihilate Taney's forceful report of reasons for removing the deposits. His charges of specific offenses on the part of the bank were too fully supported with evidence to admit of refutation. His warnings against the manipulations of powerful moneyed corporations suggested differences of economic philosophy which lay too deep to be resolved in process of debate. In this field his report was the report of an agrarian who by generations of experience had been taught to fear the uncurbed greed of merchants and bankers. His argument was widely popular because it phrased clearly and elo-

[42] *Ibid.*, pp. 82–94.
[43] *Ibid.*, p. 187.

quently the beliefs and prejudices of the rank and file of Jacksonian Democracy, beliefs and prejudices evolved out of backgrounds in many respects similar to his own. Unable to disprove his facts, break down his logic, or uproot his presuppositions, the enemy turned to other and oftentimes less reputable methods in an attempt to wreck the administration program.

CHAPTER XIII

THE PANIC SESSION

AMONG the forty-eight members of the Senate which assembled in December, 1833, were three particularly prominent leaders, Calhoun, Clay, and Webster, who were hostile to Jackson. Clay and Webster had for many years been counsel for the Bank of the United States or for one or more of its branches. They were committed to the renewal of its charter and to the restoration of the deposits to its custody. Calhoun was suspicious of the bank, but his hostility to Jackson forced him toward the camp of its friends.

None of the three forgot his own political interests, however, and each was ludicrously reluctant to support a program sponsored by either of the others. Biddle tried persistently to persuade them to act together. "I only repeat what I have said again and again," he wrote to Webster, "that the fate of this nation is in the hands of Mr. Clay, Mr. Calhoun and yourself. It is in your power to save us from the misrule of these people . . . but you can only do it while you are united." [1]

The three were fully aware of their importance to Biddle. They made full use of their advantages, although they at times met their match in dealing with Biddle, who among people of his own class was no amateur at the game of politics. In the midst of discussions of parliamentary strategy, for instance, Webster informed Biddle that he had recently declined an offer to appear as counsel in a case against the bank. If it was wished, however, that his relation with the bank should continue unchanged, it would be well for the bank to send him the usual fee. [2]

[1] Biddle to Webster, Dec. 15, 1833, President's Letter Book, Biddle MSS.
[2] Webster to Biddle, Dec. 21, 1833, Biddle MSS.

Biddle replied smoothly that of course he did not wish to see Webster engaged against the bank, but that it seemed unwise to send retainers at the time, "for a reason which furnishes perhaps the best illustration of the necessity of abating the nuisance which now annoys us." The fact of retaining Webster as counsel would instantly be perverted. If he were hired by the board of directors the fact would be known to the editor of the *Globe* within forty-eight hours, and it would be known within a week even if done by officers of the bank without an order from the board. It would be announced immediately, or "treasured up to be used on the first occasion, when any vote of yours gave displeasure to that gang." [3]

Biddle was too shrewd to attempt direct bribery with Webster. The technique which he did use, however, was probably more effective. He merely suggested that Webster, who was never well supplied with money, should use his position in the Senate to put through the bank program, so that he might collect from the bank for professional services!

The debates in Congress over the removal of the deposits began December 10 and continued almost without interruption for three months, and intermittently thereafter until the close of the session at the end of June. A preliminary skirmish took place when Clay secured the adoption of a resolution to call upon the President for an official copy of the "Paper Read to the Cabinet." Old Hickory declared he had yet to learn what constitutional right the Senate had to ask for his communications to his cabinet, and refused to send the document. He won a round of applause by his reply, but Clay was left in the position to attack the President for arrogance, and to imply that official access had been denied to a document which had wrought injury to the public welfare.

In both houses of Congress Jackson was attacked for dismissing Duane and assuming responsibility for the disposition of government money. The charter of the bank conferred the power of removing the deposits not on the President but on the Secretary of the Treasury. Yet it was hard to make a convincing legal attack on this

[3] Biddle to Webster, Dec. 25, 1833, President's Letter Book (pp. 577–578), Biddle MSS.

ground, for it was recognized that the President must ultimately take responsibility for the policies of his subordinates even though some of the duties of his subordinates were prescribed by special legislation. Technically Jackson was not to be criticized for the removal of the deposits, however. True, he had taken responsibility for the measure in his "Paper Read to the Cabinet," but that document was not officially before Congress, whereas the report in which Taney took responsibility had been officially presented, and was the legitimate source of information.

Clay was not amused by the insistence that the order for removal was signed by R. B. Taney. He did not look to the hangman as accountable for the infliction of death, but to the tribunal sanctioning it.[4] George McDuffie declared in the House of Representatives that Taney was nothing more than a "pliant instrument" of Jackson.[5] Speaking in such a way as to leave no doubt that reference to Taney was intended, though without mentioning his name, McDuffie discoursed on "one of those miserable sycophants who literally crawled in their own slime to the footstool of Executive favor." When James K. Polk took him to task and showed that Taney had advocated the removal of the deposits before Jackson was committed to it, McDuffie pretended that he had not referred to Taney.[6] On the whole Taney seemed to have achieved his desire to be considered important enough to be soundly abused.[7]

Congress debated for weeks the question discussed at length in Taney's report as to whether the only legitimate reason for removing the deposits was the belief that they were unsafe. Webster asked Justice Story for his views. The Judge agreed with Taney that the Secretary of the Treasury could act on any reasons which seemed to him sufficient. The only check was that he must report them to Congress. Congress could order the restoration of the deposits, however, in spite of any contracts which the Secretary might have made with

[4] *Congressional Globe*, Dec. 26, 1833, p. 54.
[5] *Ibid.*, Dec. 20, 1833, p. 44.
[6] *Ibid.*, Jan. 2, 1834, p. 70.
[7] Taney to Andrew Stevenson, Nov. 16, 1833, Stevenson MSS.

the state banks.[8] The letter was doubtless a disappointment to Webster. It is not recorded that he made use of those portions of it which did not serve his purposes. He presented a report from the Senate Finance Committee declaring that the Secretary of the Treasury had not the power to remove the deposits unless they were unsafe, that the removal had caused great public distress, and that it was inexpedient and altogether unjustifiable.[9]

The Senate adopted many resolutions, introduced by denunciatory speeches from bank leaders, calling upon Taney for information of various sorts—information which, if it could not when provided be used to bolster attacks on the administration, was usually filed away without a word. A Clay resolution called for the correspondence with the deposit banks concerning the contingent drafts. Since Taney had been shrewd enough to discuss the more scandalous aspects of Ellicott's conduct at a personal interview rather than in official correspondence the documents sent to the Senate seemed to provide no ammunition for Clay, and were not used.

Pretending that in his report to Congress Taney had deliberately misinterpreted letters of Secretary Crawford, Clay secured the adoption of a resolution asking Taney to provide the correspondence in full. Taney replied by quoting the passages he had relied upon and showing that they proved his point. He stated that the original letters had been destroyed when the Treasury building was burned, but that official copies could be found in the records of Congress— from which, he intimated, Clay could get them without the help of the Treasury Department.[10]

When during the public reading of Taney's reply Clay discovered that he could make no political use of it, he suggested the inexpediency of reading the remainder; but administration senators were on the alert, and prevented the suppression. It was said that Clay then declared he had read the entire Crawford correspondence, and would pledge himself to show, at some other time, that Taney had misquoted in every instance where there was a semblance of similar-

[8] *Life and Letters of Joseph Story*, II, 155–156.
[9] *Register of Debates*, 23rd Cong., 1st sess., Appendix, pp. 155–156.
[10] *Ibid.*, pp. 98–100.

ity between Crawford's argument and his own.[11] He never attempted the impossible task of proving his statement, however. Taney would not have dared misquote in such an instance, where exposure would have been inevitable, even if he had had no other reason for being accurate.

A show of strength was brought in the Senate by action on the appointment of government directors of the Bank of the United States. Jackson sent to the Senate the names of four men who had served as directors the preceding year, and one other. A number of bank leaders immediately planned vengeance through the rejection of the nominations. Webster advised against rejection lest it embarrass the Senate by labeling it the friend of the bank,[12] but Clay was for it,[13] and Biddle insisted on using the occasion as a test of strength and as a mode of disciplining the offending directors. Webster surrendered after a time, and on February 27, 1834, the nominations of the four men who had previously served as directors were rejected by a close vote. Jackson had the hardihood to send the names back to the Senate with a message defending the conduct of the government directors, but after reposing in committee for several weeks the nominations were again rejected.

Biddle was less sure of his strength in the House of Representatives than in the Senate. Among others he had the venomous McDuffie there; he had his faithful servant Watmough, who was better at picking up rumors and circulating propaganda than at making speeches; he had the support of the sharp-tongued John Quincy Adams, and he had Horace Binney, a director and counsel for the bank, who had probably taken time to win an election to the House because of Biddle's desire to have him there. Expecting that the speech of James K. Polk would be the strongest delivered for the administration, Biddle wrote to Watmough, "When Mr. Polk finishes, I wish you could get everybody to give way for Mr. Binney to answer him—so that he may be demolished outright." [14]

11 Washington *Globe*, quoted, Richmond *Enquirer*, Jan. 4, 1834.
12 Webster to Biddle, Dec. 19, 1833, Biddle MSS.
13 Watmough to Biddle, Dec. 22, 1833, *ibid*.
14 Biddle to Watmough, Dec. 28, 1833, President's Letter Book, Biddle MSS.

Polk was not a prepossessing speaker, but he was not "demolished outright" by Binney or any other of the bank orators. Biddle concluded that he must win his battle in the Senate and resort to pressure from the public to win acquiescence in the House. He expressed to Webster the hope that the Senate would agree on a resolution against the removal of the deposits and send it to the House, where he hoped for delay until there had been some change in sentiment. "I believe the true theory of the case is—for the Senate to act as soon as possible and the House to talk as long as possible.

"But before the Senate acts," Biddle continued, "you *must make a speech,* one of your calm, solid, stern, works, that crushes, like the block of your Quincy granite, all that it falls on. I want that Jackson and Taney and Benton and all these people should fall by your hand. I wish you to do it for my sake. I wish you to do it for your own." [15]

In the meantime tides of conflicting sentiment were rolling up to influence legislation one way or the other. The people were responding to the pressure of bank credit contraction as prices fell lower and lower, bankruptcies increased, and more and more persons lost their property or their means of livelihood. Bankers, merchants, tradesmen, laborers, and farmers, looking to the government as a means of curing their ills, poured petitions upon Congress. Many of them were inspired from bank sources and were filled with bank propaganda, urging the restoration of the deposits and the renewal of the charter of the bank, and denouncing the administration in unmeasured terms. The memorials and resolutions were sent to Washington by deputations who sat in the galleries of Congress while bank spokesmen on the floors presented the petitions with indignant harangues on the growing distress of the nation.

"If we ask, who is the author of this dire calamity," ran a typical memorial, "with one voice it is answered—it is Andrew Jackson. He takes the responsibility—he does not even ask to hold his subordinate and pliant tool and pander, *Roger B. Taney,* responsible for it.

[15] Biddle to Webster, Jan. 8, 1834, *ibid.*

And why did he do this deed? . . . The true motive was, to crush the bank, in order to punish the supposed contumacy of some of its officers. This institution had kept aloof from politics, 'pursuing the even tenor of its way'—it would not 'bow the knee to Baal,' would not be an instrument in the hands of Andrew Jackson. . . ." [16]

Administration meetings were held throughout the country to defend the course pursued and denounce the bank. Administration leaders no longer asserted, as Jackson had done in his annual message to Congress, that there was no distress in the country. It was too much in evidence for further denial. They claimed that it was overstressed, however, and that both the distress and the clamor about it were stimulated by the activities of the bank and its spokesmen. The mercantile interests of the country, declared Taney, had been persuaded that they must support the bank in order to save themselves. They sanctioned resolutions therefore to the effect that unless the deposits were restored the commerce of the country would be ruined and general bankruptcy would follow. When the merchants themselves proclaimed that they were in desperate straits the people very naturally believed them, and credit was destroyed. With all his power over the currency, argued Taney, Biddle could have produced nothing more than a severe and trying pressure. But "by the aid of the merchants and politicians, he created a fearful panic, deepening in intensity every day for some months, and overwhelming with ruin many of the friends of the bank as well as its opponents." [17]

The deputations which brought memorials to Congress usually called on Jackson to urge him to restore prosperity by surrendering to the bank. Jackson received them with courtesy until he perceived their desire to provoke him into making statements which could be used against him. Thereafter he harangued them on the evil ways of the bank and told them to go to the "monster" for relief, not come to him. Nicholas Biddle was responsible for such distress as there was. Let him cease his machinations and the trouble would

[16] Richmond *Enquirer*, Feb. 4, 1834.
[17] Taney, Bank War MS., pp. 28-29.

cease. With a delegation from Philadelphia, Jackson was said to have been particularly harsh. When members hinted that the people would resort to force unless there was a change of policy he roared at them, "If that be your game, come on with your armed bank mercenaries, and, by the Eternal, I will hang you around the Capitol on gallows higher than Haman's." [18]

Such undiplomatic utterances made excellent material for pro-bank speeches and articles. Jackson was portrayed as a hard-hearted autocrat bent upon achieving his own ends at whatever cost to others, and at whatever sacrifice of the Constitution. That such propaganda was accepted at its face value by intelligent people is illustrated by the attitude of Justice Story, who felt "humiliated at the truth, which cannot be disguised, that though we live under the form of a republic we are in fact under the absolute rule of a single man." [19]

From the varied evidence available, however, it seems clear that it was another man than Jackson who sought to dominate the country by something like absolute rule. Biddle declared that nothing but public suffering would produce any effect in Congress,[20] and set about producing the necessary suffering. If the bank pursued a steady policy of restriction he had no doubt that the deposits would be restored and the bank rechartered. He felt no responsibility for the injury done to the country by such a policy. He would render no assistance which might endanger his own institution. All the other banks and all the merchants might break, but the Bank of the United States should not break.[21] If Congress would pass the desired legislation, relief would come, but not otherwise. "The bank feels no vocation to redress the wrongs inflicted by these miserable people. Rely upon that. This worthy President thinks that because he has scalped Indians and imprisoned judges, he is to have his way with the bank. He is mistaken." [22]

Senator Frelinghuysen of New Jersey boasted on the floor of the

---

[18] *Autobiography of Amos Kendall*, p. 412.
[19] *Life and Letters of Joseph Story*, II, 154.
[20] Biddle to William Appleton, Jan. 27, 1834, President's Letter Book, Biddle MSS.
[21] Biddle to Watmough, Feb. 8, 1834, *ibid.*
[22] Biddle to Joseph Hopkinson, Feb. 21, 1834, *ibid.*

Senate that the anathemas of Jackson could never reach the bank. "There sits Mr. Biddle," declared the orator proudly, "in the presidency of the bank, as calm as a summer's morning, with his directors around him, receiving his salary, with everything moving on harmoniously; and has this stroke reached him? No, sir. The blow has fallen on the friends of the President and the country." [23] On hearing of this speech Taney remarked, "Nero is said to have fiddled while Rome was burning, but I have not learned from history that even his courtiers praised him for doing so." [24]

Baltimore provided one of the many deputations which were sent to Washington, and members of it called on Taney to discuss the situation. Assuming that he was talking with friends, Taney expressed himself freely on the program of the government and the conduct of the bank. Upon returning to Baltimore the deputation reported the conversation in such a way as to put him in a bad light. To cure the economic ills of the country the government was trying an "experiment," which it would not give up under any circumstances. When he had been told that unless some relief were afforded the entire commercial community must fail, Taney had replied, "If *all* did fail, the policy of the government would not be changed."

On Taney's authority the Washington *Globe* declared that his conversation had been misrepresented. Three members of the group then published a letter asserting that they had quoted correctly. Taney then wrote a long letter to his friend Upton S. Heath, which was published in the Baltimore papers. It had never entered his mind, Taney declared, that the interview was for publication, or that detached expressions would be used in such a way as to create erroneous impressions. He had declared that he opposed the recharter of the bank, that he found it possible to carry on necessary government functions without the aid of the bank, and that the pressure in the money market had been initiated by the bank to compel the renewal of its charter.

He had told how newspapers under bank influence had spread

[23] *Congressional Globe*, Jan. 27, 1834, p. 129.
[24] Taney, Bank War MS., p. 29.

groundless rumors as to failures and bankruptcies, and groundless predictions of the suspension of specie payments by state banks. He had deplored the way in which the merchants had participated in creating this unjustified alarm. If they expected to drive the government from its course by such measures they were mistaken. The government was not responsible for the evils which they voluntarily brought on themselves. He had not professed indifference to the sufferings of Baltimore. "I was endeavoring to impress upon them the folly of coöperating with the bank in exciting an alarm for political objects, and ruining the credit of their whole community to give political power to the bank. I wished to satisfy them, that while it endangered the happiness and comfort of innumerable industrious and valuable citizens, it would fail to produce the political object it was intended to accomplish." [25]

Taney's defense seems reasonable. Yet the antagonism aroused on this occasion was doubtless among the factors which made trouble for him during the weeks immediately ahead.

In the meantime, although it was true that his deposit system was working, Taney was having trouble with the deposit banks. Some of them had overexpanded their loans on the basis of the government deposits, and all of them suffered under the pressure of the contraction policy pursued by the Bank of the United States. When funds placed with some of the banks amounted to more than half the capital stock paid in, Taney called on them for security, which they gave with great reluctance. When about the middle of December he notified them that funds in the Bank of the United States were nearly exhausted, and that it would soon be necessary to issue drafts on the new depositories for the expenses of the government, their replies were most depressing. It was almost as if they had assumed that the government deposits had become permanently a part of their capital.

As a matter of fact the funds in the Bank of the United States lasted until well into February or longer. Taney's notice was prob-

[25] Taney to Upton S. Heath, March 10, 1834, *Niles' Weekly Register*, March 22, 1834.

ably but a variation of the warnings which he found it necessary to issue to keep the deposit banks safely liquid. "I take this opportunity to impress upon you the necessity of keeping yourselves strong," he wrote to the president of one of them early in January. "Let no outcry of pressure and no clamor induce you to place yourselves in a position that may make a call on you embarrassing. . . . I am persuaded that the adherents of the Bank of the United States are induced by private understanding and advice to press on the selected banks in order that they may weaken them and distress them by sudden calls. It behooves your board to act with firmness and decision and not to suffer yourselves to be the victims of an insidious policy." [26]

The Girard Bank, the Philadelphia depository, existing virtually within the shadow of the enemy, was in difficulties almost from the beginning. "The whole force of the Bank of the United States appears to be concentrated upon this city," the cashier wrote to Taney in December.[27] Rumors appeared in the papers that the Girard Bank was about to suspend specie payments, and a bank politician made matters worse by calling attention to the fact in the House of Representatives. The institution withstood the varied attacks until the latter part of March, when the stockholders directed that it receive no more deposits from the government.

Unsuccessful attempts were made to wreck the deposit system by persuading the New York depositories to receive no more government money. The depository in Louisville withdrew from the system, informing Taney that it had accepted government funds only because of the fear that they would otherwise be sent to Cincinnati.[28] It may have seemed possible for a time that even without the defection of the New York banks enough depositories would be compelled to withdraw to make the administration program appear a failure.

Like a number of other deposit banks, the Planters' Bank, at Natchez, Mississippi, interpreted Taney's original instructions as

[26] Taney to Samuel Frothingham, Jan. 4, 1834, Gratz Coll., Historical Society of Pennsylvania.

[27] W. D. Lewis to Taney, Dec. 16, 1833, Letters from Banks, Treasury Department.

[28] A. Thurston to Taney, Feb. 17, 1834, *ibid.*

directing it to expand its loans in proportion to the government deposits received. Like others also it was caught by the excessive contraction policy of the Bank of the United States, and became panic-stricken when Taney notified it to expect withdrawals.[29] Its difficulties became so serious that Taney appointed an agent to investigate its condition, remarking that he would immediately direct the making of deposits in another bank in the locality were it not that such a measure might bring ruin on the Planters' Bank and endanger the public funds along with it.[30] Under pressure from the government the bank finally put itself in condition to honor the drafts drawn on it, and was allowed to continue as the government custodian.

With banks all over the country being forced to close their doors each bank was reluctant to honor the notes of other banks, particularly of those at a distance. This lack of confidence was injurious to business, and it threatened the defeat of Taney's plan to maintain a currency of state bank notes as sound as that provided by the notes of the Bank of the United States. The point seems to have been reached, indeed, where many of the deposit banks would have refused longer to accept government deposits if in so doing they had to assume responsibility for the face value of the notes in which the money came to them. Taney was ultimately obliged to send to certain of the western banks a list of eastern depositories in which he had confidence and ask the acceptance of their notes on the responsibility of the government.[31] The plan worked successfully in that the guarantee of the government made the notes quite acceptable, but it had the disadvantage of compelling the government to shoulder the risks which the banks themselves had been unwilling to take.

The risks were particularly great in that among the notes guaranteed were those of the Union Bank of Maryland, which was still loaded with the huge purchase of Tennessee bonds which it had

[29] See Sam Gustine, *et al.*, to Taney, Jan. 25, 1834, *ibid.* See Taney's reply, Feb. 19, 1834, Letters to Banks, *ibid.*

[30] Taney to Powhatan Ellis, March 24, 1834, Miscellaneous Letters, Treasury Department.

[31] See Taney to the cashier of the Franklin Bank of Cincinnati, April 28, 1834, and to the cashiers of the Planters' Bank of Mississippi, and the Branch Bank of Alabama, June 21, 1834, *ibid.*

made. It had also made loans to the Baltimore and Ohio Railroad all out of proportion to its capacity, and was linked in many ways with the Bank of Maryland which was on the verge of failure. Then, on March 24, 1834, came the collapse of the Bank of Maryland, with all the attendant chaos in the community. Evan Poultney, its president, transferred his visible property to Reverdy Johnson and John Glenn for the benefit of his creditors. Thomas Ellicott, president of the Union Bank, was made trustee of the assets of the defunct institution. The responsibility was later shared by two others, and Ellicott was finally forced out when it was discovered that he and his family were intimately involved in the manipulations which had constituted virtually a sacking of the bank.

When the news spread that the Bank of Maryland had closed its doors, the public at first placed the blame upon the Jackson administration, and particularly upon Taney. R. L. Colt wrote to Biddle of a rumor that Taney was in town, and that an attempt would be made to assassinate him. The panic was beyond belief, declared Colt. At an earlier date he had callously recommended that Biddle put pressure on local New York banks and create distress as a means of forcing the renewal of the charter of the Bank of the United States. For the Baltimore community where he had relatives and interests, however, he felt a greater tenderness. He urged Biddle to direct the local branch of his bank to be liberal in its discounts and lenient in calls on state banks for specie payments. Colt added that a run was being made on the Union Bank, the government depository, and that Ellicott would be unable to keep it open unless Taney came to its aid.[32]

The resemblance between the names of the Union Bank of Maryland and the Bank of Maryland added to the confusion and increased the pressure on the Union Bank. It brought the crisis to the attention of Congress, where it was rumored that Taney had transferred many thousands of dollars from other depositories to protect the

[32] This letter, like many of Colt's letters to Biddle in the Biddle MSS., is unsigned. It bears no date except that of "Monday evening." It was written either March 24 or March 31, however, and presumably the former.

Union Bank. Henry Clay secured the adoption of a resolution of inquiry about the matter and about Taney's investments in the stock of the Union Bank, it having been rumored that he had held $25,000 in the stock, and had quietly sold it to others when through his official position he learned of the condition of the bank.

On April 3 Taney replied that no Treasury drafts had been sent to the Union Bank during the period specified.[33] The answer was technically accurate, and it provided Clay with no further materials for abusing the administration. The whole truth, however, might have been somewhat embarrassing. Although no Treasury drafts had been sent to the Union Bank it was about this time that the Girard Bank of Philadelphia declined to accept additional government deposits, and it was rumored that Taney had directed the collector of customs at Philadelphia to send his collections to Baltimore,[34] where the Union Bank was the only depository. According to R. L. Colt the February statement of the Union Bank showed $53,000 in specie.[35] On March 26 Ellicott claimed possession of $262,000.[36] It is extremely unlikely that the difference was raised by revenue collections in Baltimore or by the contraction of loans and note issues in the Baltimore community, and it is highly probable that some assistance had been provided from an outside source.

Taney replied to the inquiry about his ownership of stock in the Union Bank by saying that for more than two years he had held seventy-one full shares and four half-shares, the total with a par value of $5,475, all of which, and no more, were in his possession October 1, 1833. Since that date he had sold eight full shares and four half-shares to pay a debt which he owed as trustee of his father's estate. The remaining shares were still in his possession.[37] There was nothing in the statement of which Clay could make political capital.

Distress continued to prevail in Baltimore and throughout the

[33] *Congressional Globe*, April 3, 1834, pp. 284–285.
[34] Colt to Biddle, March 24 (?), 1834, Biddle MSS.
[35] *Ibid.*
[36] Ellicott to Taney, March 26, 1834, Letters from Banks, Treasury Department.
[37] *Congressional Globe*, April 3, 1834, pp. 284–285.

surrounding area. The price of tobacco declined. There were runs on all the savings banks and on some of the commercial banks. Farmers refused to accept any bank notes except the notes of the Bank of the United States. "The experiment works badly," wrote a prominent critic of the administration. "Mr. T[aney] does not keep the wheels well greased." [38] Colt urged Biddle not to let any solvent bank in the city be compelled to stop payment, with the exception of the Union Bank, which should be made to rely on Taney.[39]

Biddle finally sent a substantial sum of money to Baltimore for the relief of the banks, and by means of it the stronger of them were able to survive. Biddle received full credit for the relief, and the popularity of the Jackson administration ebbed low. One observer wrote to Biddle that Jacksonism was almost extinct in Maryland.[40] Colt advised Biddle to grant the request of the executors of the Charles Carroll estate for a loan. "It is a curious fact," he remarked, "that all these parties were a year ago ultra Jackson. Now they are all *Whigs*. Nothing quickens some people's reasoning faculties like touching their pockets. Jackson is a wonderful opener of eyes." [41]

The fate of the Union Bank, closely linked as it was with Taney's deposit system, remained for some weeks in doubt. In the meantime events of great importance were taking place in Congress. On March 28 the Senate adopted Clay's resolution declaring that Taney's reasons for removing the deposits were "unsatisfactory and insufficient." Administration senators taunted Webster for his acceptance of this weak resolution in place of an act directing the return of the deposits. He replied that he and his friends would be green politicians not to see what was desired. No bank legislation could at this time be forced through the House of Representatives, and a Senate measure requiring House concurrence would lose prestige if rejected by the more numerous body.[42]

38 James Tongue to Virgil Maxcy, April 12, 1834, Maxcy MSS.
39 Colt to Biddle, April 14, 1834, Biddle MSS.
40 James Tongue to Biddle, April 22, 1834, *ibid.*
41 Colt to Biddle, April 22, 1834, *ibid.*
42 Benton, *Thirty Years' View*, I, 395.

On the same day, after much wrangling over phraseology, the Senate adopted another Clay resolution, declaring that "the President in the late executive proceedings, in relation to the public revenues, has assumed upon himself authority and power not conferred by the Constitution and laws, and in derogation of both." The resolution was put through chiefly by the efforts of Clay and Calhoun. It was a statement of personal condemnation which was recorded on the Journal of the Senate but was sent formally neither to the President nor to the House of Representatives. It remained, as Benton expressed it, "an intrusive fulmination on the Senate Journal." [43]

Forgetting what their rejection of his nomination had done for Van Buren, Clay and Calhoun apparently assumed that Senate condemnation would destroy whomsoever it struck, even a long-time hero like Jackson. Although he received no formal notice of the resolution, Jackson, never a stickler for forms, began the preparation of a "solemn protest against the usurpation by the Senate of the impeaching power and violation of the Constitution." He thought it might open the eyes of the people so that a constitutional amendment would be adopted shortening the terms of senators and providing for their recall at the pleasure of state legislatures.[44] Kendall was ill, and Taney, whose frail health was suffering strain such as it had rarely had to endure, was "worn out almost." [45] Attorney General Butler, therefore, had most of the responsibility for the phrasing of Jackson's indignant sentiments. On April 15 the Senate which had taken the liberty of censuring him listened to his protest with astonishment that the President should retaliate by indulgence in the same pastime. After a debate marked by such a show of outraged dignity as only the Senate can put on, it voted solemnly that the protest be not received.

The issue was immediately taken up by the press and by the country at large. Whig meetings were held to discuss and denounce the protest, Jacksonians came to the defense of their leaders, elated that

[43] *Ibid.*, p. 423.

[44] Jackson to Andrew Jackson, Jr., April 6, 1834, *Correspondence of Andrew Jackson*, V, 259.

[45] Jackson to Kendall, April, 1834, *ibid.*, p. 258.

the Whigs had provided them with an issue which they could use. Hitherto they had been for the most part on the defensive. Now they began offensive action to have Clay's resolution expunged from the Senate Journal. Clay and Calhoun had made another tactical error.

The bank continued to be handicapped by jealousy among its leaders in the Senate. Webster, Clay, and Calhoun each had a plan for the renewal of the bank charter. Webster advocated renewal for six years, with the elimination of certain abuses permitted by the old charter, including the issuing of branch notes and of notes of small denominations. He had private assurance of the support of a number of wavering friends of the administration, and Biddle was with him. He reasoned shrewdly that a short renewal, extending beyond the period of Jackson's control, would make it easier to secure renewal for a longer period at a later date.

Clay objected to the scheme, however, insisting on renewal for twenty years. There was no possibility of the adoption of such a measure, but he evidently preferred seeing the bank defeated to supporting a program arranged by a political rival.

Calhoun advocated renewal for twelve years. It required some stretching of consistency on his part to support a national bank at all, centralizing as it was in its tendencies. He could not oppose renewal altogether, however, for such a policy would align him with Jackson. He compromised by evolving a scheme whereby a bank chartered for twelve years would aid in the gradual elimination of paper currency of small denominations and in the restoration of gold coins to circulation, after which the bank would cease to exist.

The inability of the three leaders to agree on a program in spite of the efforts of Biddle to secure united action, together with the prospect of defeat in the House, prevented final action in the Senate. Webster asked leave to bring in a bill, had his motion laid on the table to make room for other business, and did not call it up again at this session.[46]

[46] Benton, *Thirty Years' View*, I, 433–436.

Benton, whose advocacy of a metallic currency had won him the nickname of "Old Bullion," was worried for a time lest Calhoun should run away with his issue. "The opposition mean to forestall me in our own work," he wrote to Taney, "and take the credit of compelling the government to do what you are going to do, that of discouraging small bank notes. I gave out this (with the reform of the gold currency) as things for which the country would be indebted to this administration. Calhoun means [to] seize the golden prize. Now what I wish is that you should begin with repressing the small notes by *instructions* and follow it up by law; for which purpose I send you an amendatory resolution to read and return; but I shall not submit it until I see you." [47]

Although the ultimate suppression of small bank notes was an important part of Taney's monetary program, he was now too much pressed on all sides to take the responsibility for the further contraction of the currency which the immediate withdrawal or suppression of small notes would involve, even though his refusal to act might result in Calhoun's winning some support which the administration had counted on. He supported Benton's plan for a revaluation of the gold dollar, however, and probably aided in drafting the resolution presented by Benton on March 29 which provided for the appointment of a committee to study and report on the relative values of gold and silver.[48] Calhoun's insistence upon linking currency reform with the rechartering of the Bank of the United States prevented his assuming effective leadership, and, although he ultimately gave support to the measures which were decided upon, as did Webster also, it was regarded as Benton's measure in the Senate.

Under the leadership of Andrew Stevenson, the speaker, and of James K. Polk, chairman of the Committee on Ways and Means, the House of Representatives was for the most part kept in line for the administration, in spite of the pressure created by bank propaganda. On March 4 Polk presented for his committee a report which

---

[47] Benton to Taney, undated but probably of late in March, 1834, *Maryland Historical Magazine*, XIII, 167.

[48] *Congressional Globe*, March 29, 1834, p. 277.

described and denounced at length the conduct of the bank. It closed by recommending the adoption of four resolutions:

1. The Bank of the United States should not be rechartered.
2. The government deposits should not be restored to it.
3. Laws should be passed regulating the making of government deposits in state banks.
4. A special committee should be appointed to investigate the conduct of the Bank of the United States to discover whether the business crisis was the result of its activities.

Polk discussed with Taney the strategy of presenting the resolutions for discussion and vote, and Taney recommended that they be taken up in the order given.[49] They were acted upon in this order, and each was adopted by a substantial majority. Stevenson appointed a committee to investigate the bank—with a majority friendly to the administration and hostile to the bank—and Polk and his committee set about preparing a report on legislation needed for regulating the new deposit system.

By asking him for detailed recommendations Polk shifted to Taney most of the burden of making the report. Taney complied with a long letter which the committee used as it stood, preceding it with a brief statement which was hardly more than a preamble.

Taney's letter [50] resembled Benton's speeches of the period at many points, indicating that the two men had coöperated in working out their arguments. Taney argued at length that the Bank of the United States had not established and could not establish a sound currency—evidently to refute Calhoun's argument that the bank should be rechartered to aid in monetary reform. If the bank were merely denied the right to issue small notes the state banks would issue them. The state legislatures, viewing the special privileges given to the competing national institution, could hardly be expected to deny to the state banks this one privilege of issuing small notes.

49 Taney to Polk, March 11, 1834, Polk MSS.
50 *Register of Debates*, 23rd Cong., 1st sess., Appendix, pp. 157-161.

Taney recommended reform in the coinage of gold so that gold would circulate once more rather than leave the country in the form of bullion as it was inclined to do. The current gold dollar was too valuable to circulate in competition with the silver dollar, in spite of the fact that silver did not constitute a satisfactory medium of exchange. A devaluation would change all this, and gold might take the place of the notes of the Bank of the United States as they were withdrawn from circulation. In addition, foreign coins should be made legal tender at their real value.

Congress should discourage the issue of small notes, Taney continued, by refusing to deposit money in banks issuing them, and by refusing to receive payments in notes of banks issuing them in denominations of less than certain amounts. Taney assumed, with altogether too much optimism, as later events were to demonstrate, that if the federal government refrained from chartering a bank it could "safely rely upon the coöperation of the several states to impose upon their banks the restrictions necessary to aid in this desirable change in the state of the currency." He believed that notes of less than five dollars might be outlawed in the near future, and that others of larger denominations might be withdrawn after the liquidation of the Bank of the United States. Notes of very large denominations would continue indefinitely to be issued by state banks, on the basis of substantial specie reserves.

These reforms, Taney declared, had an immediate relationship to the welfare of the masses of the people. The laboring classes, for instance, were paid in notes of small denominations, which might be depreciated or entirely worthless. "If the alteration suggested should be adopted, the smaller notes would soon be banished from circulation everywhere, and the laborers would, therefore, be paid in gold and silver, and that portion of society which is most apt to suffer from worthless or depreciated paper, and who are least able to bear the loss, would be guarded from imposition and injustice. It is time that the just claims of this portion of society should be regarded in our legislation in relation to the currency. So far we have been providing facilities for those employed in extensive commerce, and have left the mechanic and the laborer to all the hazards of an insecure and unsuitable circulating medium."

After recommending legislation outlining a deposit system similar to the one he had established, Taney closed by reverting again to the subject of currency reform. With pathetic optimism he predicted: "If a broad and sure foundation of gold and silver is provided for our system of paper credits, we need not hereafter apprehend those alternate seasons of abundance and scarcity of money suddenly succeeding each other, which have so far marked our history, and irreparably injured so many of our citizens."

Taney drafted a deposit bill [51] which was eventually passed by the House of Representatives. It was bitterly attacked by administration enemies, however, because it did not require the deposit banks to pay interest on the deposits. A charge of interest had no part in Taney's plans. He wished the government to be in position to require that some or even all government money be held subject to call at any time, and not lent out to borrowers. If the banks were required to pay interest they would have to lend the money in order to pay expenses. The point lost its immediate importance because of the fact that the bill was tabled by the Senate, but it ultimately played a leading part in wrecking the deposit system which Taney had set up.

The administration was successful in securing the enactment of a law changing the ratio of gold and silver to sixteen to one, and helped thereby to bring gold back into circulation. It came to grief, however, in the investigation which was to discover the responsibility of the Bank of the United States for the economic ills of the country —and which was also intended to learn as much as possible about the relations of the bank to members of Congress. The congressional committee went to Philadelphia and was received by a committee of directors of the bank, who insisted on staying in the room of the bank where the investigation was going on, sharply reminding the legislators that they were there by permission and not by right. The

[51] See Taney to Jackson, July 3, 1837, *Correspondence of Andrew Jackson*, V, 491.

committee thereupon retired to their hotel, summoned Biddle and the other directors, and demanded the books. "They summoned us to Yoke's Tavern today," wrote Biddle to Watmough with malicious glee, "for the purpose of bringing our private account books, and testifying before the committee. We went to the Tavern in mass, and presented a paper signed by all the individuals who had been summoned, stating that we did not mean to bring the books to Yoke's, and did not mean to testify. We then made the best bows we could and took our departure. Whereupon they resolved to take theirs, and accordingly adjourned to meet at Washington on Thursday. And so ends the story, the moral of which is that as the speaker packed a committee to us, we packed them back to him." [52] The majority report of the committee,[53] presented by Taney's friend, Francis Thomas of Frederick, revealed almost tearful exasperation as it told of the experiences of the committee and recommended that Biddle and thirteen directors be arrested and brought before the House to answer contempt charges.

A resolution was introduced to send the sergeant-at-arms to Philadelphia to make the arrests, while friends of the bank circulated rumors that the officer would be tarred and feathered if he made his appearance in Philadelphia. Many administration congressmen, particularly among those with state-rights leanings felt that making the arrests would be too strong an assertion of national authority. Stevenson, as speaker of the House, sensed this fact. Realizing that the resolution probably could not be put through, and not desiring to add to hostility to himself, he attempted to bring matters to a quiet close. He tried unsuccessfully to persuade the committee merely to report facts and ask to be discharged because of the lateness of the session. He tried to persuade Taney to stop pressure for further action, declaring that he spent two hours with Taney attempting to show him the error of his doings, but all without effect. "Between you and I," commented one of Biddle's traveling propagandists,

---

[52] Biddle to Watmough, May 10, 1834, President's Letter Book, Biddle MSS.

[53] *Register of Debates*, 23rd Cong., 1st sess., Appendix, pp. 187–193.

"this Mr. Taney is President and Cabinet and K[itchen] C[abinet] too. How disgraceful to our country!" [54]

Although Taney could not be persuaded, a way was found, probably by Stevenson, to keep the resolution from coming to a vote. Biddle therefore won a victory, but it was a victory of which he had no great reason to be proud, even though some of his retainers were highly elated. Biddle went down to defeat on another and more important measure, although he left no stone unturned in his efforts to win. The end of the session being near and the available time for putting popular pressure on the House of Representatives by bank propaganda having passed, Clay introduced in the Senate and secured the passage of another resolution declaring Taney's reasons for removing the deposits to be insufficient, with an added provision directing their restoration to the Bank of the United States. The House showed its independence by laying the resolution on the table. When a senator from Louisiana wrote to Biddle pleading for leniency in the control of credit in New Orleans,[55] Biddle replied with a promise of favors if the desired change of eleven votes could be brought about in the House of Representatives. He did not insist that the bank be rechartered at this time. He did not insist that the measure before the House be passed over the President's veto. All he asked was a peace offering, in the form of a majority vote to restore the deposits to his bank. "I think for instance," he continued, "I could venture to say that if such a vote were secured, the bank would feel no reluctance in giving one, or if necessary, two millions of loans to Louisiana as requested for her relief. This could be done because such a vote is peace and harmony and confidence between the bank and the Congress. In truth I know of no way in which all the interests on the western waters could be more immediately and substantially advanced than by such a vote, which it would be in the power of

[54] ———— to Biddle, June 1, 1834, Biddle MSS. The writer, who was evidently quite well known to Biddle, and who like others among the bank observers did not sign his name, had been in Harrisburg gathering information and was now in Washington for the same purpose. By persuading the Jackson men that he was one of them he was able to collect facts from them and also to make comments which might have some influence in controversial cases such as that of the proposed arrest of the bank directors.

[55] Alexander Porter to Biddle, June 11, 1834, Biddle MSS.

eleven men, who are sent to Congress to promote these interests, to give in a few days. Could not that resolution be brought up?" [56]

Among Biddle's recorded offers to provide the use of the bank's millions in return for political support this is probably the most frank. He was eager to go to Washington and conduct negotiations in person, but he claimed to be fearful of what he oddly called "misinterpretation," and it is possible that he was also afraid that the House might yet decide to make the much discussed arrests. He wrote to Webster to ask if it would be wise for him to come to Washington, and Webster replied that he could see no reason "in law or equity" why he should not come. "We all want to see you; and some of us *very much*." [57] Evidence that he was absent from the bank for several days during the latter half of June is probably sufficient to justify the conclusion that he picked up his courage and went to Washington, but there is no record of a grand celebration such as that which was held at the time when the bill for recharter was passed in the summer of 1832. Furthermore, whatever negotiations he may have entered into, the resolution directing the restoration of the deposits remained undisturbed on the table of the House of Representatives.

In the meantime the Union Bank continued to provide worries for Taney. It was reported to be in such a bad condition that the Bank of the Metropolis, at Washington, refused to receive its notes—giving the opposition the opportunity for gibes at the deposit bank currency which Taney had promised would be better than the currency provided by the Bank of the United States.[58] Colt told Biddle of the rumors that Taney had permitted Ellicott to withdraw the Tennessee bonds deposited with the Treasury Department as security,[59] and that Ellicott had borrowed $500,000 on them in New York.[60] If the rumor was not correct, Colt declared, he did not see

[56] Biddle to Porter, June 14, 1834, President's Letter Book, Biddle MSS.

[57] Webster to Biddle, June 15, 1834, Biddle MSS.

[58] Centreville (Md.) *Times*, April 26, 1834.

[59] The rumor that Taney had released the Tennessee bonds was, however, false. See Taney to R. Johnson and C. Howard May 28, 1834, Miscellaneous Letters, Treasury Department.

[60] Colt to Biddle, May 14, 1834, Biddle MSS.

how the Union Bank could continue to stand, "unless Taney comes
to their aid, and he it is [said is] sick—sick at heart I am sure he is—
if this bank were to fail the consequence to our town would be fearful indeed. I trust it will not though they certainly for their own
sakes deserve no mercy." [61] On the day following that on which
Colt made this comment Ellicott talked with Taney in a state of
such trepidation concerning the future that he tried to persuade
Taney to consent to the recharter of the Bank of the United States,
so that its pressure on the state banks would cease. During the following week Ellicott wrote Taney two letters revealing the same
fears and making the same request, intimating that unless Taney
agreed with him he might have to surrender the deposits, and upbraiding Taney because of rumors that, having lost confidence in
Ellicott, he was about to withdraw the deposits of his own accord.

"You have not, I think, taken a view of my own opinions in
advising me to adopt the course you suggest," Taney replied. "You
are aware that I have always regarded this as a struggle for the
liberties of the country, and that if the bank triumphs, the government passes into the hands of a great moneyed corporation. Its conduct, since the removal of the deposits, and especially its recent con-
tumelious conduct to the committee of the House of Representatives,
has confirmed the opinion I before entertained. With these opinions
can you urge me to recommend its recharter upon any terms? Would
it not be the betrayal of the best and dearest interests of the country,
and justly cover my name with dishonor? Can you as one of my
oldest and most trusted friends upon more reflection, seriously advise
such a course? . . . I am sure that you and every other friend that
I have in the world would rather see me trampled in the dust, than
do any act that would forfeit my own self respect."

Taney assured Ellicott that he had made no plans for ceasing to
employ the Union Bank as a depository, and that he would leave
the deposits with it as long as it was believed to be safe. He would
not blame Ellicott if the bank found it advisable not to receive more
deposits, but he would not modify his program to avoid such an

[61] Colt to Biddle, May 17, 1834, Biddle MSS.

eventuality. "I trust that you who have been among my oldest and most confidential friends will recall the counsel you have given, when you look at the position in which such a measure would justly place me." [62]

The Union Bank had been unable to dispose of the $500,000 in Tennessee bonds, and, unknown to Taney, it had tied up huge additional sums by the purchase of securities of the Baltimore and Ohio Railroad. Ellicott's conduct, together with rumors as to the condition of the bank, made Taney so uneasy that he finally appointed Reverdy Johnson and Charles Howard to make an investigation into the bank's affairs, so that he might decide whether it was safe to retain it as a depository. [63] It seems that Johnson, who was counsel for the Union Bank, again demonstrated his capacity for serving at the same time a number of masters with conflicting interests, and for keeping each to some extent in ignorance of the fact that he was working for the other. He wrote to Biddle in an attempt to get for the Union Bank a loan on the Tennessee bonds. If the loan were made he thought Ellicott would give up the government deposits and declare the conviction that the entire scheme had failed. It was possible that such a step "on the part of this choice pet" would affect the situation in Congress with reference to the restoration of the deposits to the Bank of the United States. [64]

Biddle refused to make a loan on the Tennessee bonds. He recommended that they be sold outright at any sacrifice. He advised that the Union Bank give up its contract to make additional loans to the Baltimore and Ohio Railroad, and that it dispose of its railroad holdings. Finally he advised that the bank retrieve its credit and get back its position in the community by refusing to accept further government deposits. It would be best for the Bank of the United States if the Union Bank should fail, he declared, but personally he hoped it would survive. [65]

[62] Taney to Ellicott, Taney MSS., Maryland Historical Society.

[63] Taney to Johnson and Howard, May 28, 1834, Miscellaneous Letters, Treasury Department.

[64] Johnson to Biddle, May 29, 1834, Biddle MSS.

[65] Biddle to Johnson, June 2, 1834, President's Letter Book, *ibid.*

Johnson wrote to Biddle again, agreeing that the Union Bank ought to give up the government deposits. Doubtless using information acquired from Taney while acting as his agent to investigate the condition of the bank, Johnson told Biddle that if the bank did not surrender the deposits he thought it probable that the Treasury Department would take them away. Catering to Biddle's prejudices, he added that "its being done by the Department would argue volumes against their favorite system, and render their whole scheme now glaringly absurd." He offered pleasing information likewise by saying that the public had lost confidence in Ellicott to such an extent that he would probably be forced out of the presidency of the bank, and he promised to keep Biddle posted on coming events.[66]

In spite of his virtually betraying both Taney and Ellicott to Biddle, Johnson got no assistance for the Union Bank. Neither did he get the loan of $10,000 which he solicited for the General Insurance Company,[67] of which he was president. The Union Bank did not reject additional government deposits, probably because it could get no compensation from Biddle for doing so. Johnson and Howard made a report to Taney which was not sufficiently detailed.[68] He insisted on a more thorough report, and insisted that the board of directors be notified that unless certain reforms were instituted it would be necessary for the Treasury Department to select another depository in Baltimore and terminate its contract with the Union Bank.[69]

In spite of the disloyalty of friends and agents he kept the Union Bank sufficiently in line, by pleading, threats, and investigations, to continue it as a depository until he was himself supplanted in the Treasury Department and until the "panic session" of Congress came to an end. No other deposit bank ever caused him as much worry as this one, managed though it was by a man who had had much to do with the development of Taney's own ideas on banking and public finance,

---

[66] Johnson to Biddle, June 4, 1834, *ibid.*

[67] Johnson to Biddle, June 7, 1834, *ibid.* See Biddle's reply, June 10, 1834, President's Letter Book, *ibid.*

[68] Johnson and Howard to Taney, June 20, 1834, Miscellaneous Letters, Treasury Department.

[69] Taney to Johnson and Howard, June 20, 1834, Miscellaneous Letters, Treasury Department.

and who had been influential with Jackson and Kendall as well as with Taney when the removal of the deposits was first contemplated. There is reason for believing that Taney's patience with Ellicott at last came to an end, and that he was among the indignant stockholders who in July, 1834, elected a board of directors pledged to remove Ellicott from the presidency of the bank.

The Senate had continued to heckle Taney from time to time with inquiries intended to be embarrassing. A resolution proposed by Senator Preston called for the name and salary of the agent appointed to superintend the deposit banks, with information as to the fund from which the salary had been drawn. It was evidently hoped that there was truth in the rumors that Reuben M. Whitney had been appointed to such a position, and that Taney had been illegally awarding him a salary. Taney replied that no such appointment had been made, but Webster, much to Taney's irritation, insisted thereafter both in and out of the Senate on ignoring Taney's reply and stating that the rumors were true. A resolution of Senator Chambers of Maryland called for a statement of the purposes for which drafts had been drawn on the deposits in the Bank of the United States. Taney's itemized statement showed no just cause for criticism. A resolution of Senator Southard asked what government funds had been lost in the banks of the District of Columbia which had recently stopped payment. Taney was able to show that no money had been lost which had been placed on deposit under the new deposit system.

The bank senators introduced these and similar resolutions with speeches in which they made various indignant charges against the administration, but ignored the replies and let the matters drop unless there was some point which they could use. At last, however, Clay introduced a resolution which Taney could turn to his own ends. Having made and listened to so many distress speeches as to have convinced himself that the country was well on the way to economic ruin, Clay tried to place the blame on Taney's shoulders by calling for a comparative statement of the government revenue for the first quarter of 1834 with that of 1833, and for an answer from Taney as to whether his December report had made an adequate estimate of the income of the government for the year. Upon compiling the information which he received from the custom houses, land offices, and other sources Taney discovered, perhaps somewhat even to his own surprise, that instead of being in a condition of depression the country as a whole seemed to be relatively prosperous. Imports had not fallen off, and although there had been some shrinkage in customs duties due to lower tariff schedules, the total revenue from this and other sources promised to be higher than that estimated.

Chuckling over the prospective discomfiture of the bank forces, and foreseeing that they would attempt immediately to suppress it, Taney called Benton to his office the day before the report was to be submitted, went through it with him, and discussed the strategy of gaining publicity for it. "It was our intention," says Benton in his memoirs, "that such a report should go to the country, not in the quiet, subdued tone of a state paper, but with all the emphasis, and all the challenges to public attention, which the amplification, the animation, and the fire and freedom which the speaking style admitted." [70]

When on June 16 the clerk of the Senate began reading the report, Webster, seeing that the bank forces would derive no comfort from it, moved that the reading be dispensed with and that it be referred to the Committee on Finance—of which he was chairman, and by which it would have been effectively suppressed. Benton, elated, demanded in his lordly fashion that it be read through to the end. When the reading was finished Benton arose and insisted on immediate discussion. He outlined scornfully the charges which had been made against Taney and the lamentations of nation-wide disaster which had led the friends of the bank to call for the report. The answer, he declared, had come.

"The Secretary sends in his report, with every statement called for. It is a report to make the patriot's heart rejoice! full of high and gratifying facts; replete with rich information; and pregnant

[70] Benton, *Thirty Years' View*, I, 462.

with evidences of national prosperity. How is it received—how received by those who called for it? With downcast looks, and wordless tongues! . . . A pit was dug for Mr. Taney; the diggers of the pit have fallen into it; the fault is not his; and the sooner they clamber out, the better for themselves." [71]

Benton continued his speech at length, analyzing and explaining the several sections of the report, and showing how, in spite of the distress created in many centers by the manipulations of the Bank of the United States, the evidence of basic prosperity throughout the country could not be refuted. Webster followed with a suggestion that perhaps foreigners had made the importations which had kept up the revenue, and Chambers of Maryland tried to show that there had not yet been time for the distress to show itself nationally; but the combat clearly ended in a forensic victory for Benton.

On Webster's motion the report was now laid on the table. It was printed and passed to the newspapers, and, together with Benton's speech, was circulated widely throughout the country. As interpreted by administration papers it revealed the fact that the bank had deliberately caused much of such distress as had prevailed. By proving to the terror-stricken public that the country was not in a state of ruin, as they had been taught to believe, it brought about a change in psychology, and the panic came gradually to an end. Congress, giving no more attention to distress memorials and making no more distress speeches, turned to the completion of its several tasks in order that the panic session might be brought to its close.

[71] *Ibid.*, p. 463.

CHAPTER XIV

REJECTED

THERE was no precedent in 1834 for senatorial rejection of a cabinet appointment, but the bank forces were determined that Taney should be punished by the loss of his office. Jackson was fully aware of the fact, and he withheld Taney's nomination from the Senate as long as possible in spite of the insistence of bank senators that it be sent in. A short time before submitting Taney's name to the Senate, Jackson nominated Andrew Stevenson, speaker of the House of Representatives, to be minister to London. The treatment accorded Stevenson was suggestive of that which Taney might expect. Biddle wrote to Webster that it would be "the greatest moral and political lesson which the slaves of the Executive could receive" if Stevenson was rejected.[1]

Colt urged Biddle to prevent the confirmation of the appointment, declaring that after Jackson it was a debatable matter as to whether Taney or Stevenson had done the more injury to the country, "for the acts of the first would have been reversed, if the second had not so packed his committees as to play into the hands of the Kitchen Cabinet. If the Senate confirms Stevenson I do not see how they can refuse to confirm Taney."[2] An attempt was made to show that Stevenson had made himself subservient to Jackson in order to get the London post, which had been vacant since the rejection of the Van Buren appointment in 1832. No proof of such subserviency could be secured, but, pursuant to plan, Stevenson was rejected nevertheless.

Since Clay's ill-fated call for the report on the public revenue

[1] Biddle to Webster, May 28, 1834, President's Letter Book, Biddle MSS. See also Biddle to George Poindexer, May 22, 1834, *ibid.*

[2] R. L. Colt to Biddle, May 30, 1834, Biddle MSS.

Taney had been left pretty much unmolested by his political enemies. Biddle had thought of asking a friendly judge in a federal court to issue a mandamus directing Taney to return the deposits to the Bank of the United States, but gave up the idea as not feasible. Colt doubted whether the "Old Man" would allow Taney to obey the mandamus, and was unwilling to advocate a measure which might result in the overthrow of the Constitution.[3] No action was taken, but the self-restraint of the enemy represented no leniency of attitude toward Taney. On June 23, within a week of the close of the session, Jackson submitted Taney's name to the Senate, and on the following day the nomination was rejected, by a vote of twenty-eight to eighteen.

There was no debate and no statement of reasons for the rejection. During the session he had been attacked from all angles. He had been criticized as a former member of the party responsible for the alien and sedition laws. He had been accused of participation in the Baltimore mob disturbance of 1812. It was said that he had opposed the Missouri Compromise. It was intimated or declared outright that he lacked intelligence, honesty, and ability to deal with financial matters, that he had imbibed jesuitical tendencies from his religion, and that he was so weak in character as to be the mere tool of the man under whom he served. It was said that he had quoted inaccurately in his messages to Congress, had made illegal expenditures of government funds, and had brought the country to a state of financial ruin.

His friends, in Congress and out, in speeches and through the press, defended him ably and well on every charge. His enemies had been so unsuccessful in making their accusations hold that they finally deemed it best to retire him from office without formal charges of any kind. In their eagerness to serve the bank, members of the Senate had cried "Crucify him, crucify him," declared the *Globe*. And when it was asked, "What evil hath he done?" they stopped their ears to reason and justice and cried more furiously than ever, "Crucify him, crucify him!"[4]

The two senators from Maryland, Chambers and Kent, were

[3] *Ibid.*
[4] Washington *Globe*, quoted, the Richmond *Enquirer*, July 8, 1834.

among those who voted to reject the nomination. At least four of the opposition senators voted against the mandates of the legislatures of their states. The *Globe* contended that they should have heeded the sentiments of their legislatures. Some years earlier, as a Federalist leader, Taney had argued that a United States senator should be regarded as an independent legislator, and not as a mere delegate of the body which had elected him. The records do not show whether his sentiments on the subject had changed. Perhaps he would have said that it was better to be a mouthpiece of a legislature than a tool of the Bank of the United States.

Although expecting the nomination to be rejected, Jackson received the news with disgust. "Nicholas Biddle now rules the Senate, as a showman does his puppets," he wrote to Edward Livingston.[5] Taney submitted his resignation immediately. Jackson replied in a letter undoubtedly intended more for the eyes of the public and of posterity than for those of Taney. In it he paid high tribute to Taney's services to the country, and declared that "as it is the martyrs in any cause whose memory is held most sacred, so the victims in the great struggle to redeem our Republic from the corrupting domination of a great moneyed power will be remembered and honored in proportion to their services and their sacrifices." [6]

It was subsequently reported that six of the Senators who voted against Taney because of pressure from the Bank of the United States notified him and Jackson that they would support him for any other office for which he might be nominated.[7] Taney, as if suspecting that the offer was made to expose him to ridicule by means of another rejection, is said to have remarked that he could not trust his honor to the keeping of those who had already forfeited their own.[8]

At any rate, Taney's name was not submitted for another office, and he retired to his home to recover his energies and contemplate

[5] Jackson to Livingston, June 27, 1834, *Correspondence of Andrew Jackson*, V, 272.
[6] Jackson to Taney, June 25, 1834, Tyler, *Memoir of Roger Brooke Taney*, pp. 222–223.
[7] Philadelphia *Aurora*, July 19, 1834.
[8] Wilmington (Del.) *Watchman*, quoted, Richmond *Enquirer*, Aug. 5, 1834.

his work of the preceding nine months. Undoubtedly he found it good on the whole, although he could have named flaws in it which the diligent agents of the bank had not discovered. His deposit system was working relatively smoothly, and difficulties connected with the few depositories which had caused trouble were being overcome. The panic was for the most part a thing of the past. Within a few weeks the Bank of the United States, no longer hopeful of gaining anything by it, ended its policy of intensive contraction. Before the end of the session Congress had passed the act changing the monetary ratio of gold and silver, and in a short time the mint at Philadelphia was turning out stacks of new gold coins. Taney and Jackson were elated in the belief that coin would soon supplant paper money for all ordinary purposes. "Mr. Taney, Benton, and Polk, deserve not only golden medals," declared Jackson, "but the gratitude of their country." [9] Levi Woodbury, the close-mouthed New Englander, was transferred from the Navy Department to the Treasury Department to carry out the general policies which Taney had initiated. On the whole, rejected though he had been, Taney was justified in feeling a sense of victory rather than of defeat.

An incident which occurred about the time of Taney's retirement illustrates the care he took to avoid any basis, however slight, for slurs upon his personal integrity. An acquaintance in the custom house in New York had come across some of the long, black cigars of the type which Taney smoked, and sent him two boxes as a gift. Taney had set them aside unopened. Now at his leisure he wrote, graciously regretful, that he could not accept the gift, but would be willing to keep the cigars and pay for them. He had made it a fixed rule, he explained, to accept no present of any kind from any person deriving compensation from his department. "You will, perhaps, smile at what you may think my fastidiousness about such a trifle as your cigars. But I have thought it the true rule for a public man, and that it ought to be inflexibly adhered to in every case, and without any exception in the smallest matters." [10] He could not be persuaded to

[9] Jackson to William Findlay, Aug. 20, 1834, *Correspondence of Andrew Jackson*, V, 286.
[10] Taney to Samuel Thomson, June 28, 1834, Tyler, *op. cit.*, p. 236.

accept the gift even though he was now a private citizen, and sent ten dollars to cover their cost.[11]

Taney declined the first proffer of public honors made after his return to private life. Administration leaders invited him to come to Philadelphia, the camp of the enemy, to participate in the celebration of Independence Day. Doubtful perhaps of his ability to do himself credit on the public platform, he pleaded a previous engagement, and sent a toast to the people of Pennsylvania. Benton, for whom a platform had no terrors, appeared in his stead, and lauded in true Benton style the removal of the deposits and the men responsible for it. Toasts were offered for Taney at Philadelphia and at a great number of other places throughout the country on the same day, and appeared in the newspaper columns for weeks thereafter.

It had been rumored that the banking crisis had made Taney so many enemies in Baltimore that he would not dare return to his former home. He and his party had friends there still, however, and early in July the executive committee of the Jackson party, stressing the high admiration of the people for his conduct in office, asked the privilege of holding a public dinner for him when he returned to the city. Taney accepted with warm appreciation. "I go to Baltimore on Monday," he wrote to Jackson, who was now on his way to the Hermitage. "My friends there are making preparations to meet me at the city line, and are to have a barouche and four horses to convey me into the city, escorted by a number of my friends, and then I am to meet our friends generally. You know this is my first trial in this way, and I am not sure that I am very well fitted for such scenes, and under any other circumstances would excuse myself. But at present it seems to be a matter of duty, and is moreover I acknowledge not a little gratifying. Some day in the next week they are to give me a dinner and I suppose I must make a speech. Although I have no desire to become a table orator, yet I am quite willing to make a speech at this time." [12]

[11] See Thomson to Taney, July 3, 1834, and Taney to Thomson, July 11, 1834, *ibid.*, pp. 237-238.

[12] Taney to Jackson, July 18, 1834, *Correspondence of Andrew Jackson*, V, 273.

On July 21 Taney approached Baltimore at the appointed hour, was met at the city line by a reception committee, and with great pomp was transferred to a barouche drawn by four gray horses. Accompanied by some three hundred persons on horseback and a number of carriages he was driven to Columbian Gardens, receiving along the way and at his destination the applause of the hundreds who had remained loyal to him and Jackson. At the Gardens, Upton S. Heath delivered an address of welcome, to which Taney made a brief reply, stressing his gratitude to his Baltimore friends for their generous welcome. His country had demanded his services at a time when they could not be refused. He accepted the greetings of his friends as a mark of approbation for his conduct.[13]

Resolutions were offered praising Taney and the work he had done, and after other speeches they were adopted, with shouts of applause for the returning hero. Taney thought his friends "in the highest spirits and full of animation." [14] Some of his former associates, however, were conspicuously absent. John V. L. McMahon, George Winchester, and members of the Carroll and Harper families, who in 1828 had been loyal Jacksonians, had in the midst of the bank war deserted his cause. Virgil Maxcy, in private apparently more loyal to Calhoun than to Jackson, had remained quietly concealed from the storm in his position as Solicitor of the Treasury. Those who welcomed Taney's return to Baltimore could provide numbers and noise, but they could not boast of the "quality" of Taney's one-time Federalist associates.

A dinner was planned for the following Thursday. Van Buren, unable to accept an invitation, sent a toast to Taney—"a whole-hog toast," it was, he wrote to Jackson.[15] Levi Woodbury, William T. Barry, and John Forsyth, who had succeeded McLane as Secretary of State, replied to their invitations with regrets, but also with expressions of high respect for Taney—which was probably the purpose for which the invitations were sent. McLane, through Biddle's

[13] Baltimore *Republican*, quoted, Washington *Globe*, July 31, 1834.
[14] Taney to William M. Beall, July 22, 1834, Taney MSS., Maryland Historical Society.
[15] Van Buren to Jackson, July 22, 1834, *Correspondence of Andrew Jackson*, V, 275.

influence [16] now president of the Morris Canal and Banking Company, was in Baltimore the day before the dinner was held, and was also honored with an invitation. He regretted his inability to attend in a cool note which made no mention of Taney except such as was necessary to identify the dinner.

On Thursday evening fifteen tables, seating one hundred persons each, were arranged beneath a canopy in Columbian Gardens, overlooked by portraits of Jackson, Washington, and Lafayette. Attorney General Butler, Benton, Francis Thomas, Isaac McKim, John Nelson, and many others were present to do honor to Taney, and so many of lesser repute came also that there were not enough seats for all. As a precaution against disorder no spirituous drinks were served, except the wine, beer, and cider provided for toasts. After the dinner, in response to a generous greeting, Taney expressed "in his peculiarly plain and forceful language" his gratitude for the compliment paid to him. He declared modestly that he had only done his duty. He referred to the crisis created by the Bank of the United States, and warned his friends that the war was not yet over, and that the bank was gathering strength for a new and final encounter, when it hoped to find the country lulled into fancied security. He closed with the toast, "The People of Baltimore: Always faithful to the cause of freedom."

Benton delivered the principal speech of the evening, discussing the struggle with the bank and the part which Taney had played in it. While he was talking a storm came up, dramatically punctuating his speech with flashes of lightning and crashes of thunder. Suddenly it rained, and a strong wind tore through the gardens, blowing down trees and breaking the canopy away from its moorings. The people fled in chaos, to reassemble for toasts in the adjoining tavern. In spite of the storm the meeting was heralded as a huge success.[17]

Taney's friends in Frederick likewise wished to honor him with a dinner. He accepted the proposal with eagerness, asked that a time

---

[16] *Autobiography of Martin Van Buren*, p. 617.
[17] See the Baltimore *Republican*, quoted, Washington *Globe*, July 28, 1834.

be selected when his friends from the surrounding community could be present, and suggested a notice of the dinner in the local papers. "I am as you know no great *diner out*," he wrote to William M. Beall, "and my habits have not altered since you knew me. And the only places at which I could consent to accept such invitations are my two homes, Frederick and Baltimore." [18] Taney had been deeply hurt by that fact that some people in Frederick with whom he had formerly been intimate had continued to support the bank in spite of the unjustifiable attacks made upon him by Clay and others. He was delighted, however, that of the nineteen signers of the invitation from Frederick seventeen were persons whom the Baltimore *Chronicle*, an opposition paper, had listed as among his opponents.[19]

The date was set for August 6. Taney planned to set out on the preceding day from Washington, where his family still resided. He and Frank Key would drive in his own carriage to the home of Elisha Beall, William Beall's father, some nine miles from Frederick, where they would spend the night, and proceed toward Frederick for the formal greeting on the following morning.[20]

On the morning of the appointed day Taney was met at the Monocacy bridge, near Frederick, by a welcoming committee consisting of Francis Thomas, Roderick Dorsey, and George W. Ent, and an escort of more than one hundred persons on horseback. Hearing the sound of the bugle and the report of a cannon on Barracks Hill, the residents of Market Street rushed to their windows and the townsmen gathered along the street to watch and cheer the return of a local citizen who had won fame in national affairs. In front of the Central Hotel, Taney and Thomas mounted a platform which had been erected for the occasion. Thomas, who three months earlier as chairman of the congressional investigating committee had been humiliated by Nicholas Biddle, now delivered an address of welcome to the man who had removed the government deposits from Biddle's bank.

---

[18] Taney to Beall, July 22, 1834, Taney MSS., Maryland Historical Society.

[19] Baltimore *Republican*, quoted, Washington *Globe*, Aug. 8, 1834.

[20] Taney to Beall, July 25, 1834, copy, in possession of Miss Nannie Floyd, Frederick, Md.; Taney to Beall, Aug. 1, 1834, MS., in possession of Mrs. L. R. Lee, Washington, D.C.

Taney replied with simple and friendly eloquence, expressing his gratitude to his fellow citizens of the Frederick community for the honor with which they received him. It had been with reluctance and only as a matter of duty, he declared, that he had accepted the position which he had recently held. Having advised the measures which the President was taking, he could not do other than stand by the "grey-haired patriot now at the head of the government." Complimenting Thomas on his own conduct, Taney closed his brief address, and withdrew from the platform amid the resounding cheers of the multitude.[21]

Shortly after two o'clock a procession of three or four hundred people was formed in front of the hotel, to march to the music of a full band along Market Street and up Court Street to the Court House square, where seventeen tables, laden in fine style, had been prepared by Jacob R. Thomas. A portrait of Washington, draped with the Star Spangled Banner, marked the head table, while on the right and left respectively were portraits of Jackson and Jefferson. Abraham Shriver presided over the meeting. John Schley was first vice president, and sat at the head of the first table. Joseph Taney sat at the head of another table. Frank Key was conspicuous among the many visitors.

The multitude at the tables, said the local Jackson paper, included "many of our oldest and most respectable citizens—men who have long stood aloof from the excitement of the most violent party conflicts—and men who had long maintained a position of neutrality in politics; these together with the deep and pervading enthusiasm which animated, and gave life to the whole, are some of the evidences of the cordial and hearty confidence and affection with which the Jackson Republicans of Frederick received Mr. Taney." [22] It was said to have been such a demonstration of popular sentiment as had never before been seen in the county, although some marked the vacant countenances and chop fallen visages of "the whole host

[21] Frederick *Citizen,* quoted, Washington *Globe,* Aug. 18, 1834.
[22] *Ibid.*

of hatred" that stood by, and some of the participants in the celebration showed signs of discomfort.

After the dinner thirteen regular toasts were offered, to the accompaniment of music and cheers. One of them was given to Key, who like Taney had been asked to return and receive the plaudits of his former neighbors. Key replied by calling to mind the experiences which had led him to compose the national anthem. A toast to "The Democracy of the Entire Union" had been sent by Benton, together with a letter praising Taney as leader of the struggle with the bank, and refuting the charge that Taney had been the "passive instrument of the President." "I know," Benton concluded, "that since his rejection, he has refused to receive his own choice of some of the highest offices which the President and the *Senate* could bestow. Such a man does not prostitute himself for office; nor will he be charged with it, except by those who are themselves capable of the prostitution which they ascribe to him." [23]

When a toast was offered in honor of Taney he arose to face the vast audience of applauding friends, untroubled by the sense of panic which so often paralyzed his best efforts on the platform. He delivered an address which for simplicity, clarity, and comprehensiveness is unexcelled by any other of his productions which are on record. From his knowledge of them as neighbors, clients, and jurors he gauged the shrewdness and simplicity of the members of his farmer audience. For his explanation of the issues of the bank war he chose words which all would understand, and illustrations which would register sharply in their minds. He did not go deeply into the more complex problems of banking, though even in this field he gave a striking demonstration of what familiar words of from one to three syllables can be made to do.[24]

Taking up the subject of political alignments, Taney ridiculed the attempts of the Jackson opponents, the National Republicans of the

---

[23] Benton to the Committee, Aug. 2, 1834, Richmond *Enquirer*, Aug. 29, 1834.

[24] The speech, copied from the Frederick *Citizen*, is in the Washington *Globe*, Aug. 25, 1834, the Richmond *Enquirer*, Aug. 29, 1834, and, in part or in full, in many other papers of the period.

North and the Nullifiers of the South, to conceal their identity by taking the name of Whigs, at the same time labeling the Jacksonians as Tories. Why had they changed their names? Taney had an explanation: "Gentlemen, many of you I know have been jurors. I now see around me many well-remembered friends, before whom, in other times, I have had the honor of arguing cases. When you sit as jurors, and it appears in evidence that the party on trial has often changed his name, I incline to think it generally brings suspicion on his character and motives. If you found that he had sometime ago passed in the South under one name, in the North and West under another—and that he had recently at Washington assumed a third, it would, I am sure, beget a suspicion that he had perpetrated something under the former names, for which he did not like to be responsible. And if in his last name he represented himself as belonging to the family of some well known and respectable citizen, the suspicion against him would be strengthened. . . . I leave you to judge how far the recent determination of the 'Nationals' and the 'Nullifiers' to drop the names of baptism, by which they were heretofore known, and take upon themselves the ancient and honored name of the family of the '*Whigs*' is calculated either to alter their old principles, or give any additional confidence in their designs.

"But it is said that this is a new state of things, calling for a new formation of parties, and therefore for a new name. That the question is not bank or no bank, but that they have banded together to resist Executive usurpation, and to restore the Constitution and the laws. But, it unfortunately happens that these 'Whigs' complain of no Executive usurpation, except where the bank is concerned; no violated Constitution, or broken laws, but in relation to the bank. Ask them of what usurpation General Jackson has been guilty? They will answer, 'In his conduct to the bank, and to the secretary who refused to remove the deposits.' How has he violated the Constitution? How broken the laws? Still they answer, 'In his conduct to the bank, and to the secretary who refused to remove the deposits.' And if you ask them what remedy they propose for these Executive usurpations?—How is the violated Constitution to be purified, and the broken laws to be healed? The answer is ready—'Restore the deposits to the bank.' This is the healing bond for every wound.—And thus it seems, that Executive usurpation—violated Constitution—broken law —is the old story, under a new name. It is still *Bank, Bank, Bank!* It is still the old song, sung so often during the last winter, with the chorus of *'Restore the deposits and all will be well!'* The new name of 'Whig,' therefore, marks no new principle of action, and has opened no new ground of contest. . . .

"In one thing, indeed, I agree with the 'Nationals' and 'Nullifiers,' otherwise called 'Whigs!'—and that is, that the question which now agitates the country, is not simply a question as to the recharter of the bank, and to end with the grant or refusal of an act of incorporation without any other material result. The source of the controversy lies much deeper. The bank is the center, and the citadel of the moneyed power. For the first time in the history of our country, as I have already said, moneyed men, as an associated class, have united together and openly endeavored to obtain possession of the government, by using their money to control the elections. Now, for the first time, the issue is made up, and the question boldly and distinctly presented to us, whether this noble country is to be governed by the power of money in the hands of the few, or by the free and unbought suffrages of a majority of the people. . . . Until this bank was created and began to feel its strength, the possessors of extraordinary wealth were content, like other citizens, to act as individuals in our political concerns; and to have, as individuals, their just influence in the affairs of the nation. But the vast capital of the bank, its extensive and exclusive privileges have enabled it to concentrate the money power of the country. And, feeling its strength, its ambition has been awakened, and it is striving to seize on the government, in order to perpetuate its enormous and exclusive privileges, at the expense of the rest of the community. It has entered the lists as representing a peculiar and separate class. And it brings forward its demands in the spirit and temper, which, in all ages, have marked the moneyed aristocracy, when they believed themselves strong enough to govern. It never appeals to the high and generous feelings of the people.

It must govern by other means. If the poor laborer dare to think for himself, he is contemptuously dismissed from his employment, and, with his family, left to starve—the debtor is pressed for money he is unable to pay—the trader, with but moderate means, is denied the usual facilities necessary for the successful prosecution of business— the mechanic is cut off from his ordinary employment—the needy, wherever they may be found, are tempted with loans of money— and the ambitious with the hope of advancement—and for those who presume openly to oppose its power, it has a thousand instruments to minister to its vengeance. Its favorite weapons are corruption and fear."

Taney brought his speech to a close with a final warning against the chartering of another national bank, anywhere, for any purpose, except for local purposes in the District of Columbia—and the District was for the time being adequately supplied with banking facilities. "Let us not talk of compromise. There can be no compromise between the antagonistic principles. Yield but an inch, and you will be driven to the wall; and instead of the rich inheritance of liberty which you received from your fathers, you will bequeath to your descendants slavery and chains—the worst of slavery, that of submission to the will of a cold, heartless, soulless, vindictive, moneyed corporation."

The friends of Taney and of the administration were, for just cause, delighted with the speech. It was circulated and discussed far and wide,[25] with almost the measure of attention given to Jackson's communications, which were received by his followers much like letters from home. Its style was a subject of universal comment, and all were struck by what the *Globe* characterized as the contrast between Mr. Webster's studied, artificial concoction of false apothegms, and Mr. Clay's libelous, declamatory denunciations, on the one hand, and Mr. Taney's firm and honest exposition of the true condition of public affairs. Taney, who claimed not to be a public speaker, had won a forensic triumph.

[25] See the editorial in the *Globe* of Aug. 25, 1834, and the reprints of the comments of other newspapers in the issues of Sept. 4, 10, 15, and 25.

Taney remained in Frederick for two days, visiting happily with his friends, and then returned to Washington. He was pleased with his visit, he wrote to William M. Beall,[26] except for one thing. He had been embarrassed in the presence of two of his former friends, Wootton and Hammond.[27] In former years they had coöperated with him as Federalists. They had later aligned themselves with the National Republicans, but party differences had not until recently been permitted to interfere with friendship. When Taney visited Frederick, however, he refused an invitation to dine with one of them, and, although he had a good excuse, Taney was unable to conceal the fact that the old friendship was gone.

The recent struggle with the bank, he wrote to Beall, had not been a mere partisan struggle. A great combination had been formed to destroy him personally. "It was supposed by the men who formed this design to destroy me that I had personal friends in Frederick, who differed with me as party men but who would not consent to see injustice done to me—in the mere spirit of malignity. They feared they might lose some of their own supporters if they carried out their plan of individual persecution and Chambers [28] (as I have understood) was directed to write to Frederick and ascertain whether those who were considered my personal friends, would continue to support Mr. Clay, Mr. Webster and Mr. Calhoun notwithstanding their attempts to disgrace and ruin me—in my private pursuits as well as my public character. The answer was *that they would.* And I have no doubt that Hammond and Wootton were in some way sounded but without their knowing it before the answer was given. It would be easy to extract from honest and unsuspicious men like them in the course of conversation what they would do in case of my rejection. I am quite sure that both of them would be opposed to such an act of personal malevolence towards me. But the men who planned and executed it did not care what their wishes were provided they would still continue to support them. For it would still be under-

[26] Taney to Beall, Aug. 10, 1834, Beall MSS.
[27] Probably Dr. Singleton Wootton and "Gentleman Nat" Hammond.
[28] Ezekiel F. Chambers, United States senator from Maryland.

stood from the result of the election and so represented abroad that the people of Frederick County where I had so long lived cared nothing about me and thought I deserved the mark of disgrace which they have endeavored to fix upon me. Under such circumstances I could not with justice to myself accept at this time the hospitality of Wootton. It would be an admission on my part that he was right in supporting Mr. Clay in his attempt to destroy me."

Deeply concerned as he was about the outcome of the autumn elections in Maryland as a vindication of his own conduct, Taney had originally intended to permit no public dinners to be given for him except at his "two homes," Baltimore and Frederick. A report came to him, however, that Webster had recently delivered a speech at Salem and had published it again referring to him as the "pliant instrument" of the President. Flattered perhaps at the reception of his own speech at Frederick, and receiving an invitation to a dinner at Elkton, he decided to take the occasion to answer Webster. Van Buren, with his intimate knowledge of politicians and their methods, had advised Taney to ignore the personal attacks made upon him in Congress. "The attack of Mr. Webster however made a new case," Taney wrote to Van Buren, "and I thought it due to myself and the public to place him in his true position." [29]

On September 4 Taney addressed an enthusiastic audience at Elkton.[30] Referring to Webster's Salem speech, he called attention to the fact that his nomination as Secretary of the Treasury had been rejected by a silent vote. If a member of the Senate had charges to bring against his character, that was the time to bring them. Since no charges had been brought, he had a right to expect that no senator who had voted against him would after the close of the session follow him with a spirit of hostility into private life. Yet Webster had chosen to malign him in a public address. Rather than attempt to refute Webster's charges, Taney thought it proper to show how little Webster's statements of fact or opinion were to be relied upon. He

[29] Taney to Van Buren, Sept. 16, 1834, Van Buren MSS.
[30] See the speech in full, *Niles' Weekly Register*, Oct. 18, 1834.

told how, in the face of an official statement from the Treasury Department, Webster had continued to declare falsely in the Senate that Taney had illegally employed an agent to superintend the deposit banks, and had permitted his speech to be published in a local paper.

"Here then," continued Taney, "is a senator, in his place in the Senate, professing to state the contents of an official communication, made to the body of which he is a member, and representing it not merely incorrectly, but in direct and unequivocal opposition to the truth. He knows that thousands will probably read his statement who will never see the report; and instead of recalling what he has said, and offering some excuse for this extraordinary conduct, he takes occasion, after the session has closed, to unite himself with the known purchased instruments of the bank in bestowing opprobrious epithets upon the individual whom he had in his place in the Senate flagrantly wronged as an officer, by stating untruly the contents of his official report, and making that statement the foundation of charges against him. Neither my habits nor my principles lead me to bandy terms of reproach with Mr. Webster or anyone else. But it is well known that he has found the bank a profitable client, and I submit to the public whether the facts I have stated do not furnish grounds for believing that he has become its 'pliant instrument,' and is prepared, on all occasions, to do its bidding, whenever and wherever it may choose to require him. In the situation in which he has placed himself before the public, it would far better become him to vindicate himself from imputations to which he stands justly liable, than to assail others."

Leaving these personal matters, Taney continued with topics which he had discussed in his Frederick speech, stressing more heavily, however, the prospect of the return of gold to ordinary use as currency. It would ever be one of the proudest recollections of his life, he declared, that it was under his administration of the Treasury Department that measures were taken which would restore the golden currency to the country and rescue the people from the power of a heartless moneyed corporation. "The free and plentiful circulation of gold will soon give us a stable and safe currency; and the time I am persuaded is not distant when the banks will cease to issue notes of the smaller denominations; and when this is the case, and we are emancipated from the tyranny of a national bank, we shall have no reason to apprehend the fluctuations and disasters to which the sudden expansions and contractions of our paper currency have heretofore been liable, and from which we have suffered so severely."

The Elkton speech, though not such a work of art as the one delivered at Frederick, was well received. Colt sent a copy to Biddle and suggested that he get someone to criticize it,[31] but apparently no serious attempt was made at a rebuttal. Webster wisely remained silent rather than give added publicity to Taney's charges by attempting to refute them. It probably would have been better for Taney to have exercised the same self-restraint in the first place, for nothing was gained by presenting evidence that the man who had called him a "pliant instrument" was himself both a "pliant instrument" and a liar. Taney's own friends never believed the accusations against him, and his enemies were not to be convinced by his arguments. In terms of the evidence the charge of servility on Taney's part is seen to have been obviously false.

It is unfortunate that this fiction has been widely credited, like that other more notorious fiction that he said the black man had no rights which the white man was bound to respect. Taney was himself partly responsible. He professed again and again his loyalty to the "grey-haired patriot," and never admitted the shrewdness with which he not only persuaded Jackson to remove the deposits, but persuaded him also that it was largely his own idea. It was for the most part Jackson, rather than Taney, who was being manipulated, though there is little evidence that Taney ever permitted Jackson to become aware of the fact. Taney had been so determined on the achievement of certain ends that even though his manner suggested subordination and even subservience to Jackson's superior judgment there was on the whole little that was subservient or pliant about his

[31] Colt to Biddle, Sept. 30, 1834, Biddle MSS.

conduct. Or perhaps it might be said that he was pliant as to the part he was to play, and in some degree as to the methods to be used in defeating the bank, but that there was no pliancy in his determination that the defeat of the bank should be achieved.

Taney wrote to Van Buren that he was pessimistic as to the probable results of the Maryland elections, which were to take place in October, even though Maine and New York were showing evidence of new strength for the party. The bank would spend money freely to carry the state, if for no other reason than for the pleasure of beating him, and money was highly effective in a state such as Maryland, which had a rotten borough system. Besides, there was a vexatious question about the division of Frederick County which was getting more attention there than the really important issues, and which might cause defeat for the party. His friends had told him, however, that they would carry Baltimore by more than their usual majority.[32] He proved to be right about Frederick County but wrong about Baltimore, for the opposition carried both, and the Jackson party elected only seventeen members of the House of Delegates. The Bank of the United States was said to have participated extensively in the elections, winning the favor of the western counties of the state by a loan of $200,000 to the Chesapeake and Ohio Canal Company at the strategic moment.[33]

Biddle was of course elated. "Your triumphs in Baltimore," he wrote to Robert Gilmor, "which seem to be echoed back from all parts of the state, are most happy omens of the success of the good cause throughout the country, and are hailed with great satisfaction among us."[34] The *National Intelligencer*, gloating over Taney, printed the following communication as a "Decisive Reproof":

Roger B. Taney is a native of Calvert County, in Maryland, and a descendant of one of the most ancient and respectable families of the state. He continued to reside there until about the age of twenty-four or twenty-five years, and was elected twice or three times as a delegate to the General

[32] Taney to Van Buren, Sept. 16, 1834, Van Buren MSS.

[33] See the Washington *Globe*, Oct. 18, 20, 22, and 24, 1834; and the Richmond *Enquirer*, Oct. 31, 1834.

[34] Biddle to Gilmor, Oct. 9, 1834, President's Letter Book, Biddle MSS.

Assembly. For upwards of twenty years he pursued the practice of law in Frederick, the residence of his choice, and rose to eminence in his profession. During that long period, he stood at the head of the federal party in that county, and enjoyed a popularity that very few have been able to attain. With a laudable desire to extend his professional fame and increase his private fortune, he removed to Baltimore, where, for several years, he divided the highest honors of his profession with the distinguished and lamented Wirt, possessing the unlimited confidence and esteem of his personal friends, and idolized by his political party. At the moment of his acceptance of the office of Attorney General, he was undeniably the most popular citizen of Baltimore.

Now, behold *"the fruits of a single error."* Taney, the amiable and retiring citizen, the eminent lawyer, the favorite of the people, listened to the suggestions of vanity and ambition, and yielded to the seductions of office. He abandoned the substantial happiness of private life, and the profits of his lucrative profession, and entered into the service of a debased and debasing junto. The menials of the kitchen smeared him over with flattery, and he *descended to their level.* The principles of his early life were forgotten; he worshiped the idol in the high places: he threw himself before the Car of Juggernaut and was crushed, a willing victim, under its wheels. What are the results? Calvert, his native county, last year politically divided, has condemned the unlawful seizure of the public treasure, by a majority of more than THREE to ONE! *Frederick,* where for more than twenty years he flourished without a rival, last year numbered a majority of four hundred for Jacksonism, has now recorded, by an overwhelming majority, a verdict of condemnation against corruption and its unhappy victim, in reply to his pathetic and beseeching appeal for sympathy and support!! But BALTIMORE, the hitherto unwavering and unshrinking adherent of the Hero, and steadfast supporter of all his measures, has stamped the final, emphatic, and indelible seal of reprobation upon the pliant and willing instrument of the kitchen cabinet.

Poor Mr. Taney! Poor Mr. Taney!

MARYLAND.[35]

Although the bank forces were victorious in Maryland they were defeated in much of the remainder of the country. The administration would be much stronger in the new House of Representatives, and the Jackson party state legislatures promised to dilute the bank membership of the Senate with loyal Jacksonians. "The last nail is

[35] Washington *National Intelligencer,* Oct. 14, 1834.

drove in the coffin of modern Whigism," [36] Jackson exulted in a letter to Taney. A Pennsylvania friend of Biddle's deplored the losses sustained by the institution and hoped that the results of the elections would not shake its stability. "All hope now lies on bribery!" he declared. "I think some of the members of Congress might be sounded successfully! You understand." [37] It is not unreasonable to assume that Biddle did understand, though the fact would never be inferred from his pious letter to a man in New York stating concerning the bank, "I have always made it a point of duty never to permit its interference in any manner with our political concerns." [38] As the next session of Congress approached, Biddle made plans for another struggle for the recharter of his bank, and for properly rewarding those of his enemies who might be appointed to office by seeing that they were rejected by the Senate.

Although he received invitations, Taney attended no more dinners and made no more speeches after his Elkton appearance. Suffering from a cold and weary of celebrating a public victory crowned by a personal defeat, he returned to Baltimore to begin the restoration of his law practice. He was grievously disappointed when his state failed to vindicate his conduct by returning majorities for his political party. His party had been poorly organized, he wrote to Jackson, while the opposition had spent huge sums of money on the election. "The bank and the whole moneyed interest in Baltimore, were determined cost what it would to wreak their vengeance on me, and to procure such a result in Maryland as would be most mortifying to me, and such as they hope may affect my character and standing in other states." [39] He found this hostility carrying over into his professional pursuits. He professed an unshaken confidence in the virtue and intelligence of the people, and the belief that they would ultimately do what was right, but as far as the immediate future was concerned his own prospects were thickly clouded with gloom.

[36] Jackson to Taney, Nov. 8, 1834, Taney MSS., Maryland Historical Society. The letter is printed, with grammar corrected, in the *Maryland Historical Magazine*, IV, 304.
[37] David Gulliver to Biddle, Oct. 16, 1834, Biddle MSS.
[38] Biddle to S. M. Stillwell, Oct. 30, 1834, President's Letter Book, *ibid.*
[39] Taney to Jackson, Oct. 12, 1834, Jackson MSS.

CHAPTER XV

FROM DEFEAT TO VICTORY

DURING the two years which he served as Attorney General, Taney was able to continue much of his private practice. As Secretary of the Treasury, however, he had to drop it completely. When his salary from the government came to an end, therefore, he was faced with the necessity of rebuilding the practice which he had lost. Ordinarily his employment in the offices which he had held under the federal government would have added to his prestige to such an extent as to enable him quickly to reëstablish himself in a profitable business. However, the disturbances in Baltimore created by the bank war, and also perhaps his scathing denunciations of the subservience of local merchants to the Bank of the United States, had made him bitter enemies among those able to pay the counsel fees he had been accustomed to receiving. Instead of having, as of old, a host of friends eager to turn business in his direction, he found attempts being made to block him at every point.

He suffered from a severe cold, he wrote to Jackson, and from an attack of rheumatism which made it impossible to move about without great pain. His recovery was retarded by the necessity of attending court every day. "For in the vindictive spirit which prevails here towards me among many of the moneyed men of this place, I am obliged to give strict attention to my professional concerns, in order to sustain myself against the influence which is seeking to prevent me from reëstablishing myself in my former practice." [1] He ended the term of the local court in a state of exhaustion. Mrs. Taney and the daughters, who until this time had remained in Washington waiting for their Baltimore house to be vacated by its tenants, hurried home to take care of him.

[1] Taney to Jackson, Oct. 20, 1834, *Correspondence of Andrew Jackson*, V, 299.

Jackson and those around him were loath to see Taney struggling to rebuild a private practice under such difficulties. They needed him in Washington. There was no reason why he could not be taken care of politically in one office or another. It was at some time urged upon him that he put himself in line for the vice presidency under Van Buren, who was being groomed to succeed Jackson. He was not financially able to accept that position, however. Furthermore, he could see nothing desirable in it unless it led to the presidency, and he estimated that by the time Van Buren had served two terms he would be at that time of life when repose and quiet would be far more agreeable than the constant turmoil of active political life.[2]

In spite of his professed lack of interest in political office, administration leaders in Washington continued to call on Taney for advice and assistance on various matters. Woodbury was having trouble with the Bank of the United States about the bank's claim to fifteen per cent damages on the French protested bill, to which Taney as Attorney General had declared that the bank had no legal or moral right.[3] Biddle, refusing to surrender the claim, collected for himself by withholding from the government the dividends due it on the stock which it held in the bank. The ordinarily close-mouthed Woodbury called Biddle to account in language so unrestrained that Colt indignantly pronounced it a disgrace to the government. He was convinced that even Taney and Kendall could have had nothing to do with the production of such a letter.[4]

Biddle was undisturbed by Woodbury's strong language, however, and Woodbury, faced with the necessity of putting up a fight and of preparing a statement on the subject for the President's message to Congress, asked the Attorney General for a copy of Taney's opinion that the bank had no right to the damages claimed. Unable to find it in the files, Attorney General Butler wrote to Taney for a copy.[5] When after two weeks Taney had not replied Jackson also wrote

[2] Taney to William M. Beall, March 23, 1836, MS. in the possession of Mrs. L. R. Lee, Washington, D.C.

[3] *Ante*, pp. 220–229.

[4] Colt to Biddle, Dec. 13, 1834, Biddle MSS.

[5] Butler to Taney, Oct. 1, 1834, *Niles' Weekly Register*, Jan. 3, 1835.

telling him that the opinion was much wanted, and urging him to come to Washington to help prepare the message to Congress.[6]

Taney replied that he had given the opinion to a member of the Committee on Ways and Means, who had never returned it. He told of his illness and professional difficulties, and promised to visit Jackson as soon as he was able, and to write out a new opinion if the old one was not found.[7] On his way through Baltimore, Van Buren stopped to discuss with Taney a portion of the President's message under preparation. He reported to Jackson that Taney's health was improving, and that he would be in Washington in time to work on the message.[8] Jackson was much pleased with the news. "Remember I have a bed and room for you," he wrote to Taney.[9]

Taney went to Washington some time in November. There he brought together the papers relating to the bank's claim for damages, and wrote out his opinion showing why the bill of exchange in question was not the kind of bill referred to by the law giving the right to damages.[10] Wrangling over the point continued, however, for a number of years. It reached the Supreme Court in 1844, when Taney was Chief Justice. Because of illness and because of his connection with the controversy Taney did not sit in the case. Other judges also were absent. The court decided in favor of the bank by a vote of four to one.[11] Taney, in Baltimore, wrote out an opinion giving the history of the case as he knew it and disagreeing with the opinion of the court. He then took the unprecedented step of having his opinion published in the appendix to the official reports, to the disgust of Justice Story, who thought Taney's conduct indelicate and improper, and wanting in respect for his fellow judges.[12] The issue came before the court again three years later, when there had been some changes in personnel. This time the decision was against the

---

[6] Jackson to Taney, Oct. 13, 1834, *Maryland Historical Magazine*, IV, 303.

[7] Taney to Jackson, Oct. 20, 1834, *Correspondence of Andrew Jackson*, V, 299.

[8] Van Buren to Jackson, Nov. 5, 1834, *ibid.*, p. 305.

[9] Jackson to Taney, Nov. 8, 1834, *Maryland Historical Magazine*, IV, 304.

[10] See Taney to Butler, Nov. 25, 1834, *Niles' Weekly Register*, Jan. 3, 1835.

[11] *Bank of the United States* v. *United States*, 2 Howard 711 (1844).

[12] See Story to John McLean, Aug. 16, 1844, McLean MSS., and Story to James Kent, Aug. 31, 1844, Story MSS.

bank by a vote of five to two.[13] Taney and Woodbury were both members of the court at this time, but neither of them sat in the case, and neither recorded an opinion. Taney's earlier irregular conduct—quite uncharacteristic of him as a judge—may have had something to do with the later decision, though the changes in the personnel of the judges sitting appear to have been much more important. At any rate, the bank was finally defeated on the issue.

Soon after Taney went to Washington, Colt reported to Biddle that "Taney is down there and no doubt helping to concoct the message." [14] Taney did help, particularly with that portion of the message beginning, "Created for the convenience of the government, that institution has become the scourge of the people." [15] In addition to reiterating and further supporting old charges against the bank the message showed how, after the close of the last session of Congress, the bank had abandoned its policy of unparalleled contraction of loans. The abandonment of the policy at this time seemed to the writers final and conclusive proof that the bank had been motivated solely by the belief that rapid contraction would create sufficient distress to force the restoration of the government deposits. In terms of all the evidence available it seems clear that Taney and his collaborators were not far wrong in their appraisal of the motives of the bank.

Many people otherwise friendly toward the Bank of the United States had disapproved of the way in which Biddle and the directors treated the congressional investigating committee. A few days after Taney's rejection the Senate attempted to soften the criticisms by directing its Committee on Finance to investigate the bank during the summer. The committee consisted of Webster, John Tyler, Thomas Ewing, W. P. Mangum, and William Wilkins. Wilkins was the only friend of the administration among them. Knowing the type of report which might be expected, he refused to serve. After trying vainly to persuade another administration man to serve, Web-

---

[13] *United States* v. *Bank of the United States*, 5 Howard 382 (1847).
[14] Colt to Biddle, Nov. 29, 1834, Biddle MSS.
[15] See *Messages and Papers of the President*, III, 97ff.

ster, as if to give a semblance of fairness to the investigation, left the gathering of evidence to his colleagues, with John Tyler in charge. Tyler, though opposed to the removal of the deposits, was not regarded as in other respects friendly to the bank.

The committee made its investigation during the summer, with the full coöperation of the bank as far as it went. Although he did not appear publicly in the matter, and did not write any of the report, Webster gave advice in the selection and arrangement of materials.[16] Tyler read the report[17] before the Senate on December 18, 1834, occupying the floor for two and a half hours. It was an attempt at an elaborate vindication of the bank on all points, and was highly critical of Jackson, Taney, Van Buren, and Benton. It did reveal flaws in the armor of the administration, although it had flaws of its own which were quickly exposed. Since the impression prevailed widely that it was a whitewash report, it constituted no important victory for the bank, but it provided material for further wrangling during succeeding weeks. It was probably in part responsible for the fact that Tyler reached the Presidency some years later, where he surprised his supporters by vetoing a bill to charter a Bank of the United States.

In spite of the report the bank found itself weaker in Congress than during the preceding year. Samuel Jaudon, the cashier, spent some time in Washington to aid in pressing the measures desired by the bank, but he finally wrote to Biddle that he could do nothing, and was returning to Philadelphia.[18] Indeed, the bank forces were successful during the term in little else than defeating the appointment of enemies to office. As a result of the urging of Taney, Kendall, and others, Jackson nominated Henry D. Gilpin, a former government director of the bank, to be governor of Michigan Territory. The Senate refused to "advise and consent." John T. Sullivan, another of the former directors whom Biddle had characterized as snoopers for the government, was nominated to be paymaster of the Army, and was treated to a similar fate. The position of minister to

---

[16] See Webster's letters to W. P. Mangum, Oct. 9 and Nov. 4, 1834, and to John Tyler, Nov. 27, 1834, Mangum MSS.

[17] *Register of Debates*, 23rd Cong., 2d sess., Appendix, pp. 185–208.

[18] Jaudon to Biddle, Feb. 25, 1835, Biddle MSS.

England had been vacant since the rejection of Van Buren in 1832. Jackson made no attempt to fill it at this time, however. He was convinced that the "lame duck" Senate would confirm no appointment which he would be willing to make, and he decided calmly to wait until the meeting of the next Congress, which promised to be much more friendly to the administration.

Supreme Court vacancies, however, could not be left indefinitely. Justice Johnson, from a southern district, had died during the preceding summer, giving Jackson the opportunity to make his third appointment to the court. John McLean had turned out to be a Whig, opposed to most of Jackson's policies and intensely desirous of the office of President. There was doubt as to Henry Baldwin's sanity, and he was a fanatical friend of the Bank of the United States. Many Democrats thought Jackson should redeem himself with the new appointment, and begin packing the court with Democrats as the Federalists had packed it in earlier years. "Johnson's death," wrote F. P. Blair to Jackson, "and the probable resignation of Duvall and the Chief Justice before the end of your term, will probably enable you to impose a strong Republican control over this bench of Lords, especially if you have the making of a Chief Justice, who is something like a president of a bank, all in all sufficient and prevailing in their privy councils." [19]

For the position now vacant Jackson chose James M. Wayne, of Georgia, who had supported him during the nullification controversy and during the bank war, but who had not been sufficiently outstanding among the leaders to incur in any high degree the enmity of the bank. The nomination was confirmed by the Senate, and Wayne took his seat on the bench at the beginning of the term in January, 1835.

Gabriel Duvall, so deaf that arguments before the court meant little or nothing to him, had long been expected to resign. There was jealous and vindictive speculation as to his successor. "Of course Taney cannot have this place," Colt wrote to Biddle.[20] It seems that Duvall had clung to his position because of the belief that in the

[19] Blair to Jackson, Aug. 18, 1834, *Correspondence of Andrew Jackson*, V, 284.
[20] Colt to Biddle, Nov. 29, 1834, Biddle MSS.

event of his resignation it would go to some one—probably McLane
—who had ability as a lawyer but whom he thought too much of
a politician to be a member of the Supreme Court. If Taney had had
anything to do with implanting this idea in his mind there seems to
be no evidence to that effect. The clerk of the court, a member of
the Carroll family, discovered that Jackson had determined to protect Taney from his enemies by appointing him to the position if the
opportunity was given. The clerk passed the information along to
Duvall, whereupon the Judge resigned,[21] about January 10, 1835.

The records do not reveal discussions of the appointment between
Jackson and Taney. Quite possibly they were conducted orally, while
Taney was in Washington aiding in the preparation of the message
to Congress. At any rate, Jackson sent Taney's name to the Senate
for the position of Associate Justice of the Supreme Court on January 15. The nomination was discussed for an hour on that day, but
no action was taken. A newspaper correspondent concluded that
Taney would hardly reach the bench. The editor of a Jackson paper
threatened that if Taney were rejected it would be an outrage that
would be repaired.[22] An opposition paper in Boston, on the other
hand, hoped that "the Senate will not only apply the veto to the
pretensions of this man, but that it will pass a decided resolution to
oppose the elevation of any man who is not perfectly sound in regard
to the fundamental principles of the Constitution, as expounded by
Daniel Webster." [23] Other comments on opposing sides followed in
similar vein.

In the Maryland House of Delegates John L. Dorsey, a Whig
but nevertheless a friend of Taney, offered a resolution saying that
in the opinion of the legislature Taney's nomination ought to be
confirmed. The House, however, not only failed to adopt the resolution, but directed by a vote of fifty to sixteen that it be expunged
from the journal.[24] The four delegates from Frederick County, the
two from the city of Baltimore, and the three who were present from

---

[21] Tyler, *Memoir of Roger Brooke Taney,* pp. 239–240.
[22] Richmond *Enquirer,* Jan. 20, 1835.
[23] Boston *Columbian Sentinel,* quoted, Washington *Globe,* Feb. 11, 1835.
[24] *Journal of the Proceedings of the House of Delegates,* Dec. sess., 1834, p. 213.

Calvert County, all voted to expunge. It was harsh treatment from Taney's own state, and particularly from the localities in which he had lived. It is not surprising that his letters of the period reveal a sense of persecution.

He had friends among the respectable conservatives of the country, including Chief Justice Marshall. The Chief Justice wrote to Senator Benjamin Watkins Leigh of Virginia that if Leigh's mind was not already made up on the nomination he had some information in Taney's favor.[25] The hostility of the Senate, however, and of the Bank of the United States, was intense. John Sergeant of Pennsylvania, who was in Washington arguing cases and gathering political information for the bank, reported to Biddle the general belief that Taney would be rejected. Some senators had told him in secret of a plan to alter the judicial circuits so that Maryland would be included in the circuit of one of the judges now sitting, with the result that the new judge would be appointed from another state.[26] Webster favored this type of strategy, and was not at all sure that the nomination could be defeated otherwise. "If we could get rid of Mr. Taney on this ground," he wrote, "well and good; if not, it will be a close vote." [27]

Jackson seems to have relied on the support of those senators who had opposed Taney's nomination as Secretary of the Treasury but promised to support him for any other office for which he might be named.[28] A reporter declared that if they should permit Taney to be rejected the President would have the means of exposing their infidelity to their own words "in a manner that would add disgrace to any other set of men on earth." [29]

[25] Tyler, *op. cit.,* p. 240.

[26] Sergeant to Biddle, Jan. 30, 1835, Biddle MSS. See Frelinghuysen's resolution, *Senate Journal,* IV, 465.

[27] Webster to Jeremiah Mason, Feb. 1, 1835, *Writings and Speeches of Daniel Webster,* XVI, 252.

[28] According to the Wilmington (Del.) *Watchman,* quoted, Richmond *Enquirer,* Aug. 5, 1834, John M. Clayton, of Delaware, was one of the group. A letter of Taney's of a later date suggests that Clayton got pledges for Taney but was unable to hold them.—"I have every confidence in Mr. Clayton but I cannot forget in what manner pledges made to him by opposition senators on a former occasion were openly broken or openly evaded."—Taney to Van Buren, March 15, 1836, Van Buren MSS.

[29] Portland *Eastern Argus,* Feb. 3, 1835.

The last day of the session arrived, and still no final action had been taken. The day passed, the evening session talked itself away, and still no action. The administration had probably discovered that it could not count on enough votes to confirm, and had decided to see the session end without a formal decision, assuming that the opposition would not press the matter. Jackson, with members of his cabinet, was in his room in the Capitol considering and signing bills as the clock ticked past the hour of twelve, when the session was supposed to come to an end.

The Senate clock had been stopped, however, and while Jackson worked on, perhaps congratulating himself on a qualified victory in that he had at least escaped overt defeat, Webster called up the nomination for action. He moved that it be indefinitely postponed —a motion which was tantamount to a rejection. A vote was taken, the doubtful senators violated their pledges or congratulated themselves that they had made no pledges as to indefinite postponement, and, twenty-four to twenty-one, Taney again went down to defeat. The secretary of the Senate carried notice of the action to the President. Old Hickory threw down his pen, roared that it was more than an hour past twelve o'clock and he would receive no more messages from the scoundrels, and stalked out of the building.[30]

The months immediately following the rejection of Taney's nomination to the Supreme Court constituted in his life a period of uncertainty which was filled with varied but for the most part not highly significant activities. He argued one case before the Supreme Court, presumably at the invitation of Reverdy Johnson, his colleague in the case. He argued three cases before the Maryland Court of Appeals, two of which were for members of the Duvall family and one for the state. He probably appeared in other cases before the lower courts.

Administration leaders continued to ask his advice on various mat-

[30] See the *Senate Journal*, IV, 484; Benton, *Thirty Years' View*, I, 598. See also the "Spy in Washington," in the New York *Courier and Enquirer*, Jan. 23, 1836, quoted, Washington *United States Telegraph*, Feb. 8, 1836.

ters. When it was decided to remove William T. Barry from the Post Office Department because of his utter inefficiency Taney was doubtful of the political wisdom of placing Amos Kendall at the head of the Department, but later admitted that he had been mistaken, and that the appointment was popular. He discussed with Van Buren plans for the party convention to be held in Baltimore in May, at which it was assumed that Van Buren would be nominated for the presidency, and he doubtless had much to do with the arrangements which were made.

He began at this time what was to constitute many years of intermittent discussion of a proposed history of the bank war and of the Jackson administration. He thought it would render the country some service to present a connected history of the contest, and besides he did not wish to "leave the bank agents and their hired writers to send their own account of it to future generations." [31] He thought the book should have a picture of the President which in future ages his countrymen would delight to look upon. Justice could never be done to him unless it was known what untiring efforts had been made by men in high stations to turn him from his purpose, such as the attempt to persuade him to send a milk-and-water and halfway veto of the bank bill in 1832, "instead of the manly and noble message with which he met the crisis." [32]

Jackson asked Taney's advice about a matter to be discussed in the message to the next Congress. No legislation had yet been passed with reference to the state bank deposit system, which was still operating for the most part as it had been when Taney left the Treasury Department. Jackson, Taney, and others had taken the position that the system was an emergency arrangement which ought to have the sanction of Congress, either as it stood or with such changes as Congress saw fit to make. The enemies of the system at first blocked any legislation of the kind and later insisted on provisions objectionable to the administration, such as that requiring the banks to pay interest on the money deposited with them. Woodbury

[31] Taney to Van Buren, May 12, 1835, Van Buren MSS.
[32] Taney to Van Buren, June 2, 1835, *ibid.*

ultimately indicated willingness to make the concession, and Jackson wrote for Taney's opinion.

Taney vigorously criticized the proposal. The Bank of the United States had not paid interest, and there was no reason why the state banks should be placed at this disadvantage. Furthermore, he felt that the depositories should keep the government money ready for withdrawal at all times. This they could not do if required to pay interest, for they would have to lend it out to pay expenses, and would therefore have an excuse for interfering with the fiscal program of the government. The demand that the state banks pay interest, Taney declared, was but another move on the part of the Bank of the United States to reëstablish itself. It was an attempt to fetter the state depositories, and prevent the system from working smoothly. "Indeed," he concluded, "the struggle of the moneyed aristocracy to obtain power never ceases and can never be expected to cease until the nature of man is changed and he becomes a purer being than he now is." The deposit system had worked so well that he was now inclined to believe that no additional legislation was needed. "It is gratifying to look at the prosperous condition of the country and its overflowing treasury and to compare it with the assertions and predictions of ruin and bankruptcy made at the time the change was adopted. The experience of two years has been triumphant." [33]

Congress at the ensuing session dealt with these and other economic matters in which Taney was deeply interested, but most of his attention was doubtless given to a measure more intimately related to his personal welfare. It is possible that Jackson planned at first to present his name a second time for the Supreme Court vacancy, trusting to the infiltration of new administration senators to bring about confirmation. Another possibility was offered, however, through the death of Chief Justice Marshall, early in July, 1835.

No appointment was made to either of the vacant positions until near the end of the year. Justice Story would have liked to succeed to the chair of his beloved chief, and many conservative members of the bar would have been delighted with the promotion. He differed

[33] Taney to Jackson, Nov. 21, 1835, Jackson MSS.

from Jackson on too many constitutional questions, however, and he never really expected the honor. Webster's name was frequently suggested, but he had even less chance than Story, for in addition to holding doctrines similar to those of Story he had conducted himself during the bank war in such a way as to lead the administration to characterize him as devoid of "truth, honor, and patriotism." [34]

Administration papers generally assumed that Taney would succeed Marshall, but they said little on the subject except occasionally to ridicule the idea that some such person as Webster would be appointed, or to defend Taney against opposition criticism. Little was said in disparagement of his legal ability, but it was said that his work as Secretary of the Treasury would "damn him to everlasting fame." [35] John Quincy Adams sourly disapproved of the appointment likely to be made.[36] Taney was widely criticized on the ground that he was a Catholic, and therefore subservient to a "foreign potentate." It seems probable, however, that the charge was made more for propaganda purposes than because the persons making it themselves took it seriously.

On December 28, 1835, Jackson sent Taney's name to the Senate for the position of Chief Justice of the United States. Along with it he sent the name of Philip P. Barbour of Virginia for the position of Associate Justice. The nominations were referred to the Judiciary Committee. They were reported out on January 5, with the recommendation that they lie on the table—presumably to await the enactment of legislation rearranging the judicial circuits. On the following day the Senate passed almost unanimously a bill creating two new circuits in the West. One of them was to be served by an eighth justice (the court now consisted of seven members), and the other was to be provided with a justice by merging two of the eastern circuits into one. By this arrangement Maryland and Virginia were to be thrown into the same circuit. Since two justices were not customarily appointed from the same circuit the bill, if it became a law,

[34] Washington *Globe*, Aug. 21, 1835.
[35] Allan Nevins (ed.), *Diary of Philip Hone*, I, 164.
[36] *Memoirs of John Quincy Adams*, IX, 243–244.

would give just grounds for opposition to the appointment of either Taney or Barbour.

While the nominations lay on the table awaiting the action of the House of Representatives on the judiciary bill the newspapers speculated on the effect of the bill on the nominations. Predictions differed as to which of the two men would be confirmed if the bill was passed. The odds seemed to be on the side of Barbour, who, although an ardent Jacksonian and an enemy of the bank, had not recently incurred such bitter enmity as that directed at Taney. No action was taken for more than two months, but occasional skirmishes kept discussion alive. The two Whig senators from Maryland were opposed to Taney's nomination. Neither of them, therefore, was the logical person to present a petition signed by members of the Baltimore bar urging confirmation. It was presented instead by John M. Clayton, Whig senator from Delaware, who seems to have tried unsuccessfully to secure confirmation at the preceding term for Taney's nomination as Associate Justice. Webster struck back at him by securing the removal of the injunction of secrecy from the Senate action at the preceding term, showing that finally Clayton and others supposed to be friendly to Taney had voted for the indefinite postponement of the nomination.[37]

In the meantime Taney was engaged in professional business at Annapolis, apparently not greatly worried about his prospects, for the administration seemed to have a safe majority in the Senate and he knew that Jackson, Van Buren, and others would defend his interests. His immediate task was that of prosecuting a claim before the Maryland legislature. A mob of the unfortunate persons who had lost their savings in the defunct Bank of Maryland, resentful that such money as was left seemed tied up indefinitely in court proceedings, destroyed the houses and furniture of Reverdy Johnson, John Glenn, and others who had been connected with the bank. Although Johnson had permitted his name to be used as a director it was never proved conclusively that he was a participant in illegal transactions, but the mob was not given to making hair-line distinctions.

[37] *Journal of the Executive Proceedings of the Senate*, IV, 505.

Taney, believing himself under obligation to Johnson for reports on the conduct of Ellicott and the Union Bank, and being hostile to mob action in any event, undertook to make to the legislature a claim for damages out of an allotment due the city. The business took more time than he had expected, and on March 4, when nearly two months had passed, he had not yet been permitted to make his formal argument.[38] On March 7 he explained the case in a letter to Van Buren. He feared that because of the delay his confirmation as Chief Justice might precede the time when the argument could be made, and thereby prevent his making it at all. By anonymous letters the destruction of his own house had been threatened if he continued with the case. Therefore, he wrote, "It would be very agreeable to me, if my friends would postpone acting on (and I suppose I may now say confirming) my nomination until this argument is over. The confirmation at this moment, before the argument, would look as if my friends had interposed to prevent the argument, and might subject me to the unworthy suspicion of having procured the action of the Senate to avoid meeting the responsibility which has been menaced. You will I am sure see at once that I owe it now to my own character to make the argument." [39]

On the following day he wrote in similar fashion to J. Mason Campbell, his son-in-law,[40] and he wrote again to Van Buren that if efforts were being made by his friends to press matters to a conclusion in the Senate the efforts were mistaken ones. He would make his speech on Thursday, "and I may say to *you* that as soon after that day as my friends think right, I should be glad to have the matter disposed of finally. For this thing of being half a lawyer and half a judge is both unpleasant and unprofitable, and the delays and doubts which my enemies have kept up so long, has been the only serious annoyance they have ever been able to give me. . . . When I can come to Washington without incurring the suspicion of coming to

[38] Taney to J. Mason Campbell, March 4, 1836, Gratz Coll., Historical Society of Pennsylvania.
[39] Taney to Van Buren, March 7, 1836, Van Buren MSS.
[40] Taney to Campbell, March 8, 1836, Etting Coll., Historical Society of Pennsylvania.

electioneer with the Senate, I shall take an early day to pay my respects to my friends there." [41]

A few days later Taney wrote to Van Buren repeating much that he had said in earlier letters, and announcing that the date for his appearance had again been postponed. He wrote to Frank Key in similar vein. He told Key also of an impression among the Jackson members of the legislature that Jackson sympathized with the mob, and asked him to see if he could get from the President a statement to the contrary. Jackson authorized the statement that he considered the destruction of property an outrage, and thought the owners should be fully indemnified.[42]

Key was one of those persons driven by a deep desire to be helpful, and unfortunately he did not stop with his consultation with Jackson. He talked with Senator Clayton about Taney's predicament, and discovered that the nomination was to be taken up immediately. On Clayton's advice he wrote to the senators from Georgia suggesting that the matter be postponed three days longer to enable Taney to make his argument in Annapolis. It is not surprising that Taney was alarmed when he learned what Key had done. It was one thing to inform trusted friends that he did not wish the confirmation of his appointment hastened to enable him to avoid the necessity of appearing in the case; it was quite another thing to have letters in circulation asking the postponement of the confirmation of his appointment as a judge so that he might argue a case intimately connected with party politics. Enemies like Clay, Webster, and Calhoun might make use of such letters to defeat the nomination altogether.

Deeply agitated, Taney wrote to Van Buren of what Key had done. "I am greatly surprised and deeply mortified," he continued, "at the utter heedlessness with which my sincere and excellent, but most injudicious friend, Mr. Key has put to hazard by his conduct all the prospects of my future life, and that too for a matter in which I have no interest and in which I have already made greater sacrifices of feeling and interest than the parties had any right to ask

---

[41] Taney to Van Buren, March 8, 1836, Van Buren MSS.
[42] Key to Taney, March 14, 1836, Tyler, *op. cit.*, pp. 244–45.

for. I have no desire that my nomination should be postponed an hour on account of my engagements at Annapolis, and I do most anxiously desire not to be surrendered by my friends to the mercies of my adversaries. . . . Excuse me for the trouble I give you in my affairs, but I wish to place them in hands that are not only friendly but judicious." [43]

In the meantime the bill for reorganizing the judicial circuits had made no headway in the House of Representatives, and the administration had gained strength through new accessions to the Senate. Illinois and Louisiana had each sent a senator who could be counted on. When the Virginia legislature instructed the Virginia senators to vote to expunge the censure of Jackson from the Senate Journal, John Tyler resigned his seat because of unwillingness either to obey or to disobey. He was replaced by William C. Rives, a loyal Jackson man. On March 14, the day when Rives took his seat, Taney's friends determined to force consideration of the nomination. In spite of Taney's fears, Key's embarrassing attempt to play politics seems to have had no effect whatever.

The struggle began with a motion of Thomas Ewing, Whig senator from Ohio, to take up a bill to appropriate to the several states the proceeds of the sale of public lands. James Buchanan objected, urging the consideration of executive business. Ewing objected on the ground that some senators were absent because of illness. An administration member countered with the statement that he would be absent at a later date, and wished the executive business to be taken up while he was present. Ewing and Calhoun attempted further to force the consideration of the land bill, but were defeated by a vote of twenty to twenty-six. After attending to routine matters the Senate went into executive session, spent the remainder of the day in a discussion of which no record was kept, and adjourned, on Webster's motion, without reaching a decision.

On the following day, March 15, Ewing won by a vote of twenty-four to twenty-three the right to discuss the land bill. He spoke until 2:30 in the afternoon, when he yielded the floor to permit

[43] Taney to Van Buren, March 15, 1836, Van Buren MSS.

another Whig senator to move adjournment. The motion failed. Buchanan urged that consideration of the land bill be postponed until the following day, but Ewing refused to yield. He talked half an hour longer, when the Whigs lost on two other motions for adjournment. They gave up, and the Senate proceeded in executive session behind closed doors. Taney's nomination was confirmed, twenty-nine to fifteen. Barbour's nomination was then taken up, and was confirmed after defeat of Webster's motion that consideration be postponed until after the House had passed upon the judiciary bill. The nomination of Amos Kendall, who had been serving as Postmaster General for almost a year on an interim appointment, was also confirmed before the disgusted Whigs could get an adjournment.

A number of Whig senators, including Kent and Goldsborough from Maryland and Clayton from Delaware, were conveniently absent when the vote on Taney's nomination was taken. The two former, as a matter of state pride, were perhaps unwilling to oppose confirmation when it seemed assured in spite of their efforts. Clayton and others probably hoped for Taney's success but thought it politically unwise to give him active support. Hugh L. White, formerly friendly to Taney and to Jackson, voted against confirmation, presumably angling for Whig support for his presidential aspirations.

Although each of the nominees confirmed received the votes of more than half the total membership of the Senate, the *National Intelligencer* lamented the fact that the lateness of the hour had prevented fuller attendance. The *Globe,* gloating over the fact that some Whigs had been absent because of unwillingness to vote against Taney, reminded its rival that the votes were taken before the fashionable dinner hour. "And when was it," the *Globe* demanded, "that the opposition ever let the shades of night prevent them sitting, when they wished to record their votes against a cabinet minister? Did they not sit as late to put them on record against Mr. Stevenson? They put their veto on Mr. Taney last year, after one o'clock at night." [44]

[44] Washington *Globe,* March 19, 1836.

Newspaper comments varied according to party alignments. Whig papers, which spoke for the more conservative membership of the bar, were aggrieved and disappointed. Democrats were elated.[45] Massachusetts Whigs were humiliated that John Davis, Webster's colleague, had voted to confirm.[46] Webster magnanimously excused him on the ground that had Taney been rejected a worse man might have been chosen.[47] Little attempt was made to reply to the final outburst of criticism. The *Globe* made an exception in the case of the prediction of a New York paper that Taney would always be known as the man who had illegally removed the deposits, violated the charter of the bank, and created panic and bankruptcy in the land, and was paid for doing so with the office of Chief Justice. The *Globe* replied that on the contrary the high office would be respected because of the virtue of its incumbent. "There never lived a man of purer purposes, of gentler, kinder manners; of more distinguished patriotism; or who blended better, moderation and firmness; professional learning with a knowledge of mankind; strict attention to official duties with a devotion to all the obligations imposed on him by his private relations. Mr. Taney is beloved by all who know him intimately. We believe he never had an enemy but those that have been made by his politics; and as his principles are of the most liberal cast, the intolerance shown him on this score is the strongest proof of his high deserving." [48]

On March 16 Taney received letters from many of his friends, from which he learned that in spite of Key's well-meaning interference he had now become Chief Justice of the United States. On the following day he wrote to Jackson of his deep gratitude for the way in which Jackson had always supported him, culminating in his appointment to the one office under the federal government which he had ever wished to attain. He would rather owe the honor to Jackson than to any other man in the world. He was glad to owe

[45] See the compilation of comments, Charles Warren, *Supreme Court in United States History*, II, 1–18. (The two volume edition is used.)
[46] See the Baltimore *Republican*, April 5, 1836.
[47] Webster to Davis, April 7, 1836, Davis MSS.
[48] Washington *Globe*, April 2, 1836.

his confirmation to the strength of his friends, rather than to the forbearance of men who had so long and perseveringly sought to destroy him. He was pleased that Kendall, who had fought with him in the bank war, was also out of reach of the vengeance of the enemy.

Finally, looking forward to the time when he might administer the oath of the presidential office to Van Buren, Taney took delight in the fact that "it will be the lot of one of the rejected of the panic Senate, as the highest judicial officer of the country to administer in your presence and in the view of the whole nation, the oath of office to another rejected of the same Senate, when he enters into the first office in the world, and to which it is now obvious that an enlightened and virtuous people are determined to elect him. The spectacle will be a lesson; which neither the people nor politicians should ever forget." [49]

When he replied a few days later to a letter of congratulation from his old friend William M. Beall of Frederick, Taney gave similar expression to his delight at his victory. He had had time, moreover, to reflect somewhat upon the change which the appointment would make in his future life. "My political battles are over," he wrote, as if with a touch of wistfulness as well as pleasure, "and I must devote myself to the calm but high duties of the station with which I am honored." [50]

Edward Livingston sent his congratulations on Taney's victory "over corrupt influence and party malignity," and told of his firm conviction that public good would be derived from the appointment.[51] In reply Taney spoke further of the responsibility which the office placed upon him. While the nomination was pending, he wrote, and he saw his old adversaries in the Senate opposing him in their usual spirit, he perhaps thought more of the conflict than of the office and the duties which it would bring with it. "For the three statesmen, as they call themselves, who lead in the Senate (or rather

[49] Taney to Jackson, March 17, 1836, *Correspondence of Andrew Jackson*, V, 390.

[50] Taney to Beall, March 23, 1836, MS. in the possession of Mrs. L. R. Lee, Washington, D.C.

[51] Livingston to Taney, March 17, 1836, MS., Princeton University Library.

have led) not only manage to elevate to high offices those whom they most hate, but they contrive to enhance the pleasure, by adding to the office itself the pleasure of victory over injustice—and that too committed in the temper and tone of the most vindictive personal hostility. But that is now past and I must hasten to forget it and as I look to the high duties of the station to which I am called, I feel sensibly the heavy responsibility which rests upon me. And it is cheering at such a time to receive from you whose good opinion I so much value, and with whom I have been so intimately associated in times of trial, assurance of your confidence and approbation." [52]

His nomination having been confirmed, Taney could not with propriety make the argument which he had prepared for delivery before the House of Delegates. He turned his materials over to John V. L. McMahon, and himself appeared as a citizen of Baltimore to urge that compensation be granted for the property destroyed by the mob. On March 22 the legislature passed a bill which in effect required the city of Baltimore to pay the full amount of the losses. Even though Taney had not argued the case it was much as if he had done so, and had won it, the last case in which he was ever to appear as counsel.

At eleven o'clock on the morning of March 28 Elias Glenn, United States district judge, Nathaniel Williams, district attorney, and the marshal and the clerk of the court, waited on Taney at his home and accompanied him to the circuit court room. In the presence of a crowd of friends and members of the bar Taney produced his commission, and was sworn in as Chief Justice of the United States and presiding judge of the fourth circuit. Judge Glenn resigned soon afterward, and his position was conferred upon Taney's friend Upton S. Heath, who thereafter was Taney's colleague for many years. On April 8 the United States circuit court for the fourth circuit commenced its regular session in Baltimore, with Taney presiding.

[52] Taney to Livingston, March 24, 1836, Livingston MSS, in possession of John Ross Delafield, New York, N. Y.

CHAPTER XVI

AFTERMATH

THE Jacksonians were sufficiently well represented in the Congress which met for the first time in December, 1835, to defeat all hope of the recharter of the Bank of the United States before the expiration of the old charter on March 3, 1836. They were not able to defeat the bank completely, however. Regarding the situation in Congress as temporarily hopeless, the bank forces lobbied a bill through the Pennsylvania legislature by which the Bank of the United States would be able to continue its existence as the United States Bank of Pennsylvania. Instead of continuing the withdrawal of the notes of the bank during the last months of its existence under the charter from the federal government, Biddle provided for the extension of note issues which, in Taney's estimation, was responsible for the orgy of currency expansion in which state banks throughout the country indulged during the months which followed.[1] Although not as powerful as when acting under the national charter the bank continued to be one of the strongest banking institutions of the country and continued to be a menace to the program of the Jackson, or Democratic, party.

Problems connected with the disposal of government revenues continued to puzzle the administration, and, in spite of the fact that the deposit system worked out by Taney and continued by Woodbury seemed to work well, the problems grew increasingly complex. The remainder of the national debt was being paid off, and less revenue would be needed in the future. Yet the tariff, pursuant to the provisions of the compromise act of 1833, would continue to provide substantial sums until 1842. Additional amounts, increasing

[1] See Taney to Jackson, Oct. 27, 1836, *Correspondence of Andrew Jackson*, V. 431–432.

in size, were coming in from the sale of public lands, which were being bought not merely by settlers but also by speculators gambling on the prospect of higher prices later on. The excess of government income over expenditure offered the prospect that money in unprecedented amounts would pile up in government depositories, and that the administration in power might have the use of this money for selfish purposes. Good policy therefore seemed to require that Congress enact legislation to protect and to guard against the misuse of the government funds.

In his message to Congress on December 7, 1835,[2] Jackson called attention to the need for a deposit law, although he would have been satisfied with an act merely sanctioning the system already in effect. He mentioned the prospect of surplus revenue to the amount of $10,000,000 by the first of January, and advised the reduction of taxes and tariff duties as far as practicable, and the expenditure of money on the navy and such construction works as could be constitutionally supported by the federal government. He spoke of the huge sum of $11,000,000 derived from the sale of public lands during the preceding year, though he did not mention and may not have been aware of the fact that much of the amount was paid in the notes of banks overissuing in a rising tide of speculation, with the threat of catastrophe ahead. He took pride in the fact that gold had been flowing into the country since the recent coinage legislation, and that approximately two-thirds of the states had taken measures to forbid the issuing of small notes, but he did not take into account the printing of millions of dollars in notes of larger denominations. Neither did he foresee the recession of a boom in England which would soon bring severe pressure upon American merchants and bankers.

Henry Clay had for a number of years advocated distributing to the states the proceeds from the sale of public lands, to be used to pay for public improvements. Many of the states had recently engaged in a riot of competitive spending on highways, canals, and railroads, and were badly in need of money. Clay reintroduced his

---

[2] *Messages and Papers of the Presidents*, III, 147ff.

distribution bill at this session, with the full support of the Bank of the United States, which was a heavy investor in state securities, and forced it through the Senate, only to meet insuperable opposition in the House of Representatives.

Calhoun opposed Clay's plan, doubtless in part because his rival was its author. He opposed it also because he was interested not in land revenue as such, but in taking from the control of the administration all surplus revenue whatsoever. "The leading question of the session," he wrote to a political friend, "will grow out of the surplus revenue which is far greater than the administration are willing to admit. . . . The question is, whether the present and accruing surplus, should go back to the states as a fund for internal improvement, or shall remain in the hands of the Executive as a fund to corrupt and govern the country."[3]

Calhoun introduced a bill to regulate deposits—those deposits not to be turned over to the states. Discovering that the administration might support his bill, however, thereby entangling him with his political enemies, he announced his intention of abandoning the bill and leaving the deposit question wholly to the responsibility of the administration. Under the leadership of Silas Wright, Van Buren's friend from New York, the administration then offered a substitute by way of amendment to the bill. Under it the federal government was to invest the surplus revenue in state securities.

Calhoun then offered an amendment not acceptable to the administration, providing that the surplus should be deposited in the treasuries of the states, on condition that it be returned when needed. Seeing that the bill could not be discussed without entanglement with the knotty distribution question, Wright decided not to call it up, whereupon Calhoun did so. It was rewritten by a special committee and passed by a vote of thirty-eight to six, in spite of the vigorous opposition of Wright and Benton.[4]

The section of the bill dealing with the surplus revenue provided

[3] Calhoun to Hon. E. Brown, Dec. 20, 1835, MS. in possession of Albert S. Brown, Frederick, Md.

[4] For the history of the bill see Calhoun to James H. Hammond, June 19, 1836, *Correspondence of John C. Calhoun*, pp. 358–361.

that the surplus in excess of $5,000,000 should be deposited with the states in proportion to their representation in Congress. No interest was to be paid. If the Secretary of the Treasury needed money to meet appropriations he was not to demand it from the states. Instead he would offer five per cent certificates for sale, on which the states would pay the interest. The states could redeem the certificates or could let them run indefinitely. It was obvious, therefore, that under the fiction of making deposits the money was to be transferred permanently to the states.

Support of the bill in both houses was so nearly unanimous that while it was pending in the House Jackson was under tremendous pressure from those of his friends who wished to vote for the bill but were reluctant to act in the face of his veto. Taney visited Washington while the bill was pending. He was opposed to the bill on constitutional grounds and on grounds of the government's need of the money, and because of the orgy of spending and corruption which would be engendered in the states. Yet it seemed improbable that Jackson could by any means defeat the strong support of the bill, and Taney was reluctant to advise Jackson, in the last year of his administration, to make a fight in which defeat seemed inevitable. He promised to write out an argument against the bill, however, to be used if Jackson saw fit. After his return to Baltimore he phrased a legal argument against the bill in the form of a veto message. It was not to be taken as an attempt to persuade Jackson in the matter, he insisted. "Your own clear judgment will I am sure point out what is best to be done." [5]

The argument [6] demonstrated the unconstitutionality of the collection of revenue by the federal government for the use of the states. "The taxing power is not conferred in unlimited terms," it stated, "but the words used show too plainly to be mistaken, that the revenue which this government is authorized to raise was intended to be used for national purposes only, and whenever it shall exceed

[5] Taney to Jackson, June 20, 1836, Jackson MSS.

[6] This document, dated June 20, 1836, is printed in the *Correspondence of Andrew Jackson*, V, 404–409.

what may be usefully and constitutionally employed in the exercise of its legitimate duties it is bound to reduce it." If the compromise on the tariff resulted in the collection of more revenue than was needed by the government, the collection of the excess was in violation of the Constitution, and the compromise must give way for a reduction in rates. "No compromise between different parties and different interests can enlarge the power of the government, and give to it rights which it does not take under the grant of powers contained in the Constitution."

On June 21, the day after the date of Taney's argument, and possibly before Jackson received the argument, some of Jackson's friends persuaded him to sign a modified bill. As redrafted it provided that deposits should be placed with the states on agreement of the states to return them on call from the Secretary of the Treasury. On its face, therefore, the arrangement was now for deposits with the states, rather than for loans to them, and the constitutional difficulty was resolved. Fundamentally the difference was of little importance, since political opposition to the recall of the deposits would be so great that it would be simpler to get the money needed by additional taxation than by withdrawal.

When he heard of the proceeding Taney wrote to Jackson that he had undoubtedly done right in signing the bill in view of the fact that on its face it provided for deposits with the states, which were constitutional, instead of loans or investments in state securities, which were not. He thought the bill objectionable on the score of policy, but since Jackson had hitherto confined his use of the veto power to issues in which constitutional questions were involved, and since he had frequently asked for legislation on the subject of the deposits, it was well to let Congress take the responsibility.

Taney was convinced, however, that the friends of strict construction would find themselves in serious difficulties as a result of their support of this measure. "They will find it impossible to get the money back from the states, for the universal impression is that it is never to be recalled. And if they do not bring it back from the states, they will be compelled to sanction a principle, which is directly at war with that construction of the federal Constitution for which they have been so long contending. For it will be no easy matter to set limits to the powers of a government which may raise what money it pleases, and apply it indirectly to what purposes it pleases, by depositing it with a state or corporation or an individual, with an understanding that it is never to be recalled. I have not seen a single political friend who does not regret the course which has been taken in Congress, while every one admits that in the shape in which the bill came to you and the vast majorities by which it was passed, you were unquestionably right in not vetoing it." [7]

No deposits were to be made with the states until January 1, 1837, when one-fourth of the surplus in excess of $5,000,000 was to be moved. The other fourths were to follow on the first days of April, July, and October. The act of Congress created more immediate disturbances, however. No deposit bank was permitted to retain government money in excess of three-fourths of its capital stock paid in. Woodbury found it necessary to reduce deposits in thirteen of the thirty-five deposit banks,[8] and to select others to care for the excess funds. The shifting of substantial sums made temporary contractions necessary, and had a depressing effect upon the credit situation.

The difficulties of the government were increased in that more banks had to be supervised. Furthermore, a requirement that the banks pay two per cent interest had been made part of the act. It was necessary that the banks be permitted to lend out the money if they were to pay interest, and the government was no longer in its former position of being able to require that heavy reserves be kept. On the whole the outlook for the deposit system was far from promising.

On July 11 Jackson aided the deposit banks indirectly by his decision to issue the order which became famous, or infamous, as the Specie Circular. Speculation in public lands had been growing more and more intense, with sales running to $5,000,000 a month. Most of the payments streaming into the government land offices

---

[7] Taney to Jackson, June 27, 1836, *Correspondence of Andrew Jackson*, V, 409–411.
[8] See the Woodbury circulars of June 24, 1836, Letters to Banks, Treasury Department.

were made in bank notes, and the fact that these notes were being issued in quantities wholly unjustified by the reserves behind them was becoming more and more apparent. Benton had tried to get legislation to check the boom, but without result, partly because many legislators were among the profiteers. Benton drafted the circular which Jackson signed, largely without the support of his cabinet, providing that with certain exceptions nothing but specie should be accepted in payment for public land.[9]

The order raised a storm of protest as it halted the land boom, cut off the speculative profits of dealers, and drew westward specie from eastern banks which had been doing "land office business" in promises to pay. At the same time, fortunately, it turned specie into the deposit banks which received such revenue as continued to come from the sale of land, thereby aiding them in preparing for the downward sweep of the business cycle which was inevitable unless the era of speculation was to go on indefinitely.

In November, 1836, Van Buren was victorious in his race for the Presidency, on a program promising support for the Jackson policies. Taney suffered the humiliation of seeing Maryland support the Whig candidate, William Henry Harrison, although the rotten borough districting of the state was doubtless largely responsible. Popular indignation at the working of the system at this time resulted in the institution of reforms at the next session of the legislature.

During the preceding October, Jackson wrote to Taney that he was thinking of writing a farewell address. He asked for Taney's ideas as to what should go in it, and whether it should be made a part of his regular message to Congress or be left until the close of the session.[10] Taney advised the latter course. The topics discussed should not be mixed with the everyday business of the government. "Your farewell address," he wrote, "should be exclusively devoted to those great and enduring principles upon which our institutions

[9] See Benton, *Thirty Years' View*, I, 676–678.
[10] Jackson to Taney, Oct. 13, 1836, *Correspondence of Andrew Jackson*, V, 429.

are founded, and without which the blessings of freedom cannot be preserved." [11]

Some two weeks later, in reply to another letter from Jackson, Taney promised to have some suggestions written out for the farewell address by the first of January. Jackson had not asked Taney to aid in the preparation of his annual message. A number of paragraphs in Taney's letter of October 27, however, are so phrased as to appear to be suggestions for the message. He had no doubt that the Specie Circular had saved the West from bankruptcy and ruin, and had been beneficial to the East through inducing the banks to adopt a cautious policy sooner than they would otherwise have done, so that they were better able to meet the calls now made upon them. The pressure on the money market in England must in any case have been felt in the United States sooner or later, but the evil was largely due to the increase of paper money issues, initiated by the Bank of the United States during its last months under its national charter. The consequence was "to create a rage for wild and mad speculations, which in the nature of things, unless checked in some way or other, must grow worse and worse and extend wider and wider, until it will bear no further expansion, and then the bubble bursts and ruin follows." Taney was convinced that the Bank of the United States had attempted to produce this situation in order to influence the presidential election.

Taney repeated his criticisms of the deposit law enacted by Congress, and took occasion to criticize the merchants of the country, for whom he had never had great admiration. They were blaming the Specie Circular for their growing business difficulties, as they had blamed the removal of the deposits three years earlier. "In both cases," he declared, "they are the chief authors of their own difficulties, and they are obviously as a class more easily led astray by their political leaders than any other class of our citizens."

There would always be currency fluctuations, he contended, until the constitutional currency of gold and silver was restored. "I had hoped that the state governments would have seen their true inter-

[11] Taney to Jackson, Oct. 15, 1836, *ibid.*, p. 430.

ests and have entered more promptly and effectually upon the work of reformation. But I now fear that their general coöperation will hardly be obtained from the influence exercised in some of them by the paper-making corporations and speculators; and that it will become necessary for Congress to take some measures which may effectually prevent the issue of small notes. The currency will not be entirely stable until no note under twenty dollars can be issued and for my own part I should prefer to go up gradually to fifty." [12]

Jackson's annual message contained many of the ideas expressed in Taney's letter, although Jackson wrote that it lacked some of the energy with which he was accustomed to speaking on these subjects.[13] In spite of his defense the Senate hotly attacked the Specie Circular, and a bill phrased for the purpose of rescinding it was passed by a vote of forty-five to five. Benton fought the bill with all his might, warning against the menace of paper money issues. "I am one of those who promised gold, not paper," he declared in final protest. "I promised the currency of the Constitution, not the currency of corporations. I did not join in putting down the Bank of the United States, to put up a wilderness of local banks. I did not join in putting down the paper currency of a national bank, to put up a national paper currency of a thousand local banks. I did not strike Caesar to make Anthony master of Rome." [14] But Old Bullion might as well not have spoken at all. The Senate was tired of his speeches. After much debate and delay the House of Representatives also gave its sanction, but at so late a date that the bill met its death when Jackson withheld it until after the end of the session.

On another issue Jackson won a much coveted victory in the Senate, the last of a series of victories over the friends of the Bank of the United States. The bank itself had ceased to exist as an agent of the federal government. Taney, twice rejected by the Senate which had stood faithfully by the bank, was now Chief Justice of the United States. Amos Kendall was Postmaster General, in spite of enemies in

[12] Taney to Jackson, Oct. 27, 1836, *ibid.*, pp. 431–432.
[13] Jackson to Taney, Dec. 6, 1836, *Maryland Historical Magazine*, IV, 304.
[14] Benton, *Thirty Years' View*, I, 703.

the same group. Andrew Stevenson had at last been confirmed as minister to England. Van Buren was President-elect of the United States. The Senate Journal, however, still held the record of the censure of Jackson for his conduct in relation to the deposits, in spite of efforts to get it expunged. On January 16, 1837, Benton forced a vote on the issue. It was debated throughout the day, with administration enemies doing most of the talking. As darkness came the great chandelier was lighted, illuminating the chamber where the floor was crowded with members and privileged persons, and the galleries packed with spectators. At last Calhoun, Clay, and Webster each made a final indignant speech against the proceeding which had become inevitable, and by a vote of twenty-four to twenty-one it was decided to blot the censure from the records. On Benton's request the manuscript Journal was opened, and the clerk drew a black border around the offensive resolution and wrote across it "Expunged by order of the Senate, this 16th day of January, 1837." [15]

On February 9, hearing that the Supreme Court was about to adjourn, Jackson invited Taney to take a room with him as soon as the term was over.[16] Taney accepted the invitation, and completed his work on the farewell address which was to be released to the public as of March 4, 1837.[17] The address did not attract either then or later the attention that was desired for it, but it has points of interest as a revelation of the ideas of Jackson, and, perhaps even more, of Taney. It called attention to the fact that forty years had passed since the delivery of Washington's farewell address, during which a great experiment in government had proved a success. It called attention to dangers still besetting the government, however, in systematic efforts to create discord and to place party lines upon geographical distinctions. Without mentioning the word "nullification" it declared that the preservation of the Union depended on the enforcement of federal laws until declared void by the courts or repealed by Congress. Resistance could not be justified except in im-

[15] *Ibid.*, pp. 727–731.
[16] Jackson to Taney, Feb. 9, 1837, Taney MSS., Maryland Historical Society.
[17] See the *Messages and Papers of the Presidents*, III, 236–260.

probable instances so extreme as to make death preferable to submission.

Without directly mentioning the growing abolitionist agitation
which was proving highly offensive to the South, the address urged
that citizens of every state studiously avoid everything calculated to
wound the sensibility or offend the just pride of the people of other
states. Each state had the right to regulate its own concerns in its
own way, and "every state must be the sole judge of the measures
proper to secure the safety of its citizens and promote their happiness."

The extension of the powers of the federal government beyond
the lines marked by the Constitution was also listed as a point of
danger, as in the collection of revenue for distribution to the states.
Another danger would lie in the efforts of industrial interests to
restore high tariffs. Other dangers inevitably grew out of a paper
money system and the monopoly powers which it was instrumental
in placing in the hands of the few. The address warned against the
reëstablishment of a national bank—with an additional comment,
significant of events then current, that if moneyed interests were
defeated at this point they might regain their influence through
state banks unless the people were constantly on the alert.

The address closed with a personal touch: "My own race is nearly
run; advanced age and failing health warn me that before long I
must pass beyond the reach of human events and cease to feel the
vicissitudes of human affairs. I thank God that my life has been
spent in a land of liberty and that he has given me a heart to love
my country with the affection of a son. And filled with gratitude for
your constant and unwavering kindness, I bid you a last and affectionate farewell."

Taney's family came to Washington for the Van Buren inauguration, and joined him at the President's house. Jackson, although
quite feeble at the time, declared that nothing should prevent his
seeing the august spectacle at the Capitol. He wished to see the great
moral phenomenon of one citizen who had been proscribed as minister to London becoming President, sworn in by another who after

being twice rejected by the Senate had been made Chief Justice of the United States—and both changes effected by the force of public opinion in a free country.[18]

On March 4 Jackson and Van Buren drove to the Capitol in a carriage made from the timber of the frigate *Constitution,* escorted by the Potomac dragoons and a volunteer corps of infantry. On the eastern steps of the Capitol, Taney administered the oath of office to the first of the many Presidents who were to stand before his uplifted hand. When the ceremony was over, shouts and cheers arose, not so much for the new President as for the gray-haired private citizen who, battered and enfeebled by eight strenuous though victorious years, wended his way slowly down the steps to his waiting carriage.

On March 6 Jackson said affectionate farewells to his friends in Washington, and with his adopted son he took a train for Baltimore, where he visited at Taney's home. When he left Baltimore, Taney accompanied him for some distance as he proceeded slowly westward, applauded all along the line by friends and foes. "I must tell you that myself and four sons had the honor of shaking the bone of Old Hickory at Sykesville on Thursday last," wrote an estranged Marylander. ". . . He is quite infirm but spoke to all very affectionately and Sir, I must say I like the man with all my heart, but am sorry to think I know he has been led astray by others." [19] At some point in Maryland, probably at Frederick, making promises to meet at the Hermitage which were destined not to be fulfilled, Taney and Jackson said good-by. As Taney made his way sadly toward Baltimore, Jackson rode off toward the setting sun, never again to return.

The Van Buren administration began its life beneath the storm cloud of one of the worst business depressions the country has experienced. As he passed through the communities beyond the mountains, Jackson heard more and more of bankruptcies, closed banks, high

[18] Richmond *Enquirer,* quoted, Washington *Globe,* March 13, 1837. See also Jackson to Nicholas P. Trist, *Correspondence of Andrew Jackson,* V, 462–463.

[19] William Brown to Charles Brown, MS. in possession of Albert S. Brown, Frederick, Md.

interest rates, and acute distress. He wrote repeatedly to Van Buren directly or through F. P. Blair, urging him to watch the deposit banks lest the government money be lost. He urged likewise, however, that Van Buren must not retract on the measures of his administration, must not, above all things, rescind the Specie Circular. Only the bank crowd and the speculators were against it, he declared.

About the middle of March, Webster made a speech in New York denouncing the monetary policies of the Jackson party and demanding that the Specie Circular be rescinded. The demand was embodied in resolutions, and a committee was appointed to take them to Washington. Van Buren listened to the committee and then replied courteously—in writing, lest he be misquoted or misinterpreted as Jackson had been—that the demands must be refused.

Nicholas Biddle, finding or making an occasion to visit Washington, called on Van Buren in the hope that the new President would coöperate with him more easily than his predecessor. Van Buren received him politely, but made no reference to business matters. Thereupon the bank papers announced that Biddle had afforded the President the opportunity to confer with the head of the largest banking institution in the country on the existing state of things, and that the President had remained profoundly silent on the great and interesting topics of the day.

Unable to influence Van Buren directly, Biddle began a flirtation with Joel R. Poinsett, the Secretary of the Navy. Poinsett responded tentatively, and Biddle advised the repeal of the Specie Circular order and suggested that the administration make peace with his bank. He would then make arrangements with selected state banks throughout the country to act as his agents, and the old deposit system would be restored.[20] While making this proposition, however, he wrote to a South Carolina politician that the good of the country required the expulsion of the people now governing the country. The office of president had no attraction for himself, he declared. "Its dignity has been degraded by the elevation to it of unworthy men—and as to mere power, I have been for years in the daily

[20] Biddle to Poinsett, May 8, 1837, President's Letter Book, Biddle MSS.

exercise of more personal authority than any President habitually enjoys." [21]

Before Poinsett had had time to reply the crash came. On May 10, 1837, the New York banks suspended specie payments, and were followed by most of the banks throughout the country. The Bank of the United States surrendered along with the rest. Biddle declared it was not forced to suspend, but did so to conserve its strength pending a change in administration policies, when it would coöperate in restoring prosperity.[22] Nearly all the deposit banks suspended. Since the deposit law required that government money be placed only in specie-paying banks, Woodbury had to direct collectors to keep their collections in their own hands. Since most of the government-owned specie was in the deposit banks, expenditures had to be made largely in the irredeemable and often depreciated notes which the banks were willing to pay out, causing immense dissatisfaction and giving impetus to a political revolt against the administration. To deal with the crisis Van Buren was forced to call a special session of Congress, to meet the first Monday in September.

Taney watched developments with deep concern. Before the suspension he wrote to Van Buren advising against any modification of the banking and currency program of the preceding administration.[23] Afterward he expressed the belief to Jackson that the Bank of the United States stimulated the speculative mania to produce an explosion in the West which would result in the renewal of its charter. The bank, however, was nothing more than the whole class of the moneyed aristocracy with its following of greedy speculators and ambitious politicians. The root of all evil was paper currency. Without it the moneyed aristocracy would have no more than its fair share of power. He was convinced that no currency should be issued in denominations of less than fifty dollars.

He blamed the danger to the public funds upon the deposit law recently enacted by Congress. It required the banks to pay interest,

[21] Biddle to Thomas Cooper, May 8, 1837, *ibid.*
[22] See quotations, Benton, *Thirty Years' View*, II, 21–23.
[23] Taney to Van Buren, April 1, 1837, Van Buren MSS.

so that they had to be permitted to lend out the money instead of keeping it for the call of the government. The limitation on the amount to be placed in each bank required the selection of so many depositories that it was not possible to keep an adequate check on all of them, and they were so numerous that being chosen as a depository was not regarded as an honor as formerly, and had not the former restraining effect. "I could almost wish," Taney sighed, "that I was again at Washington with you at the head of the government to see it out." [24]

Bank papers and speakers jeered at the failure of the fiscal program of the government. Webster, denouncing the Specie Circular and demanding the recharter of the Bank of the United States, was applauded as a man created in God's own image.[25] Justice McLean wrote sarcastically that Van Buren had indeed carried *out* the policies of his predecessor.[26] When Biddle heard the government was planning to cut all connection with banks and keep the revenue in subtreasuries he remarked that this was the newest and therefore the favorite foolery. He thought Congress would have nothing to do with this or any other experiment, and would either charter a national bank or do business with his Pennsylvania bank.[27]

Van Buren wrote to Taney of the difficulty of arranging a program for Congress, and asked his advice on a number of points, promising to guard the privacy of the correspondence. Taney replied in a thoughtful letter of more than three thousand words. He thought the government should require the importing merchants of the country to pay duties in specie, and not extend the time for payment—on which an extension had already been granted after the suspension of specie payment by the banks. There was a close alliance between the Bank of the United States and the mercantile group. The merchants who had overtraded and speculated, including the mass of the leading merchants, now got credit from the bank on their duty bonds, and made money by the suspension. The banks of the country now as

---

[24] Taney to Jackson, July 3, 1837, *Correspondence of Andrew Jackson,* V, 491–494.
[25] Wilmington *Gazette,* Aug. 4, 1837.
[26] McLean to Biddle, July 10, 1837, Etting Coll., Historical Society of Pennsylvania.
[27] Biddle to John Rathbone, Jr., July 14, 1837, President's Letter Book, Biddle MSS.

in 1817 could not well resume payment until the merchants also were compelled to resume.

Opposed though he had been to the distribution of the surplus revenue among the states, Taney advised Van Buren to pay the fourth installment which was yet due. The government money was in the deposit banks. The government could not get specie from them, but the states would take the notes with which the banks would pay. If the money were not withdrawn in this form the government would find itself encumbered for years with the item of unavailable funds which it could never recover from the deposit banks. It would be better to clear its books. If the merchants were required to redeem their duty bonds, the expenses of the government could be met without new taxes or loans. He advised against issuing Treasury notes to circulate as money. They would constitute another form of the insidious paper currency.

Perhaps prejudiced in favor of the system which he had set up, Taney opposed the resort to subtreasuries as places of deposit. He felt that it would greatly increase the patronage of the government. If the corruption which had so long struggled for power should once succeed in placing one of its instruments in the executive chair, every increase of its power to purchase support would add to the difficulty of dislodging it. The people, furthermore, would have greater confidence in the safety of the public money if it was deposited in banks in the proper manner than if kept by political officers.

"My plan would be this," Taney continued. "Let Congress authorize the Secretary of the Treasury to select as many banks as he may find necessary as depositories, make the deposit a *special deposit* to be all in specie, not to be touched for any purpose but upon the order of the proper officer of the government, take security for the faithful keeping and disbursement of the money, and inflict penalties for a violation of duty. In a word place the public money in deposits in truth and in fact, and do not as was done by the present law, under the name of deposit, loan it to the banks on interest, so as to make them borrowers and not depositories. But few banks would be necessary upon this plan, and the government would have to pay them a moderate commission for the receipt and disbursement of the money, not exceeding annually some certain sum to be named in the law."

Lest he be suspected of selfish motives in the matter, Taney referred to the charges which Clay had once based upon his possession of stock in the Union Bank of Maryland, and assured Van Buren that he now held not a single share in any bank, and owed no bank a single dollar. He closed his letter by reminding Van Buren of the delicacy of his position, and urging that it be made known only to those worthy of confidence.[28]

Much as he may have valued Taney's opinion, Van Buren was under such pressure from contending groups that few of his recommendations to Congress were those which Taney had made. The decisions made by Congress were for the most part still less in harmony with Taney's ideas. The friends of the Bank of the United States attributed the panic to the government's desertion of that institution, and found its cure in penitent return to the bank. Clay demanded to know whether the overtrading and extension of bank facilities were not the necessary and immediate consequences of the removal of the deposits and the overthrow of the bank. "And is not this proven," he asked, "by the vast multiplication of banks, the increase of the line of their discounts and accommodations prompted and stimulated by Secretary Taney and the great augmentation of their circulation which ensued?" [29]

Webster scornfully recalled Jackson's and Taney's assurances that the notes of the deposit banks would furnish the country with as good a currency as it had ever enjoyed, and probably a better, which would accomplish all that could be wished in regard to domestic exchanges. "The substitution of state banks for a national institution, for the discharge of these duties, was that operation, which has become known, and is likely to be long remembered, as the 'experiment.' . . . But the 'experiment' came to a dishonored end in the early part of May." [30]

[28] Taney to Van Buren, July 20, 1837, Van Buren MSS.
[29] *Congressional Globe*, 25th Cong., 1st sess., Appendix, p. 179.
[30] *Ibid.*, p. 168.

Calhoun deserted Clay and Webster, with whom he had had little in common except hostility to Jackson. He felt that Van Buren could be compelled to rely upon the support of the South, and that the time had come to break the control of the North over southern industry and commerce.[31] He supported the administration bill to keep government revenues in the hands of public officers, in what came to be known as subtreasuries.

The subtreasury bill passed the Senate at the special session, but was tabled by the House of Representatives. A new bill was introduced at the beginning of the regular session. Biddle aided in the attempt to defeat what he called an insane scheme to "break down all the great interests of the country." [32] The bill passed the Senate but was defeated in the House of Representatives, and the opposition made a counter attack and brought about the rescinding of the Specie Circular. In the meantime, in spite of the opposition of the Bank of the United States, the New York banks had resumed specie payments. Biddle prevented such action on the part of his own bank and many others, however, until after his victory in Congress. The repeal of the Specie Circular and the defeat of the subtreasury bill, Biddle declared, were results exclusively of the course pursued by the Bank of the United States.[33] His cause had been weakened by the desertion of the two and a half per cent patriots in New York, but still he had succeeded.[34]

Biddle won another victory over the administration. An arrangement had been made by which his bank was to pay the government for its stock in the old Bank of the United States with three bonds, maturing on the first day in October in 1838, 1839, and 1840 respectively. The government, because of inadequate appropriations, needed the money at once, but was unable to sell the bonds. Biddle offered to advance the money on the first and second of them, and perhaps on the third, if the money could be credited to the government and paid out as needed for government expenses. His offer was accepted,

[31] Calhoun to J. E. Calhoun, Sept. 7, 1837, *Correspondence of John C. Calhoun*, p. 377.
[32] Biddle to Clay, Feb. 3, 1838, Biddle MSS.
[33] Biddle to Samuel Jaudon, June 29, 1838, President's Letter Book, Biddle MSS.
[34] Biddle to Jaudon, Aug. 3, 1838, *ibid.*

so that to the amount of the bonds his bank again became the government depository, and resumed the performance of its former functions.

By a mixture of implied threats and promises Biddle attempted to prevent Van Buren from advocating a subtreasury bill in his annual message of December 3, 1838, but without success.[35] There was no break with Biddle, however, and in the latter part of February ensuing he received an invitation to dine with the President. Apparently his influence with the administration was growing. At this point something happened of which the explanation is not clear. Without warning, making reference to the condition of his health, and to the fact that the bank was now so prosperous that his services were no longer needed, Biddle resigned as its president. In the following summer it suspended specie payments, and dragged down with it a large percentage of the banks of the country. When the stockholders forced an investigation they discovered that most of their property was gone, as the result of misuse or misappropriation by officers.

Biddle claimed that the bank had been in good condition when he left it, but although there was evidence of staggering abuses after the date of his resignation there was also evidence that the loose policies instituted by him had been at the base of the disaster. The bank permanently closed its doors, and was the object of lawsuits for many years thereafter. Biddle and others were indicted for conspiracy to defraud the stockholders. They were arrested but were released on writs of habeas corpus from friendly judges. They were never punished.[36]

"The great Regulator too has fallen," Taney wrote to Jackson, "and we have both lived to see everything we said and did verified and justified. What would have been the condition of the United States now if its whole revenue was in its vaults?"[37] Pleased with this evidence of justification, he set about preparing an account of the dismissal of Duane from the Treasury Department, to be pre-

[35] See Biddle to John Forsyth, Nov. 27, 1838, and Forsyth to Biddle, Nov. 29, 1838, *ibid.*
[36] See Benton, *Thirty Years' View*, II, 365-373.
[37] Taney to Jackson, Nov. 4, 1839, Jackson MSS.

served for the future in refutation of an expanded version of Duane's account which had recently been published.

The failure of the bank gave impetus to the subtreasury bill, and it became a law near the end of the 1839–40 session. It was not a sweeping victory, however, for the years of depression had made inroads upon the Democratic party, and the future was ominous. The Whigs, the friends of central banking, made the most of their opportunities. For the election of 1836 they nominated William Henry Harrison, a war hero, forbade him to discuss issues, and put on a campaign of ballyhoo. They elected him to the presidency, with John Tyler, a Virginia state-rights Whig, as Vice President. It was of the irony of fate that Harrison died a month after his inauguration, leaving the presidency to a man who, although he had made a report in 1834 defending the Bank of the United States against the Jackson administration, had always believed the chartering of a national bank to be unconstitutional.

When the Whig Congress passed a bill chartering a Fiscal Bank of the United States, Tyler vetoed it, and the party was unable to pass it over the veto. The Whigs were enraged at the President, and deserted him when they learned they could not control him. They repealed the subtreasury act, but got no farther with their program, and another subtreasury act was passed during the ensuing administration of James K. Polk.

Taney was "most agreeably disappointed" with Tyler's veto of the bank bill, having judged him chiefly by his Senate report in 1834.[38] He felt that he and Jackson had now been amply vindicated. In part at least he probably became reconciled to the use of subtreasuries as depositories instead of state banks. In the matter of the establishment of a specie currency, however, he had to admit the failure of his program. The people had not the hardihood to face that rigid discipline, and were destined to go on bruising themselves against the inevitable results of excessive issues of paper money.

The defeat of the national bank party, however, made it impossible for many years for one coterie of bankers to sit at their desks

[38] Taney to Jackson, Sept. 30, 1841, *ibid.*

and play with the destinies of all the people of the country. Such a defeat was no mean achievement to reflect upon in less active years in a dignified judicial position. To be sure, new alliances of moneyed men in future years won for themselves much of the power which Biddle had lost, and used it no less ruthlessly in their own interests, but Taney and his colleagues of the bank war can hardly be held responsible for the conduct of future generations. Should the shades of Taney and his fellow warriors now gather before the unkempt building in Chestnut Street, Philadelphia, once known as "Nick Biddle's Marble Palace," who is to say they would not be justified in returning to their resting places with a comforting sigh of "Well done"?

Chapter XVII

THE NEW SUPREME COURT

The relatively high prestige which belonged to the Supreme Court of the United States at the time of Taney's appointment had been acquired for the most part during the years when John Marshall was Chief Justice. John Jay, the first Chief Justice, had preferred the position of governor of New York, and resigned from the bench to accept it. Oliver Ellsworth, Marshall's immediate predecessor, had resigned because of his preference for a diplomatic post. Alexander Hamilton, preferring private practice, had refused to accept the position of head of the court. Evidently he had no conception of the way in which that institution could be used to establish his ideas more firmly in the constitutional law of the country. No one, it seems safe to say, had at the time of Marshall's appointment a clear conception of the position of prominence which the court was to take in the federal government.

The growth of its prestige was coincident with and a part of the growth of the prestige of the legal profession in the United States. Lawyers and the English common law, which was their principal stock in trade, had been in low repute with the masses at the time of the Revolution. The need for the settlement of innumerable doubtful titles to property in the new country had, however, necessitated much litigation, and necessary litigation had created a demand for trained lawyers. Since the demand for outstanding legal ability was greater than the supply, the aristocrats of the bar were generally in position to choose whom they would serve, and at what price. Clients were individuals, or partnerships, or small corporations, employing legal aid spasmodically as they needed it. With the limited exception of the Bank of the United States, there were no great corporations practically monopolizing the services of the more eminent lawyers. The clients did not have lawyers so much as the lawyers had clients. The Frenchman, De Tocqueville, making a survey of America during the Jackson period, came to the conclusion that the legal profession constituted the only real aristocracy in the United States, the only barrier against the leveling influences of mass rule.

Naturally enough, the clients who employed high-priced lawyers were usually the possessors of substantial amounts of property. It was to protect or to acquire property that lawyers were retained. It is therefore not surprising that lawyers, like clients, were highly property-conscious; that property and legal ability and the rising aristocracy were becoming more and more closely allied; and that the alliance was distrustful of and to a degree hostile to the unpropertied masses, and to those who preached the preservation of human rights as against the rights of property. The rise of the legal profession in the United States, therefore, was coincident with and a part of the rise of a class, within what, in terms of democratic theory, was supposed to be a classless society.

The unfolding of the powers and the development of the reputation of the Supreme Court was a part of the same movement. Chief Justice Marshall's first great judicial opinion, in *Marbury* v. *Madison*,[1] is not immediately relevant, though in claiming for his court the power to determine the constitutionality of acts of Congress he paved the way for the use of that power by his successors to protect property from federal legislation. The more important of his later opinions are usually hailed as providing the basis for strengthening the national government. Such, however, was their immediate purpose in only a limited degree. Most of them do not assert the power of Congress to legislate, or the power of the federal Executive to administer. They assert, instead, that the states *may not* legislate in a fashion hostile to property. The addition to the strength of the national government is chiefly in the exercise of a veto power by the judiciary.

To choose a few examples, the result of one case[2] was to prevent

[1] 1 Cranch 137 (1803).
[2] *Fletcher* v. *Peck*, 6 Cranch 87 (1810).

a state legislature from recapturing property granted away by a corrupt predecessor. Another claimed for the Supreme Court the power to review cases decided by the highest courts in the states when federal questions were involved.[3] Another sanctified the creation by Congress of a national bank, which was essentially a great private financial institution, on the ground that it was an instrumentality of the federal government, and then denied to the states the power to tax the notes of that institution.[4] Another translated corporation charters into contracts which the states were forbidden to impair.[5] Another struck down state bankruptcy laws relieving debtors from obligations incurred before the laws were passed.[6] Another devitalized similar laws applying to obligations incurred after the laws were passed to the extent of holding that the debtor was relieved only in the courts of the state in which the bankruptcy laws were passed.[7] Another went a long way in the direction of the argument of Daniel Webster that the states might not legislate on interstate or foreign commerce even if there was no conflict with an act of Congress.[8] Another denied the right of the states to tax goods which had been imported until after sale or the breaking of the original package.[9] Another killed a state law under which the state borrowed money by issuing notes which were small enough to circulate as money.[10]

So the story goes, in terms of the better known decisions of the Marshall period. He wrote the opinions of the court in all but two of them, and on them the celebrity of John Marshall largely depends. It is true that where the conduct of the external affairs of the United States was involved, as in the acquisition of territory,[11] he interpreted broadly the positive powers of the federal government. Such powers were not at issue, however, in most of the important

[3] *Martin* v. *Hunter's Lessee,* 1 Wheaton 304 (1816).
[4] *McCulloch* v. *Maryland,* 4 Wheaton 316 (1819).
[5] *Dartmouth College* v. *Woodward,* 4 Wheaton 518 (1819).
[6] *Sturges* v. *Crowninshield,* 4 Wheaton 122 (1819).
[7] *Ogden* v. *Saunders,* 12 Wheaton 213 (1827).
[8] *Gibbons* v. *Ogden,* 9 Wheaton 1 (1824).
[9] *Brown* v. *Maryland,* 12 Wheaton 419 (1827).
[10] *Craig* v. *Missouri,* 4 Peters 410 (1830).
[11] *American Insurance Company* v. *Canter,* 1 Peters 511 (1829).

cases which came before him. The question was as to whether or not the court should so use its prerogative of interpreting the Constitution as to prevent state interference with property, in the enforcement of laws supposed to have been enacted for the public good. In voicing a sturdy "Thou shalt not," the court won from property its vaunted reputation as the guardian of the Constitution, and made itself the kingpin of the lawyer-property alliance.

It is not to be inferred that Marshall was a thoughtful student of John Locke's ideas concerning property, or that he was a glowing apostle of Adam Smith. Marshall did not read widely even in his own field, and he seems to have been almost wholly unlearned outside it. All he did was give persuasive utterance to the prevailing beliefs of the propertied classes of his times, in the terminology of constitutional law. Few or none of his ideas were new. Those which can not be found in the *Federalist* or in other writings of Hamilton were part of the current notions of those people who had property which they wanted protected but otherwise let alone.

The popularity of John Marshall, therefore, and the prestige acquired by the Supreme Court during his régime, resulted largely from the fact that he wrote into constitutional law the beliefs and prejudices of a class, the class, incidentally, from whose records and in terms of whose judgments most of the history of the period has been written. Outside that class he and his court were anything but popular, as is shown by the wrathful outpourings of Thomas Jefferson, Judge Spencer Roane and others during his early years as Chief Justice, and by the criticisms of the partisans of Old Hickory during the Jackson period.

Some of the opposition came doubtless from that ever present group who are critical because property is in the hands of the wrong people, with the implication that the right people are themselves. Some of it came from the holders of one kind of property, who believed that other kinds were being protected and nurtured at their expense, as for example the landholders of the South who saw themselves injured by the manipulations of a national government with pro-industrial and pro-banker leanings. Opposition came likewise from the great debtor and small-property class who had little expectation of achieving great wealth under any régime, and from their doctrinaire friends who rejected the theory that unqualified protection of property produced inevitably the highest possible total of human welfare.

Strong though the opposition was, Marshall so dominated the opinions of his brethren on the court that it was not until near the closing years of his life that a reversal of the trend of decisions was seriously threatened. With the coming of old age, however, he lost some of the captivating persuasiveness by which he had hitherto carried his brethren with him, and opposition within the court became more and more apparent. The accession to power of Jacksonian democracy revealed the strength of the advocates of change, and the prospect that Jackson would fill vacancies on the bench with men of his own point of view suggested the coming of a new order in judicial decisions. Conservatives of course resisted the tendency toward change. Able lawyers who supported it were regarded as little more than renegades—as witness the treatment of Taney—and the blatantly satisfied clamored for the perpetuation of the constitutional interpretations worked out by John Marshall and the Godlike Daniel.

The worst was feared, of course, when Taney, the arch-enemy of the Bank of the United States and critic of the merchant class, with heretical notions as to the interpretation of the Constitution and as to the authority of the court, was chosen as Marshall's successor. Would the court, under his guidance, surrender its guardianship over the rights of property and leave it at the mercy of state legislatures dominated by the masses of the people?

The answer to this question was to come gradually in terms of a long line of decisions on various topics, some related and some highly divergent. Those decisions fall into three major groups. The first group had to do with the interpretation of the rights of corporations, with the question as to whether the court should interpret corporation charters broadly, as it had hitherto interpreted the Constitution itself, or whether, in the interest of the public, they should be interpreted narrowly. The second group of decisions had to do with the interpretation of the commerce clause of the Constitution. The question was not usually one of whether or not Congress had a certain power over interstate or foreign commerce. It was usually a question as to whether the states could enforce regulatory laws which affected such commerce, but which did not conflict with any act of Congress. The third group of decisions had to do with property in connection with the "peculiar institution" of the South, that is to say, with slavery. It is in terms of the dramatic judicial controversies over these subjects, together with sketches of personal and political backgrounds, that the chapters dealing with Taney's work as Chief Justice are presented.

The Supreme Court was composed of seven members during Taney's first year as its head, and of nine members thereafter. None of the judges resided permanently in Washington. Although one of them occasionally brought his wife with him when he came to the capital each January for the annual term of the court it was more usual to come alone. For many years arrangements had been made in advance for all the judges to live at the same boarding house and take their meals at the same table. This intimate living arrangement, indeed, which made possible the discussion of the work of the court at all hours, may have been largely responsible for the captivating influence which John Marshall exercised over the minds of his brethren. Certain it is that he thoroughly approved of this mode of living, and his many letters mentioning the subject show his desire to have the custom continued as long as he retained his position.

As if by inertia the judges, or those of them who could live peacefully together, continued to live in this fashion for a number of years after Taney's appointment, until a time, around 1850, when because of the presence of wives or for some other reason it was thought best that each should choose his own residence. The cost of living may have added to the attraction of the traditional arrangement, and in addition to the arduousness of long-distance travel may have been a reason for leaving wives at home. Members of the bachelor group could get accommodations for from sixteen to seventeen dollars a week, while a man and wife had to pay forty.[12]

The judges moved about from year to year among the several boarding houses which catered to their trade. In the autumn of 1837 the clerk of the court was in doubt as to whether to choose the accommodations offered by Dawson's on the hill, or those of the Misses Polk.[13] In 1839 Taney was at Elliott's, on Pennsylvania Avenue, as he told his son-in-law in a letter asking for a box of his long, black cigars.[14] In 1841 he lived at Mrs. Turner's, likewise on the Avenue.[15] Accommodations varied greatly in quality, as Taney found to his discomfort. "I have not been fortunate in our boarding arrangements," he wrote in 1840, again to his son-in-law. "My room is very good. I would not desire a better one, but all the rest of the house is more comfortless than you can well imagine. I do not speak of the chambers of the other judges for they are all pretty good, but of the dining room, food, servants &c. &c. You can imagine nothing more abominably filthy." Yet the woman in charge had just lost her husband, he hastened to say, and had a house full of children. The judges therefore took their evils good humoredly. Nothing must be said against the house to injure its reputation in Baltimore, for he was convinced that the woman did as well as she was able.[16]

Taney received a salary of $5,000 annually, while his colleagues received $4,500. They were paid less than the Secretaries of State, War, and Navy, who received $6,000, and more than the Postmaster General and Attorney General, who received $4,000. In addition to their work in Washington each of the judges had to preside over circuit courts in the several circuits to which they were assigned. The policy of requiring them to ride circuit had long been a source of controversy. The judges and their friends claimed that it was unreasonable to require elderly men, after serving in the Supreme Court, to ride hundreds of miles over rough roads and through rough country

[12] See W. T. Carroll to Smith Thompson, Dec. 15, 1837, MS., N.Y. Historical Society.
[13] *Ibid.*
[14] Taney to J. Mason Campbell, Feb. 8, 1839, MS., Huntington Library.
[15] Washington *Globe,* Feb. 26, 1841.
[16] Taney to J. Mason Campbell, Feb. 9, 1840, Campbell MSS.

to preside over local courts when they ought to be in Washington or elsewhere adding to their knowledge of law.

The opposition replied that an important task of the Supreme Court was the application of local law in cases involving citizens of different states, and that service in the circuit courts provided excellent opportunities for learning about local conditions and local law. It was feared that if the judges established themselves in Washington and lost contact with the circuits they would become more than ever the tools of a national government for interfering with the powers of the states.[17]

Taney held two terms of the circuit court in Baltimore each year, and one each in New Castle and Dover, Delaware. The Delaware terms required strenuous trips by stagecoach over a total of more than three hundred miles. In addition he had to go to Washington each January for the regular term of the Supreme Court, and in August for a vestigial term at which he alone was required to be present. The Washington trip could now be made over the Baltimore and Ohio Railroad, and was not difficult except for the fact that he found the crowded condition of the cars oppressive in winter time.

Difficult as it was, Taney's burden was light as compared with that of his brethren. Whereas he estimated his annual travels at 458 miles,[18] Justice Story listed 1,896 miles, besides innumerable trips from his home in Cambridge to Boston.[19] Justice Barbour, who lived at Richmond, made an estimate of 952 miles.[20] Justice Wayne, who lived in Savannah, found a total of 2,370.[21] Justice Thompson, from Poughkeepsie, estimated at 2,590.[22] Justice McLean, of Richmond, in Ohio, covered 2,500 miles.[23] Justices Catron and McKinley, who were added to the Supreme Court in 1837 and were assigned to

---

[17] The Federalist party, in 1800, just before it lost control of Congress, provided for the creation of new circuit court judgeships and for the relief of the Supreme Court judges from circuit duty. The motives were largely partisan, however, and the fact that the new positions were filled with lame-duck Federalists led to the repeal of the law.

[18] Taney to John Forsyth, Sept. 9, 1838, Miscellaneous Letters, Department of State.

[19] Story to Forsyth, July 28, 1838, *ibid.*

[20] Barbour to Forsyth, July 28, 1838, *ibid.*

[21] Wayne to Forsyth, July 31, 1838, *ibid.*

[22] Thompson to Forsyth, Aug. 1, 1838, *ibid.*

[23] McLean to Forsyth, Aug. 3, 1838, *ibid.*

new circuits in the West, estimated their prescribed travels at 3,852 and 10,000 miles respectively.[24]

The difficulties of travel were often distressing and at times insuperable. McLean told of a trip through Indiana when the mud was so deep as to be almost impassable to a carriage of any description, on which the mails and passengers had to be conveyed in common wagons. McKinley declared that "upon some of the roads there are no private conveyances; and the time allowed for holding the courts would render it impossible to perform the traveling by any private mode. I have never yet been at Little Rock, the place of holding the court in Arkansas, but from the best information I can obtain it could not be conveniently approached in the spring of the year, except by water, and by that route the distance would be greatly increased." Catron complained that when he had made the trip to Washington, gone back westward down the Ohio River to St. Louis, and returned to Tennessee, he had been away from his home in Nashville for six or seven months.[25]

Taney's judicial duties began on April 8, 1836, when he first presided over the United States circuit court in Baltimore, doubtless under the eyes of many who were eager to see if the advocate and the partisan would be submerged in the judge. Daniel Webster, in a mood of unusual frankness, once expressed doubt as to his own ability to be a judge. He had mixed so much study of politics with the study of law that although he had some respect for himself as an advocate he was not confident of possessing the accuracy and precision

[24] Catron to Forsyth, Aug. 4, 1838; McKinley to Forsyth, Aug. 10, 1838, *ibid.*

[25] The alignment of the circuits was a cause of no little friction among the judges. Many attempts were made to bring about realignments so as to equalize burdens, but the task proved virtually impossible. A letter from Taney to McLean (May 5, 1840, McLean MSS.) reveals the fact that Catron and Baldwin attempted to lobby through Congress a bill to make changes advantageous to themselves. Catron letters of a later date show his deep interest in the making of readjustments (Catron to Garrett D. Wall, Feb. 25 and 26, 1841, Dreer Collection, Historical Society of Pennsylvania). Only on the subject of the court reporter did the judges reveal a greater capacity for internal wrangling. In 1843, after a long period of discontent, Baldwin, Wayne, Catron, and Daniel, taking advantage of the absence of Story and McKinley, brought about the dismissal of Richard Peters as reporter and chose Taney's friend Benjamin C. Howard in his stead. Story felt deeply wounded by the strategy employed. (See Catron to James Buchanan, Aug. 4, 1842, Buchanan MSS.; Taney to J. Mason Campbell, Jan. 27, 1843, Campbell MSS.; Story to McLean, Feb. 9, 1843, McLean MSS.; and Charles Warren, *Supreme Court in United States History*, II, 106–107.)

which the bench required.[26] Taney may have had similar moments of self-questioning, and, although he must have known as well as Webster that the administration of law could not be completely severed from politics, he did set watch upon all his political utterances and activities which might become known to the public.

He exercised notable self-restraint and shrewd political caution in his charge to the grand jury at the opening of the circuit court. From the time of the organization of the federal courts it had been the custom of the judges to deliver to grand juries long discourses on broad principles of jurisprudence and on the nature of the federal system. Since the federal judiciary had been the stronghold of the Federalist party, the charges had often been resolved into proclamations of party principles, much to the disgust and resentment of the opposition. Taney announced to his first grand jury that he had a few words to say, not in compliance with the custom of delivering charges, of which he disapproved, but to give his reason for dispensing with the usage. He thought the court should enter at once with promptness and industry upon the performance of its duties, disencumbered of all unnecessary forms. The age had passed which called for particular instructions from the court. The intelligence of the jurors was adequate for their duties, and if they needed technical information the district attorney could provide it for them. It was unnecessary that the court should discourse on the wide field of jurisprudence when the only cases for the jury were a few infractions of criminal law. He therefore merely advised that the jury examine testimony with diligence, finding a bill when and only when they were clearly convinced of guilt, remembering that "our liberties and the permanency of our free institutions could only be secured by maintaining the supremacy of the laws, securing to the innocent the enjoyment of their rights, and visiting the violator of the law with the punishment due to his guilt." [27]

Taney was in a sense acting politically in this abnegation of a

[26] Webster to Hiram Ketchum, Dec. 18, 1840, *Writings and Speeches of Daniel Webster*, XVIII, 96.

[27] Baltimore *Gazette*, quoted, *Niles' Weekly Register*, April 16, 1836. See also Tyler, *Memoir of Roger Brooke Taney*, pp. 270–271.

privilege which had become a tradition with his predecessors. Since it had been exercised largely by Federalists for Federalist purposes, their enemies were on record as opposing it. Taney's gesture of self-restraint was hailed as a Democratic gesture by the spokesmen of the Jackson party. On the other hand it was much less obnoxious to political opponents than a positive assertion of Democratic principles would have been.

Taney and Upton S. Heath, his friend of the bank war period and now a United States district judge, sat together in the circuit court. It was said that Taney presided in a manner courteous but firm, which won the approval of the public and more particularly of the bar.[28] Most of the cases decided were unimportant. In one of them,[29] however, Taney's interpretation of law was significant. The case was a suit by sailors to recover wages from an owner who had lost his freight through an illegal capture, but had won back part of the value of the freight in a suit for damages.

The law of the sea was not particularly friendly to the interests of sailors. It had been molded through its centuries of development not by sailors in the interest of sailors, but by judges whose training and associations generally led them to sympathize with the viewpoint of the propertied classes. They had worked out the principle that "freight is the mother of wages," which meant that sailors were entitled to wages only if the freight carried was delivered, or compensation recovered for it. The principle was justified by the assumption that sailors would not work hard enough and risk their lives for vessel and cargo unless their wages were at stake. A sailor could not even protect his prospect for wages by insurance, for if he were thus assured of compensation he might defend against pirates with abated zeal, or he might wrestle less valiantly in the midst of storms.

Furthermore, if a cargo was lost and the owner was recompensed by insurance, he was under no obligation to pay wages to his sailors. Since the compensation of the owner came from insurance, and since sailors could not insure their wages, the collection of wages from the

[28] Boston *Statesman*, Jan. 28, 1837.
[29] *Ardrey* v. *Karthaus*, Federal Cases, No. 511.

money paid to this owner would be doing indirectly that which could not be done directly, and would therefore shock the sense of justice possessed by the spokesmen of the law. It would also deplete the purse of the owner, and it might also be bad for insurance companies, in that sailors might not in the future strive hard enough to protect cargoes which were covered by insurance!

In the case before Taney the cargo had been condemned by the British, during the War of 1812, after Spain had illegally permitted it to be captured in her waters. The owner won compensation not in full but in part, and not from an insurance company but from Spain. The owner refused to pay wages, perhaps on the theory that sailors should be taught not to permit cargoes to be captured by the enemies of their country. It is not surprising, in view of his knowledge of the blatant selfishness of mercantile interests, that Taney refused in this case to follow the analogy of the insurance cases, declaring that he could see no principle of justice which required him to do so. Nor is it particularly surprising that he held that the wages must be paid in full even though the owner had not been recompensed in full, and had been put to great expense to make the collection.

In his discussion Taney adhered closely to the legal points involved, and refrained from elaborating on what he called principles of justice. There was nothing startling in the decision itself or in the way in which the opinion was written. Yet there was a suggestion of an emphasis upon the rights of non-propertied people which was alien to the decisions of John Marshall and most of his colleagues, and which bore promise of a new trend in the development of law.

Taney sat with his brethren of the Supreme Court for the first time on January 9, 1837, when he was slightly less than sixty years of age. As if in token of the changing order the semicircular court room in the basement of the Capitol had been redecorated. Back of each of the seven mahogany desks was set a new mahogany armchair covered with velvet. Light sifted feebly through the windows back of the seats of the judges, to melt down upon the cushioned sofas arranged for spectators in the middle of the room.[30] At twelve o'clock Taney and five of his colleagues, Justice Wayne being absent, garbed themselves in the robes of office and took their places, Taney in the central position belonging to the Chief Justice and his associates arranged on either side of him alternately according to seniority.

Taney impressed spectators as tall, narrow of face, with clear black hair and an elasticity of step that hardly suggested his three-score years. There was something of portent, perhaps, in the fact that beneath his official robe he wore ordinary democratic garb, instead of the knee breeches customarily donned by his predecessor for the occasion.[31] He was the first Chief Justice, it was said, to depart from precedent and give judgment in trousers.[32]

Joseph Story, who sat at Taney's right, was two and a half years younger. He was of medium height, slightly portly of build, with expressive features, spectacles on nose, high and broad forehead, and hair that hung down over the collar of his robe. He had been a member of the court since 1811, and had been a closer friend of Marshall's and probably more deeply in sympathy with his ideas than any other of his colleagues. He had undoubtedly coveted the succession for himself, while knowing full well that Andrew Jackson would never confer it upon him. He was a voluminous writer on legal subjects, dabbled in poetry, was a fluent conversationalist, and had great personal charm. He viewed the passing of the old order of things, however, with a despair that shrouded the remaining eight years of his life with gloom.

At Taney's left sat Smith Thompson, sixty-nine years of age, gray-haired, and spare almost to the point of emaciation. He had been a member of the court since 1823, when James Monroe chose him for the position rather than Martin Van Buren, who coveted it. He had recently married a young wife, whom he gallantly attended in the midst of the social life of the capital.[33]

---

[30] See William Elliott, *The Washington Guide* (1837), p. 97; E. F. Ellet, *Court Circles of the Republic*, p. 192; and contemporary newspaper comment.

[31] See *Perley's Reminiscences*, I, 85.

[32] "The Supreme Court," *United States Magazine and Democratic Review*, Jan., 1838.

[33] Boston *Atlas*, quoted, Boston *Statesman*, Jan. 28, 1837.

At Story's right sat John McLean, fifty-two years of age, well built, with clear-cut features and an expression suggesting strength of character and of intellect. He had been a member of the court since 1829, when Jackson, seeking to reward him for not supporting John Quincy Adams, his former chief, for the presidency but unwilling to retain him as Postmaster General because of his reluctance to remove old employees to make way for deserving Jacksonians, had offered him the vacant position on the bench. McLean's friends had long ago succeeded in convincing him that he was of presidential timber, and his reputation as a judge had suffered and was to continue to suffer because he was never able to keep that subject out of his mind. He was friendly to Nicholas Biddle and to the Bank of the United States. He aligned himself with the Whigs, although he would probably have willingly led any party strong enough to make him president. In most respects he was probably closer to Story than any other member of the court.

At Thompson's left sat Henry Baldwin, fifty-seven years of age, the logical but emotional and at times intellectually unbalanced Pennsylvanian whom Jackson had appointed in 1830. A reporter, knowing something of Baldwin's reputation, wrote: "I expected to find a little, cross, crabbed old man. He is, on the contrary, a large, full favored, black haired, quaker looking gentleman, of the most prepossessing exterior—industrious, attentive, careful, and I should think, exceedingly agreeable and obliging." [34] He was not always as agreeable or obliging as he seemed, however, as some of his colleagues and as the court reporter, Richard Peters, might have told.

At McLean's right was a vacant seat which would be occupied by James M. Wayne when he arrived from Georgia. Wayne was the youngest, perhaps the handsomest, and socially the most versatile member of the court. He had received his appointment from Jackson in 1835. At Baldwin's left sat Philip P. Barbour, fifty-three years of age, whose appointment and confirmation dated with those of Taney. He was an old-fashioned state-rights Virginian, with many years of political experience and with a brief experience as a federal district judge. He was not impressive in appearance, and he was to

[34] *Ibid.*

be the first of the group to leave the bench, but during the five terms which they served together there is reason for believing that no colleague had closer friendship with Taney than did he.

The meeting of the court on the first day of the term was, as usual, but a matter of form, and was adjourned when Taney had announced that he would begin the call of the calendar on the following day, postponing the calling of cases involving constitutional questions, however, until the entire membership of the court was present. There were about sixty cases on the docket, in only a few of which constitutional questions were involved. These few were the important cases, however, the cases which would give some basis for predicting the changes which the new personnel of the court would make in the trend of constitutional development.

Of these the most important was the Charles River Bridge Case,[35] which had been argued before the Supreme Court six years earlier, but which, because of the absence of judges and lack of agreement among those present, remained yet to be decided. The case had its roots far back in history, yet it had intimate connection with the most controversial constitutional and economic problems of the day. In 1650 the legislature of Massachusetts, assuming the control over public ferries which under the common law belonged to the government, had given aid to the new institution for higher education established at Cambridge by granting to the president of Harvard College the power, by lease or otherwise, to dispose of the ferry which crossed the tidewater Charles River between Charlestown and Boston.

The college had kept the ferry and received the profits from it until 1785. In that year a number of men, setting forth the inconvenience of transportation by ferries over the Charles River, petitioned the legislature to be incorporated for the purpose of erecting a bridge across the river in the place where the ferry was then kept. The petition was granted, and the company was empowered to erect the bridge and to collect tolls from passengers for a period of forty years, during which time two hundred pounds were to be paid an-

[35] *Charles River Bridge* v. *Warren Bridge*, 11 Peters 420 (1837).

nually to Harvard College, in lieu of the profits which might have been received had the ferry not been discontinued. At the end of the forty years the bridge was to become the property of the state, except that the state would still be obligated to make a reasonable annual payment to the college.

The bridge was built, at considerable financial risk to the builders, for because of climatic and soil conditions there were reasonable doubts as to whether a bridge across what was virtually an arm of the sea would remain in place long enough to pay for itself. The bridge was opened to traffic, and so profitable and so convenient did it prove, that as the population of the region increased it was desired to build other bridges in the vicinity. In 1792 the legislature chartered another company to build a bridge across the same river between Cambridge and Boston. The proprietors of the first bridge protested against the building of the second on the ground that it would divert some traffic and revenue from the first, even though it was some distance away. The legislature, without admitting that it was under legal obligation to do so, compensated the proprietors of the first bridge by giving them an added thirty years in which to collect tolls.

The population of Boston and its business with the surrounding country continued to increase, as did the profits of the first bridge, known always as the Charles River Bridge. Shares which had a par value of $333.33 sold in 1805 at $1,650 and in 1814 at $2,080. Whereas the original capitalization had been $50,000, the bridge company in 1823 claimed that the value of its property was $280,-000.[36] The time came when few shares of stock were in the hands of the original investors, most of them being held by persons who had bought them at high prices, and who, when the public protested against the continued payment of tolls after profits amounting to far more than the original capital with interest had been earned, claimed that they had the right to returns on their own high investments. The owners of stock, most of them Bostonians, smugly resisted the demands made by the traveling public for concessions in the form of improved services and reduced tolls.

[36] See Charles Warren, *History of Harvard Law School*, I, 510-513.

Repeated attempts were made to persuade the legislature to authorize the building of a new bridge closely adjoining the old one, and finally, in a concerted political movement in which the masses organized to protect their own interests as against those of the holders of investment property, the battle was won. The legislature of 1828 chartered a company to build the Warren Bridge, which was to be only sixteen rods from the old bridge on the Charlestown side and fifty rods on the Boston side. The Warren Bridge was to be surrendered to the state as soon as sufficient tolls had been collected to pay for its construction, or in any case within a maximum period of six years from the time at which the collection of tolls was begun. Thereafter its use was to be free to the public. It was obvious that a free bridge which was so close to one which was charging tolls, would get all the traffic, no tolls would be collected on the toll bridge, and the value of the stock of the toll bridge would be destroyed.

The old bridge company attempted unsuccessfully to secure an injunction against the construction of the Warren Bridge, and carried the case to the Supreme Court of the United States on the ground that the act of the legislature chartering the Warren Bridge unconstitutionally impaired the contract in the charter of the Charles River Bridge, by setting up a competitor which prevented it from earning tolls. When the case was argued in 1831 Marshall, Story, and Thompson seem to have agreed with this contention, and Story's opinion was apparently written out; [37] but because of absences and disagreements either on the merits or on jurisdictional questions they were unable to get a decision.

Six years had now passed, and three of the old judges had been replaced by Jacksonian appointees. The Warren Bridge had been erected, had earned in tolls the amount of the cost of its construction, and had been for ten months a free bridge, drawing to itself all the passengers who might otherwise have paid tolls to the old corporation. The outcome was a victory for the traveling public over

[37] Story to Mason, Nov. 19, 1831, Warren, *Supreme Court in United States History*, I, 773, note 2.

what were loosely called vested rights. It threatened ominously the defeat of the claims of investors to the bountiful fruits of successful enterprise, provoking the warning that unless capitalists were protected in their winnings they would in the future refuse to invest in desirable but risky enterprises in which their capital might be lost. Profits, large or small, were, in other words, the just rewards for risk. Law ought to give protection to such rewards. When law was vague, and precedents confusing, conflicting, of nonexistent, judges, in obedience to what were called principles of justice, ought to give full protection to these rights of property.

The controversy over the rights of the Charles River Bridge arose during the period when people were just coming to realize the value of the corporate form for instituting such enterprises as the building of bridges, roads, and canals. The Supreme Court, with Marshall as spokesman, had in 1819 labeled as contracts the grants of privileges and property made in corporate charters, and held that the Constitution forbade their impairment by state legislation.[38] Taney and the other new members of the Supreme Court were not hostile to the creation of public improvements. On the contrary Taney had been among those who were most eager to improve economic conditions in Maryland by building first roads, then canals, and finally railroads.

As a member of the state Senate, however, he had observed the cupidity of those who lobbied for incorporation and for special privileges. He was so convinced of the inefficiency or untrustworthiness of corporations which then seemed large but which today would seem petty, that he advised that the building of the Chesapeake and Ohio Canal be financed and supervised by the government rather than attempted by private enterprise. He admitted a feeling of revulsion at the grasping and short-sighted selfishness of the mercantile classes of the country, and his experience with the Bank of the United States convinced him that moneyed corporations, unless kept within narrowly defined limits, were a menace to the welfare of the country.

[38] *Dartmouth College* v. *Woodward*, 4 Wheaton 518 (1819).

On September 5, 1833, about three weeks before he became Secretary of the Treasury, Taney had given a legal opinion concerning issues closely approximating those now before the Supreme Court. The Camden and Amboy Railroad and the Delaware and Raritan Canal companies had persuaded the New Jersey legislature of 1832 to incorporate in charter provisions the agreement that without the consent of these companies no company should for a stated time be incorporated to build a railroad for service between Philadelphia and New York or to compete in any way with the Camden and Amboy.[39] Taney and Judge James Kent of New York, probably Daniel Webster, and possibly other noted lawyers of the day were asked for opinions as to whether one legislature could thus limit the powers of its successor. Kent expressed the opinion, concurred in by Webster, that such a legislative stipulation ought to be sternly construed, "as one that may be exceedingly inconvenient to the public welfare."[40]

Taney admitted that if such a provision was included in a valid contract it must be considered binding under the contract clause of the Constitution. He declared, however, that the power to bind the state not to create corporations to build internal improvements was such an integral part of the power of sovereignty that no legislature could be assumed to have it unless it was specifically conferred by the state constitution. He admitted that others disagreed with him. "But with every respect for the distinguished men who have sanctioned such legislation in the general government, or in the states, I cannot think that a legislative body, holding a limited authority under a written constitution, can by contract or otherwise limit the legislative power of their successors. . . . The existence of such a power in a representative body has no foundation in reason, or in public convenience, and is inconsistent with the principles upon which all our political institutions are founded. For if a legislative body may thus restrict the power of its successors, a single improvident act of legislation, may entail lasting and incurable ills on the people

[39] Published in *Niles' Weekly Register*, Nov. 2, 1833.
[40] See James Bradley Thayer, *Cases on Constitutional Law* (1895) II, 1641.

of a state. It may compel them to forego the advantage which their local situation affords, and prevent them from using the means necessary to promote the prosperity and happiness of the community." It was his opinion, therefore, that the monopoly provisions of the act of 1832 should have no status when passed upon by the courts, and that a company could legally be chartered to build a competing railroad.

Taney's opinion "made much sensation from its imputed denial of what, without reflection, are apt to be thought not only vested but sacred rights." [41] It revealed an absence of respect for privileges and rights extracted from legislatures by propertied groups which in later years, when such groups had become more firmly entrenched in the economic life of the country, would have done much to blacklist the name of any lawyer, of whatever character and ability, for a position on the Supreme Court. It may, indeed, have been one of the causes of opposition to Taney, although because of the more dramatic aspects of the bank war, it seems to have been pretty much or completely submerged.

In an official opinion given during the preceding year [42] Taney had emphasized a fact which business men were accustomed to ignoring; namely, that when a corporation was formed and special privileges were given the gift was supposed to be for the benefit of the public, and not for the exclusive benefit of the corporations. He emphasized the same fact in 1836, after he was confirmed as Chief Justice, in analyzing for Jackson the act which provided for the rechartering of the banks of the District of Columbia: "Every charter granted by a state or by the United States, to a bank or to any other company for the purposes of trade or manufacture, is a grant of peculiar privileges, and gives to the individuals who compose the corporation, rights and privileges which are not possessed by other members of the community. It would be against the spirit of our free institutions, by which equal rights are intended to be secured to all, to

[41] Charles J. Ingersoll, quoted, "Judicial Control over Charters of Incorporation," *United States Magazine and Democratic Review*, Jan., 1839.

[42] *Norfolk Drawbridge Company and the United States*, May 16, 1832, 2 Official Opinions of the Attorneys General 512.

grant peculiar franchises and privileges to a body of individuals merely for the purpose of enabling them more conveniently and effectually to advance their own private interests. No charter could rightfully be granted on that ground. The consideration upon which alone, such peculiar privileges can be granted is the expectation and prospect of promoting thereby some public interest, and it follows from these principles that in every case where it is proposed to grant or to renew a charter the interests or wishes of the individuals who desire to be incorporated, ought not to influence the decision of the government. The only inquiry which the constituted authorities can properly make on such an application, is whether the charter applied for, is likely to produce any real benefit to the community, and whether that benefit is sufficient to justify the grant." [43]

Although the quotation just given had not been made public, enough was known of Taney's attitude and of his own experience and that of two of his colleagues with the Bank of the United States to provoke the belief that the new Supreme Court would read law and precedents with a consideration for the welfare of the general public, and would scrutinize the claims of propertied groups with a critical attitude, which had not characterized Marshall and his colleagues. Six weeks before the court met, Charles J. Ingersoll, in giving his opinion that the State of Pennsylvania had the power to repeal the charter of the Bank of the United States which Biddle and his friends had extracted from the legislature, declared that the decisions of the Supreme Court applying the contract clause of the Constitution had left the whole subject in doubt and difficulty. "By recent appointments there is now a majority of that bench, not involved in these perplexing contradictions, and when these clauses of the Constitution come once more to be considered by the Supreme Court, the public may expect a final harmonious and satisfactory interpretation of them." [44]

[43] The manuscript from which this paragraph is quoted is in the Jackson MSS., filed with the materials of June 20, 1836. It is in Taney's handwriting. It is unsigned, except that his initials are added to a memorandum which he wrote on the back, and is undated except for a penciled date in another hand. From the context the date must be approximately correct.

[44] Ingersoll letter, Nov. 24, 1836, in *Niles' Weekly Register*, Dec. 3, 1836.

The bridge case was to be argued by four Massachusetts lawyers. Warren Dutton and Daniel Webster represented the Charles River Bridge; and Simon Greenleaf, a teacher at Harvard Law School, and John Davis, the Whig senator who had voted to confirm Taney's nomination as Chief Justice, represented the Warren Bridge. The counsel were kept waiting pending the arrival of Justice Wayne, who, according to Greenleaf, had remained at home with Senator Cuthbert to work for the election of a member of Congress.[45] At length, on Thursday January 19, all members of the court were present, and Dutton opened the argument. The era of long arguments before the Supreme Court had not yet ended. Dutton spoke through Thursday, Friday, and into Saturday morning. Greenleaf spoke for two hours on Saturday and three on Monday. Davis spoke during the remainder of the Monday session and for three hours on Tuesday. Webster spoke through the remainder of Tuesday and probably all day Wednesday, and the records show that the case was still before the court on Thursday.

There is no diary to reveal Webster's feelings at the prospect of addressing respectfully and presenting a constitutional argument before the man whom in another capacity he had maligned. It was reported that his speech was a masterly effort of argument and ingenuity, and that painting could have conveyed no better idea of the positions of the bridges than did his description. Greenleaf noted, however, that Webster was very uneasy and moody during the whole defense, and a letter from his son indicates that he predicted that he would lose this case and that it would be his last case before the Supreme Court. Justice Story remarked that Webster's closing was in his best manner, but with a little too much *fierté* here and there.[46] Unfortunately for our interest in such personal matters there seems to be no evidence at all as to Taney's feelings at being addressed by the man whom he had accused of being a "pliant instrument" of the Bank of the United States.

The vital point to be decided by the Supreme Court was the ques-

[45] Greenleaf to Charles Sumner, Jan. 24, 1837, Warren, *History of Harvard Law School,* I, 532–533.

[46] See materials quoted, Warren, *Supreme Court in United States History,* II, 22–23.

tion as to whether the Charles River Bridge charter gave contract rights which were impaired by the act chartering the Warren Bridge. The legislators who had granted the first charter had been faced with such questions as whether one bridge could be successfully and permanently erected, but had given no thought as to what should be done if other parties desired to erect another bridge a few rods away, and in the charter had said nothing at all on the subject. The original grantees now asked the court to hold that exclusive rights to the traffic between Charlestown and Boston were given by implication, while their opponents contended that no rights were given by a charter save those which were conferred in express language.

Counsel on both sides analyzed at length the principles and precedents on the subject of the interpretation of public grants, and the power of government to interfere with them by eminent domain or otherwise, and then turned to what for the public and to a large extent even for the lawyers and the judges were the realities of the case— the effect which the decision would have upon the security of property rights and upon general welfare throughout the country. Dutton declared that in Massachusetts alone the title to more than ten millions of dollars in corporate property would be determined by the decision, for if the decision went against his clients the public might as easily secure legislation which would render valueless the property of other corporations as they had that of the proprietors of the Charles River Bridge.

In a closing plea he warned: "Popular prejudice may be again appealed to; and popular passions excited by passionate declamations against tribute money, exclusive privileges, and odious monopolies: and these, under skillful management, may be combined and brought to bear upon all chartered rights, with a resistless and crushing power. . . .

"I have as much respect for, and confidence in legislative bodies as reason and experience will warrant; but I am taught by both that they are not the safest guardians of private rights. I look to the law; to the administration of the law, and, above all, to the supremacy of the law, as it resides in this court, for the protection of the rights of persons and property, against all encroachments by the inadvertent legislation of the states. So long as this court shall continue to exercise this most salutary and highest of all its functions, the whole legislation of the country will be kept within its constitutional sphere of action. The result will be general confidence, and general security." [47]

Thus counsel for the plaintiffs appealed to the Supreme Court as if its prime function were to act as a super-guardian to the propertied interests of the country. They used a type of appeal which in a later era fell upon highly receptive ears, resulting in the elaboration of a due process clause to curb the activities of state legislatures which were more or less responsive to popular demands. Counsel for the Warren Bridge, on the other hand, with a copy of Taney's Camden and Amboy opinion of September 5, 1833, in their possession,[48] argued that the claim set up was against common right. "They contended that the legislature possessed only limited powers;—that the power of laying taxes, of providing for the common defense, of providing safe and convenient public ways, and of taking private property for public uses, or sacrificing private rights to public necessities, were essential to the existence of all government whatever; and were entrusted to the legislature to be exercised for the public good, and not to be sold or conveyed away; and each legislature must necessarily assemble with the same powers, in these respects, as were held by its predecessors." [49]

The proprietors of the Charles River Bridge were in no worse condition, Davis declared, and had no higher claim to indemnity than other losers by public improvements. Railroads took traffic from highways near which they were built, thus depriving the latter of tolls which had been anticipated, and reducing the value of stages, wagons, and other property. Some communities were deprived of

---

[47] 11 Peters 460–461.

[48] Greenleaf placed a copy of this opinion in the library of Harvard Law School, along with the notes of his argument in the bridge case.—James Bradley Thayer, *Cases on Constitutional Law* (1895), II, 1641.

[49] From a statement of the argument in the Worcester *Republican*, Feb. 22, 1837, which was supposed to have been written by Greenleaf.

business and the value of their real estate depreciated, but there could be no legal indemnity for such losses, and, since public convenience demanded such improvements, they could not be obstructed from such causes. As a matter of strategy in winning their case, however, and doubtless also for personal reasons, counsel for the Warren Bridge avoided the denunciations of the possessors of vested rights, and the demands for radical legal changes which had characterized the popular movement culminating in the chartering of the Warren Bridge. They avoided everything "peoplish," as Greenleaf expressed it, and argued that the decision which they sought was called for by a correct interpretation of existing law.[50]

On February 14 the decision of the Supreme Court was announced, and on that and the following day three opinions were read. Taney's opinion, for a majority of the court, upheld the claims of the Warren Bridge. McLean attempted to prove that justice was on the side of the Charles River Bridge, but that the Supreme Court had not jurisdiction to decide the case. Story, in an opinion first written six years earlier, swept aside all quibbling on the score of constitutionality, and defended the claims of the Charles River Bridge. Taney passed over as unnecessary to the decision many of the arguments of counsel, held that the case turned exclusively upon the interpretation of a contract, that the contract should be construed narrowly, and that when so construed it did not confer the rights claimed by the plaintiffs. In words ominous to the representatives of entrenched property interests, he declared it to be well settled by the decisions of the Supreme Court that a state law might devest vested rights and yet not violate the Constitution, unless it impaired the obligation of a contract. Relying heavily upon an opinion in a recent English decision [51] and on other cases there cited, he stated the principle that public grants were to be construed strictly, and any ambiguity in the terms of such contracts was to be decided in the interest of the public. Our system of jurisprudence was based on that of

---

[50] Greenleaf to Charles Sumner, Jan. 24, 1837, Warren, *History of Harvard Law School*, I, 532.

[51] *Proprietors of the Stourbridge Canal* v. *Wheeley*, 2 Barn. & Adol. 792.

England, and there was no good reason for departing from it in this respect.

"The object and end of all government," declared Taney, "is to promote the happiness and prosperity of the community by which it is established; and it can never be assumed, that the government intended to diminish its power of accomplishing the end for which it was created. And in a country like ours, free, active, and enterprising, continually advancing in numbers and wealth; new channels of communications are daily found necessary, both for travel and trade; and are essential to the comfort, convenience, and prosperity of the people. A state ought never to be presumed to surrender this power, because, like the taxing power, the whole community have an interest in preserving it undiminished. And when a corporation alleges, that a state has surrendered for seventy years, its power of improvement and public accommodation, in a great and important line of travel, along which a vast number of its citizens must daily pass; the community have a right to insist, . . . 'that its abandonment ought not to be presumed, in a case, in which the deliberate purpose of the state to abandon it does not appear.' "

The continued existence of a government would be of no great value, Taney believed, if by implications and presumptions it was disarmed of the powers necessary to accomplish the ends of its creation, and the functions it was designed to perform transferred to the hands of privileged corporations. No one would question that the interests of the great body of the people of the state would, in this instance, be affected by the surrender of this great line of travel to a single corporation, with the right to exact toll and exclude competition for seventy years. "While the rights of private property are sacredly guarded," he declared in a sentence sharply revealing his point of view, "we must not forget that the community also have rights, and that the happiness and well being of every citizen depends on their faithful preservation."

Summarizing the provisions of the charter and of subsequent legislation affecting it, Taney declared that it would indeed be a strong exercise of judicial power which would, by a sort of judicial coercion, raise an implied contract and infer it from the nature of the charter. Such a decision would affect conditions of transportation all over the country. In preceding years franchises had been granted to build roads, other franchises had been granted to competitors, canal companies had been chartered and had taken business away from the highways, and railroad companies were taking business both from the highways and from the canals. If the precedent was established of reading monopoly rights into the old charters by implication, modern improvements would be at the mercy of the old corporations.

The country would "be thrown back to the improvements of the last century, and obliged to stand still, until the claims of the old turnpike corporations shall be satisfied; and they shall consent to permit these states to avail themselves of the lights of modern science, and to partake of the benefit of those improvements which are now adding to the wealth and prosperity, and the convenience and comfort, of every other part of the civilized world. Nor is this all. This court will find itself compelled to fix, by some arbitrary rule, the width of this new kind of property in a line of travel; for if such a right of property exists, we have no lights to guide us in marking out its extent, unless, indeed, we resort to the old feudal grants, and to the exclusive rights of ferries, by prescription, between towns; and are prepared to decide that when a turnpike road from one town to another has been made, no railroad or canal, between these two points, could afterwards be established. This court are not prepared to sanction principles which must lead to such results."

Justice Story, dissenting, declared that the opinion which he had originally formed had not been shaken but rather confirmed by the recent argument of the case. Relying not so much upon modern cases as did Taney, but rather upon voluminous researches into the common law of England of centuries past, he sought to establish the claims of the plaintiffs. "I stand upon the old law," he declared; "upon law established more than three centuries ago, in cases contested with as much ability and learning as any in the annals of our jurisprudence, in resisting any such encroachments upon the rights and liberties of the citizens, secured by public grants. I will not consent to shake their title deeds by any speculative niceties or novelties."

As for the effect of the decision of the case upon the prosperity of the country, he saw less danger in the assertion of the legal rights of old turnpike and canal corporations than in the prospect that men of property would refuse to invest in public improvements if the courts showed themselves other than diligent in the protection of vested property rights. Story, like most of the business leaders of the country before and since, adhered to what might be called the seepage theory of economics, to the theory that if government, including the judiciary, was sufficiently zealous and effective in protecting property for the benefit of those who held title to it, those persons would engage in productive enterprise, and a goodly share of the wealth produced thereby would seep down through the otherwise less capable or less fortunate classes of the people, and the country as a whole would prosper.

Taney, with a point of view which had become sharply defined during his experiences in the bank war, but which perhaps in some of its aspects dated back to the time when transatlantic merchants sapped the wealth of rural Maryland by dictating the low prices at which tobacco must be sold if sold at all, had not Story's faith in the seepage of wealth in such a way as to bring about the greatest good of the community. His opinion in this case does not show how far he would have had government interfere with property for the benefit of the community. It demonstrates, however, his intention to resist the use of government for the benefit of vested interests when other groups would be made to suffer thereby; and, to repeat, he saw in this instance possibilities of such suffering which Story, imbued with a different social philosophy, could not or would not recognize.

Two other cases, *Briscoe* v. *The Bank of the Commonwealth of Kentucky*[52] and *New York* v. *Miln*,[53] received with the Bridge case

[52] 11 Peters 257.
[53] 11 Peters 102.

most of the public attention given to the work of the Supreme Court during this term. The first arguments in both of these cases had likewise been made before Chief Justice Marshall. Marshall, speaking for a majority of his court, had held in *Craig* v. *Missouri* [54] that small denomination notes issued by the State of Missouri and circulated as money were bills of credit which the Constitution forbade the states to issue. He had been likewise of the opinion in the Kentucky case that notes issued by a bank owned and controlled by the State were bills of credit, and could not legally be issued. The decision had been left over until the new régime in the court, however, and now McLean, speaking for a majority, read an opinion holding that the notes were not bills of credit, since they were issued by a bank instead of by the State, even though the State owned the bank.

Story's lone dissent reveals starkly the tenaciousness with which he clung to a régime and a personnel which had gone. A majority of the judges who heard the first argument had been of the opinion that the act in question was unconstitutional. "Among that majority was the late *Mr. Chief Justice* Marshall—a name never to be pronounced without reverence." The second argument, he declared, had been upon precisely the same grounds as the former. After explaining at length his reasons for believing the decision to be wrong, he declared that he did so because of his belief that the public had the right to know the opinion of every judge who dissented from the opinion of the court on a constitutional question. "I have another and strong motive," he continued; "my profound reverence and affection for the dead. *Mr. Chief Justice* Marshall is not here to speak for himself; and knowing full well the grounds of his opinion, in which I concurred, that this act is unconstitutional; I have felt an earnest desire to vindicate his memory from the imputation of rashness, or want of deep reflection."

Taney voted silently with the affirmative in the Kentucky case, as he did also in the New York case, in which Story again attempted to preserve the reign of the dead hand. The latter case dealt with important issues of commerce and police powers, in the discussion of

[54] 4 Peters 410 (1830).

which Taney was in the future to find himself many times deeply embroiled.[55] Briefly, the court had to decide whether or not New York could constitutionally require the masters of ships to make reports of such matters as the age, health, and last legal residence of immigrants whom they brought into the country. Counsel argued as to whether such a law was a regulation of foreign commerce, and if so, whether the power of Congress to regulate foreign commerce was exclusive, so as to prevent the enactment of valid state laws on the subject. Barbour, speaking for a majority of the court, held that the act was not a regulation of commerce, but was a police measure such as a state had the power to enact. Thus began in earnest the battle to determine definitions of police and commerce powers which were to be involved in most of the important decisions of the court during the next quarter of a century.

As was to be expected, Democrats and Whigs differed sharply in their appraisals of the work of the court during the term. Democrats approvingly prophesied the restoration of the Constitution, "without shocks or reversals, by such quiet, conciliatory and unassailable adjudications as those pronounced in the cases just mentioned." [56] Taney's opinion in the Bridge case received high praise. "It is a most able document," declared a democratic magazine, "bearing on its face those features for which all the intellectual productions of that distinguished statesman and jurist are remarkable. He clears the very intricate subject before the court of all irrelevant matter, with the unerring instinct of genius; and as he pursues his unbroken chain of clear, logical reasoning, spreads light all around, leaving no cloud to confound or mislead those who may come after him. Indeed the present Chief Justice escapes from irrelevant matter with as much ease as Judge Marshall or the most distinguished of the English judges." [57]

Whigs, on the other hand, were distressed and disapproving. The reporter of a Boston paper, who had listened to the arguments in the

---

[55] For further discussion of the issues involved see Chapter XIX.
[56] "The Supreme Court," *United States Magazine and Democratic Review*, Jan., 1838.
[57] "The Supreme Court of the United States," *ibid.*, June, 1840.

important cases and to the opinions as they were delivered by the judges, expressed the belief that the system of constitutional law built up by Marshall and his associates was to be gradually, though not openly and avowedly, enclosed in black lines. Federal restraint would be removed from state legislatures, and investments in corporate property would have no guarantee of legal protection.[58] The tone and character of the decision in the Bridge case, declared the *North American Review*, "chime in with doctrines, which tend, or may be urged, deplorably, to the subversion of the principles of law and property." [59]

A New York newspaper lamented that "the fruit of all the accumulated wisdom and all the profound research and meditation of Jay, Ellsworth, Chase, Marshall, Washington, Story, and Thompson, is to be set at naught by such small lights as have been recently placed on the bench—such shallow metaphysical hair splitters as P. P. Barbour." [60] The editor of the *American Monthly Magazine* was so inarticulately enraged at a Democratic defense of the court that his article was hardly more than a jumble of denunciatory adjectives.[61] The *New York Review*, a leading Whig magazine, lamented of deep shadows cast over fairest and proudest hopes. In reading the decisions of the Supreme Court under the new dynasty, "we perceive at once an altered tone and a narrower spirit, not only in Chief Justice Taney, but even in some of the old associates of Chief Justice Marshall, when they handle constitutional questions. The change is so great and so ominous, that a gathering gloom is cast over the future. We seem to have sunk suddenly below the horizon, to have lost the light of the sun, to hold our way *per incertam lunam sub luce maligna*." [62]

Daniel Webster, defeated, assured Story that his opinion in the Bridge case left the opposition not a foot nor an inch to stand on. "The intelligent part of the profession will all be with you. There is

[58] Boston *Daily Advertiser*, Feb. 21, 1837.
[59] *North American Review*, Jan., 1838.
[60] New York *Commercial Advertiser*, Jan. 25, 1838.
[61] *American Monthly Magazine*, March, 1838.
[62] *New York Review*, April, 1838.

no doubt of that; but then the decision of the court will have completely overturned, in my judgment, one great provision of the Constitution." [63] He was wrong as to the ultimate position of the bar, for the decision was in time to be fully accepted and approved, but he never changed his own opinion. "When I look back after a long lapse of years," he declared in 1845, "and read the judgment of those judges . . . I must say that I see, or think that I see, all the difference between a manly, honest, and just maintenance of the right, and an ingenious, elaborate, and sometimes half shamefaced apology for what is wrong." He staked his reputation as a lawyer that the decision could not stand.[64]

Chancellor James Kent, of New York, one of the best known jurists in the country, read the decisions of the Supreme Court for the term, and wrote to Story to vent in confidence his grief and mortification. "It appears to me," he declared, "that the court has fallen from its high station and commanding dignity, and has lost its energy, and spirit of independence, and accuracy, and surrendered up to the spirit of the day, the true principles of the Constitution." He had reperused the Bridge case with increased disgust. It violated a great principle of constitutional morality, and destroyed the sanctity of contracts. "Now we feel with a pang the loss of Marshall. Now we sadly realize that we are to be under the reign of little men—a pigmy race and that the sages of the last age are extinguished." As for the Kentucky case, "It absolutely overwhelms me in despair, and I have no hopes left especially when I consider that we have two new judges—very feeble lights added to your bench. . . . I am astonished that Judge Thompson should have deserted you, *but he had married a wife and could not come to the rescue.*[65] I have lost my confidence and hopes in the constitutional guardianship and protection of the Supreme Court." [66]

By the clamor of his Whig friends Story was persuaded that he

[63] *Life and Letters of Joseph Story*, II, 269.

[64] Warren, *History of Harvard Law School*, I, 540.

[65] *Ante*, p. 359.

[66] Kent to Story, June 23, 1837, Story MSS., Massachusetts Historical Society. Printed in part in *Life and Letters of Joseph Story*, II, 270.

had the approbation of those persons whose good opinion was worth having. Taney's opinion was not deemed satisfactory, even by those who were not against the decision of the court. Justice Baldwin had published a pamphlet in which he discussed the constitutional issues involved in the important cases of the term, on which he had voted with the majority of the court. Story read it calmly. Chief Justice Marshall had approved the doctrines which he laid down in his *Commentaries,* and by that fact he was quite consoled, even though another judge expressed disapproval.

But though convinced that he was right, he faced the future with sadness. "I am the last of the old race of judges. I stand their solitary representative, with a pained heart, and a subdued confidence. Do you remember the story of the last dinner of a club, who dined once a year? I am in the predicament of the last survivor." [67] He doubted gloomily that in his day any law of a state or of Congress would be declared unconstitutional, and he made up his mind to resign, only to be persuaded by his friends to remain on the bench a while longer.[68] He remained a member of the court for eight years, during which time friction continued between him and most of his colleagues on important constitutional issues, for, although he was younger in years than many of them, he had lost the flexibility of thought and emotion which should have enabled him to adjust more or less happily to the new régime.

[67] Story to Harriet Martineau, April 7, 1837, *Life and Letters,* II, 277.
[68] Story to McLean, May 10, 1837, *ibid.,* pp. 272–273.

CHAPTER XVIII

THE RIGHTS OF PROPERTY

"WHILE the rights of property are sacredly guarded," Taney declared in the Charles River Bridge decision, "we must not forget that the community also have rights, and that the happiness and well being of every citizen depends on their faithful preservation." The doctrine was new in the official utterance of the Supreme Court. It revealed a hitherto unconfessed awareness that scrupulous guardianship over property might be carried to the point of injuring the community instead of protecting its welfare. The Bridge case, however, gave only general clues as to the attitude which the court under Taney's leadership would take toward rights in specific kinds of property. That attitude was revealed only gradually, in a series of decisions handed down over a period of years. It proved to be not a clear attitude supported by all the judges toward all kinds of property, but a series of attitudes toward different kinds of property, worked out as compromises among judges with different points of view.

One of the first of these decisions turned upon an important question as to the legal rights of corporations—with the question as to whether a corporation of one state could engage in business in another state, either with or without the consent of the latter.[1] Many persons interested in the growth of business enterprise in the United States insisted that a corporation of a state could go wherever a citizen of that state could go, and, like the citizen, should be free to engage in business wherever it went. Other persons, fearful of the growth of corporate power, argued that a corporation had no power outside the range of the laws of the state by which it was created, or

[1] *Bank of Augusta* v. *Earle*, 13 Peters 519 (1839).

at least that it could not do business outside that state without the consent of the state to which it sought to migrate.

The issue came up in connection with the perennial attempts of the states to solve their banking problems. Alabama had found it advisable to assume ownership or management of most of the banks within its borders. To protect these banks the corporations of other states were by law forbidden to engage in banking in the state. The law did not state clearly whether the business of banking included the buying and selling of bills of exchange. Since there was at this time no adequate supply of any kind of money which was equally acceptable in all parts of the country, and since it was not possible to make payments by writing checks on banks at a distance, most transactions between different sections of the country were conducted by the use of bills of exchange.

Since cotton, the chief product of Alabama, had to be exported elsewhere for manufacture, and since most of the goods consumed were imported, the use of bills of exchange had to be heavily relied upon. The state banks declared that the business was banking, and that under the state law they had a monopoly of it. The banks of other states found the business too profitable to surrender to the Alabama institutions. The rights in dispute became a court issue when debtors refused to pay bills of exchange held by the Bank of Augusta, the Bank of the United States, now operating under a Pennsylvania charter, and one other company.

In the federal circuit court in Alabama, Justice McKinley took the extreme position that a corporation of one state could not so much as make a contract in another state, either directly or by agent. The decision was a threat of death to all interstate business by corporations. It was a portent of the continuation of the days of agricultural simplicity wherein transactions were small and limited to the resources of individual owners and partnerships. Justice Story declared that it "frightened half the lawyers and all the corporations of the country out of their proprieties." [2] He wrote to McLean that

[2] Story to Charles Sumner, June 17, 1838, Warren, *The Supreme Court in United States History*, II, 50.

if the decision were well founded it would ruinously affect corporations throughout the Union. He thought the decision bad law and bad economics. He remained of the persuasion that powerful banking institutions operating across state lines were essential for the good of the country, and thought nothing could be more mischievous than the prevailing system of little banks.[3] It was evident, however, that he feared the Jackson Democrats composing a majority of the court would not agree with him, and that the Supreme Court would affirm the McKinley position.

Among the lawyers who presented the case for Alabama was Charles J. Ingersoll, an inveterate foe of corporations and particularly of the Bank of the United States. He portrayed with evangelical fervor the ominous growth of corporations in the United States, and the threat which it bore for the rights and the property of the people. He urged the court to interpret narrowly the rights and privileges conferred upon corporations, and thought the case of such importance as to justify the assumption that he had the whole country as his client.

Counsel for the banks suing for the right of doing business in Alabama predicted national disaster if McKinley's decision were upheld. A deeper wound would be inflicted upon the commercial business of the United States than it had ever sustained, declared David B. Ogden. Daniel Webster denounced what he regarded as attempts on the part of the anti-bank press to influence the decision of the Supreme Court. McKinley's decision, he declared, was in principle "anti-commercial, and anti-social, new and unheard of in our system, and calculated to break up the harmony which has so long prevailed among the states and people of this Union." He argued that the corporations of one state were guaranteed the privilege of doing business in other states by the constitutional provision that "citizens of each state shall be entitled to all the privileges and immunities of citizens of the several states." Pushed to its logical conclusion his argument would have left corporations virtually free from effective state control.

[3] Story to McLean, May 25, 1838, McLean MSS.

Although in private he expressed despondently his conviction that the Supreme Court had undergone hopeless deterioration, he closed his address in the presence of an enthralled audience with a plea that, worthy of itself, the court would stand in the way of threatened disaster: "It is for you, Mr. Chief Justice and judges, on this, as on other occasions of high importance, to speak and to decide for the country. The guardianship of her commercial interests; the preservation of the harmonious intercourse of all her citizens; the fulfilling, in this respect, of the great object of the Constitution, are in your hands; and I am not to doubt that the trust will be so performed as to sustain at once high national objects and the character of this tribunal."

Justice McKinley, unconvinced by the arguments of Webster and his colleagues, adhered stubbornly to the position which he had taken in the lower court. Baldwin went most or all the way with Webster in the contention that a state could not prevent a corporation of another state from doing business within its borders. Taney saw the injury to banks and commercial interests in general, and indirectly to the country as a whole, which would result from a decision that a corporation could do no business across state lines. On the other hand he saw the menace of corporation despotism in Webster's argument that a state must provide at least a passive welcome to corporations created elsewhere and subject to restraints which under the circumstances could hardly be effective. Superb craftsman that he was, therefore, he wrote for a majority of the court an opinion which pursued a middle path between the two positions. That opinion, delivered on the last day of the term after his recovery from several days of illness, was one of the clearest that he ever put on record. Most or all the materials utilized were accumulated by counsel on one side or the other. The synthesis, however, was in every sense his own, bearing throughout the stamp of his thinking and the configuration of his literary style.

He rejected the argument that a corporation was a citizen of a state, even though made up of citizens. Therefore it was not entitled to the rights in other states which were guaranteed to citizens by the

Constitution. He admitted, with McKinley, that since a corporation had existence only by virtue of the laws of a state it could have no existence outside the jurisdiction of those laws. Therefore it could not migrate to another state. He parted company with McKinley, however, by arguing that, although a corporation could not migrate beyond the state of its creation, it could do business in other states through its agents if the other states permitted. He showed how in international relations many countries, by comity, permitted the agents of foreign corporations to do business within their borders. Since the states of the Union were related more closely than were foreign states, the power of corporations to do business in similar fashion ought to be recognized. Furthermore, although a state had the undoubted right to prevent such business, the principle of comity should be adhered to by the courts, and in the absence of a clear prohibition the right to do business ought to be assumed.

The opinion was a masterpiece of strategy, in that, while it recognized the power of a corporation to do business outside the home state, it recognized also the right of the other state to exclude it. Since the other state had the power of exclusion it could also admit under condition, and could use the power of conditional admission as a means of exercising control over the visiting corporation. In this manner Taney defined for many years to come the constitutional law of "foreign" corporations. "The terse and quotable style of the opinion," says a recent authority, "its philosophical flavor, and its clear-cut reasoning combined to give even the dicta of the Chief Justice an authority which was to stand unquestioned for half a century." [4]

It is true that in relatively recent years judges jealous of state interference with corporations have modified and distorted the doctrine which Taney announced. When a state admits a corporation created elsewhere on certain conditions, the courts will scrutinize the conditions which the state has prescribed, and may hold them "unconstitutional," permitting the corporation to remain in the state even

[4] G. C. Henderson, *The Position of Foreign Corporations in American Constitutional Law*, p. 42. See this volume for the further development of the doctrines of the decision.

though it might not have been admitted in first place except for the belief that it could be required to live up to the conditions of admission. Taney's decision still holds, however, in the sense that a state may still exclude foreign corporations not engaged in interstate commerce, and the courts have not yet extended the doctrine of "unconstitutional conditions" far enough to defeat all control by conditional admission.

The decision was widely misunderstood, both by the friends and by the foes of the banks involved. Democratic and anti-bank newspapers denounced the court for delivering a blow at the rights of the states, in language similar to that long used when the court was predominantly Federalist in personnel.[5] A Pennsylvania paper prepared to battle for the inalienable rights of the people, and announced its intention to strike first at the life judiciary of the United States, the "judicial noblemen of America." [6]

Whig papers, on the other hand, were deluded into the belief that the court had aligned itself fully with them. The decision, declared one of them, would increase the confidence of the people in the purity, wisdom, and independence of the court. The Washington *Globe*, the administration organ at the national capital, had been repelled in its insolent attempts to dictate to the court, and Ingersoll's tissue of sophistries had been scattered to the wind.[7]

Justice Story, greatly relieved that the court had not affirmed the McKinley decision, wrote to Taney that his opinion had given general satisfaction to the public, and added, "I hope you will allow me to say that I think it does great honor to yourself as well as to the court." [8] The decision, added to that in the Kendall case in the preceding year, did much to refute the earlier beliefs that Taney and his Jacksonian colleagues would use the court under all circumstances to serve the ends of the Democratic party and as a tool in the warfare against corporations. The thoughtful observer must, however, have recognized a change in trend from the Marshall court, though such

[5] See Warren, *op. cit.*, II, 57–62.
[6] Harrisburg *Pennsylvania Reporter*, March 22, 1839.
[7] New York *Commercial Advertiser*, quoted, Salem *Essex Register*, March 14, 1839.
[8] Story to Taney, April 19, 1839, Tyler, p. 288.

recognition required a refinement of perception which clamorous critics did not possess.

The records create the impression that Taney continued distrustful of corporations as aggregations of wealth which were apt to be dangerous, but accepted them as necessary instruments of the society in which he lived. Deeply pragmatic in his thinking, he found a place for them in his interpretation of law, without making drastic concessions or freeing them from effective governmental control. He was similarly pragmatic in other decisions affecting business, property, and property rights. He had his own conceptions of what was best, and he molded his legal interpretations accordingly. He did not shrink at substituting his own interpretation of the common law for that of the state courts,[9] seeming to regard that law not as flowing merely from the power of sovereign states but as what has been called a "brooding omnipresence," [10] giving sanction to his own conceptions of what ought to be.

Property in land and mortgages, the kind of property with which Taney had been most familiar as a product of a plantation country, had for him a sanctity not possessed by interloper corporations or by liquid wealth in the hands of banking and mercantile classes. Attempts of states to interfere with mortgage claims to relieve the stress of deflation in a depression period found him adamant in opposition. The depression of the 1830's, like that of a century later, produced legislation in defense of the rights of debtors threatened with the loss of their property. The first case of the kind to come before Taney's court arose out of two Illinois laws, one of which provided that property could not be sold on foreclosure unless it brought a certain proportion of the appraised value, and the other gave the debtor the right to repurchase the property within a given period of time at a given rate.

The laws were the product of the conditions brought about by the

[9] Note his concurrence in *Swift* v. *Tyson*, 16 Peters 1 (1842), and his opinion in *Martin* v. *Lessee of Waddell*, 16 Peters 367 (1842).

[10] See Justice Holmes in *Southern Pacific Co.* v. *Jensen*, 244 U. S. 205, 222 (1917).

panic of 1837 and the disturbances which followed. Values had collapsed and buying power had disappeared. People who had borrowed by means of mortgaging their property when prices were high and business was booming found themselves unable to pay the principal and oftentimes even the interest. When the mortgaged property was sold on foreclosure it went to the highest bidders for insignificant sums, leaving nothing to the mortgagors and often failing to cover the amount of the mortgages. Chaos reigned among bewildered people, who turned to the legislatures for protection against what operated as the confiscation of their property.

For some reason the creditors were unrepresented by counsel when the case testing the validity of the remedial legislation reached the Supreme Court, and the debtor interests were supported only by a written brief. The fact is surprising, in view of the extent of the rights involved on both sides. The court passed upon the case, however, and, in an opinion by Taney from which only McLean dissented, it held that the laws interfering with foreclosures impaired the obligations of contracts, and were in violation of the contract clause of the Constitution.[11] Although the laws did not deny the rights of creditors which were conveyed by contract, they did interfere with court enforcement of the contracts. This interference with the legal "remedy," Taney declared, had the effect of impairing the contract itself, and was therefore unconstitutional.

Justice Story, who was absent when the case was decided, informed Taney of his full concurrence in the opinion.[12] To McLean, who dissented, he wrote pointedly that he was entirely satisfied with the opinion of the court.[13] There were times, he declared, in which the court was called upon to adhere to every sound constitutional doctrine in support of the rights of property and of creditors. It seemed odd that McLean refused to concur with the court, in view of the conservative ideas on property rights which he was known to hold. The case had come up from his circuit, and he, perhaps more than

[11] *Bronson* v. *Kinzie*, 1 Howard 311 (1843).
[12] Story to Taney, March 25, 1843, Tyler, *Memoir of Roger Brooke Taney*, p. 289.
[13] Story to McLean, April 14, 1843, McLean MSS.

his brethren, was familiar with the crying need which had given rise to the laws in question. Furthermore, the fact cannot be ignored in any realistic appraisal that McLean's perennial hopes of achieving the presidency made him sensitive to what his debtor constituents would think of him if he decided in opposition to their interests. Under the circumstances his courage may have been inadequate for the support of his convictions. At any rate he disagreed with the conclusion reached by the court, and continued to do so for a number of years, even though he felt compelled to follow it in subsequent circuit court cases.

Taney's decision that debtors must be required to observe the letter of their contracts, however much they were damaged in doing so, was of course consistent with his belief that every man should pay his debts, and with his belief that business cycles need not be feared if the country were to rely exclusively on a specie currency, and were to regulate properly the banking system. In terms of his assumptions, interference with contracts was the wrong method of curing the ills of an economic crisis.

The subsequent experience of nearly a century, however, has failed to demonstrate a method of regulating currency and credit which will prevent the disaster of the recurrent oppressions of debtors when the business cycle sweeps downward. When in 1934 the Supreme Court was called upon to appraise legislation similar to that disapproved by Taney, it upheld it by a bare majority.[14] The case was not exactly identical with that of 1843, as two cases are seldom exactly identical, but Taney's opinion called forth all the ingenuity of Chief Justice Hughes in making distinctions, and it provided much comfort and the basis for most persuasive arguments for the spokesman of the four dissenting judges.

Taney's opinion, therefore, can be appraised in different ways. It might be said that he did not forget the "rights of the community," which he regarded as entitled to protection along with property rights, but believed that there were more just and more effective ways of protecting community rights than by enforcing laws inter-

---

[14] *Home Building & Loan Association* v. *Blaisdell*, 290 U. S. 398 (1934).

fering with mortgage claims. The relevant comment is that no such methods have been made to work, and that for the protection of the community a majority of a succeeding generation of Supreme Court judges have rationalized the acceptance of a remedy similar to that which Taney rejected.

Another plausible interpretation is that, while Taney was keenly aware of a distinction between property rights and community rights when the property rights involved were claimed by corporations or by mercantile or banking interests, he ignored his own warning and failed to see the distinction when the rights involved were those of individuals in tangible property, which were guaranteed by title or contract. Such rights, which to the landholders from whom he descended had characteristics of sanctity, and which as a lawyer he had been accustomed to regard as fundamental, may have seemed to him inseparable from the community rights which were easily distinguished from the rights of corporations.

Indeed, it is not impossible that Taney would have seen the case in a different light had the creditor seeking to foreclose the mortgage been a moneyed corporation of another state, clearly portrayed by opposing counsel as extending its tentacles throughout the Union to gather in for its own selfish purposes the economic resources of the people. Instead the controversy was between two individuals. One of them was seeking to enforce a right which in terms of the contract was clearly his. It was asking a great deal, it proved to be asking too much, to expect Taney to approve of legislative interference with the enforcement of contracts the observance of which he had always regarded as fundamental to social stability and order. If his conceptions were too old-fashioned for the promotion of social justice, he was not the first nor the last against whom this charge could legitimately be made. At any rate, the decision gave stability to contract rights, and it quieted the last of the fears that the court would eventually overthrow the major doctrines of Taney's predecessor.[15]

[15] See for example the *National Intelligencer*, March 16, 1843.

During the years when Taney was Chief Justice the number, size, and influence of business corporations increased rapidly. It was apparent that they were becoming increasingly important fixtures in American economic life. It was necessary, therefore, that they be accepted by the legal system, and that their position before the law should be defined. One of the significant decisions of Taney's court, handed down during his absence but apparently approved by him, gave corporations the right to remove cases from state to federal courts when suing or being sued by citizens of other states than those in which they had been created.[16] The decision conferring this important right, indeed, was more friendly to corporations than the position of Chief Justice Marshall had been,[17] though the latter had regretted the narrowness of the doctrine to which he had committed himself.

Some of the judges accepted the decision with great reluctance, and Justice Daniel, who was apparently absent at the time it was rendered, refused to accept it even after it had been many times repeated. With all the prejudices of his agrarian and state-rights background he protested that corporations had no right under the Constitution to be parties to suits in the federal courts. In falling into this error, he declared, and in repeating it time after time, "this court has been led on from dark to darker, until at present it is environed and is beaconed onward by varying and deceptive gleams, calculated to end in a deeper and more dense obscurity. In dread of the precipices to which they would conduct me, I am unwilling to trust myself to these rambling lights; and if I cannot have reflected upon my steps the bright and cheery day-spring of the Constitution, I feel bound nevertheless to remit no effort to halt in what, to my apprehension, is the path that terminates in ruin." [18]

Daniel's opinions may have been more consistent with those of the founding fathers than were the opinions of a majority of his brethren. The latter, however, maintained themselves more fully in public

[16] *Louisville . . . R. R. Co.* v. *Letson,* 2 Howard 497 (1844).
[17] *Bank of the United States* v. *Deveaux,* 5 Cranch 61 (1809).
[18] *Marshall* v. *B. & O. R. R. Co.,* 16 Howard 314, 345 (1853).

respect, or at any rate in the respect of the dominant economic groups with which they came in contact, by giving judicial sanction to what seemed inevitable economic trends. Daniel's voice was a voice from the dead past. It was doomed to be lost in the uproar and clamor of a new age, wherein the centralization of economic power in corporate organizations had achieved an irresistible impetus.

Taney, less stubborn than Daniel in his resistance to unwelcome change, sanctioned the development of constitutional law in such a way as to give protection to the basic rights of corporations. Unlike those of his brethren who were friendly to the development of corporate enterprise, however, he interpreted those rights as narrowly as possible, and refused to recognize them if there was reasonable doubt concerning their existence. When a corporation made claim that a state had granted it some privilege or right, such as exemption from taxation, the case of the corporation had to be clear indeed to win his support. On the other hand, if there was no doubt that a right had been conferred by contract, he held the state bound by the contract clause of the Constitution, even though the grant had been unwisely made. The states had the right to govern themselves, even to the extent of making foolish bargains. It was not the function of the federal government to prevent the states from making mistakes, or to shield them from the results. "The principle that they are the best judges of what is for their own interest, is the foundation of our political institutions." [19]

Taney's opinions show full awareness of the extent to which the legislative grants of corporate privileges were secured through corruption and otherwise unethical manipulation. The acceptance of these evils, however, seemed to him preferable to having the federal government sit in judgment over state morality. The unfortunate effect of his position was that corporations were permitted to take unfair advantage of the public provided only that they were careful of the phraseology of the contracts which they persuaded legislatures to

[19] *Ohio Life Insurance & Trust Co.* v. *Debolt,* 16 Howard 415 (1854). Among others see *Piqua Branch Bank* v. *Knoop,* 16 Howard 369 (1854), *Dodge* v. *Woolsey,* 18 Howard 331 (1856), *Planters' Bank* v. *Sharp,* 6 Howard 301 (1848), and *Perrine* v. *C. & O. Canal,* 9 Howard 172 (1850).

sign. A contract, once made, took on characteristics of inviolable sanctity, without much reference to the conditions of its making.

During a period of recurrent hostility to corporations the commitment of the Supreme Court to the enforcement of contracts unwisely made by state legislatures had importance far beyond that of the cases immediately involved. It established the Supreme Court as the peculiar defender of corporation rights, and suggested to corporation lawyers the desirability of interpreting other general phrases in the Constitution so as to give the Supreme Court a veto power over hostile legislation. When at the close of the Civil War, after Taney's death, the Fourteenth Amendment was made a part of the Constitution, the court was immediately bombarded with interpretations of the "privileges and immunities," "due process," and "equal protection" clauses which would make it the final judge of a great mass of state legislation. By a bare majority the court for a number of years refused to make the desired use of these clauses. Finally, however, after some changes in personnel, the court began to give way, and to use the "due process" clause to defeat state legislation hostile to property rights, particularly to the rights of corporations.

The account of this development belongs primarily in the story of the lives of the judges who succeeded Taney and his colleagues.[20] It can be fully understood, however, only in connection with the fact that the judges of the Taney régime permitted the use of the Constitution to enforce upon the people the bad bargains made by unwise, inefficient, or corrupt legislatures. It is certain that Taney would not have sanctioned the due process fanaticism of the later generation of judges, but he was partly responsible for the development of the idea in the minds of those who helped to make the court the devoted guardian of corporate rights which it became.

[20] See, for example, the relevant chapters in the author's *Stephen J. Field: Craftsman of the Law.*

Chapter XIX

THE CONTROL OF COMMERCE

ONE of the most difficult tasks which circumstances forced upon Taney and his court was the interpretation of the constitutional provision, "The Congress shall have power . . . to regulate commerce with foreign nations, and among the several States, and with the Indian tribes." The question was not usually as to whether Congress could, if it chose, regulate a particular kind of commerce. Congress during this period enacted few commercial regulations which were challenged before the courts. The point at issue was more likely to be whether a given business affected by a state regulation was interstate or foreign commerce, and, if so defined, whether the state regulation was unconstitutional merely because Congress possessed the unused power of control.

The question was important in view of the fact that if Congress left commerce pretty much alone, and the courts interpreted the constitutional provision to prevent state interference with business related to interstate or foreign commerce, such business would be largely free from government control. The courts, therefore, were in danger of becoming the tools of those businesses whose interest it was to escape regulation.

At the time when Taney became Chief Justice the Supreme Court had not passed directly on the question as to whether the failure of the federal government to exercise its commerce power left the states free to act on the same subject. The matter was debated in connection with the famous Steamboat Case of 1824.[1] Daniel Webster, in arguing this case, one of the most important of his career, and John Marshall in writing the opinion of the court, held that a com-

[1] *Gibbons* v. *Ogden,* 9 Wheaton 1 (1824).

mercial law of a state was void when in conflict with an act of Congress regulating interstate or foreign commerce. They interpreted "commerce" to include such intercourse as was involved in the carrying of passengers as well as the transportation of salable commodities. But in spite of Webster's insistence that even in the absence of a federal law the state regulations would be void, Marshall declined to pass upon this point. A federal law was involved, and although he seemed to look with approval upon Webster's argument he treated the further question as merely hypothetical and as not requiring an answer at the time.

Three years later, in the Original Package case,[2] Marshall rejected the arguments of Taney and Reverdy Johnson and held that a state could not tax the first sale of imported goods while in the original package. He suggested that the same principle would apply to the sale of articles brought merely from another state. He seemed on the point of committing himself to Webster's position that under no circumstances could a state regulate or interfere with interstate commerce. The doctrine was not clear in his own mind, however, and he blurred it two years later by holding that a state might authorize the building of dams across navigable streams if the commerce power of Congress had been left dormant.[3]

The precedents were therefore vague and somewhat confused when during his first term Taney's court was called upon to interpret the commerce clause. The case was that of *New York* v. *Miln*.[4] It concerned a New York law requiring commanders of ships to report names, ages, occupations, and other data as to passengers brought in from foreign ports or from other states. Six of the seven judges who then constituted the court decided that the act was not in violation of the Constitution.[5] Taney, busy writing the opinion in the Bridge case, asked Thompson to write the opinion in the commerce case, which was almost equally important.

---

[2] *Brown* v. *Maryland,* 12 Wheaton 419 (1827).

[3] *Willson* v. *Blackbird Creek Marsh Co.,* 2 Peters 245 (1829).

[4] 11 Peters 102 (1837).

[5] For data on the disagreements of judges in this case see the statements of Wayne and Taney in the Passenger Cases, 7 Howard 283, 429–436, 487–490 (1849).

Thompson wrote an opinion holding that the law could be justified as a police measure, if it was a police measure; or as a regulation of commerce if it was a commerce regulation. It was in conflict with no federal law, he declared, and in the absence of federal legislation the states might to some degree regulate interstate and foreign commerce. When the opinion was read in conference, Story, McLean, Baldwin, and Wayne, a majority of the court, refused to sanction Thompson's commerce argument. All but Story agreed with the police power argument, but Thompson refused to prune out the objectionable portion of his opinion.

Since the six judges who were willing to uphold the measure as a police regulation were divided three to three on the commerce question the deadlock was broken only by directing another judge to write the official opinion, leaving Thompson to file his own merely as a personal expression. This time the task was given to Barbour. Barbour complied, holding that the law was a state police measure for the promotion of public welfare which took effect after transportation had ceased.

The opinion was evidently discussed in some haste at the conference just preceding the close of the term, and the fact that Barbour had worked in some phrases not acceptable to his brethren was not then discovered. He had declared that passengers arriving at their destination were not in commerce, like goods still in original packages, for persons were not "subjects of commerce." In terms of this argument it would have been possible for the states to set up anti-immigration barriers along their coast lines, as some of them at times would have liked to do. The argument had implications also for tangled questions in another field, as to whether the transportation of slaves across state lines was commerce or not, and whether it might be interfered with by state or federal governments.

Barbour read the opinion in court on the last day of the term. The judges present to whom a portion of it was objectionable apparently thought it was too late to say anything about the matter, though Wayne voiced his indignation in another case many years later. Baldwin was not present at the official reading. He heard that the opinion contained objectionable phrases, and asked Taney to have changes made. Taney replied that Barbour had already left the city, and no change could be made without his concurrence. The opinion therefore went to press as it stood, and was regarded as having the sanction of the court in its entirety until the time when Wayne saw fit to denounce a portion of it.

There is little evidence to show how much manipulating Taney did in connection with the case. It was later made clear that he thought the New York law constitutional even though a state regulation of commerce, as well as because it was a legitimate exercise of the police power. He may have called on Thompson to write the opinion for this reason, but the reason was more probably the fact that Thompson was a citizen of the state in which the law was enacted. He also believed, with Barbour, that persons were not "subjects of commerce," and he may have had something to do with the fact that this idea was made a part of the opinion, and remained a part of it in spite of Baldwin's protest.

It was in connection with the issues of slavery that the breadth of the commerce power was again debated at length before the Supreme Court.[6] The case arose in connection with an attempt to collect payment for slaves from other states which had been sold in Mississippi. Thousands of slaves had been marketed there in the years preceding, producing a huge amount of debt to citizens of other states, which because of bad business conditions the planters found it hard to pay. To prevent the injurious withdrawal of capital from the state the Mississippi constitution was amended in 1832 to forbid the importation of slaves as merchandise after May 1, 1833. The amendment did not state whether it was self-acting or whether an act of the legislature was necessary to make it effective. No legislative act was passed. In 1839, however, a debtor refused to pay for slaves which he had purchased, on the ground that they had been imported in violation of the state constitution, and on an agreed statement of facts the case arising out of the dispute was taken from the federal

[6] *Groves* v. *Slaughter*, 15 Peters 449 (1841).

circuit court in Louisiana to the Supreme Court of the United States.

Eminent counsel appeared on both sides. Henry D. Gilpin and Robert J. Walker, United States senator from Mississippi, argued that the contract to purchase the slaves was invalid, and Walter Jones, Henry Clay, and Daniel Webster argued to the contrary. "The solemn temple of justice," wrote an observer, "was filled with an admiring auditory consisting of a large proportion of well-dressed ladies who occupied the seats within the bar." [7] The court listened attentively while counsel debated not merely the question of whether the constitutional provision had become operative or not, but also the deeper and more fundamental question as to whether, if the provision was operative, it was in conflict with the power of Congress to regulate interstate commerce.

The court decided the case on the narrower point, holding that because of the absence of a legislative act the constitutional prohibition against the importation of slaves had not become operative. It was therefore not necessary to discuss the more heated issues concerning the right to sell slaves across state lines, and the exclusiveness of the power of Congress over interstate commerce. A number of judges insisted on expressing themselves on these controversial points, however, and from their accessory discussions the case derives its chief significance.

It was McLean, the most eager of the judges to maintain influence in national politics, who provoked the unnecessary strife. Some doubts remain as to the details. John Quincy Adams, who was in the court room, recorded the statement that Taney read an opinion in the case. Thereupon McLean, to the surprise of his colleagues, took from his pocket and read a counter opinion, to which Thompson, Baldwin, and McKinley replied, each differing from all the others. [8] The opinion of the court, as published, stands not in Taney's name but in that of Thompson. It may be that Adams' memory played him false. It is possible, however, that since McLean had insisted on discussing points not necessary to the decision, Taney turned over to

[7] Allan Nevins (ed.), *The Diary of Philip Hone*, II, 523.
[8] *Memoirs of John Quincy Adams*, X, 442.

Thompson the opinion of the court, so that he might be unhampered in replying to McLean.

At any rate, in the official reports Thompson spoke for the court. McLean, declaring that basic questions had been fully argued before the court, insisted on expressing his opinion on them. Taney, differing from McLean, felt that McLean's action had forced him to state his difference on one point, and to emphasize the fact that the commerce question had never been settled by the court. Baldwin felt that extraneous topics ought not to be discussed by the court, but because McLean and Taney had expressed opinions he added his own, differing with each of them. McKinley and Story dissented from the opinion of the court. Altogether it seemed as complex a tangle as the eight judges sitting in the case could well have worked themselves into.

McLean took the Whig position that a state had no power to regulate interstate commerce even in the absence of federal regulation, and wrote as if this point had already been decided by the court. He was an abolitionist, however, and catered to the abolitionist sentiment of his state and other sections of the country. He was evidently not interested in preserving to Mississippi the power to boost the price of local products by excluding slaves from other states, or even the power to check the growth of indebtedness by forbidding purchases. He was deeply interested, however, in preserving the power of a state to do away with slavery within its borders, and to forbid the shipment of slaves into its territory from other states. He tried to avoid inconsistency, therefore, by arguing that, while a state could not interfere with interstate commerce, slaves were persons as well as articles of purchase and sale, and in their capacity as persons they might be excluded.

Although the fact had not been made public, Taney held the belief that the states could regulate interstate commerce in the absence of federal regulation. He did not state his position even now, but he made pointed reference to the fact that the question had not been settled by the court, as McLean implied; and he made an astonishingly inaccurate prediction that the court would never have to pass upon it. Without a supporting argument he expressed briefly the opinion that each state might decide for itself, without interference from the federal government, whether or not it would admit slaves from other states.

Baldwin believed that the states could not regulate interstate commerce, and that slaves were merchandise and therefore articles of commerce even though they were also persons, and that because they were articles of commerce a state could not prohibit their shipment in interstate commerce. McKinley and Story, dissenting, held that the Mississippi constitution voided the contract of purchase, even though the slaves were brought from outside the state. Story believed that the states had no power over interstate commerce,[9] but he may have believed that Mississippi acted on the slaves as persons rather than as commerce. McKinley did not state his position on either of the doctrines. Catron was absent at the argument of the case, and was unable to join officially in the fray.[10]

Prior to the decision in this case the differences among the judges on the several controversial points had not become matters of public knowledge. Now the questions were torn open and the chaos of judicial thinking was revealed, a chaos not to be dispelled until observers were given much additional evidence of judicial disharmony. Incidentally, the dramatic portrayal of the way in which issues of slavery were entangled with issues of constitutional law was suggestive of other stormy scenes yet to be enacted by the Supreme Court.

The next of the important commerce cases touched only indirectly the subject of slavery, although in his argument Daniel Webster called attention to laws in the South restricting the rights of free negroes from other states, and declared it high time that the court gave an opinion on the basic questions involved.[11] The issue, instead, was one of prohibition, or at least of temperance. Massachusetts had

[9] Story to R. J. Walker, May 22, 1841, MS., New York Historical Society.

[10] For the respective positions of the judges at this time on the issues in question see the chart on the following page.

[11] Baltimore *American*, quoted, Charleston *Courier*, Feb. 8, 1845.

forbidden the unlicensed sale of alcoholic beverages in quantities of less than twenty-eight gallons. The board having power to license the sale of smaller quantities was under no compulsion to do so, and in districts where prohibition sentiment was strong the law had the effect of prohibiting retail sales.

CHART

POSITIONS OF THE JUDGES ON THE EXCLUSIVENESS OF THE POWER OF CONGRESS OVER INTERSTATE COMMERCE, AND ON THE POWER OF THE STATES TO PROHIBIT THE IMPORTATION OF SLAVES

	The power of Congress over interstate commerce excludes the exercise of such power by the states.	States may prohibit the importation of slaves.
TANEY	The question has not yet been settled by the court, and should not be discussed unless necessary to the decision of a case. Such a case may never arise. (His answer, when subsequently given, was "No.")	Yes.
STORY	Yes.	Yes. (He did not say how he harmonized the two positions.)
THOMPSON	No answer here. (Probably would have said, "Not in all cases.")	**Yes.**
McLEAN	Yes.	Yes; in their capacity as persons, not as commerce.
BALDWIN	Yes.	No.
WAYNE	No answer here. (Later said "Yes.")	Yes. (No explanation of position.)
BARBOUR	No answer. (Position had probably been "No.")	No answer. (Position had probably been "Yes.")
CATRON	No answer. (Probably would have said, "Not in all cases.")	No answer. (Presumably would have said, "Yes.")
McKINLEY	No answer.	Yes.

Samuel Thurlow was convicted of selling "two quarts of spirituous liquors, and no more, against the peace of said Commonwealth." His counsel, Webster, Choate, and Hallett, took the case to the Supreme Court. They argued that the state law was invalid, because in conflict with federal laws and treaties which provided for the importation of liquors from certain foreign countries. Only seven judges were present at the time of the argument. They agreed that the law was valid, but they could not agree on reasons for their belief. The case was therefore continued to the ensuing term for argument before a full bench, giving the public the impression that the court was divided four to three as to the judgment. Because of a vacancy on the bench the case was postponed again. It was reargued finally in 1847 with two other similar cases, one from Rhode Island and one from New Hampshire, and the three, popularly known as the License Cases,[12] were decided together.

The decision revealed the continuation of chaos in judicial minds. Nine judges agreed that the three laws were valid. To demonstrate this fact, however, six judges wrote nine opinions, no one of which had the full concurrence of a majority of the court. Taney discussed the three cases in one opinion. The Massachusetts and Rhode Island cases were practically alike. They dealt with the retail sale of "broken" packages of liquor imported from abroad under federal laws and treaties. While such goods were in foreign commerce and under federal control, Taney declared, they were not subject to state interference. According to the doctrine of *Brown* v. *Maryland*, however, they ceased to be articles of foreign commerce when the original packages were broken. Although that decision had been in opposition to his argument as counsel, he now accepted it as the best method of determining when the foreign aspect of the commerce came to an end. Since the sales affected by the law were of broken packages, they did not directly affect foreign commerce, and there was no constitutional barrier to the enforcement of the law.

The New Hampshire case provided greater difficulties. It had to do with liquor brought from another state and sold in the original packages. No federal law was involved. The business, in terms of the original package doctrine, was obviously in interstate commerce, and Taney, in order to uphold the law, had to declare for the first time his belief that a state might regulate interstate commerce in the absence of federal regulation. McLean argued that the federal power over interstate commerce was exclusive, but contended that the state law was valid not as a regulation of commerce but as an exercise of the police powers of the state. Taney, seemingly in reply to McLean or to the arguments of counsel, rejected the contention. Police

---

[12] *Thurlow* v. *Massachusetts, Fletcher* v. *Rhode Island, Peirce* v. *New Hampshire,* 5 Howard 504 (1847).

powers, he declared, were but powers of sovereignty, and for the purposes of the case at hand they were not to be distinguished from other sovereign powers. The validity of the state law in question depended on whether the states had retained the sovereign power of regulating interstate commerce. He believed that the grant of power to the federal government was not an absolute and entire prohibition to the states, but merely conferred upon Congress the superior and controlling power.

The positions of the several judges varied all the way from the argument of McLean, that states could never regulate interstate commerce, to that of Daniel that states might regulate any business within their borders, even in spite of the original package doctrine. In bewilderment persons interested in the issues awaited another decision, in the hope that it might clarify some of the confusion. The next important decision came in the Passenger Cases, two cases one of which came from New York and the other from Boston.[13] Each of the laws involved provided for the raising of revenue for so-called police purposes connected with immigration or immigrants, by taxing each foreign passenger arriving at a port of the state.

Mixed motives had brought about the enactment of the laws. Recent years had witnessed a flood of immigration to the seaboard states. Large numbers of the immigrants were so impoverished and bewildered on their arrival in the new world that they became or were in danger of becoming public charges. Many were petty criminals or for other reasons were regarded as objectionable neighbors. By taxing immigration the states sought at the same time to curb it and to raise money to pay its costs.

People considered the laws from various points of view. Some favored any source of revenue which caused no pain to native Americans. Some thought the country would be better off without any more foreigners. Others were opposed to any measure which might check the flow of cheap labor. Some southerners were interested in the fate of these laws because of the analogy betwen them and the

[13] *Smith* v. *Turner, Norris* v. *City of Boston,* 7 Howard 283 (1849).

southern laws for inspecting vessels and checking the immigration of free negroes. Whatever the conflicting attitudes, however, the cases were watched with deep interest in the different sections of the country.

The New York case was argued in 1845, when the membership of the court was incomplete, and was returned to the calendar for reargument. The two cases were argued separately in 1847, and returned to the calendar. They were argued together in 1849, and decided. There were changes of counsel from case to case and from argument to argument, but Daniel Webster, smartly dressed in his blue coat and buff vest with brass buttons,[14] followed them through from beginning to end. He considered the points involved more important than in any case which he had argued since the Steamboat Case in 1824, when Chief Justice Marshall had welcomed his broad interpretation of the Constitution.

He was convinced that he was right in his contention that the state laws in question were in conflict with the Constitution, but he was uneasy about the court. He feared the judges were too much inclined to find apologies for irregular and dangerous acts of state legislatures. It was no court for constitutional questions. It "wants a strong and leading mind"—by which presumably he meant a mind which would interpret the Constitution as he saw it and as Marshall had seen it. John Van Buren, an opposing lawyer, urged the court to be responsive to the will of the people. He congratulated the judges on the overthrow of the "mastodon of construction" by which during the Marshall period the rights and sovereignty of the states had been trampled underfoot. Webster chose to understand Van Buren as congratulating the court for yielding to the popular impulses of the day. This might be a compliment, he declared, but it was a compliment he would not address to any court for which he entertained a feeling of respect.[15]

Webster was victorious by the narrow margin of one vote, when five of the nine judges held the state laws to be unconstitutional.

[14] New York *Tribune*, Dec. 27, 1847.
[15] *Ibid.*, Dec. 27, 28, 1847.

Each of the five, however, McLean, Wayne, Catron, McKinley, and Grier, insisted on stating his own views in his own way. In spite of the concurrence of some of them with the opinions of others, therefore, and in spite of Wayne's summary of the points on which he believed all five to agree, the reporter was unable to find any opinion which could be listed as the opinion of the court. The only legal point which he felt safe in stating in his headnotes was that the laws imposing taxes on alien passengers were null and void because in conflict with the Constitution.

Of the four dissenters Taney, Daniel, and Woodbury wrote opinions, and Nelson concurred with Taney. The eight opinions of the nine judges revealed a seemingly hopeless inability to agree on a general interpretation of the commerce power. They piled up such a maze of confusing arguments that it would be wearisome to attempt to follow them out. Taney's dissenting opinion, however, was so clear and forceful as to be significant in spite of the fact that it was not accepted by the court.

He believed it to be settled law that a state might expel undesirable persons from its borders; and if it could expel them it could exclude them in the first place. Likewise he believed, and he thought that five judges in the License Cases had agreed, that a state might make port and harbor regulations for the convenience of trade and the security of health, unless in conflict with an act of Congress. He disagreed with the contention of the majority that federal laws and treaties gave aliens the right to enter a state in spite of state laws.

He denied that immigrants were free from state control because of their status as imports. The Supreme Court had decided in *New York* v. *Miln* that persons were not "subjects of commerce." This opinion, written by Justice Barbour in 1837, stood embarrassingly in the way of the arguments of the majority. To weaken its influence Wayne resorted to unusual strategy in his opinion, by giving an account of the events connected with the decision in *New York* v. *Miln*, attempting to prove that the contention that persons were not subjects of commerce had never had the concurrence of a majority of the court.

The majority opinions in the Passenger Cases and Taney's dissent were read in court on the same day, but the remaining dissents were left over until the following day. Taney spent the evening industriously preparing a refutation of Wayne's statement, and on the next day he read it in court. Wayne then added more material to his own opinion to prove that Taney had refuted his argument in no essential point. The dispute over the historical facts was never satisfactorily settled. There was obvious weight, however, in Taney's contention that they should never have been mentioned at all, since if the authority of one opinion could be unsettled in after years in this fashion the same thing could be done with respect to any other.

The court was not called upon to decide whether a state could exclude a citizen of another state from its territory. To prevent misunderstanding, however, Taney declared that such a measure would be unconstitutional. In a statement in which he and his admirers in after years took pride, he declared that every citizen of the United States had certain rights, among which was the right to come and go as he pleased. "For all the great purposes for which the federal government was formed," he continued, "we are one people, with one common country. We are all citizens of the United States; and, as members of the same community, must have the right to pass and repass through every part of it without interruption, as freely as in our own states. And a tax imposed by a state for entering its territories or harbors is inconsistent with the rights which belong to the citizens of other states as members of the Union, and with the objects which that Union was intended to attain. Such a power in the states could produce nothing but discord and mutual irritation, and they very clearly do not possess it."

For negroes, however, the statement offered no comfort. Among the rights enumerated was the right "to pursue and reclaim one who has escaped from service." While it may have seemed that Taney had asserted the right of a free negro to go from one state to another in spite of the laws of the latter, such was not his intention. He was speaking of the rights of citizens. He had held long since that within the meaning of the Constitution a negro could not be a citizen at all.[16]

The decision of the majority of the court was regarded as a blow to the interests of the South, in spite of Wayne's assertion that the slave states still had the power to exclude free negroes from their territory. The Washington correspondent of the Charleston *Mercury* wrote to his paper that the decision virtually annulled the inspection laws of his state, and the *Mercury* interpreted the decision to mean that free negroes could no longer be excluded.

Webster was elated by his victory, which paralleled the victory of a quarter of a century earlier in the Steamboat Case. He regretted the lack of unanimity among the judges, but consoled himself with the belief that Marshall and Story would have been with him had they been members of the court at the time. He was pleased also with Taney's admission that the laws were unconstitutional in so far as they applied to citizens of other states.

It was in the Pilot Case,[17] decided in 1852 by a bare majority of the court, that a rule was worked out for interpreting the commerce power which seemed to dispel some of the confusion. After the adoption of the Constitution, Congress had provided by law that the harbors and ports should continue to be regulated by laws of the states. A Pennsylvania law subsequently enacted provided that all vessels of certain descriptions coming into port should employ pilots, or if they refused to do so should nevertheless pay half the regular fee, for the use of the Society for the Relief of Distressed and Decayed Pilots. Cooley refused to pay the fee, on the ground that the state law regulated foreign commerce which was subject only to federal control, a control which could not be delegated to the states.

Had there been no intervening change in the personnel of the court it seems probable that the case would have been decided to the accompaniment of a series of conflicting opinions such as characterized its predecessors. A new judge, however, Benjamin R. Curtis, offered

16 *Ante*, pp. 153–154.
17 *Cooley* v. *Board of Wardens of the Port of Philadelphia*, 12 Howard 299 (1852).

a formula for eliminating some of the chaos. He was a lawyer of prestige; he had the ability to phrase legal materials neatly with a minimum of commitments, and he had not been on the bench long enough to incur the hostility of his brethren in connection with the issues of the controversy. Four of them united with him, therefore, in the acceptance of a compromise doctrine which had been mentioned by other judges but which a majority had not previously been willing to accept.

The decision was that if the interstate or foreign commerce to be regulated was an essentially local matter, and required local rather than national rules, such as pilotage rules in a particular harbor, the states might legislate on the subject until Congress interfered. If on the other hand the subject required a national, uniform rule, the states could not interfere even in the absence of legislation by Congress.

Taney was one of the five who accepted the opinion. McLean and Wayne, whom Curtis characterized privately as "the most high-toned Federalists on the bench," [18] dissented on the ground that the states had no power at any time to regulate interstate and foreign commerce. Daniel, on the other hand, as might be expected, disagreed on the ground that the states had full power to regulate such matters as pilotage, and could not be interfered with by the federal government. McKinley was absent.

The principle was now established, but from the very beginning [19] the court had difficulty with its application, difficulty which was not to be blamed wholly upon the dissenting judges. There was no way of determining clearly whether or not a given business was purely local, or whether it should be governed by a national uniform rule, and in the many cases which arose in after years the judges were notoriously unable to agree. The final outcome has been that, in harmony with the general tendency toward centralization, less and less business has been labeled as local and subject to local regulation.

[18] See B. R. Curtis to George Ticknor, Feb. 29, 1852, *Memoir of Benjamin Robbins Curtis*, I, 168.
[19] See *Pennsylvania* v. *Wheeling & Belmont Bridge Co.*, 13 Howard 518 (1852).

With this curtailment of the powers of the states the business has been left unregulated, save as the federal government has ultimately stepped in to provide control.

To understand the nature and significance of the work of Taney and his colleagues in connection with the commerce clause of the Constitution, it is necessary to remember that they were not called upon to define the power of the federal government to use the clause as a justification for broad regulation of business and industrial activity. These problems did not arise in force until after many decades. The questions of the Taney period had rather to do with the power of states to legislate in the interest of their citizens when interstate or foreign commerce was in some way involved.

The exclusive character of the federal power was at this time usually asserted not because federal control was desired, but to block state regulation, and therefore all the regulation that was threatened. Hence the development of doctrines as to the exclusiveness of federal power was coincident with the development of powerful business organizations, which, after getting as many concessions as possible from government, desired only to be let alone. The development of the doctrines of nationalism, as contrasted with those of state rights, was for the most part synonymous with the unfolding of theories of *laissez faire* industrialism in the United States.

In certain ways, it is true, the national government had already become to a degree the servant of large business interests, as in laying protective tariffs and chartering a national bank. Consequently it is not surprising that Daniel, a Virginia agrarian who opposed extensive state interference with the activities of the people, was even more deeply and intensely hostile to the development of national power. Taney was more paternalistic than Daniel in his conception of the functions of government. He recognized more fully than Daniel the need for state legislation for the promotion of public welfare. He was hostile to the use of the national government as a tool of business interests, but he was not opposed to federal legislation, or to the extension of federal authority in other ways,[20] if local institutions were not interfered with.

The paternalism by which he differed from his agrarian colleague may have been due to each or any of a variety of causes. His contact with urban society may have taught him the need for government protection of public welfare to a degree not apparent to Daniel. He may have been more of a humanitarian and less of a doctrinaire in temperament. His devotion to the institutions of Catholicism may have accustomed him to more of authoritarian interference with individual liberties than many of his fellows had learned to accept. At any rate, however, the two were in firm agreement on one point. The states were to be left free to deal with slavery in their own territory as seemed to them best, without interference and without restriction from the federal government. No doubt this issue had much to do with the development of the ideas of each of them as to the interpretation of the commerce power.

More credit has been given to Taney in recent years for the development of the concept of police power than he is entitled to, and more than he would have been willing to accept. The concept is now used largely to justify state legislation which conservatives regard as of doubtful reasonableness, and as at least on the verge of taking liberty or property without due process of law. It is therefore regarded with favor by those who are liberal in their attitude toward social legislation, and the fact that a judge has played a part in working out the concept is regarded as evidence of distinction.

Taney did not so regard it, however. In *New York* v. *Miln* and certain other cases he accepted it as a compromise basis for holding certain state laws to be constitutional, but he seems to have regarded it as nothing more than a compromise and an excuse for permitting certain legislation to stand, which, indeed, it was. He preferred to rely on the power of sovereignty, and to hold that if the states had

[20] See for example his extension of the admiralty jurisdiction of the federal courts in the *Genesee Chief* v. *Fitzhugh*, 12 Howard 443 (1851).

not clearly surrendered powers by the Constitution the right to legislate was not to be limited by the Supreme Court.

Indeed, the nationalists on the court seem to have had more to do with the growing use of the doctrine than did those who insisted generally on the existence of broad powers in the states. McLean, for instance, found it particularly helpful in resolving the inconsistency between his assertion that the federal government had exclusive control over interstate commerce, and his insistence on the other hand that a state had the power to forbid the sale of liquor shipped in interstate commerce. He labeled such interference as the exercise of police power, and attributed it to a different source from the power to regulate commerce. In his attempt to find an excuse for certain exceptional items of state legislation, while limiting the breadth of state powers in general, he had far more influence than Taney in working the police power doctrine into constitutional law.

Taney's position, essentially, was that the sanctifying label of "police power" was not needed to justify the exercise of powers possessed by sovereign states and never surrendered. Had he lived in a later period he would doubtless have resisted hotly the use of "due process of law" as a Trojan horse to gain for great business interests entrenchment against the authority of the states. Had he resorted to the police power doctrine, however, he would have recognized its use as a "retreat to previously prepared positions," which is to say, a surrender of ground which was given up only because it could not be held.

One impression given by the commerce cases as well as by other cases of the period, is, as Webster suggested, that the court lacked a strong and leading mind. Perhaps there were too many strong minds, or too many stubborn judges, but at any rate no member of the court dominated it as Marshall had dominated the court of his period. Perhaps Taney tried, and failed. There is more reason for believing, however, that he wished the court to exist as a democracy rather than the voice of one man, and that he was sufficiently skeptical of legal dogmas to believe that there were many potentially "right" ways of working out judicial decisions and giving content to principles of constitutional law, rather than merely one. Within a short time after he began his work as Chief Justice the court recaptured the prestige which had been threatened by the appointment of himself and other Jacksonians. There is no evidence that any general lack of respect for the court grew out of its lack of unanimity in the commerce cases. The loss of respect came later, in connection with division over the dynamic issues of slavery. True, there would have been more unanimity in the commerce decisions had not slavery issues been in the background, but the latter did not for a time come far enough into the foreground to take the place of all else. Slavery was not yet the all-absorbing topic.

Chapter XX

RUMBLINGS OF THE DISTANT DRUM

IN THE mass of disputes settled by the Supreme Court during Taney's first term on the bench there was a series of cases which, like dark clouds over the horizon, radiated the threat of approaching storm. They had to do with questions concerning property rights in slaves. Controversies over other kinds of property were settled as a matter of routine, usually without the persistence of private or public rancor. Conflicts over slave property were different, however, in that back of the question as to who owned a slave was the more fundamental question as to whether any man could own property in the body and in the labor of another. There were sharp differences of opinion, sectional and cultural, which require analysis in terms of their historical backgrounds in order to fit them into a picture of Taney and his court at the time when forebodings of national disaster began to be widely felt.

As noted elsewhere, the first generation of many of the distinguished families of the American colonies, including the Taneys, came to the new world as indentured servants, submitting to ownership by other men to pay their passage and provide the necessities for ultimately independent life. Little stigma was attached to such servitude. It was a preliminary and oftentimes a necessary step in the process of attaining to a position of prosperity and of ultimate aristocracy.

In the South, however, as the necessary capital was acquired, people invested more and more in negroes who could be held as slaves for life, rather than in indentured servants of their own race who might be harder to control and in any case would demand their freedom soon after they were adjusted to life amid pioneer conditions. Labor came more and more to be performed by degraded hands, and the performance of manual labor came to be regarded as evidence of a position in the social scale which was at least unpleasantly low. The descendants of indentured servants who had been respected in their time found it convenient to conceal the economic histories of their ancestors.

Indeed, the social standards of a slave economy became such that a white man cast reflection upon his status if he performed routine manual labor even on his own property. A gentleman owned slaves for such purposes. His business was to manage, to direct, to command, and, as a man of generous and cultured attainments, to play the part of the gentleman. Those white people who remained slaveless, because of lack of funds or other reasons, and yet continued to reside alongside their more prosperous neighbors, came to be regarded by those neighbors and even by the slaves of the region as inferior people. Because of this social discrimination and because it was increasingly difficult for non-slaveholding white planters to compete successfully with black gang labor in raising cotton, many of these people drifted away from the fertile tidewater and piedmont regions to seek homes in more congenial surroundings, leaving the economic and social system of the South more completely in the hands of the owners of slaves.

In this way the South came completely under the dominance of a civilization incorporating the ideals of the planting aristocracy, with slave labor as one of its fundamentals. Succeeding generations adjusted themselves for the most part unquestioningly to the accepted social pattern. Justification at home was unnecessary. The criticisms of outsiders were regarded as the effusions of aliens whose understanding and motives were suspect, and, unless they made trouble among the slaves, were worthy only of a sort of gentlemanly scorn.

In the North, although individual merchants had added to their incomes by running slave ships, and although slaves had been kept for household purposes, black property had on the whole much less value than in the South. Whereas the South could profitably use the routine labor of untutored negroes in the production of one or two major crops, the North, surviving by means of more complex and varied activities, had to have more training and initiative even for its manual labor. In the face of incipient industrialism, therefore, and of growing diversification of labor, slavery died out in the North. The philosophy of the dignity of labor, having its roots among such diverse sources as the Calvinist background of the people, the desire of employers to keep their workers, and the desire of workers to retain their social rank among conditions which they found it difficult to escape, prevailed throughout the section. Success at acquiring property through work and through trade became convincing evidence of high rank in society.

In the two regions, therefore, together with their westward extensions, which were linked together by the Constitution, there were two sharply contrasting civilizations. At first, when they had approximately equal strength, they made mutual concessions and gave evidence of respect for each other in spite of a certain amount of rivalry. As their differences became more apparent, however, and as the North outstripped the South in population and in wealth, each became more highly critical of the other. Increasing numbers of northerners scorned the immorality of a society based on slavery, while southerners scoffed at the crudeness of a life based on trade and on the performance of menial tasks by white men for whose welfare employers assumed no responsibility. With the growth of sectional suspicion and hostility each section increased its efforts to dominate the national government for the protection of its own interests, with the result of making suspicion and hostility still more intense.

At the time when Taney made his speech in the celebrated Gruber case, in defense of the Methodist minister who attacked the institution of slavery, many people in the South were free to admit that serious problems grew out of their "peculiar institution." No small number of them liberated their slaves, only to discover that newly emancipated slaves were unequipped to care for themselves in a *laissez faire* world, and were apt to create disturbances among slaves and in society in general. They tried hard to solve the complex race problems by plans for colonizing free negroes in Africa. They passed humanitarian legislation for protection of the rights of negroes, at the same time at which they were attempting to make it more difficult for slaves to escape from their masters.

The Nat Turner insurrection, in 1831, might be said to mark the end of tolerant and thoughtful consideration of the problems of slavery by the people of the South. The northern abolitionists who were circulating antislavery sentiments which might have the effect of provoking further slave uprisings were less numerous than they were believed to be; but they were vociferous, and doubtless constituted a real menace. Southerners who had hitherto attempted to face their problems without bias now felt the necessity of defending their institutions against all criticisms. The levying of protective tariffs hostile to the interests of the South demonstrated what the North might be able to do concerning slavery through its control of the federal government. Northern leaders, pleased with the growing strength of their position, glorified the Constitution and the Union. The South evolved the doctrine of nullification. Catastrophe may or may not have been inevitable, but the threat of it was ominous.

It was to be expected that an issue representing a fundamental cultural and economic cleavage in the country should find its way ultimately into controversies to be decided by the Supreme Court. The prospect of such an event was a legitimate cause of uneasiness, for the prestige and authority of court decisions rest not merely upon the power of government to enforce them, but also upon the popular assumption that they ought to be enforced. When cases turned upon a fundamental cultural rift within the country, upon a fundamental disagreement as to what government was under obligation to do, judicial decisions had not that assurance of general support from the people of all sections which made their enforcement a mere matter of routine. It was best, therefore, that major sectional issues be avoided by the court as long as possible.

A slave case was decided during Taney's first term.[1] It was relatively insignificant, but the fact that Taney's judicial career was

[1] *United States* v. *The Ship Garonne*, 11 Peters 73 (1837).

virtually ushered in by a slave case has to some seemed a sinister portent. It was in connection with the *Amistad* Case,[2] however, decided in 1841, that the Supreme Court captured from the wrangling House of Representatives the spotlight which played upon the discussion of heated slavery issues. It concerned a cargo of negroes which slave merchants had brought from Africa. The negroes had been sold in Havana in violation of Spanish laws, and shipped by the purchasers from Havana to another port in Cuba.

During the voyage the negroes revolted, killed the captain, made prisoners of the two alleged owners, and ordered the latter to steer the ship in the direction of Africa. While creating the impression of obeying orders the two men steered for the coast of the United States, and the vessel, the *Amistad,* was captured by a United States naval brig off the coast of Connecticut. A federal court, which may or may not have been influenced by the abolitionist sentiment of the locality, decided that no treaty with Spain obligated the government to surrender the negroes to the Spanish claimants, since they had been imported into Cuba in violation of Spanish laws. The case was appealed to the Supreme Court, however, by the federal government. The taking of the appeal was perhaps to be attributed to the southern viewpoint of Secretary of State John Forsyth, and perhaps in part to the desire of President Van Buren at this time to ride the fence on the slavery issue.

The case stirred excited and partisan discussion. Northern sentiment was for the negroes, while that of the South was decidedly in favor of the claimants. The Charleston *Courier* declared that northern writers and reviewers had hitherto prejudiced the case, but they would be unable to influence the Supreme Court, which breathed a different atmosphere and was not affected by fanaticism nor overawed by clamor. The court, therefore, would no doubt pay some attention to treaties with Spain, and would deliver the slaves to their owners.[3] To the indignation of northern papers, the Washington *Globe,* the administration paper, printed an able defense of the claims of the

[2] *United States* v. *The Schooner Amistad,* 15 Peters 518 (1841).
[3] Charleston *Courier,* Jan. 13, 1841.

owners, at the time of the beginning of the term of the court.[4] This was a dangerous and discreditable attempt to influence the court on the side adverse to humanity, declared an Albany paper.[5] On the other hand the prediction was made in Charleston that even if the Supreme Court decided that the negroes were to be surrendered, the northern people would not permit it.[6]

The case attracted all the more attention because John Quincy Adams was retained to aid in the defense of the negroes. His growing capacity for biting sarcasm and bitter denunciation was one of the striking phenomena of the decade. The case enabled him to demonstrate in the court room the techniques which he used in the House of Representatives, denouncing to his heart's content the policy followed by the Van Buren administration. His argument was extraordinary, declared Justice Story, "extraordinary, I say, for its power, for its bitter sarcasm, and its dealing with topics far beyond the record and points of discussion." [7]

The court decided in favor of the negroes. Story, writing the opinion, made only the necessary commitments. He declared that our treaties with Spain provided only for the return of slaves who were legally held, and that neither under Spanish law nor under international law were these negroes, born free but kidnaped in their native land, to be classified as slaves. He declared further that "upon the eternal principles of justice and international law" the United States could not make with Spain a treaty by which free Africans were deprived of their liberty.

Story left undiscussed a number of sharply controversial questions raised by counsel. It had been contended, for instance, that whatever their previous status had been, the negroes became free when they arrived in the free state of Connecticut, and that no federal treaty could supersede the state laws in the matter. Taney had taken this position a decade earlier in an opinion as Attorney General, but the

---

[4] *Ibid.*, Jan. 23, 27, 1841.

[5] Albany *Gazette*, quoted, Boston *Liberator*, Feb. 12, 1841.

[6] Charleston *Courier*, Feb. 20, 1841.

[7] Story to Mrs. Story, Feb. 28, 1841, *Life and Letters of Joseph Story*, II, 348.

court as a whole was evidently unwilling to commit itself so far.[8] It was contended by government counsel that the government derived the power to make treaties on the subject from the fact that the transportation of negroes was foreign commerce. The opposition denied that this was true, pointing to the statement in *New York* v. *Miln* that persons were not subjects of commerce. On this point, likewise, Story was silent.

It is apparent from his opinions stated on other occasions that Taney believed the negroes to be subject solely to the laws of the state in which they happened to be, that he thought them not subject to the treaty making power as far as the sovereign rights of the state were concerned, and that he held persons not to be articles of commerce. It is quite possible that his judgment was guided by these beliefs rather than by his interpretation of the texts of particular treaties, or by Story's "eternal principles of justice and international law." Taney probably concurred with Story in his disapproval of the kidnaping of negroes for slavery purposes, but with the growth of sectional friction he became wary of federal interference with slavery in any way. His concern was in having it left to the states in which it was found. He was quite willing that those states hostile to it should abolish it within their borders. He felt even more deeply, however, that states not wishing to abolish it should be left unhampered in dealing with it as they saw fit.

Many southerners were of course displeased by the decision of the Supreme Court in the *Amistad* Case, but Story judiciously stated the position of the court in such a way as to commit the court no further than necessary and give cause for only a minimum of criticism. In *Groves* v. *Slaughter*,[9] decided at the same term, an attempt seems to have been made likewise to keep the court as free as possible from the increasing strife over slavery issues. It was found possible to avoid passing on questions as to whether a state could impede interstate commerce in negroes, by a decision that the state constitutional provision involved had not become operative. Unfortunately Mc-

---

[8] 2 Opinions of the Attorneys General 475. For discussion see Chapter VIII.
[9] 15 Peters 449 (1841). For discussion see preceding chapter.

Lean insisted on discussing the questions in a concurring opinion, drawing a subtle distinction by arguing that a state could not regulate interstate commerce, but could exclude slaves in their capacity as persons rather than as articles of commerce. By McLean's argument Taney felt obliged to express his opinion that a state had complete control over slavery within its borders, and might prevent other slaves from being imported. Other judges permitted themselves to be drawn into the debate, and expressed still other points of view.[10]

The case therefore placed the Supreme Court definitely in the arena of conflict. From this time onward it was taken heavily into account in appraising the strength and the weapons of opposing forces, and decisions of the court on the controversial issues were watched with anxiety.

Among the slavery problems producing friction between the North and the South none were more irritating and perplexing than those having to do with slaves who had escaped from their masters and fled northward. During the period of the Articles of Confederation, as antislavery sentiment grew in the North, there was a tendency to regard slaves escaping into free states as entitled to their freedom. At the drafting of the Constitution the southern representatives demanded guarantees of their property rights in fugitive slaves. A compromise provision was adopted to the effect that, "No person held to service or labor in one State, under the laws thereof, escaping into another, shall, in consequence of any law or regulation therein,

[10] The Supreme Court customarily followed the decisions of state courts as to whether or not constitutional provisions required supporting legislation to make them effective. The Mississippi courts had not at this time settled the question concerning the provision upon which the case turned, and the Supreme Court had to decide for itself. At a later date the highest court in Mississippi, contrary to the Supreme Court decision, held that the constitutional provision had become effective without supporting legislation. The Supreme Court, in *Rowan* v. *Runnels*, 5 Howard 134 (1847), had to decide whether it would now follow the state interpretation of its constitution, as it normally would have done, or whether it would adhere to its own previous decision. In an opinion written by Taney, with only Daniel dissenting, it followed its own decision. Following the state decision would not merely have added to the strife over slavery questions, but also have made it possible for citizens of Mississippi to repudiate huge sums in debt to residents of other states from whom they had purchased slaves. It seems probable that beliefs as to the sanctity of contracts had quite as much to do with the judgment arrived at by the court as did the more specific slavery aspects of the case.

be discharged from such service or labor, but shall be delivered up on claim of the party to whom such service or labor may be due." In this manner the Constitution was made the defender of the rights of slave owners. Pursuant to this constitutional provision Congress enacted the Fugitive Slave Law of 1793, providing for the restoration of fugitive slaves to their masters, after ownership had been demonstrated before a state or federal magistrate.

In a spirit of evangelism, however, many citizens of free states organized so-called underground railroad lines to aid slaves in escaping, thereby of course deeply irritating the foiled pursuers from the South. Old state laws were enforced and new ones were enacted to aid escaping slaves. Some of them required that a negro should not be removed by an alleged owner until the claim had been determined by a jury. On its face the requirement seemed fair, and only intended to discover whether the claimant was the legal owner. Juries were quite apt to have abolitionists among their number, however, or at least persons sympathetic enough to be unwilling to send unfortunate negroes back into slavery. Jury trial therefore often had the effect of depriving legal owners of their property. It was likewise true, on the other hand, that as slaves increased in value traders went into northern states and laid claim to free negroes or kidnaped them outright and sold them into slavery. There was need for laws to protect the rights of the unfortunate class.

The state of Pennsylvania had ample experience with fugitive slaves, with false claims to ownership, and with kidnaping. It had detailed legislation covering the rights of negroes within its borders. Since there were few federal magistrates in any of the states, the enforcement of the federal Fugitive Slave Law depended largely upon the coöperation of state officers. These officers acted under the restrictions of state laws, however, and were often personally abolitionist in sentiment. The southern states therefore complained bitterly of the difficulty of getting their property out of Pennsylvania.

In response to the criticism the legislature in 1826 passed a law intended to prevent the taking of negroes not legally owned by the claimants, but to prescribe a manner in which lawful owners might make their claims effective. Evidence of ownership was to be presented to a magistrate, who was to direct that the negro be brought before him. If he was convinced that the claim was well founded he was to issue a certificate authorizing the removal of the negro from the state. A heavy penalty was provided for issuing a certificate otherwise than in accordance with this procedure.

The constitutionality of the law was challenged in *Prigg* v. *Pennsylvania*,[11] which reached the Supreme Court in 1842. A negress had escaped from her owner in Maryland and fled into Pennsylvania. Discovering her whereabouts, the owner sent Edward Prigg to capture her and the child born to her during her absence. Pursuant to the Pennsylvania law Prigg took the negroes before a magistrate. The magistrate, perhaps sympathetic with the slaves, or fearful of issuing the certificate without additional proof of ownership, refused to authorize their removal. Prigg then seized the negroes and took them into Maryland without a certificate.

A Pennsylvania indictment for kidnaping was issued against him, and a demand was made upon the governor of Maryland for his surrender for trial. The governor admitted the legality of the claim, but made an unsuccessful attempt to secure the withdrawal of the demand. The Maryland legislature adopted a report declaring that the rights of the slaveholding states were endangered, and proposing a deputation to the Pennsylvania legislature to demand the withdrawal of the indictment and modification of the Pennsylvania laws to protect the rights of the owners of fugitive slaves.[12]

To determine the constitutionality of the Pennsylvania law and to remove the interstate friction, amicable arrangements were made for a suit. Prigg submitted to trial. He was found guilty. The Supreme Court of Pennsylvania affirmed the judgment *pro forma,* and the case was brought before the Supreme Court of the United States.

Story, writing the opinion of the court, had no difficulty in demonstrating the unconstitutionality of the Pennsylvania law, because of the fact that certain of its provisions interfered with the enforcement

[11] 16 Peters 539 (1842).
[12] Charleston *Courier,* Jan. 23, 1838.

of the federal Fugitive Slave Law. On this point, which was all that was necessary for the decision of the case immediately at hand, his colleagues were in unanimous agreement. He went further, however, and declared that since the Constitution gave the federal government the power to deal with fugitive slaves the states could not pass laws on the subject even if not in conflict with federal laws, or even, indeed, if intended to aid the federal government's program. He doubted, furthermore, whether state officers could be required to enforce federal fugitive slave laws, and whether the states were required to provide the means for making such laws effective. This was true because the obligations of a state to protect slave property were only such as the Constitution laid upon it. Slavery was protected only by municipal regulations, and had no sanction in international law.

Some of Story's friends were unable to understand why he, an enemy of slavery, would write the opinion of the court striking down a state law for the protection of fugitive slaves. His own pious explanation was that he would never hesitate to do his duty as a judge, under the Constitution and laws of the United States, whatever the consequences might be.[13] A more plausible explanation, however, lay in his belief that he had won a "triumph for freedom" in persuading the court to permit him to say as its spokesman that slavery had no sanction in the principles of international law, but only in the positive legislation of particular governments.[14] Slave property differed for him in this respect from other property, which was apparently protected by some body of fundamental principles which lay behind and supplemented or even superseded positive law—some "brooding omnipresence in the sky," in the language of Justice Holmes.

Ephemeral as Story's victory may have seemed to those holding a different conception of law, it was very real in so far as it produced the conclusion that a state was under no obligation to aid in the enforcement of federal fugitive slave laws, and had no power to enact supplementary legislation. Taney, who fully agreed that the

---

[13] Story to Ezekiel Bacon, Nov. 19, 1842, *Life and Letters of Joseph Story*, II, 431.

[14] See Charles Sumner to S. P. Chase, March 12, 1847, Chase MSS., Library of Congress. See also *Life and Letters of Joseph Story*, II, 381-398.

obstructive Pennsylvania law was unconstitutional, had no use for those of Story's arguments which were unnecessary to the decision of the case. He declared that the Constitution contained no prohibition of state legislation protecting property rights in fugitive slaves. On the other hand, the federal Fugitive Slave Law assumed the coöperation of state officers, and would be ineffective without it, since there were not enough federal officers available for the execution of its provisions.

Some of the states had assumed that they had obligations to aid in returning fugitives from other states to their owners. Maryland, for instance, had laws requiring the arrest of negroes unable to give proper account of themselves, and providing that they should be held while advertisements were circulated for the attention of possible owners. These were not mere police power laws, enacted to drive objectionable people from the state. The negroes in question might be committing no objectionable act, and might be trying to get out of the state as quickly as they could reach the northern border. The purpose of the laws was the protection of the property rights of the owners, which by the Constitution was enjoined upon the states as a duty. If Maryland was forbidden to enforce such enactments her territory must soon become an open pathway for fugitives escaping from other states.

Nowhere in the course of his argument did Taney suggest that the slave might have rights to freedom which society, or the federal government, or the states, ought to protect. He concerned himself solely with the legal rights of the master over the slave. These rights, he believed, were entitled to protection from the federal and state governments by virtue of the legal and the compact nature of the Constitution. There is no reason for assuming that he was in 1842 any less kindly disposed toward individual negroes than he had been during preceding decades. Kindness toward negroes, however, was a matter of personal volition. It might be taken as evidence of character, it might justify public approbation, it might be a manifestation of religion, but it had nothing directly to do with law. Existing law dealt with the negro in his traditionally degraded condition, degraded oftentimes to the level of slavery. It was the function of judges to apply the law, and not to teach morality or preach religion.

Justice Thompson wrote an opinion agreeing that the burden of responsibility for enforcing the constitutional provision was on the federal government. He contended, however, with Taney, that the states might legislate concerning fugitive slaves as long as their laws did not conflict with those of Congress. McLean wrote a long opinion concurring with Story on many points but emphasizing the powers of states to prevent the seizure of free negroes under the pretense of recapturing slaves. He believed that state officers were under obligation to aid in enforcing the federal Fugitive Slave Law.

Baldwin thought the constitutional provision so complete in itself that no legislation at all was needed. Wayne agreed with Story on all points but wrote a long opinion of his own, emphasizing the fact that much state legislation nominally in aid of the recovery of slaves had actually stood as a hindrance. Catron and McKinley were silent. Daniel wrote an opinion agreeing in substance with that of Taney.

The decision was in part unsatisfactory both to the North and to the South. The North heard with resentment that it could not constitutionally enforce laws such as those requiring jury trial in fugitive slave cases, which were intended to hamper the recovery of slaves. The South, on the other hand, was told that its laws aiding the recapturing of slaves were unconstitutional, and that the states to which their property had fled were under no obligation to render them assistance.

The Supreme Court came in for bitter criticism from all sides, and all the more because of the diversity of the opinions expressed. The effect of the criticism, however, was only temporary. The prestige of the court was seriously damaged only with extreme abolitionists, who were ready to denounce any man and any institution which was not ready to put abolitionism before everything else. The major significance of the decision lies in the fact that many of the northern states took advantage of the advice that they might forbid their officers to aid in the enforcement of the federal Fugitive Slave Law, thereby rendering it ineffective. As a result the representatives of the South, who had formerly done everything possible to prevent congressional discussion of the "peculiar institution" of their section of the country, now had to bring the subject up in order to secure the adoption of an effective federal law. Once the subject was opened to clamorous and acrimonious debate there was no silencing the discussion, and the distant rumblings of disaster grew louder and louder until the storm burst upon the country in the form of secession and civil war.

CHAPTER XXI

THE SPOILS OF OFFICE AND CHANGING PERSONNEL

ALTHOUGH appointed for life, and supposedly unaffected by changes in the political scene, the judges of the Supreme Court were intimately affected by the shifting fortunes of party strife, and deeply interested in them. They were interested as a matter of course because of their previous political connections; they were interested in the principles sponsored by opposing candidates; they were occasionally bent on securing appointments for friends, and some of them had presidential aspirations.

In addition, they were deeply concerned about the way in which a presidential election might affect their own little group, an exclusive club of nine men, chosen for life. Since most of the members were elderly it happened but seldom that four years passed without the loss of one or more, whose places were filled by presidential appointments and senatorial confirmation, oftentimes without reference to the desires of the members previously chosen. The new men might fit in well and bring distinction by their learning, or they might possess limited capacity with ideas unpopular with their fellows, and cause unpleasant friction within the group. Their selection was therefore watched with great anxiety, and the election of the Presidents who would make the appointments was a matter of concern.

Jackson's later appointments were made not merely in attempt to place his friends in high office but also to place men in this strategic position who were "right" on matters of principle. His selections were therefore anything but popular with men not imbued with Jacksonian principles. When at the very end of his administration the Senate enlarged the court from seven to nine Jackson sent to the Senate the names of John Catron of Tennessee and William Smith of Alabama. "What judges they will make!" Henry Clay remarked in disgust.[1] Chancellor Kent appraised them as "very feeble lights." [2] Justice McLean believed they would add little to the bench, and Justice Story agreed with him, remarking that an increase of numbers without an increase of strength and ability was a positive disadvantage.[3] Story evidently retained his unfavorable opinion, while Taney on the other hand was pleased, at least with Catron. "The more I have seen of him," Taney wrote to Jackson, "the more I have been impressed with the strength of his judgment, legal knowledge, and high integrity of character. He is a most valuable acquisition to the bench of the Supreme Court." [4]

Catron had some private doubts as to his ability to perform the duties required by the court, but they disappeared with the experiences of his first term. The legal questions, he wrote to Jackson, depended more on common sense than on any deep legal knowledge, "and I find that political tendencies are just as strong on all constitutional and political questions as they are in any other department of the government." [5]

When Smith refused to serve, because the position would interfere with his active career in politics, Van Buren had the opportunity to make his first appointment. He chose John McKinley of Alabama, a man of moderate ability who achieved neither distinction nor notoriety. It seemed as if Van Buren would have no further opportunities of the sort. The judges continued in apparently good health, and, largely because of the business depression, his experience as President was limited to one term. Barbour died suddenly, however, just before the end of the term, and Van Buren sent to the Senate the name of his friend Peter V. Daniel of Virginia, then a judge of the United States district court.

Action on the nomination was postponed while attempts were

---

[1] Clay to Francis S. Brooke, March 7, 1837, Clay MSS. For a list of the appointments of Taney's colleagues see the Appendix.
[2] Kent to Story, June 23, 1837, Story MSS.
[3] Story to McLean, May 7, 1837, McLean MSS.
[4] Taney to Jackson, Sept. 12, 1838, Jackson MSS.
[5] Catron to Jackson, Feb. 5, 1838, *ibid.*

made to merge the Virginia district with other eastern or southern districts, to provide for more adequate service in the Southwest. The Whig senators, led by Henry Clay, sponsored the proposed changes with enthusiasm, since their adoption would take time and would doubtless result in preventing action on Daniel's nomination until after March 4, when Harrison, the new President, would be expected to confer the position upon some member of the Whig party. The bill made no progress, however, partly because of the opposition of Virginians who were unwilling to see their state lose a position on the Supreme Court, and the nomination was pressed. On the evening of March 2, when a vote was about to be taken, Clay picked up his hat, bade the presiding officer of the Senate a mocking good night, and walked out with his supporters, leaving less than a quorum in the hall. The sergeant-at-arms attempted to bring them back, but they refused to obey. Finally, near midnight, after an exasperating wait, enough Democrats were located to constitute a quorum, and the nomination was confirmed.

The Whigs sharply criticized Van Buren for his haste in replacing the deceased Barbour, but Van Buren was not much disturbed. He wrote to Jackson that he had an opportunity of appointing a man to the court at the moment of leaving the government who was a Democrat and would stick to the true principles of the Constitution. He was not distressed by the raving of the Federalists over the selection.[6]

Daniel's Democracy did not make him a commoner, for he was a great admirer of the landed aristocracy and of the old families of Virginia, and was proud of his marriage connection with the Randolphs. He was anti-nationalist, however, and anti-corporation and anti-bank. "The influence of corporate monopolies," he had once written to Van Buren, "spread as it has been like a pestilence, by the rearing of a bank in almost every village; powerful as it unquestionably is, will I hope be made to yield to the integrity and common sense of the people."[7] He identified banks, corporations, and monop-

[6] Van Buren to Jackson, March 12, 1841, Van Buren MSS.
[7] Daniel to Van Buren, Jan. 23, 1838, *ibid.*

olies with city life, and took pride in the fact that Virginians were essentially an agricultural people.[8] He believed not merely in state rights but also in limiting narrowly the functions of government of every kind. The protection of life, property, and reputation was the only protection in which government could justly intermeddle.[9]

It was evident, therefore, that Story, already miserable because of the changes wrought in the court by Democratic appointments, had nothing to hope for from the accession of Daniel. During the years which he served, down to 1860, Daniel was the extreme agrarian on the court, the extreme enemy of corporations, and the extreme defender of doctrines of state rights and *laissez faire*. He is of more than usual interest because of his position as an extremist, even though he was not a man of outstanding ability. The work of the court as a whole is often thrown more sharply into perspective when seen in contrast with Daniel's prejudices.

The Whigs came into power March 4, 1841, with William Henry Harrison, a figurehead leader, as President. Webster, as Secretary of State, promised to be the dominating character in the cabinet, and Clay stood out as party leader in the Senate. The reëstablishment of a national bank and other aims of the Whig program seemed about to be realized when, one month from the date of his inauguration, the President died. John Tyler, a state-rights Whig whose Whiggism consisted largely of opposition to Andrew Jackson and his followers, became President, and the plans of the party leaders to govern the country through an amiable military gentleman were ruined. Tyler proved to have a mind of his own, demonstrating his independence during his first year in office by vetoing a bill to charter a national bank. The complete break between the President and his party was revealed when most of the cabinet resigned. Webster, however, remained for some time in the position of Secretary of State. He perhaps did so partly for the purpose of completing diplomatic negotiations already begun. Another motive, however, prob-

[8] Daniel to Van Buren, May 23, 1838, *ibid.*
[9] Daniel to Van Buren, July 6, 1843, *ibid.*

ably lay in the fact that Clay had become so clearly the head of the Whig party as to leave no position of proper dignity for Webster, who refused to consider himself a mere subordinate. It was better to capture such glory as he could get from his present position, even though he had no party support.

Justice McLean was offered the position of Secretary of War, and Webster assured him that the nomination would be confirmed. Webster declared McLean was needed both on the court and in the cabinet. "You cannot be in both places; but if you are tired out by long journeys, and sick of bills, answers, and demurrers, no one will be happier than myself to meet you in the circle of heads of departments." [10] McLean decided against changing places. His decision may have been governed by the fact that although he was not a Clay man he was opposed to the major policies of the President. He was in favor of a national bank, and was a nationalist in most matters. He may also have doubted the wisdom of giving up a permanent position for an office in the cabinet of a President largely without a party.

Clay resigned from the Senate to organize opposition to Tyler more effectively and to prepare for the next presidential campaign. Story read one of Clay's political speeches with great enthusiasm. "It abounds with passages of great eloquence, and statesmanlike views, and lofty principles," he wrote. "I am a Whig, and although I do not pretend to mingle in the common politics of the day, there are great measures, upon which I have a decided opinion and which I would not disguise if I could. I am for a national bank, a protective tariff, a distribution law of the public lands and a permanent bankrupt law. All these measures are in my judgment indispensable to the public prosperity and peace of our country. In promoting these measures I know no man, who has labored more perseveringly, or with more zeal, ability and honorable devotion than yourself at all times. I as one, feel grateful to you for these labors; and I trust that my country will for many years to come possess the services of one,

[10] Webster to McLean, Sept. 11, 1841, McLean MSS.

whose eminent talents have so justly obtained the approval of the most enlightened minds in our public councils." [11]

He would rejoice, Story wrote to McLean, if the service of good men and true like McLean should be demanded by the people, "for without it, there can be no security or value in our republican institutions." [12] He feared the time would not come, however, until after the period of another administration.

So unpopular was Tyler with the Whigs that they began to express hopes that no Supreme Court judges would die until a new President had been elected. When Thompson fell ill, toward the end of 1843, Daniel Lord declared: "If we could keep him alive for a couple of winters, even if unable to sign his name, we would hold fasts and prayers for it. The change we fear, at his death now, is fearful to us in every prospect. We are sure of one thing, however, that the judge is as resolute in holding on to life as we can be earnest in wishing him to be." [13] Six weeks later when Story wrote from Washington of Taney's serious illness, he commented, "His constitution is exceedingly feeble and broken; but I trust and hope that he will be spared until times assume a better aspect" [14]—and continued with a discussion of the bright prospects for Clay's election as President.

Taney survived this and many other crises, but Thompson did not. He died December 19, 1843, and a second court vacancy was created when Baldwin died the following April. Tyler had a friend sound out Silas Wright to see if Van Buren, the man who appeared to be his strongest rival for the presidency, would accept the appointment to Thompson's place. Wright's answer was that if Tyler desired to give the country a broader, deeper, and heartier laugh than it had ever had, and at his own expense, he could do it by making the nomination.[15]

Tyler gave up the plan, and nominated instead John C. Spencer,

[11] Story to Clay, Aug. 3, 1842, Clay MSS.
[12] Story to McLean, Oct. 9, 1843, McLean MSS.
[13] Daniel Lord, Jr., to J. J. Crittenden, Dec. 16, 1843, Crittenden MSS.
[14] Story to W. W. Story, Jan. 30, 1844, Story MSS.
[15] Warren, *Supreme Court in United States History*, II, 108–110.

a New York Whig who had stood by him instead of Clay. The Clay Whigs achieved revenge by rejecting the nomination. Tyler then offered the position to both John Sergeant and Horace Binney of Pennsylvania, and each in turn refused to accept. He offered it twice to Silas Wright, the Democratic leader in the Senate, but Wright likewise declined, probably not so much because he did not want the position as because of the probability that the nomination would not be confirmed. Tyler then appointed Reuben H. Walworth, Chancellor of the State of New York, who was an able man but was said to have been recommended because of the desire to get rid of a "querulous, disagreeable, unpopular Chancellor." [16]

While Walworth's nomination was pending Baldwin died, leaving a second vacancy. "How nobly it might be filled," sighed Story. "But we are doomed to disappointment." [17] If he could have the son of ex-Chancellor Kent as his colleague he would feel ready to depart in peace. In addition to his nationalist convictions, however, the attitude of the elder Kent had not been such as to render himself and his family popular with Tyler. In 1842 he had expressed his contempt for Tyler and his indignation at Webster for remaining in his cabinet by saying, "The profligate apostacy of Tyler did not disturb me so much (for he is a fool) as that of the former great champion of the Constitution." [18] "I look upon the administration of our general government as rotten to the core," he wrote about the time of Baldwin's death, "and great chiefs and statesmen are contending for power with much less dignity and with as much profligacy as did the Roman demagogues in the last stages and agonies of the Roman Republic. But I have no doubt Mr. Clay will be elected and give us better times. Nothing can be so degrading and detestable as the conduct of the weak, vain, perfidious wretch that at present wields power to the dismay and scourge of the nation." [19]

Story fully agreed. He thought that Kent's son and one other

16 Thurlow Weed to J. J. Crittenden, March 17, 1844, Crittenden MSS.
17 Story to Kent, April 25, 1844, *Proceedings, Mass. Historical Society*, 2nd Series, XIV, 424.
18 Kent to Story, Oct. 5, 1842, *ibid.,* p. 419.
19 Kent to Story, April 18, 1844, *ibid.,* p. 420.

were the only persons who should be considered for appointment to the Supreme Court from New York, but "what can we hope from such a head of an administration as we now have but a total disregard of all elevated principles and objects. I dare not trust my pen to speak of him as I think. Do you know (for I was so informed at Washington) that Tyler said he never would appoint a judge 'of the school of Kent.'" [20]

In Baldwin's place Tyler appointed Edward King of Pennsylvania. The Whig Senate, however, laid the two nominations on the table on the last day of the session, quite obviously with a view to keeping the positions vacant until after the election of the following November, when in the case of success they would plan further obstructive action so that the positions could ultimately be filled by a Whig President.

In the meantime the lines of battle were forming. Although there were other aspiring candidates among the Whigs, such as Judge McLean and John M. Clayton, Clay had little trouble in making himself the standard-bearer of his party. Theodore Frelinghuysen of New Jersey, who in 1834 had made the famous "marble palace" speech on the floor of the Senate glorifying Nicholas Biddle and the Bank of the United States, was placed on the ticket with him. The Democrats were divided into many factions led by James Buchanan, John C. Calhoun, Lewis Cass, George M. Dallas, Richard M. Johnson, Martin Van Buren, Levi Woodbury, and others. Calhoun and Van Buren at first seemed the most formidable contestants. Calhoun was eager and confident. "If my friends should think my service will ever be of importance at the head of the Executive," he declared, "now is the time. It has never come before, and will pass away forever, with the occasion." [21] He felt that sentiment in his favor was developing, and that all his friends needed to do was to use the mails and the press to prevent this development from being forestalled. He declared that his object, as for many years past, was to restore the old state-rights republican doctrines of 1798. Upon

[20] Story to Kent, April 25, 1844, *ibid.*, p. 424.
[21] Calhoun to Armistead Burt, Nov. 28, 1841, *Correspondence of John C. Calhoun*, p. 497.

their restoration he believed the existence of free popular institutions to depend. The first step in the restoration was the overthrow of Clay's American system, and for that purpose it was necessary to expel the Clay forces from power.[22]

The Van Buren forces were similarly zealous, however, and it was the Van Buren strength which seemed to be steadily increasing rather than that of Calhoun. The latter ultimately declined to be a candidate, left his friends to do the best they could for the South in the selection of another candidate, and upon the death of Secretary Upshur accepted the position of Secretary of State in Tyler's cabinet, from which position he labored effectively for the annexation of Texas, which would mean the admission of another slave state into the Union. Clay had announced his opposition to the annexation of Texas. Van Buren, had he announced his support of the project, would probably have assured his nomination and election. Instead he announced his personal opposition, although he agreed to be bound by the vote of Congress in the matter. In this manner he sealed his fate as far as the support of the South was concerned. Even so he was defeated at the convention only by the adoption of the two-thirds rule, for which it was said that some of the jealous northern candidates voted for the deliberate purpose of defeating him. The convention ultimately compromised on James K. Polk, who had announced himself as in favor of the annexation of Texas, with George M. Dallas as his running mate. So passed Van Buren's only real chance of returning to the presidency. His old friend Benjamin F. Butler threw himself upon his bed and cried like a child at his defeat.[23]

The friends of Van Buren for the most part gave their support to Polk. Judge Daniel, long a friend of Van Buren to whom he owed many political favors, announced his support of the party in spite of the fact that he had not approved the annexation of Texas, and had no personal acquaintance with Polk. He did so, he wrote to Van Buren, because of his belief that a Democratic victory might avert

[22] Calhoun to J. H. Hammond, Nov. 27, 1842, *ibid.*, pp. 519–520.
[23] John Bigelow, MS. Diary, p. 48, entry of June 9, 1844.

or retard the effects of sectional friction over slavery, protect the interests of the South, and curb the power of the moneyed aristocracy. He hotly resented the attitude of those northerners who regarded the slave areas as the "plague spot upon the nation," and declared that if these sentiments came to prevail the southerners would withdraw from the Union and "leave these exclusively beautiful and moral and clean and immaculate, to their own purity." [24]

The campaign was fought on a grossly low plane. The Whigs denounced the Democrats as irreligious, ignorant, and corrupt. While "Native Americans" were being courted by and were aligning themselves with the Whigs, the Democrats were naturalizing the despised immigrants in droves to secure their votes. The Whigs played up anti-Catholic sentiment, and the Democrats capitalized Catholic resentment. Judge Story was deeply shocked. "I utterly despair of a republican government," he wrote to McLean. "My heart sickens at the profligacy of public men, the low state of public morals, and the utter indifference of the people to all elevated virtue and even self respect. . . . Is not the theory of our government a whole failure?" [25]

With loud lamentations and prophecies of national ruin the Whigs went down to defeat, frustrating once more the hopes of Clay. Taney was elated and sent warm congratulations to Polk. "We have passed through no contest for the presidency more important than the one just over," he wrote; "nor have I seen any one before in which so many dangerous influences were combined together as were united in support of Mr. Clay. Your triumphant success gives me increased confidence in the intelligence, firmness and virtue of the American people; and in the safety and stability of the principles upon which our institutions are founded. I need not say with what pleasure I shall again meet you in Washington, and see you entering upon the high station to which you have been so honorably called." [26]

In similar elation Taney wrote to Jackson that the spirit of 1828

[24] Daniel to Van Buren, Oct. 17, 1844, Van Buren MSS.
[25] Story to McLean, Aug. 16, 1844, McLean MSS.
[26] Taney to Polk, Nov. 20, 1844, Polk MSS.

and 1832 had been abroad in the election, and the country would now have peace for many years. The dangerous and evil influences combined in support of Clay could hardly be brought to bear in support of another candidate. He thanked God that Jackson had lived to witness this great triumph. "You will readily imagine what pleasure I shall feel in administering the oath of office to the 'Young Hickory' as he has been called. It will remind me of the proud day when in your presence, and that of thousands of friends I administered it to Mr. Van Buren." [27]

On New Year's Day, Taney wrote to Jackson that he had just paid an official call at the President's Mansion, "where I have so often seen you; and in the room where I was accustomed to find you; and perhaps I looked at them with the more pleasure because I know they are soon to be occupied by one of your most firm and faithful friends." Although he had abstained from taking part in political movements since he had been on the bench, he told Jackson, he had found it difficult to remain quiet during the preceding campaign. He felt anxious for the success of Polk's administration. He hoped that Calhoun, now Secretary of State under Tyler, would voluntarily withdraw with the close of the administration. He feared that Calhoun would not do so. "You always said that with all his talents he had no judgment, and I am every day more and more convinced of the correctness of your opinion." [28]

With all his friendship for Jackson, Taney never wrote to him of intimate problems connected with the court, and he made no mention at this time of the vacancies to be filled. Yet he must have been relieved and elated by the fact that Henry Clay would not soon have the opportunity of appointing to his court two judges with nationalist leanings, abolitionists, perhaps, and servants of the "moneyed aristocracy." With two vacancies to begin with it was conceivable that even with a normal rate of fatalities among the judges a Whig President might within the run of one administration gain control

27 Taney to Jackson, Nov. 20, 1844, Jackson MSS.
28 Taney to Jackson, Jan. 1, 1845, *ibid.*

of the court. Daniel, less reticent than Taney, regretted that Silas Wright had refused the appointment, for the court needed able men. "The permanence of that body enables it to give direction to the whole government; and hence the vital importance of infusing into it sound principles upon every opportunity which may occur; of calling into it men who will fairly and plainly expound the Constitution and laws, and who will not think themselves called on either by an esprit de corps, or by party bias, or for party ends, to quibble and distort the text or the context of the one or the other in order to grasp it, or to maintain power, either in the court or in any other department of the government. The filling up of the vacant seats on the Supreme Court Bench, I regard as perhaps the most important function of the incoming administration." [29]

Judge Catron was a close friend of Polk. Richard Peters, still smarting from his dismissal as reporter of the Supreme Court as a result of the efforts of Catron and others, prayed fervently that Taney's life might be spared during the next four years. "Catron will succeed him, if he should, while Polk is President, be called to a better world." [30]

There was now no reason why the Whigs should attempt to keep the court positions vacant until after March 4. For various reasons the appointments of Walworth and King were blocked, however, and in February Tyler substituted the names of Samuel Nelson of New York, and John M. Read of Philadelphia. The Senate failed to act on Read's nomination, but confirmed that of Nelson, a lawyer of recognized ability who was at the time Chief Justice of the highest court of his state. He took his seat on the 5th of March following, and remained a member until eight years after Taney's death. Contemporary records of his point of view are scanty, save in showing that he was a Democrat, and that he stood for the protection of the property rights of slaveholders. His father seems to have been a slaveholder, and to have remained so as long as the laws of his state permitted. It was reported by a resident of his home town that when

[29] Daniel to Van Buren, Nov. 19, 1844, Van Buren MSS.
[30] Peters to McLean, Dec. 6, 1844, Warren, *op. cit.*, II, 117–118.

the father wished to send young Sam to the Academy he sold a negro girl to raise the money. "It is said the Judge could scarce keep his feathers sleek when told by his playmates that he was feeding on a negro wench." [31]

On March 4, 1845, the dignitaries of the new administration and of the old assembled beneath spreading umbrellas on a platform at the east front of the Capitol, where Taney administered the oath of office to "Young Hickory." Some of the formerly active Democratic politicians now on the Supreme Court seem to have found it hard to remember that for them political activity was a thing of the past. When he came to Washington for the annual term of the Supreme Court beginning in December, 1844, Catron took charge of arrangements for Polk's temporary residence in Washington, and thereafter gave advice on appointments, the inaugural address, and general administration policies. He administered the oath of office to his friend James Buchanan, the new Secretary of State—for Polk, like Taney, had seen the inadvisability of retaining Calhoun in the cabinet, and had tactfully informed the latter of his decision. Shortly after the election Daniel, who had no acquaintance with Polk and who had not kept in touch with Jackson, wrote to Jackson asking him to support with Polk the cause of a friend who needed a political job.[32] Thereafter, writing to Polk or to the Attorney General, he on various occasions attempted to influence appointments and policies, with what success the evidence is not clear.

Taney also had appointments to recommend for offices connected with the federal courts. His greatest desire was that his son-in-law, James Mason Campbell, should be made district attorney for Maryland. His friend Upton S. Heath, the federal district judge at Baltimore, gave aid by writing to Taney a letter recommending Campbell for the position, which letter Taney could use as he saw fit.[33] Taney spoke to Polk about the matter, and later, enclosing Heath's

[31] John Bigelow, MS. Diary, p. 222, May 10, 1851.
[32] Daniel to Jackson, Dec. 29, 1844, Polk MSS., 2nd Series.
[33] U. S. Heath to Taney, March 4, 1845, *ibid.*

letter, he wrote a long letter of his own, which reflects not merely his interest in his son-in-law but also his reactions to political methods, with some evidence as to the way in which those reactions had been determined by his experiences as a member of a former cabinet.

"Mr. Campbell," Taney wrote, "whom I mentioned to you for the place of District Attorney, is, it is true, my son-in-law; and I feel the deepest interest for him, and am very sensible that the appointment is of great importance to him, not merely as respects the emoluments of the office, but also in the position it would give him in the profession. Yet I think I can judge as impartially of his qualifications and claims as if he were a stranger. And I say with confidence that he is perfectly qualified for the office, from his talents, his legal learning, his habits of business, and his unblemished character, and that from his steady and uniform political course, during his whole life, and his standing and character he would be quite as acceptable to the friends of the administration in this city and throughout the state, and to the community generally as either of his competitors. I say this because I understand that many names have been laid before you in favor of other candidates. But you are well aware I am sure, of the facility with which names are given, and letters written on such occasions; and that the number exhibited is generally the evidence of nothing more than superior activity or importunity, not of superior fitness or popularity. By my advice Mr. Campbell has abstained from soliciting a multitude of names, and has forwarded to you only a few, whose standing and character he presumes you know, and in whose statements he supposes you would feel justified in placing confidence. . . .

"I mark this letter *private* in order the more certainly to bring it to your own eye. But in a day or two I shall address a letter to Mr. Buchanan upon this subject, because it seems but respectful to him that my recommendation should be made known to the Department through which the appointment of District Attorney is made—and I am therefore not willing to recommend in a private letter to you an appointment, which I do not at the same time take the responsibility of recommending openly and publicly at the proper department." [34]

On the following day in a letter to Buchanan he stated somewhat more briefly the same things which he had said to Polk, without, however, mentioning the fact that he had written to Polk.[35] He also urged with Polk the appointment of another relative, Philip Barton Key, the son of his deceased brother-in-law and almost lifelong friend. Frank Key had been driven from the office of federal attorney for the District of Columbia by the incoming tide of Whigs in 1841. The son urged that he be placed in the position formerly occupied by his father, and Taney presented the matter orally with Polk.[36] He also wrote letters of introduction to the Secretaries of State and Treasury for his old friend William M. Beall of Frederick.[37]

However worthy the causes of Campbell, Key, and Beall may have been, Taney was not notably successful as a lobbyist. The explanation may have been that his withdrawal from active politics had destroyed so much of his political influence that he could make an appeal to Polk only on the basis of an old friendship, and that friendship was not enough. The reason may have lain in other matters which the records do not disclose. Polk and his cabinet may have believed that the Chief Justice of the United States was out of his place when trying to influence appointments, even in the interest of worthy relatives and friends, although there seems to be no factual evidence to support the position. At any rate, Campbell and Beall received no recognition from the government. Key, however, was after a time appointed to the position which his father had held, and retained it until he was shot down some years later by a congressman with whose wife he had been too intimate.

Story had nothing to ask of the new régime. For years he had mourned the passing of the old order, the disappearance of the "table round" once presided over by John Marshall. In addition to

[34] Taney to Polk, March 24, 1845, *ibid.*
[35] Taney to Buchanan, March 25, 1845, Buchanan MSS.
[36] P. B. Key to Polk, June 26, 1845, Polk MSS., 2nd Series.
[37] Taney to Beall, April 7, 1845, MS., Taney House, Frederick, Md.

his regret and exasperation he was pained by the dilemma of being constantly forced to dissent from the decisions of his brethren or appearing to concur in opinions and doctrines with which he did not at all agree. He had long talked of resigning, and would doubtless have done so had Harrison lived to make a Whig appointment in his place, but he disliked creating a vacancy to be filled by a man who had vowed he would not appoint a judge "of the school of Kent," which to all intents and purposes was the school of Marshall and Story. He had looked forward eagerly to the election of Clay. "If Mr. Clay had been elected, I had determined to resign my office as a Judge, and to give him the appointment of my successor. How sadly I was disappointed by the results of the late election I need not say." [38] He considered whether he ought to go on for another four years, but a combination of poor health and dissatisfaction with his job led to the decision to bring his judicial career to a close.

The Whigs gave mournful approval to Story's decision. Clay was not surprised at Story's disgust with his service on the court. Among the greatest causes for regret for the loss of the election, he declared, was the result that the Whigs could not fill the court vacancies. Richard Peters declared that the bench was no longer fit for Story. Only McLean, he declared, was now left of the school to which Story belonged. Taney was an eminent and a good man, but he would always feel the influence of Jacksonism. Chancellor Kent declared that the loss of Story from the bench would be immense, but he had done his part. The court had degenerated from a succession of great and estimable men to a "melancholy mass," for the decisions of whom he felt habitual scorn and contempt. Doing his part in perpetuating a false conception of Taney, he added, "I can never think well of a man who consented to do what his predecessor thought it dishonest to do, that is, to remove the U. S. Bank deposits to gratify the malignant persecutions of a savage despot, and in palpable violation of contract." [39]

[38] Story to Ezekiel Bacon, April 12, 1845, *Life and Letters of Joseph Story,* II, 527.
[39] Kent to Story, June 17, 1845, *Proceedings, Mass. Historical Society,* 2nd Series, XIV, 420-421.

In the autumn of 1845, while he was winding up his circuit work preparatory to resigning, Story died. His death was an occasion of profound regret to the vast number of people who respected him for his learning in law and for the part which he had played in working out orderly interpretations of the Constitution. It was a sad occasion also for the many who knew him personally and liked him for the rich, warm side of his personality which was revealed in contacts with friends and admirers, and which was in sharp contrast to the maudlin whining in which he, in common with other Whigs, indulged when faced with the fact that men of their social philosophy were no longer accepted as political and philosophical leaders of the nation.

Perhaps his greatest strength had lain in his belief in the principles which infused his decisions and the volumes of commentaries which remained as monuments to his memory. Perhaps here also, however, lay his greatest weakness. As is the tendency among aristocrats, he believed so firmly in the principles accepted by his class that any modification in the working out of those principles seemed to him a modification in the direction of disaster. He and those who thought like him had not the mental and emotional elasticity necessary for adjustment to a new order, nor the ability to see that change might be socially desirable. They could conceive of nothing of corruption flowing from too much Marshall, Story, Clay, and Webster, and they could see nothing good apt to come from an order dominated by Jackson, Van Buren, Tyler, Taney, Catron, and Daniel. The fact that Taney, Catron, and Daniel were ultimately to bring suffering upon themselves and aid in bringing disaster upon the nation by a similar lack of elasticity in no sense blots out the fundamental weaknesses of the school of Story.

In spite of their differences of opinion Taney and Story had for the most part been on friendly terms. They had corresponded frequently, and Story had often visited the Taney home in Baltimore. In a letter to Richard Peters, Taney told of his regret at the passing of another member of the court. "What a loss the court has sustained in the death of Judge Story! It is irreparable, utterly irreparable in this generation; for there is nobody equal to him. You who have seen me sitting there for so many years between Story and Thompson, will readily understand how deeply I feel the loss of the survivor of them, especially so soon after the death of the other; and I feel it still more deeply, as the time approaches when I must again take my seat there under such altered circumstances." [40] In a gracious reply to resolutions offered before the Supreme Court, Taney paid in public a similar tribute to the fine qualities of his deceased colleague.[41]

In Story's place Polk appointed Taney's former cabinet colleague, Levi Woodbury of New Hampshire. Woodbury had been in politics most of his life, having served as governor and member of the highest court of his state, United States senator, Secretary of the Navy, and Secretary of the Treasury. He had been one of the Democratic competitors for the presidency. He continued to be talked of for that office in spite of his appointment to the court. Although he was from the North he had advocated the annexation of Texas, and he approved the conduct of the Mexican War which in large part resulted from it. It was thought for a time that he might become a compromise presidential candidate, in spite of the fact that he was at odds with the Van Buren faction of the party.[42] He was not nominated, however, and protected his judicial reputation from aspersions of playing politics by his characteristic reticence, at which Taney, in their earlier days of association, had been amazed and perhaps irked as well. Catron referred to this trait in connection with a political situation, saying, "My brother Woodbury has never in word or motion shown any symptoms as to what side he is on, in the present agitation going forward, and is the most valuable example of prudence, in the court, or in all society I think. Nor do his women leak anything." [43] He was an able lawyer and judge, but his career was cut short by death in 1851.

Polk had also to fill the vacancy created by the death of Baldwin. He appointed George W. Woodward of Pennsylvania, but Wood-

[40] Taney to Peters, Nov., 1845, Tyler, *Memoir of Roger Brooke Taney*, p. 290.
[41] Preface to 4 Howard.
[42] New York *Tribune*, Jan. 29, 1848.
[43] Catron to Buchanan, undated, filed with 1849, Buchanan MSS.

ward, because of alleged antagonism to the immigrant element in his state, was rejected by the Senate. Buchanan, the Secretary of State, could have had the nomination had he desired it. He claimed at times to desire it, saying that he "preferred a place on the Supreme Bench to any other under the government; that he would rather be Chief Justice of that court than to be President of the United States." [44] For the time being, however, he seems to have felt that he could serve the administration better by remaining in the cabinet. Whether he reasoned that the frail Chief Justice might die, and that by waiting he might be appointed to the higher position, does not appear.

He advised Polk to reappoint Tyler's nominee, John M. Read of Pennsylvania. Read had formerly had Federalist leanings, however, and Polk was suspicious of him. "I have never known an instance of a Federalist who had after arriving at the age of thirty professed to change his opinions, who was to be relied on in his constitutional opinions. All of them who have been appointed to the Supreme Court Bench, after having secured a place for life became very soon broadly Federal and latitudinarian in all their decisions involving questions of constitutional power. General Jackson had been most unfortunate in his appointments to that bench in this respect. I resolved to appoint no man who was not an original Democrat and strict constructionist, and who would be less likely to relapse into the broad federal doctrines of Judge Marshall and Judge Story." [45]

After the rejection of Woodward, Polk sent to the Senate the name of Robert C. Grier of Pittsburgh, and this nomination was confirmed. Grier was a descendant of a line of Presbyterian ministers, a graduate of Dickinson College, an able lawyer, and had been for some years a judge in a local state court. Although he had a Federalist ancestry he had been a Democrat from an early date, having supported Andrew Jackson in 1824. He had opposed the Bank of the United States on grounds of constitutionality and of expediency. A leading political sponsor had not neglected to advise Polk that Grier was "right" on the slavery question, saying that he was "known as a

[44] Allan Nevins (ed.), *Polk, The Diary of a President, 1845–1849,* p. 27.
[45] *Ibid.,* p. 37.

warm if not violent opponent of abolition." On one occasion, it was said, a minister in the Presbyterian church of which Grier was an elder read from the pulpit notices of an abolition meeting. At the close of the service Grier arose and demanded to know who had placed the notices in the pulpit, and declared that the pulpit should not be made a town crier's office for such purposes, purposes which were unconstitutional and seditious, and were to be repudiated by all good Christians and loyal citizens.[46]

In expressing his gratitude to Polk for the appointment Grier pledged himself to a conscientious devotion of all his faculties to his judicial duties,[47] and it is not to be denied that on the whole, until his faculties began to fail him some years after the death of Taney, he performed his duties well. He meddled dangerously in politics on one occasion, and his anti-abolitionist leanings, coupled with the more vigorous proslavery zeal of a number of his brethren, aided in precipitating a crisis, but the responsibility belonged with others quite as much as with him.

The death of Woodbury in 1851 made necessary the choice of another justice from New England. The Whig party was again in power, under Millard Fillmore. The thoughts of Webster, the Secretary of State, turned immediately to Benjamin R. Curtis, an eminent Whig lawyer of Boston, who had loyally supported Webster when the latter had offended abolitionist sentiment by coming to the defense of the Compromise of 1850. Webster wrote to President Fillmore recommending the appointment of Curtis, and on the same day Fillmore wrote to Webster asking if the Curtis appointment would be advisable. He wished to combine the appointment of a good Whig and a good lawyer, he declared. "I believe that Judge McLean is the only Whig now upon the bench; and he received his appointment from General Jackson. I am therefore desirous of obtaining as long a lease, and as much moral and judicial power as possible, from this appointment." [48] The appointment was made, and

---

[46] Benjamin Patton to Polk, March 30, 1845, Polk MSS., 2nd Series.

[47] Grier to Polk, Aug. 8, 1846, *ibid.*

[48] Fillmore to Webster, Sept. 10, 1851, B. R. Curtis (ed.), *Memoir of Benjamin Robbins Curtis*, I, 155.

Curtis soon afterward antagonized his Free Soil neighbors by denying the right of jurors to pass upon the constitutionality of the Fugitive Slave Law in disregard of the instructions of the court.

He proved an able judge. The issues of slavery remained to plague him, however, and although he was not an abolitionist he was also unable to align himself with the majority of his brethren who were more sympathetic with southern interests than he. In spite of the fact that he gave other reasons for his act, the decision in the Dred Scott case undoubtedly had much to do with his resignation from the court and his return to private practice, when he had served for a period of only six years.[49]

When McKinley died, in 1852, Fillmore hoped again to add to the strength of the Whigs on the court, although this appointment was to be made from the South. Unfortunately for his plan his party had now lost control of the Senate, and he was unable to secure the confirmation of either of the three men whom he proposed. Shortly before President-elect Pierce took office Catron and Curtis went to him as representatives of the court to request the appointment of John A. Campbell of Alabama, who had many times demonstrated his superior qualifications before the court. The appointment was made, and was speedily confirmed, and to a considerable degree received the approval of all parties.

It is a significant fact, however, that Campbell was an ardent southerner in all respects, including his attitude toward slavery. He had opposed the acquisition of territory from Mexico, not because he thought it wrong to take it, but because of his conviction that it would not make good slave territory. "I regard the subject of the acquisition of new territory," he wrote to Calhoun, "mainly as it may affect the balance of power in the federal government." [50] He worked with his brethren with great ease and ability, and is said to have been Taney's choice as the man best fitted to succeed him as Chief Jus-

[49] See Chapter XXIV.
[50] Campbell to Calhoun, Nov. 20, 1847, *Correspondence of John C. Calhoun*, p. 1140.

tice.[51] His pronounced southern bias, however, which revealed itself in the crisis decisions, led to his withdrawal to give aid to his seceding countrymen, leaving Taney still presiding over the panorama of changing personnel of the Supreme Court.

[51] George W. Duncan, "John Archibald Campbell," *Alabama Historical Society Transactions,* 1904, V, 113.

Chapter XXII

LIGHTS AND SHADOWS OF THE AFTERNOON

The traditional assumption, fictitious though it be, that judges are but passive mouthpieces of the law has created the impression that their lives apart from their profession are without color, significance, or interest. The care with which judges keep from the public the records of their informal opinions and conduct adds to the impression. It may be that some of them become so desiccated in their devotion to the machinery of justice as to justify the impression, but it is not true of all, and it was not true of Taney, in spite of the chronic ill health from which he suffered. The afternoon years of his life had shadings and variety entirely different from those revealed directly by his formal opinions.

Part of the variety, of course, fell ultimately into a routine of its own, as in making formal calls, attending formal dinners, funerals, and the laying of cornerstones, making official expressions of sorrow at the death of prominent persons, introducing friends to American diplomats abroad, and ministering to the hunger of seekers after autographs. In spite of the routine aspect, however, Taney performed his many parts with such graciousness as to create warm personal relationships with the people whom he met, without at the same time attracting undue attention to himself.

The members of the Supreme Court were much in demand at dignified social functions. During Taney's period as Chief Justice his colleagues gradually abandoned the custom of living together in one house, and brought their families with them to private residences or hotels. Mrs. Taney, however, like her husband always frail in health, never accompanied him to Washington, but left to him alone the social responsibilities of the family. He derived only a limited enjoyment from the frills of Washington. In his younger days he had not, in his own words, been a great "diner out," and he did not become one now. He attended those functions which he thought he mighty enjoy, and such others as it seemed necessary to attend, if the condition of his health did not provide an adequate excuse for sending regrets. "In the evening we went to President Tyler's," he wrote to Mrs. Taney early in 1845, speaking of his colleagues and himself. "There must have been, I think, a thousand people there,— well-dressed, well-behaved people; for none others were there. You know the President and I are good friends, and he and Mrs. President received me with great kindness; and I met there more old friends, and spent a more pleasant evening, than I expected; except only that I was greatly oppressed, as I always am on such occasions, by the crowded state of the rooms." [1]

The development of this friendship with Tyler was typical of many of Taney's experiences when he came into close personal contact with men who had formerly been his political enemies. Tyler had fought Taney's bank policies and had opposed his confirmation as Secretary of the Treasury. In his subsequent report to the Senate he had criticized Taney with a sharpness which the latter did not soon forget. As President, however, Tyler had surprised the Chief Justice by vetoing a bill to charter a national bank, and made enemies of many of the Whigs who had likewise been Taney's enemies. Official duties brought the two men together, and each found in the other much that was admirable. In delivering an address in Baltimore some years later Tyler offered what might be called an apology for his early treatment of Taney:

"And now let me do an act of justice to myself, on this, the first occasion which has ever presented itself, in regard to the part I bore on the nomination of that distinguished Secretary. Had I then known him as I have since in his exalted office of Chief Justice of the United States, maugre any discrepancy of opinion which might have existed between us, there was no office, however exalted, either in the gift

[1] Taney to Mrs. Taney, Feb. 24, 1845, Tyler, *Memoir of Roger Brooke Taney*, pp. 472–473.

of the executive or the people, for which I would not promptly have sustained him." [2]

Henry Clay similarly admitted his error, though less publicly, a few years after Taney became head of the Supreme Court. He called at Taney's temporary residence in Washington, entering with embarrassed recollection of their former relationship. He was received with great kindness and with no evidence of rancor. Reverdy Johnson, one of Taney's frequent visitors, reported that as Clay took his leave he grasped Taney's hand, deeply moved, and said: "Mr. Chief Justice, there was no man in the land who regretted your appointment to the place you now hold more than I did; there was no member of the Senate who opposed it more than I did; but I have come to say to you, and I say it now in parting, perhaps for the last time, I have witnessed your judicial career, and it is due to myself and due to you that I should say to you what has been the result; that I am satisfied now that no man in the United States could have been selected more abundantly able to wear the ermine which Chief Justice Marshall honored." [3] In his many letters to Taney thereafter, declared Taney's contemporary biographer, Samuel Tyler,[4] Clay seemed by his kindness and courtesy to strive for his generous forgiveness.

Between Taney and two others of his former political enemies, Webster and Calhoun, no such warmth of feeling seems to have developed. Webster, however, showed his respect for Taney while Secretary of State by consulting him many times on public matters, even though he continued in his private letters to sputter about the fact that the Supreme Court was not what it had been in former times. Taney complimented Webster in 1846 to the extent of saying that when animated he was the first of living orators.[5] Following their deaths in 1852 Taney had to express for the Supreme Court its regret at the passing of Clay, Webster, and John Sergeant, each

---

[2] Lyon G. Tyler, *Letters and Times of the Tylers*, I, 497–498, note.

[3] Speech of Reverdy Johnson before the United States Senate, March 31, 1864, *Congressional Globe*, 38th Cong., 1st sess., p. 1363.

[4] *Op. cit.*, p. 317.

[5] S. M. Maury, *The Statesmen of America in 1846*, p. 87.

of whom had been allied with the enemy in the bank war. He did it graciously, concluding with the statement that, while they were maintaining their distinguished position before the judicial tribunals, "they were able at the same time to place their names among the leading and eminent statesmen of the day, exercising a strong and wide influence upon the great political questions which were agitated during the period in which they lived." [6] There was nothing in his comment to suggest in any way the survival of any of the bitterness of the old struggle.

In view of their common interest in the South it is somewhat surprising that no warmth of sympathy ever developed between Taney and Calhoun. True, there was not the same opportunity for friendship, since Calhoun, unlike Clay and Webster, did not appear frequently before the Supreme Court. Yet they could hardly have escaped meeting each other occasionally, since the one was Chief Justice of the United States and the other senator or Secretary of State. Through it all Taney seems never to have fully trusted the South Carolina nullifier in spite of his recognized ability, and he seems to have continued to regard him with a certain amount of political enmity. The court adjourned on the occasion of Calhoun's death, but Taney, in his letter to his wife on that day, remarked merely that the judges would of course be expected to attend the funeral. He made no allusion to the event as one of either public or private sorrow. His letter contained evidence of feeling on other subjects, but on this none whatsoever. [7]

Interests outside the fields of law and politics gave variety to Taney's life in Washington. For a number of years he had followed developments in astronomy and perhaps in other natural sciences. His interest was deepened when the Smithsonian Institution was organized under a law which made the Chief Justice of the United States a member of the board of regents. During the early years of its life both Congress and the board of regents were sharply divided as to the purpose of the Institution. One faction insisted that it

---

[6] Supreme Court Reports, 14 Law. Ed., 300.
[7] Taney to Mrs. Anne Taney, April 1, 1850, S. Tyler, *op. cit.*, pp. 470–471.

should concentrate on a library for general reading purposes. The other insisted strongly that the funds available be used to finance scientific research and reports thereon. Taney aligned himself with the intellectually aristocratic group in voting that the money be used for scientific purposes. He was chancellor at the time when the issue was fought out—that office belonged ordinarily to the Vice President but devolved upon the Chief Justice when the vice presidency was vacant. As presiding officer he seems to have demonstrated that his abilities as a political strategist had not atrophied from lack of use. His faction won in the struggle, and Joseph Henry, secretary of the Institution, was permitted to continue its management in the interest of science.[8]

In spite of his varied interests, however, much of Taney's life in Washington was obviously lonely. His chief consolation was in writing to and receiving letters from his family in Baltimore, and in discussing with them matters more personal and intimate than were proper as ordinary topics of conversation. For instance, he had been injured in an accident during the term of 1839, not seriously but in such a way as to leave one eye blackened. "I was shut up in the house for four days with my black eye," he wrote to Alice, his youngest daughter, "for although it did not give me one pain it looked so badly, that I was ashamed to walk the streets. But now I walk every evening a little before the sun goes down, as far as the war office, and often take a look at our old house." [9]

On another occasion he wrote of his disappointment that his son-in-law had been unable to come to Washington. "Although I could have seen but little of you," he wrote, "from our separate engagements, yet it would be a great pleasure to see you here at all, where the sight of a home face never greets me, and where the days are dark and laborious and the nights long. I, however, continue to wear along through them as well as when I left home." [10] A letter to Mrs. Taney of another date sounds the same note: "I write you a brief note, my dear wife, to tell you that I have safely arrived. . . . Having just left

[8] See, for example, the New York *Times*, Feb. 28, March 4 and 17, 1854, and the annual reports of the Smithsonian Institution for the period.

[9] Taney to Alice Taney, Feb. 24, 1839, Campbell MSS.

[10] Taney to J. Mason Campbell, Jan. 15, 1848, *ibid.*

you all, my room is lonely and sad today, and I feel much more disposed to lie down and think of you all at home than do anything else. This bright weather will, I hope, continue, and enable you to exercise and be more in the open air. How glad I should be to walk with you." [11]

Taney's sensitive fondness for his family is clearly apparent throughout his life, and his need for periodic retirement from contacts with the public while winning his way back to health after being exhausted by his labors made him peculiarly dependent on his wife and daughters. Throughout her life Mrs. Taney devoted herself almost exclusively to her home. Some mention is made of her in connection with local charities, and at least one of Taney's colleagues learned to know her well enough to be fond of her,[12] but she seldom appeared in society. The cause may have lain in her own frequent illness, or in the lack of funds necessary for social display, or in the conviction that her vocation was to make life richer and more endurable for her husband.

The daughters remained a part of the home even after growing to maturity. Two of them never married. The four who married did so at ages well past the period at which most young women took life partners, and they remained thereafter in Baltimore, perennial visitors if not dwellers in the home. They added to the warmth and cheeriness to which Taney returned with so much delight.

The home was to Taney a place of refuge wherein the formalities of judicial life were unnecessary, and where the harshness and strife and pettiness of the outside world had no place. The least violation was a matter of deepest disturbance. During his many years as a politician he developed a great deal of imperturbability in the face of newspaper criticism. Yet when a paper reported and distorted personal conversation which took place in his home he was hotly indignant.[13] He was enraged when a neighbor encroached upon his home

[11] Taney to Mrs. Anne Taney, April 1, 1850, S. Tyler, *op. cit.*, pp. 470–471.

[12] See P. V. Daniel to Mrs. Ann(e) Taney, March 13, 1849, Etting Coll., Historical Society of Pennsylvania.

[13] See Taney to Christopher Hughes, Dec. 14, 1841, Hughes MSS., and the article on Hughes in the New York *Herald*, Dec. 4, 1841.

by building a privy on land at the rear of his house where the title was in dispute, and extending a vent above the dividing wall.[14]

More deeply offensive to him was another kind of invasion of the privacy and integrity of his family, through a marriage which turned out badly. His daughter Sophia, frail in health and retiring of disposition, had married Colonel Francis Taylor. He had distinguished himself in the war with Mexico, but in personal relationships he evidently proved something of a scoundrel. After the birth of a child—which was named for Taney—he seems to have decided to get rid of both the wife and child, writing to her on the subject, as he declared, "after prayerful recollections."

He wrote also to Taney to urge him to consent to the arrangements he had proposed to Sophia. Language came near failing Taney as he attempted to express his opinion of his son-in-law. "It would be the coolest piece of impudence you ever saw," he sputtered, "if the man had any sense. But he has no moral sense. No sense of propriety. No sense of honor—and not as much sens-sibility as belongs to the higher grades of the mere animal creation. Poor Sophia. How I grieve for her. An evil past our cure—past hope, when the man is a hypocrite in religion." [15]

Sophia and her young son returned to Taney's home, she hiding herself in shame from public gaze.[16] When her husband died some time later he seems to have left them nothing, and Taney had to bear the financial burden of their care.

Although it was the personal disaster to his daughter rather than the money matter which Taney felt most deeply, financial problems continued to worry him throughout his life. A salary of five thousand dollars was by no means sufficient to support in aristocratic fashion a wife and six grown daughters. Yet it remained at this level until 1855, when it was increased only to sixty-five hundred dollars. The expenses of the family were increased by the fact that physicians were regular callers in the home. In this field the best was demanded,

[14] See Semmes, *John H. B. Latrobe and His Times,* p. 203, and the copy of a deed, Taney to St. George W. Teackle, Dec. 1, 1858, Latrobe MSS.

[15] Taney to J. Mason Campbell, June 26, 1855, Campbell MSS.

[16] Taney to J. Mason Campbell, July 13, 1855, *ibid.*

and in spite of the size of his fees Dr. Thomas Buckler was a frequent visitor to a number and perhaps to all of the Taneys.

None of the daughters married well enough to be of assistance. James Mason Campbell, the young Baltimore lawyer who married Anne, the eldest, was Taney's favorite among his sons-in-law, but Campbell achieved distinction only within a very narrow range. William Stevenson, the Baltimore merchant who married Elizabeth, and Richard T. Allison, the purser in the navy who married Maria, likewise did not distinguish themselves except that the latter became a major in the Confederate army, and they lightened the Taney burden only to the extent of supporting their own wives. Ellen was an invalid much of her life, and never married. Alice, the youngest, though much has been said of her loveliness, was twenty-eight years of age in the fatal year of 1855, and was still unmarried, and so living at the expense of her father.

The Campbell family, indeed, at times added to Taney's financial worries. The family letters reveal the fact that he again and again signed notes to enable Campbell to borrow money. On one occasion Campbell seems to have been unable to get money unless Taney himself borrowed it direct. He urged Taney to borrow it from the Union Bank, but this Taney refused to do. "It is with more sorrow than I can well express," he declared, "that I refuse you anything you ask. But in my official position, I have an insuperable repugnance to ask pecuniary favors from those who may come before me as suitors in my court. . . . I will as I am sure you know, do anything in my power to relieve you from embarrassment, except that of asking to borrow money for myself, which would create the impression that I was living beyond my income and in need of pecuniary favors, which I have always thought no judge could do without losing caste more or less, and disturbing in some degree the public confidence in his entire independence. Think of some other way, and let me know how I can aid you." [17]

The Campbell children basked in the warmth of their grandfather's affection. His frequent letters written when he was away

[17] Taney to J. Mason Campbell, Feb. 7, 1846, *ibid.*

from home were often addressed to them, and were phrased in the personal intimacy in which children would take delight. He was especially devoted to Taney Campbell, who was named for him, and about whose experiences at riding he was eager to hear and to give advice. It is a matter for deep regret that both this grandson and the son of Sophia, who was also named for Taney, failed in any way to lend distinction to the family name, but permitted it to sink into comparative oblivion.

Of Taney's life in Baltimore outside the range of his family few records remain. It is known indirectly that he continued to make and retain friends. For one of these, David M. Perine, he performed a service which he performed rarely after he became Chief Justice, that of educating his son for the bar. His course of study was easily prescribed. It included Blackstone's *Commentaries*, Kent's *Commentaries*, Story's *Conflicts of Laws*, Phillipps' *Evidence* or Starkie's *Evidence*, Fontblanque's *Treatise on Equity*, and Story's *Commentaries on Equity Jurisprudence*. Directions for study were clear:

"The student should not be content with reading these books only. They should be studied over and over again, and some of the leading cases to which they refer turned to and examined, whenever he feels any difficulty in the application of the principle stated in the text. The reports will not only illustrate the point, but will show how learned men are accustomed to apply and distinguish cases in the arguments of the court." [18]

[18] Taney to T. H. Perine, Sept. 22, 1848, Perine MSS.

When his pupil had graduated to the bar Taney professed inability to advise him in selecting a library. "The selection of books for your Law Library," he wrote, "I find to be a difficult task, and one that I am unable to perform to my own satisfaction. The books with which I [am] familiar, are adjudged cases, which are always expected to be referred to by yourself and not abridgments or treatises. But you want in your library, books that will facilitate your researches, and enable you to prepare an argument or form an opinion in the shortest possible time; and for this purpose you need abridgments and treatises on the various branches of the law. Many books of this kind have been published since I was at the bar. Some no doubt of much value, and many of very little. And a lawyer in full practice is much better able to point out those that are worth buying than I can be because as I have said it is the reports that are cited in the argument and not the treatise or abridgment which was used in the preparation. . . . I am afraid if I undertook to select I might encumber you with works which were useful in my day at the bar, but have been since superseded by more valuable works on the same subject."—Taney to T. Harwood Perine, Aug. 14, 1852, Perine MSS.

March 17. 1855

My Dear Grandchildren

I thank you for your birthday present It is very acceptable. The Segars I am sure will prove good, and I shall think them still better and enjoy them the more because they shew that you remembered me today —

Your truly affectionate Grandfather .

R. B. Taney

To
Alice & Taney Campbell

Though he had to be careful what he said, both in public and to his friends, Taney retained his interest in politics. Unlike Chief Justice Marshall he continued to vote except when absent from home at election time. He deeply resented the organized movement against foreigners in the country, which was in part a movement against Catholics. He feared that the impetus which it had achieved in Philadelphia would carry it on to Baltimore. "I fear," he wrote to Campbell, "there are many among us, whose Christianity consists in hating others, and in whom the love of persecuting those whom they hate, is stronger than their zeal for political principles." [19] When at a later date the Know Nothing movement did get under way in Baltimore, he blamed Protestant clergymen for it. "Clergymen have gotten it up," he declared, "and direct it behind the scene. I could name several churches in Baltimore in the vote against Catholics." [20]

All this was said in strict privacy, of course. In similar privacy he discussed the possibilities of war with England over Oregon. With the prejudices of a typical southerner in the matter he was opposed to the extension of the United States into the far Northwest. He believed that the mass of the people had too much sense to go to war for such a bubble as Oregon—worse than a bubble, he thought it, for it was his solemn conclusion that the acquisition of Oregon would be one of the worst misfortunes that had ever befallen the United States. It would inevitably create new and discordant interests, and endanger the stability of the Union. "You know however," he cautioned in conclusion, "that I do not talk about these matters nor involve myself with them." [21]

Eager as he was to serve his friends whenever they called upon him, Taney was frequently embarrassed by petitions for support in getting political jobs. Nevertheless, with the exception of Campbell, his son-in-law, and Philip Barton Key, his nephew, he usually declined to intervene. Even in connection with these relatives he was reluctant to urge appointments unless the positions desired had some relation to the courts. At Campbell's plea he once wrote a note recommending him for a state position. He then gave Campbell a strong hint that he must not be asked to do it again. "I must hereafter take

[19] Taney to J. Mason Campbell, Oct. 13, 1844, Campbell MSS.
[20] Taney to J. Mason Campbell, Oct. 6, 1854, Etting Coll., Historical Society of Pennsylvania.
[21] Taney to J. Mason Campbell, Jan. 22, 1846, Campbell MSS.

firmer ground on this subject," he declared, "and refuse to say a word. And I am the more inclined to this course, because when politicians are pressing around the Governor who have been prominent in supporting his election and upon whom he must rely to support him in his administration of the government, it is absurd to suppose that my recommendation ought to have any influence; and it ought not to have influence in the mere distribution of executive patronage, when most commonly there are a dozen applicants fit for the office, and nearly equally qualified and when it is the chief object to select from them the one most likely to give satisfaction to his political friends." [22]

When one of his Maryland friends requested his aid in connection with a state appointment he graciously but firmly declined to give it. Since his appointment to the bench, he declared, he had thought it best to abstain altogether from interfering in appointments to offices in either the federal or state governments. True, he had once interfered in behalf of Mr. Ridgely, the state librarian, whose removal from office would have caused great suffering to his family and loss to the office itself, but he could make no further exceptions. [23] He

[22] Taney to Campbell, Jan. 15, 1848, *ibid.*

[23] Taney to J. B. Boyle, Jan. 1, 1842, Boyle MSS., in possession of J. Carbery Boyle, Winchester, Md.

Taney discussed the difficulties of his position more at length in reply to a request made some years later by another member of the same family: "I have received your letter and from my long and intimate acquaintance with yourself and family, as well as the friendship which subsisted so long between Mr. Boyle's father and myself, and my sincere respect and regard for him, it would give me real pleasure to render him any service that I could properly offer. But since my appointment to the Bench of the Supreme Court, I have uniformly refused to interfere in appointments to be made by the Executive, unless they were connected with the Courts and the administration of justice in them. I have found it absolutely necessary to come to this determination. For my position in the government has led to the belief that my recommendation would have weight, and this impression has brought upon me a multitude of applications for recommendation, and would have made me almost daily a solicitor for Executive favor for a friend if I had not resolved to interfere in no case except as above mentioned. For if I recommended one friend I could not refuse to recommend another who was equally worthy and had equal claims upon me without giving just cause of offense. And if I recommended all whom I knew and really would be glad to serve, I should be mixed up with Executive patronage and appointments more than would be desirable and becoming in my judicial position. You therefore and Mr. Boyle must pardon me for declining to interfere in behalf of his son, although if I recommended in any case it would give me pleasure to do so in his behalf.

"But the weight of a recommendation from me is entirely overrated. I am so much engrossed with my judicial duties that I rarely see the President or any member of the cabinet.

demonstrated in this and other instances, however, the rare ability to refuse a request, and at the same time to extract the sting from the act of doing so. It was one of the important elements in his capacity to make and to keep personal friends.

Throughout the years of his mature life Taney's annual retreats into the open country enabled him to restore his depleted energies and prepare for his work with renewed vigor. During the early period in Frederick he and Mrs. Taney delighted in trips on horseback into the mountains of Virginia. Taney suffered greatly from the heat in midsummer.[24] To secure as much comfort as possible the family went for a few weeks each summer to the home of Mrs. Taney's parents at Terra Rubra or its vicinity, where delightful reunions were held with the family of Frank Key. After he became Chief Justice the Taneys rented a summer home a few miles from Baltimore. Then, during the 1840's, they began to make seasonal visits to summer resorts, from which were written many of the personal letters which throw light upon the intimate aspects of their lives.

Jordan's Springs, at some distance from Winchester, was for some years their gathering place.[25] Then for some reason they changed to

---

It is well known that I have been so long separated from any active concern in political life, that I cannot be supposed to be as well acquainted with the relative merits of rival applicants, as those who are actively engaged in political life. And if new regiments are raised and officers appointed, the recommendations of the Senators and Members of Congress friendly to the Administration, will probably have more weight than those of any other persons. Far more than mine, because they will be naturally presumed to have a better knowledge of the relative merits and standing of the different applicants from their respective states. . . .

"I have written you this long letter, in order that you may understand the motives which induce me to decline interfering in a matter of so much interest to you and Mr. Boyle. But I have thought it a matter of public duty in the judicial station in which I am placed to adopt and adhere to the resolution I have mentioned."—Taney to Mrs. E. Key Scott, Dec. 19, 1857, Boyle MSS.

[24] "I suffer so much from exposure to hot sun, that I have put off from day to day my intended visit to Frederick in the hope that the weather may change."—Taney to William M. Beall, Sept. 22, 1829, MS., copied by Mrs. L. R. Lee, of Washington, D.C.

[25] In addition to the comments already quoted, the following excerpts from the letters written at Jordan's Springs are of interest:

"Mrs. Taney and the girls arrived safely and to our great joy this evening, Sophia having borne the journey very well, but Mrs. Taney I am sorry to say not so well. She is suffering with a headache, but it does not appear to be a bad one, and I hope, as it has been occasioned by fatigue that it will go off when she has rested, and that she will be well tomorrow. She desires me to say to Anne that she will write to her as soon as she has recovered from

Old Point Comfort, near Norfolk, where they enjoyed the bathing and the sea air. "We are all more and more pleased with our trip here," Taney wrote during the summer of 1849, his first at Old Point. "Our accommodations are everything we could desire. The scenery and the walks beautiful, and the bathing exceedingly pleas-

---

her journey—which she hopes will be in a day or two. I am rejoiced to hear from her that dear little Taney is recovering, and that the rest of you are all very well. Stevenson will tell you who are new here, and I am glad to tell you that Ellen, Maria and myself are all better than when we left home. You have I think done wisely in determining to remain in the country until after the election and also in refusing to make speeches. The excitement is now so high that nothing will take but very bitter speeches—and no one when the excitement is [over] thinks with any pleasure upon speeches of that sort and most commonly would be glad that he had not made them."—Taney to J. Mason Campbell, Sept. 27, 1844, Campbell MSS.

"Mrs. Taney has been in bed today with a headache. . . . The rest of us are well, and we think are growing stronger, and praying that the good weather may continue so as to enable us to remain here. . . . Mrs. Taney appears to have improved so much that I am not willing to bring her again to Baltimore while the weather [is] favorable to residence here."—Taney to J. Mason Campbell, Oct. 13, 1844, *ibid.*

"We are all doing very well here. Mrs. Taney had one severe headache last week, but she is better since than she was before; and yesterday morning after breakfast we walked to the Backbone, and remained there until after 12 o'clock; and although we found the sun hot and oppressive on our return she has not suffered from it, and is ready for a walk there again this evening. She looks much better than when we left Baltimore, and I think we are all better, and you will judge how much Sophia has improved when I tell you she joins in the dancing in the evening [and] seems to enjoy it as much as any of them. We have I suppose about an hundred here. . . .

"I trust that you all continue well and that Taney's nurse has recovered, and that the dear little fellow has not suffered in the late warm weather."—Taney to Campbell, Aug. 12, 1845, *ibid.*

"I rejoice to hear that you all continue well and that the dear little boy is weaned and that his mother has not suffered. It is nice that you have been in the country this summer for it has been exceedingly warm here until within two days past and I suppose, with the aid of the mosquitoes, it must have been not only oppressive in Baltimore but dangerous to health. Elizabeth writes us sad accounts of the mosquitoes at my house, and in that neighborhood."—Taney to Campbell, Aug. 30, 1845, *ibid.*

"I hope to be at home the latter end of this week, but I am not certain. For Carmichael is sick and I cannot think of leaving him here. . . .

"In this uncertainty about our movements I wish to provide in time for the payment of the premium on my life insurance. That in New York does not fall due until about the middle of November and I need not therefore be in any hurry about it. But the one in Baltimore is I think payable on the 12th of this month which is next Sunday. . . .

"We are all doing well here except Sophia, who has not improved at all. . . . Mrs. Taney and Ellen appear to me to have gained more in the last ten days than in all the previous part of the season. Yet this cold weather of today makes us all willing to return although we are not impatient about it. I would have been glad to have been at home at the election, but as things I see have all gone well my absence was of no consequence. I should have been deeply mortified if Giles had lost his election for the want of my vote."—Taney to Campbell, Oct. 6, 1845, *ibid.*

ant and safe. There are not many visitors here yet but they are beginning to drop in. . . . And the excellent arrangements made under the orders of General Bankhead and the neatness and cleanliness of the whole place, afford every security against disease that human prudence and foresight can provide." [26]

Invigorated by rest and exercise at this new vacation spot, and prodded by a request from Francis P. Blair,[27] Taney turned during this season to a task which he had often contemplated but had never been able to undertake, that of writing an account of the bank war. Four months after his arrival at Old Point he took up his quill pen and began the story:

"I have always intended to write an account of the part I took in opposition to the renewal of the charter of the Bank of the United States. But infirm health and the fatigue of official duties have heretofore compelled me to postpone it; and I have found it necessary to pass the vacations which are allowed me during some of the summer months in recreation and exercise in order to recover strength for the renewal of my judicial labors. Yet I have always felt that justice to myself and to General Jackson, and to the truth of history required of me the work I now commence. I know not whether I shall be able to complete it, but being at this time in the country with my family at a quiet place, and without any engagements of business for a few weeks it will give me pleasant occupation to pass a few hours every day in recalling to memory and narrating the incidents of that memorable struggle made by the bank to compel the government to renew its charter." [28]

In a document of one hundred and fifty-eight manuscript pages he wrote the account of his bank war experiences, much of which has been reproduced or summarized herein. It never reached the stage of a polished draft, its organization was not of the best, it incorporated minor inaccuracies, and there were evidences of prejudice at many points. Nevertheless, taken in connection with others of the

[26] Taney to Campbell, June 8, 1849, *ibid.*
[27] See Blair to Martin Van Buren, Nov. 6, 1849, Van Buren MSS.
[28] Taney, Bank War MS., p. 1.

materials gathered by Taney, it is to be considered as one of the most significant documents now remaining to throw light on the dramatic events of the bank war period.[29]

Taney was not able during the autumn of 1849 to carry the account through the entire period of the bank war. He returned to Old Point the following summer expecting to continue the story. The initial zest had been dissipated, however, and minor obstacles stood in the way of composition. "I think I told you," he wrote to J. Mason Campbell, "that I would bring with me a plentiful supply of paper, pens, etc. and amuse myself while here in writing Memoirs which I have so long talked about. But an old man's habits become a part of his nature. I have always been accustomed whenever I sit down to write anything, to have a comfortable chair, a roomy and firm table and good pens:—most commonly ready made to my hand. And these conveniences have become essential, and I feel unwilling to write even a letter, upon the little cramped up shaking table in my room, with bad pens which I cannot make better, (for I could never acquire the art of making a pen) and with an inkstand which holds about ink enough to write one letter of reasonable length and nothing more. And so I have not written a word on the Memoir and have put off writing to you from day to day. . . ."[30]

He did not return to his writing during that summer nor during

---

[29] Taney's manuscript came near to being permanently lost. Some years ago, however, at a public sale in Savannah, Georgia, a locksmith purchased an old safe. He found inside a mass of old letters and other manuscripts. He destroyed the letters, but by some miracle of self-restraint he saved a bound manuscript which proved to be Taney's longhand account of the bank war, together with some pages of clear copy evidently made from it by Samuel Tyler, who, however, used little of it in his biography of Taney. It is now in the Library of Congress.

[30] "This letter however," Taney continued, "is written with more pleasure because I am able to tell you, that the sick have all improved here. Our first week was a sad one. For the first two days we were most uncomfortable in our rooms, and moreover we ventured upon diet which is always unsafe for invalids, and unsafe for anybody when cooked as it generally is in a large hotel. And they were all except Maria more or less sick for some days, and Mrs. Taney and Alice worse than any of the others. But Doctor Steinecker soon put matters right, and they have been ever since improving, and all are quite well, and pleased with their trip, and enjoying the bathing and walks on the beach with bright spirits. Mrs. Taney has not had a headache since she came here, and her strength appears to me to improve every day. The only difference in my own health is that I am cheerful and inspirited by looking at the improved health and happier spirits of those I love. Fortunately although my room is not fixed up so as to be convenient for writing in, yet it is most agreeable in every other re-

those which immediately followed. In 1854, however, he was again prodded into action by the publication of Van Santvoord's *Lives of the Chief Justices of the United States,* which included a friendly but sketchy account of his own life. Struck by the lack of biographical material available, and by the fact, whether for better or for worse, that his life was intertwined with the history of the country, he took up the story. "The high offices I have filled," he declared, "and the stirring and eventful political scenes in which I was engaged before I received the appointment I now hold, and in which my position compelled me to take a prominent part, may naturally create a desire to know more about me than can be found in Mr. Van Santvoord's life. Yet I am sensible that he has written it in the kindest spirit, and has used every means in his power to obtain information from those whom he supposed might be able to give it."

He was aware, Taney continued, that scarcely anyone but himself could do more than Van Santvoord had done. He belonged to a generation which had passed away. He had come to the conclusion that, even if the public were indifferent as to his life and character, the account should nevertheless be written because of his connection with men and events of preceding decades. He was aware that autobiography was seldom impartial, and he could not hope to be free from the general infirmity of self-love, but he would try to write of his own life as if it were that of a third person. It would be pleasant, while recuperating at Old Point Comfort, to spend an hour or two each day in recalling to memory the times that were gone.[31]

He continued writing through the weeks which followed, beginning with his ancestors and carrying the story down to the time of

---

spect, cool, quiet and with a beautiful view of the water, and my time never hangs heavy on my hands.

"But not a day passes that I do not wish for you and Anne and the dear children. . . . You will readily suppose how I think of Taney and the girls, when I see Brown's children on the broad beautiful beach picking up pebbles and wading in the water. . . .

"Carlisle writes Mr. Ward that he will be here early in August, and I shall be truly glad to see him, for this is the very place to lounge and talk of old times. . . .

"The salt water has not made my hand steadier, as this scrawl abundantly shows."—Taney to Campbell, July 27, 1850, Campbell MSS.

[31] Taney, "Early Life and Education," in Tyler, *Memoir of Roger Brooke Taney,* pp. 17–19.

his removal to Frederick in 1801. He worked with a sense of trepidation, for cholera, one of the death-dealing plagues which periodically terrorized the country, was again abroad in the land. Word came that a man who had recently put up at a Baltimore hotel had died while on a steamboat bound for Norfolk, and that the boat carried the body of another man who had died in Baltimore of the same disease. In deep anxiety Taney wrote to Campbell to inquire about the family. He was relieved that Campbell had been seen on the street by a friend, and had been well. He was relieved also by the fact that the Baltimore paper said nothing about the disease, though the papers were not to be fully trusted. "I have always found the city papers unfaithful to the public in this respect," he continued, "and unwilling and reluctant to tell the whole truth for fear of hurting the interests of the city."

He presumed that cholera, like other diseases, was produced by unwholesome dirt or improper exposure, and that the two victims had suffered from their own imprudence. There was no disease at Old Point, he hastened to assure Campbell. It was delightful there. "How often in these moonlight nights and soft sunny days, we wish you were all here with us." All was well, indeed, save that Mrs. Taney had seriously injured her foot by letting a heavy tumbler fall on it, and by neglecting it thereafter, so that she was now unable to exercise during the fine weather.[32]

The Taneys returned to Baltimore, and winter came without the serious spread of the cholera which had been feared. The year in court proved unusually exhausting. "I am out of health and soon fatigued," Taney wrote from Richmond. "Perhaps Old Point may do something for me if I can get through the court here. But I am sensible of a sad falling off in my strength this spring." [33] The Campbells were preparing to make their annual trip to Newport, Rhode Island. As Taney looked forward eagerly to his return to Old Point, his youngest daughter, Alice, begged to be permitted to go to Newport with the Campbells. Campbell broached the subject with Taney, and

[32] Taney to Campbell, Oct. 6, 1854, Etting Coll., Historical Society of Pennsylvania.
[33] Taney to Campbell, June 22, 1855, Campbell MSS.

the latter replied with as close an approach to brusqueness as he seems ever to have used with the family:

"I have not the slightest confidence in [the] superior health of Newport over Old Point, and look upon it as nothing more than that unfortunate feeling of inferiority in the South, which believes every thing in the North to be superior to what we have. Yet I am willing that Alice shall go with you if she wishes it and her mother wishes it, and it will not cost more than $100. I would take that much from my increased salary but am unable to spare more without injustice to others. And it must be distinctly understood, that nothing additional must come from you. Until I see you have provided for your wife and children, I will accept nothing from you for mine." [34]

Taney became so ill that he had to go to bed for three days before he finished his work at Richmond. He had been overworked, he wrote to Campbell, and the fatigue of the journey to Old Point brought a relapse, so that he was in bed again for days. Yet he wrote about life at Old Point with no forebodings of disaster, no awareness that his attitude toward Alice's desire to go to Newport, which had been such as to prevent her going, was to cost the life of one of those whom he dearly loved. Mrs. Taney was improving. Ellen and Maria were quite well. Alice, who had not yet joined them, had had a delightful visit with Elizabeth at some point outside Baltimore. Sophia was in Baltimore, shrinking from the disgrace which "that mean miserable hypocrite," her husband, had brought upon her. Taney hoped she would come to Old Point, "For I am afraid every day of hearing that the little boy is made sick by the summer heat of the town." The weather had been cool at Old Point, and it had been necessary to close the doors and windows against the wind, "which was rather too strong for one who loves gentle breezes as much as I do." It had been so cool as to keep the figs from ripening, but he was doing well, and last evening had walked around the fort on the outside without fatigue, a distance of a mile and a half. All of them enjoyed the sea bathing every day.[35]

[34] Taney to Campbell, June 26, 1855, *ibid.*
[35] Taney to Campbell, July 13, 1855, *ibid.*

Soon, however, evidences of fearfulness became apparent in the letters. Rumors were drifting in concerning an epidemic of yellow fever. It had broken out in New Orleans, had been carried to Norfolk on ocean-going vessels, and was spreading back into the country. No one knew the cause. Taney attributed the disease to dirt. Bishop McGill, of the Roman Catholic church in Richmond, proclaimed that the Almighty had sent the yellow fever as punishment for the attacks of the Know Nothings upon Catholics.[36] It was of the irony of fate that the Taney family, wherein certainly no members of the Know Nothing party were to be found, even though the women were not Catholics, trembled alike with the heathen at the news of the spread of the menace.

"The ravages of the pestilence in Norfolk and Portsmouth have not abated," Taney wrote at the end of the month of August, "and the scene there must be awful. . . . There has been no case on the Point. And the apprehensions and anxieties of Mrs. Taney and the girls is much abated. . . . I have just returned from witnessing the grand parade of the troops here. This being the last day of the month is inspection day, and of course there was a full turn out. And with the number now on the Point, the muster is quite an imposing spectacle. I left Ellen and Alice (who went with me) with some friends as they wished to see the end of it.

"I have set about no work here, although I almost every day think of it. I have certainly a propensity to be idle and work hard only as a matter of duty, when the work can be no longer delayed. I excuse myself to myself on this occasion by the uneasiness and painful excitement which the state of things in Norfolk and Portsmouth produced in Mrs. Taney and the girls. Indeed apart from any apprehension of personal danger, it has been impossible not to feel saddened and depressed, when so many were suffering and dying near you and every day told of new victims to the disease. One's thoughts must frequently be called away from matters of mere business, and he would be a hard man, and one whom I should neither love nor respect who could coolly fix his thoughts on any other sub-

[36] Baltimore *Clipper*, Sept. 29, 1855.

ject for hours together, and feel no interruption from the agony and sufferings of the multitudes so near him." [37]

Two weeks later Taney reported that the pestilence had given no certain signs of abatement. "But we hope the abundant rain and the sea breeze may operate favorably upon it. It has been a terrible and awful scourge without example in this country. . . . We do not think that there is the least danger that the infected atmosphere can extend to this place. . . . The place is perfectly healthy and the weather fine and pleasant, and we are all I think improving, notwithstanding the sad and depressing influence of the scenes around or near us." [38]

Another week passed, and still no special cause for worry had appeared. Taney, voracious smoker that he was, realized that he would need more cigars for the month or six weeks which he might yet spend at Old Point, and placed an order for a quarter-box of two hundred and fifty to last him through that period. The heat of summer seemed to be over, and the weather was pleasant. "We all continue well here," he wrote to Campbell, "Mrs. Taney certainly much stronger, but I grieve to say that her difficulty in speech and defect of memory still remains, and I fear is not materially better. The constant uneasiness she unfortunately feels about the fever, and the sad amounts of suffering and death which she is continually hearing must be in some measure injurious to her health. Yet she has never wished to leave here, and indeed would be unwilling to go in any of the steam boats between this place and Baltimore or Richmond, as all of them have been filled with persons flying from the infected towns." [39]

Three or four days later Mrs. Taney, apparently already a victim of paralysis, suffered a severe stroke. In panic Taney wrote to Campbell urging that medical aid be sent from Baltimore. Not trusting the mail service, he sent another note by private conveyance. "I wrote to you by mail today to tell you of the illness of my dear wife," he said pitifully, "and to implore Doctor T. Buckler to come and see

[37] Taney to Campbell, Aug. 31, 1855, Campbell MSS.
[38] Taney to Campbell, Sept. 15, 1855, *ibid.*
[39] Taney to Campbell, Sept. 22, 1855, *ibid.*

her. Fearing the letter may miscarry I write this note to give you this sad intelligence." [40] Mrs. Taney grew worse in spite of medical aid, and Alice suddenly fell seriously ill. On September 29 Mrs. Taney died. It was believed at the time that paralysis was the cause, but it was reported later that after death the evidences of yellow fever were present in the body.[41] A few hours later, on the morning of the following day, Alice also died, unquestionably the victim of the marauding disease, leaving Taney crushed beneath another terrible blow.

There was no possibility at this time of moving the bodies, the victims of the dread contagion, to a cemetery at any distant place. Accordingly they were temporarily interred in a grave on Colonel Segar's farm, near Old Point. Some time later, at Taney's request, his friend David M. Perine had the bodies moved to Frederick, where they were reinterred in the lot of the Potts family in Mt. Olivet cemetery, along with Mrs. Taney's parents.

The broken-hearted family boarded a boat for Baltimore. Taney was leaving Old Point, the scene of many happy summers and of one terrible tragedy, never to return, and the writing of the story of his life, which had been begun there, was never to be resumed.

So great had been Taney's devotion to and dependence upon his wife [42] that now, at seventy-eight years of age, there was real danger that he would collapse completely when deprived of her companionship. It was here that his religion, an intimate spiritual reality rather than a mere commitment to creed, came to his aid. When a few days after his return to Baltimore a friend stopped at his house to take him for a drive he courteously refused to go. "The truth is, Father,"

[40] Taney to Campbell, Sept. 26, 1855, *ibid.*

[41] Baltimore *Sun*, Oct. 4, 1855.

[42] The following letter, written in 1852 on the anniversary of their marriage, has been much quoted: "I cannot, my dearest wife, suffer the 7th of January to pass without renewing to you the pledges of love which I made to you on the 7th of January forty-six years ago. And although I am sensible that in that long period I have done many things that I ought not to have done, and left undone many things that I ought to have done, yet in constant affection to you I have never wavered—never being insensible how much I owe to you—and now pledge to you again a love as true and sincere as that I offered on the 7th of January, 1806, and shall ever be Your affectionate husband, R. B. Taney."—Taney to Mrs. Anne Taney, Jan. 7, 1852, Tyler, *op. cit.*, p. 317.

he said to the Catholic priest who happened to be with him at the time, "that I have resolved that my first visit should be to the Cathedral, to invoke strength and grace from God, to be resigned to His holy will, by approaching the altar and receiving holy communion." [43]

"I have indeed passed through most painful scenes," he wrote a few days later to his cousin Ethelbert Taney, "and have not yet gained sufficient composure to attend to business. But it has pleased God mercifully to support me through this visitation, and to recall my bewildered thoughts, and enable me to feel this chastisement comes from Him, and that it is my duty to submit to it with calmness and resignation. And I do not doubt that, severe as the trial is to those who survive, it is, in the mysterious ways of Providence, introduced in justice and mercy to the living and the dead." [44]

He never swerved in his loyalty and devotion to the Catholic Church as far as his personal conduct was concerned. "Most thankful I am," he wrote in another letter to Ethelbert Taney, "that the reading, reflection, studies, and experience of a long life have strengthened and confirmed my faith in the Catholic Church, which has never ceased to teach her children how they should live and how they should die." [45] Yet he was broadly tolerant of those who had different beliefs and affiliations from his own, save when, as in the case of the Know Nothings, they organized themselves for political attacks upon Catholics. Although one of his daughters, Sophia, became a Catholic of her own accord, he did not attempt to persuade either them or his wife to accept his religion, and he protected them against the proselyting efforts of members of his own church. His attitude toward their religion is not easy to discover. In view of his devotion to them and of his firm belief in a future life it seems clear that he could have been happy only in the belief that they, by their separate religious paths, would arrive at the same goal as he. If holding such a belief constituted in any sense disloyalty to his own church it seems probable that to this extent he was disloyal.

[43] John McElroy to Samuel Tyler, March 2, 1871, Tyler, *op. cit.*, pp. 476–477.
[44] Taney to Ethelbert Taney, Oct. 22, 1855, *ibid.*, pp. 473–474.
[45] *Ibid.*, p. 475.

Now that Mrs. Taney was gone it was no longer worth while to maintain a residence in Baltimore. The Campbells could provide Taney with a home when he was holding circuit court in Baltimore, and he needed a home of his own in Washington, where Ellen, and Sophia too at times, could take care of him. Accordingly the Baltimore house was sold in December, 1855. Early in January, a month after the term of the Supreme Court had opened, Taney ventured in Ellen's company to make the trip to Washington, and Maria, whose husband was then at sea, followed to aid in making them comfortable.

"I escaped a relapse which I much apprehended from the sudden and extreme cold weather which came on the evening I left you," Taney wrote soon afterward to Campbell. "But I have gained no strength, and can hardly expect to do so until I can get out and exercise. But there has not been a day since I came here that I could venture out, and today I see no prospects of its improving. Until I can get some exercise in the fresh air I am unfit for business, and feel constantly a sensation of lassitude and depression which unfits me for the bench. Perhaps I may be able to take my seat in court some time next week. . . .

"You remember the little iron cup which Taney gave me for my segar ashes," he concluded. "If it is at your house bring it with you.

"We are all as well as when we left you, and find our quarters comfortable." [46]

The location of these quarters is not clearly indicated, but they may have been those visited about this time by one of Taney's young admirers, who described them with indignation at a government which paid a salary so low as to require the Chief Justice to resort to such a habitation. He found Taney living with his family over a candy shop on Pennsylvania Avenue, between Fourth and Fifth streets. Taney's office was partitioned off by a calico curtain from another apartment in which the family cooking was done. "Of course there was an impressiveness and an air of refinement which emanated from the dignity of his person and which no mean surroundings

[46] Taney to Campbell, Jan. 16, 1856, MS., Boston Public Library.

could overcome, and there was also the stamp of superiority given by the law books which filled the pine-wood shelves. But more forcibly there was indelibly engraved upon the mind of the young lad the conviction of the penuriousness of the country which demanded of the leading law officer of the state a lifelong devotion, and exacted from him an unsullied and unblemished integrity, together with entire abstention from any speculations to advance his worldly concerns, . . . while it at the same time lodged that self-same officer in what was little better than a garret, and left him cause for anxiety even for the mere subsistence of his family after his death." [47]

During most of the remaining years of his life Taney lived at 23 Blogden's Row, on Indiana Avenue, near the Court House. That section was respectable enough at the time, as respectability went in what was then a drab and sprawling city. The streets immediately adjoining were unpaved, but so were all the streets except Pennsylvania Avenue. They served in winter as muddy wallows for the hogs which ran at large, and in summer they threw up a blanket of dust which covered the trees and houses. There were no sewers. The only drainage was on the surface. A shallow stream, called the Tiber, crossing Pennsylvania Avenue at Second Street, carried off refuse to the Potomac save when the incoming tide moved it back into the city. Water for household use was drawn by pumps from wells at various street corners, apparently with little awareness of the pollution which it had inevitably undergone.

Such was the physical condition of the capital city, in which Taney had spent part of each year since his arrival in Washington to take a place in the cabinet of Andrew Jackson, and in which he was now to make his home for the remainder of his life. He was able to attend court only a small portion of the term during which he removed there, though within that portion he heard the first argument of the Dred Scott case. When summer came he and Ellen and Sophia and little Roger set out for a new place of recuperation, going this time to Fauquier White Sulphur Springs, in Virginia. He wrote a cheery

[47] Simon Sterne, "The Salaries of the United States Supreme Court Judges," *The Counsellor*, Jan., 1892.

letter to one of his granddaughters,[48] who was now at Newport, but a later letter to Campbell reflected more of gloom:

"As respects our health here," he reported, "my own has improved, and I think continues to improve, and I am now able to walk a mile without much fatigue. But at my time of life and broken constitution I have no right to expect again anything like the good health of earlier life. And when I say I have improved and am improving, it is only by comparison with the state of utter prostration to which I was reduced when I came here. Ellen I am sorry to say has not improved as much as I hoped for. . . .

"I have no news to tell you here, except that I understand a Know Nothing meeting is to be held here on the 29th and 30th of this month at which General Houston of Texas and Mr. Marshall of Kentucky are to address the meeting. I never go to the Hotel except to my meals and therefore talk with no politicians. But from the recent elections I think Mr. Buchanan will be the President. Yet I have always supposed that Fillmore would get the vote of Maryland. For the only difference between him and Mr. Buchanan is his pledge to proscribe Catholics and foreigners. And there is no state in which the clerical influence has been so generally and strenuously exerted to inform the Protestant mind against those who belong to the Catholic Church as in Maryland. In the eyes of the clergymen I am Mordecai the Jew sitting at the King's gate, and their zeal will hardly flag while I remain there." [49]

The family had been negligent in seeing that good photographs were taken of Taney and his wife in their mature years, for distribution to the many friends who desired them. Taney had had no interest in broadcasting his likeness for purposes of notoriety, and in 1852 had refused to donate a picture to be reproduced in a book of portraits of the seventy-five most distinguished men in the country. He expressed his gratitude for the honor, but added: "I have no ambi-

[48] Taney to Alice T. Campbell, Aug. 5, 1856, Campbell MSS.
[49] Taney to Campbell, Aug. 28, 1856, Campbell MSS.

tion to be distinguished in that way; nor any vanity that would be gratified by the association you propose." [50]

A year later, however, he permitted Horatio Stone, at the instance of a number of members of the bar, to work out in marble a bust which is now in the conference room of the Supreme Court. Samuel F. B. Morse, who was regarded as an authority on such matters, praised it for its fidelity of reproduction. To him it revealed "that firmness of will, tempered with benevolence of heart, and also, that earnest, yet mild inquisitiveness so characteristic of his physiognomy, and a meditativeness which, if it has not moulded the lineaments of his face into smooth forms of a feminine beauty, has yet stamped upon them indelibly the more fitting and sublime beauty of intellect." [51]

After the death of his wife, of whom no good pictures had been made, a number of photographs were taken of Taney in different poses. Few of them, however, reflect the personality of a man in the vigor of life. His life, perhaps, was too much of the mind, of the spirit, to be portrayed adequately in any unanimated sketch of a frail physique. At any rate, most of the pictures taken of the aging and decrepit man reveal nothing of the invincible spirit which in spite of a worn-out body continued to drive him on until the day of his death.

Nevertheless, the pictures had significance for the friends who knew him, and he distributed many of them. At the request of a friend he had a likeness taken for presentation to two judges of the Court of Queen's Bench, in England. It is significant of his humble friendliness to people in all walks of life that from the same negative he had two other pictures made, had them put in gilt frames, and inscribed them to Madison Franklin and Martha Hill, the negro man and woman who as free persons had served him for many years.

In this process of perpetuating the record of his own life he revived again his interest in the mementos and records of the past, though

[50] Taney to R. Van Dien, Jan. 31, 1852, MS., New York Historical Society.
[51] S. F. B. Morse to Hamilton Fish, March 28, 1854, New York *Times*, May 30, 1854.

not sufficiently to lead to the continuation of his autobiography, the materials for which were turned over to Samuel Tyler for biographical synthesis. He received with delight a photograph of the Brooke coat-of-arms, from his mother's family, and was eager to know its history—whether it had been brought to America by Robert Brooke, the first settler, and through what branches of the family it had since passed.

"This memorial of my mother's family," he wrote, "is the more acceptable because ever since my childhood it has been said of me, that in face and figure and manner I resembled her family more than any of my brothers or sisters, except a sister who died shortly after she had grown to womanhood. And your letter reminds me of family traits in the duration of life, which seem, in some degree to have been exemplified in my person. I am however now verging upon the longest period of time, allotted here to any of my family and race; and am thankful that I have been spared some of the distressing infirmities which advanced age often brings with it." [52]

These varied experiences of Taney's later years, although not immediately connected with his work as a judge, cast revealing illumination upon his life. Of the complete story of his life one final segment, part personal and part professional, remains yet to be presented. It has to do with the slavery crisis as he participated in it, and with the effects of his participation upon the country and upon his own life during the closing years.

[52] Taney to Mrs. H. B. Chesley, Sept. 25, 1859, Conarroe Coll., Historical Society of Pennsylvania.

Chapter XXIII

STORM CLOUDS OF SECTIONAL STRIFE

To RETURN to the story of the increasingly embittered conflicts which grew out of the issues of slavery [1] is to resume the tracing of events which led inevitably, or which seem now to have led inevitably, into the maelstrom of civil war. Viewed superficially, these events appear to have little relevance for the present day, except for explanation of the happenings of a dead past. The general background of the Civil War has so much its own peculiar coloring, and its issues seem so foreign to situations likely to arise again, as to seem largely without significance in connection with the problems of a later period.

The uniqueness of the developing sectional conflict, arising out of divergent economic interests and divergent conceptions of property, and rights, and justice, out of divergent cultures as a whole, is so apparent that it cannot be ignored in any accurate portrayal. The significance of the struggle, however, is even wider than the explanation of dramatic happenings in a closed chapter of American history, since it is not in the past alone that evolving cultures are molded by economic systems, and since the past has no monopoly of major struggles in courts of law and elsewhere over rights in particular kinds of property. The assertion of the right of southerners to hold property in slaves touched something too fundamental in the social order to be wholly unique, as did also the insistence of abolitionists that all men were entitled to a certain minimum of freedom, of immunity from control by others.

Such problems must arise in some manner in any society as long as inequalities of capacity and opportunity continue to occur among men. In a well ordered society the problems are solved, temporarily

[1] See Chapter XX.

at least, before the festering wounds of individual and class friction have stirred the frenzy culminating in social disaster. When problems can be solved only by fundamental changes in the economic and cultural order, however, there is always the possibility that the changes may come too slowly, or may be engineered and correlated by unskilled hands, and that the ship of state may flounder through the storm only at the expense of immeasurable suffering. In view, therefore, of the dangers surrounding any living and changing society it is possible to find something more than uniqueness and drama in the events which led to war to the death between the social orders of the North and the South.

Members of Congress desirous of preventing sectional friction had for many years attempted to escape the necessity of debating the issues of slavery in public. They had been by no means successful, and the Supreme Court had added to their difficulties by its decision in *Prigg* v. *Pennsylvania*. The states learned from that decision that they were under no obligation to aid in the enforcement of the Fugitive Slave Law, and a number of northern states enacted "personal liberty laws" by which the support of state officials and the use of state jails and other property were denied to the federal government and to alleged owners in connection with the recapture of slaves. The South sputtered angrily at these developments, but sputtering did no good. Relief was to be secured only from Congress, by the setting up of machinery for the recapture of fugitive slaves which would be adequate without the coöperation of the states. It was inevitable that such legislation should be bitterly opposed by abolitionist leaders, and that the rancor of sectional disagreement should air itself freely on the floors of Congress.

The war with Mexico and the expectation that Mexican territory would be seized by the United States provoked further discussion of slavery issues. Some northern leaders fought the annexation of territory both because it would be carved into additional slave states and because the new states would be predominantly agricultural and would provide representation hostile to the interests of the more highly industrialized section of the country. Some hot-headed southern leaders clamored for the seizure of much or all of Mexico, not aware of the fact recognized by Calhoun and others that much of Mexico would not lend itself well to the conditions of a slave economy.

To curb the territorial aspirations of the South, industrialists and abolitionists supported the proposition of David Wilmot, member of Congress from Pennsylvania, that slavery should not be permitted in any territory acquired from Mexico. The Wilmot Proviso, in other words, was to become an act of Congress defining the boundary of slave territory. It was to take its place alongside the Missouri Compromise of 1820, which provided that in the vast area known as the Louisiana Purchase the territory of Missouri should be admitted into the Union as a slave state, but that thereafter slavery should be prohibited in any other state which might be formed north of the line marking the southern border of Missouri.

The South had reluctantly accepted the Missouri Compromise but southern leaders were angered by the much discussed Wilmot Proviso. They opposed it on various grounds, including that of constitutionality, and began to proclaim their doubts as to the constitutionality even of the Missouri Compromise. The mood and temper of the South were well represented in the Supreme Court in Justice Daniel. His point of view is revealed in his letters to Van Buren, whose attitude toward the Wilmot Proviso he was seeking to discover. "I have ever regarded what has been called the Missouri Compromise, as utterly without warrant from the Constitution," Daniel declared. "The people of this nation may in practice observe it if they so please, but so far as any authority for it is to be sought in the Constitution no foundation for it whatever can be discovered there. Congress never had the power to ordain or establish it. . . .

"There is another aspect of this pretension now advanced, which exhibits it as fraught with dangers far greater than any that can flow from mere calculation of political influence, or of profit, arising from a distribution of territory. It is that view of the case which pretends to an insulting exclusiveness or superiority on the one hand, and denounces a degrading inequality or inferiority on the other: which says in effect to the southern man, Avaunt! you are not my equal, and hence are to be excluded as carrying a moral taint with you. Here is at once the extinction of all fraternity, of all sympathy, of all endurance even: the creation of animosity fierce, implacable, undying. It is the immitigable outrage, which I venture to say, there is no true Southron from the schoolboy to the octogenarian, who is not prepared for any extremity in order to repel it." [2]

Daniel's resentment at northern disapproval, odd as it seems at first in connection with a class which had long been conscious of its aristocracy, was characteristic of the attitude of many southern leaders. It was as if, beneath mannerisms of assumed superiority, doubts as to their own status stirred restlessly with the criticisms of their northern neighbors, and threatened to break to the surface. At any rate, wrangling over slavery issues grew more bitter as the Mexican War came to an end, with the acquisition of California and a vast and largely unsettled area known as New Mexico.

A compromise was proposed by which territories would be organized by act of Congress without reference to slavery. The right to hold slaves in the incorporated areas would be determined by the territorial courts, from which appeal or writ of error would be allowed to the Supreme Court of the United States. Northern leaders were afraid of the proposed arrangement. It is not clear whether they doubted that the law was on their side, or whether they suspected that in any case the Supreme Court would be swayed by southern and pro-slavery prejudices and uphold the right of owning slaves in the territories.

A number of southern leaders likewise feared the proposal. They admitted in private that, in the absence of federal legislation on the

---

[2] Daniel to Van Buren, Nov. 1, 1847, Van Buren MSS.

On another occasion Daniel characterized the support of the Wilmot Proviso as "the over-throw of the great national compact; as the extreme of injury and oppression; oppression in its most galling form, because it declares to me that I am not regarded as an equal; the sharer of a common birthright—that the compatriots of Washington, Jefferson, Madison, Monroe, of Henry, of Mason, of the Randolphs, the Lees, of Giles, of Brent, and of many other worthies, are a disfranchised and degraded caste. Oppression which all that is holy in duty and obligation binds the patriot to repel at any and every cost. This, my dear Sir, is a subject of greatest grief to me."—Daniel to Van Buren, Nov. 19, 1847, *ibid.*

subject, the laws of Mexico at the time of the acquisition would govern property rights—and those laws did not permit slavery. John A. Campbell of Alabama, then in private practice but later a member of the Supreme Court, warned Calhoun that in order to legalize slavery in the newly acquired area positive legislation must be secured from Congress.[3] The argument seems highly plausible, much more plausible than the opposing argument which he used nine years later in the Dred Scott case. Nevertheless, many southern politicians were willing to leave the law as it stood and trust to the Supreme Court for the protection of slavery interest, and they boldly taunted northern Whigs for their unwillingness likewise to leave the matter to the court.

The compromise was not accepted. Had it been agreed upon, it is a matter for speculation as to whether the court, on a basis of doubtful law at the very best, would have read slavery into the newly acquired area. From later decisions it seems that it might have done so. This crisis was not as threatening in 1848 as it was later to appear, however, and a majority of the judges might not so easily have concluded that the country could and must be saved by a decision which would block abolitionist encroachment on the territorial claims of the slaveholders.

Congress continued its debates over fugitive slave laws and slavery in the territories, to which hotly controversial topics were added the abolition of the slave trade, and the abolition of slavery itself in the District of Columbia. Calhoun, tottering on the edge of the grave but ably seconded by other southern leaders, including Jefferson Davis, the future president of the southern Confederacy, threatened disunion unless the North gave heed to the grievances of the South. The ties which bound the two sections together, he declared, were snapping, strand by strand. Catastrophe could be avoided only by legislation and a constitutional amendment which would restore the balance of power. Legislation which had excluded slavery from cer-

[3] Campbell to Calhoun, March 1, 1848, C. S. Boucher and B. P. Brooks (eds.), "Correspondence Addressed to John C. Calhoun, 1837–1849," in the *Annual Report of the American Historical Association* for 1929, pp. 430–434.

tain parts of the country, and which by erecting tariff barriers had injured the prosperity of the South, had led to the crisis. Now all discriminations against the South must be removed. Slavery must be permitted to seek its own habitation, and adequate machinery must be set up for the recapture of fugitive slaves.

Among the leaders at the opposite extreme were two younger men who were prominent defenders of the rights of fugitive slaves, both before the courts and elsewhere, and who were able propagandists for abolition.[4] Salmon P. Chase of Ohio had won the title of "attorney general for free negroes." William H. Seward, former governor of New York, was no less zealous in the cause. He declared in Congress that the Constitution devoted the territory of the nation to justice, welfare, and liberty, and that a "higher law than the Constitution" devoted it to the same ends. He thereby created for the abolitionists an effective slogan, and offended with heresy the ears of the friends of slavery and the legalists who were interested not so much in slavery as in the textual interpretation of law and the maintenance of the stability of the Constitution. He denounced the attempts to secure the adoption of a new fugitive slave law, and demanded the abolition of slavery in the District of Columbia. He and Chase scorned the threat of secession, although the threat was made more real by the fact that a southern convention had been called to meet in Nashville in the near future, in June, 1850.

Two of the country's best known but now aged leaders sought a compromise between the positions of the hot-headed propagandists at either extreme. Henry Clay proposed what seemed a reasonable program, if any program was to be agreed upon. California was to be admitted to the Union as a free state. The remaining territory acquired from Mexico was to be admitted as slave or free, depending on the desires of the population. An effective fugitive slave law would be passed for the protection of southern property. The slave

---

[4] They had been counsel in *Jones* v. *Van Zandt*, 5 Howard 215 (1847), and seemed quite as interested in using the case as a vehicle for spreading abolitionist propaganda as in winning for their client. See Seward's letters to Chase, Dec. 26, 1846, Jan. 15, 1847, and Feb. 2, 1847, Chase MSS., Library of Congress. See also J. W. Schuckers, *The Life and Public Services of Salmon Portland Chase*, pp. 64–65.

trade would be prohibited in the District of Columbia, but slavery itself would be permitted to exist there.

With the aid of Daniel Webster and other moderate leaders who felt that the issues of slavery were less important than the preservation of the Union, the program was adopted, during the year 1850, though not until after great bitterness of feeling had been stirred. It was fervently hoped that the compromise would bring an end to the sectional strife. Unfortunately, feelings had run too deep to be smoothed merely by legislation. Abolitionists and northerners not interested in direct interference with slavery were angered by the new Fugitive Slave Law, which legalized the recapture of slaves without jury trial and without the assistance of the states. In spite of the law, friends of escaping negroes continued to aid in their transit northward toward Canada, where they would be reasonably safe, to the exasperation of the pursuing owners.

The enforcement of the Fugitive Slave Law was entrusted to federal magistrates, and, ultimately, to the judges of the Supreme Court when they sat as circuit judges. Their duties, of course, did not add to their popularity with the abolitionists, but they refused to be swayed by the sentiments of the opposition. In a charge to a grand jury Woodbury immediately took the position that it was the function of judges to enforce law rather than to make it, and gave the act his official support. Nelson took a similar position. Grier, who had always been stirred to wrath by abolitionist activities, vigorously denounced in court a Pennsylvania personal liberty law. It forbade obedience to the Constitution, he declared, and encouraged race riots.[5] He insisted on the fullest enforcement of the Fugitive Slave Law, and publicly denounced the politicians who opposed it.[6]

When the execution of process under the new law was forcibly resisted in Pennsylvania, Grier wrote to learn whether, in case it happened again, he could rely upon the support of federal troops. President Fillmore announced to Webster, the Secretary of State, and

[5] Grier to James Buchanan, April 2, 1850, Buchanan MSS.
[6] Grier to William Robinson, Nov. 22, 1850, Washington *National Intelligencer*, Dec. 12, 1850.

presumably told Grier, that he knew of no higher law which con-
flicted with the Constitution which he had sworn to support, and that
he would not tolerate nullification.[7] Even McLean, with all his sympathy for the abolitionists of his section, had no kind words for
Seward's doctrine of a higher law. It was utterly destructive of all
law, he declared, and would overturn the basis of society. The Fugitive Slave Law must be enforced.[8]

Salmon P. Chase admitted despondently that the judges of the
Supreme Court would hold the Fugitive Slave Law to be constitutional. "They were appointed to do so," he declared. "The slaveholders have seen to it for years that every judge was sound on the
slavery question. But their decision wont make it constitutional. Nor
is it constitutional." [9] Thus, although resistance to the law was gradually quelled by threat of armed force, the opposition of political
leaders did not cease, and at the same time it remained apparent that
the hunger of the South for more slave territory was unappeased.

The growth of population in that portion of the Louisiana Purchase north of Missouri provoked additional hostility. By the Compromise of 1820 the southern leaders had agreed that when states
were carved from this area they would be admitted to the Union as
free states. The rivalry between the two cultures for dominance had
now become so intense, however, that the South refused to support
the admission of a new free state. Interests deeply concerned with
western development but not particularly concerned with the issues
of slavery, sought another compromise. Under the leadership of
Stephen A. Douglas of Illinois, support was organized for the Kansas-
Nebraska Act, by which the new states were to be admitted not necessarily as free states, but as free or slave, depending on the votes of
the people of the respective areas.

Although Douglas was not the spokesman of the conservative
slavery interests, those interests found it to their advantage to support his proposal. The Kansas-Nebraska Act was adopted, in 1854,

[7] Fillmore to Webster, Oct. 23, 1850, *Letters of Daniel Webster* (Van Tyne edition), pp.
436–437.
[8] Alexandria *Gazette*, Sept. 19, 1850, quoted, A. J. Beveridge, *Abraham Lincoln*, II, 112.
[9] Chase to ———, Dec. 21, 1850, Chase MSS.

repealing the Missouri Compromise. The abolitionist leaders were frantic in their rage at what they called the bad faith of the South in abrogating the agreement adopted years earliers to maintain peace between the sections. Southern leaders replied that there was no violation of good faith, in that the Kansas-Nebraska Act merely extended the principle of the Compromise of 1850 by which the slavery question in the new states was to be settled by the votes of the residents. Furthermore, they declared, Congress had no control over the subject, the Missouri Compromise had been unconstitutional, and it had therefore carried no obligation. While both sections of the country poured settlers into the territories in frantic attempts to resolve the issues by the piling up of votes, the constitutional questions continued in heated debate. It was inevitable that sooner or later the Supreme Court should be asked to pass upon them.

In a case decided by the Supreme Court early in 1851 an attempt had been made to secure from the court a definition of the power of the federal government to prohibit the geographical extension of slavery. A resident of Kentucky owned certain slaves whom he wished to have trained as musicians. He hired them out to a man who took them from point to point to play for compensation at public entertainments, and supervised their training. Among other places he took them into Ohio. The state of Ohio had been carved out of the Northwest Territory, in which the Ordinance of 1787 had provided that slavery should never exist, and which under its own laws was a free state.

No attempt was made under the Ordinance or under the Ohio laws to interfere with the trainer's control over the negroes under his charge, and he returned them to their owner in Kentucky without mishap. Some time later, however, the negroes escaped from their master. They were carried across the Ohio River by a man named Strader. Strader was prosecuted under a Kentucky law which prescribed punishment for assisting slaves in escaping from their masters. Strader defended on the ground that these negroes were not slaves. They had previously become free, he contended, when they had been taken with the consent of their owner into free territory in Ohio. Strader lost in the lower court, and appealed to the Supreme Court of the United States.

Taney, speaking for the court in a clear opinion, rejected Strader's argument.[10] The Ordinance of 1787 had been superseded by the Constitution and by the act of Congress admitting Ohio to the Union, he declared, and the slavery issue in Ohio was now one for Ohio and not for the federal government. Furthermore, he continued, it was not necessary to decide whether the negroes had been free during the period when they were in Ohio under the direction of their trainer. They had returned voluntarily to Kentucky, where they were subject to Kentucky laws; and under those laws they were slaves. Strader had therefore been aiding slaves when he helped them to escape, and was subject to punishment.

The question of federal power therefore remained undetermined. Although abolitionist critics were hacking away at the reputation of the court, it seems probable that a decision at this time on the controversial points would have been generally accepted, in spite of the inevitable acrimonious protests of the defeated interests. Yet admittedly the court acted wisely in not presuming to decide more points than were necessary to the decision of the particular case before it. It was a major tragedy that it did not exercise the same self-restraint six years later in the handling of the Dred Scott case, which even now was on its way through the lower courts.

This famous controversy was begun in a lower state court in Missouri in 1846. A negro, Dred Scott, began a suit against the widow of his deceased master to establish the freedom of himself, his wife, and their two children. In 1834 Dr. John Emerson, a surgeon in the United States Army, took Dred Scott, his slave, to a military post at Rock Island, in Illinois. For two years the negro was held in slavery at this place, in spite of the fact that Illinois was included in the territory to which the Ordinance of 1787 had reference and despite the existence of state laws forbidding slavery. In 1836 he was taken to Fort Snelling, in the northern part of the Louisiana Purchase, where

[10] *Strader* v. *Graham*, 10 Howard 82 (1851).

he was held as a slave in spite of the provisions of the Missouri Compromise. At this post he was married to Harriet, a negress owned by an army officer at the fort, whom Dr. Emerson purchased in order that the negro family might be kept together.

In 1838 Dr. Emerson returned to Missouri with Dred Scott and his wife and a daughter who had been born to them, and continued to hold them as slaves, together with another daughter who was born after the return to Missouri. Dr. Emerson died, and suit was brought against his widow in a state court, on the ground that his residence at the several points in free territory outside Missouri had made Dred Scott a free man. The case dragged through the court for a period of between three and four years, and was then decided in favor of the negro. The decision occasioned no great surprise, for there were a number of precedents for it in the courts of the state.

Mrs. Emerson, however, appealed the case to the state supreme court. The three to two decision arrived at in 1852 reflected the bitterness produced by the Compromise of 1850. It reversed the lower court, holding that whatever the legal status of the negro had been while outside the state, his voluntary return to Missouri had subjected him again to Missouri laws, under which he was a slave.

Mrs. Emerson had in the meantime married Dr. C. C. Chaffee, a Massachusetts abolitionist, whose chief interest in Dred Scott, now a shiftless elderly negro, and in the case itself, was in discovering whether a negro became free automatically when taken by his owner into free territory. An attempt was now made to get at the issue by having a suit brought for Dred Scott in a federal court. To protect Chaffee's reputation as an abolitionist and to conceal the friendly character of the suit it was thought best to transfer title to the negro to Mrs. Chaffee's brother, John F. A. Sanford [11] of New York. In the latter part of 1853 Roswell M. Field, an abolitionist lawyer of St. Louis, as counsel for the negro, brought suit against Sanford in the federal district court in St. Louis to secure the freedom of Dred Scott and his family.

The facilities of the federal courts were available in cases of this

[11] The name is incorrectly spelled "Sandford" in the reports.

kind only when the plaintiff and the defendant were citizens of different states. The declaration presented to the court by Field contained the averment that Dred Scott was a citizen of Missouri, and Sanford a citizen of New York. Counsel for Sanford, acting nominally in defense of Sanford's property in the slave but actually aiding in opening up the questions to be settled, submitted the "plea in abatement" which was to be the subject of endless discussion in the months and years which followed. It was contended in the plea that the court had no jurisdiction in the case because, as the term "citizen" was used in the Constitution, Dred Scott was not a citizen of Missouri. His inability to be a citizen, it was contended, was due not merely to his own status as a slave, but to the fact that negroes in general in the United States were either slaves or the descendants of people who had come into the country as slaves, and were therefore a degraded people. The Constitution, in providing access to the federal courts to citizens of different states, did not include degraded people within the concept.

Field demurred to this plea, contending that the fact of Dred Scott's race and origin did not prevent his being a citizen of a state, and did not deny him access to the federal courts. The judge, agreeing with Field on this point, overruled the plea in abatement, and the case was argued on the merits before a jury. When the facts had been submitted the judge instructed the jury that Dred Scott was not entitled to his freedom, and the jury so decided. The case was taken to the Supreme Court on writ of error, and was filed during the term which began in December, 1854.

There was a possibility that the Supreme Court would merely follow its decision in the case of the Kentucky negro musicians, and hold that, whatever the status of Dred Scott had been while he was outside Missouri, he was subject to Missouri laws after his return. Such a decision would leave the major questions unsettled while Dred Scott would be held in slavery—for the highest court in the state had already decided that under the laws of Missouri he was a slave.

This case differed somewhat, however, from that involving the negro musicians. That controversy had been between two white men whose right to sue in the courts resorted to was unquestioned. In the Dred Scott case, on the other hand, quite apart from the merits of the case, the right of one of the parties to sue was questioned merely because of the fact that he was a negro. Furthermore, since the sectional friction intensified by the repeal of the Missouri Compromise was revealing itself in persistent wrangling over the constitutionality of federal laws excluding slavery from United States territory, the court was under pressure to pass upon this question. It was thought that the court might decide it if given an opportunity, even if the case before it did not absolutely require such a decision. In view of the prestige which the court had, there was reason for believing that the decision, whatever its nature, would be generally accepted, and would aid in removing the friction.

The court was behind with its work, and the case was not reached until February, 1856, when Taney returned to the bench after the illness and other disturbances which followed the death of Mrs. Taney. It was argued from February 11 to 14, by Montgomery Blair of St. Louis, son of Francis P. Blair, for the negro; and by Henry S. Geyer, formerly of Frederick County, Maryland, and now United States Senator from Missouri, and Reverdy Johnson of Maryland, for Sanford.

Except in a few abolitionist papers, particularly Horace Greeley's New York *Tribune,* the argument did not receive a great deal of attention. The *Tribune* reported a gentleman as saying that the case was not strongly put on either side, and particularly on the "right" side.[12] James S. Pike, writing much of the *Tribune's* Washington correspondence during the following weeks, kept the story alive by recounting the various and conflicting rumors as to how each of the judges stood on the several complex questions involved in the case. In his earlier accounts he admitted that all statements were mere conjectures, but as the court continued to hold secret sessions about the case his reports took on more of assurance. They never squared completely with Campbell's statement many years later as to the posi-

[12] New York *Tribune,* Feb. 15, 1856.

tions of the several judges,[13] but the report sent out after one of the conferences was so nearly accurate that Taney came to the indignant conclusion that the information could have come only from one of the judges present.[14]

There is no absolute proof as to the source of the information, if indeed it was given. McLean, however, was more apt to be in close touch with the abolitionist paper than was any other of the judges. He was in closest sympathy with the aims of the paper, and at this time he was panting for the leadership of the newly organized Republican party which was soon to select its presidential candidate, and was eager to make use of the slavery issues. If among the judges there was a culprit, therefore, it seems most probable that it was McLean.

At any rate, the judges continued divided not merely upon whether Dred Scott had been free while out of Missouri, but also upon the question raised in the court below by the plea in abatement, as to whether any negro could be a citizen of a state so as to be able to sue in a federal court. They were also in disagreement as to whether the latter question was properly before them, or whether as far as this case was concerned it had been taken out of their hands by the decision in the court below. Repeated discussions in conference failed to bring the judges together. It gradually became apparent that if the case was decided at this time almost every member of the court would write an opinion differing in some respect from the opinions of his brethren. These opinions would appear just in time to be used by all factions in the presidential campaign of 1856, adding to partisan and sectional chaos instead of aiding in quelling it. All things considered, Taney was doubtless relieved when Nelson, declaring himself in doubt on certain points, requested that the case be reargued. The request was granted, and the second argument was scheduled for the following term, when the election would be over.

The *Tribune* had been fearful lest the case be decided in such a way that the minority could not effectively dissent as to the constitu-

[13] 20 Wallace x, xi.
[14] Catron to James Buchanan, Feb. 6, 1857, Buchanan MSS.

tionality of such federal measures as the Missouri Compromise [15] —for it evidently learned at an early date that a majority of the court would hold that measure unconstitutional if it passed on the question. Hard-hitting dissents, however, would provide excellent materials for campaign purposes, and could be made to advance the abolitionist cause.

"There is such a thing as a minority left on the bench," the *Tribune* declared, "notwithstanding the court has been denounced as the 'citadel of slavery'; and unless all the impressions are erroneous, Judge McLean will fortify their positions with an opinion that cannot fail to confound those who are prepared to repudiate the judgments of southern courts and the practice of southern states. Judge Curtis it is believed will also contribute a powerful exposition of the case, and of all the incidental questions connected with it, and Judge Grier will concur with both. Of course, the South will go in a body, and probably carry Judge Nelson with them." [16] There were too many southern judges. Chief Justice Taney was "not without a certain share of sectional bias, which has grown upon him, with increasing infirmities. He has almost added ten years to the age of the psalmist and now seems to linger upon the brink of the grave." Other judges were well advanced in years, and because of the crisis issues to be passed upon by the court the filling of vacancies under the next administration would be a matter of great importance. [17]

In anger and exasperation the *Tribune* denounced the court for its "convenient evasion" of a decision at this time by directing a reargument of the case at the next term. The purpose, the paper declared, was to restrain the expression of the convictions of those judges who were known to be ready to vindicate the constitutionality of the Missouri Compromise. "The black gowns have come to be artful dodgers. The minority were prepared to meet the issue broadly and distinctly; but the controlling members were not quite ready for such an encounter of authority as could be produced; or perhaps not in-

[15] New York *Tribune*, Feb. 29 and April 9, 1856.
[16] *Ibid.*, April 12, 1856.
[17] *Ibid.*, May 14, 1856.

clined to open the opportunity for a demolition of the fraudulent pretenses that have been set up in Congress on this question." [18]

If the *Tribune* was right as to the basic reasons which led to the postponement of the decision, and it was probably right at least in part, it is hard for the casual observer to discover any great amount of odium in the use of a device for keeping the court out of what promised to be a bitterly fought presidential campaign. Editor Greeley, however, had no interest in the preservation of judicial decorum, but had a fanatical devotion to his issues, and great hopes for the new Republican party. He permitted his zeal to direct such violent attacks on James Buchanan, the aged and corpulent Democratic nominee for the presidency, as to stir frantic rage in the bosom of Buchanan's friend, Judge Jeremiah S. Black, of the Pennsylvania Supreme Court. "No greater service could be rendered to the cause of truth," declared Black, "than by putting Greeley where he ought to be. He is a liar and the truth is not in him. He is a mush toad spotted traitor to the Constitution. And he is a knave beyond the lowest reach of any comparison I can make. Shall this political turkey buzzard be permitted to vomit the filthy contents of his stomach on every decent man in the country without having his neck twisted?" [19] The "political turkey buzzard" continued his outpourings without restraint, however, both as to the Supreme Court and as to opposition candidates.

McLean, foiled in his plans to get campaign material before the country in the form of a judicial opinion in the Dred Scott case, was aided by the *Tribune* in spreading his views indirectly. A political letter written to him was published, together with his reply, after the reply had been reworked by his political managers. His correspondent, Joseph C. Hornblower of New Jersey, referring to a McLean letter published some years earlier, asked if he was right in concluding that under McLean's construction of the Constitution there would be no more slave states and no further extension of slavery. McLean replied that since the Missouri suit had been post-

[18] *Ibid.*, May 15, 1856.
[19] J. S. Black to J. Reynolds, June 9, 1856, Black MSS., Library of Congress.

poned he could not properly say anything about it. Nevertheless, he was glad that Hornblower approved of his views already publicly avowed as to the constitutional power of the federal government over slavery in the territories. He was convinced that the violence and bloodshed, the civil and fraternal war now going on in Kansas were "the fruits of that ill-advised and mischievous measure, the repeal of the Missouri Compromise, which, from the first, I have earnestly deprecated." He favored the immediate admission of Kansas into the Union under a free constitution, and believed that peace could thus be brought to the territory and to the country.[20]

In spite of the strategy of advertising his views in this manner, however, McLean's ambitions were again frustrated. The Republican nomination went to a younger, handsomer, and more dashing man, John C. Frémont, the "Pathfinder" of the Far West. Frémont was opposed by James Buchanan, the Democratic nominee, a "northern man with southern principles," and by Millard Fillmore, the nominee of the southern wing of the "American," or Know Nothing, party and of the Old Line Whigs.

Taney, spending the summer quietly at Fauquier White Sulphur Springs, anxiously watched the progress of the campaign. He dreaded the possible success of the abolitionist Republican party of the North, and he dreaded equally a victory for the anti-Catholic "Americans," whom he regarded as enemies of the South. They would permit themselves to be ruled by northern interests, and for selfish purposes would retain their offices instead of attempting to preserve the integrity and independence of the South by seceding from the Union. He wrote to his son-in-law of the gloom with which he viewed southern prospects:

"As far as the South is concerned, I think it matters very little if Buchanan is defeated, whether Frémont or Fillmore is chosen. But there will be no dissolution of the Union in either event. The Constitution will undoubtedly be trampled under foot, and the Union will be one of power and weakness, like the Union of England and

---

[20] See Hornblower to McLean, May 13, 1856, and McLean to Hornblower, June 6, 1856, in the *Tribune,* June 16, 1856.

Ireland, or Russia and Poland. But how can the southern s.
divide, with any hope of success, when in almost every one of them
there is a strong and powerful party, acting in concert with the
northern Know Nothings, and willing to hold power from the
North, if they may be enabled thereby, to obtain the honors and
offices of the general government, and domineer in their own states.
. . . The South is doomed to sink to a state of inferiority, and the
power of the North will be exercised to gratify their cupidity and
their evil passions, without the slightest regard to the principles of
the Constitution. There are many bold and brave men at the South
who have no vassal feeling to the North. And they will probably
stand to their arms if Frémont is elected, or further aggressions made
under Fillmore. But what can they do, with a powerful enemy in
their midst? I grieve over this condition of things, but it is my deliberate opinion that the South is doomed, and that nothing but a firm
united action, nearly unanimous in every state, can check northern
insult and northern aggression. But it seems this cannot be." [21]

The day was postponed when the South must take up arms to
preserve itself from northern domination, through the election of
Buchanan to the presidency, although Taney suffered the discomfort of seeing his own state cast a majority of its votes for Fillmore.
Buchanan's victory was due to a variety of complex causes. He and
his friends attributed it, however, to popular hostility to sectionalism,
to abolitionism, and to all movements on the part of northerners
which antagonized the South by efforts to prevent the spread of
slavery. He probably believed quite sincerely that by dealing with
northern agitators with an iron hand he could eliminate the friction
which was threatening to destroy the Union, and immediately after
his election he assured Justice Grier that this would be his program:
"The great object of my administration will be, if possible to destroy
the dangerous slavery agitation and thus restore peace to our dis-
tracted country." [22]

[21] Taney to J. Mason Campbell, Oct. 2, 1856, Campbell MSS.
[22] Draft of a letter from Buchanan to Grier, Nov. 14, 1856, written as an answer to and
filed with a letter from Grier to Buchanan of Nov. 10, 1856, in the Buchanan MSS.

Franklin Pierce, the outgoing President, sounded the same note in his last annual message to Congress, delivered December 2, 1856. He summarized the history of antislavery agitation in the country, denounced the Missouri Compromise and other attempts to prevent the spread of slavery, and attributed the victory of Buchanan to the determination of the people to have no more of sectional strife. Many other leaders agreed in sentiment with the President and the President elect. A national campaign had been fought in which a sectional alignment had appeared more clearly than ever before. Threats of secession had been heard in times past, but never until this year had the possibility of their being carried out seemed so real. Something had to be done to eliminate the issue which was tearing the country asunder. Since the intemperate agitation of the abolitionists was a major source of danger, that agitation must be suppressed. Since the repeal of the Missouri Compromise was one of the crying points of the agitation a great boon was hoped for in the form of a declaration from the Supreme Court that the Missouri Compromise had been unconstitutional, and that the federal government had no power to exclude slavery from the territories. Such was the state of affairs when, in December, 1856, the Dred Scott case came up for reargument.

CHAPTER XXIV

DRED SCOTT AND AFTER

The Dred Scott case was reargued, December 15 to 19, 1856, by the same lawyers as before, with the addition of George Ticknor Curtis, brother of Justice Curtis, for the negro. The arguments were more elaborate and perhaps more skillfully arranged than at the first presentation, but they added nothing essentially new. More attention was given to the case by outsiders, however. Congressmen, particularly those with abolitionist leanings, watched its progress with uneasiness, and the abolitionist press reported it with great detail, together with speculation as to the attitudes of the several judges.

For several weeks thereafter nothing was done about the case. Taney, probably believing that it would attract less publicity if decided after the ardor of the presidential campaign had had time to cool, refrained from calling the case up for discussion in conference. He even avoided taking his colleagues into his confidence, perhaps because of his irritation at the leaks from the bench at the preceding term. Further delay was caused by the absence of Justice Daniel. His young wife caught fire in her home, and was so badly burned that she died. Daniel, prostrated with grief, did not return to the bench until well along in February.

In the meantime President elect Buchanan came to Washington on business connected with his incoming administration. He was still imbued with the idea of putting an end to the controversy over slavery, which to him meant the suppression of abolitionist agitation. Determined to deal firmly in his inaugural address with the issue of slavery in the territories, he wrote to Catron, who had long been his personal friend and was less punctilious about mixing in politics than was Taney, asking him whether the Dred Scott case would be decided before the date of the inauguration. "It rests entirely with the Chief

495

Justice to move in the matter," Catron replied. "So far he has not said anything to me on the subject of Scott's case. It was before the judges in conference on two several occasions about a year ago, when the judges expressed their views pretty much at large. All our opinions were published in the N.Y. *Tribune,* the next day after the opinions were expressed. This was of course a gross breach of confidence, as the information could only come from a judge who was present. That circumstance I think, has made the Chief more wary than usual." The death of Daniel's wife, Catron added, had no doubt caused delay, but there was little reason for it since Daniel would undoubtedly deliver an opinion of his own and at great length. Catron thought Buchanan entitled to the information he sought, and promised to try to get it.[1]

Four days later, on Tuesday, Catron wrote to Buchanan that the case would be decided in conference on Saturday, but that no opinion would be announced before the end of the month. Furthermore, the decision probably would not help Buchanan with his inaugural, since the question of the power of Congress over slavery in the territories probably would not be determined. Catron expressed the personal opinion, however, that the Missouri Compromise had been in conflict with the treaty by which the Louisiana Purchase had been acquired, and therefore unconstitutional.[2]

In conference the judges debated at length the plea in abatement which had been rejected by the court below. According to that plea the lower court should have dismissed the case for want of jurisdiction, on the ground that no negro could be a citizen in the constitutional sense and entitled to sue in a federal court. The judges disagreed as to the correctness of the argument. They also disagreed as to whether the plea was properly before them, and subject to their decision in this case, since it had not arisen on the pleadings.

If it was not before them the case would have to be decided on the merits, or on some other question affecting jurisdiction. The merits of the case were then likewise debated at length. A majority of the

---

[1] Catron to Buchanan, Feb. 6, 1857, Buchanan MSS.
[2] Catron to Buchanan, Feb. 10, 1857, *ibid.*

judges came to the conclusion that the case could be decided without passing on the power of Congress to exclude slavery from the territories. It could be held, following the analogy of the Strader case, that whatever the status of the negro had been while he was outside Missouri, his return to the state had made him subject to its laws. Under those laws the highest court of Missouri had adjudged him to be a slave, and the Supreme Court, according to custom, would accept the state court's interpretation of state laws. Nelson was appointed to write, and did write, an opinion to that effect.

Had this plan been fully carried out, the furore raised by the New York *Tribune* and others would have been the product of wasted effort, since almost nothing would have been settled except the fate of one family of negroes about whom nobody was very much concerned. McLean, however, and perhaps Curtis as well, was determined that publicity should no longer be denied to his views on the power of Congress over slavery in the territories, and his brethren discovered that he intended to include in his dissenting opinion an argument to show that the Missouri Compromise had been constitutional. The line of argument, later followed in the two dissenting opinions, was plausible. The decision of the Missouri Supreme Court that Dred Scott was a slave, even after his residence at the localities described outside the state, was in conflict with earlier decisions of that court. The earlier decisions, rather than the last one, represented the settled law of the state, and must be followed by the Supreme Court of the United States. According to the earlier decisions, if Dred Scott had been free while outside the state, he remained free after his return. It was necessary, therefore, to discover whether the negro had been free, and to determine this fact it was necessary to inquire whether the Missouri Compromise, which prohibited slavery within the specified area, had been constitutional.

The members of the court who were deeply sympathetic with the South in the sectional struggle were concerned about the propaganda effect of the dissenting arguments that the Missouri Compromise had been constitutional, particularly if these arguments were not countered in opposing opinions. Some of these judges, Wayne in particular, it seems, had believed all along that the court should express itself fully on the controversial points, rather than dodge them by a narrow decision such as that which had been planned. They felt that if the court agreed that federal legislation excluding slavery from the territories was unconstitutional, a center of abolitionist agitation would be removed, the South would gain a sense of assurance about its welfare, and sectional peace would be restored.

Learning the line of argument to be followed by the dissenters, Wayne therefore proposed a change of plans, whereby Taney was to take over the opinion of the court, and to discuss fully all the issues involved. A majority of the judges agreed to the change. Nelson, who was absent at the time, later served notice that he would file as his own the opinion which he had prepared as the opinion of the court.[3]

At this point Catron wrote again to Buchanan to advise him how best to make political capital out of the new developments, suggesting that in his inaugural he speak as follows:

"The question involving the constitutionality of the Missouri Compromise line is presented to the appropriate tribunal to decide; to wit, To the Supreme Court of the United States. It is due to its high and independent character to suppose, that it will decide and settle a controversy which has so long and seriously agitated the country: and which *must* ultimately be decided by the Supreme Court. And until the case now before it (on two arguments) presenting the direct question, is disposed of, I would deem it improper to express any opinion on the subject."

Catron did not state directly what the decision would be, but its nature could easily be inferred. He informed Buchanan that the majority of his brethren would be forced by two dissenters to pass upon the Missouri Compromise question. He was dissatisfied, however, with the position of Grier, who, although convinced of the absence of federal power over slavery in the territories, was inclined "to take the smooth handle for the sake of repose," and hold merely

[3] See J. A. Campbell to Samuel Tyler, Nov. 24, 1870, Tyler, *Memoir of Roger Brooke Taney*, pp. 382–384.

that the negro was not free because of the fact that he had acquired no domicile while absent from Missouri. Catron advised Buchanan to write to Grier urging that the case provided a good opportunity for settling agitation by a Supreme Court decision one way or the other.[4]

Buchanan replied to Catron's letter evidently saying that it was of the utmost importance that he know when the decision of the court was to be made public, since he had to prepare in advance an inaugural address for delivery on a definite date. Knowing now what the decision was to be, he hoped it would be made public before the inauguration. Catron replied that he recognized the necessity which Buchanan was under, and was anxious to have the opinion delivered. Most of the judges were ready, or nearly ready. He was still worried about Grier. "I want Grier *speeded*," he urged. "I think whatever you wish may be accomplished." [5]

Buchanan did write to Grier, who showed the letter to Wayne and Taney. Grier replied to Buchanan that the three of them agreed with him that the court ought to pass on the troublesome question. They also agreed that Buchanan ought to know the history of the case, which Grier traced as outlined above, saying that although it was contrary to the usual practice they thought it due him that he should be told. Nelson and himself had at first refused to pass upon the Missouri Compromise, and Nelson might still remain neutral. As for himself, however, he thought that if the question was to be decided by the court it ought to be decided with all the prestige the court could give it. To prevent the Mason and Dixon line from marking the line of division in the court he had talked with Taney and agreed to concur with him. The opinion would not, however, be delivered before the 6th of March. The reason for the postponement, he added in a postscript, was the weak state of the Chief Justice's health.[6]

[4] Catron to Buchanan, Feb. 19, 1857, Buchanan MSS.

[5] Catron to Buchanan, Feb. 23, 1857, *ibid.*

[6] Grier to Buchanan, Feb. 23, 1857, *ibid.* Much newspaper and other material with reference to these events, including parts of some of the letters here cited, is quoted in Chapter XXVI of Warren's *The Supreme Court in United States History*. Other accounts, some good and some bad, in histories, biographies, and special articles, are too numerous to mention.

In this manner the President elect was fully informed as to the essentials of the case well in advance of the date of his inauguration, and of the date of the public announcement of the decision. Details of the friction between the judges, which have human interest if not historical importance, perhaps did not reach him. The story in later years found its way by word of mouth from Curtis that Taney had to exercise the rôle of disciplinarian in the midst of heated discussions in the conference room. On one occasion the judges in their excitement rose from the conference table arguing and gesticulating. "Brothers," snapped Taney, "this is the Supreme Court of the United States. Take your seats." "We sat down like rebuked schoolboys," said Curtis.

In the meantime Congress awaited the decision anxiously, and abolitionist members attacked the prestige of the Supreme Court and made proposals for reorganizing it so as to make it more amenable to the sentiments which they held. The court, so often the victim of similar attacks, seems not to have regarded them as possessing more of menace than in times past. Or perhaps it felt that if they were more dangerous than usual they should be quelled by a decision showing that threats against it, whether from Congress or from any other source, were without avail. At any rate, instead of heeding the portents of disaster, it listened, probably with pleased and complacent attention, to a farewell address from the retiring Attorney General, Caleb Cushing, as he dwelt eloquently on the position held by the court in our political system and on the honor due to the present members.

Cushing saw eye to eye with Taney in the case about to be decided; he had given an official opinion covering many of the points as they arose in another connection, and it is said that Taney consulted with him in the preparation of his Dred Scott opinion.[7] Presumably therefore, when on the morning of March 4, just preceding the hour for the inaugural ceremony, he addressed the court as "the incarnate mind of the political body of the nation," he knew approximately what the fateful decision was to be. He could well charac-

[7] C. M. Fuess, *Life of Caleb Cushing*, II, 154–155.

terize the court as the pivot point on which turned the rights and liberties of all, or as the central light of constitutional wisdom around which they perpetually revolved.

Unaware as were the judges of the storm about to break upon them, Cushing bespoke for the court the confidence of the country as the conservators of the sanctity and integrity of the Constitution. "As the supreme appellate tribunal of the country," he declared, "your honors possess not only its loyal acquiescence in your judgments, but the deference for them which follows a long line of illustrious magistrates, from the Jays and the Ellsworths, who organized our judicial system, through the Marshalls, who developed our federal independence. To you and your venerable chief—and venerable not more in years than in the accumulated wisdom of a long life of high duties—to you I say, worthy successors of the Fathers of the Republic, our country looks with undoubting confidence as the interpreters and the guardians of the organic laws of the Union." [8]

After the address the court adjourned to participate in the inaugural ceremony to take place in front of the Capitol. Taney was joined on the platform by President Pierce and President elect Buchanan, to whom he was to administer the oath of office. In the view of the assembled audience Taney spoke briefly with Buchanan in casual conversation or about some matter connected with the ceremony. The incident was unfortunate, for out of it evolved the ridiculous story that here on the platform Taney whispered to Buchanan a statement of what the Dred Scott decision was to be, whereupon Buchanan modified his prepared address to make political use of the information. The story was repeated with telling effect in ensuing campaigns, in spite of the fact that if Buchanan and the court had wished to communicate with each other, as they did, there were other means much more convenient than by hurried conversation in the presence of a large audience.

Buchanan expressed in his inaugural address the conviction that he owed his election to the inherent love of the people for the Constitution and the Union, implying, of course, that his opponents had

[8] Washington *National Intelligencer*, March 5 1857.

been the enemies of both. He was pleased with the way in which public excitement had subsided in acquiescence in the choice of the majority. He approved the extension of the principle of majority rule to the territories, so that by majority vote the people resident therein might decide for or against slavery. He admitted that there was difference of opinion as to whether this power could be exercised during the period of territorial government or only as the territories became states, but he thought this a matter of little practical importance. At this point he inserted a paraphrase of the statement which Catron had written for him:

"Besides, it is a judicial question, which legitimately belongs to the Supreme Court of the United States, before whom it is now pending, and will, it is understood, be speedily and finally settled. To their decision, in common with all good citizens, I shall cheerfully submit, whatever this may be." [9]

From the abolitionist press this portion of Buchanan's address received the most attention. "You may 'cheerfully submit'—of course you will," the *Tribune* answered in derision, "to whatever the five slaveholders and two or three doughfaces on the bench of the Supreme Court may be ready to utter on this subject; but not one man who really desires the triumph of freedom over slavery in the territories will do so. We may be constrained to obey as law whatever that tribunal shall put forth; but, happily, this is a country in which the people make both laws and judges, and they will try their strength on the issues here presented." [10] It was of course not true that five of the judges were holders of slaves at this time,[11] as the *Tribune* implied, but the abolitionist organ concerned itself little about a minor twisting of the facts if its cause could be served thereby.

On March 5 Taney remained at home to complete the writing of his opinion in the Dred Scott case. On March 6, as soon as the court

[9] *Messages and Papers of the Presidents*, V, 431.
[10] New York *Tribune*, March 5, 1857.
[11] See A. J. Beveridge, *Abraham Lincoln*, II, 477.

assembled for business, in a low and feeble voice which was to call forth sneering comments from the abolitionists, he began the reading of the opinion.[12] Countless criticisms of the document have been published during the years which have passed since that fateful occasion. Most of them have denounced as almost criminal the circuitous method which Taney used in deciding the case; most of them have demonstrated what they considered flaws in his logic, and in earlier years they deliberately misquoted him.

If the purpose of an appraisal is to condemn the man, or the cause, or the culture which he was attempting to protect, the methods used in many of the analyses perhaps leave little to be desired. Even those comments which do not misquote Taney, and which are obviously drafted in an attempt to preserve other portions of his judicial career from adverse criticism, are inadequate as to this case. They tend to leave the impression that in the Dred Scott case Taney permitted narrow prejudices to dictate an opinion largely without support in facts and logic, unethical in the breadth of its discussion, and in these respects unprecedented in the annals of the Supreme Court.

If on the other hand the purpose of the appraisal is to make possible a sympathetic understanding of what Taney was attempting to do, the materials must be handled in a somewhat different manner. First and foremost it is necessary to remember his devotion to the South, of which he was a product, and his belief that, if the trend of events continued, the South was doomed. At the time of the adoption of the federal Constitution neither the North nor the South had a population sufficiently large to permit it to control the federal government. In the years which had passed, however, the North had outstripped the South in numbers, and it seemed more and more inevitable that the federal government should become the tool of the North, to which the South, in an increasing degree would be compelled to submit.

Such a condition had not been contemplated by the framers of the Constitution, and such domination of the South, in Taney's estima-

[12] *Dred Scott* v. *Sandford,* 19 Howard 393 (1857).

tion, was "unconstitutional." He preferred secession by force of arms to submission to it. His deepest fear seems to have been that when a northern political party directly assumed the reins of government the South would not act with sufficient unanimity to make rebellion effective.[13] Since one of the major causes of sectional strife was the subject of slavery in the newly settled territory of the United States, territory which would be carved up into new states, the destruction of the Union or the subjugation of the South could at least be postponed if that issue could be removed.

It was unthinkable that the South, already sinking into a minority section, should passively surrender the hope of securing the admission of new states dominated by the culture of the South, of which slavery was an integral part. On the other hand the North as a whole did not desire an open break with the South, and the feeling was widely prevalent that the strife over slavery was not worth its cost in ill will, and perhaps in business. The aggressive and loquacious abolitionists were still a minority group, and Buchanan was not alone in his belief that peace would be brought to the country if they were silenced.

The abolitionists had made a tremendous stir about the repeal of the Missouri Compromise, by which slavery had been excluded from certain territory, and continued to use it as propaganda material. If it could be demonstrated that the Missouri Compromise was unconstitutional, an effective abolitionist weapon would be destroyed. The Supreme Court had considered the question at length in connection with the Dred Scott arguments, but rather than pass upon a question charged with such high explosives they arranged to decide the case on a narrower point. Then the majority judges discovered that the two dissenters planned to demonstrate positively that the Missouri Compromise had been constitutional. Such a demonstration would add to the effectiveness of abolitionist propaganda, rather than detract from it, would add to the drawing of sectional lines, and hasten the subjugation or the secession of the South.

It was this prospect which Taney, Wayne, Daniel, and others set

[13] See the preceding chapter.

out to defeat. By outvoting and perhaps outarguing the two dissenters they planned to defeat the abolitionists and avoid disaster. It may be argued, and of course has been argued, that, however dire the straits of the country, the plotting of strategy to save it is not properly a judicial function. This may be true. Nevertheless, the fact remains that most of the Supreme Court decisions which stand out as landmarks in the minds of students of American history and of American constitutional law have been policy-making decisions. This has been true all the way from the régime of John Marshall to that of Charles Evans Hughes. The ultimate approval or disapproval of these decisions is determined by approval or disapproval of the policies established, and not by their relation to precedents.

It is inconsistent to denounce Taney for deciding questions broadly in the hope of benefiting the country, while praising others, Marshall for instance, for doing the same thing. This does not mean that an admirer of Marshall must necessarily be an admirer of Taney, but rather that the distinction must be made where it belongs. The question is not one as to narrowness or breadth of decision, but as to the nature of the order which the particular judge is seeking to preserve. People with a rabid abolitionist point of view believed that, in so far as southern culture rested upon slavery, it was not worth preserving. Taney believed that southern culture and southern independence were worth saving, whether it meant the preservation of slavery on the one hand, of which privately he was no zealous advocate, or civil war on the other. He wrote his opinion in the Dred Scott case in an attempt to aid in preserving it.

Taney's long and involved opinion was written in such a way as to lead to the judgment that the court below should have dismissed the case for want of jurisdiction, because Dred Scott had no constitutional right to sue in a federal court. His argument can be boiled down to three seemingly simple points:

1. Negroes, having been regarded as persons of an inferior order at the time when the Constitution was adopted, and not as "citizens," were not intended to be included in the term "citizen" as used in the Constitu-

tion, and were not included when the Constitution gave to citizens of different states the right to sue in federal courts.

2. Apart from the question as to whether *any* negro could be a citizen in the constitutional sense, it was obvious that no slave could be such a citizen. It was admitted on the record that Dred Scott had been taken from Missouri as a slave. He had not become free by virtue of residence in territory covered by the Missouri Compromise, since the Missouri Compromise was unconstitutional, so that unless he had some other claim to freedom he was still a slave, not a citizen, and not entitled to sue in a federal court.

3. Whatever the temporary effect of Dred Scott's residence in Illinois, he had returned to Missouri, where his status was determined by Missouri law. The Missouri courts had held that he was a slave. Therefore he was not a citizen, and could not sue.

The first point had been raised by the plea in abatement in the court below. Taney found himself in difficulties immediately, in that, as disclosed by the concurring opinions, only Wayne and Daniel agreed with him that the plea in abatement was before the Supreme Court. Others presumably agreed with him in private as to the inability of negroes to be citizens, but because of differences as to technical problems of procedure, or because they felt that the discussion of the first point might embarrass the discussion of the second, in which they were more deeply interested, they did not concur in this portion of Taney's opinion. This was true in spite of the fact that Taney referred to his opinion as the opinion of the court.

Taney's argument in support of his first point had not been cooked up by him in a moment of desperation in effort to establish the point, as was charged by abolitionist critics. He had made it clearly and discussed it at length twenty-five years earlier, in an official opinion as Attorney General of the United States.[14] In an opinion delivered in the United States circuit court in Baltimore in 1840 he had similarly portrayed the position of the negro in colonial Maryland.[15] The argument was neither original nor unique with him, and he made no pretense that it was. William Wirt, as Attorney General

---

[14] Opinion of May 28, 1832, on a South Carolina law respecting colored mariners, and a supplement submitted June 9, 1832. For discussion, see Chapter VIII.

[15] *United States* v. *Dow*, Taney's Decisions, p. 34.

of the United States, had in 1821 denied the right of the negro to citizenship, and Caleb Cushing, in the same office, had in 1855 taken the same position. It had been so often asserted as virtually to be taken for granted by able southern lawyers.

Taney doubtless overstated his point when he described as "universal" the attitude toward the negro which he outlined. If there were exceptions, however, as ably indicated by Justice Curtis, Taney nevertheless seems to have presented a fairly accurate portrayal of relations between the two races in communities where both lived in considerable numbers. In some communities after the American Revolution it is probable that the few negroes in residence were treated substantially as equals. In other communities, where both slaves and indentured servants were held, it is possible that the badge of inferiority had not been firmly fixed on all negroes because of the condition of most of their race. Curtis showed that in certain localities free negroes had had the legal right to vote. He made no attempt to demonstrate the fact, however, that public sentiment had permitted the general exercise of that right.

He did not effectively meet Taney's argument, furthermore, that the privilege of voting did not necessarily prove citizenship. Taney demonstrated the fact that aliens were occasionally given voting privileges, whereas on the other hand many citizens had no such privileges at all. A major difficulty, indeed, grew out of the fact that the concept of "citizen" was exceedingly vague. It was a term to which the judges attempted to give content for the purpose of supporting their respective arguments, rather than a concept with a clear-cut and definable meaning.

Turning to his second major point, Taney argued that the lower court should have dismissed the case for want of jurisdiction not merely because Dred Scott was a negro, but because he was a slave. To prove want of jurisdiction on this ground he had to discuss the questions which had been raised on the merits of the case. He stirred thereby the wrath of the opposition, who claimed that having demonstrated the absence of jurisdiction on one ground he had no right to examine into the merits to make the same point on another ground.

Or rather, as far as Taney's discussion of his second point was concerned, they tended to ignore the fact that he was still dealing with jurisdiction, and claimed that, having decided that the court had no jurisdiction, Taney had gone on to a discussion of the merits as if the court had jurisdiction.

The Missouri Compromise had not entitled Dred Scott to his freedom, Taney declared, because Congress had no power to prohibit slavery in the territories. In an argument which at best seems somewhat strained he admitted that Congress had the power to acquire territory, but held that Congress could govern it only to the extent of nurturing it into statehood. During that period the territory was held in trust for all the people and must be governed for the benefit of all, and not for one class. People of one section of the country could not be excluded from the territory by the denial of the right to hold the kind of property which was essential to their way of life, and in this respect slave property was not different from property of any other kind.

As a suggestion, rather than as a necessary link in his argument, Taney dragged in a phrase which at the time was relatively innocuous, but which in later years was to become a potent weapon for defeating legislation to which the court was opposed. "An act of Congress," he declared, "which deprives a citizen of the United States of his liberty or property, merely because he came himself or brought his property into a particular territory of the United States, and who had committed no offense against the laws, could hardly be dignified with the name of due process of law." The due process phrase had been used prior to this time chiefly as a restriction upon judicial process rather than on the content of legislation. In the minds of those opposed to the broad exercise of the judicial veto Taney performed no service to his country when he thus prominently called attention to the use to which the phrase could be turned.

Having shown that Dred Scott could not claim freedom and citizenship and the right to sue in a federal court because of the Missouri Compromise, Taney turned to the question as to whether residence in Illinois had conferred freedom and the rights claimed. He answered briefly with the statement that whatever Dred Scott's status had been while in Illinois, the Missouri Supreme Court had held him to be a slave under Missouri laws after his return. Without dwelling on the arguments of McLean and Curtis to the contrary, Taney stated briefly the conclusion that the decision represented the settled law of the state. Dred Scott was therefore a slave, and not a citizen, and not able to sue in a federal court. The case was therefore remanded to the court below, with directions to dismiss it for want of jurisdiction.

This third point was substantially that which Nelson made in the opinion which he had written as the opinion of the court. It was all that was really necessary to the decision of the case. The first and second points, about which all the furore was raised, could have been omitted altogether. On the other hand they did have relevance to the subject of jurisdiction, and Taney was plausible, to say the least, in his contention that the Supreme Court had the power to examine not merely into one error but into all the errors made by the court below. The anger of the opposition is understandable, for they did not want a majority of the court to assert itself in opposition to the rights of negroes and the constitutionality of federal prohibitions of slavery. This is all the more reason, however, for guarding against their obvious bias when appraising Taney's opinion. Their characterization of Taney's discussion of his second point as illegitimate because delivered as *obiter dictum*, and as a treatment merely of the merits of the case after having decided against jurisdiction, is not to be accepted without the reserve which the facts justify.[16]

Wayne had written an opinion of his own covering all the points, but decided to concur in Taney's, and merely filed a brief supporting statement. He justified the breadth of the decision on the ground that the peace and harmony of the country required the settlement of the important points discussed. Nelson filed the opinion which he

[16] For a clear discussion of these and other points see Edward S. Corwin, "The Dred Scott Decision in the Light of Contemporary Legal Doctrines," *American Historical Review*, October, 1911.

had prepared for the court as a whole. Grier filed an opinion expressing his concurrence as to the constitutionality of the Missouri Compromise, and concurring also in Nelson's opinion. Daniel filed a long opinion making the same major points as those made by Taney.

Campbell filed a long opinion denying the power of Congress over slavery in the territories. His statement was inconsistent with, and seems less clear and persuasive than the opinion on the subject which he had expressed to Calhoun nine years earlier.[17] Whether he had really changed his mind on the point of law, or whether he wrote as he did because of political expediency, is a matter for speculation. Catron thought the plea in abatement was not before the Supreme Court. He sought to prove, in an argument not noted for its strength, that the Missouri Compromise was unconstitutional because in conflict with the treaty by which Louisiana Territory was acquired.

McLean and Curtis of course dissented, each of them at length. Although it won the approval of abolitionist newspapers and of the many political friends among whom he circularized it, McLean's opinion was discursive and loose-jointed, and not at all the forceful legal and political document which the *Tribune* had expected it to be. It bore, however, the stamp of the contentious politician. Taney's method of getting at the questions raised by the merits of the case under cover of examining jurisdiction was, McLean declared, "rather a sharp practice." Nothing said by the court not bearing directly on jurisdiction could be considered as authority. "I shall certainly not regard it as such."

Whereas McLean's opinion seemed to be made up of stinging but often disjointed utterances, that of Curtis was compact, forceful, and direct. He also charged that Taney had passed upon questions which he had no right to discuss after a denial of jurisdiction, and declared he would hold no judicial opinion binding if expressed on a question not legitimately before the court. He declared that the recent decision of the Missouri Supreme Court differed from preceding decisions, and did not represent the settled law of the state. Therefore it was not necessary to hold that Dred Scott was a slave merely

---

[17] Campbell to Calhoun, March 1, 1848, *Correspondence Addressed to Calhoun*, p. 430.

because he was now in Missouri. He argued that Congress had full power to exclude slaves from the territories, and that under the Missouri Compromise Dred Scott had become a free man. He debated at length the question of citizenship, and denied that the position of negroes was so degraded at the time of the adoption of the Constitution as to prevent their being "citizens," and to prevent their bringing suits in federal courts. Like Taney's, the Curtis opinion had the weakness of resting oftentimes upon the meaning of vague phrases, but it offered exceedingly able opposition to the several arguments of the majority members of the court.

The story has been often told of the way in which the Dred Scott decision back-fired upon those who hoped by means of it to quell the agitation which threatened to destroy the Union. For a decade or more the abolitionist leaders had been hacking away at the prestige of the court. Their outburst of vituperative wrath was now heard by thousands who had already been taught to suspect the integrity of the court when slavery issues were at stake. Thousands were shocked at the false statement, made from press and pulpit, that Taney had said the negro had no rights the white man was bound to respect.

Horace Greeley and his employees on the New York *Tribune* led the attack. They poured forth the venom which they had been secreting since the preceding year when the court had kept the decision out of party politics by postponing it until after the conclusion of the presidential campaign. Taney's opinion, declared the *Tribune,* was long, elaborate, and jesuitical, with arguments based on historical falsehoods. The decision was entitled only to the weight to be given to the judgment of a majority of the persons congregated in any Washington barroom. No wonder Taney's voice had sunk to a whisper as he promulgated a decision based on a mere collation of false statements and shallow sophistries, got together to sustain a foregone conclusion. What he had to say had been still more feeble than his voice.[18]

Other Republican papers were similarly bitter in their denuncia-

[18] See the *Tribune* of March 7, 1857, and for many issues thereafter.

tion. Alongside their more violent outpourings they published less picturesque though not necessarily less prejudiced analyses by able lawyers. The violence of the denunciation was deplored in other papers, but their comments lacked the drive of emotion and carried less weight than those written without restraint. The press of the South, characterized by similar violence and prejudice, defended the court and its decision; but defense from this source was in the North but further cause for condemnation. From the pulpit the court and the decision were assailed, often with little understanding of the legal issues, but nevertheless always with great vigor.[19]

The term of the court came to an end with the reading of the opinions in the Dred Scott case, but friction among the judges remained in evidence, especially between Taney and Curtis. Curtis filed his opinion immediately in the office of the clerk of the court, and gave a copy to a Boston paper for publication, where it was used in criticism of the arguments of the majority of the court, which had not yet been officially made available. He left Washington for a vacation in Virginia. Upon returning to his home in Massachusetts he learned that the other opinions had not been published, except as summarized by reporters from the oral deliveries in court, and he heard the rumor that extensive changes were being made in Taney's opinion.

He wrote to the clerk of the court requesting a copy of Taney's opinion, but was told that the opinions were not yet printed, and that a rule had been adopted by the judges forbidding the giving out of the opinions until they were officially published in Howard's Reports. Curtis protested that the rule should not be held to apply to a member of the court, but Taney assured the clerk that it applied to Curtis as well as to everybody else. When Curtis asked for an explanation Taney replied that Curtis' father-in-law had announced his intention of publishing the Curtis opinion in pamphlet form, and on the ground of his relationship to one of the judges had asked for

---

[19] For extensive quotations from the contemporary comments from the varied sources and for bibliographies of additional comments, see Charles Warren, *The Supreme Court in United States History*, II, 302–319, and A. J. Beveridge, *Abraham Lincoln*, II, 486–499.

a copy of Taney's opinion to publish along with it. Taney had refused, and he intimated to Curtis that he thought the whole proceeding quite bad form. Before leaving Washington, therefore, he had consulted with Wayne and Daniel, the only members of the court remaining in the city, and they had agreed on a written order to the clerk prohibiting the delivery of opinions to any person except the court reporter. Since Curtis had already published his own opinion, and had declared in it that he regarded the opinion of the court as extrajudicial and not binding, Taney reminded him that he had no right to object to the order which had been issued.[20]

Curtis denied any intention of aiding his relative in getting a copy of the opinion of the court for publication. His motive, he declared, lay in the fact that he had heard that the opinion from which he had dissented had subsequently been materially altered. He doubted the power of the court in vacation to make an order of the kind mentioned without giving all the judges an opportunity to debate on it. Had he been consulted he would have advised the immediate giving out of authentic copies of all the opinions, to prevent the great misunderstandings and gross misrepresentations which Taney deplored.[21]

Taney wrathfully perused Curtis' letter while preparing to leave for Richmond to hold circuit court. Because of his duties in Richmond, performed under the handicap of ill health, he was unable to reply until nearly a month later, after his return to Washington, by which time the opinions had been officially published. His wrath still unappeased, he declared that he had no desire to continue the unpleasant correspondence which Curtis had been pleased to commence, and was glad to notice that Curtis' letter called for no reply. Nevertheless, it would be unfair to the other judges and to himself, he continued, to ignore certain passages in Curtis' letter. As his reason for desiring a copy of the opinion of the court Curtis had given the rumor that it had been materially changed after delivery. Had Curtis inquired of him directly about the matter, as he should have done, a direct reply would have been given.

[20] Taney to Curtis, April 28, 1857, *Memoir of Benjamin Robbins Curtis*, I, 213–215. Most of the materials here summarized are to be found contiguously in this volume.
[21] Curtis to Taney, May 13, 1857, *ibid.*, pp. 217–220.

The report, Taney declared, had no foundation in truth. "There is not one historical fact, nor one principle of constitutional law, or common law, or chancery law, or statute law, in the printed opinion, which was not distinctly announced and maintained from the bench; nor is there any one historical fact, or principle, or point of law, which was affirmed in the opinion from the bench, omitted or modified, or in any degree altered, in the printed opinion." The only changes made had been in the insertion of proofs and authorities to support the truth of historical facts and principles of law which he had thought unquestioned until he heard them denied in the dissenting opinions.

After a long discussion which revealed the bitterness of his feelings about the way in which the several opinions had been used for political purposes, growing in part out of the way in which they had been reported, he brought his letter to a close which culminated in an outburst of personal indignation: "I have now done. I had, indeed, supposed that, whatever difference existed on the bench, all discussion and controversy between members of the tribunal was at an end when the opinions had been delivered; and I believed that this case, like all others that had preceded it, would be submitted calmly to the sober and enlightened judgment of the public in the usual channels of information, and in the manner in which it has heretofore been thought that judicial decorum and propriety required. But if it is your pleasure to address letters to me charging me with breaches of official duty, justice to myself, as well as to those members of the court with whom I acted, makes it necessary for me to answer and show the charges to be groundless; and a plain and direct statement of the facts appears to be all that is necessary for that purpose." [22]

It is easy to understand Taney's angry mood, provoked as it had been by the assaults made upon his opinion, upon him and his brethren as persons, and upon the dignity of the court; and provoked also by the fact that he had added to sectional strife instead of restoring peace to the country by passing upon constitutional ques-

[22] Taney to Curtis, June 11, 1857, *ibid.*, pp. 221–225.

tions which might easily have been avoided. Furthermore, he was probably right in assuming that the early and widespread publication of Curtis' dissenting opinion had played a prominent part in the forming of public sentiment on the case.

Nevertheless, it is apparent from reading the correspondence in full that his heated feelings had led him to put the worst possible construction on Curtis' actions, and that in some respects he was quite unfair to Curtis. The latter replied with great restraint, admitting that the correspondence had grown unpleasant, but declaring that it had been made so by Taney and not by himself. He had not meant to charge Taney with official misconduct. As for the additions which Taney had made in the way of proof of facts already stated in the opinion, Curtis intimated that he would have much desired to see them, in spite of Taney's contention that they added nothing new. He made a private notation of an estimate that at least eighteen pages had been added by Taney in refutation of his dissenting opinion, none of which Curtis saw until the publication of the official reports. He denied sharply that he had published his opinion for political purposes as Taney had intimated, declaring that his sole purpose had been to avoid misconstruction and misapprehension.[23]

Taney replied with a brief expression of pleasure that nothing in Curtis' last letter called for more than an acknowledgment of its receipt, and added that he was not aware that there was anything in either of his own letters that was not strictly defensive in character.[24]

Curtis was by this time thoroughly dissatisfied with his position as a member of the court. With reference to constitutional questions about which he felt deeply he was in a hopeless minority, and perhaps felt that he could serve his cause better by resigning than by remaining on the bench. This is not to say that he had become an abolitionist. The use of his dissenting opinion by the rabid Free Soil party, with which he had never been aligned, may have given him more discomfort than pleasure. It seemed to him, however, that the

[23] Curtis to Taney, June 16, 1857, *ibid.*, pp. 226–228.
[24] Taney to Curtis, June 20, 1857, *ibid.*, pp. 228–229.

court was committed not to impartiality, which he had tried to achieve, but to active aid of the southern cause.

He had another plausible reason for resigning. He had found the salary of six thousand dollars a year quite inadequate for the standard of living which he wished to maintain. He was one of the most prominent lawyers in the country, and could earn far more as a practitioner than as a judge. He discussed the several matters with his friends, and in spite of the protests of many of them decided to send in his resignation, giving inadequate compensation as his major reason.

Jeremiah S. Black, the Attorney General, wrote an acceptance in which he lauded Curtis as a man and as a judge, and sent the letter to Buchanan for inspection. Buchanan indignantly blue-penciled the laudatory remarks. "I return your letter to the late Judge Curtis," he wrote in a note to Black. "I do not think it ought to contain what I have stricken out. I know I entertain no such opinion of him as is therein expressed, and your communication to me of what had passed between him and the Chief Justice does not serve to enhance him in my estimation." [25] The letter was sent to Curtis over Black's signature, and without the comments of which Buchanan disapproved. Another judicial career came to an end, and the way was paved for political battles over another appointment to the Supreme Court.

In his letters to Curtis, Taney did not attempt further justification of his legal arguments in the Dred Scott case, nor did he attempt to show further that he had been right in his appraisal of the position of negroes in the United States. To the violent attacks made upon him from all sides he made no reply. It was a sympathetic appraisal, made by a stranger, that called forth a private supplementary statement showing more clearly his ideas on the great race problem. Samuel Nott, a Congregational minister in Massachusetts, published a pamphlet discussing the position of the American negro, and analyzing and defending Taney's opinion. Thanking Nott for a

[25] Buchanan to Black, Sept. 15, 1857, Black MSS., Library of Congress.

copy of the pamphlet, Taney wrote that if anything could allay the unhappy excitement daily producing so much evil to the African as well as to the white race it was discussion of the subject in the temper in which Nott had treated it.

"Every intelligent person," Taney continued, "whose life has been passed in a slaveholding state and who has carefully observed the character and capacity of the African race, will see that a general and sudden emancipation would be absolute ruin to the negroes, as well as to the white population." Before the present excitement had been stirred emancipation had been encouraged in Maryland and Virginia, and many negroes had been set free and had been permitted to continue in residence in the state. In the greater number of cases which Taney had observed, though not including the slaves whom he himself had liberated, freedom had been a serious misfortune to the negroes, and they had experienced privation and suffering which they would not have been called upon to endure as slaves.

Relations between slaves and masters were usually kind on both sides, he declared, unless the slaves were tampered with by ill-disposed persons. The slaves were free from distressing wants and anxieties. They were taken care of in infancy, in sickness, and in old age. True, there were painful exceptions. But this would always be the case where weakness was faced with a combination of power, bad passions, and a mercenary spirit. The presence of slavery or of race differences was not necessary to the existence of such evils. In the states which he knew best, care had been taken to give slaves every possible protection against abuse. The giving of such protection had been rendered more difficult, however, by the agitation which for some years had produced discontent and ill feeling on the subject of race.

Taney hoped that Nott's review of the Dred Scott decision would correct some of the misrepresentations which had so industriously been made, some of them, he feared, by persons who must have known better. He could not consistently defend himself in public, however, and he requested that his letter should not be published. "Not that I am not perfectly ready," he explained, "on all proper occasions to say publicly every thing I have said in this letter. But in the judicial position I have the honor to occupy, I ought not to appear as a volunteer in any political discussion; and still less would it become me out of court and off the bench to discuss a question which has been there determined. . . . I am not a slaveholder. More than thirty years ago I manumitted every slave I ever owned, except two, who were too old, when they became my property, to provide for themselves. These two I supported in comfort as long as they lived. And I am glad to say that none of those whom I manumitted disappointed my expectations, but have shown by their conduct that they were worthy of freedom; and knew how to use it." [26]

The letter supports the belief that Taney had a deep understanding of relations between the white and colored races, and adds to the evidence of his belief that the Dred Scott decision ought to contribute to the welfare of both. It belies the contemporary abolitionist and Republican picture of him as a malevolent old man who had prostituted himself before diabolical slavery interests, and distorted both law and history for the destruction of human liberty.

He wrote the letter from Fauquier White Sulphur Springs, where he had gone to recuperate during the hot weather. Ten days later he wrote from the same place to Franklin Pierce, who was likewise a victim of abolitionist criticism. "You see," Taney commented on the storm of abuse provoked by the Dred Scott decision, "I am passing through another conflict, much like the one which followed the removal of the deposits. And the war is waged upon me in the same spirit and by many of the same men who distinguished themselves on that occasion by the unscrupulous means to which they resorted.

"At my time of life when my end must be near, I should have rejoiced to find that the irritating strifes of this world were over, and that I was about to depart in peace with all men; and all men in peace with me. Yet perhaps it is best as it is. The mind is less apt to feel the torpor of age, when it is thus forced into action by public duties. And I have an abiding confidence that this act of my judicial

[26] Taney to Rev. Samuel Nott, Aug. 19, 1857, Massachusetts Historical Society *Proceedings*, 1873, pp. 445–447.

life will stand the test of time and the sober judgment of the country, as well as the political act of which I have spoken." [27]

Although he adhered to his determination to make no public comment on the Dred Scott decision, it is evident that Taney had some difficulty in exercising this self-restraint in the face of the published criticisms. He in part found vent for his feelings in private letters, but they were not wholly adequate. Eighteen months after the decision was announced, still feeling the sting of current criticisms, he wrote out a supplement to his opinion in the case. It had been among the most important cases in the history of the Supreme Court, he stated in the introduction. While the subject was still fresh in his mind he was preparing a statement in proof of facts asserted in the opinion about the position of negroes in England. If the questions were to come before the court again in his lifetime the statement would save the trouble of again investigating the proofs.

He had learned from the newspapers that the United States circuit court in Indiana had recently decided that a negro born in the United States, whose ancestors had not been brought here as slaves, was a citizen of the United States and entitled to sue in federal courts. Such a ruling was inconsistent with the opinion in the Dred Scott case. The court had held that slavery had fixed the badge of inferiority upon the entire race, and not merely upon those negroes whose ancestors had been slaves. Therefore no negro, whatever the condition of his own ancestors, could be a citizen in the sense in which the word was used in the Constitution. He introduced many pages of supporting evidence, and rephrased many arguments previously presented, in the effort to prove his point.

The concluding paragraph suggests either that Taney was writing to justify himself in his own eyes against the criticisms to which he would make no public reply, or that he was preparing a justification for the eyes of posterity. "I have seen and heard of various comments and reviews of the opinion," he declared, "published since its delivery, adverse to the decision of the court. But I have seen none that I think it worth while to reply to, for they are founded upon

[27] Taney to Pierce, Aug. 29, 1857, Pierce MSS., Library of Congress.

misrepresentations and perversions of the points decided by the court. It would be a waste of time to expose these perversions and misrepresentations. For if they were exposed, they would nevertheless be repeated, and new ones invented to support them. They are for the most part carefully and elaborately put together in a volume published at Boston soon after the opinion appeared in the report, and which from the beginning to the end is a disingenuous perversion and misrepresentation of what passed in conference, and also of what the court has decided. They cannot mislead the judgment of any one who is in search of truth, and will read the opinion; and I have no desire to waste time and throw away arguments upon those who evidently act upon the principle that the end will justify the means." [28]

One of the most vindictive attacks made on the court was that of William H. Seward, in the United States Senate, in March, 1858, at the time when slavery interests were pressing a bill to admit Kansas as a slave state. He pictured the Dred Scott case as one trumped up and managed by slavery interests from beginning to end. The court, acting with the incoming President, had seized a matter of extraneous and idle forensic discussion and converted it into an occasion for pronouncing the invalidity of the Missouri Compromise. The judges and the President alike forgot that judicial usurpation was more odious and intolerable than any other among the manifold practices of tyranny. Came inauguration day, when the President took his seat upon the portico, attended by the Supreme Court attired in robes which yet exacted public reverence. All unknown to the watching multitude the insidious whispering between the Chief Justice and the new President revealed that the court decision would be as the latter desired, whereupon he arose and blandly promised to submit to the decision, whatever it might be.

Taney was so enraged by Seward's attack that he told Samuel Tyler some years later that had Seward been nominated and elected President in 1860 he would have refused to administer the oath of

[28] "Supplement to the Dred Scott Opinion," Tyler, *op. cit.*, pp. 578–608.

office.[29] Reverdy Johnson, who had been counsel in the case and who has been thought by some to have had a profound influence over Taney, wrote a public letter in which he replied to Seward's charges and denounced with high indignation the impeachment of the honor and integrity of the court. The charge, he declared, that judges had pandered to party or executive influence, was a slander so gross and revolting that it could ultimately only disgust the public mind.[30]

Johnson's indignant letter was regarded by many as an inadequate rebuttal of the charges made against the court and the President. In any case the charges were doubtless too potent as political weapons to be abandoned even if disproved. Ere long the rail-splitter from Illinois was calling attention to a series of events sponsored by Stephen A. Douglas, Franklin Pierce, Taney, and Buchanan. Douglas had put forth the doctrine of squatter sovereignty in connection with the Kansas-Nebraska Act. Pierce, in his last annual message to Congress, had endorsed the Dred Scott decision in advance. Buchanan, in his inaugural address, had exhorted obedience to the decision, whatever it might be. Taney had written the opinion in the case.

All this, declared Lincoln, looked like the cautious patting and petting of a spirited horse, preparatory to mounting him, when it was dreaded that he might give the rider a fall. Lincoln could offer no proof that these four men had connived to the end of fastening slavery upon the territories. Yet, he declared, illustrating in terms of one of the homely figures of which he was a master, when the work of Stephen, Franklin, Roger, and James fitted so closely together, matching in every conceivable way, it was impossible not to believe that they had understood each other from the beginning, and had worked together on a common plan.[31]

Lincoln was probably wrong in his intimation as to the degree of coöperation among "Stephen, Franklin, Roger, and James." There was a certain amount of coöperation between "Roger and James,"

[29] *Ibid.*, p. 391.
[30] *Ibid.*, pp. 385–391.
[31] See Beveridge, *Abraham Lincoln*, II, 580–581.

however, in that Taney had consented to Grier's informing Buchanan as to the history of the case. Therefore, although Taney may not have whispered to Buchanan about the case while sitting on the inaugural platform, as crudely charged by Seward, the indignation of Taney and his friends was hardly justified. Lincoln did not advocate disobedience to particular decisions of the Supreme Court. He did insist, however, that the principles asserted by the court in such controversial decisions might be changed in other decisions, perhaps by a court with different personnel, and he pledged his efforts in behalf of the change.

So it was that the case, entangled on all sides in complex and conflicting human emotions, became an instrument in a party struggle which was to culminate in civil war. In its absolutely immediate effect the decision was of little importance. It resulted in the defeat of efforts to secure the freedom of a dilapidated old negro, who was set free by his master anyway as soon as the legal battle was over. Its immediate effect even as far as the Missouri Compromise was concerned was only to declare unconstitutional a statute which had already been repealed.

The ultimate effects, however, were of deeper significance. The court had labeled the entire negro race as so degraded at the time of the adoption of the Constitution that the rights and privileges of citizenship were not intended to be conferred. This meant, among other things, that negroes in southern states could not seek protection in federal courts presided over by judges appointed by presidents with abolitionist sympathies. The decision on the Missouri Compromise meant that, however great the congressional majority of northern interests might become, no federal law could be passed to exclude slavery from the territories.

Such curbing of the power of the North in spite of its increasing numerical majority, and such protection of southern interests, were undoubtedly the intention of Taney and his colleagues. They were attempting to determine national policy, to settle constitutional law in such a way as to prevent the catastrophe which would result if one section of the country attempted to dominate the institutions of the other. In view of the growing power of the North, they regarded their efforts as purely defensive, and not as aids to southern aggression. They failed, because northern majorities and sectional ill will had already developed too far to be restrained by mere judicial pronouncements of law. Their efforts can be understood, however, only through a sympathetic appraisal of what they attempted to do.

There is irony in the fact that the decision was most bitterly attacked by the class of people who in the past had favored the development of a strong federal judiciary, and who were to favor it in the future. No act of Congress had been declared unconstitutional by the Supreme Court since John Marshall's decision in *Marbury* v. *Madison*, in 1803. After the accession of Taney and other Jackson and Van Buren appointees Justice Story had lamented the probability that never again would a state or federal law be declared unconstitutional. Yet to many of the friends of a strong judiciary the Dred Scott decision was the most unwelcome decision in the history of the court. From their point of view the power of judicial veto had been exercised over the wrong kind of law.

CHAPTER XXV

NULLIFICATION

MANY Whigs, Republicans, and Free Soilers were indignant at Curtis for resigning from the Supreme Court and leaving McLean as their sole representative. They felt certain that Buchanan's appointment, even though made from New England as it was supposed to be, would only add to the strength of the majority which had sanctioned the Dred Scott decision. The opposition press, therefore, held itself in readiness to attack vigorously any nomination which Buchanan might make. The President considered and then rejected the idea of appointing Isaac Toucey of Connecticut, who for some reason was unpopular as Secretary of the Navy. Rufus Choate of Massachusetts had some support, but he seems not to have desired the position. Choate, Reverdy Johnson, and Charles O'Conor recommended John J. Gilchrist, formerly chief justice of New Hampshire and now of the United States Court of Claims, but he too failed to satisfy.[1]

Buchanan almost gave up the hope of finding in all New England a man whom he was willing to appoint, and considered the choice of William L. Yancey of Alabama. Finally, however, he determined upon Nathan Clifford of Maine, who had been Attorney General of the United States under Polk. The abusive powers of the Republican press were immediately turned full blast upon the appointee, with the New York *Tribune* taking the lead. He would never dissent from any decision that it might please the slave breeders to require, the *Tribune* predicted.[2] That paper artfully exposed a rift

[1] "I should prefer a seat on the Bench of the Supreme Court to my present position," Gilchrist wrote to Franklin Pierce, "because I do not think it so anxious a place, the salary is better, and the thing is more fixed and permanent."—Gilchrist to Pierce, Sept. 16, 1857, Pierce MSS.

[2] New York *Tribune*, Dec. 11, 1857.

within Democratic ranks by eulogizing Caleb Cushing and declaring that Buchanan had been "guilty of a sin and a shame in overlooking the qualifications of Mr. Cushing for the bench of the Supreme Court, and in nominating such a man as Clifford, who is just about equal to the trial of a case of assumpsit upon a promissory note in the court of a justice of the peace. Whatever else may be said of General Cushing, he certainly does know a little law." [3]

Republicans in the Senate sought to make capital of the fact that Taney and some of his colleagues had been silent about the nomination instead of giving it support. Soon afterward, perhaps as a result of Democratic persuasion, they were reported as saying that Clifford would make a respectable and able judge. [4] The *Tribune* scoffed at the report that Taney favored the appointment. "The old Judge is too much of a courtier toward the powers that be to criticize their public acts in a disagreeable manner, and doubtless he has, in reply to those who would tease him upon the subject, declared that the appointment would do very well. But the members of the bench always look upon the appointment of new associates with great interest. They do not wish to see the character of their tribunal lowered by an infiltration of feeble intellect. They had much rather find it improved by an infusion of fresh vigor. A good appointment is, therefore, welcomed as tending to heighten the position of the court and increase the weight of its decrees, while an appointment of an inferior caste is felt to lower both. It is of no use to pretend, therefore, that Mr. Clifford's elevation is satisfactory to Judge Taney." [5]

Clifford's nomination was confirmed by a narrow majority. Clifford was not a man of outstanding ability, but his many years of routine work as a member of the Supreme Court were to demonstrate that the charges of incompetence were quite unfounded. The *Tribune* took comfort in the argument that since most of the judges were men of low caliber it was well for purposes of adaptation that the new member should be of the same grade. All that was now

[3] *Ibid.*, Dec. 23, 1857.
[4] *Ibid.*, Dec. 29, 1857.
[5] *Ibid.*, Jan. 6, 1858.

needed to establish the perfect homogeneity of the court was to get rid of Judge McLean.[6]

It was unfortunate for the prestige of the court that while the attacks provoked by the Dred Scott decision were continuing unabated it was necessary to pass upon a highly contentious issue of nullification. The issue arose not in South Carolina, which with Calhoun as its teacher had learned its lesson well, but in Wisconsin. A great many residents of Wisconsin had made up their minds that the Fugitive Slave Law of 1850 should not stand in the way of continued assistance to slaves escaping northward through the state. In March, 1854, Sherman M. Booth, firebrand editor of the Milwaukee *Free Democrat,* aided a negro in escaping from a United States deputy marshal. Booth was taken before the federal commissioner at Milwaukee, and was ordered held for trial for violation of the Fugitive Slave Law.

There being no federal prison available, he was held in a local jail. He applied for a writ of habeas corpus, not to the federal court in the district, in which he was to be brought to trial, but to a judge of the state supreme court, contending that the federal Fugitive Slave Law was unconstitutional. In spite of the obvious irregularity of the proceeding the abolitionist state judge issued the writ and directed that Booth be released. The marshal appealed to the state supreme court as a body, where the order to release Booth was confirmed. The marshal then sued out a writ of error to the Supreme Court of the United States.

While this case was pending in Washington, Booth was brought to trial before the federal district court at Milwaukee. In the midst of the excitement that usually characterized such trials in abolitionist states, he was found guilty and sentenced to prison for one month, and fined one thousand dollars. He was to remain in prison until the fine was paid. He was again incarcerated in a state or local prison, and immediately applied to the acquiescent Wisconsin supreme court for a writ of habeas corpus, contending that his federal sentence had been illegal because the federal Fugitive Slave Law was unconstitu-

[6] *Ibid.,* Jan. 14, 1858.

tional. That court granted the writ, held that the Fugitive Slave Law was unconstitutional, and ordered Booth's release. The jailer therefore set him at liberty.

In spite of the barriers which the state court attempted to put in the way, this case was likewise appealed to the Supreme Court of the United States. The two Booth cases, one to review the state court's release of Booth when he was being held before trial by order of the federal commissioner, and the other to review his release by the state court after his trial and conviction, were argued and decided together. Before the date set for argument, January 19, 1859, attempts were made to secure the withdrawal of the court's jurisdiction in such cases. Its jurisdiction on writs of error to state courts was conferred not by the Constitution itself, but by the Judiciary Act. Emasculating amendments were introduced in both houses of Congress, providing opportunities for the continuation of the abuse resulting from the Dred Scott decision.

Legislative proposals for curbing the power of the court were not new, but in a sense those made at this time were unique. During the régime of John Marshall it had been for the most part the representatives of the South who had orated against judicial usurpation. Now it was men from the North who denounced the encroachments of the federal judiciary on the sovereignty of the state. It was a Congressman from Ohio, and not one from the former habitation of Calhoun, who demanded the repeal of an important provision of the Force Act, passed at the instance of Andrew Jackson to meet the threat of nullification in South Carolina.[7]

None of the bills proposed became laws, however, and on the date scheduled J. S. Black, Attorney General of the United States, presented the Booth cases before the Supreme Court. He attempted to prove that the Fugitive Slave Law was constitutional, and argued that a state had no right in any event to liberate a prisoner held by the authority of the United States. He contended that the state judges might even be attached for contempt, but stated that the government would not ask that such a step be taken. Booth, who all this

[7] Warren, *The Supreme Court in United States History,* II, 332–336.

time had been at liberty, ignored the case, as did the Wisconsin authorities, pretending to believe that the Supreme Court had no jurisdiction in the matter.

Having learned a lesson from bitter experience in the Dred Scott case, the court carefully kept from the public the evidence of any disagreements in which the judges may have indulged over the cases from Wisconsin. They agreed unanimously on the judgment. Taney wrote the opinion of the court,[8] and they permitted this opinion to stand alone, unqualified by the presence of concurring statements. Taney's opinion was so clear, so forceful, and so persuasive as to be called by the historian of the court "the most powerful of all his notable opinions." [9] It asserted without qualification the power of the federal government to enforce its laws without state interference. No one would suppose, Taney declared, "that a government which had now lasted nearly seventy years, enforcing its laws by its own tribunals, and preserving the union of the states, could have lasted a single year, or fulfilled the high trusts committed to it, if offenses against its laws could not have been punished without the consent of the state in which the culprit was found."

The Constitution, he continued, had been formed not merely to guard against dangers from abroad, but also to secure unity and harmony at home. It had been necessary to cede to the federal government many of the rights of sovereignty which the states had hitherto possessed, and to make that government supreme within its sphere, with the power to enforce its own laws in its own tribunals, without hindrance from the states. "And it was evident that anything short of this would be inadequate to the main objects for which the government was established; and that local interests, local passions or prejudices, incited and fostered by individuals for sinister purposes, would lead to acts of aggression and injustice by one state upon the rights of another, which would ultimately terminate in violence and force, unless there was a common arbiter between them, armed with power enough to protect and guard the rights of all, by appropriate

[8] *Ableman* v. *Booth*, 21 Howard 506 (1859).
[9] Warren, *op. cit.*, II, 336.

laws, to be carried into execution peacefully by its judicial tribunals."

A system of federal courts had been necessary, and, within that system, it had been necessary to establish a court of final appeal. One of the most revealing paragraphs of Taney's opinion was that in which he discussed the nature of the tribunal over which he had presided for more than twenty years. The establishment of the court had been regarded as of such importance that it had not been left to the discretion of Congress, but had been provided for in the Constitution itself.

"This tribunal, therefore, was erected, and the powers of which we have spoken conferred upon it, not by the federal government, but by the people of the states, who formed and adopted that government, and conferred upon it all the powers, legislative, executive, and judicial, which it now possesses. And in order to secure its independence, and enable it faithfully and firmly to perform its duty, it engrafted it upon the Constitution itself, and declared that this court should have appellate power in all cases arising under the Constitution and laws of the United States. So long, therefore, as this Constitution shall endure, this tribunal must exist with it, deciding in the peaceful forms of judicial proceeding the angry and irritating controversies between sovereignties, which in other countries have been determined by the arbitrament of force." [10]

It was doubtless with current criticisms very much in mind that Taney wrote this appraisal. He did not discuss directly the withdrawal of the jurisdiction of the court in cases appealed from state courts, which had been proposed in Congress. Congress had the power to limit the appellate jurisdiction of the court, and might have curbed its usefulness by so doing. Taney did not deny this fact. His opinion was so written, nevertheless, as to give the impression that the jurisdiction in question was necessary for the survival of the government. It had been conferred by the first Congress, because of the duty laid upon Congress by the Constitution. He did not say

[10] Other decisions in earlier years had shown his unwillingness to use the federal courts as a means for encroaching on the sovereignty of the states, as for instance in *Rhode Island* v. *Massachusetts* 12 Peters 657 (1838); 4 Howard 591 (1846). Note a somewhat different exercise of restraint in *Luther* v. *Borden,* 7 Howard 1 (1849).

that it would be a violation of duty, and perhaps unconstitutional as well, to withdraw the jurisdiction of the Supreme Court in appeals from state courts, but that implication is to be found in his language. It is very clear that he would have regarded such a step as a disastrous one to be taken.

Having decided that a state court had no power to release any prisoner held by the authority of the United States, Taney could have avoided all discussion of the constitutionality of the Fugitive Slave Law. The question had been passed upon by the state court, however, and was before the Supreme Court on the record. To let it be known that the court had no doubts on the subject, Taney stated briefly that it was the judgment of the court that the law was fully authorized, in all its provisions, by the Constitution of the United States. Since the opinion stood alone, presumably receiving the sanction of all the judges, including McLean, Taney was not generally criticized for passing upon the constitutionality of the Fugitive Slave Law when he could have avoided the subject. It is obvious, however, that in deciding this case broadly Taney, with the concurrence of his brethren, used judicial powers as he had been criticized for using them in the Dred Scott case.

In normal times Taney's careful analysis of the relation between the state and federal governments, and his assertion of the supremacy of the federal government within its sphere, would have been hailed as an outstanding act of statesmanship, particularly in the North and among people with federalist leanings. The times were not normal, however, and abstract doctrines of sovereignty were submerged in the more highly emotional issues of abolitionism. Abolitionists and Republicans generally denounced the decision, while it was hailed by Democrats and proslavery interests. In so far as the court, by its conduct in the Dred Scott case, had destroyed confidence in its own integrity, it had itself to blame for the fact that this decision, even though unanimous and fully in harmony with past pronouncement from the same bench, was widely regarded as another political decision. Unless the powers of the court are to be interpreted with extreme narrowness, however, much of the blame is to be attached not to the court but to the strategy and the systematic malignity of abolitionist and Republican factions which for the sake of a political issue made every effort to blacken the reputation of the court.

The New York *Tribune*, still the leader of the critics of the court, trusted that the people of Wisconsin would not submit to the decision.[11] The Wisconsin legislature threatened resistance by adopting resolutions characterizing the decision as the assumption of jurisdiction and an act of arbitrary power unauthorized by the Constitution. The decision was therefore "without authority, void, and of no force." The federal government, the legislature continued, was not the final and exclusive judge of its own powers. The states had the right to judge of its infractions of the Constitution, and should meet all unauthorized acts with positive defiance.[12]

Having won the decision which he sought, Attorney General Black was now faced with the unpleasant necessity of bringing about Booth's reimprisonment. Rather than add to the intensity of the storm in Wisconsin he waited for months before taking action. Although the case was decided March 7, 1859, it was not until August 4 that he wrote to A. J. Upham, the federal district attorney at Milwaukee, directing him to seek from the district court an order for the rearrest. Booth was to be kept where he could not be released by force, and any order for his release from a state judge was not to be obeyed. "You will take care, however," Black urged, "to show no wanton disrespect to the judicial or other public authorities of Wisconsin. Do nothing to provoke hostility, and advise the marshal to be equally on his guard against anything which may furnish an excuse for opposition to the laws." Black requested that the mandates in the Booth cases be laid before the Wisconsin supreme court, in the somewhat frail hope that the court would file them and take steps to carry them out.[13]

Wisconsin was in the midst of an exciting political campaign, and an administration adviser urged the postponement of the arrest by

[11] New York *Tribune*, April 1, 1859.
[12] See Tyler, *Memoir of Roger Brooke Taney*, pp. 397–398.
[13] J. S. Black to A. J. Upham, Aug. 4, 1859, Attorney General's Letter Book.

federal authorities, lest it be "converted into a fire brand of trouble and excitement." [14] Upham presented the mandates to the state court, where they were taken into advisement, and when told to use his own judgment he postponed his request to the federal district court for an order for Booth's recommitment until the November term.

The times continued unpropitious for the arrest, because of the furore produced by the tragic John Brown raid at Harper's Ferry. Upham applied for the warrant for Booth's arrest, but the district judge postponed action in the hope that the state supreme court would carry out the federal mandates. [15] That court, however, provided another disappointment. One of the three judges declined to vote because he had been counsel for Booth, and the other two disagreed, so that no action was taken.

In fear and trembling the federal authorities finally took Booth into custody. [16] Since state jails, in charge of state sheriffs, could not be relied upon for the confinement of the prisoner, they locked him in a room in the federal building in Milwaukee, apparently expecting a mob to take him away at any moment. For a time there was no serious trouble. Booth had served about one-fourth of his one-month sentence before his release five years earlier, and was due to be released on March 21, 1860, if by that time he had paid his fine of one thousand dollars and costs. He refused to pay the fine, claiming inability to do so. Upham, being as eager to get rid of Booth as Booth was eager for freedom, advised him to apply to the President for a remission of the fine. Booth was too independent to make any such plea, and continued to reside in the federal building after the date for the expiration of his sentence. A state court commissioner issued a writ of habeas corpus, but the federal marshal refused to surrender the prisoner. [17]

The federal district attorney and the federal judge gave support to a public petition for the release of Booth, but the President refused

14 H. C. Hobart to Black, Sept. 22, 1859, Black MSS.

15 A. G. Miller to Black, Dec. 6, 1859, *ibid.*

16 See A. J. Upham to Black, Dec. 16, 1859, Attorney General MSS.

17 J. N. Lewis to Black, April 6, 1860, *ibid.*

to grant the petition without a petition directly from Booth declaring that he was unable to pay the fine. Booth still refused to ask any favors of the detested administration, and continued for a total of about five months as the unwelcome guest of the government. On July 4 a mob attempted to release him, but gave way in the face of armed resistance. At the time of a Republican convention in the city another unsuccessful attempt was made. The state supreme court began the consideration of another petition for a writ of habeas corpus. To the discomfort of the Democrats, the Republicans assiduously persuaded the people that Booth was illegally and maliciously held prisoner by the administration, and made political capital for the coming election.[18]

Doubtless to the secret relief of the federal authorities, Booth was finally liberated by a band of abolitionists. He toured the state making speeches and defying his former captors. Although it was said that the marshal offered one hundred dollars for Booth's recapture, he never had to pay out the money. The election brought into power a Republican administration, and Booth was lost in the oblivion of friendly surroundings. He reappeared once in 1861 when a reconstituted state supreme court upheld a judgment against his printing press as a penalty for rescuing a slave.[19] This, however, was at a time when Republicans were in power in the national as well as state government, and had no need for nullification as a means for the achievement of Republican ends.

The events which preceded and followed the decision of the Booth cases illustrate the growth of uncompromising abolitionist sentiment in many localities in the North to the point of defiance of the federal government. Such sentiment boded ill for the success of any plans designed to enable the North and the South to live peaceably together under the same government. In the South, where the nullifying principles of Calhoun were more familiar, the same attitude of desperation was making itself felt. The same insistence

[18] A. G. Miller to Black, July 20, 1860, *ibid.*
[19] *Arnold* v. *Booth,* 14 Wisconsin 195 (1861).

was heard, more and more clearly, that rather than permit local interests to be crushed beneath the domination of an unsympathetic government it would be better to defy that government outright.

The attitude revealed itself in many ways. For instance, a persistent minority strenuously maintained that the continued prestige of the South in the Union demanded the seizure of more territory easily adaptable to southern culture, from Cuba, or Mexico, or Central America. The filibustering expeditions of William Walker and others used this desire as a basis for propaganda. By their violations of federal laws and treaties they brought the administration even more worry than did the abolitionists of Wisconsin. Justice Campbell, wholly committed to the preservation of southern culture but aware likewise of the danger of attempting to seize foreign territory, made himself thoroughly unpopular in Mobile by his attempts to enforce the laws.[20]

Southern defiance of the federal government was also threatened in connection with the laws forbidding the importation of slaves. Such importation had long been forbidden, but with the rise in the price of slaves, the South, in the face of bitter northern criticism, demanded the repeal of the prohibitory laws. Abolitionist critics countered with demands for legislation which would prohibit the use of the American flag in the slave trade between Africa and Cuba, and which would classify the slave trade as piracy. The New York *Tribune* maliciously suggested that Taney would support such legislation, since he was interested in raising slaves for sale, and could get more for his products if the price was not cut through the competition of imports.[21]

Southern feeling on the subject was illustrated by the comment of a Charleston Whig member of Congress. A Congressman was not considered entirely safe, he declared, unless willing to advocate the slave trade, and to hold every man who worked at the North as no

[20] See the Mobile *Register*, Nov. 20, 1858, quoted, Washington *National Intelligencer*, Dec. 2, 1858. See also the Campbell-Black correspondence in the Black MSS. and Attorney General MSS.

[21] New York *Tribune*, Dec. 2, 1858.

better than a slave.[22] With such sentiment prevailing, the importation of slaves became more and more open, and the clamor grew for the repeal or nullification of federal laws prohibiting the slave trade. With nullification thus threatening both in the North and in the South, on diametrically opposite issues, the ultimate collapse of the Union seemed more and more inevitable.

There had been no little talk of southern secession in 1856 when the election of Frémont to the presidency seemed among the possibilities. In 1860 the election of the Republican nominee seemed clearly in prospect, and many southern leaders could offer no hope for the preservation of the Union. The candidate, it was true, was a relatively unknown man from Illinois, and not the positively offensive Seward or Chase, but it was assumed that the crude rail-splitter would be no better than his party and would direct the government for the benefit of northern interests. The Democrats virtually guaranteed the election of Lincoln by dividing into two hostile parties. The northern and moderate members supported Stephen A. Douglas, while the southern and uncompromising slavery Democrats aligned themselves with John C. Breckenridge.

Taney had preserved a careful silence concerning the strife among the Democrats which had been acute since the break between Douglas and Buchanan in 1857. A major cause of the break had been the dispute over Douglas' popular sovereignty argument, wherein he contended that slavery could not by law be kept out of the territories, but that nevertheless it could not practically exist there without positive support which the federal and territorial governments were under no obligation to give. Justice Grier scorned Douglas' ideas as to the obligations of the government,[23] and it is probable that Taney also thought the government duty-bound to legislate for the protection of slave property in the territories.

Although there is reason for believing that Taney favored Breckenridge as among the several candidates, he kept silent as to his preference. A Douglas paper, perhaps with a view to influencing the

[22] George S. Bryan to John P. Kennedy, April 10, 1858, Kennedy MSS., Peabody Institute.
[23] Grier to J. S. Black, Sept. 15, 1859, Black MSS.

Catholic vote in Maryland, announced that Taney was for Douglas. One of Taney's old friends asked permission to deny the statement. Taney replied firmly that any comment which he might make would be regarded as made not merely by an individual but by him as Chief Justice. "It would be most unseemly in that officer to take any notice in any way of anonymous publications in newspapers, upon exciting political questions, in which his name is improperly used." [24]

With the passage of time the election of Lincoln became more and more clearly inevitable. Democrats began looking about them to see what they could conserve from the impending defeat. Fearing that Taney, now eighty-three years of age, would not survive the next four years, some expressed the hope that he would resign to permit Buchanan to appoint the next Chief Justice before leaving office. When it was suggested that Taney's need for income was too great to permit him to resign the proposal was made that a gift be collected for him from members of the bar.[25] The gift was not made —Taney probably would not have accepted it in any case—and he did not resign, in spite of the frequent rumors that he was about to do so. Finally what appears to have been a semi-official statement was published to the effect that although his body was feeble his mind was as clear as it had ever been, and that he would die in the harness.[26]

The meeting of the Supreme Court for the December term of 1860 was the first to be held in the old Senate chamber, directly above the basement room hitherto occupied by the court. The meeting in the more attractive quarters was saddened, however, by the fact that Daniel had died during the vacation. He was the first of the judges to die in a period of eight years, but a number of those left were growing feeble, and Daniel's departure was a warning of what the near future doubtless had in store.

There were other causes for sadness. It was clearly apparent that the President who had sought to bring peace to the country by sup-

[24] Taney to G. W. Hughes, Aug. 20, 1860, Tyler, *op. cit.*, pp. 405–408.
[25] A. G. Miller to J. S. Black, Sept. 13, 1860, Black MSS.
[26] New York *World*, Dec. 6, 1860.

pressing slavery agitation, had only added to the strife, and that the efforts of the Supreme Court to aid him had become the implements of sectional warfare. When after the election the South openly prepared for secession, Buchanan, bewildered and despondent, did nothing to stop it. Reverdy Johnson, pausing at the conclusion of an argument before the Supreme Court, denounced secession and the weak-kneed attitude of the government toward it. He continued to pronounce, as it were, an obituary upon the nation and upon the Supreme Court. This, he predicted, might be the last time the court would sit peacefully on a Constitution acknowledged and obeyed by all. He prayed that Heaven might stay the arm of the madman before it struck the fatal, parricidal blow.[27] Later in the month a lawyer from Texas caused a sensation in the court room by predicting that before the mandate in the case went down the highest court in his state would have decreed that the Supreme Court had no jurisdiction to enforce over it the Constitution and laws of the United States.[28] Such pronouncements caused an atmosphere of gloom to surround the court throughout the term.

In the face of the crisis most of the judges maintained a troubled silence. Campbell alone seems to have tried actively to do something about it. Feeling that Buchanan's policy of inaction was disastrous for the Union, he urged him to take a positive stand by sending commissioners to the southern convention. "I believe that a final settlement of this slavery question should be made," he wrote to Franklin Pierce, "or that disunion should follow. Agitation can not be carried on further, without a civil war. The question is for both sections, shall we part in peace or shall we make a constitutional settlement of every open question. I think that a constitutional settlement, at all events, is better—far better—than a sudden and violent disruption."[29]

When he returned to press his point Campbell found Buchanan nervous and hysterical, and was unable to do anything with him.[30]

[27] Washington *National Intelligencer*, Dec. 15, 1860.
[28] *Ibid.*, Dec. 29, 1860.
[29] Campbell to Pierce, Dec. 19, 1860, Pierce MSS., Library of Congress.
[30] Campbell to Pierce, Dec. 29, 1860, *ibid.*

He then tried to exert influence through Jeremiah S. Black, one of the few men who seemed to be able to get action from the President. Campbell wished the President to come out in favor of some arrangement whereby the slavery question could be permanently settled. He referred with approval to proposals made by Crittenden, Douglas, Seward, and others for a constitutional amendment to define the position of slavery. He thought them all feasible, though that of Crittenden—which went farthest in granting the demands of the slaveholders—would be more acceptable to the South. The amendment, Campbell believed, should be placed beyond the reach of future amendments except at the instance of the state directly affected, to prevent the controversy from starting all over again.[31] The desired action from the President was not secured, however, and matters continued to go from bad to worse.

Southern statesmen in Washington continued to hold federal offices while aiding in preparations for secession and for such resistance to federal authority as might be necessary. To many northerners such acts seemed treasonable, even though treason was narrowly defined in the Constitution to include only levying war against the country and giving aid and comfort to its enemies. Conviction could be based only on the testimony of two persons to the same overt act, or confession in open court. Technically speaking, there was as yet no war, and the southern statesmen had as yet participated in no "overt act" against the federal government. In spite of the preparations being made, therefore, it was too soon to make accusations of treason.

Many abolitionists, however, were not to be deterred by legal technicalities. A New York lawyer, for instance, F. C. Treadwell, prepared an affidavit mentioning by name a long list of southern statesmen and charging them with treason and other crimes. He demanded that they be arrested and held to answer before the Supreme Court or such other tribunal as the court should designate, and that James Buchanan, Jeremiah S. Black, Joseph Holt, and

[31] Campbell to Black, Jan. 4, 1861, Black MSS.

Lieutenant-General Winfield Scott be called to testify.[32] He presented the affidavit to Taney.

What a storm would have been raised had the President and members of his cabinet and the commander of the army been ordered to testify as to treason committed by outstanding political leaders of the South! Without doubt the President would have ignored any summons issued by the court, but the controversy would have added to the chaos amid which the discredited Buchanan administration was leaving office. Taney, knowing all this, and understanding also that treason as constitutionally defined had probably not been committed, and in addition lacking sympathy with the purpose of the affidavit, did the only thing with it which he could have done. He directed the clerk of the court to return it to Treadwell, remarking that it was not a proper document to be submitted to the court.[33]

In spite of the fact that he could hardly have done otherwise, however, Taney's conduct provided one more basis for abolitionist criticism, and one more argument for the contention that he and his court were working not for the nation but for a treasonable faction. The prestige of the court was that much further depressed, and the subsequent decisions of the court or of its members when on circuit were viewed with all the more suspicion when dealing with matters connected with the sectional controversy. The worst had not yet come, however, as far as Taney was concerned, for out of the partisan controversy in Maryland a controversy was about to develop by which his reputation with zealous abolitionists was still further damaged.

[32] New York *Herald*, Jan. 25, 1861.
[33] *Ibid.*, Jan. 24, 1861.

Chapter XXVI

CIVIL WAR AND MILITARY RULE

LIKE the nation as a whole, the state of Maryland was divided against itself, "half slave and half free." The population ranged all the way from uncompromising abolitionists on the one hand to equally uncompromising secessionists on the other. Most of the people, perhaps, belonged to the intermediate group which had sympathies both with the North and with the South, dreaded disunion, and hoped that Maryland might escape participation in war. Some of them, recognizing that the interests of Maryland were different from those of both North and South, believed that in the event of the destruction of the Union Maryland should align herself with a central confederacy, rather than with the states at either extreme. "I fear," declared Benjamin C. Howard, "that our country is destined to be cut up into parallel slices as you would slice up a loaf of bread." [1]

Howard thought the border states should get together in convention, perhaps remain in the Union if Mr. Lincoln did not drive them out, and act together in any case. Governor Hicks seems for a time to have had much the same idea. He wrote to Governor Burton of Delaware, proposing that the two states unite in a central confederacy opposed both to the North and to the South. Burton replied, however, that Delaware must remain allied with the North. [2]

Governor Hicks was prominent among those who brought about the convention, held in Washington in February, 1861, to seek a way to save the Union. Unfortunately the convention was unable to

[1] Howard to John P. Kennedy, Dec. 26, 1860, Kennedy MSS., Peabody Institute.
[2] Hicks to Burton, Jan. 2, 1861; Burton to Hicks, Jan. 8, 1861. Advertised, *American Art Association Catalog*, May, 1923.

agree on a program satisfactory to all sections of the country. In the midst of the futile wrangling over the Dred Scott decision and other topics a member introduced the embarrassing fact that Taney, in the Gruber case in 1819, had declared that slavery was a blot on our national character. When Reverdy Johnson in surprise and discomfiture demanded the authority for the statement he learned that a Boston minister had recently quoted Taney's defense of Gruber from the pulpit.[3] The matter was much discussed thereafter. Although there was no absolute contradiction between the early argument and Taney's Dred Scott opinion, it required no little explaining to demonstrate this fact. There was inconsistency, of course, between the argument and the contention of many southerners that slavery was an institution decreed by God himself.

The date was approaching for the inauguration of the first Republican President. Abraham Lincoln left his home in Illinois and made his way eastward, delivering speeches from which unfortunate phrases were extracted by his rabid enemies for propaganda purposes. He went to New York, returned southward to Philadelphia, and planned to stop for a greeting in Baltimore. The bitter enmity of the pro-southern leaders in Baltimore, however, and the unruly character of the populace, made it appear altogether dangerous for Lincoln to present himself there. On the advice of Seward and General Scott he therefore passed through Baltimore secretly at night, to the disappointment of his friends and the exasperation of his enemies. The latter shrieked their derision, branded Lincoln as a coward, and prepared to make trouble at the first opportunity.

One day late in February a sensation was created at the Capitol when the homely westerner made his appearance there. Accompanied by Seward, by whom Taney had been so violently traduced, he visited the Supreme Court in the conference room. It is probable that he met there for the first time the Chief Justice who was so like him in gaunt homeliness and in his human qualities, and yet so different from him in theories of government. No record remains, unfortu-

[3] L. E. Chittenden, *Report of the Debates and Proceedings in the Secret Sessions of the Conference Convention*, p. 236.

nately, of the mutual appraisals made by the writer of the Dred Scott opinion and by the man who had criticized it and had talked suggestively of a conspiracy among "Stephen, Franklin, Roger, and James."

They met again on March 4, on the inaugural platform at the front of the Capitol. Shortly before one o'clock on that day the diplomatic corps and the local statesmen who had already taken their places arose as the doorkeeper of the Senate announced the Supreme Court of the United States. The judges, led by Taney, moved slowly to the red plush chairs brought for them from the Senate chamber. A few minutes later the President elect entered the Capitol at a side door, and went to the President's room to be relieved of the dust of the city. Then, towering in his long black coat and grasping his high top hat, he proceeded with Buchanan to the platform.

Quickly came the stage in the ceremony at which Lincoln was to tell the eager audience what he expected to do to preserve the Union. He stepped forward toward the desk, with his manuscript in one hand and in the other what was a most useless hat—whereupon came one of those almost pathetically friendly gestures which people like to remember. Stephen A. Douglas, for many years Lincoln's able political rival, had taken a place on the inaugural platform to provide for his huge following an example of loyalty to the incoming administration. As the awkward rail-splitter vainly sought to free his hands his dapper and graceful rival slipped inconspicuously forward, took the hat, and held it while the address was delivered.

Taney listened with deepest attention as Lincoln, in a manner conciliatory yet firm, gave assurance that it was not his purpose to interfere with slavery in the slave states, but that it was his purpose to execute the laws and to defend the property of the government. Under the Constitution, he declared, no state had the right to secede. It had been maintained that no state would desire to secede if it were possible otherwise to maintain its constitutional rights. He denied that any group was threatened with the loss of any right clearly guaranteed by the Constitution. The difficulties arose out of questions not clearly met by the Constitution, such as the power of

Congress to prohibit slavery in the territories, or the obligation of Congress not merely to tolerate slavery in the territories but also to protect it there.

It was assumed by some that the Supreme Court was to settle these questions. He did not deny that the decisions of the court were binding upon the parties to the cases decided, or that they were entitled to great respect and consideration in parallel cases by other departments of the government. "At the same time," he continued, "the candid citizen must confess that if the policy of the government upon vital questions affecting the whole people is to be irrevocably fixed by decisions of the Supreme Court, the instant they are made in ordinary litigation between parties in personal actions the people will have ceased to be their own rulers, having to that extent practically resigned their government into the hands of that eminent tribunal. Nor is there in this view any assault upon the court or the judges. It is a duty from which they may not shrink to decide cases properly brought before them, and it is no fault of theirs if others seek to turn their decisions to political purposes."

One section of the country believed that slavery was right, and ought to be extended. The other believed that it was wrong, and ought not to be extended. This was the only substantial dispute before the country. The fugitive slave clause of the Constitution and the law for the suppression of the slave trade were perhaps as well enforced as any law could ever be in a community where it was imperfectly supported by the moral sense of the people. Even though enforcement was not perfect, it was better than it would be if the two sections separated, for in that case one of them would revive the slave trade, while the other would refuse to surrender fugitive slaves.

Urging the people to think calmly and well before they brought disaster on the country by secession, the new President concluded with his eloquent peroration: "I am loath to close. We are not enemies, but friends. We must not be enemies. Though passion may have strained it must not break our bonds of affection. The mystic chords of memory, stretching from every battlefield and patriot grave to every living heart and hearthstone all over this broad land, will yet swell the chorus of the Union, when again touched, as surely they will be, by the better angels of our nature." [4]

As the cheers of the crowd died away, Taney, trembling with emotion, stepped slowly forward, raised his hand and phrased the oath of office, which Lincoln repeated after him. The ceremony was over. Taney grasped the hand of this, the last man whom he was to induct into the presidential office, and congratulated him warmly on his address. Then the new President rode away to the White House to begin officially his futile efforts to stem the tide of secession.

In spite of the conciliatory tone of the message, confirmed secessionists regarded the program of holding and defending government property and collecting government revenues as a declaration of war. The South was out of the Union or was going out, and would not permit the government of another nation to hold forts within southern borders or collect revenues at southern ports. It was reported that Justice Campbell now regarded the situation as hopeless, and than he would soon resign from the Supreme Court.[5]

The opposition press in the southern and border states sharply criticized Lincoln's discussion of the Supreme Court, labeling as rank heresy his exaltation of the will of the majority above the judicial interpretation of the Constitution. It was a deliberate attempt, declared a Baltimore paper, to put numbers above right, to put opinion above law, to subordinate the Supreme Court to the illegitimate exercise of power by the government. The message, declared the same paper, showed that the President would *tolerate* slavery in the border states, and that was all. It was doubtful as to whether the party behind him would make even this concession to the rights of the South.[6]

While the new administration was being organized the Supreme Court carried to completion its work for the term. On the last day of the term, March 14, it handed down two decisions which attracted

[4] *Messages and Papers of the Presidents*, VI, 5–12.
[5] New York *Evening Post*, March 5, 1861
[6] Baltimore *Sun*, March 9, 1861.

much attention. One of them was in the long sequence of scandal-laden cases in which Myra Clark Gaines sought to recover property in Louisiana. The other was an important slave case, though it had significance in other respects as well. It arose from the attempt of Kentucky to extradite from Ohio a free negro who, while living in Kentucky, had violated Kentucky laws by aiding a slave to escape. He had fled to Ohio, and the governor of that state had refused to surrender him, on the ground that aiding fugitive slaves was not an extraditable offense. Kentucky brought suit against the governor to compel the surrender of the criminal.

All the judges again united in a single opinion, as they had done in the Booth cases, with Taney as their spokesman.[7] Taney denied the argument of counsel from Ohio that a man could be extradited only if his act was an offense in the state to which he had fled, as well as in the state seeking to capture him, delving into American history to show why the general rule prevailing in international law did not apply to extradition between states within the Union. It seemed therefore that the court must grant the request for a mandamus. Not so, however. The Constitution provided briefly that offenders should "be delivered up." The act of Congress defining procedure declared that "it shall be the duty" of the executive to arrest and surrender him. The obligation applied to all offenders who were sought by the states from which they had fled, declared Taney, but it was only a moral obligation, not a legal one. Although the federal government had the authority to empower state officers to do certain acts it could not command them, and in this case it had not attempted to do so. If Governor Dennison refused to do his duty the court could not issue a mandamus to compel him to do it.

The decision saved the court from much embarrassment. It put the abolitionist governor of Ohio in the wrong, yet avoided the necessity of issuing a mandamus which probably would not have been obeyed. From the point of view of good public policy furthermore, as well as of good constitutional theory, it was probably best to refrain from asserting the legal obligation to surrender any fugitive

[7] *Kentucky* v. *Dennison,* 24 Howard 66 (1861).

whenever another state demanded it. Northern critics, naturally enough, resented the implied criticism of the governor of Ohio, and denied that there was even a moral obligation to surrender the negro.

The New York *Evening Post* abusively declared that the court should have done nothing more than disclaim jurisdiction. "A good part of Judge Taney's opinion is therefore extra-judicial—the individual opinion of an old lawyer, who is either too conceited or endowed with too little power of discrimination to perceive what part of his views of a particular subject are pertinent to the case before him, and what are not. The real decision in the case is that the court has no jurisdiction, and therefore the application for a mandamus must be dismissed. All the rest, all the parade of reasonings and conclusions on other points, has no more of the nature of a judicial decision than if it had been a letter addressed by Judge Taney to the publisher of a newspaper. It is the talk of a man who has certain opinions which he wishes to get before the world, which he hopes his judicial position will persuade the country to receive as oracles, and who is resolved to express them in his seat on the bench without regard to the fitness or propriety of the occasion." [8]

The criticism was grossly unfair, unless it was to be made against all the innumerable court opinions which said more than was absolutely necessary for the decision of the cases at hand. All the questions discussed by Taney had been legitimately raised and fully argued. In passing upon them Taney and his colleagues were merely doing as they and their predecessors had done from the time when the court was created, and as their successors were to do. If the policy was wrong it was wrong at all times, and not merely as applied to a few cases decided just preceding the Civil War.

The vacancy caused by Daniel's death remained unfilled when the court adjourned, although there was daily discussion as to what would be done about it. Less than a month later another vacancy resulted from the death of McLean, the senior member of the court, who had served for twenty-two years. Campbell remained with the

[8] New York *Evening Post*, March 16, 1861.

court for a time in spite of rumors as to his resignation. He attempted to act as a mediator between the southern leaders and Seward, Lincoln's Secretary of State, whom he believed to be acting for the President in negotiations concerning the evacuation of Fort Sumter. Seward proved to be acting only on his own initiative, however, and when the administration refused to support him in commitments made through Campbell the latter was discredited with the southern leaders and left in a most embarrassing position. Giving up the situation as hopeless, and feeling that if a choice must be made his loyalty belonged to Alabama rather than to the Union, he resigned from the Supreme Court, leaving it crippled by a third vacancy.

He departed leaving a note of friendly farewell for Taney. "In taking leave of the court," he wrote, "I should do injustice to my own feelings if I were not to express to you the profound impression that your eminent qualities as a magistrate and jurist have made upon me. I shall never forget the uprightness, fidelity, learning, thought and labor, that have been brought by you to the consideration of the judgments of the court, or the urbanity, gentleness, kindness and tolerance that have distinguished your intercourse with the members of the court and bar. From your hands I have received all that I could have desired and in leaving the court, I carry with me feelings of mingled reverence, affection and gratitude." [9]

In the meantime exciting events occurred which turned public attention from such minor matter as Supreme Court appointments, but which ultimately, through bringing about the suspension of the writ of habeas corpus, embroiled Taney in a controversy with the administration. The bombardment and surrender of Fort Sumter marked the beginning of military hostilities. In response to the President's call for volunteers troops began to move toward Washington. A vociferous and energetic portion of Baltimore and vicinity were determined that the city and state should have nothing at all to do with the war, or should support the South. Troops moving through Baltimore were stoned, and their way was blocked. Bridges

[9] Campbell to Taney, April 29, 1861, *Maryland Historical Magazine*, V, 35.

along the Baltimore and Ohio Railroad were destroyed to prevent the further transportation of northern troops through the state. A number of delegations, one of them headed by the governor, went to Washington to urge that troops be headed some other way.

Sabotage on the part of disloyal persons became so general and so dangerous that on April 27, 1861, the President directed General Scott to suspend the writ of habeas corpus, either personally or through his officers, if it proved necessary for the public safety. The purpose was to make it possible to imprison persons on suspicion and hold them in confinement without the prospect of their being released by means of writs of habeas corpus from judges who might themselves be southern sympathizers. The suspension was a delicate step, particularly in view of the fact that it had no authorization from Congress. The Constitution provided that the writ should not be suspended "unless when in cases of rebellion or invasion the public safety may require it." Who might suspend it under these circumstances was not stated, but from the position of the clause in the Constitution it could be reasonably inferred that the power was with Congress, rather than with the President.

Almost immediately the issue came before Judge William F. Giles, in the United States district court in Baltimore. He issued a writ of habeas corpus for the release of a minor who had enlisted in the army without his parents' consent. A deputy marshal presented the writ to Major W. W. Morris, at Fort McHenry, who read it and handed it back declaring that he would see the court and the marshal damned before he would deliver up one of his men.[10]

The Baltimore newspapers played up the story, and Judge Giles, to prevent misunderstanding, made a statement to the press. This was the first time within his experience of thirty-three years at the bar and on the bench, he declared, that the writ of habeas corpus had failed to procure obedience in Maryland. It had not been suspended by a competent authority, and no circumstances had arisen under which it could have been legally suspended. "The court sincerely hopes," he concluded, "that in a crisis like the present wiser counsels

[10] Affidavit of U.S. Deputy Marshal James Gettings, May 2, 1861, Attorney General MSS.

may prevail at the post, and that no unnecessary conflict of authority may be brought in between those owing allegiance to the same government, and bound by the same laws." [11]

Major Morris wrote to differ as to the justification for the suspension of the writ. For two weeks, he declared, Baltimore had been under the control of revolutionary authorities. Soldiers had been attacked and murdered in the streets, and no arrests had been made. Supplies intended for Fort McHenry had been stopped, and the intention to capture the fort had been boldly proclaimed. The flag over the federal offices had been cut down by a man wearing a Maryland uniform. The Maryland legislature, a body elected in defiance of the law, was debating the forms of abrogating the federal compact. "If this is not rebellion, I know not what to call it. I certainly regard it as sufficient legal cause for suspending the writ of habeas corpus."

In the hands of an unfriendly authority, he continued, the writ of habeas corpus might depopulate the fort and place it at the mercy of the "Baltimore mob" in much less time than it could be done by all the appliances of war. Furthermore, in view of the ferocious spirit of the community toward the army, he would himself be highly averse to appearing publicly and unprotected in the city to defend the interests of the body to which he belonged. If the judge had never known the writ to be disobeyed it was only because such a contingency in public affairs had not hitherto arisen.[12]

When the marshal attempted to serve Major Morris with an order to appear and show why a writ of attachment should not issue against him, he refused to receive the order. He declared that he would obey no order of any kind issued by this court or by any other court.[13] Judge Giles wrote to Morris deploring the suspension of the writ, and expressing the opinion that it could be legally suspended only by act of Congress, whatever the circumstances.[14] The ability to use force was all on the side of the Major, however, and

[11] Baltimore *Exchange,* May 4, 1861.
[12] Morris to Giles, May 6, 1861, Attorney General MSS.
[13] John W. Watkins to Giles, May 8, 1861, *ibid.*
[14] Giles to Morris, May 7, 1861, *ibid.*

the district judge had not sufficient prestige to make a serious public issue of the disobedience of the orders of the court.

It was with this case in the background that another case arose involving the same legal problems, when Taney was called upon to take action, presumably chiefly because of the additional prestige which his decision would give to arguments of the type which Judge Giles had advanced. General Keim, of Pennsylvania, had been ordered to put a stop to secessionist activities between Philadelphia and Baltimore. Among other things he called for the arrest of the captain of a secessionist company operating in Maryland. The result was the arrest of John Merryman, a country gentleman, the president of the state agricultural society, and an active secessionist. He was confined in Fort McHenry. On the same day, May 25, 1861, he petitioned for a writ of habeas corpus partly on the ground that he was not the captain of any company—which technically was true, although he was lieutenant in a company of cavalry, and had supervised the destruction of a number of railroad bridges. The petition was presented to Taney, who, it seems probable, went to Baltimore chiefly for the purpose of receiving it.

On May 26 Taney issued a writ of habeas corpus, directing General George Cadwalader to bring Merryman before the Chief Justice of the United States on the following day at the circuit court room in the Masonic Hall. The order added to the already intense excitement. A reporter, phrasing well the vindictive attitude of extreme abolitionists toward Taney, declared that his purpose was "to bring on a collision between the judicial and military departments of the government, and if possible to throw the weight of the judiciary against the United States and in favor of the rebels." Taney was at heart a rebel himself, the reporter continued. He had recently expressed the wish that "the Virginians would wade to their waists in northern blood." The fact that he volunteered to go to Baltimore to issue a writ in favor of a rebel showed the alacrity with which he served the cause of the rebellion.[15]

With the mind of the North prepared for Taney's decision by this

[15] New York *Times*, May 29, 1861.

kind of propaganda, and with southern sympathizers eagerly hoping that Taney could and would curb the growing power of the military forces of the Union, the case was called, on the morning of March 27. Instead of appearing in court, and bringing Merryman with him, General Cadwalader sent a statement to be read by his aide-de-camp, Colonel Lee, an officer decked out in full uniform with a red sash and wearing a sword. The statement reviewed the facts of the case, called attention to the President's order for the suspension of the writ of habeas corpus, and requested the postponement of the case until the President could be consulted.

In effect, although it was done in courteous language, the military authorities told the court they would obey a court order only if the President saw fit to direct them to do so. Taney countered with a stern reply. "General Cadwalader was commanded to produce the body of Mr. Merryman before me this morning," he declared, "that the case might be heard, and the petitioner be either remanded to custody or set at liberty if held on insufficient grounds; but he has acted in disobedience to the writ, and I therefore direct that an attachment be at once issued against him, returnable before me here at twelve o'clock tomorrow, at the room of the circuit court." [16]

An audience of some two thousand people assembled on the following day to witness the outcome of the struggle between the Chief Justice and the military authorities. Leaving the Campbell home in the company of his grandson, Taney remarked that he might be imprisoned in Fort McHenry before night, but he was going to court to do his duty. As he took his place he announced that he acted alone rather than with Judge Giles because of the fact that he was sitting not as a member of the circuit court, but as Chief Justice of the United States. One reason for the distinction, undoubtedly, was the belief that it would lend added weight to the decision.

When Taney called for the return upon the writ of attachment the marshal replied in writing that he had not been allowed to enter Fort McHenry to serve the writ, and that he had sent in his card but

[16] The proceedings appear at length in the contemporary newspapers and other records of the period, and are presented and discussed in the Tyler and Steiner biographies.

had received no reply. "It is a plain case, gentlemen," Taney declared, "and I shall feel it my duty to enforce the process of the court." He had ordered the writ of attachment because the detention of the prisoner was unlawful on two grounds. First, the President could not constitutionally suspend the writ of habeas corpus nor authorize any military officer to do so. Second, if a military officer arrested a person not subject to the rules and articles of war the prisoner must be turned over to the civil authorities. He would write out his opinion at length, and file it in the office of the clerk of the circuit court.

It would have been well for his reputation for judicial calmness had Taney stopped with the reading of his prepared statement. Unfortunately he forgot himself in the excitement of the moment, and made additional comments. Because the military force was superior to any force the marshal could summon, the court would not be able to seize General Cadwalader. If he were before the court it would inflict punishment of fine and imprisonment. Under the circumstances he would write out the reasons for his opinion, and "report them with these proceedings to the President of the United States, and call upon him to perform his constitutional duty and enforce the laws. In other words, to enforce the process of this court." [17]

It is hardly surprising, therefore, that reporters wrote "sensation" after this notice that the Chief Justice would carry war into the camp of the Executive. It was "sensation" of enthusiastic approval on the part of the crowd, and was similarly pleasing to most Baltimore papers and to some few Democratic papers elsewhere. Union presses, however, stormed wrathfully at the "hoary apologist for treason," and were not less abusive than they had been after the Dred Scott decision. The New York *Tribune*, for instance, continued day after day to rearrange the stock of expletives in Horace Greeley's vocabulary into varied scorching characterizations, and other papers differed only in matters of vocabulary and figures of speech.

Taney had been too much and too often abused to be greatly dis-

[17] As quoted in the Baltimore *American*, May 29, 1861.

turbed by the outburst. Indeed, in defending the writ of habeas corpus, one of the great traditional bulwarks of individual liberty, and in resisting military encroachments on the rights of southern sympathizers, he seems to have acted from a profound sense of mission. "Mr. Brown, I am an old man, a very old man," he replied to the Baltimore mayor's congratulations on his decision, "but perhaps I was preserved for this occasion." He believed, indeed, that the government had considered the possibility of imprisoning him. Although that danger seemed to have passed, he warned Mayor Brown, a southern sympathizer, in what proved to be an accurate prediction, that the time of the latter would yet come.[18]

Taney immediately wrote out his opinion in the case, filed it with the clerk of the circuit court, and directed that a copy be sent to the President. "It will then remain for that high officer," he concluded, "in the fulfillment of his constitutional obligation, to 'take care that the laws be faithfully executed,' to determine what measures he will take to cause the civil process of the United States to be respected and enforced." [19] He elaborated his argument that only Congress, and not the President, could suspend the writ of habeas corpus. He contended that the civil administration of justice in Maryland was unobstructed save by the military authority itself, and that under these circumstances the military had no right to supersede the performance of civil functions.

This document, prepared in defense of the reign of law as against arbitrary military rule, has after the calmer appraisal of more remote periods been hailed as a masterpiece of its kind. Indeed, although it was not specifically mentioned, many of its principles were sanctioned by the Supreme Court shortly after the close of the war, with the personal and political friend of President Lincoln as its spokesman.[20] Immediately contemporary reactions, however, were those which were to be expected. The opinion was loudly praised by friends of the South, and heartily denounced by the friends of the administration.

---

[18] George W. Brown, *Baltimore and the 19th of April 1861*, pp. 90–91.
[19] Ex parte *Merryman*, Federal Cases, No. 9487.
[20] See Ex parte *Milligan*, 4 Wallace 1 (1866), opinion by Justice David Davis.

A few days after Taney's altercation with the commander at Fort McHenry, Judge Samuel Treat, of St. Louis, had a similar experience in a federal district court, when an officer refused to produce a man for whom a writ of habeas corpus had been issued.[21] Treat sent a copy of his opinion to Taney, and Taney replied by sending Treat a copy of his own opinion in the Merryman case. "It exhibits a sad and alarming condition of the public mind," he wrote to Treat, "when such a question can be regarded as open to discussion; and no one can see to what disastrous results the inflamed passions of the present day may lead. It is however most gratifying to one trained in the belief that a government of laws is essential to the preservation of liberty to see the judiciary firmly performing its duty and resisting all attempts to substitute military power in the place of the judicial authorities."[22]

Replying in similar fashion to a congratulatory letter from Franklin Pierce, Taney added that the "paroxysm of passion into which the country has suddenly been thrown appears to me to amount almost to delirium. I hope that it is too violent to last long, and that calmer and more sober thoughts will soon take its place: and that the North, as well as the South, will see that a peaceful separation, with free institutions in each section, is far better than the union of all the present states under a military government, and a reign of terror preceded too by a civil war with all its horrors, and which end as it may will prove ruinous to the victors as well as the vanquished. But at present I grieve to say passion and hate sweep everything before them."[23]

If it was true, as reported,[24] that Taney received a letter from the President concerning the Merryman case, neither party made the fact public. On July 4, however, in his message to the special session of Congress, the President made an official though indirect reply to Taney. He stated that the legality and propriety of authorizing the suspension of the privilege of the writ of habeas corpus had been

[21] In re *McDonald*, Federal Cases, No. 8751.
[22] Taney to Treat, June 5, 1861, Treat MSS., Missouri Historical Society.
[23] Taney to Pierce, June 12, 1861, Pierce MSS.
[24] New York *Herald*, June 2, 1861.

questioned. The attention of the country had been called to the proposition that one who was sworn to "take care that the laws be faithfully executed" should not himself violate them. His answer and his justification lay in the fact that all the laws were being resisted in nearly one-third of the states. "Must they be allowed to finally fail of execution," he asked, "even had it been perfectly clear that by the use of the means necessary to their execution some single law, made in such extreme tenderness of the citizen's liberty that practically it relieves more of the guilty than of the innocent, should to a very limited extent be violated? To state the question more directly, are all the laws *but one* to go unexecuted, and the government itself go to pieces lest that one be violated?" He did not, however, believe that the Constitution had been violated. He suggested a brief argument to that effect, leaving a more extended argument to be presented on the following day in an official opinion by the Attorney General.[25]

It is futile to argue whether the President or the Chief Justice was *right* in the matter, for back of their legal differences were fundamental differences of opinion on matters of public policy. Lincoln preferred to interpret the Constitution so as to avoid the appearance of violating it, but he preferred violating it in one particular to permitting the Union to be destroyed. Taney regarded the dissolution of the Union as less disastrous than the reign of coercion which would be necessary to save and maintain it. Lincoln won, and the Union was saved. Men who are the products of the surviving culture, the culture of the North, are not inclined to question that the saving was worth the cost. Yet no one familiar with the destructiveness of the war and with the subsequent decay of the finer aspects of the culture of the old South will deny the greatness of the cost, or wonder that Taney, farseeing as he was, was appalled by it.

One point at issue between Taney and the military authorities was never officially stated clearly. The authorities assumed not only that ordinary legal and judicial processes were too slow to be effective in

[25] *Messages and Papers of the Presidents*, VI, 25. For the Bates opinion see 10 Official Opinions of the Attorneys General 74.

the crisis, but also that the normal effectiveness of these processes would be warped by the prejudices of the judges. It was of little significance that no one had resisted federal judicial officers, if the officers were themselves disloyal. The point was one of importance even though not clearly stated, for although Taney and Giles presumably would not have conducted themselves in a frankly illegal manner they had definite prejudices and sympathies, and, as was true of other judges, their prejudices and sympathies affected the principles of law which they chose to emphasize in given cases. Had Taney felt about the issues of the war as did the President and the Attorney General, for instance, he might have pursued the legal arguments employed by them without destroying his own reputation as a careful logician and as an authority on constitutional law. He felt so differently, however, as to prefer the death of the Union to the medicine which the President prescribed as necessary to save it. Loyal unionists, quite naturally, were unwilling to trust judges who held or were suspected of holding such ideas.

Because of its nearness to the capital city of the nation, Maryland had to be prevented from seceding. Leaders guilty of overt acts were imprisoned and held by military authorities. This, however, was not enough. The large numbers of secession aristocrats of Baltimore and vicinity were able, without tangible violation of law, to keep alive the resistance to the government and to plot arrangements for an alliance with the Confederacy. After trying to control them by peaceful means Attorney General Bates remarked in disgust that they were so far perverted and so deeply committed to the cause of the enemy that it was useless to argue with them. "To keep them quiet," he concluded, "we must make them conscious that they stand in the presence of coercive power." [26]

To make them conscious of coercive power the authorities arrested Mayor Brown and the police commissioners of the city without making any specific charges against them, and lodged them in Fort McHenry. Finding this an effective method for getting rid of

[26] Bates to N. P. Banks, June 16, 1861, Attorney General's Letter Book.

embarrassing persons, the government used it to get rid of influential members of the legislature and other disloyal persons of prominence. The prisoners included a grandson of Frank Key, a son of General William H. Winder, and others of Taney's friends or the sons of his old friends. Most of them were shifted to Fortress Monroe, and then to other places of confinement as expediency required, without ever being charged with particular offenses. Finally, in the latter part of 1862, when Maryland was safely under the control of loyal persons, the exiles, fuming and raging, were permitted to return to their homes.

Persons who had participated in the burning of railroad bridges or in other direct attempts to sabotage the government program were accused before grand juries, and indictments were found against them. In due time some sixty treason cases, including that of Merryman, were listed on the docket of the federal circuit court. After being held for a time many of them were released pending trial, though on exceedingly high bail. There was much curiosity and anxiety as to what Taney would do with these treason cases, at the November term of the court, at which he sat with Judge Giles. He disappointed the sensation seekers, however, and doubtless served the interests of the alleged criminals as well, by continuing the cases to the April term, intimating that the questions involved would in the meantime be decided by the Supreme Court.

Cases involving the questions at issue were not reached at the ensuing term of the Supreme Court. Taney fell ill, and was unable to attend the circuit court at the April term. The Maryland treason cases were therefore postponed again, doubtless to the deep relief of the accused, for southern influence had now been so effectively suppressed by military power that the Union extremists ran unchecked. Jury trials would probably have been conducted in an atmosphere of intolerance toward the prisoners in spite of all that sympathetic judges might be able to do on their behalf.

In the autumn of 1862 Taney was still in poor health, and he felt unable to attend the November term of the circuit court. It is clear that his sympathies were with the persons accused of treason, and that he felt unable to guarantee them a fair trial under the circumstances. He may therefore have welcomed an excuse for absenting himself from court, in so far as his absence provided a reason for further postponing the cases. He feared, however, that pressure would be put on Judge Giles to hear the cases while sitting alone. He therefore wrote to Giles to show that the district judge, sitting alone in the circuit court, could not try cases which might lead to capital punishment. If both judges sat, and the case involved a new and doubtful question in criminal law, the question could be certified to the Supreme Court. If the district judge sat alone, however, the question could not be so certified, and the decision of the judge would have to stand. Taney thought there was ample evidence that Congress had not intended in a case of life and death to give such power to a district judge.[27]

Giles' sympathies were so similar to those of Taney that in the conduct of treason trials he would doubtless have done his best for the defendants. Under the circumstances, however, he might have been unable to save them, and he may have welcomed Taney's argument showing that he could not conduct the trials while sitting alone.

In the meantime William Price, the new district attorney in Maryland, was planning a vigorous prosecution of the treason cases. "You are aware from the constitution of the court," he wrote to Attorney General Bates, "[that] if the Chief Justice should be on the bench, the treason cases will have to be made very plain and conclusive if we expect a conviction." [28] When he discovered that Taney would be absent, and that the presence of a member of the Supreme Court would be necessary at the trials, he tried ineffectively to have arrangements made whereby another judge could be designated to sit with Giles.[29]

Giles himself effectively blocked Price's plans in one particular. There was no record of the testimony on the basis of which the indictments for treason had been found, but Price had expected to get

---

[27] Taney to Giles, Oct. 7, 1862, S. P. Chase MSS., Historical Society of Pennsylania.
[28] Price to Bates, Sept. 1, 1862, Attorney General MSS.
[29] Price to Bates, Oct. 15, 1862, *ibid.*

the evidence from the notes kept by one of the grand jurors. Before surrendering his notes, however, the man consulted Giles, who told him that giving out secret information in this way would be in violation of his oath [30]—whereupon Price, deeply exasperated, was left to get his information as best he could.

By circumstances and devices of one sort or another the cases were kept pending until another year and more had passed. In the spring of 1864 Taney discussed them in a letter to Justice Nelson. He doubted that he would be able to go to Baltimore, but declared his intention to postpone the cases further if he did go. To him the official orders issued by military authorities almost every day, and the arrest of civilians without assignment of cause, showed that Maryland was under martial law and that the civil authority was utterly powerless. The court could not under the circumstances give a fair and impartial trial, since witnesses and jurors would feel that they might be imprisoned for anything they said displeasing to the military authority, and the court would be unable to protect them. If the party was acquitted he might nevertheless be rearrested and imprisoned, and the court could neither protect him nor punish the offenders. "I will not place the judicial power in this humiliating position," Taney declared, "nor consent thus to degrade and disgrace it, and if the district attorney presses the prosecutions I shall refuse to take them up." [31]

The cases were further postponed in some way without this act of outright defiance of the administration. In another six months Taney was in his grave, and six months after that the war was over. Although the persecution mania and the self-interest of Republican "radicals" carried distress and disorder throughout the South for many years, neither Merryman nor any other of the Marylanders charged with treason during the first year of the war was brought to trial. For this fact the credit or the blame belongs in no small part to Taney. In view of his belief that the maintenance of the Union

[30] Price to Bates, Jan. 16, 1863, *ibid.*

[31] Taney to Samuel Nelson, May 8, 1864, from a copy provided by Edward S. Delaplaine, Frederick, Md.

was not worth the cost in tyranny, repression, and blood, his position on this and allied matters is easy to understand. Furthermore, it is by no means clear that the cause of the Union would have been served better had the disloyal sons of Maryland been tried and convicted of treason and made to pay the penalty. Just so much would the terrific social cost of the war have been increased, to add to the bitterness and hatred which hung like a cloud over the country for many years to come.

Taney's efforts to prevent the prosecution of the southern sympathizers accused of treason have not hitherto been generally known. His opinion in the Merryman case, however, by which he attempted to outlaw a part of the military régime of which the prosecutions were a part, has come to be regarded as one worthy of the deepest respect. It stands as a courageous defense of the rights of citizens against the usurpations of military brusqueness and tyranny, and against repressive rule of any kind by executive authority. It is regarded as a noble and fitting monument to Taney's memory.

THE opening of the Supreme Court for the December term in 1861 was a dreary affair. The three vacancies had not been filled. The President reported to Congress that he had delayed action in the matter because it would be unfair to the South to make all the appointments from the North, and it was improbable that able southern men could at this time be persuaded to serve. Three of the six judges who remained had been seriously embroiled in the sectional controversy since the close of the preceding term. Taney had been soundly abused because of his opinion in the Merryman case. Because of a grand jury charge disliked by southerners Catron's property had been confiscated and he had been forced to make a hurried departure from Nashville. Grier had offended the administration in a federal circuit court in Pennsylvania by refusing to sit in cases in which southern privateers were tried for piracy.

Others had been only slightly less involved. Nelson had for a time participated with Campbell in negotiations with southern leaders in attempt to prevent war, and had somewhat besmirched his reputation by the connection. Wayne had remained with the court in spite of the fact that he was from Georgia, but his circuit had now deserted him through secession. Only Clifford, from Maine, the latest appointee, seems not to have been involved in any personal way. Benjamin C. Howard, the court reporter, had resigned to enter Maryland politics in opposition to the Union party. The court filled his place with Jeremiah S. Black, whose attitude toward impending events was indicated by his opinion that the government could not constitutionally use force to prevent states from seceding, and by his characterization of Lincoln as "very small potatoes and few in a hill." [1]

No cases were decided at this term which had important bearing upon the war issues. The case most closely related to the struggle was that of Nathaniel Gordon, whose ship had been seized in 1860 with a huge cargo of slaves from Africa. The slaves were sent back, and Gordon was tried in a New York federal court for violation of the law prohibiting the slave trade. He was convicted and sentenced to death. He had many influential friends who assured him that the President would be persuaded to do something for him. The President granted a respite of two weeks, on the ground that because of the false hopes raised by his friends the prisoner was not yet prepared to die, but refused to interfere further. Gordon appealed to the Supreme Court to restrain further proceedings, but Taney, in a unanimous opinion in which he avoided discussion of the merits of the case, decided that the Supreme Court had no jurisdiction. [2]

Because of the ill health of various members it happened at times during the term that the court had to adjourn because of the absence of a quorum. The President gave aid in January, 1862, by appointing Noah H. Swayne of Ohio to one of the vacancies. He was an able Republican lawyer, and thereafter served in part as a contact man between the court and the administration. The other appointments were postponed while Congress discussed the realignment of the circuits, abusing the existing membership of the court as it did so. When a law was finally enacted, in July, 1862, President Lincoln appointed Samuel F. Miller, an abolitionist Republican from Iowa, to one of the positions. In December following he appointed his personal and political friend, David Davis of Illinois, to the other position. The appointments were confirmed with but little opposition.

The administration now had three judges whose loyalty was unquestioned. The fact that these three constituted only a minority of the court, however, was cause for discomfort, and as a matter of pre-

[1] Black to C. A. Buckalew, Jan. 28, 1861, Black MSS.
[2] Ex parte *Nathaniel Gordon*, 1 Black 503 (1862).

caution the addition of another was contemplated. The project gained support from the fact that none of the existing circuits assigned to Supreme Court judges reached as far as California. That state was now sending to the Supreme Court cases dealing with land title controversies which involved complex problems of local law. Californians urged their need for representation on the court, and, to stimulate loyalty to the Union, many congressmen were disposed to make a concession by creating a position to be filled with a unionist judge.

While these plans were being considered the famous prize cases came up for argument, and for twelve days the judges listened to debates on the legality of the blockade of southern ports and the confiscation of blockade runners as prize. If the struggle was a bona fide war there was no question as to the right to apply the blockade against foreign ships. It had been contended, however, that if this was a war the opponent must therefore be a belligerent entitled to recognition as such by other nations. This the administration was eager to prevent. On the other hand if it was not a war, the laws of war could not be applied through instituting a blockade. The administration had attempted to treat the conflict as a mere insurrection, for the purpose of preventing foreign recognition of the Confederacy and of limiting the rights of southerners taken into custody. On the other hand, in the matter of the blockade it had sought all the advantages of the principles of international law which applied to conflicts between sovereign states.

The Supreme Court was in position greatly to embarrass the government in either of two ways. It might hold that the conflict was not a war and not covered by the laws of war, and that the prizes had been illegally taken and foreign trade with southern ports illegally broken up. Such a decision would make the government liable for huge sums in damages, and its psychological effect would be such as seriously to cripple the conduct of the war. On the other hand the court might hold that the Confederacy was an independent sovereign power, and, although holding the blockade to be legal, it might do it in such a way as to encourage the recognition of the Confederacy by foreign governments. Such a decision would be only less serious than the other.

Six lawyers appeared for the government, but the management of the case was left largely in the hands of Charles Eames, an international lawyer of reputation. After the arguments were concluded Attorney General Bates learned with a sinking heart that Eames had made himself highly unpopular with the court. He had recently defended unsuccessfully a general who had been cashiered from the army for disobedience. Taney remarked that he no longer wondered at the general's conviction. He deserved to be convicted for trusting his case to such a counsel. Representing himself and Davis, Justice Swayne called on Bates to report the reaction of the court and to recommend that Eames should not be again employed in government cases.[3]

One of Eames' associates was more successful. After Richard H. Dana had concluded his argument Justice Grier exclaimed in delight, "Well, your little *Two Years before the Mast* has settled that question; there is nothing more to say about it!"[4] This was a portent of victory, for, since it was felt that Swayne, Miller, and Davis could be counted on, it was necessary only to win Grier and one other. There was perhaps an item of menace in the fact that Taney's close friend and an able lawyer, James M. Carlisle, was one of the opposition counsel.

The opinion of the majority of the court,[5] which was read on March 10, 1863, by Grier for himself, Wayne, and the three Republican appointees, was all the administration could have desired. The Civil War was not less a war because it was called an insurrection, Grier declared. It was properly conducted according to the laws of war, and the proclamation of blockade and the taking of prize was legitimate. He did not admit, however, that the Confederacy was a sovereign power—to whose recognition by other gov-

[3] H. K. Beale (ed.), *The Diary of Edward Bates*, p. 281. (Published as Vol. IV of the *Annual Report of the American Historical Association for the Year 1930*.)
[4] C. F. Adams, *Richard Henry Dana*, II, 269-270.
[5] *Prize Cases*, 2 Black 635 (1863).

ernments the United States could not object—but held that the United States might claim sovereignty over the South and belligerent rights at the same time.

Nelson wrote a vigorous dissent in one of the cases. He did not deny that the government had recourse to the laws of war, but held that a blockade could not be legally proclaimed until after war was declared, and that only Congress could declare war. The capture of prize before Congress gave its sanction, in July, 1861, had therefore not been legal. Together with Taney, Catron, and Clifford, Nelson held that the vessel whose owner Carlisle represented had been illegally taken because proper notice had not been given to it. The point had little significance for the further conduct of the war, however, and received but little attention.

Grier's opinion stood as precedent for the many prize cases which were subsequently tried in the district courts of the United States. Many district judges probably outdid themselves to be loyal to the Union, and foreign adventurers suffered heavily. The British smarted painfully from their losses. Earl Russell, speaking in the House of Lords, apparently unaware that Taney had not differed basically from the majority of the court, deplored the fact that prize cases could not be taken directly to the Supreme Court instead of being left to the lower courts. "I believe," he continued, "that the judge now at the head of the United States Supreme Court though a man above eighty years of age, retains the full vigor of his faculties, that his memory is furnished with a knowledge of all the cases applicable to the questions that come before him, and his decisions would be received with respect, not only in America, but in this country." [6]

It is significant that it was in the period of uncertainty between the argument and the decision of the Prize Cases that Congress made provision for an additional circuit and for an additional member of

[6] The New York newspaper which published Russell's statement added that Taney was now ninety-four years of age. He was in fact only eighty-six. His only comment to the friend who sent him the clipping was: "Judging from the extracts given from Earl Russell's speech he is better informed as to my age than Mr. Wood. And if I had reached the age of ninety-four years, I fear the public could hardly be persuaded that I was any longer fit for the headship of this court."—Taney to G. S. S. Davis, July 11, 1863, MS., New York Historical Society.

the Supreme Court, making ten in all. To that position the President appointed Stephen J. Field of California, whose membership in the Democratic party was obscured by the fact that he had been influential in keeping California in the Union, and by the further fact that David Dudley Field, his brother and an effective agent in his behalf, had helped to bring about the nomination of Lincoln and was influential with the administration.[7] From the time of Field's appointment until Catron's death shortly after the close of the war the court had a larger membership than ever before or since. Since there were diverse reasons for making the appointment it may be argued that this was not a bona fide instance of packing the court for the sake of a point of view, but the fact remains that one of the reasons grew out of doubts as to the loyalty of the older members.

Notwithstanding preparation in the form of the appointment of new and unquestionably loyal judges, most of the important constitutional questions raised by the war were not decided by the Supreme Court until the war was over, when Taney was no longer Chief Justice. A number of his circuit court opinions, however, and other opinions not the official expressions of any court, show that he was persistently critical of the centralization of power and the arbitrary exercise of power by which the war was carried on.

At the April term, 1863, he upheld a decision of Judge Giles against the confiscation of a vessel for trading with the enemy when conflicting regulations of government departments were involved.[8] In another case at the same term he reversed a decision in which Judge Giles had upheld the seizure of a cargo destined for enemy country. He denounced the use of spying techniques and deceptions of various kinds by the detective employed by the government. The detective had made friends with the children of the suspected person, had ingratiated himself into the home under false pretenses, made use of forged papers of various kinds, and had in various ways made use of sneaking techniques highly obnoxious to a southern gentleman

[7] See the author's *Stephen J. Field: Craftsman of the Law*, pp. 115–118.
[8] Summary of the case of the Schooner *Reform*, Attorney General MSS.

of Taney's type. In deciding the case he declared he could see no benefit to the government comparable with the evil in the sanction of such conduct by a court of justice.[9]

In still another case decided at the same term Taney declared unconstitutional a regulation issued by Salmon P. Chase, the Secretary of the Treasury. In an attempt to stop trade with the enemy Chase had forbidden the shipment of goods from Baltimore to any point in Maryland south of the railroad between Washington and Annapolis without a permit.[10] In issuing such regulations, Taney declared, the Executive Department was unconstitutionally usurping legislative power. They could not be sustained, however, he continued, even if made directly by Congress. It had been repeatedly decided by the Supreme Court in years past that the government could not interfere with the internal and domestic trade of a state. It could take proper means to prevent trade or intercourse with the enemy, but it could not disregard the limits of its own powers or the rights reserved to the states and the people.

"A civil war or any other war," Taney added, "does not enlarge the powers of the federal government over the states or the people beyond what the compact has given to it in time of war. A state of war does not annul the 10th article of the amendments to the Constitution, which declares that 'the powers not delegated to the United States by the Constitution, nor prohibited by it to the states, are reserved to the states respectively or to the people.'

"Nor does a civil war or any other war absolve the judicial department from the duty of maintaining with an even and firm hand the rights and powers of the federal government, and of the states, and of the citizen, as they are written in the Constitution, which every judge is sworn to support."

This important constitutional opinion was unfortunately omitted from the volume reporting Taney's circuit court decisions, and is very little known. It illustrates again his efforts to prevent the use of

[9] *Claimants of . . . Merchandise* v. *United States*, Tyler, pp. 436–443. Taney's indignation suggests Justice Holmes' characterization of wire tapping as "dirty business."—*Olmstead* v. *United States*, 277 U. S. 438, 470 (1928).

[10] *Carpenter* v. *United States*, Baltimore *Sun*, June 20, 1863.

war conditions as justification for the arbitrary violation of the rights of the people, at a time when the prevailing hysteria led freely to outrages of this sort. The situation derives additional interest from the fact that Taney was placing the ban of unconstitutionality upon regulations framed by the man who within a year and a half was to succeed him as Chief Justice of the United States. The disgruntled district attorney declared his belief that Taney could not be sustained,[11] but the case was never pronounced upon by the Supreme Court.

Taney clashed with Chase on other matters connected with the conduct of the war. Congress had provided for a tax of three per cent on the salaries of all officers of the government. Chase interpreted the law as applying to the salaries of federal judges, in spite of the constitutional provision against the reduction of the salaries of judges during their term of office. Taney knew from personal experience that judicial salaries were too low even in normal times, and that they were particularly deficient during the period of war-time inflation. He knew also of the difficulties which inadequate salaries placed in the way of getting the best men for positions in the lower courts. Not illogically, therefore, he regarded the tax measure as another blow at constitutional government.

Since judges usually declined to sit in cases involving their own economic interest, there seemed no way to get an official opinion on the constitutionality of the measure. Rather than have his silence interpreted as acquiescence, however, Taney wrote to Chase vigorously attacking the law, and asking that his letter be filed in the public records of the Treasury Department. "Having been honored with the highest judicial station under the Constitution," he explained, "I feel it to be more especially my duty to uphold and maintain the constitutional rights of that department of the government, and not by any act or word of mine have it to be supposed that I acquiesce in a measure that displaces it from the independent position assigned to it by the statesmen who framed the Constitution." [12]

[11] William Price to T. J. Coffey, July 7, 1863, Attorney General MSS.
[12] Taney to Chase, Feb. 16, 1863, Tyler, *op. cit.*, pp. 432–434.

Chase made no reply to Taney, and did not grant the favor of filing his letter in the public records of the Department. Some weeks later he sent it to Attorney General Bates, saying that a number of the judges of the Supreme Court and other federal courts had claimed that the tax on their salaries was unconstitutional. Bates endorsed Chase's letter "No reply to be given," and, with Taney's letter, tucked it away in his own official files, where it still remains.[13] Taney, having been ignored by Chase, asked and received the permission of the Supreme Court to have a copy of the letter entered on its records. Nine years later, when Taney was in his grave, another Secretary of the Treasury came to the conclusion that the tax on the salaries of judges had been illegally collected, and the amounts paid were refunded.

Had a case been brought before him Taney would have denied the constitutionality of the part of the war program sponsored by Chase which had to do with the control of the currency. Since the defeat of the efforts of Nicholas Biddle and his friends to secure the recharter of the Bank of the United States there had been no national bank in the country. That part of the Taney-Jackson program which called for a specie currency and the exclusion of paper money had not been carried out, however, and the notes of state banks continued to provide much of the circulatory medium. The system had never been wholly satisfactory, for the state banks were poorly regulated, and continued to overissue in times of prosperity and to pull their patrons down with them in times of depression.

The Civil War called for unprecedented achievements on the part of those who had to arrange for financing it. The state banks were unequipped to meet the emergency, and in a short time were forced to suspend specie payments. The federal treasury, in order to protect such specie as it had, was forced to do likewise. Yet the government had to make huge purchases, and had to pay either with irredeemable state bank notes or with other irredeemable notes issued by itself.

The latter alternative seemed better. It was feared, however, that

[13] Chase to Bates, March 26, 1863, Attorney General MSS.

since the notes were not redeemable in coin people would hesitate or refuse to take them, and that they would depreciate in value for that reason. To prevent the depreciation Congress adopted the additional feature of Chase's program by making the government notes, or greenbacks as they were commonly called, a legal tender for all public and private debts.[14] It was assumed that the people, knowing that they could compel their creditors to accept the notes as money, would therefore be perfectly willing to receive them.

The power of Congress to make the notes legal tender was seriously questioned, and a decision of the Supreme Court was awaited with trepidation. It was perhaps fortunate for the program of the administration that prior to the close of the war no case reached the Supreme Court in which it was necessary to pass upon the question. During the long days on which he sat at home too feeble to go to court Taney prepared himself for such a case by writing out his opinion on the subject. Discussing the problem at length, he attempted to show that the legal tender provision was unconstitutional. The power of Congress to coin money was not the power to print paper money. The power to borrow was not the power to force irredeemable notes on private creditors.[15]

No occasion arose for the delivery of this opinion either in the Supreme Court or in the circuit court, and it remained unpublished. It is of interest that Chase himself, however, after he had left the Treasury Department and taken Taney's place on the bench, came to a conclusion similar to that which Taney had worked out.[16] The fact is significant as suggesting that, although Taney's lukewarm attitude toward the winning of the war probably had something to do with his position, there were other substantial grounds for opposition to the legal tender acts.

Taney also wrote out an opinion called "Thoughts on the Conscription Law of the U. States," [17] pronouncing the conscription act

[14] Except for customs duties and interest on the public debt.

[15] From a manuscript copy in the New York Public Library, made by M. L. York from Taney's original manuscript.

[16] *Hepburn* v. *Griswold*, 8 Wallace 603 (1870).

[17] Manuscript copy in the New York Public Library, made by M. L. York from Taney's original manuscript.

unconstitutional. He set forth again the doctrine as to the relation between the federal and state governments which he had outlined in the Booth cases. Two separate governments, he declared, were to exercise powers of sovereignty over the same territory and the same people at the same time. Yet a line of division was marked between them, and each was altogether independent of the other within its own sphere of action. The conscription act was an encroachment by the federal government upon the sovereignty of the states. Under the act the officers and men in the state militia might be taken by the federal government, with the effect of destroying the militia as such. All the civil officers of the states except the governor might be taken in the same way, leaving none to preserve and use the machinery of government. Taney believed that the Constitution allotted to the federal government no such power.

The opinion was filed away and never used. Perhaps Taney never expected to use it. Apparently his method of thinking on legal topics had so long been that of writing out his ideas in the form of court opinions that he found it easiest to use the same technique even in the privacy of his home. He did not attempt to make an issue of the matter when his colored servant, Madison Franklin, was drafted. He was so feeble that he could not conceive of getting along without the servant who had been with him for many years. His physician knew the negro had heart disease which disqualified him for the duties of a soldier, and proposed to make arrangements to have him excused. In spite of the fact that he was pressed for money, however, Taney preferred to pay for a substitute and in this way make an immediate end of the matter.[18]

By proclamation of the President all slaves within the area in rebellion against the government were made free on January 1, 1863—in so far as the government of the United States could make them free. The constitutional power of the President to destroy property rights in this fashion was widely questioned, and many predicted that the Supreme Court would declare the proclamation unconstitutional at the first opportunity. It is clear that Taney must have so regarded

---

[18] Tyler, *Memoir of Roger Brooke Taney,* p. 482.

it, and he may have spent long hours working out an opinion on this subject as well as upon others connected with the conduct of the war. Advocates of abolition were quite unwilling to trust to his decision. "The proclamation of 1863," declared a Washington paper, "was to be filtered through the secession heart of a man whose body was in Baltimore and whose soul was in Richmond. It was to pass the ordeal of the bench of judges the majority of whom came out of the wickedness of Buchanan and Polk and Franklin Pierce—the only two of whom who refused to concur in the Dred Scott decision being no longer in the court. God help the negro who depended on Roger B. Taney for his liberty." [19]

In this fashion the venomous attacks upon the court and particularly upon Taney continued throughout the period of the war. Among the members of the court itself, whether new or old, he was held in deep affection, as he had been throughout his life among those who knew him best. His mind continued to function clearly, but his body grew steadily weaker, until his physician remarked on his resemblance to a disembodied spirit.[20] The many letters to his friends show his belief that his life was nearing its close, a belief usually expressed in connection with a gloomy prophecy that he would never again see the government restored to what it had been before the days of military domination.

When the court adjourned in March, 1862, Taney asked each of his brethren to call and see him before leaving Washington. At his home he took affectionate leave of them, saying he had a presentiment he would die very soon, and he did not expect to see them again.[21] He was back at work the following winter, however, and in the summer of 1863 he wrote to a friend that he hoped to linger along to the next term of the court—which was the term at which ten judges were to sit. "Very different, however," he commented sadly, "that court will now be from the court as I have heretofore

---

[19] Washington *National Intelligencer*, Dec. 29, 1863.
[20] Tyler, *op. cit.*, 457.
[21] *The Diary of Edward Bates*, p. 243.

known it. Nor do I see any ground for hope that it will ever again be restored to the authority and rank which the Constitution intended to confer upon it. The supremacy of the military power over the civil seems to be established; and the public mind has acquiesced in it and sanctioned it. We can pray for better times, and submit with resignation to the chastisements which it may please God to inflict upon us." [22]

His lamentation was not unlike that of Justice Story many years earlier when he grieved over the passing of the old order. In so far as he anticipated the permanent supremacy of the military over civil power Taney's capacity for prophecy was no more accurate than Story's prediction that no state or federal act would ever again be declared unconstitutional by the Supreme Court. His instincts were sound, however, in leading him to the conclusion that the culture of which he was a product would never flourish again.

Although he was able to attend court only a few days during the term of 1863–64 Taney continued to survive, to the exasperation of those Republicans eager to participate in the choice of his successor. "No man ever prayed as I did that Taney might outlive James Buchanan's term," profanely remarked Senator Benjamin F. Wade, "and now I am afraid I have over done it." [23] Taney watched with keen interest the military and political movements connected with the war, and discussed them with his friends. When able to do so he accompanied his colleagues to make the customary call on the President at the beginning of each term of the court. His resentment toward the man who ignored his opinion in the Merryman case was but thinly concealed, however, when he refused to make a similar call on January 1, 1862. "I expect some friends tomorrow," he wrote to Justice Wayne, "and as there is no established etiquette which requires the court to wait on the President on the 1st of January, as a matter of official courtesy, I am sure my brethren will excuse me for not joining them tomorrow." [24]

[22] Taney to D. M. Perine, Aug. 6, 1863, Tyler, *op. cit.*, p. 454.
[23] J. G. Nicolay and John Hay, *Abraham Lincoln*, IX, 386.
[24] Taney to Wayne, Dec. 31, 1861, *Maryland Historical Magazine*, XIII, 167.

He subscribed to and read thoroughly one or more New York papers, and the *Globe* and *National Intelligencer* in Washington. He took also the London *Times,* a number of literary reviews, and one or more Catholic papers. To Samuel Tyler he lamented his narrow means, saying he would like to take another newspaper but could not afford it.[25] Though unable at times to sit up he was always able to read, and spent many hours lying in bed with a cigar clamped between his tobacco-stained teeth and newspapers and magazines spread out before him. It was his great pleasure, when entertaining friends whom he could fully trust, to lie there drawing at one of his ever-present cigars and discussing such issues of the day as he could talk about without violating judicial ethics. Even with Samuel Tyler, however, his chosen biographer, he never forgot that there were some things which a judge did not discuss.

He became too feeble to go often to Baltimore, where most of his friends, like himself, had deep sympathy for the South. Life in Washington was lonesome for him. When a grandson of John Eager Howard, of Revolutionary War fame, had come to Taney to say good-by upon leaving to join the Confederate army, Taney had wished him well. "The circumstances under which you are going," he said, "are not unlike those under which your grandfather went into the Revolutionary War." [26] Major Allison, the husband of one of his daughters, was serving with the Confederate forces. To Taney as well as to other members of the family his welfare and his cause were doubtless the objects of deep solicitude. A man harboring such sentiments could have little in common with the major portion of the inhabitants of the armed camp which Washington had become. The more moderate persons connected with the administration, who might have liked Taney had they come to know him, shunned him because of the belief that he was the malevolent old despot so frequently portrayed by abolitionist and Republican propaganda.

"There was no sadder figure to be seen in Washington during the years of the Civil War," wrote a contemporary resident, "than that

[25] J. B. Ellis, *Sights and Secrets of the National Capital,* p. 267.
[26] Steiner, *Life of Roger Brooke Taney,* p. 503.

of the aged Chief Justice. His form was bent by the weight of years, and his thin, nervous, and deeply-furrowed face was shaded by long, gray locks,[27] and lighted up by large, melancholy eyes that looked wearily out from under shaggy brows, which gave him a weird, wizard-like expression. He had outlived his epoch, and was shunned and hated by the men of the new time of storm and struggle for the principles of freedom and nationality." [28]

He was sheltered by the love of his family, but at the same time burdened with expenditures which it seemed that he would not be able to meet. David M. Perine asked the privilege of taking up his deficit, but he was unwilling to accept charity from even the best of friends. One cause for the difficulties was the loss of income from investments. Scrupulously eager to avoid investments which might be thought to influence his judicial decisions, he had spent several thousand dollars for securities issued by the state of Virginia. With the beginning of the war Virginia ceased to pay interest to the holders of securities residing in states which had not seceded, and it seemed as if the principal as well as the interest might be lost.

Persons in Richmond who had warm feelings for Taney thought an exception might be made in his case as to the payment of interest, and broached the subject to Perine, who acted as his agent in the matter. Taney told Perine he could not receive the money. Some people would believe that the money was paid by the Virginians because of the office which he held. "Malignity would not fail to impute unworthy motives to them and to me; and in the present frenzied state of the public mind, men, who do not know my Virginia friends or me, would be ready to believe it. I mean to stand, in relation to this debt, upon the same ground with the other Maryland creditors, and cannot consent to any exception in my favor." [29]

In the spring of 1864 Attorney General Bates remarked that Taney, Wayne, Catron, and Grier were obviously failing, and that he thought they would resign from the Supreme Court if Congress

---

[27] Other accounts indicate that his hair retained throughout his life its color of almost jet black.

[28] Mrs. J. A. Logan, *Thirty Years in Washington*, p. 413.

[29] Taney to Perine, July 18, 1861, Tyler, *op. cit.*, pp. 481–482.

would provide for an adequate pension.[30] A bill for this purpose was much discussed but it failed to pass, and no resignations were submitted. Taney, almost too feeble to walk, remained most of the time at his home, in one of the stucco houses in Blogden's Row in Indiana Avenue, where he lived with Ellen, his semi-invalid daughter. In the room in which he lay in bed, smoking and reading, he hung photographs of Maria and of her husband who was absent in the service of the Confederacy. As if eager to surround himself with the likenesses of the persons most dear to him, he wrote to Taney Campbell asking for photographs of Anne and J. Mason Campbell to hang beside those of Maria and Major Allison.[31]

Under the loving care of his daughters Taney lived placidly through the summer of 1864, but in the autumn the chronic intestinal disease which had plagued him for years began to achieve dominance. His regular physician, Dr. Grafton Tyler of Georgetown, was called in. He shook his head and arranged a consultation with Taney's former physician, Dr. James C. Hall, now retired from practice. When the old gentleman entered the room Taney, himself the gentleman to the last, deplored his inability to arise and receive his old friend. Dr. Hall could do nothing, and Dr. Thomas Buckler, the eminent physician who had served the family for many years in Baltimore, was summoned. All three physicians agreed, however, that the career of the aged Chief Justice was at last coming to its close.

Dr. Hall remained with him for a time, and Taney, undisturbed by his own condition, listened while the Doctor read about the election soon to be held in Maryland. The people were to vote on the adoption of a state constitution under which all slaves in the state would be set free without compensation to their owners. The old order was indeed changing while the candle of life was flickering to extinction. A letter of William Schley was read suggesting that the oath of allegiance proposed by the President and provided for in the new constitution might be taken even though conscience disapproved.

---

[30] *Diary of Edward Bates*, p. 358.

[31] Taney to R. B. Taney Campbell, March 1, 1864, from description of the "J. H. Benton Sale," American Art Association catalogue, 1920.

Taney condemned the idea. There should be no compromise of principles.[32]

Although he had not been told of the verdict of the doctors Taney perceived that the end was near. "My dear child," he said gently to Anne, his eldest daughter, on the morning of October 12, "my race is run. I have no desire to stay longer in this painful world, but for my poor children." He asked to receive the last rites of his church, and calmly gave directions for the preparations that were needed. In the afternoon came again the violent pains from which he had suffered for many days. That evening—in the words of Mrs. Campbell—"I think it was about ten o'clock when being helped from one side to the other to relieve his pain, he suddenly raised his head, all trace of suffering gone, his eyes bright and clear, said 'Lord Jesus receive my spirit,' and never spoke again. He lived for more than an hour afterward with the same sweet peaceful face and though we stood round his bed we did not know he was gone until we saw the Doctor closing his bright uplifted eyes." [33]

Taney had requested that his funeral be conducted quietly without display, sensing no doubt the lack of fitness in a public ceremony held in a city so deeply hostile to the things in which he believed. No attempt was made, therefore to have the body lie in state in the court room, or to bring together the dignitaries of the government in his honor. The death occurred late Wednesday evening. Plans were made to move the body to Frederick by special train early Saturday morning. On Friday the President and his cabinet discussed the question as to whether they should attend. Lincoln, Seward, and Dennison decided to be present at the brief ceremony to be held in Washington; Bates thought it his duty to go to Frederick; and Welles, Fessenden, Stanton, and Usher refused to make any gesture in honor of the deceased.

The diary comments of Gideon Welles and Edward Bates show the striking contrast between the attitudes of the political opponents

[32] Baltimore *Sun,* Oct. 15, 1864.
[33] Anne Arnold Campbell to Miss Margaret Birnie, Oct. 13, 1864, MS., in the possession of Edward S. Delaplaine, Frederick, Md.

who had come to know Taney well and those who had not. Welles had never called upon Taney while living, and had no honors for him beyond those which belonged to him by virtue of his office. "That he had many good qualities and possessed ability, I do not doubt; that he rendered service in Jackson's administration is true, and during most of his judicial life he was upright and just. But the course pursued in the Dred Scott case and all the attending circumstances forfeited respect for him as a man or a judge." [34]

Bates had come to Washington harboring all the prevalent prejudices against Taney. His office of Attorney General, however, necessarily brought them together. After his first conversation with the Chief Justice he remarked grudgingly that the meeting had been more pleasant than he had expected.[35] As the months passed the forced acquaintance ripened into friendship. Taney sent Bates a photograph of himself, and the latter received it gratefully. Instead of awaiting Taney's death with callous eagerness, as did some of his Republican colleagues, he watched the condition of his health with genuine concern. "He was a man of great and varied talents," he wrote in his diary when he learned that Taney was gone; "a model of a presiding officer; and the last specimen within my knowledge, of a graceful and polished old fashioned gentleman.

"The luster of his fame, as a lawyer and judge, is for the present dimmed by the bitterness of party feeling arising out of his unfortunate judgment in the Dred Scott case. That was a great error; but it ought not and will not, for long, tarnish his otherwise well earned fame. He cannot be forgotten, for his life is interwoven with the history of his country, and, in a greater or less degree, must give tone and color to the eventful age in which he lived." [36]

Bates was therefore among those who gathered at the Taney home in Washington early on Saturday morning, and, showing that he was not merely making a gesture of formal courtesy, he arranged to accompany the family and friends to Frederick as well. There is rea-

[34] *The Diary of Gideon Welles*, II, 176–177.
[35] *The Diary of Edward Bates*, pp. 204–205.
[36] *Ibid.*, p. 418.

son for believing that many others would have experienced similar changes in attitude toward Taney had they had the privilege of his friendship. It was one of the tragedies of his entire life that, possessing a superb capacity for friendship with those with whom he came in intimate contact, he had not the energy to make himself known throughout a wider circle.

A few minutes before seven o'clock on Saturday morning the family and friends took a last look at the features of the deceased. A special train of two cars conveyed the body and the attendant mourners to Frederick, Taney's home for twenty years in the prime of his life. There, in St. John's Catholic Church, which sixty years earlier Taney and John Dubois had struggled to build and which was now draped in mourning, a requiem mass was sung and a funeral sermon was delivered by Father Maguire, who for a time had ministered to Taney in Washington. After the service the body was carried across the street to the little noviciate cemetery, to a newly dug grave beside that of Taney's mother, who for fifty years had been sleeping there. In that spot they were to remain until the abandonment of the cemetery, when they were removed to the larger Catholic cemetery, where they were again placed side by side.

Taney's wife, with two of the daughters, now sleeps beside her own parents in the lot of the Potts family in the Mt. Olivet cemetery at Frederick. Thus matters of religious dogma, which could not separate the devoted husband and wife while they lived, separated their bodies when they were gone. He who ponders the question will decide for himself whether the separation at this late date was a matter of importance.

As directed by Taney's will, J. Mason Campbell and David M. Perine took charge of the estate. After the distribution of certain articles and sums and the payment of debts they set the remainder aside as a trust fund, the income of which was to be used for Ellen, who was unmarried, and for Sophia, who was widowed and had a young son to support. It seemed for a time that little would be left after the payment of debts except ten thousand dollars in life insurance. The Virginia securities ultimately regained some of their value, however, and yielded a few thousand dollars. A small additional sum was provided when the Secretary of the Treasury in a later administration decided that Taney had been right as to the unconstitutionality of a tax on the salaries of federal judges, and refunded the amount collected.

The fund was by no means sufficient for the support of the two women, and they had to take unimportant and poorly paid positions in the Treasury Department, at a time when it was by no means good form for respectable and well-bred women to work in ordinary positions for the government. Regarding the situation as too tragic to be ignored, prominent lawyers called a meeting of the bar of the Supreme Court in February, 1871, at which a committee was formed to raise funds for the family.[37] For some reason, however, perhaps because of the death of Ellen later in the same year, the matter was allowed to drop.

Newspaper comments on Taney's death varied all the way from those which repeated old falsehoods about the Dred Scott decision and delivered harangues based upon them, through other comments which muted their criticisms and found a few kind things to say, to those which lauded him as a gentleman and as a great judge.[38] It was perhaps not to be expected that editors who had stimulated the circulation of their papers for years by periodic denunciations of Taney should now appraise him without bias merely because he had died. Most of the articles, indeed, were so repetitious of innumerable others which had preceded them as not to be worthy of even casual mention.

The comment of the New York *Tribune*, for years the leader of Taney's newspaper critics, seems to have represented a synthesis of the ineradicable bias of the editor with a sincere desire to be just and fair. Taney's death occurred simultaneously with the coming of a new era in Maryland, the writer noted, in that the people had

[37] See *The Taney Fund. Proceedings of the Meeting of the Bar of the Supreme Court of the United States.* 1871.

[38] For a bibliography and summary of newspaper comments and bar proceedings, see Charles Warren, *The Supreme Court in United States History*, II, 388–398.

adopted the constitution outlawing slavery. His life had begun during the darkest hours of the Revolution, and its end had been synchronized with the disintegration of the slave power, of which he was a votary and a pillar. "He belonged to a dispensation now happily closed; it is no more just than generous to question his integrity, nor the sincerity, whatever we may think of the quality, of his patriotism. He was the product of circumstances which (we trust) will mold the character of no future Chief Justice of the United States; but it were unjust to presume that he did not truly and earnestly seek the good of his country." [39]

Bar proceedings in praise of Taney were published by his friends at many points throughout the country. Benjamin R. Curtis, his former colleague on the Supreme Court, was perhaps the most prominent of the speakers who came to the defense of his memory, and told of his excellent qualities as a man and as a judge. Reverdy Johnson and orators of lesser fame likewise came to his defense.[40]

In private letters Republican critics gloated over the demise of the aged Chief Justice. "So old Taney is at last dead," wrote Charles Francis Adams. ". . . The darling wish of Taney's last days is doomed not to be realized. It was not reserved to him to put the veto of the law on the Proclamation of Emancipation." [41] Friends wrote jubilantly to Salmon P. Chase to congratulate him on his appointment as Taney's successor, and to predict that right would now prevail, and that on the Supreme Court there would be no more truckling to the slave power.[42]

Among his most bitter enemies in the United States Senate his death brought no abatement of vindictiveness. "The name of Taney," decreed Charles Sumner, the embodiment of the northern spirit of revenge, "is to be hooted down the page of history. Judgment is beginning now; and an emancipated country will fasten upon him the stigma which he deserves. . . . He administered justice at last

---

[39] New York *Tribune*, Oct. 14, 1864.

[40] Among others see the speeches published in Tyler, *op. cit.*, pp. 486–516.

[41] C. F. Adams to Henry Adams, Oct. 15, 1864, *A Cycle of Adams Letters*, II, 205–206.

[42] See for instance David Urner to Chase, Dec. 7, 1864; and E. A. S. Standard and Oliver Johnson to Chase, Dec. 7, 1864, Chase MSS.

wickedly, and degraded the judiciary of the country, and degraded the age." [43] The occasion was the discussion of a bill to provide for a bust of Taney to be placed in the court room. Taney's friends indignantly defended his reputation against the assaults of Sumner and others, but Sumner, declaring that Taney should not be represented as a saint by any vote of Congress if he could help it, succeeded in defeating the bill. For nine years thereafter his zeal was similarly rewarded. Finally, upon the death of Chase, an appropriation was voted without debate for busts of the two Chief Justices.

Busts, statues, and portraits have been unveiled in many places since that time, to the accompaniment of sincere and laudatory comments. Praise on such occasions is expected, of course, and only such persons are chosen to speak as have words of praise to deliver. The peroration to one such address is significant, however, because of the time and the place, and because of the man who delivered it. "With the passing of the years and the softening of old asperities," declared Chief Justice Charles Evans Hughes at the unveiling of a bust of Taney at Frederick in 1931, "the arduous service nobly rendered by Roger Brooke Taney has received its fitting recognition. He bore his wounds with the fortitude of an invincible spirit. He was a great Chief Justice." [44]

Eight years after Taney's death Samuel Tyler of Frederick, his chosen biographer, published a *Memoir of Roger Brooke Taney, LL.D.* It contains as much of Taney's autobiography as was completed during his sojourns at Old Point Comfort, and a rich store of letters and other materials dealing with Taney's life. Much valuable material was omitted, however, and, as was almost inevitable in those times of emotional stress, the book was written with a narrow bias in Taney's favor and against his political enemies. Numerous additional articles have been written in similar vein.

Most of the bias of historians was against Taney, however, rather than for him. Those writing immediately after the close of the war

---

[43] *Congressional Globe*, 38th Cong., 2nd sess., p. 1012.
[44] Charles Evans Hughes, "Roger Brooke Taney," *American Bar Association Journal*, XVII, 785-790.

treated him hardly less venomously than the abolitionist newspapers had done. Those of a later period often tried to be fair. They were for the most part northerners, however, and, so sublime was their confidence that the North was right and the South wrong in the sectional struggle, they were unable to do anything but condemn all actions based on sympathy with the South. Their point of view was perhaps most clearly stated by Professor John W. Burgess. The history of the period should be written by northerners, he declared, because the victors could and would be more liberal, generous, and sympathetic than the vanquished. Furthermore, the northern view was, in the main, the correct view. The men of the South must acknowledge that they were in error in their attempt to destroy the Union, and it was unmanly of them not to do so. "Any interpretation of this period of American history which does not demonstrate to the South its error will be worthless, simply because it will not be true." [45]

The same attitude, though not so clearly outlined, was implicit in the writing of James Ford Rhodes' *History of the United States*, and in many other respected products of historical research. It proved an effective barrier to the understanding and appreciation of Taney, for it assumed without question that many of the ideals for which he stood were false. He was condemned without a hearing, or at least in advance of a hearing. The same had been true in earlier years in connection with his struggle with the Bank of the United States. Leading historians, including Channing, McMaster, Bassett, and others, accepted in general the Whig account of the bank war, assumed that Taney was the "pliant instrument" of Andrew Jackson in the performance of a task that was carried out for the sake of petty politics rather than for the good of the country, and so announced their conclusions without further investigation. His attempts as Chief Justice to interpret the Constitution to protect human rights, or "community rights" as against property rights, and to deviate from *laissez faire* doctrines to the extent of justifying state laws needed by local

[45] John W. Burgess, *The Middle Period, 1817–1858*, pp. x–xi.

communities but opposed by conservative interests, have gone largely unrecorded.

An authentic portrayal of Taney's life, his character, and his influence must be worked out as a result of an entirely different approach. Among others it must take into account the following facts, which have been detailed herein at considerable length: Taney's ideas as to the nature of the good society evolved out of his heritage as a member of the landed aristocracy of the South. The southern culture provided a way of life which for the aristocracy was by no means unattractive, and, if it gave little heed to abstract principles of liberty as far as slaves were concerned, it provided a living and a system of discipline for the simple and untutored black people whose condition would otherwise have been precarious.

A necessary adjunct to the southern culture but oftentimes a menace to its well-being nevertheless, was the merchant and trader through whose hands southern products had to pass on the way to the market. For generations the southern planters, unable to help themselves, paid heavy tribute to the merchant-shipper-middleman-creditor class. A well warranted distrust of the greed of this class, the coöperation of which was necessary for the prosperity of the South, was bred into the fiber of southern society through generations of hard experience. As the linkage of this class with the northern part of the country became more and more obvious, and as it increased its power through the growth of banking and industrial interests, sectional rivalry began to test the bonds of union between the North and the South.

In his position as a leading citizen in a community the interests of which were predominantly rural and agricultural Taney had some decades of experience with the efforts of his own class to protect itself against predatory financial interests. He approached the war with the Bank of the United States not as a narrow politician nor as a mere theorist on money and banking problems, but as a man who knew both the aims and strategy of the opposing forces. His purpose was largely defensive. He set out to protect the country from a powerful organization of the forces from whose predatory instincts

the South, and agricultural interests everywhere, were traditional
sufferers. The history of the bank war itself demonstrated the fact
that his fears were not the products of a depraved imagination but in
many respects were eminently justified. Although historians bred in
the camp of the enemy have consistently condemned his acts, ignored
the qualities of his judgment, and labeled him erroneously as the
"pliant instrument" of an ignorant and prejudiced President, the
people were slow to forget the lesson learned, and for many years
staunchly opposed a renewal of the aggregation of power in a national
banking system.

Taney's appointment as Chief Justice of the United States was a
political appointment. It was rightly so, since in the larger sense the
position was political. His predecessor, Chief Justice Marshall, had
used the position to work into constitutional law the political principles of the now defunct Federalist party. He had made the Constitution sanction the centralization of power in the federal government,
and he had used the federal judiciary to curb state interference with
the aggregations of wealth which Taney regarded as the potential
enemies of the community. Taney became Chief Justice as a part of
a governmental régime basically opposed to many of the principles
for which Marshall stood, and the more significant aspects of his
judicial career are those in which he attempted to redirect the trends
for which his predecessor was largely responsible.

Taney was only superficially inconsistent when he failed to adhere
to the party organization and to the doctrines of the Whigs, the
legitimate successors of the Federalist party of which he had been a
member. The Federalist organization had been the party of aristocrats, of whatever kind, and the Taneys had without question been
of the aristocracy of their section. The Whigs, however, represented
aristocracy in shipping, in banking, and in industry, but not predominantly in land. Through the combination of the increasingly powerful
forces of liquid wealth, farmers, whether rich or poor, aristocratic or
lowly, were compelled to act together in their own interest and to
align themselves more and more with undifferentiated debtor groups
and small propertied groups in general.

Their organization, therefore, easily became an organization for "democracy," in contrast to the "aristocracy" of liquid wealth. Consequently, even though during his first years in Frederick Taney may have phrased many stinging paragraphs about Thomas Jefferson, the doubter in religion and the lover of revolutions, it was a natural movement by which he gradually shifted in the direction of what has come to be known as Jeffersonian Democracy. It is significant that the works of Jefferson, and not those of John Adams, or Alexander Hamilton, or other leading Federalists, were left on his shelves at the time of his death.

In interpreting narrowly the legal rights of corporations Taney reversed the policy of the Marshall court, but acted with complete consistency as far as his own previous conduct was concerned. If he was at all inconsistent in any of his decisions affecting corporations, indeed, it was in making occasional concessions to them, such as in recognizing their right to sue in federal courts, and in certain cases in protecting them against state laws said to impair the obligation of contracts. In so doing he was perhaps recognizing that the growth of corporations had achieved an impetus not to be blocked by court decisions, and making an adjustment to the inevitable by finding them a place in constitutional law. Such concessions to growing propertied interests added to his reputation as a judge, whether justifiably so or not. His popularity with his brethren and with the lawyers who appeared before the Supreme Court, his knowledge of law, and his efforts to achieve order in court procedure, likewise added to his reputation. Had he died at some time before March 6, 1857, he would have gone to his grave to the accompaniment of unanimously laudatory obituaries.

The fact that he died in virtual public disgrace was the result of his refusal to make another concession to the inevitable. To him it was unthinkable that the rapidly growing North should be permitted to impress its culture upon the South, not by slow permeation but by domination exercised through the federal government. He saw clearly that culture was inseparably linked with economic life, that barriers against the spread of slavery into the territories would prevent the territorial spread of southern culture and encourage that of the North, that the North would ultimately dominate the federal government, and that it would use its power throughout the country for the economic and cultural benefit of the section in which it evolved.

The South would be injured not so much because its culture would not remain static as because change would be forced upon it from without. Had the southern states of their own volition set about the gradual abolition of slavery and the making of adjustments necessary to the change, the movement would doubtless have had Taney's deepest sympathy, although he was aware of the difficulties in the way of such a program. It was coercion from the North which he feared, coercion based on the assumption that the southerners were an immoral people. A coerced South would not be the South at all. To survive it must remain independent, even though independence might be maintained only through secession.

He was a defender of state rights in part because of his belief that most internal problems were sufficiently local to justify state rather than national regulation. Another reason was the fact that during his régime the assertion of the power of the federal government often took the form not of positive regulation by Congress, but of using the grant of powers to the federal government as an excuse for holding state laws unconstitutional. While resisting this method of defending *laissez faire* he might have welcomed the extension of the legislative power of Congress over items of public welfare in which sectional interests were not divided. His argument against the constitutionality of the Missouri Compromise did not evince a broad jealousy of congressional legislation, but of the use of the power of Congress to aid the North in its competitive struggle with the South. Had the South been equally or more numerously represented in the federal government he might have shown definite nationalist tendencies, although presumably he would not have justified the use of that government to defeat state regulatory measures and aid business enterprise. To what extent he would have justified its use as an implement for encroaching upon the culture of the North is a matter for speculation.

It is perhaps futile to speculate on what would have happened had circumstances been different. The South was defeated, and under the coercion of the victors most of the richness of its culture was destroyed. In view of the arrogance of northern beliefs and the rapaciousness of northern interests it seems probable that Taney was right in his conclusion that the South was doomed if it remained in the Union. Had the Confederacy been permitted to establish itself it might have preserved a rich and vital culture which in its own way gradually removed the worst evils connected with it, and southern territory might not have become the waste lands of northern missionary zeal, inhabited throughout vast areas by a civilization brooding over its own decay. Within his field of action Taney labored to avert this disaster. Those rejecting the biased argument that the victory of the North proved that the South deserved its fate will, at the very least, accord him sympathy and admiration.

APPENDIX

List of Associate Justices of the Supreme Court at the time when Roger B. Taney became Chief Justice of the United States, and of persons appointed while he held office.

Name	Appointed by		Served until
Joseph Story	James Madison	1811	died, 1845
Smith Thompson	James Monroe	1823	died, 1843
John McLean	Andrew Jackson	1829	died, 1861
Henry Baldwin	" "	1830	died, 1844
James M. Wayne	" "	1835	died, 1867
Philip P. Barbour	" "	1835	died, 1841
William Smith	" "	1837	declined
John Catron	" "	1837	died, 1865
John McKinley	Martin Van Buren	1837	died, 1852
Peter V. Daniel	" " "	1841	died, 1860
John C. Spencer	John Tyler	1844	rejected
Reuben H. Walworth	" "	1844	postponed, withdrawn
Edward King	" "	1844	postponed, withdrawn
Samuel Nelson	" "	1845	died, 1873
John M. Read	" "	1845	not acted upon
George W. Woodward	James K. Polk	1845	rejected
Levi Woodbury	" " "	1845	died, 1851
Robert C. Grier	" " "	1846	resigned, 1870
Benjamin R. Curtis	Millard Fillmore	1851	resigned, 1857
Edward A. Bradford	" "	1852	not acted upon
George E. Badger	" "	1853	postponed
William C. Micou	" "	1853	not acted upon
John A. Campbell	Franklin Pierce	1853	resigned, 1861
Nathan Clifford	James Buchanan	1857	died, 1881
Jeremiah S. Black	" "	1861	rejected
Noah H. Swayne	Abraham Lincoln	1862	resigned, 1881
Samuel F. Miller	" "	1862	died, 1890
David Davis	" "	1862	resigned, 1877
Stephen J. Field	" "	1863	resigned, 1897

BIBLIOGRAPHY

No ATTEMPT is made to present a complete list of the materials available and needed for an understanding of Roger B. Taney and the period in which he lived. For the convenience of the reader, however, most of the works cited in the footnotes are brought together here, along with a limited number of others which have been of value.

ADAMS, CHARLES FRANCIS, *Richard Henry Dana*. 2 vols., Houghton Mifflin, 1890.

ADAMS, JOHN QUINCY, *Memoirs, Comprising Portions of His Diary from 1795 to 1848*, ed. by Charles Francis Adams. 12 vols., Lippincott, 1876.

BASSETT, JOHN S., *Life of Andrew Jackson*. 2 vols., Doubleday, Page, 1911.

BATES, EDWARD, *Diary*, ed. by H. K. Beale. Government Printing Office, 1933.

BENTON, THOMAS HART, *Thirty Years' View*. 2 vols., Appleton, 1858.

BEVERIDGE, ALBERT J., *Abraham Lincoln, 1809–1858*. 2 vols., Houghton Mifflin, 1928.

—— *Life of John Marshall, 1755–1835*. 4 vols., Houghton Mifflin, 1916–1919.

BIDDLE, GEORGE W., *Constitutional Development in the United States as Influenced by Chief Justice Taney*. University of Michigan Studies in Political Science, 1889.

BIDDLE, NICHOLAS, *Correspondence*, ed. by Reginald C. McGrane. Houghton Mifflin, 1919.

BLACK, JEREMIAH S., *Essays and Speeches*, ed. by Chauncey F. Black. Appleton, 1885.

BOUCHER, C. S., AND BROOKS, B. P. (eds.), *Correspondence Addressed to John C. Calhoun, 1837–1849* (*Annual Report of the American Historical Association*, 1929).

BOWERS, CLAUDE, *Party Battles of the Jackson Period*. Houghton Mifflin, 1924.

BRIGANCE, WILLIAM N., *Jeremiah S. Black*. University of Pennsylvania Press, 1934.

BROWN, GEORGE W., *Baltimore and the 19th of April, 1861*. N. Murray, 1887.

BRYAN, W. B., *History of the National Capital*. 2 vols., Macmillan, 1916.

BUCHANAN, JAMES, *Works*, ed. by John Bassett Moore. 12 vols., Lippincott, 1908.

BURGESS, JOHN W., *The Middle Period, 1817–1858*. Scribner, 1897.

BUTLER, WILLIAM A., *Retrospect of Forty Years, 1825–1865*, ed. by Harriet A. Butler. Scribner, 1911.

CALHOUN, JOHN C., *Correspondence*, ed. by J. Franklin Jameson. (*Annual Report of the American Historical Association*, 1899.)

—— *Works*, ed. by Richard K. Crallé. 6 vols., Appleton 1854–1860.

—— See also BOUCHER AND BROOKS (eds.).

CARSON, HAMPTON L., *The Supreme Court of the United States*. J. Y. Huber Co., 1891.

CATTERALL, RALPH C. H., *The Second Bank of the United States*. University of Chicago Press, 1903.

CHANNING, EDWARD, *History of the United States*. 6 vols., Macmillan, 1905, 1926.

CHITTENDEN, L. E., *Report of the Debates and Proceedings in the Secret Sessions of the Conference Convention*. Appleton, 1864.

CLAY, HENRY, *Private Correspondence*, ed. by Calvin Colton. 4 vols., A. S. Barnes & Co., 1856.

—— *Works*, ed. by Calvin Colton. 7 vols., Putnam, 1904.

CONNOR, HENRY G., *John Archibald Campbell*. Houghton Mifflin, 1920.

COODY, ABIMELECH. (See VERPLANCK.)

CORDELL, EUGENE F., *The University of Maryland, 1807–1907*. 2 vols., Lewis Publishing Co.

CORWIN, EDWARD S., *Doctrine of Judicial Review*. Princeton University Press, 1914.

—— "The Dred Scott Decision in the Light of Contemporary Legal Doctrines," *American Historical Review*, October, 1911.

—— *Twilight of the Supreme Court*. Yale University Press, 1934.

COTTON, JANE B. (ed.), *Maryland Calendar of Wills*. 8 vols., W. J. C. Dulany Co., 1901.

CURTIS, BENJAMIN R., JR. (ed.), *Memoir of Benjamin Robbins Curtis*. 2 vols., Little, Brown, 1879.

CURTIS, GEORGE T., *Life of James Buchanan*. 2 vols., Harper, 1883.

—— *Life of Daniel Webster*. 2 vols., Appleton, 1870.

DELAPLAINE, EDWARD S., *Chief Justice Taney—His Career as a Lawyer*. Reprinted from the *American Law Review*, July-August, 1918.

—— *Life of Thomas Johnson*. Hitchcock, 1927.

DUANE, W. J., *Narrative of Correspondence Concerning the Removal of the Deposites*. Philadelphia, 1838.

EARLE, SWEPSON, *The Chesapeake Bay Country*. Thomson-Ellis Co., 1923.

ELLET, ELIZABETH F., *Court Circles of the Republic*. J. D. Dennison, 1869.

ELLIS, J. B., *Sights and Secrets of the National Capital*. United States Publishing Co., 1869.

ESSARY, JESSE F., *Maryland in National Politics*. John Murphy Co., 1915.

FUESS, CLAUDE M., *Life of Caleb Cushing*. 2 vols., Harcourt, Brace, 1923.

—— *Daniel Webster*. 2 vols., Little, Brown, 1930.

GREELEY, HORACE, *The American Conflict*. Chase, 1866.

GRIFFITH, THOMAS W., *Annals of Baltimore*. W. Wooddy, 1833.

GROVE, WILLIAM J., *History of Carrollton Manor*. Marken & Bielfeld, 1928.

HENDERSON, GERARD C., *Position of Foreign Corporations in American Constitutional Law*. Harvard University Press, 1918.

HODDER, FRANK H., *Some Phases of the Dred Scott Case*. Reprinted from *Missouri Historical Review*, Vol. XVI.

HONE, PHILIP, *Diary*, ed. by Allan Nevins. 2 vols., Dodd, Mead, 1927.

HOWARD, GEORGE W., *The Monumental City*. M. Curlander, 1889.

HUNGERFORD, JAMES, *The Old Plantation*. Harper, 1859.

HUNT, CHARLES H., *Life of Edward Livingston*. Appleton, 1864.

JACKSON, ANDREW, *Correspondence*, ed. by John S. Bassett. 6 vols., Carnegie Institution, 1926-1934.

JEFFERSON, THOMAS, *Works*, ed. by Paul L. Ford. 12 vols., Putnam, 1904–1905.

—— *Writings*, ed. by H. A. Washington. 9 vols., Taylor & Maury, 1854.

KENDALL, AMOS, *Autobiography*, ed. by William Stickney. Shepard & Dillingham, 1872.

KEY-SMITH, FRANCIS SCOTT, *Francis Scott Key*. Washington, 1911.

KING, CHARLES R. (ed.), *Life and Correspondence of Rufus King*. 6 vols. Putnam, 1894–1900.

LEWIS, WILLIAM D. (ed.), *Great American Lawyers*. 8 vols., John C. Winston & Co., 1907–1909.

LODGE, HENRY CABOT, *Daniel Webster*. Houghton Mifflin, 1883.

LOGAN, MRS. J. A. (ed.), *Thirty Years in Washington*. A. D. Worthington Co., 1901.

McMASTER, JOHN B., *History of the People of the United States from the Revolution to the Civil War*. 8 vols., Appleton, 1927–1929.

McMaster, John B., *History of the People of the United States During Lincoln's Administration*. Appleton, 1927.

Madison, James, *Writings*, ed. by Gaillard Hunt. 9 vols., Putnam, 1900–1910.

Martin, David, *Trial of the Rev. Jacob Gruber, Minister in the Methodist Episcopal Church*. David Martin, 1819.

Martineau, Harriet, *Retrospect of Western Travel*. 2 vols., Saunders & Otley, 1838.

—— *Society in America*. 3 vols., Saunders & Otley, 1837.

Maury, Sarah M., *The Statesmen of America in 1846*. Carey & Hart, 1847.

Mikell, William E., "Roger Brooke Taney" (in William D. Lewis, *Great American Lawyers*, IV, 77–194).

Morris, Gouverneur, *Diary and Letters*, ed. by Anne C. Morris. 2 vols., Scribner, 1888.

Nicolay, John G., and Hay, John, *Abraham Lincoln*. 10 vols., Century, 1890.

Parton, James, *Life of Andrew Jackson*. 3 vols., Masons, 1860.

Pickering, Octavius, and Upham, Charles W., *Life of Timothy Pickering*. 4 vols., Little, Brown, 1867–1873.

Pickering, Timothy, *A Letter . . . to James Sullivan, Governor of Massachusetts*. Greenough & Stebbins, 1808.

Polk, James K., *Polk: The Diary of a President*, 1845–1849, ed. by Allan Nevins. Longmans, Green, 1929.

Poore, Benjamin Perley, *Perley's Reminiscences of Sixty Years in the National Metropolis*. 2 vols., W. A. Houghton, 1886.

Rhodes, James Ford, *History of the United States from the Compromise of 1850*. 8 vols., Harper, 1893–1906.

Richardson, James D. (ed.), *A Compilation of the Messages and Papers of the Presidents, 1789–1897*. 10 vols., Government Printing Office, 1896–1899.

Rowland, Kate M., *Life and Correspondence of Charles Carroll of Carrollton*. 2 vols., Putnam, 1898.

Scharf, John T., *Chronicles of Baltimore*. Turnbull, 1874.

—— *History of Baltimore City and County*. L. H. Everts, 1881.

—— *History of Western Maryland*. 2 vols., L. H. Everts, 1882.

Schuckers, Jacob W., *Life and Public Services of Salmon Portland Chase*. Twentieth Century, 1874.

Semmes, John E., *John H. B. Latrobe and His Times*. Norman, Remington Co., 1917.

Sioussat, Mrs. Annie Leakin, *Old Baltimore*. Macmillan, 1931.

SMITH, WILLIAM E., *The Francis Preston Blair Family in Politics*. 2 vols., Macmillan, 1933.

SPARKS, EDWIN E. (ed.), *Lincoln-Douglas Debates of 1858*. F. A. Owen, 1908.

STEINER, BERNARD C., *Life of Roger B. Taney*. Williams & Wilkins, 1922.

STORY, WILLIAM W., *Life and Letters of Joseph Story*. 2 vols., Little, Brown, 1851.

STRICKLAND, WILLIAM P., *Life of Jacob Gruber*. Carlton & Porter, 1860.

SUMNER, CHARLES, *Works*. 15 vols., Lee & Shepard, 1870–1873.

SUMNER, WILLIAM G., *Andrew Jackson*. Houghton Mifflin, 1882.

"The Supreme Court," *United States Magazine and Democratic Review*, January, 1838.

"The Supreme Court of the United States," *United States Magazine and Democratic Review*, June, 1840.

SWISHER, CARL B., *Stephen J. Field: Craftsman of the Law*. Brookings Institution, 1930.

TANEY, R. B., *An Address to the People of Frederick County*, Feb. 27, 1817.

THAYER, JAMES B., *Cases on Constitutional Law*. 2 vols., C. W. Sever, 1895.

TOCQUEVILLE, ALEXIS DE, *Democracy in America* (Reeves edition, ed. by Francis Bowen). 2 vols., Sever & Francis, 1862.

TYLER, LYON G., *Letters and Times of the Tylers*. 3 vols., Whittet & Shepperson, 1884.

TYLER, SAMUEL, *Memoir of Roger Brooke Taney*. John Murphy & Co., 1872.

The Unjust Judge: A Memorial of Roger Brooke Taney. Baker & Goodwin, 1865.

VAN BUREN, MARTIN, *Autobiography*, ed. by John C. Fitzpatrick. Government Printing Office, 1930.

VAN SANTVOORD, GEORGE, *Sketches of the Lives and Judicial Services of the Chief-Justices of the Supreme Court of the United States*. Scribner, 1854.

VERPLANCK, GULIAN C., *Letter to the Hon. Saml. L. Mitchell*, . . . By Abimelech Coody. Literary Exchange, 1811.

WARDEN, ROBERT B., *An Account of the Private Life and Public Services of Salmon Portland Chase*. Wilstach, Baldwin, 1874.

WARREN, CHARLES, *History of the American Bar*. Little, Brown, 1911.

—— *History of Harvard Law School*. 3 vols., Lewis Publishing Co., 1908.

WARREN, CHARLES, *The Supreme Court in United States History*. 2 vols., Little, Brown, 1926.

WEBSTER, DANIEL, *Letters*, ed. by Claude H. Van Tyne. McClure, Phillips & Co., 1902.

—— *Private Correspondence*, ed. by Fletcher Webster. 2 vols., Little, Brown, 1857.

—— *Writings and Speeches* (National Ed.). 18 vols., Little, Brown, 1903.

WELLES, GIDEON, *Diary*. 3 vols., Houghton Mifflin, 1911.

WEYBRIGHT, VICTOR, *Spangled Banner: The Story of Francis Scott Key*. Farrar & Rinehart, 1935.

WILLIAMS, THOMAS J. C., *History of Frederick County, Maryland*. 2 vols., R. Titworth & Co., 1910.

MANUSCRIPTS

Attorney General MSS., Library of Congress.

Edward Bates MSS., Library of Congress.

William M. Beall MSS., Miss Nannie Floyd, Frederick, Md.

Nicholas Biddle MSS., Library of Congress.

John Bigelow, MS. Diary, New York Public Library.

Jeremiah S. Black MSS., Library of Congress.

J. B. Boyle MSS., J. Carbery Boyle, Westminster, Md.

James Buchanan MSS., Historical Society of Pennsylvania.

John C. Calhoun MSS., Clemson College.

James M. Campbell MSS., in possession of the author.

Salmon P. Chase MSS., Library of Congress, and Historical Society of Pennsylvania.

Henry Clay MSS., Library of Congress.

Conarroe Collection, Historical Society of Pennsylvania.

John J. Crittenden MSS., Library of Congress.

John Davis MSS., American Antiquarian Society.

Andrew J. Donelson MSS., Library of Congress.

Dreer Collection, Historical Society of Pennsylvania.

Etting Collection, Historical Society of Pennsylvania.

Gratz Collection, Historical Society of Pennsylvania.

Horace Greeley MSS., New York Public Library.

Christopher Hughes MSS., Professor Jesse Reeves, Ann Arbor, Mich.

Andrew Jackson MSS., Library of Congress.

John P. Kennedy MSS., Peabody Institute.

James Kent MSS., Library of Congress.

John H. B. Latrobe MSS., Maryland Historical Society.
Edward Livingston MSS., John Ross Delafield, New York, N. Y.
John McLean MSS., Library of Congress.
Willie P. Mangum MSS., Library of Congress.
Virgil Maxcy MSS., Library of Congress.
Jonathan Meredith MSS., Library of Congress.
David M. Perine MSS., Washington Perine, Baltimore, Md.
Richard Peters MSS., Historical Society of Pennsylvania.
Timothy Pickering MSS., Massachusetts Historical Society.
Franklin Pierce MSS., Library of Congress.
James K. Polk MSS., Library of Congress.
Benjamin Rush MSS., Historical Society of Pennsylvania, and Philadelphia Library Company.
Samuel Smith MSS., Library of Congress.
Andrew Stevenson MSS., Library of Congress.
Roger B. Taney Bank War MS., Library of Congress, and MSS., at the Maryland Historical Society and at the Taney House, Frederick, Md.
Treasury Department MSS., including Letters to Banks, Letters from Banks, and Cabinets and Bureaus.
Samuel Treat MSS., Missouri Historical Society.
United States Bank MSS., Library of Congress.
Martin Van Buren MSS., Library of Congress.
William H. Winder MSS., Johns Hopkins University, and the Force Transcripts, Library of Congress.

NEWSPAPERS

Albany *Argus,* and *Gazette;* Alexandria *Gazette;* Annapolis *Maryland Gazette,* and *Maryland Republican;* Baltimore *American, Clipper, Evening Post, Exchange, Federal Gazette, Federal Republican, Patriot, Republican,* and *Sun;* Boston *Atlas, Columbian Sentinel, Daily Advertiser, Liberator,* and *Statesman;* Camden *Journal;* Centreville *Times;* Charleston *Courier;* Detroit *Journal;* Elkton *Gazette;* Frederick *Bartgis' Republican Gazette, Citizen, Herald, Independent American Volunteer, Political Examiner, Republican Advocate,* and *Star of Federalism;* Georgetown *Federal Republican;* Hagerstown *Gazette,* and *Maryland Herald;* Harrisburg *Pennsylvania Reporter;* Mobile *Register;* New York *Commercial Advertiser, Courier and Enquirer, Herald, Post, Times, Tribune,* and *World;* Philadelphia *Aurora,* and *National Gazette;* Richmond *Enquirer;* Salem *Essex Register;* Washington *Globe, National Intelligencer,*

National Journal, and *United States Telegraph;* Wilmington *Watchman;* Worcester *Republican.*

PUBLIC DOCUMENTS

Archives of Maryland.
Baltimore County Land Records.
Baltimore County Wills and *Administration Papers.*
Calvert County Rent Rolls.
Calvert County Wills and *Administration Papers.*
Frederick County Land Records.
Maryland General Assembly
 Votes and Proceedings of the House of Delegates, 1780–1835.
 Votes and Proceedings of the Senate, 1780–1835.
Circuit Courts of the United States
 Federal Cases.
 Reports of Cases . . . in the Circuit Court of the United States for the District of Maryland, 1836–1861 (Taney's decisions, ed. by J. Mason Campbell).
Supreme Court of the United States
 Minute Books, 1825–1864.
 Peters' Reports, vols. 11 to 16.
 Howard's Reports, vols. 1 to 24.
 Black's Reports, vols. 1 to 2.
 Wallace's Reports, vol. 20.
United States Congress
 Register of Debates in Congress, 1831–1837.
 Congressional Globe, 1833–1865.
 Journal of the Executive Proceedings of the Senate, 1831–1864.
Official Opinions of the Attorneys General, 1831–1864.

INDEX